The Student's Companion to Social Policy

The Student's Companion to Social Policy

Third Edition

Edited by

Pete Alcock, Margaret May and Karen Rowlingson

Blackwell
Publishing

© 1998, 2003, 2008 by Blackwell Publishing Ltd

BLACKWELL PUBLISHING
350 Main Street, Malden, MA 02148-5020, USA
9600 Garsington Road, Oxford OX4 2DQ, UK
550 Swanston Street, Carlton, Victoria 3053, Australia

The right of Pete Alcock, Margaret May and Karen Rowlingson to be identified as the authors of the editorial material in this work has been asserted in accordance with the UK Copyright, Designs, and Patents Act 1988.

First edition published 1998
Second edition published 2003
Third edition published 2008 by Blackwell Publishing Ltd

1   2008

Library of Congress Cataloging-in-Publication Data is available

ISBN: 978-1-4051-6901-1 (paperback)

A catalogue record for this title is available from the British Library.

Set in 10 on 12.5 pt Sabon
by SNP Best-set Typesetter Ltd., Hong Kong
Printed and bound in Singapore
by Markono Print Media Pte Ltd

The publisher's policy is to use permanent paper from mills that operate a sustainable forestry policy, and which has been manufactured from pulp processed using acid-free and elementary chlorine-free practices. Furthermore, the publisher ensures that the text paper and cover board used have met acceptable environmental accreditation standards.

For further information on
Blackwell Publishing, visit our website at
www.blackwellpublishing.com

Contents

Contributors

Pete Alcock is Professor of Social Policy and Administration and Head of School of Social Sciences at the University of Birmingham. He is the author and editor of a number of books on social policy. His research interests include poverty and social exclusion and the role of the voluntary and community sector in welfare. He was Chair of the Social Policy Association 1995–8.

Hilary Arksey is Senior Research Fellow in the Social Policy Research Unit, University of York. Over the past 12 years she has conducted a number of research studies of carers, including their experiences of assessment and their decisions and aspirations around paid work and retirement.

Rob Baggott is Professor of Public Policy and Director of the Health Policy Research Unit at De Montfort University, Leicester. His research interests include public health, alcohol policy, health service reform, patient and public involvement and pressure groups.

Saul Becker is Professor of Social Policy and Social Care and Director of Research for the School of Sociology and Social Policy at the University of Nottingham. He has also held chairs at Loughborough and Birmingham Universities. His main research interests include informal family care (particularly children who are carers – 'young carers'), community care, vulnerable children and their families, and research methodology in social policy. He was the Chair of the Social Policy Association 2004–8.

Peter Beresford is Professor of Social Policy and Director of the Centre for Citizen Participation at Brunel University. He is Chair of Shaping Our Lives, a Trustee of the Social Care Institute for Excellence and Visiting Fellow of the School of Social Work and Psychosocial Science at the University of East Anglia. With Suzy Croft, he has written widely on the subjects of citizen involvement and empowerment.

Alice Bloch is a Senior Lecturer in the Department of Sociology at City University. Her research interests are in the areas of migration, forced migration and asylum policy. Her main teaching interests are in refugee studies and migration and she is course director for the MA in Refugee Studies.

Catherine Bochel is a Senior Lecturer in Social Policy at the University of Lincoln where she teaches on a range of policy-related courses. Her research interests include the policy process, participation and local government, on which she has published widely.

Michael Cahill is Reader in Social Policy at the University of Brighton. He is the author and editor of a number of books on the environment and social policy, and on new approaches to the study of social policy with reference to the impact of globalization, and the changing nature of citizenship in contemporary welfare systems.

Claire Callender is Professor of Higher Education Studies at Birkbeck, University of London. Her research is about access and equity in higher education, focusing on student funding. She has written widely on this topic and undertaken research for some of the most significant inquiries into student funding in the UK. In recognition of her expertise, she was selected as a Fulbright New Century Scholar for 2007–8.

John Clarke is Professor of Social Policy at the Open University. His research and teaching have centred on the social, cultural and political struggles around the remaking of welfare states. These concerns have ranged from the impact of managerialism and consumerism on state policy and practice, through to wider questions of globalization, neo-liberalism, the reworking of alignments between nations, states and welfare to the unsettled relationships between changing publics and changing public services.

Jochen Clasen is Professor of Comparative Social Policy in the School for Social and Political Studies at the University of Edinburgh. He has researched and written widely in the areas of social security, labour market policy and cross-national analysis of welfare states, particularly across European countries. His teaching centres on European social policy and the political economy of the welfare state. He is co-chair of ESPA*net*.

Bob Coles is a Senior Lecturer in Social Policy at the University of York. He has a long-standing interest in youth policy and developed a degree specializing in children and young people at York. He helped establish youth policy as a sub-area within social policy and developed the links between policy, research and practice. His research has focused on vulnerable young people, including work on Connexions funded by the Joseph Rowntree Foundation, for which he also acted as research adviser on their youth research programme.

Guy Daly is Associate Dean, Faculty of Health and Life Sciences, Coventry University. He has an academic and professional background in health and local government services. His areas of teaching and research include governance, community care, service user involvement, local government, housing and social and public policy generally. He is also active in the area of local governance, having been an elected councillor, a school and colleges governor and a board member of an urban development corporation and a housing association.

Howard Davis is Principal Research Fellow and Research Manager at The Local Government Centre, Warwick Business School. He has been centrally involved in projects advising on and/or evaluating the modernization and improvement of local government – commissioned by both national and local government bodies. His work also includes research on the use of competition and procurement approaches in local government in international contexts, with particular reference to improving the delivery of local and public services in Central and Eastern Europe.

Alan Deacon is Professor Emeritus of Social Policy at the University of Leeds. He has written widely on welfare reform in Britain and the United States, and was a member of the ESRC Research Group on Care, Values and the Future of Welfare. He was Chair of the Social Policy Association from 2001 to 2004.

Hartley Dean is Reader in Social Policy at the London School of Economics and Political Science. Before his academic career he was a welfare rights worker in a multiethnic inner-

London neighbourhood. His research interests and several publications have focused on poverty and social exclusion, survival strategies of marginalised social groups, discourses of welfare, welfare rights, social citizenship and rights of redress.

Nick Ellison is Professor of Sociology and Social Policy at the University of Leeds. Core research and teaching interests include welfare politics and welfare state change with particular reference to the impact of 'globalization', and the changing nature of citizenship in contemporary welfare systems.

Tony Fitzpatrick is Reader in the School of Sociology and Social Policy, Nottingham University, and was Treasurer of the Social Policy Association 2003–6. He has published many books and articles dealing with the relevance to social policy of new technologies, environmentalism and social democracy, among other social and political theories.

David Gladstone is currently Honorary Visiting Fellow in the School for Policy Studies at the University of Bristol. An historian by training, his teaching and research interests are in aspects of – and the interrelationship between – British social policy past and present. He has authored and edited several books and book series.

Jon Glasby is Head of Health and Social Care Partnerships at the Health Services Management Centre, University of Birmingham. A qualified social worker by background, he leads a national programme of research, teaching and consultancy to support more effective inter-agency working between health and social care. He is also a board member of the UK's Social Care Institute for Excellence (SCIE).

Caroline Glendinning is Professor of Social Policy and Assistant Director of the Social Policy Research Unit, University of York. She leads SPRU's Department of Health-funded research programme on 'Choice and Independence across the Lifecourse'.

Howard Glennerster is Professor Emeritus at the London School of Economics, where he taught for thirty-five years. His continuing research is on the economics and finance of social welfare in this and other countries and its history. He is particularly concerned with the funding of healthcare and education.

Stephen Harrison is Professor of Social Policy in the School of Social Sciences at the University of Manchester. He is currently on a long-term secondment to the National Primary Care Research and Development Centre. His research interests include health policy-making, implementation and evaluation, and empirical research in healthcare organizations. He was formerly Professor of Health Policy and Politics at the University of Leeds.

Linda Hantrais holds a chair in European Social Policy in the Department of Politics, International Relations and European Studies at Loughborough University. Her main research interests are in cross-national comparative research theory, methodology and practice, with particular reference to socio-economic change, social and family policy in Europe.

Colin Hay is Professor of Political Analysis at the University of Sheffield. His research interests are diverse, including at present the comparative political economy of contemporary Europe, welfare reform and political disaffection in advanced liberal democracies and analytical techniques in contemporary political science.

Michael Hill is Emeritus Professor of Social Policy, University of Newcastle upon Tyne. He has taught comparative social policy at Goldsmiths College and at the University of Brighton since his retirement from Newcastle. He has also made visits to universities in Taiwan,

Hong Kong, South Korea and Japan. His research interests range from policy-making and public policy processes, current developments in welfare services and benefits, particularly pensions, to comparative social policy – on all of which he has published widely.

John Hills is Director of the Centre for Analysis of Social Exclusion and Professor of Social Policy at the London School of Economics. He is author or editor of a number of books on aspects of social policy. His research interests include income and wealth distribution, social security, pensions policy, housing and the distributional effects of government policy. He was a member of the Pensions Commission from 2003 to 2006.

Chris Holden is Lecturer in Social Policy at the School of Health Sciences and Social Care, Brunel University. He has published widely on corporate provision of health and social care and international trade in health services, as well as more broadly on the political economy of welfare in the context of globalization. He is a member of the Executive Committee of the Social Policy Association.

John Hudson is Lecturer in Social Policy in the Department of Social Policy and Social Work at the University of York. His research and teaching interests include the information society, e-government, policy analysis, comparative political economy of welfare and socio-economic aspects of football.

Jeremy Kendall is a Senior Lecturer in Social Policy at the School of Social Policy, Sociology and Social Research (SSPSSR), University of Kent. His research interests include the policy process; the third sector, civil society; and the mixed economy of social policy. He has taught social research methods, economics and health economics, and aspects of British and European social policy, and is pioneering the delivery of teaching on European social policy and civil society at the University of Kent's Brussels campus.

Patricia Kennett is a Senior Lecturer in Comparative Policy Studies at the School for Policy Studies, University of Bristol. Her research interests include globalization, governance and institutions; citizenship and the welfare state; comparative welfare systems and social policy.

Hilary Land is Emeritus Professor of Social Policy and Honorary Senior Research Fellow in the School for Policy Studies, University of Bristol. She has had longstanding interest in family policies broadly defined and is currently studying changes in how responsibilities for care are shared between the generations as well as between men and women.

Jane Lewis is Professor of Social Policy at the London School of Economics. Her research interests lie in the fields of gender, families and social policies; the history of social policies; and the role of the third sector. She has written widely on family structure and family change.

Ruth Lister is Professor of Social Policy in the Department of Social Sciences, Loughborough University, where she teaches on a wide range of social policy modules. Her main research interests are poverty, citizenship, gender, children and welfare reform. She has published widely in these areas and in social policy more generally. She has sat on various independent commissions, including the Commission on Poverty, Participation and Power and the Fabian Commission on Life Chances and Child Poverty.

Ruth McDonald is Research Fellow at the National Primary Care Research and Development Centre, University of Manchester. Her research interests concern issues of change and resistance in organizations. Wherever possible she has explored these from inside the organization(s) concerned, examining, amongst other things, the unintended consequences of change and its implications for individual identity. Recent research topics include the 'empowerment' of staff in a primary care trust, threats to patient safety in the operating theatre and the new general medical practice contract. All of which is a far cry from her old job as an NHS finance director.

Stephen McKay is Professor of Social Research at the Institute of Applied Social Studies at the University of Birmingham, and heads a research centre devoted to wealth, welfare and well-being. He conducts research on poverty, inequality, family change and the role and effects of social security policies. Most of this research takes a quantitative approach. His teaching interests follow similar themes on the role of income maintenance policies, including pensions.

Tony Maltby works at the Centre for Research into the Older Workforce at NIACE. His main research interest is in the social policy of employment, work and income in later life, with a central interest in the concept of workability and its applicability to the UK. His move to CROW extends his interests to include training, education and lifelong learning issues.

Nick Manning is Professor of Social Policy and Sociology, and Director of the Institute of Mental Health, University of Nottingham. His recent research interests include unemployment, poverty, ethnicity and health in Russia and Eastern Europe, and medical sociology and mental health policy. He has written books on healthcare, social problems and comparative social policy.

Margaret May is Principal Lecturer in Human Resource Management at the London Metropolitan Business School, where she teaches on a range of management and business courses. Her main research interests are in employment policy, occupational welfare and employee relations, welfare management and comparative policy. She was Chair of the Social Policy Association from 1999 to 2001.

Jane Millar is Professor of Social Policy and Director of the Centre for the Analysis of Social Policy, University of Bath. Her research interests include family policy and the policy implications of family change; income support and labour market policies for unemployed people and lone parents; poverty, inequality and social exclusion; gender and social policy; and comparative social policy.

Alan Murie is Professor of Urban and Regional Studies at the Centre for Urban and Regional Studies, School of Public Policy, University of Birmingham. He has been a leading contributor to housing research and policy debates for more than twenty years. He has published widely on housing and related issues.

Tim Newburn is Professor of Criminology and Social Policy and Director of the Mannheim Centre for Criminology at the London School of Economics and President of the British Society of Criminology. At the LSE he teaches sociology and criminology to undergraduate and postgraduate students. His major areas of research interest concern policing and security, comparative criminal justice and penal policy, and youth crime and youth justice.

Janet Newman is a Professor of Social Policy at the Open University. Her research and publications focus on analyses of governance, policy and politics including work on the managerial reforms of the 1990s, analyses of the politics and policies of New Labour, and changing configurations of power associated with the 'modernization' of European welfare states. Recent research includes work on power, participation and political renewal, and citizen-consumers.

Robert M. Page is currently Reader in Democratic Socialism and Social Policy at the University of Birmingham. He has written and edited fifteen books on a wide range of topics in social policy. His main research interest is in the political history of the welfare state from 1940 to the present day.

Richard Parry is Reader in Social Policy in the School of Social and Political Studies at the University of Edinburgh, where he teaches on Scottish, UK and European social policy and on public policy and management. His recent research projects have been on the role of the Treasury in social policy, the impact of devolution on the civil service through-out the United Kingdom and a cross-national comparison of the cost of public administration.

Robert Pinker is Emeritus Professor of Social Administration at the LSE and an interna-tional consultant with the Press Complaints Commission. His research interests lie in the fields of social policy theory, the impact of civil war on social welfare and the role of self-regulatory institutions in civil society.

Lucinda Platt is Senior Lecturer in Sociology at the University of Essex. She teaches British and comparative social policy, social stratification and inequality, and quantitative research methods. Her research focuses on child poverty, with a particular focus on historical context, and on ethnic minorities and disadvantage. She has published on poverty and ethnicity, child poverty, social mobility, social security, disability and social capital.

Martin Powell is Professor of Health and Social Policy in the Health Services Management Centre, University of Birmingham. His main research interests and publications are in the areas of historical and geographical aspects of social policy, health policy, new social democracy, partnerships, decentralization and equality.

Mark Priestley is Reader in Disability Studies at the Centre for Disability Studies, Uni-versity of Leeds, and administrator of the international discussion forum on disability research. He has taught disability studies since the mid-1990s and was previously a lec-turer in rehabilitation work. He has written extensively on disability theory, politics and policies, and his current interests include life-course and comparative perspectives.

Carol Propper is Professor of Economics of Public Policy at the University of Bristol. Her main research interests and publications are in the field of health economics. Her research interests include the impact of competition and choice on health outcomes, whether public sector workers respond to financial incentives and the links between low income and child health and behaviour.

Tess Ridge is Lecturer in Social Policy at the University of Bath. She teaches courses on childhood sociology and social policy and family sociology and social policy. Her research interests are childhood poverty and social exclusion, children and family policy, especially financial support for children and families.

Karen Rowlingson is Professor of Social Policy and Director of Research at the Institute of Applied Social Studies, University of Birmingham. Her research interests include social security and taxation policy, personal finances, poverty and inequality, wealth and asset-based welfare, and family change. Her teaching interests cover all these fields as well as qualitative and quantitative research methods.

Rob Sykes is Principal Lecturer in Social Policy in the Division of Applied Social Sciences at Sheffield Hallam University where he teaches comparative social science, comparative policy-making and comparative politics. His main research interests lie in the area of comparative social policy especially in Europe and East Asia and the study of globalization and political change.

Peter Taylor-Gooby is Professor of Social Policy, University of Kent, and Director of the ESRC's Risk Network. His main interests lie in cross-disciplinary work on risk, comparative cross-national work on European social policy and work on theoretical developments in social policy. He believes strongly that progress is to be made by developing empirical tests of theoretically based ideas.

Alan Walker is Professor of Social Policy and Social Gerontology at the University of Sheffield, a position he has held for more than twenty years. His main research interests are in the following fields: the sociology of ageing and old age, the social policy implications of population ageing, social policy in Europe, China and East Asia, and social quality. He currently directs the New Dynamics of Ageing Research Programme, funded by five research councils, and previously directed the ESRC's Growing Older Programme.

Anne West is Professor of Education Policy in the Department of Social Policy at the London School of Economics and Political Science. She is also Director of the Centre for Educational Research. Her research has focused on recent education policy, in particular market-oriented reforms and associated equity issues; she has a particular interest in school admissions policies. Her other research interests relate to financing education and comparative education policy. She teaches education policy on undergraduate and postgraduate programmes at the LSE.

Fiona Williams is Professor of Social Policy at the University of Leeds. Until recently she directed the ESRC Research Group on Care, Values and the Future of Welfare. She has written widely on gender, 'race' and ethnicity in social policy, and is currently researching the employment of migrant workers in home-based care in Europe. Her teaching and research interests focus on the place of care in contemporary society, including the changing nature of family lives and personal relationships, and the development of a political ethic of care.

Sharon Wright is Lecturer in Social Policy at the University of Stirling. Her research interests are in the processes of making and implementing social policy, service delivery, unemployment, active labour market policies, social security and poverty. Her teaching includes understanding social policy; gender, work and welfare; poverty, income and wealth; and qualitative research methods. She is co-convenor of the Scottish Social Policy Network.

Nicola Yeates is Senior Lecturer in Social Policy at the Open University. She has published widely on issues of globalization as it relates to social policy. She co-convenes the International and Comparative Social Policy group of the Social Policy Association.

Acknowledgements

The editors and publisher gratefully acknowledge the permission granted to reproduce the copyright material in this book:

Figure 57.1 "Social sector spending among country grouping classified by income," from p. 118 in P. Keyy and V. Saiz-Omenaca, *The Allocation of Government Expenditure in the World 1990–2001*, unpublished paper, United Nations, Department of Economics and Social Affairs, Division for Social Policy and Development in UN, 2005. Reprinted with the permission of United Nations Publications.

Every effort has been made to trace copyright holders and to obtain their permission for the use of copyright material. The publisher apologizes for any errors or omissions in the above list and would be grateful if notified of any corrections that should be incorporated in future reprints or editions of this book.

The editors would also like to thank Sarah Dancy and Ben Thatcher for assisting in compiling the final manuscript, and Justin Vaughan, our Commissioning Editor at Blackwell, for his help.

Introduction

This *Student's Companion to Social Policy* is a resource book that will be of practical use to students of social policy throughout their undergraduate or postgraduate study of the subject. It aims to acquaint students with the study of social policy by covering all the main themes and issues likely to be included in any curriculum in the UK, and indeed in many other countries. Readers are introduced to current theoretical and ideological debates, service areas, key policy issues and the broader international context. Each chapter includes a short guide to further sources, which points to some of the literature that pursues the issues addressed in the chapter in more depth and also alerts readers to major web-based sources. The *Companion* will be of value to students studying social policy on its own, as part of another undergraduate or postgraduate programme (for instance, sociology, politics or applied social science) or as part of a professional course in a related field (for instance, social work, nursing and health studies, public and voluntary sector management or criminology).

This third edition of the *Companion* has been much expanded and updated from the previous editions. New chapters have been added to take account of developments in academic debate and policy issues and existing authors have updated their original contributions. In some cases previous authors have been replaced with others

leading in research and teaching in those areas. The organization of the book has also been changed to create a simpler, eight-part structure, with all contributions grouped into coherent sections. The sections dealing with generic issues of learning and teaching have been omitted from this edition, because these matters are now well provided for by learning support units in universities, in a range of specialist texts and learning materials which have become available over recent years and, in particular, through the work of the HEFCE-funded subject centre for Social Policy and Social Work (SWAP). In their place, there is now further substantive coverage of policy provision.

There has also been a change in the editors of this third edition. Angus Erskine has retired from academic work since the second edition was produced and he has been replaced as third editor by Karen Rowlingson. The current editors and the publishers would like to thank Angus for all his work on the earlier editions. We are pleased that Karen has been able to join us, and her role has meant that the editorial process has been able to remain much the same for this latest edition.

All the contributors to this book, both old and new, are scholars and teachers in the forefront of social policy studies in the UK. They were selected on the basis that their expertise in their particular areas would provide readers with an authoritative introduction to a range of thinking and scholarship. Because the book has been prepared as a handbook and guide, rather than as a single text which focuses on one or two main themes, not all readers will necessarily want to read it from cover to cover. Indeed, most readers are likely to use it as a source of reference for consultation; and so the chapters have been written so that they can be read in any order, separately or in groups.

Since the appearance of the first edition of the *Companion*, *The Blackwell Dictionary of Social Policy* has also been published. This provides a sister volume to the *Companion*, offering short definitions of all key terms and concepts and longer discussion of major items. We hope that readers will be able to use the two together; and partly for this reason we excluded from the second edition, and again from this third edition, the Glossary that appeared in the first edition of this book.

Part I introduces students to the concepts and approaches that underpin the study of social policy – and its (inter)relationship with other disciplines. These include a brief history of the development of the subject and the ways in which it is studied and researched, together with discussion of a number of the key concepts which students are likely to encounter in their studies.

Part II provides readers with a guide to the theoretical and ideological context of social policy. Readers are introduced to the central themes and perspectives which provide the intellectual foundations to debates about the focus and aims of the subject.

Part III explores the social, political and economic context in which policies are developed and implemented, including key issues such as social division, economic context, family structures and political processes.

Part IV focuses on the provision and delivery of social policies. The different providers of welfare are examined by looking at the five main sectors of welfare – state, commercial, occupational, voluntary and informal – setting these in the context of a brief examination of the ways in which welfare is financed and how citizens are able to secure access to it.

Part V provides a discussion of different dimensions of the governance of welfare, including management and delivery and the role of users in determining welfare policy. The different geographical organization of welfare within the UK is explained, as well as the role of the supranational agencies, including in particular the European Union.

Part VI comprises chapters which examine the key areas of welfare service provision, with each providing up-to-date summaries of policy developments and policy planning in that area.

Part VII focuses on the provision of services to particular social groups, and analyses the extent to which these groups are advantaged or disadvantaged by different aspects of policy provision.

Part VIII explores the international context of social policy. There is an introductory chapter on the development and importance of comparative study, followed by a number of chapters summarizing the differing policy experiences of different groups of nations across the world.

As editors we are very grateful for the work put into this volume by the contributors. The *Companion* first set out to produce a collection of chapters written by some of the most distinguished teachers and lecturers in social policy in the UK, and in this third edition we have followed this with an expanded range of contributions. We asked all our contributors to write in as accessible a way as possible, while introducing complex issues in a short space. In this edition we extended this by asking all contributors to provide readers with a short bullet point summary of key points at the beginning of each chapter, and to conclude with some brief speculation on emerging issues.

Authors in social policy are no different from other authors, however; some write sharply and clearly, others are more difficult to follow and pack difficult ideas together. This collection reflects the range of styles of writing and the range of ideological and political positions that students of social policy are likely to encounter. All the chapters, of course, also only provide a short summary of a wide range of issues and information in their area. The aim therefore is to encourage readers to investigate further and read more widely.

We were successful in persuading our authors to contribute to the *Companion* because it was prepared with the support and backing of the Social Policy Association (SPA) – the professional association for academics in Social Policy (see Appendix). While we, as editors, made the difficult and contentious decisions about what should be left out, what should be included and who should be asked to write, the SPA's support was essential in persuading many of our contributors to take part. We should also like to thank Justin Vaughan and Ben Thatcher at Blackwell for their support in the production of this new edition, and the anonymous reviewers of the proposals for revision who all gave us such helpful advice. We hope that what we have produced is worthy of all this support and will continue to be of value to the social policy community as a whole. Any shortcomings in the collection as a whole are, however, our responsibility.

Pete Alcock
Margaret May
Karen Rowlingson

Part I

Concepts and Approaches

Chapter 1

The Subject of Social Policy

Pete Alcock

Overview

- Social policy is an academic subject which both overlaps with cognate subjects and has a discrete disciplinary base.
- It has changed its name from social administration to social policy to reflect a broadening concern with the theory as well as the practice of welfare.
- The welfare reforms in the UK in the period following the Second World War were critically important in establishing the policy context for subsequent policy development.
- Social policy analysts adopt a range of different theoretical perspectives, leading to differing conclusions about the viability and desirability of different policy measures.
- Much social policy has been developed by national governments, but policy also has local and supranational dimensions.

What Do We Study?

The study of social policy comes into the category of the academic social sciences. It is different from other areas of social science, such as sociology, economics and politics, however, because it is based upon a distinct empirical focus – support for the well-being of citizens provided through social action. Nevertheless, social policy draws on the methods used and the understanding developed within these other areas of social science. Thus, although on the one hand we can see social policy as a discrete academic *discipline*, which is studied and developed in its own right, on the other we can recognize that it is also an inter-disciplinary *field*, drawing on and developing links with other cognate disciplines at every stage and overlapping at times with these in terms of both empirical foci and methods of analysis. To put this another way, the boundaries between social policy and other social science subjects are porous, and shifting; and students and practitioners of social policy may also be working within or alongside these other areas or cooperating closely with others who do.

The term 'social policy' is not used only to refer to academic study, however; it is also used to refer to the social actions taken by policy-makers in the real world. So social policy refers both to the activity of policy-making to promote well-being and to the academic study of such actions. This may seem a bit confusing at first – whereas soci-ology students study *society*, social policy students study *social policy* – but it is a con-fusion that we all soon learn to live with.

This confusion is also true of the disci-pline versus interdisciplinary field debate, referred to above. The subject of social policy has the core features of an academic discipline, with its own theoretical debates and empirical foci, and it is recognized as such in the management and planning of higher education in the UK. At the same time, however, the study of social policy is developed and extended through interdisci-plinary collaboration. This may seem odd in principle; but it is not a problem in prac-tice. Thus students studying social policy may well find themselves in the same departments, or on the same degree pro-grammes, as others studying different sub-jects such as sociology; or they may be studying social policy as part of profes-sional education and training, for instance in social work. This variety and collabora-tion are to be welcomed, and students on these different courses will learn much from each other through learning together; but this does not mean that social policy can be subsumed within sociology or social work. Similarly, those engaged in social policy research often work alongside others such as economists or statisticians; but the focus of their concern is distinct – on investi-gating the development or delivery of policy, rather than on economic modelling (as economists) or data analysis (as statisticians).

The later chapters in this book explore in more detail some of the key concepts and perspectives which have underpinned the study of social policy, the major issues which inform policy development and the important areas of policy practice. Much analysis of social policy focuses on the poli-cies and practices of national government. Within the UK, however, the devolution of policy-making and the local development and administration of significant aspects of welfare provision are of major significance, as discussed in Part V. In Part VIII the book also explores the international context of policy development and the importance of comparative analysis and global trends to any understanding of social policy in the one country. Here, however, we will focus on the development of social policy as an academic subject in the UK, for it has a particularly interesting history, involving even a change of name from *social admin-istration* to *social policy*.

The Development of Social Policy

The development of social policy in the UK can be traced back over a hundred years to the end of the nineteenth century. This is because it is closely linked to the develop-ment of the Fabian Society and to the influ-ence of Fabian politics on policy development in Britain. The Fabian Society was estab-lished in 1884, and was strongly influenced by the work of Sidney Webb, a civil servant who later became a Labour MP. It devel-oped critical analysis of the social and economic problems found in late nine-teenth-century British capitalism and cam-paigned for the introduction of social protection through the state to combat these. Fabian politics were closely linked to the establishment and growth of the Labour Party in Britain, which Webb and others saw as the political vehicle through which policy innovation and reform could be achieved. The early development of Fabian social policy thinking also drew on new research evidence emerging from some of the earliest empirical studies of social prob-lems in the country by people like Charles Booth and B. Seebohm Rowntree, whose research revealed that the extent and depth of poverty in Britain at the end of the nineteenth century were both serious and widespread. This challenged conserva-tive political assumptions that economic markets could meet the welfare needs of all;

and the Fabians used it to argue that policy intervention through the state was needed to provide those forms of support and protection which markets could not.

In fact, of course, it was some time before the Labour Party did achieve political power in Britain, and important reforms were introduced before this by the Liberal governments of the early twentieth century. The context for these reforms was influenced significantly by a review of the Poor Laws, the mainstay of nineteenth-century welfare policy, by a Royal Commission established in 1905. The work of the commission was an important step in the development of debate about social policy reform in Britain, in part because the commissioners themselves could not agree on the right way forward and so produced two separate reports:

- a Minority Report, which was largely the work of Beatrice Webb, who was married to Sidney and herself a prominent Fabian;
- a Majority Report, which was largely the work of Helen Bosanquet, who, with her husband Bernard, was a leading figure in the Charity Organization Society (COS), a body which co-ordinated voluntary action to relieve poverty.

Both reports stressed the need for policy reform to improve welfare provision. But, whilst the minority Fabian report saw the public provision of state services as the means of achieving this, the majority COS report envisaged a continuing central role for voluntary philanthropic activity. This debate about the balance between state and non-state provision of welfare continued to influence the development of social policy throughout the rest of the twentieth century, as the chapters in Part IV of this book reveal; and the concern to secure the appropriate mix between public and voluntary provision remains a key element in social

policy planning at the beginning of the twenty-first century.

What is particularly significant for our purposes about the policy debate between the Webbs and the Bosanquets, however, is that this did not influence only the development of social policy reform, but extended also into the study and evaluation of policy as it developed. Despite their political differences, both the Webbs and the Bosanquets were concerned to promote the study of social policy as well as the development of welfare reform. And this took concrete form with the establishment by the Webbs of the London School of Economics (LSE) and the incorporation within it of the COS's School of Sociology to form a new Department of Social Sciences and Administration in 1912. This was the first, and most important, base for the study of social policy. Its first new lecturer was Clement Attlee (later Prime Minister in the reforming Labour government after the Second World War); and later members included W. H. Beveridge (architect of the modern social security system, and Director of the LSE from 1919 to 1937), R. H. Tawney (who developed theoretical analysis of poverty and inequality) and T. H. Marshall (whose idea of 'social citizenship' has been used by many as a theoretical basis for understanding the development of social policy in modern society).

The LSE has continued ever since to provide a leading base for the study and evaluation of social policy. In 1950 it appointed Richard Titmuss as the first Professor of Social Administration in the UK, and during the 23 years before he died he became a leading figure in the academic study of social policy throughout the developed world. Titmuss's major contributions to the development of the study of social policy have now been collected together into a single volume (see Guide to Further Sources), and his writing remains at the centre of academic debates about theory and practice today. Some of the contributors to this *Companion* come from the LSE's current Department of Social Policy; but the study of social policy has now extended much further than this. Over the last fifty years, social policy teaching and research have spread to most other universities in Britain, and have been taken up more widely in schools and colleges too. There are also major research centres in a number of universities, and other independent agencies and think-tanks providing specialist research and consultancy in particular fields or from different perspectives.

What is more, as we shall see shortly, this wider development of teaching and research has promoted debate and controversy over the aims and methods of study and over the direction of, and priorities for, research and policy reform – and this has provided a challenge to the Fabianism which dominated debate within social policy until the 1970s.

- Much of the early teaching of social policy was geared to the training of social workers and others to act as providers within existing welfare services – it was focused upon how to administer welfare, rather than upon what welfare should be administered.
- Much of the early research work concentrated on measuring poverty and other social problems in order to provide evidence of the need for policy intervention – it was focused upon measurement of social need, rather than upon definitions of need or debate about the appropriateness of seeking to respond to it.

These broader questions became much more important as social policy expanded and developed in the latter quarter of the twentieth century. However, in the middle of the century such questions seemed to a large extent to be answered by the introduction of a 'welfare state' by the Labour government of 1945–51. At this stage, the debate about the direction of reform appeared to have been won conclusively by the Fabian supporters of state welfare, and the focus of academic study upon the training of state welfare workers and the empirical measurement of new welfare needs appeared to have been established as the orthodoxy for all.

The Welfare State and the Welfare Consensus

The creation of what has come to be called the welfare state in the years immediately following the Second World War remains the major development in social policy in the UK and is central to the study of it, although in fact the depiction of these reforms as a 'welfare state' is a controversial and contested one. It begs questions about what we mean by this and why these particular reforms should be seen as achieving it; and these questions are matters of significant debate and disagreement. Nevertheless, the post-war welfare state thesis has been widely promulgated – and for important and obvious reasons.

Part of the reason for the electoral success of the Labour government in 1945 was its manifesto commitment to introduce state provision to meet major welfare needs – and to do this on a comprehensive basis, replacing the piecemeal and partial provision which had been developed in the earlier part of the century. This message had been prefigured in Beveridge's famous report on the need for comprehensive social security reform, published in 1942 and included in Labour's manifesto promises. Beveridge had written about the 'Five Giant Social Evils' which had undermined British society before the war: ignorance, disease, idleness, squalor and want. He argued that it was in the interests of all citizens to remove these evils from British society, and it was the duty of the state, as the representative body of all citizens, to act to do this.

In the years following the war, comprehensive state provision to combat each was introduced:

- free education up to age 15 (later 16), to combat ignorance;
- a national health service (NHS) free at the point of use, to combat disease;
- state commitment to securing full employment, to combat idleness;
- public housing for all citizens to rent, to combat squalor;
- national insurance benefits for all in need, to combat want.

All of these required the development of major state services for citizens and they resulted in a major extension of state responsibility – and state expenditure. Many of the reforms were enacted by the post-war Labour government; but despite their Fabian roots they were not supported only by Labour. Indeed, the state education plans had been introduced by a Conservative member of the coalition government (R. A. Butler) in 1944, and the Conservative governments of the 1950s supported the spirit of the reforms and maintained their basic structure. This cross-party consensus on state welfare was so strong that it even acquired an acronym – Butskellism – made up from the names of the Labour Chancellor (Gaitskell) and his Conservative successor (Butler).

For Fabian social policy, therefore, the post-war welfare state could be seen as the culmination of academic and political influence on government and, after this, analysis and debate focused more on the problems of how to administer and improve existing state welfare than on the question of whether these were appropriate mechanisms for the social promotion of well-being. However, this narrow Fabian focus within post-war social policy did not last for long. It was soon under challenge from other perspectives which queried both the success and the desirability of state welfare.

Theoretical Pluralism

From the 1970s onwards, the focus of social policy began to move beyond the narrow confines of Fabian welfare-statism. This was symbolized most dramatically by a change (at the annual conference in 1987) in the name of the academic subject from 'social administration' to 'social policy', primarily because it was felt that social administration was associated too closely with a focus upon analysis of the operation of existing welfare services, whereas social policy encompassed a more general concern with analysis of the political and ideological bases of welfare provision. This change was representative of more general trends within academic and political debate to embrace a wider range of conflicting perspectives challenging the orthodoxy of Fabianism, and to move academic study towards a more open theoretical pluralism in which questions of *whether* or *why* to pursue state welfare became more important than questions of *how* or *when*.

The new left

The predominant focus of Fabianism on the success and desirability of state welfare was challenged in the 1960s and 1970s by critics on the left. Drawing on Marxist analysis of capitalist society, they argued that welfare services had not replaced the exploitative relationships of the labour market; and that, although they had provided some benefits for the poor and the working class, these services had also helped to support future capitalist development by providing a secure base for the market economy to operate. Unlike the Fabian socialists of the early twentieth century, these new left critics did not necessarily see the further expansion of the existing state welfare base of social policy as resolving this dilemma. Indeed, for them, state welfare was in a constant state of contradiction, or conflict, between the pressure to meet the welfare needs of citizens and the pressure to support the growth of capitalist economic markets.

The new right

In the 1970s and 1980s, rather different criticisms of state welfare began to appear from the right of the political spectrum. Right-wing proponents of free market capitalism, most notably Friedrich von Hayek, had been critical of the creation of the welfare state in the 1940s, but at the time these had been marginal voices in academic and political debate. In the 1970s, as the advent of economic recession revealed some of the limitations of state welfare, these voices became both more vocal and more widely supported – especially after the move to the right of the Conservative Party following the election of Margaret Thatcher as leader in 1975. The essence of the new right critique is that the development of extensive state welfare services is incompatible with the maintenance of a successful market economy, and that this problem will get worse as welfare expands to meet more and more social needs. For them, the desirability of state welfare itself is called into question.

New social movements

The failings and limitations of state welfare also came under challenge in the late twentieth century from perspectives outside the traditional left/right political spectrum. Most significant here was the challenge by feminism to the unequal treatment of men and women in the development and delivery of welfare services. As feminists pointed out, the provision of welfare was 'gendered'. Others have also challenged traditional analysis of state welfare to address a wider range of social divisions and social issues in analysing social policy. Anti-racists have pointed out that welfare services can

be discriminatory and exclusive; disability campaigners have suggested that the needs of certain social groups can be systematically ignored; and environmentalists have argued that existing service provision is predicated upon economic development which cannot be sustained over the longer term.

The new pragmatism

The new radical voices which began to influence social policy towards the end of the twentieth century have had widely varying, and sometimes mutually conflicting, implications. They challenged state welfare and the orthodoxy of Fabianism, but they were also critical of the new left and the new right. At the beginning of the twenty-first century these differing perspectives have resulted in a theoretical pluralism which has not only transformed academic study but has also shifted the focus of policy-making itself. The Labour governments of the new century have openly eschewed the policy programmes of the Fabian left and the new right, and have appealed instead for a 'third way' for social policy in which private and public welfare are openly combined. There is much debate about what is meant by this new Third Way politics (see chapter 12); but its embracement of the legacy of theoretical pluralism has resulted in a more pragmatic approach to policy planning – captured in the phrase 'what counts is what works'.

Emerging Issues: The Future of Social Policy

At the beginning of the twenty-first century, therefore, social policy has developed from its Fabian roots at the LSE and its support for the welfare state reforms of the early post-war years to embrace a wide range of diverse – and conflicting – theoretical debates about both the value and the success of public welfare provision and a wider conceptualization of the policy context as the product of local and global action as well as national politics. Social policy is now characterized by theoretical and geographical pluralism. It is also characterized by 'welfare pluralism': the recognition that state provision is only one feature of a broader mixture of differing forms and levels of welfare service.

We can capture these new pluralisms within social policy as the product of a shift in the focus of study from the *welfare state* to the *welfare mix* – and this is a shift which is likely to develop further during the early part of this century. As all social scientists know, social forces, and hence social policies too, are dynamic. The legacy of the past will continue to structure the agenda for study in the future; but change is always taking place. And in social policy, trends for future change are already being set:

- We are moving beyond state-based welfare, to focus not only upon public services but also upon partnerships between the state and other providers

of welfare and well-being and on the role of the state as a subsidizer and a regulator of the actions of others.

- We are moving beyond the provider culture, to focus not only upon questions of who provides welfare services but also on examination of who uses and benefits from these and how access to such benefits is determined, or prevented.

- We are moving beyond a focus upon policy development within the nation-state to embrace also the impact of global forces and global actors on social policy and the importance of comparative analysis of issues of welfare and well-being.

These changes will accentuate further the overlap and the collaboration between social policy and the study of other cognate subjects such as sociology, economics, politics and law. However, it is just such interdisciplinary flexibility which has always been a central feature of the study of social policy – that this is likely to develop and to grow is a sign of continuing academic vitality and strength.

Guide to Further Sources

There are no textbooks dealing with the history and development of the discipline of social policy, but M. Bulmer, J. Lewis and D. Piachaud (eds), *The Goals of Social Policy* (Unwin Hyman, 1989) is an interesting review and history of the work of the leading department at the London School of Economics. The major work of Richard Titmuss, undoubtedly the founding father of the subject, is now gathered together, with commentaries, in P. Alcock, H. Glennerster, A. Oakley and A. Sinfield (eds), *Welfare and Wellbeing* (Policy Press, 2001).

More recently, however, a number of authors have sought to provide introductory guides to the discipline. The most well established is M. Hill, *Understanding Social Policy*, 7th edn (Blackwell, 2003), which provides a service-based review of welfare policy. P. Alcock, *Social Policy in Britain*, 3rd edn (Palgrave, 2008), takes a broader approach, covering also key questions of structure, context and issues. J. Baldock, N. Manning, S. Miller and S. Vickerstaff (eds), *Social Policy*, 3rd edn (Oxford University Press, 2007), is a collection which covers both contextual issues and service areas. K. Blakemore, *Social Policy: An Introduction*, 3rd edn (Open University Press, 2007) uses key social policy questions to provide a different perspective on provision in different service areas. C. Bochel,

H. Bochel, R. Page and R. Sykes, *Social Policy: Issues and Development* (Prentice Hall, 2005) is a broad and accessible collection on topical issues in social policy.

A collection of topical essays on UK policy issues is also provided by N. Ellison and C. Pearson, *Developments in British Social Policy*, 2nd edn (Palgrave, 2003). Finally, the Social Policy Association produces an annual collection of topical essays, *Social Policy Review* (Policy Press). A useful website providing introductory material on social policy is maintained by Paul Spicker at: <http://www2.rgu.ac.uk/publicpolicy/introduction/main.htm>.

Chapter 2

Methods and Approaches in Social Policy Research

Saul Becker

Overview

- Social policy is a research-informed and research-orientated discipline. Research methods and approaches, and research evidence, form an essential part of the foundation on which the discipline's knowledge and practice base is built.
- Students of social policy need to have a good understanding of the wide range of approaches and methods in social policy research, including how to read critically and make judgements about the quality of published research, and how to conduct their own investigations.
- Social policy draws from the full range of social science research approaches, quantitative and qualitative methods, and research designs with established procedures for how to review the existing literature, and for collecting and analysing data, within an ethical framework.
- There is no universally superior research design or research method – they are only as good as their suitability to the research question(s) being asked.

The Research Foundation for Social Policy

Social policy, as an academic subject and as a field of social action and practice, requires the rigorous linking of theoretical analysis with empirical inquiry. Thus, social policy is a research-informed and research-orientated discipline. The research methods, designs and approaches used in social policy, and the evidence generated from research inquiries, are the foundation on which the discipline (its multilayered analysis, theory and knowledge) and its application (policy-making, implementation, action, social change, evaluation) are built.

Social policy is to a large extent the study of policy practice in order to contribute to policy reform. It combines both descriptive and prescriptive elements. For social policy analysis and practice to be robust and trustworthy there is a need – as in all academic subjects and areas of practice – for knowledge and action to be based on a foundation of reliable research evidence generated through the appropriate application of research designs and methods of data collection and analysis, collected within an ethical framework.

Students of social policy are expected to have a good knowledge of research methods and approaches. They need to:

- be aware, and make use of, the more significant sources of data about social welfare and the main research methods used to collect and analyse data;
- seek out, use, evaluate and analyse qualitative and quantitative data derived from social surveys and other research publications;
- understand the strengths, weaknesses and uses of social research and research methods;
- develop a critical ability to assess, summarize, synthesize and comment on different forms of research evidence;
- undertake investigations of social questions, issues and problems, requiring skills in problem identification; collection, storage, management, manipulation and analysis of data; the construction of coherent and reasoned arguments and the presentation of clear conclusions and recommendations (Social Policy Association 2007).

While there are other important sources of 'evidence' that contribute alongside research to the knowledge and practice base of social policy, knowledge that is generated from research is the only 'way of knowing' that provides a systematic procedure for establishing the reliability and trustworthiness of the knowledge base and for assessing the superiority of one claim over another (Becker and Bryman 2004). While welfare service users' experiences (see chapter 33) and service providers' perspectives have an important place alongside research in the policy-making and analysis process (because they tell us how policy is experienced in the real world by those on the receiving end of policy and by those implementing policy), there is nonetheless debate as to whether these perspectives carry the same authority as research evidence when it comes to laying the foundations for social policy as an academic discipline.

Research evidence, then, unlike other forms of knowledge, can be systematically tested, refuted or verified using long-established research procedures. To 'count' as research, an inquiry must be conducted in a systematic, disciplined and rigorous way, making use of the most appropriate research designs and methods to collect and analyse data and to answer specific research questions. These transparent and systematic procedures, and the evidence they generate, distinguish research knowledge from other ways of knowing (such as beliefs founded on personal experience, or views based on ideology or religion). Sources of 'experiential' knowledge, from welfare service users, providers of welfare and others, can themselves be subjected to rigorous research inquiry and scrutiny, to determine the extent, representativeness and reliability of the views and their appropriate place within the knowledge base for social policy and practice.

To this end, social policy research needs to test actively existing and alternative forms of knowledge in circumstances where they are most likely to be challenged or refuted. Where research conducted to the highest standards of inquiry cannot prove that these other sources of evidence are wrong, then the social policy knowledge base can be considered to be stronger, more robust and more reliable than before. That is why social policy locates research and research evidence at the centre of its activities: research informs teaching, analysis, theory-building, policy-making, practice and further research. As with all academic disciplines, social policy research conducted in UK universities is periodically scrutinized by panels of subject experts to identify and distinguish the quality of research outputs and publications. The outcome of these Research Assessment Exercises (as they are known) leads to those social policy researchers who are producing the highest quality research being given additional resources to continue to conduct and to develop their investigations.

A distinction is sometimes made between research *for* policy, and research *of* policy, although much social policy research is simultaneously of both types. Research *for* policy is concerned to analyse, understand and inform the various stages of the policy process (from before the formulation of policy through to its implementation). Research *of* policy is concerned with how social problems and issues are defined, agendas set, policy is formulated and decisions are made, and how policy is delivered in the real world, evaluated and changed.

Approaches, Methods and Designs

Social policy draws from the full range of approaches, research designs and methods that are used in the social sciences. In terms of *approaches*, these can include, for example, feminist research, user participatory research, action research, evaluation research and post-structuralist approaches to research. These approaches each have their own assumptions about the nature of the social world and the researcher's and research participant's place within it, and about knowledge creation and the research process itself. These assumptions help to inform the way in which the research is carried out, the selection of methods, the data analysis techniques and the way in which research is written up and reported. Some research-based publications give an explicit statement of the approach and assumptions that are being adopted, while in other publications this is far less transparent.

A *research method* is a technique for gathering data, like a questionnaire, interview or observation. A *research design* is a structure or framework within which data are collected (for example, an experimental or longitudinal design). Research methods can serve different designs. Thus, a method of data collection such as a questionnaire can be employed in connection with many, if not all, research designs. Decisions about appropriate research methods are in a sense subsidiary to decisions about an appropriate design, since it is the research design that provides the framework for answering research questions.

Whatever the approach, design or methods used in a study, *all* research needs to be conducted in a systematic and rigorous way if it is to be a reliable knowledge base for social policy analysis and practice. There are established procedures in the social sciences and social policy by which research ideas and questions are formulated, for reviewing the existing body of knowledge on a subject, and for collecting and analysing data and drawing conclusions. The choice of research design and method(s) will also be critically informed by what is already known about an issue and what still needs to be found out.

An early stage of the research process involves a review of the available literature. This needs to be as comprehensive as possible – there may be answers here already to the questions that are of current concern. It is important to have some explicit and transparent way of distinguishing between different publications and for deciding which to include in the literature review, not least because of the sheer volume of information that is now publicly available and the need to recognize that not everything can or should be read or included. Researchers need a way of distinguishing between existing studies based on 'quality' and other criteria. 'Systematic reviews' are one way of conducting literature searches and reviews. These are comprehensive literature reviews with studies chosen in a systematic way and summarized according to explicit criteria. These forms of review are valued highly in medicine and healthcare research and are increasingly being used, in developing forms, within social policy.

Depending on the specific research question(s) to be addressed, in some cases just one research method may be used within an overall design or approach. This could be a quantitative method, such as a large-scale questionnaire survey, or a qualitative method, such as in-depth interviews. In other cases there may be an integration of different methods, which can bring with it specific research advantages and improve the comprehensiveness of the data and analysis. This multi-strategy research is commonly referred to as a 'mixed methods' study, and it is important to be able to explain and justify why different methods are being integrated in the way that they are rather than the alternative of using a single method or other approach. Mixed methods research has become more accepted, common and popular in social policy and has helped to bridge the gap that has sometimes divided quantitative and qualitative researchers in other social science subjects.

Each research design and method, or combination of methods, has its own strengths and limitations, and those conducting research, and students of social policy, need to be aware of the appropriateness or otherwise of the approaches, designs and methods used in any published inquiry. Students need to develop a critical ability to 'read' research-based publications, not just for their findings and conclusions, but also to make judgements about whether or not the research methods have been used appropriately. Which studies are the most trustworthy? Which studies are of the highest quality? In answering these and other questions, students need to know about quantitative and qualitative methods and what counts as quality in social policy research.

Quantitative and Qualitative Research

Quantitative and qualitative research approaches each have a distinctive cluster of concerns, preoccupations and assumptions. *Quantitative* research adopts an objectivist position with respect to the nature of social reality. This means that social phenomena and social reality are generally construed as 'out there' for social actors, as entities that confront them as out of their scope of influence. In thinking of social reality in an objectivist manner, quantitative researchers display a commitment to a natural science model of the research process, since the natural order is frequently conceptualized as a pre-existing phenomenon awaiting the analytic tools of the scientist. Thus, there is a commitment to provide rigorous measures of concepts that drive the research and an interest to demonstrate causal relationships between variables. Statistical tests are commonly used. There is also a concern to allow generalization from the research to a wider population, and for the study to be replicable by others seeking to confirm or to refute the findings. The approach taken by quantitative researchers also typically involves a deductive approach to the relationship between theory and research, involving the drawing of research questions from an established body of existing knowledge which are then tested for their soundness. Finally, quantitative research has well-developed and internationally understood criteria that are sometimes employed for assessing the quality of research, centring on reliability, validity, generalization and replication. While these are widely regarded as important principles, they are not, however, universally observed. It is rare for published social policy research to discuss these criteria explicitly.

By contrast, *qualitative* research tends to be associated with a constructionist position, which pays greater attention to the role that individuals play in constructing their social networks and their influence over them. There is a strong focus on actors' meaning: qualitative researchers aim to understand the behaviour, values, beliefs and so on of the people that they are researching from the perspective of the participants themselves. There is an emphasis on description, context and process. There is also a degree of flexibility in the way in which the research is conducted. Qualitative research adopts an inductive approach to the relationship between theory and research, whereby concepts and theory are generated out of the data, rather than as in the quantitative approach, whereby concepts and theoretical ideas often guide the collection of data. Finally, while there are criteria for determining the quality of qualitative research, there is less agreement about these than is the case with quantitative research.

The decision as to whether to conduct a quantitative, qualitative or mixed methods study in social policy will be determined by many factors, most importantly what it is that needs to be found out and the specific research question(s) to be addressed. How a social issue or a social problem is perceived, and the social policies in place (or not in place) to respond to it, will also influence the type of research that will be conducted. For example, where policies already exist to respond to the needs of lone parents (for example, 'New Deals' designed to assist them into the paid labour market), then these policies can be evaluated to determine whether they work or not, whether they are better than doing something else (or nothing at all) or whether they provide good value for money.

Where an issue has not yet been defined widely as a social issue or social problem (for example, the hidden and problematic nature of children's unpaid caring roles and responsibilities within the family), then other research approaches will need to be used to highlight the issue, perhaps for the first time. Qualitative studies are particularly appropriate here, as they can take us inside a 'hidden world', give a voice to those who are invisible and raise the profile of the issue amongst policy-makers, the media and others. In the case of new or emerging social issues, it is often difficult to conduct a large-scale survey and would be virtually impossible (and inappropriate) to utilize an experimental research design.

At other times, secondary analysis of existing large-scale datasets can help to quantify the extent and characteristics of a problem or even enable it to be reconceptualized. Secondary analysis is when researchers analyse data that they did not themselves collect. For example, Abel-Smith and Townsend's secondary analysis of government data, published in 1965 as *The Poor and the Poorest*, enabled poverty to be reconceptualized and its extent to be measured, and this has had enduring consequences for the ways in which we understand poverty and social exclusion today.

Research data, particularly expensive resources, need to be archived systematically for their potential to be fully exploited through secondary analysis or by future generations of researchers wanting to build upon former findings. It is important that publicly funded research has systems in place to archive data for future interrogation and use.

Ethical considerations underpin all social policy research. For example, it is unacceptable to conduct research that would harm research participants or place researchers themselves in danger. Data must be collected and stored in a way that is safe and secure, and which protects the anonymity of participants. Participants should give their informed consent to taking part in research rather than being coerced, bribed or misled. There are ethical codes and protocols for conducting research in social policy, and other research governance frameworks, and it is important that these are adhered to in all inquiries. It would be seen as an indicator of the quality of a social policy research study where there is evidence that ethical procedures have been followed. Students need to be aware of the ethical implications of their own studies and be able to recognize good or poor ethics in published reports.

'Quality' and 'Hierarchies' in Social Policy Research

If research is to provide a reliable foundation for social policy teaching, analysis and practice, then it goes without saying that the quality of that research must be of a high standard. There is some debate, however, about what counts as 'quality' in social policy research (Becker, Bryman and Sempik 2006). There are some criteria of quality that command widespread support and consensus amongst social policy researchers and research users, while for other criteria there is considerable dissension. However, most social policy researchers do place a high value on research evidence that is written in a way that is accessible to the appropriate audience, that has a research design which clearly addresses the research question(s), that is transparent in explaining the ways in which the data were collected and analysed, that gives an explicit account of the research process, that makes a contribution to knowledge and that includes confirmation that informed consent and the safety of participants have been assured.

In social policy, unlike medicine, healthcare and research in some other natural sciences, there appears to be little consensus or support for a discipline-based 'hierarchy' of research designs or methods, whereby the quality of research can be inferred simply from the method or design used. In medicine and much healthcare research, systematic reviews of randomized controlled trials, meta-analyses, and randomized controlled or quasi-experimental trials are regarded as 'gold standard' approaches to research, commanding status and authority, and forming the research foundation for these subjects' knowledge base. In social policy, there is less reverence for these experimental designs or for statistical meta-analyses, and there is little agreement that these methods and approaches

are by themselves indicators of high quality.

Indeed it is other methods, particularly in-depth interviews and longitudinal studies, which are often more highly regarded by social policy researchers. These same methods would command much lower status in medical and healthcare research. What this indicates is that different research methods are regarded differently across disciplines, and within social policy itself there is considerable debate about which methods and approaches, and criteria, are indicators of high quality (Becker, Bryman and Sempik 2006). The important message from this is that there is no universally superior research design or research method – they are only as good as their suitability to the research question(s) being asked.

Some academics have argued that social policy research needs to make greater use of experiments and trial methodology, rather than rejecting these as inappropriate or unethical. Experiments can contribute to the kinds of knowledge that academics, policy-makers, professionals and the public are interested in. Reliable information about the effectiveness of social policy and social interventions is hard to come by using other means, because experiments offer a robust design for assessing cause and effect. There is a growing interest in the use of experiments in social and public policy, as seen in the growth of a network of researchers, coordinated from York University, which is committed to developing the use of these approaches.

Rather than adopting a 'hierarchy' approach to the use of research methods, social policy academics appear to be more inclined to draw on specific designs, methods or approaches (or combinations of these) which they consider to be the most appropriate for the particular research question(s) that they are addressing. This 'continuum approach' (Becker and Bryman 2004: 57) acknowledges the varying strengths and limitations of different research designs and methods and acknowledges that all designs and methods have an appropriate use and relevance. Systematic reviews, randomized controlled trials and other experimental designs would be considered by many to provide reliable forms of evidence on 'cause and effect', while ethnography and other qualitative methods provide the most appropriate forms of evidence on experiences and processes – especially as understood by research participants themselves. This continuum approach also facilitates the integration of methods, breaking down what has been seen as a 'paradigm war' between those committed to quantitative or qualitative approaches.

Emerging Issues

Social policy will continue to develop and mature as a subject (chapter 1) with research, and knowledge from research, being central to these developments and transformations. There is likely to be a growing interest within social policy to develop and highlight research approaches and methods that might be seen as more 'social policy specific', for example, cross-national research techniques. There will also be an interest in devising appropriate criteria to help judge the quality of published social policy research studies. These criteria may include a list of 'things to look out for' when reading research publications (for example, evidence that informed consent was given by participants; that the research is ethical; that the design and methods were used appropriately; and so on), which students of social policy would also no doubt find of use. But there will also be a growth in 'metrics' indicators of quality, in particular to be used across the university system to judge the quality of research, under the auspices of future Research Assessment Exercises (RAE). All indicators of quality, particularly metrics, are likely to be controversial and disputed, with some researchers in social policy set to gain prestige or valuable research income from a favourable RAE outcome.

The Social Policy Association may develop its own set of ethical guidelines and protocols, to sit alongside those of other learned bodies (for example, the British Sociological Association) and relevant research groups (the Social Research Association). Students of social policy will be encouraged in their degree programmes to develop their research knowledge, skills, critical analysis and evaluation, particularly as these are transferable and will be valued highly in the marketplace.

However, there is likely to be some challenge about the weight that social policy gives to research evidence as a foundation for the discipline, vis-à-vis other forms of knowledge, including welfare service users' perspectives. In other academic areas, such as social work, users' perspectives are permeating throughout, including in direct teaching to students and representation on ethics or other committees. To what extent social policy goes in this direction waits to be seen.

Guide to Further Sources

There are literally hundreds of textbooks on research methods in the social sciences, but only one (at the time of writing) that has been specifically written for social policy students. This is S. Becker and A. Bryman (eds), *Understanding Research for Social Policy and Practice: Themes, Methods and Approaches* (Policy Press, 2004), which provides an overview of all the main research methods and approaches, with research examples and illustrations from a wide range of social policy areas, including Abel-Smith and Townsend's work, *The Poor and The*

Poorest (G. Bell and Sons, 1965). An excellent 'generic' research methods text is A. Bryman, *Social Research Methods*, 2nd edn (Oxford University Press, 2004), which also signposts the reader to other research methods texts. H. Davies, S. Nutley and P. Smith (eds), *What Works? Evidence-Based Policy and Practice in Public Services* (Policy Press, 2000) is a useful book on the relationship between research and policy-making.

For those interested in issues around how to determine 'quality' in social policy research, then S. Becker, A. Bryman and J. Sempik's report, *Defining Quality in Social Policy Research* (Social Policy Association, 2006), provides the first study of how social policy researchers conceptualize 'quality' and offers a framework for discussion. It can be downloaded free from the SPA website at: <http://www.social-policy.com/documents/spaquality06.pdf>. The subject benchmark for social policy identifies what research skills and knowledge social policy students are expected to have – Social Policy Association, *Social Policy and Administration* (Bristol: QAA, 2007). The SPA website also has other useful research resources: see <www.social-policy.com>. The Social Research Association's Code of Ethics can be found at: <http://www.the-sra.org.uk/ethical.htm>.

Chapter 3

History and Social Policy

David Gladstone

Overview

- It is easy to argue that a present- and future-centred subject like social policy has little need of an historical perspective.
- By contrast, this chapter suggests that an understanding of welfare in past time is important in providing an awareness of changes and continuities in relation to risk, resources and responsibility.
- New environmental hazards, demographic patterns and working practices may suggest new 'diswelfares'. But a view over time suggests that continuity as well as change is important in understanding threats to well-being.
- Resources – or responses to risk – show a considerable variety of agencies at work in the past as well as the present. Together they comprise what is often called the mixed economy of welfare.
- There are also longstanding historical continuities in the ideological debate about who should be responsible for responding to risk. Should it be individuals themselves or government action?

Introduction

Those who study social policy are often more concerned with the present and the future than with the past. They engage with current issues about the supply and distribution of welfare. They discuss how social policies might be improved and made more effective and efficient in the future. Why, then, study the past? What can an historical perspective contribute to social policy as an academic subject and as a programme for action? Those themes are central to this chapter.

What is History?

The *Shorter Oxford English Dictionary* defines history as the study of past events. That definition suggests that history is both an academic study or discipline as well as a narrative or chronology of past events. As an academic discipline, history's origins are comparatively recent and are usually attributed to a nineteenth-century German scholar, Leopold von Ranke. Ranke's contribution lay, first of all, in emphasizing that the task of the historian was to understand the past and to provide a narrative of past events. His second contribution was methodological. For Ranke, understanding the past meant uncovering as many documents as could be found and using them as evidence from which to create or construct a narrative history of change.

Documentary or written materials remain an important source of historical evidence. But the range of sources which historians use in their attempts to recreate the past has widened immeasurably since Ranke's time. They now include interviews (often recorded) in which individuals recall experiences and events in their own past, as well as a whole variety of visual and material artefacts from which the past can also be recreated. Jordanova (2000) lists a wide range of examples: seals, maps, photographs, drawings, prints, paintings, jewellery, costume, tools and machines, archaeological remains, buildings, town plans, films: many of them, in her phrase, are 'transparent windows onto past times'. For those interested especially in the history of welfare, children's toys, the legacy of the large barrack-like buildings in which the poor, the mad and the criminal were incarcerated, and the class-segregated housing developments of towns and cities are just such transparent windows onto past times. The past, in other words, is not confined to the written records of previous centuries or generations. It is, in a variety of ways, all around us as a component of our present.

The increasing diversity of sources is, in part at least, a reflection of the growing specialization that has taken place within academic history itself. Whereas history used to be the study of kings and queens, battles, wars and great national events, it is now a much more multifaceted view of the past. One of the most significant developments over the past half-century has been the growth of social history. Once crudely defined as 'history with the politics left out', social history provides a distinctive perspective on the past. As Harold

Perkin, one of its foremost protagonists, expressed it:

> We want to know not only what laws were made or battles fought or even how men [sic] got their living, but what it felt like to be alive, how men [sic] in history – not merely kings and popes, statesmen and tycoons – lived and worked and thought and behaved towards each other.
>
> (*The Structured Crowd*,
> Harvester Press, 1981, p. 24.)

In that quest, the history of welfare is an important ingredient, for it addresses issues of risk and responsibility as part of the way in which state and citizen, men and women, parents and children, and people of different social classes, ethnic origin and economic and political power behaved towards each other in past time.

Specialization in research – whether by period or theme – has resulted in the diversity of history as an academic subject. But it is also necessary to acknowledge that there are a variety of perspectives on the past: not one history, but many histories. As Jordanova (2000) notes, there is 'a diffused awareness of the past that varies from person to person, group to group, country to country'. In part, this is the result of the ideological and experiential baggage which individual scholars bring to their historical inquiry and investigation. That represents a challenge to Ranke's notion that there could be an agreed narrative of events because the widest possible selection of relevant documents had been examined. As Dorothy Porter has noted: 'History writing is no longer dominated by one ideological vantage point even within Western societies where a new multi-cultural mix ensures that a huge variety of historical perspectives has been able to gain legitimate authority' (*Health, Civilization and the State*, Routledge, 1999, p. 4). Furthermore, we are now much more aware that the documentary evidence that has survived from the past was generally written and recorded by those in powerful positions of authority. As such, it is official history. Thus, for example, while much documentary evidence exists concerning the Poor Law, one of the key agencies of British social welfare in the past, there is comparatively little recording the experiences and reactions of those who were on the receiving end of its policies as paupers, whether living at home or in a workhouse. The sources of historical evidence, that is to say, are more often 'top-down' records of policy-makers and administrators rather than 'bottom-up' accounts of the impact of their decisions on the lives of ordinary people.

At the beginning of the twenty-first century the historian's task is thus much more specialist and diverse than it was in the Germany of Ranke two centuries ago; and postmodernism is simply the latest challenge to attempts to reconstruct the past of human experience. Yet the past remains a central feature of the way in which we understand and make sense of the present, not least in welfare and social policy. Present-day ideological and political debates about rights and responsibilities, organizational and administrative arrangements and demarcations between service sectors, as well as the language and terminology of welfare all resonate with echoes of the past. The past may be, in H. E. Bates's phrase, 'a foreign country', but the historical perspective is one which no present-day explorer can afford to ignore. Those who are ignorant of history, as George Santayana observed, are doomed to repeat it.

Themes in Welfare History

It is possible to identify three distinct yet interrelated themes in the historical approach to welfare – risk, resources and responsibility. These themes also link past and present in the study of social policy.

Risk

What were the risks or threats to their well-being to which individuals were exposed in the past? How similar or different are present-day diswelfares? The historian Paul Johnson defines social risk as 'the probability weighted uncertainty that derives from the changing and dynamic world in which people live'. In other words, it constitutes what the social policy tradition tends to define as social problems. Johnson's analysis highlights four categories of risk. Each will now be examined in turn.

Health   It is now well established by demographic historians that death rates only began to fall significantly from the beginning of the twentieth century. In the preceding century there was a high level of infant deaths (until 1900 about 150 in every 1,000 children died in their first year), an average life expectancy of 40 years and a much greater risk of premature death for those living in the expanding industrial towns and cities. The contrast with present-day statistics suggests a considerable improvement or reduction of risk measured by nineteenth-century standards, an improvement which historians explain in different ways. Some see it as the consequence of a general improvement in the financial and material conditions of the population; others as the result of more comprehensive and accessible health services, in the sense both of public and environmental health improvements and of the wider range of medical and clinical treatments that are now available.

Life course   In this category, Johnson highlights the vulnerability of large families with several dependent children and the poverty of old age consequent on declining physical powers and enforced withdrawal from the labour market. Both these categories of risk were identified by B. Seebohm

Rowntree, one of the early social investigators at the beginning of the twentieth century, in his discussion of the life cycle of poverty based on his research in York. With the high infant mortality rates of the nineteenth century, a large number of children represented an insurance for care of their parents in old age; while, as life expectancy improved, so too did the poverty that invariably accompanied the final phase of the life course. The abolition of child and family poverty was one of the priorities of the New Labour government elected in 1997. Similarly, it is now generally recognized that there are two nations in old age: those who have the benefit of occupational pensions and those who are dependent on the state retirement pension.

Economic and occupational Economic risks are very much determined by the availability and remuneration of paid employment. In the second half of the nineteenth century, on average some 4.5 per cent of male workers were unemployed, but of greater significance at that time was underemployment. Workers in many trades and industries were hired and paid by the day on a casual basis. Such irregularity of employment had considerable effects on household finances which became more precarious when the main wage-earner was ill, became disabled or died. Though the unemployment rate has fallen in recent years, the experience of unemployment still impacts on individual self-worth, as well as the economic and social well-being of the household unit.

Environmental The final type of risk in Johnson's analysis is that which results from living in a physically hazardous world. This category ranges, therefore, from all types of accident to industrial pollution and environmental hazard on a grander scale, such as that occasioned by climate change. It has been observed that it is those near the bottom of the social scale who are most exposed to hazards at work – something

which accords very closely with the historical evidence on the nineteenth century. One study of coal-mining, for example, notes that between 1869 and 1919 a miner was killed every six hours, seriously injured every two hours and injured badly every two or three minutes.

Resources

Historians have not only researched the risks and threats to welfare in the past; they have also mapped the strategies of survival and sources of available support. That evidence shows the existence of a mixed economy welfare system in the nineteenth century, in which a developing diversity of agencies, formal and informal, played an often overlapping role.

Household strategies, often initiated by women who deprived themselves in the interests of their husbands and children, were an important resource, as were the earnings of children even after the introduction of compulsory elementary schooling in 1880. Mutual support networks existed in working-class communities and faith-based organizations also provided support for some. Self-help organizations, such as savings banks and commercial insurance, provided a means for those with a regular and reliable income to save against the eventuality of hazards and risks. This was especially important at a time when most medical treatment required payment and when the accident or death of the principal wage-earner could create considerable financial difficulties for the household unit. The trade union movement and the friendly societies, controlled by those of the working class themselves, provided a range of benefits for their members and their dependants at times of unemployment, ill health or death, based on the payment of weekly subscriptions – although the benefits of membership were limited to those who were able to pay the weekly dues. Membership of such organizations thus became one of the defining characteristics of the so-called *respectable* working class.

Philanthropic charity expanded dramatically during the nineteenth century, coordinated to some extent by the Charity Organization Society (see chapter 1). Philanthropy encompassed housing schemes, schools and specialist hospitals (such as Great Ormond Street Hospital for Sick Children), as well as many of the voluntary societies which still exist today (such as the children's charity Barnardo's). At the time, some critics deplored the unorganized spread of philanthropic endeavour, seeing it as an encouragement to dependency and pauperization, although more recent criticism has stressed the intrusions made into working-class households by the middle-class 'lady' visitors of many local charitable associations.

The state – both centrally and locally – became more proactively involved in aspects of welfare during the course of the nineteenth century. The long-established system of state-provided financial assistance – the Poor Law – was reformed in the interests of the emerging industrial society in 1834, and parliamentary legislation was also introduced in relation both to public health and elementary education. But despite the activity of the encroaching state, the level of intervention and public spending remained small and much welfare provision remained largely localized and amateur.

By contrast, the twentieth century was characterized by more extensive state-provided welfare and a growing professionalization of welfare activities. A variety of social legislation passed by the Liberal government between 1906 and 1914 encompassed the provision of school meals, school medical inspection and old age pensions, as well as the creation of a national scheme of sickness and unemployment insurance which was progressively expanded during the inter-war years. But it was the classic welfare state developed between 1944 and 1948 in legislation passed by the wartime coalition and post-war Labour government that provided a more comprehensive coverage of risks – from the cradle to the grave – of the British population. The 5 July 1948 was the appointed day for the introduction of the National Health Service and the schemes of post-war social security and financial assistance. It was described by the Prime Minister Clement Attlee as 'a day which makes history'.

The introduction of a more comprehensive system of state-provided welfare meant something of a readjustment in the roles of other suppliers in the mixed economy of welfare. But though their roles may have been redefined over the past sixty years in relation to changing state activity, each of the sources of formal and informal assistance and support continue to operate; and Britain's welfare system today is made up of a diversity of responses to risk, just as in the past.

Responsibility

Historians do not only describe change, they also seek to explain it. In that task, Britain's welfare system is a fertile area for investigation of both particular policy changes and more general and significant transformations. At the general level is the comparative historical study, which locates the development of welfare states in Europe and America in the context of political mobilization (the voter motive in the conditions of mass democracy) and specific levels of economic development (i.e. when sufficient resources are available to yield the tax revenues necessary to fund public welfare services), whereas more detailed studies of particular policy changes indicate a wide range of change agents. In the middle are theories drawn from a number of historical case studies which explain change in more conceptual terms such as:

- Legitimacy: is this an area in which government is legitimately involved?

- Feasibility: is the proposed change feasible in terms, for example, of resources?
- Support: is the change in question likely to enhance rather than diminish government support?

Such a framework indicates the inevitably political and value-laden nature of welfare state change and takes the historian into the history of ideas and political debate. What an historical perspective suggestively indicates is that current discourse around the respective welfare responsibilities of state and citizen is in fact by no means new. Political discussion has been around for the past century and more, and over that time a number of distinct ideological positions have been developed, many of which still influence policy debates today (see Part II). These different ideological positions raise important questions for the historian about the changing role of the state in welfare and the factors which can explain the greater comprehensiveness of the classic welfare state of the 1940s, the much discussed 'crisis' of the welfare state in the 1970s which provided the springboard for the Thatcherite agenda of rolling back the frontiers of the state, and the third way between state and market promoted by Labour at the beginning of the twenty-first century.

One final issue that needs to be considered in the context of responsibility is the objective of state welfare. Whereas earlier writers on Britain's welfare past tended to portray it as an essentially beneficent activity, more recent critical commentators have emphasized the functional necessity of public welfare in a capitalist economy, and its role in regulating the poor.

Emerging Issues: The Historiography of the Welfare State

Early studies written in the aftermath of the creation of Britain's classic welfare state in the mid-twentieth century, with titles such as *The Coming of the Welfare State*, tended to be Whiggish in character – that is they characterized the emergence of comprehensive state welfare as a unilinear progression from the 'darkness' of the nineteenth-century Poor Law to the 'light' of the Beveridge Plan of 1942 and the post-war welfare state. These Whiggish accounts saw comprehensive public welfare as part of a generally beneficent process, although, as we mentioned earlier, more modern commentators would dispute that welfare provision has been an unqualified benefit for all.

Such a 'welfare state escalator' view of history has therefore largely been replaced in more recent accounts by the mixed economy approach. This recognizes the continuance of the diversity of welfare suppliers, the growth of state intervention and the changing role of the state (from direct service provider to financier and regulator of other agencies) and the moving frontier between providers that has characterized both the present and the past of welfare. It is this dynamic that has made these historical studies of social policy, drawing on a wider range of sources, more stimulating than previous teleological accounts.

Increasingly, too, more recent studies of welfare have pushed back beyond the nineteenth and twentieth centuries. The Poor Law, it is true, has a long history dating from the sixteenth century, and historical studies of welfare have ranged over its total time frame. But there is now much more attention to a wider range of risk and resources in earlier historical periods which encompasses households and families, philanthropy, community and informal networks.

Furthermore, the British experience is now increasingly set within a wider geographical context of comparative study. Such research has challenged both the notion of the primacy of Britain's welfare state (itself a German term of the 1920s) and located the British experience within a broader discussion of welfare state regimes. It is appropriate, therefore, to end with Jane Lewis's observation:

> Rather than seeing the story of the modern welfare state as a simple movement from individualism to collectivism and ever increasing amounts of (benevolent) state intervention, it is more accurate to see European countries as having had mixed economies of welfare in which the state, the voluntary sector, employers, the family and the market have played different parts at different points in time.
>
> (Lewis J, 'The voluntary sector in the mixed economy of welfare', in D. Gladstone (ed.), *Before Beveridge: Welfare Before the Welfare State*, IEA Health and Welfare Unit, 1999, p. 11)

Guide to Further Sources

D. Gladstone, *The Twentieth Century Welfare State* (Macmillan, 1999) is a review of twentieth-century welfare from the mixed economy perspective. H. Glennerster, *British Social Policy since 1945* (Blackwell, 2006) is an authoritative account and the third edition includes a discussion of recent policy directions. R. Lowe, *The Welfare State in Britain since 1945* (Palgrave, 2005) is a detailed study of the period of the classic welfare state set within a useful theoretical perspective, covering Thatcherism and New Labour in Part III. R. Page and R. Silburn, *British Social Welfare in the Twentieth Century* (Macmillan, 1999) provides a well-selected series of essays reviewing political ideas, sectors of the welfare state, and welfare outside the state across the last century.

B. Harris, *The Origins of the British Welfare State* (Palgrave, 2004) is a comprehensive and well-documented study of social welfare between 1800 and 1945. Although its primary focus is the introduction and development of state-provided services, it also discusses other suppliers. P. Johnson, 'Risk, redistribution and social welfare in Britain from the poor law to Beveridge', in M. Daunton ed., *Charity, Self-Interest and Welfare in the English Past* (UCL Press, 1996; 2nd edn, 2000) examines how a variety of welfare instruments were used to reduce the incidence of social risk between the late nineteenth century and the Second World War. L. Jordanova, *History in Practice* (Arnold, 2000) is a stimulating and wide-ranging study of recent historical scholarship and what is involved in studying history.

The most relevant website is <www.historyandpolicy.org>. The Institute of Historical Research's web site, <www.history.ac.uk>, contains good links to other sites and sources.

Chapter 4

Social Needs, Social Problems, Social Welfare and Well-being

Nick Manning

Overview

- Social welfare refers to the various social arrangements that exist to meet the needs of individuals and groups in society, and to tackle social problems.
- Basic definitions of need include subjectively-felt need, needs defined for us by others, usually experts or professionals, and needs as revealed, perhaps in surveys, in comparison with other people in the same social group.
- Measuring needs remains a contested problem, with some favouring a bedrock of objective basic necessities and others arguing that personal perception is fundamental.
- Social problems, which are related to, but not the same as, social needs, are also the concern of social welfare institutions. C. Wright Mills famously observed that one person suffering from unemployment may be in acute need, but it is only widespread unemployment that is a social problem.
- The word 'policy' implies that social policy is part of the political processes and institutions of modern society; social needs, social problems and social welfare are similarly political.
- Individual well-being is a new focus of concern, but this too is a contested concept, open to subjective, objective, political and comparative definitions, and subject to the pressures of both professional and mass media fashions.

Introduction

The study of social policy focuses on the way in which social welfare is organized to meet the needs of individuals and groups, for healthcare, shelter, food, clothing and so on. It is also concerned with the way in which social problems are recognized and dealt with. In this chapter, I will examine the growth and structure of social welfare provision, introduce some basic definitions of need, review the debates that have developed about this concept and examine the way it is used in practice. I will also discuss ideas about social problems, the way these are related to needs and to social welfare provision, and the considerable debates about this. Finally, there is a brief introduction to the idea of well-being.

What is Social Welfare?

Social welfare refers to the various social arrangements that exist to meet the needs of individuals and groups in society, and to tackle social problems. Our use of the term 'social policy' in modern times implies that social welfare means government welfare. This is not at all the case. Welfare for most people is still provided through other social mechanisms than the state, of which there are three main types: family and friends, the market, and non-governmental organizations (NGOs) such as voluntary organizations, mutual associations and charities. Social policy as an area of study is concerned with the way in which all these institutions affect the welfare of individuals and groups, and is taken up in more detail in some of the chapters in Part VII.

Box 4.1   Types of social welfare institution

- family
- market
- NGOs (non-governmental organizations)
- the welfare state

Social policy is a branch of social science. From this point of view, the basic conditions for the existence and survival of individual people are necessarily social. No individual, however resourceful, could survive for long in isolation. Human beings, in contrast to many other animals, are not capable of mediating directly with nature without mechanisms of cooperation and a division of labour between individuals. This is illustrated well by the long period of dependence that children need for them to become adults. The family, then, may be taken as the archetypal social welfare institution, both in fact and as an ideal. Markets, governments and NGOs are, by comparison, modern developments.

Families not only meet a whole variety of social needs at various stages of our lives, but they are at the same time the

object themselves of government and academic concern. Of course, families come in different shapes and sizes, as is discussed in chapter 21. With the lengthening of life expectancy, the steady rise in the rate of marriage dissolution and the consequent growth of sole parenthood, the classic family form of two parents and dependent children has now become a minority structure within the overall mix of households. Nevertheless, over time the majority of people will at some point experience this pattern as children, and in turn as parents themselves.

Taking an historical view, however, the modern family provides less welfare than it did two hundred years ago. Hospitals, schools, shops, workplaces, transport and leisure facilities have developed to fulfil a variety of functions which mean that social welfare provision has become a more complex and mixed system than it used to be. Much of this change occurred in the nineteenth century, when hospitals, schools, shops and factories came to prominence. Two rival mechanisms underlay these changes: the market and NGOs. The market developed in two senses relevant to social welfare. The first sense is the market in labour as individual workers shifted increasingly from agriculture towards industrial wage labour. The vicissitudes of this means of livelihood threw up new insecurities whenever the availability of, or ability to, work stopped. The second sense is the market in goods and services, such as food, clothes and medical care, that accompanied these changes, and through which families increasingly met their various needs rather than through self-provisioning. Inability to pay could have disastrous consequences for a range of needs of family members.

Alongside the market, and very often in response to its failures to provide either adequately waged work or adequately priced goods and services, NGOs developed. However, this was not always for humanitarian reasons. On the one hand, for example, mutual associations such as friendly societies were indeed designed for the mutual benefit of members when social needs arose. By contrast, however, the settlement house movement for the 'improvement' of working-class lives was also motivated by fear of upper-middle-class organizers concerning the consequences of poverty lifestyles, such as the spread of disease, for all social classes. In addition, there were also concerns about the costs of market failure, not to individual victims, but to those who might have to pick up the pieces. For example, in the later part of the nineteenth century, the provision of education was motivated by the employment needs of industrialists, and the provision of agreed compensation for industrial accidents was designed to avoid more expensive court proceedings.

For a while, the market and NGOs enjoyed considerable independence from the attentions of government, but there was a growing concern by the end of the nineteenth century to regulate their activities. In the twentieth century, regulation led to the provision of financial support and eventually to state provision of welfare services. Motives for this were again mixed. Genuine humanitarian concern for the meeting of social needs coexisted with the fear of social problems threatening the wider social order, and the realization that the costs of social reproduction (both the biological production of children for the future workforce and the daily replenishment of the capacity for work) might be better organized by the state. The climax of this process was the establishment of the British welfare state by the Labour government of the 1940s.

All these institutions of social welfare, family, market, state and NGO continue to coexist, but with regular changes in their functions and scope, most recently under the impact of processes of 'modernization' by the New Labour government. State regulation has been strengthened in these recent years, while privatization and market mechanisms have been encouraged to the point where social welfare can increasingly be thought of as a consumption good. Nevertheless, the level of state expenditure on social welfare has remained at about 25 per cent of gross national product (GNP), albeit covering a steadily changing mix in favour of social security and health services, and away from education and housing.

What are Social Needs?

While I have suggested that there were mixed motives for organizing social welfare institutions, the meeting of social needs remains their central concern. We must therefore review the definition of this crucial concept. A useful starting point is to distinguish needs from two related notions: wants and preferences. There are two important senses in which wants and needs differ. First, wants are more inclusive: we may want things that we do not need; indeed, marketing experts make great efforts to persuade us to do so. Second, we may need things that we do not want, either through ignorance or our dislike of them. Medical intervention can often be of this type. Both these distinctions from want suggest that needs are more basic or essential to us than wants.

Preferences, a concept frequently used in economic analyses, differ from needs and wants in the sense that they are revealed only when we make choices, usually in the act of buying goods or services as consumers. The argument here is that it is difficult really to know what people need or want unless they act in some way to try to secure for themselves the things in question. This action component however has its limits, for of course wants cannot be revealed in the market if we do not have the money to pay for things, and needs cannot be revealed by individuals where they are not aware of them, or there are no services to meet them. Needs, then, may well have to be discovered by those other than the individual concerned.

We should also make a distinction between needs and social needs. Needs (and problems and welfare) are 'social' in the sense that they are not merely concerned with, for example, individual causes and experiences of illness and poverty, but also with the amount and distribution of illness and poverty in different social groups, the reasons for this that arise out of the shared conditions of life for those social groups, and the social structures and processes through which they might be ameliorated. For example, it is only necessary to vaccinate a proportion of the population to stop the spread of infectious disease. In this case, the population can be seen to have a need, but any specific individual may not necessarily feel, or be defined by others as, in need. Waiting in line for an injection, we may all have felt this way as children.

Box 4.2   Needs, wants and preferences

- needs
  - felt need
  - expertly defined need
  - comparative need
- wants
- preferences

These considerations enable us to make some simple classification of types of need. First are those needs of which we are ourselves aware: felt needs. These are obvious when we feel ill, or have an accident. The second type of needs are those defined for us by others, usually experts or professionals, such as doctors or teachers, but also importantly by family and friends. The third type of need is partly an extension of the second, a focus on needs as revealed, perhaps in surveys, in comparison with other people in the same social group. Here an individual can be said to be in comparative need because others have something that they do not.

An important aspect of needs, shared by all three types, has given rise to many debates in social policy. This is the question of how needs can be measured, particularly when we move away from the obvious examples such as major medical emergencies. The classic case is that of poverty. How much income do we need? One approach, drawing on the second type of need as defined by experts, is to think about the basic essentials, such as food, clothing and shelter, and to work out the amount of money needed to buy the cheapest minimal provision of these, and to define anyone with less as poor or in need.

However, any close study of the way in which poor people live reveals that the notion of 'basic essentials' or 'cheapest minimal provision' varies with the way of life of the particular family and community in which an individual lives. Is television an essential? Is meat-eating essential? What cultural prescriptions about dress codes are essential?

An alternative approach is to use the first type of need, and merely to ask poor people what they feel they need. However, where this has been done, it seems that poor people often adjust to their circumstances and feel less in need than they 'ought' to, especially if they are older people; while others can feel poor where they 'ought' not to. Finally, we could merely define as poor those people with less than others, as in the third type of need, comparative need, for example by ranking incomes and identifying, say, the bottom 10 per cent as poor.

This problem of measurement has resulted in an oscillation in social policy debates between those who favour an objective interpretation of what is 'basic' or 'essential', for example in terms of the ability of an individual to remain alive and to retain the capacity to act as a 'person' in society (Doyal and Gough 1985), and those who argue that needs are really more subjectively defined by individuals themselves, experts, and government agencies and others who provide services designed to meet needs (Piachaud 1981).

What is a Social Problem?

Social welfare institutions are also concerned with social problems, which are related to, but not the same as, social needs. For example, as C. Wright Mills famously observed, one person suffering from unemployment may be in acute need, but it is only when unemployment becomes a more widely shared experience in a community that there may be said to be a social problem. Social problems, then, are to be distinguished from individual need.

A further distinction should be made between the mere existence of a shared set of social misfortunes in a community, whether or not they have been defined as needs, and three further elements of a social problem: the extent to which they are perceived, the judgements made about them and the values they threaten, and the actions recommended to deal with them. Needs can exist whether or not they are known about by anyone. Social problems cannot; they exist within the public domain rather than private experience. The perceptions, judgements and recommended actions are in the broadest sense of the term part of the political process of a society or community.

Box 4.3 Elements and types of social problems

- elements of social problems
  - social conditions
  - perceptions
  - judgements
  - solutions
- types of social problems
  - open/contested
  - closed/uncontested

Perceptions of social problems can occur through the eyes of experts or the general public. In the case of experts, social problems are typically defined in relatively objective terms such as the incidence of divorce, where the rate of change is a crucial issue. However, since many social issues are less amenable to objective measurement, for example the effects of family neglect on children, experts can differ widely in their claims about the objective state of a social problem. In these cases, the general public, community groups, pressure groups and so on may have widely varied views, such that a social problem is more subjectively defined. Social problems, in the extreme version of this view, become merely 'what people think they are'. Since most of our experience of and knowledge about social issues is indirect, the mass media are an important influence not only on our knowledge of social issues, but also on the way in which they are framed, judged and dealt with.

These perceptions are heavily influenced by judgements about the kinds of value felt to be under threat. This brings us to the heart of defining a social problem, since it is the sense that something is wrong that motivates any attempt to put things right. There are two aspects of this that we have to consider. First is the issue of whose values are threatened. Some issues command widespread consensus, for example that threats to life are unacceptable. The judgement that the spread of disease such as HIV-AIDS is a social problem from this point of view is relatively uncontested. Other issues, however, may be the site of sharp value conflict, for example the relevance of people's sexuality to family life in various ways.

A second important aspect of value judgements in definitions of social problems can sharply modify the effects of these value concerns. This is the issue of who is to blame for the problem. In the case of HIV-AIDS, what might have been an ordinary medical issue was transformed in this regard by very sharp dissensus over the judgements of blame made about gay men, and therefore about the nature, status and solution to the problem. Where problems are the site of value conflict, or where blame is attributed, we can speak of contested or open social problems, the solutions to which are far from clear. Where consensus and lack of blame are typical, we can think of social problems as closed or uncontested.

The solutions proffered to social problems have an intimate connection to perceptions and judgements made about them. Indeed, it has been argued that often the solution may indeed tend to determine these other aspects. An example of this process has been the development since the 1970s of a social problem of hyperactivity amongst children, at a time when a drug treatment to calm them down became available. Certainly, the ways in which a problem is perceived and judged strongly affect the kind of solution suggested. For example, there is a running battle between governments and the poverty lobby over the level and distribution of poverty. Both use conventional statistical analysis to try to demonstrate the presence or absence of poverty, and the two sides take very different positions over who should take moral responsibility for the problem. The government's solution, to create jobs through the enforced flexibilization of employment conditions, is the very cause of the problem from the point of view of the poverty lobby.

A related example has been the Labour government's attitude in the early years of the twenty-first century to the problem of income poverty amongst lone parents. Although benefits have been increased, the main solution was felt to be strong encouragement for lone parents to take up paid employment. In this instance, the UK government borrowed ideas from the USA, particularly ex-President Clinton. Benefits have been statutorily limited to a total of five years in the USA, and there is evidence that the number of lone parents claiming support has declined. Such a 'solution' to this perceived social problem may not actually increase the welfare of lone parents.

Such an approach to solving social problems illustrates the subjective nature of the perception and definition of social problems, which in earlier years was used by progressive commentators to attack official or expert opinions (for example patriarchal elements of medical opinion). Strategies such as these can be turned round by a government to deny the existence of a problem, or to argue that only certain kinds of solution are reasonable. Thus the claim that globalization demands low rates of taxation, or flexible labour markets, or the use of private finance to fund healthcare infrastructure development has helped to obscure alternative solutions.

Context

Social welfare institutions have evolved in their current form alongside the development of industrial society. As industrial societies change, so do their welfare institutions. This is most clearly observed in the countries of Russia and Eastern Europe, where a variety of neo-liberal social policy innovations have been developed, and already modified in response to economic and political forces. Western societies have not been immune to such influences, with the ubiquitous assumption of globalization used to justify significant debates and changes in the trajectory of social policies for the twenty-first century. While they are chiefly oriented to meeting social needs and tackling social problems, this has not been the only motive. Otto Bismarck, the nineteenth-century German Chancellor, and Winston Churchill both argued in favour of social welfare institutions as a buttress against the attractions of socialist ideas.

Social needs and social problems are subject to contested definitions. In both cases a major debate concerns the relative weight to be given to objective or subjective definitions. Can needs and problems be scientifically measured in some absolute sense, or are they inescapably subject to the relative social circumstances of both those in need and the particular interests of the definers? The genomic revolution, which seems to offer so many tantalizing health benefits, and yet to raise an even larger number of ethical uncertainties, illustrates well the interaction between industrial and scientific developments and public concerns. Public debate has never been more wide-ranging, buttressed through public opinion surveys, focus groups and the development of professional committees and academic departments of ethics.

These points lead us back to the nature of social policy as a subject. The word 'policy' implies that it is a part of the political processes and institutions of modern society, and that social needs, social problems and social welfare are similarly political. While some observers have come to anticipate the decline of the nation-state in the wake of an increasingly globalized world, discussed further in chapter 53, social policy issues have in reality grown in importance in regional affairs, whether at a sub-national level, or more widely in multi-country regional welfare 'blocs', most noticeably in the development of a European social model, alongside the distinctive American or Asian patterns of welfare development.

Emerging Issues: From Needs to Well-being

With the steady expansion of consumer and individualist definitions of the 'good life' that have emerged with the economic growth of the last decade or so, a new definition of needs in terms of our individual well-being has also developed. For example, healthcare is now focused on developing and sustaining good health as well as treating disease. We are encouraged to stop smoking, eat wisely and take exercise. This emphasis has also spread into concern for our personal relationships and mental health, such that stress generated by domestic or employment factors has become central to both public health and trade union actions. Economists have noted that the level of personal satisfaction reported in public surveys has risen very little over the last twenty-five years, despite record levels of income and wealth, and there is a growing call for more balanced measures of well-being than the gross national product. However, the arguments that we have reviewed in relation to defining needs and problems apply equally here. Well-being is a contested concept, open to subjective, objective, political and comparative definitions, and subject to the pressures of both professional and mass media fashions.

Guide to Further Sources

On social welfare institutions

D. Fraser, *The Evolution of the British Welfare State* (Palgrave, 2003) is the third edition of a comprehensive and balanced account of the growth of the British welfare state. N. Timmins, *The Five Giants: A Biography of the Welfare State* (HarperCollins, 2001) is a well-written and accessible revised second edition of a very successful account of the welfare state written by a journalist. The short book by J. R. Hay, *The Origins of the Liberal Welfare Reforms 1906–1914*

(Macmillan 1975) gives a very clear account of the variety of different reasons for the rapid development of state welfare in the early twentieth century.

On social needs

There are three seminal articles on social needs. J. Bradshaw, 'The concept of social need', *New Society* (30 March 1972) was a milestone statement about different types of social need. D. Piachaud, 'Peter Townsend and the Holy Grail', *New Society* (10 September 1981) presents a strong argument for the impossibility of finding an objective definition of need. L. Doyal and I. Gough, 'A theory of human needs', *Critical Social Policy*, 10 (1985) represents a cogent argument for returning to an objective basis for the definition of needs.

On social problems

N. Manning (ed.), *Social Problems and Welfare Ideology* (Gower, 1985) offers a detailed review of the theory of social problems, together with a range of case studies. M. May, E. Brunsden and R. Page (eds), *Introduction to Social Problems: Issues in Social Policy* (Blackwell, 2001) provides further exploration of the way in which social problems emerge and are tackled. E. Rubington and M. Weinberg, *The Study of Social Problems: Seven Perspectives* (Oxford University Press, 2002) presents a detailed analysis of seven different models of social problems.

Chapter 5

Equality, Rights and Social Justice

Peter Taylor-Gooby

Overview

- Equality, rights and social justice are all political slogans, endlessly contested, endlessly renewed.
- The main contrast in relation to equality is between the increasingly popular centre-left ideology of equality of opportunity and the traditional left conception of equality of outcome.
- Rights have been based on needs, capabilities (opportunities available in practice) and deserts.
- For justice, the big division is between those who base just allocations on individual contribution and circumstances and those who take social factors into account.
- In a more fluid, flexible, diverse, uncertain and globalized world, the opportunities for making claims based on these concepts multiply, while the capacity of governments to achieve them directly diminishes.

Introduction

'Equality', 'rights' and 'social justice' have been prominent among the rallying cries of those calling for radical reforms, whether in defence of individual property rights against the taxes necessary to provide common services to advance an expansionary programme based on the equal worth of all human beings (Commission on Social Justice 1994 in Franklin 1998: 40), to support social investment to meet the needs of future generations (Goodin 1998: 237) or to argue that rich nations have a moral responsibility to the poor (Sen 1999: 12). Since the concepts have been interpreted in various ways and used as ideological slogans by different groups at different times, we are faced with two main tasks in this chapter: understanding the root meanings attached to these terms, and tracing changes in the way in which they are used.

Meanings and Definitions

Equality

In mathematics, equality refers to a relationship whereby two distinguishable elements have equal value. Note that claims about equality for elements that are the same in every respect are uninteresting – if they are completely identical you cannot distinguish them anyway. Similarly, no serious reformers who use a language of equality have argued for social uniformity, although detractors sometimes wish to treat them as if they do. The egalitarian claim of welfare reformers has been that different groups should be treated as of equal value in social policy. In practice this has led to demands for equality in entitlement to benefits and services, in treatment by welfare authorities and in participation in decision-making.

The main issues arise in two areas. First, there is a problem in setting limits to the range of egalitarianism. Views on the scope of equality will depend on theories about what influences people's behaviour. The view, associated with neo-classical economic theory, that people are inclined to maximize their individual utility, implies that egalitarianism may undermine work incentives and kill the goose that lays the golden egg. If being a victim of inequality gets you welfare benefits, why bother to be anything else? The view that individuals are more influenced by culture, social relationships and behavioural norms suggests that the impact of equalizing policies will depend much more on the social framework within which they operate (Rothstein 2005: ch. 2; Gintis et al. 2005).

The second point concerns the practical rather than the moral scope of inequality. Many policy-makers have distinguished between 'equality of outcome' and 'equality of opportunity'. Policies directed at the former must aim to put people in positions of equal value, while those seeking the latter are more modest. The objective is simply to give individuals an equal starting point in an unequal society. Egalitarianism in this sense is entirely compatible with wide divergences in people's life-chances. As globalized capitalism increasingly dominates the societies in which welfare states exist and equality of outcome recedes as a practical policy goal, the main practical application of egalitarianism has been in the area of equal opportunities.

The notion is immediately relevant to education and training, and to policies in relation to the acknowledged social divisions of sex, disability and ethnicity. It has been particularly influential in the rhetoric surrounding New Labour (Franklin 1998: Introduction). It is thus surprising that the disturbing evidence of declining social mobility does not attract more attention in policy debate.

Different groups have struggled to ensure that particular divisions are recognized as meriting equal opportunity intervention. Issues of sexuality, of age, of disability, of region, of linguistic facility and sometimes even of social class are discussed as areas where equal opportunities policies should apply.

Rights

The notion of 'rights' is essentially a juristic concept referring to the legitimacy of an individual's claims. In the context of social policy the question is whether claims to social benefits and services should be backed by state force, so that social rights become an element in citizenship in the modern state. In a celebrated analysis, T. H. Marshall distinguished civil, political and social rights originating at different periods and based on individual status in relation to the legal, political and social system (George and Page 1995: ch. 6; Franklin 1998: ch. 4). Many commentators have pointed out that different patterns of rights have evolved at different speeds in different countries (see Part VIII in this book). Developments in the UK indicate a gradual shift from residence-based rights towards an exclusionary notion of citizenship based on hereditary rights.

Weber, the prominent social theorist, pointed out that the development of the modern state and its framework of social individuation and categorization made possible the establishment of a precise and formal structure of social rights. This is one of the achievements of modern civilization. At the same time, the process of categorization also subordinates the individual to a structure of authority that enforces obligations as a member of society – the individual becomes a 'mere cog in the machine', victim of an 'iron cage of bureaucracy'.

The conflict between individual rights and state authority has been one of the central themes of modern literature, from Franz Kafka's *The Trial* to Margaret Atwood's *The Handmaid's Tale*. In relation to welfare, governments have sought to impose obligations to pay taxes and to conform to particular norms in relation to work, sexuality, household and family transfers of income, childcare, retirement and residence. The welfare components of the modern state apparatus can be particularly powerful in enforcing desired patterns of behaviour. In the UK, the policies enforced by the Child Support Agency are designed to enforce transfers between separated parents (chapter 21), the New Deal and Single Gateway policies for benefit claimers to regulate job-seeking behaviour (chapter 39), pension policy imposes greater responsibility on the individual to provide for needs in old age (chapter 49) and government increasingly intervenes in promoting healthy life-style and diet (chapter 40). Social rights, far from being a simple reflection of social progress, are two-edged.

Claims in the welfare area can be legitimated as rights in a number of ways. In practice, ideas about need, about capability and about desert are most important.

- *Need-based* arguments maintain that a class of human needs can be identified, which provides the justification for an obligation on government to ensure that these are met, so far as the current stage of development allows. There are a number of problems in this approach, not least in establishing a bedrock of human needs that is secure against relativist reduction (for an important contribution by Gough, see Franklin 1998: ch. 3). The human needs approach has offered some of the most profound arguments for the legitimation of welfare as an ineluctable duty of government (see Plant 1991: ch. 5).

- The *capability-based* approach, developed in the path-breaking work of Nobel Laureate economist Amartya Sen, understands well-being in terms of the capabilities a person has, 'the substantive freedoms he or she enjoys to lead the kind of life he or she has reason to value'(1999: 87). Poverty can be understood as the deprivation of capabilities. The onus lies on government to remedy this, if possible. People's access to capabilities can be established by comparing what more or less privileged groups are able to do or enjoy in a society. The approach underlies the construction of the widely used UN *Human Development Index*, which, broadly speaking, seeks to compare the achievement of a range of capabilities in different countries. It has been expanded to examine the extent to which particular groups are systematically deprived of capabilities, for example, women in Nussbaum's influential work, *Sex and Social Justice* (1999).

- *Desert-based* claims are founded on the view that some quality or activity of a particular group imposes an obligation on society to provide them with certain services. Examples of such arguments are claims that motherhood or contribution through work or in war are deserving of social support, and that the duty to provide it should come home to the state. Such claims are typically linked to functional or reciprocal arguments or are part and parcel of a normative system.

Box 5.1 Entitlement through desert

- entitlement to social insurance benefits based on work records is more secure and, in practice, less subject to official harassment than entitlement to means-tested benefit based on need;
- support services designed to help those caring for frail elderly people are sometimes effectively rationed by reference to the status and the access to employment of the carer; receipt of the services is influenced by gender and age;
- Allocation of social housing of particular quality may involve the grading of tenants as appropriate to particular estates.

Functional arguments suggest that some activity is essential for the continuance of social order, and that therefore an obligation is owed to those who carry it out. It is difficult to specify such activities in a society subject to rapid change in the way ours is. Social theorists such as the American writer Talcott Parsons tend to identify them at the highest abstract level ('authority', 'production', 'reproduction', 'communication'; see Gough, in Franklin 1998: ch. 3). The disadvantage with such generality is that abstract categories can be applied to a very wide range of activities. These arguments parallel at a social level the issues raised in earlier discussions of individual obligation.

One result is that arguments about 'desert' are typically linked to normative systems. In our society, the principal ethics involved are the family ethic, with its attendant claims about the gender division of labour, the spheres of childhood and adulthood, appropriate forms of sexuality and the work ethic, and the implied legitimacy of the market. These ethics are subject to modification, and the growing diversity of UK society (see chapter 16 and Part VII) adds extra impetus to this process. Traditional norms of family childcare seem detachable from a strict gender division of spheres of home and paid employment. In relation to work, the boundaries between the life stage, where maintenance should

depend on work or property, and periods appropriate to retirement and education/training appear to have a certain malleability. Ideas about the desert of particular groups are of considerable importance in relation to social rights and the way in which they are put into practice (see box 5.1).

Social justice

Social justice is concerned with who ought to get what. Resource allocation in most welfare states is dominated by market systems that rest on the idea that goods are property to be owned, valued, bought and sold, and on normative systems of distribution closely linked to kin relationship. Arguments about rights and about equality have provided a basis for claims about justice which often cross-cut market and kin allocation. The most important positions of recent years have been those of Robert Nozick and John Rawls, and these illustrate the way in which individualistic and social approaches to social justice may be developed (see box 5.2).

Both approaches have been extensively discussed and criticized. Nozick's position rests on a particular individualism in relation to labour which is not compelling. Production in modern society involves the interlinked activity of many people. The correct allocation of credit for work is

---

Box 5.2   Individualist and social approaches to social justice

- Nozick argues that the core of just claims is labour – people have a right to what they have 'mixed their labour with', i.e. improved by their work. As a matter of strict justice, it is a violation of individuals' autonomy to appropriate or redistribute the goods that people have gained through their work, although individuals may as a matter of charity choose to surrender property to those they view as needy and deserving (see Plant 1991: 210–13).
- Rawls's approach rests on the notion of a 'veil of ignorance'. The central idea is that just arrangements are those which people would agree on if they did not know what position in society they themselves would come to occupy, if they had no vested interests themselves (see Plant 1991: 99–107). Rawls goes on to argue that it is in principle possible to 'second guess' the kinds of choices about the allocation of goods (and bads) that individuals would arrive at under these circumstances. Unable to be certain that they would not end up in the worst possible position in an unequal and exploited society, they would tend to legislate for a social order in which only those inequalities existed which improved the position of the worst off; for example, by raising living standards throughout the community.

---

highly controversial and is carried out in practice mainly through market institutions. The impact of a Nozickian approach, linking just distribution to work, may be to legitimate the market and to undermine any justification for welfare interventions.

The Rawlsian approach is attractive in that it rests on negotiation free from the biases that social position – class, gender, tenure, age, employment opportunities, state of health and so on – generates in the real politics of social policy. However, there are severe problems in deciding a priori what allocation of benefits and services people who were abstracted from their social circumstances would agree to. There is nothing irrational in favouring a grossly unequal world and hoping to come out as a winner; or, if one felt more charitable, in supporting the highest average standard of living, providing the worst off are not too hard hit. It is difficult to devise approaches to social justice which both take seriously the autonomy of individual citizens and lay down the definitive policies

a society must follow if it is to be labelled just – to put the seal of social justice on particular welfare arrangements.

Equality, Rights and Justice as Ideology

Equality

In the post-war decades of confident welfare expansion, the advancement of equality – in the sense of equality of opportunity – was often used to justify policy, particularly in relation to educational reform. Crosland's influential book *The Future of Socialism* (see George and Page 1995: 131–2, 144) argued that technical and economic change squared the circle. Meritocracy was both rational and just. Harold Wilson, leader of the Labour Party in the 1960s, succeeded in developing a political ideology based on this approach, which united traditionalists and modernizers among party supporters by arguing that both class struggle and class privilege were outdated by the requirement to get the best people in the right positions. Equality of outcome has never been seriously advanced as a dominant policy goal by the main left currents in British politics.

The remaking of Conservative policy associated with the charismatic leadership of Margaret Thatcher from the mid-1970s resulted in a vigorous commitment to free market principles and to a traditional family ethic. Egalitarianism has no place in this doctrine. Equal opportunity policies are seen as a corrupt and unfashionable 'political correctness'. Reappraisal on the left after four successive election defeats led first to the programme of the Commission on Social Justice (Franklin 1998: ch 2), which deprecated egalitarians as backward-looking 'levellers' and defined justice in terms of 'the need to spread opportunities and life chances as widely as possible', and more recently to the conception of a 'Stake-holders' Britain', in which equality of opportunity again plays a clear role but in which there is also a strong emphasis on individual responsibility to contribute to society. This has been vigorously proclaimed by New Labour, although, in some areas, policy fails to live up to the ideology. This is most obvious in the active promotion of new, better-resourced and selective forms of privileged schooling (chapter 41), the exclusionary treatment of asylum-seekers with worse benefit rights than citizens (chapter 51) and the acquiescence in rapid increases in income and wealth at the top end that give the most privileged groups enhanced access to vastly superior opportunities (chapter 18).

In short, the right in politics prioritizes rights, derived from market and family, over claims based on considerations of equality. The left has regarded equality as important, but as only one policy objective among several. The commitment is increasingly to equality of opportunity (with an obligation to group opportunities) and to the linking of welfare to social contribution.

Rights

Individual rights are closely linked to notions of social justice. Equality has been one of the principal foundations of rights claims in social policy debate, so that citizenship in itself is seen to justify rights to welfare. The other major foundation has been the notion of desert. In policy debate, ideas about desert, linked to work and family ethics, have become increasingly important, so that rules of entitlement to benefit are drawn more stringently, the mechanisms for ensuring that able-bodied people are pursuing employment have been strengthened and obligations to maintain children after the end of a relationship have been codified. Much reform has also been concerned to reduce state spending, in line with the general emphasis on property rights which requires collective spending decisions to be justified against a stricter criterion than is applied to individual spending.

The emphasis on desert is a central pillar of right-wing approaches to welfare. However, recent arguments about stake-holding on the left have also been concerned to emphasize individual contributions as part of a move towards more active policies. These are characterized by concern to expand opportunity and also to give due weight to individual responsibility for outcomes, rather than simply provide maintenance as in the passive receipt of benefits.

Social justice

Developments in relation to social justice follow largely from the above. The key shift is towards a more active notion of how social entitlements should be structured, in keeping with the move away from an egalitarian approach and towards one influenced by meritocracy or by ideas about property- and family-linked desert.

The impact of the New Labour approach has been to shift debate on the left from rights justified by equal citizenship to rights justified by desert. Benefit rights for unemployed people, for example, are ever more tightly linked to appropriate behaviour as 'job-seekers' or to participation in New Deal programmes. Similar requirements are being extended to single parents and some categories of sick and disabled people.

Emerging Issues

Debates about equality, rights and social justice have become both broader and narrower. On the one hand, increasing social diversity, more fluid patterns of family life and of employment, and struggles for the recognition of the rights by a broader range of groups have extended the range of claims for social policy interventions that can be made on the grounds of social justice. On the other, the ideological pressure justifying allocation on market and family-ethic principles and promoting individual rather than state responsibility is stronger than it has been for half a century. One view requires government to expand social policy, the other to spread welfare interventionism more thinly.

Social policy is overshadowed by concerns about the impact of population ageing, technological un- or sub-employment, growing international competition, tax revolt, the weakening of kinship care networks, general distrust of big government and the future sustainability of Western welfare states. The climate of policy-making is one of spending constraint and of scepticism about how far government can resolve social problems (see chapter 19). Under these circumstances it is hardly surprising that conceptual debates turn away from a highly interventionist concern with the promotion of equality of outcome to an interest in the nourishment of more equal opportunities. Moral arguments point out that equal opportunity policies may damage the interests of the most vulnerable unless we develop effective systems to protect rights. Equally, we can only determine whether the final outcomes are morally acceptable by comparison with standards of social justice. Equality, rights and social justice remain central to social policy, especially in a more globalized, diverse and uncertain social world.

Guide to Further Sources

The best (and most clearly written) guide to the main relevant currents in contemporary political philosophy remains R. Plant, *Modern Political Thought* (Blackwell, 1991), especially chs 3–7. R. Goodin, *Reasons for Welfare* (Princeton University Press, 1998) covers similar ground in more detail (see chs 2, 3 and 4). This book also reviews the moral aspects of exploitation and dependency and develops a principled case against new right arguments.

A. Sen, *Development as Freedom* (Oxford University Press, 1999), ch. 3, summarizes the capability approach; chs 4 and 5 point out the relevance to social policy. This book is particularly valuable since it is written from a global rather than a national perspective; see <http://them.polylog.org/3/fsa-en.htm> for a typically readable and incisive article relating Sen's work to other writers on social justice. M. Nussbaum, *Sex and Social Justice* (Oxford University Press, 1999) points out the relevance of the approach to gender inequality, from which it is a short step to embrace other dimensions of difference. F. Foley, *Sustainability and Social*

Justice (IPPR, 2004) extends the focus to include issues of sustainability, environmentally, cross-nationally and intergenerationally.

J. le Grand, *Motivation, Agency and Public Policy* (Oxford University Press, 2003) discusses theories of human agency (why people do what they do) and argues that social policy should be deliberately designed to respect diversity in values and motives.

B. Rothstein, *Social Traps and the Problem of Trust* (Cambridge University Press, 2005) argues that trust and social cohesion are central to ensure that a moral social policy can be sustained. H. Gintis, S. Bowles, R. Boyd and E. Fehr, *Moral Sentiments and Material Interests* (MIT Press, 2005) is hard-going, but rewarding: a principled critique of the view that we can understand how people behave in society simply by assuming that they follow self-interest.

J. Franklin (ed.), *Social Policy and Social Justice* (IPPR, 1998) is a useful source, with extracts from *The Commission on Social Justice*, and relevant material on need, citizenship, family and gender and ethnicity.

V. George and R. Page (eds), *Modern Thinkers on Welfare* (Prentice Hall/Harvester Wheatsheaf, 1995) provides succinct accounts of the views of major policy commentators and critics. The value of T. Fitzpatrick, *New Theories of Welfare* (Palgrave, 2005) is that it provides an up-to-date review of theoretical concepts in social policy that includes new developments in areas such as genetics, information and surveillance.

For the UN Human Development Report, influenced by Sen's work on capability, see <http://hdr.undp.org/>. Probably the best overall web resource on political ideas is Richard Kember's webpage at the University of Keele: <http://www.psr.keele.ac.uk/>.

Chapter 6

Efficiency, Equity and Choice

Carol Propper

Overview

- Economics provides a framework to analyse the production and use of welfare services.
- Economic analysis begins from the assumption of scarcity – we cannot have everything we want. So people and society must make choices.
- The appropriate cost of these choices to society is the opportunity cost – the resources that are forgone if the choice is made.
- Economic efficiency means making the most of scarce resources. Economic efficiency occurs when the opportunity cost of using resources in a particular activity is equal to the sum of everyone's marginal benefits from that activity.
- Efficiency is not the only goal. Other goals include fairness and choice. These goals may clash with efficiency.
- Economists see markets and choice as one way of delivering efficiency and choice in social and welfare services.

Introduction

Economic ideas and concepts are widely used in public policy. The domain of social policy is no exception: 'effective' and 'efficient' are adjectives frequently cited by politicians and policy-makers as goals for those responsible for delivering public services. Yet the ideas of economics are considerably more than buzzwords. Economic analysis provides a framework which can be – and is – used to analyse questions about behaviour as diverse as worker participation in unions, the relative welfare of nations, the tendency of bureaucracies to grow, the behaviour of politicians or why increasing wealth does not appear to bring us happiness.

Terms such as 'efficiency' and 'effectiveness' have rather more precise meaning within economics than when used by politicians or policy-makers. Economists see efficiency, equity and (sometimes) choice as ends – and ends which may be achieved through a number of possible means. These means include the market, the state and a mixed economy. This chapter presents these key economic concepts and illustrates their applicability to social policy (see also chapter 29).

Scarcity and Choice

Economic analysis begins from a single fact: we cannot have everything we want. We live in a world of scarcity. One way of seeing this scarcity is to notice that no one can afford all the things he or she would really like. This is obvious in the case of the homeless, but it applies equally to the carer who also does a part-time job and would like to have more time to devote either to that job or to the person she cares for, and to the rich rock star who goes on giving concerts in order to buy yet one more Caribbean island. It equally applies to governments, which have larger budgets than do individuals, but which can never spend as much on health services or education as the voters would wish.

Faced with scarcity, be it of money or time, people must make choices. To make a choice, we balance the benefits of having more of something against the costs of having less of something else. Because resources are finite, in making choices we face costs. Whatever we choose to do, we could have done something else. So, for example, the carer with limited time can choose between working longer hours at her job or looking after the person she cares for. Or a society which invests in building roads uses up time and material that could be devoted to providing hospital facilities. Economists use the term 'opportunity cost' to emphasize that making choices in the face of scarcity implies a cost. The opportunity cost of any action is the best alternative that is not taken. So if building a hospital is viewed by society as the next best thing to building a road, the cost of building a hospital is the opportunity cost of building a road.

In many situations the price paid for the use of a resource is the opportunity cost. So if the cost of materials and labour used in the construction of a road – say, £1 million – was the same as for the construction of something else, then £1 million is its opportunity cost. But market prices do not always measure opportunity costs and nor are all opportunity costs faced by individuals the result of their own choices. For example, when you can't get onto a train at a busy time of day, you bear the cost of the choices made by all the other people on the train. This is not a price that is quoted by the market and nor is it one that the other people on the train take into account when they get onto it.

Efficiency

Efficiency has a specific meaning within economics. When deciding how much of a good or service should be produced, we need to take into account that having the good or service gives rise to both benefits and costs, and that those benefits and the costs vary with the amount that is produced. In general, benefits are desirable and costs are to be avoided. Given this, it would seem sensible to choose that amount of the good at which the gap between benefits and costs is largest. When society has selected this amount of the good and allocated resources of production accordingly, economists say that this is the efficient level of output of this good, or alternatively that there is an efficient allocation of resources in production of this good.

In determining the level of output which is efficient, we need to take into account both the benefits from the good and the opportunity costs of producing it. As an example, I consider the consumption and production of something simple – ice cream. But the analytical framework can be equally applied to hospitals, schools, social work services and nuclear power stations.

Benefits of consumption

We would expect the benefits from eating ice cream to vary according to the amount eaten. In general, for someone who likes ice cream we would expect the total benefit to rise the more is eaten. However, this total benefit may not rise proportionately with each mouthful consumed. Let us consider the first spoonful. If the eater is really

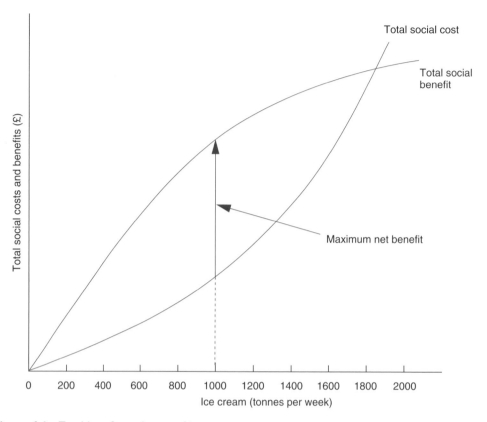

Figure 6.1   Total benefits and costs of ice cream consumption

hungry, the first spoonful will give considerable satisfaction. But as the amount eaten is increased, the satisfaction derived from each additional spoonful will begin to fall. By and large, we would expect to find that the benefit derived from each additional spoonful falls the more that is consumed. If we define the last spoonful as the marginal spoonful, we can say that the marginal benefit falls as the quantity of ice cream eaten increases. Either you become full or, because variety is nice, you would rather eat something else.

This analysis can be applied to society as a whole. Defining society's benefits as the sum of the benefits received by all individuals from ice cream, we can add up across all individuals to get the total social benefit. Similarly, we can add up each person's marginal benefit at each amount of ice cream eaten to get the marginal social

benefit. This is the increase in total social benefit as we increase society's consumption by one unit. We assume that we can add up the benefits received by different people. Often we can do this easily because benefits are measured in a single unit, say pounds. But in some cases there may be measurement problems: for example, when it is hard to value a good, or when £100 is worth much more to one person than to another.

Both the total social benefit and the marginal social benefit can be drawn on a graph. Figure 6.1 shows the total social benefit from ice cream consumption. The amount of ice cream consumed is on the horizontal axis and the benefit from this in pounds is on the vertical axis. Total social benefit rises as consumption increases, but it rises at a falling rate. It rises at a falling rate precisely because the marginal social

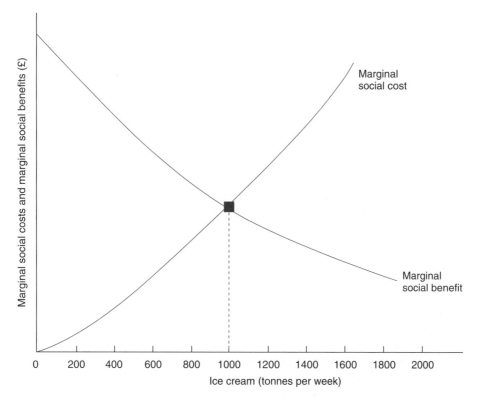

Figure 6.2 Marginal benefits and costs of ice cream consumption

benefit of consumption falls as more ice cream is eaten.

Figure 6.2 shows this marginal social benefit of ice cream consumption. The total amount consumed is on the horizontal axis and is measured in the same units as in Figure 6.1. On the vertical axis, we show the value in pounds of the marginal benefit. The marginal benefit curve slopes downwards from left to right, showing that the marginal social benefit falls as consumption of ice cream increases.

Costs of production

To determine the efficient level of production and consumption of ice cream we also need to consider the costs of production. Typically, the more of a good that is produced the more costly it is to produce. So total costs increase with production.

However, what is required to establish efficiency is the cost of producing an extra unit of output, known as the marginal cost. Studies of production generally show that there is a level of production beyond which it becomes increasingly costly to expand output. This could be for a variety of reasons: firms may have to pay overtime or use less productive machinery, or the costs of coordinating production or delivery rise as the amount of good produced rises. So the marginal cost of production increases as output increases.

Assuming that ice cream production has the same pattern, we can add up the total costs of production across all producers. This will be the total social cost. We can also add up all the marginal costs to obtain the marginal social cost for each unit of output. The total social cost of figure 6.1 shows the way that total social cost rises

with output of ice cream. The corresponding marginal social cost of production is
shown in figure 6.2.

The efficient level of output

We can use the information on how social
benefits and social costs of ice cream consumption and production vary with output
to identify that level of output at which the
difference between total social benefits and
total social costs (net social benefit) is at a
maximum. This is the efficient level of
output. From figure 6.1 we can identify this
as at 1,000 tonnes per week. Looking at
figure 6.2, we can see that this is the point
at which marginal social benefits equal
marginal social costs. This is no coincidence. As long as the marginal social cost
is below the marginal social benefit, society
will gain by producing and consuming
more ice cream. Conversely, if the marginal
social benefit is below the marginal social
cost, society would do better by putting its
resources to other uses and consuming and
producing less ice cream. Only when the
marginal social benefit is equal to the marginal social cost will it be impossible to
increase net social benefits.

The analysis of the efficient amount of
ice cream output is relevant to all goods
and services. So we can define the socially
efficient output of hospitals, home helps,
education or cars in exactly the same way.
We may have more problem in measuring
the benefits and costs, but the principle
remains the same: the socially efficient
amount of the good or service is produced
at the point where the marginal cost and
benefit are equal.

An efficient level of production is thus a
desirable end: if all goods are produced in
their efficient quantities, then net social
benefit cannot be increased by reallocating
resources. Conversely, if the level of production is not efficient, then net social benefits can be increased by producing more (or
less) of one good and less (or more) of at

least one other. Given that resources are
always finite, efficiency is thus an important social objective.

Efficiency and effectiveness

Although efficiency and effectiveness are
often used synonymously by policy-makers,
they are different. Effectiveness means producing something in the best possible way
technically, and is sometimes called 'technical efficiency'. We can check whether a
production is technically efficient by seeing
whether, given the current technology,
more output could be produced from the
present inputs. As an example, consider the
delivery of meals on wheels by one person
with one van. One service might visit houses
by order of number. If all the even houses
are on one side of the street and all the odd
numbers on the other, this will mean cross-
ing the road between each delivery. This is
likely to be less technically efficient than
delivering meals to all the odd-numbered
houses and then to all the even ones.

Efficiency goes further than (and encompasses) effectiveness. To know whether a
production process is efficient, we must
first check that it is effective. Then we have
to see whether its current technology produces the output in a cheaper way than the
alternatives. This requires looking at the
prices of inputs, whereas effectiveness does
not. So in our example it may be that once
costs are taken into account, it might be
found that it is better to change the amount
spent, and so to employ two people and
one van. Then we must check that consumers cannot make themselves better off by
choosing to buy other goods. Finally, we
must check that all the costs and benefits
involved have been taken into account.
(Technically, this is known as checking that
there are no external costs and benefits. In
the train example given above, there were
external costs – those imposed by train
users on others. In some activities – for
example, smoking cigarettes or the use of

fuels which pollute the atmosphere – these external costs may be large.)

So before we can say that something is efficient, we must first ensure that it is effective; hence the drive towards effectiveness in the use of scarce medical resources, for example. However, just because a production method is effective, it does not mean it is efficient. We need to know the costs and the benefits of the service and of alternatives to know that. For many areas of social policy, we are still at the stage of establishing effectiveness and not efficiency.

Efficiency versus Other Goals

Equity

Even though efficiency is a desirable end, it is not the only one. An efficient outcome is not necessarily a fair or equitable one. An efficient output is one for which the sum of all individuals' marginal valuations equals the marginal social costs of production. But each individual's valuation of a good or service – and so the sum of these valuations – will depend on the resources he or she has. So the efficient level of production will be defined in relation to the existing distribution of resources. If initial resources are distributed in a way that is judged as unfair, there is no reason why an efficient allocation of those resources should be fair.

An example may make this clearer. Suppose there are only two members of society, Ms A and Ms B. Given their initial resources, their likes and dislikes and the production methods available to them, the efficient level of production of ice cream is four tubs per week. These tubs could all go to Ms A, or all to Ms B, or they could share them equally. Each of these divisions of the total production is possible, but not all will be judged as fair or equitable. On the other hand, if each received only one tub, this allocation might be judged as fair, but it is not efficient. It is not efficient because we

know that the efficient level of production is four tubs. If only two tubs were produced, net social benefit would be increased by producing more and in so doing we could make both Ms A and Ms B better off.

There are many possible definitions of equity or fairness – for example, minimum standards or equal distribution for all – but we do not discuss them here. The points to note are: first, that efficiency is not the same as fairness; second, that there is often trade-off between the two (a fair allocation may be one which is not efficient); third, that efficiency embodies a value judgement just as definitions of fairness do. The value judgement underlying the definition of efficiency is that some distribution of income (often the existing one) is legitimate.

Choice

Choice is seen as an important mechanism by economists. By making choices, individuals can indicate their valuations of goods and services. If valuations are known, then the production of those services which have greater net (marginal) value will be increased and the production of others decreased, and so the outcome will be more efficient. Choice is often linked to competition: competition is one means by which individuals can exercise choices. To see this, consider the case where there is no competition in the supply of a service because there is only one supplier. In this case, individuals cannot choose the type of service they prefer, as there is only one on offer.

Of course, there are costs to making choices – individuals have to decide which product they prefer and this will mean finding out about each possible option. In some circumstances it could be the case that very small differences between goods do not merit the costs of trying to choose between them. In others, the amount of information required to make informed choices may be very high. It has sometimes been argued, for example, that the level of medical knowledge required to make informed choices in healthcare is too large for individuals to make good choices. The same argument has been advanced in debates about giving greater choice in pension arrangements. However, in general, more choice is judged to be better than less.

In the field of social policy, where choice has often been limited, increasing choice – and the allied goal of increasing responsiveness of suppliers to users' wishes – is viewed as an important goal. From an economics perspective this is viewed as a move in the right direction. However, this does not mean that the benefits of increasing choice necessarily outweigh the costs. This will depend on the particular service.

The Means of Delivering Efficiency and Choice

All societies have had methods of trying to get the most out of limited resources. In large-scale societies, two dominant mechanisms of allocation have been used. These are allocation by the government and allocation by the market. Under the former system (the so-called command economies), planning and administration were used to decide what and how goods should be produced, and to whom they should be allocated. Under the latter, allocation decisions are made by the decisions of large numbers of individuals and private firms.

Markets are seen as desirable by economists, since – in the absence of market failure – they will lead to an efficient allocation of resources without the need for coordination mechanisms and the costs of planning. In practice, of course, not all decisions in a market system are made by individuals, and not all ownership is private. Government has a large role in all market economies. However, the market mechanism currently has dominance: command

economies have largely abandoned their structures in favour of freer markets.

Emerging Issues

In the provision of public services, choice and competition have been introduced into systems where, previously, allocation was by means of administrative decision. Politicians from the left and the right see choice as a way of allowing greater parental say in where their child goes to school or of where individuals are treated for medical care. In healthcare, education, social care and social rented housing in the UK (and elsewhere), competition in supply has been introduced as a means of increasing choice, responsiveness and efficiency. Services which were previously delivered by government monopoly have been opened up to competition. So private firms collect garbage, build houses for low-income tenants and run prisons. Private suppliers compete to provide care for the mentally handicapped, and not-for-profit public education providers compete for contracts to provide education. In some countries – Canada is one – while healthcare is financed by the state, all provision is private. Thirty years ago these arrangements would have been seen in the UK as the wrong way to provide services: today, many go without comment.

On the other hand, in health, education and transport (amongst other services) there is still considerable debate about the role for the private sector as a provider, for individual choice and for competition between suppliers. Research findings make it clear that the precise institutional arrangements of choice and competition in public services matter: a reform that works well in one context cannot be transposed without adaptation to another. Nevertheless, if choice and efficiency are important goals, market mechanisms have their uses in welfare services as in other parts of the economy.

Guide to Further Sources

J. le Grand, C. Propper and R. Robinson, *The Economics of Social Problems*, 3rd edn (Macmillan, 1992) provides an economic analysis of social policy issues and assumes no previous knowledge of economics. A more advanced textbook, designed for those already studying economics, is N. Barr, *The Economics of the Welfare State*, 4th edn (Oxford University Press, 2004). For a book also aimed at economics students which discusses these issues in a US context, see J. Stiglitz, *Economics of the Public Sector*, 3rd edn (W. W. Norton, 2000).

For a review of recent evidence on the use of competition in healthcare markets see C. Propper, D. Wilson and S. Burgess, 'Extending choice in English health care: the implications of the economic evidence', *Journal of Social Policy*, 35/4 (2006). For a review of the evidence on choice in education, see S. Burgess, D. Wilson and C. Propper, 'The impact of school choice in England: implications from the economic evidence', *Policy Studies*, 28/2 (2007): 129 – 43. A non-technical review of current economic issues in the provision of public services is provided in P. Grout and M. Stevens (eds), 'Financing and managing public services', *Oxford Review of Economic Policy*, 19/2 (2003).

For a summary of many current issues in the economics of health aimed at those who are studying economics, see A. Jones (ed.), *The Elgar Companion to Health Economics* (Edward Elgar, 2006). For a discussion of the role of economic motivation in the behaviour of those who provide public services, see J. le Grand, *Motivation, Agency, and Public Policy: Of Knights and Knaves, Pawns and Queen* (Oxford University Press, 2005).

Chapter 7

Altruism, Reciprocity and Obligation

Hilary Land

Overview

- Differing assumptions about human nature underpin the principles and practices upon which social policies are based.
- Understandings of family relationships are based on assumptions about reciprocal commitments to love and care; but these have been challenged in particular by feminist critics.
- The collective obligations which underpin social policy are based on a mixture of altruism and self-interest.
- Policies based more directly on self-reliance and self-protection were promoted by neo-liberals towards the end of the twentieth century, supported by the rise in sociobiology.
- Support for altruism and reciprocity in the future may require a fundamental review of the obligations and rights of citizenship.

Human Nature

Resources in societies, whether in the form of cash, kind or services, are claimed by and distributed to individuals and households within a variety of institutions. The family, broadly or narrowly defined, is important in all societies as a system for allocating resources between the generations as well as between men and women. In market economies, alongside the market itself, there may be state welfare systems, voluntary societies, charities and religious institutions. The relative importance of each of these systems varies over time and between countries. For example, in England, charities and religious and voluntary societies play a much smaller role now than they did in the nineteenth century or than they do today in Italy or the Netherlands. The principles underlying the distribution of resources in each of these systems are often different because some claims are based on 'desert', others on 'need' – both highly contested concepts. Some are enshrined in law as obligations, which one person owes another and which the courts can enforce, punishing those who fail to honour them. These also change over time and differ between countries. In the UK, for example, until 1948 grandparents could be obliged in law to maintain their grandchildren. That is still the case in Germany. Others are less well defined and are in part the product of a society's history and culture, or what the sociologist O'Neill calls 'rituals of reciprocity that celebrate exchanges between society, nature and God, involving a covenant between them as a model of all other civic reciprocities between individuals, neighbours, families, communities and the state' (1994: 92).

The assumptions about human nature on which these principles and practices are based also differ. Some assume that individuals are motivated primarily by self-interest and selfishness, others by altruism and concern for others. Adam Smith, one of the founding fathers of political economy in the early nineteenth century, recognized both but is more often quoted in support of the former view, particularly by those on the right of the political spectrum. In 'An inquiry into the nature and causes of the wealth of nations', he wrote:

> It is not from the benevolence of the butcher, the brewer or the baker that we expect our dinner, but from their regard to their own interest. We address ourselves, not to their humanity but to their self-love, and never talk to them of our necessities but of their advantage.
> (Cited in Collard 1978: 51)

However, Smith did recognize that not all human activity could be interpreted in this way. In a less well-known quote, he wrote: 'How selfish so-ever man may be supposed, there are evidently some principles in his nature, which interest him to the fortune of others, and render their happiness necessary to him, though he derives nothing from it except the pleasure of seeing it' (in ibid.: 52) In the words of a twentieth-century economist, this means that:

> altruism implies externalities in consumption. The happiness of one individual is a function not only of the volume of goods and services consumed by himself but also of certain goods and services consumed by others. Thus many people would be distressed to know that the sick were, for financial reasons, receiving very inadequate attention.   •
> (Collard, *The New Right: A Critique*, Fabian Tract 387)

Adam Smith also recognized altruism to be particularly important within the family, for 'they are naturally and usually the persons upon whose happiness or misery his conduct must have the greatest influence' (Collard 1978: 52). However, by and large, political economy placed the family outside its domain (it is no accident that the male pronoun is used in the above quotes) and concentrated instead on developing models of human society comprising solitary and independent individuals acting rationally and freely making contracts in pursuit of their own self-interest. As the philosopher Mary Midgley has pointed out, this model derives from seventeenth-century physics, in which the ultimate building blocks of matter were conceptualized as hard, impenetrable atoms. It is a model, she writes, in which 'all significant moral relations between individuals are the symmetrical ones expressed by contract' (1985: 2). However, there are other ways of thinking about human relationships. Midgley argues:

> [If] we use a biological or 'organic' model, we can talk also of a variety of asymmetrical relations found within a whole. Leaves relate not only to other leaves but to fruit, twigs, branches and the whole tree. People appear not only as individuals, but as members of their groups, families, tribes, species, ecosystems and biospheres and have moral relations, as parts, to these various wholes.
> (Ibid.)

In this model people are not independent but interdependent, and relationships cannot be specified with reference to a contract.

Family Relations

Family relationships have always been perceived to be different from those of the marketplace and not subject in the same way to rational calculation. Reciprocity between men and women or between parents and children is informed by love or altruism rather than narrow self-interest. Many economists treat the family or household as a 'black box' and have developed models which assume a household can be treated as if it were an individual – a male individual – with identifiable interests or 'joint utilities', to use the jargon. G. S. Becker is one of a minority of economists who has shown a sustained interest in the family and in altruism, arguing that:

> Families in all societies, including modern market oriented societies, have been responsible for a sizeable part of economic activity – half or more – for they have produced much of the consumption, education, health and other human capital of the members. If I am correct that altruism dominates family behaviour, perhaps to the same extent as selfishness dominates market transactions, then altruism is much more important in economic life than is commonly understood.
>
> (*Treatise on the Family*, Harvard University Press, 1991 [1981], p. 303)

However, Becker accepts women's willingness to invest in the 'human capital' of their husbands and children rather than in their own, using a rather circular argument, namely that since on average they enter marriage with less education, training and marketable experience (i.e. less human capital) than their partners, it is rational from the point of view of maximizing the family's interest for them to use their time and effort in this way. Families invest less in the human capital of their daughters than their sons because they are expected to devote at least part of their adulthood to marriage and children, and so the cycle is repeated.

The assumptions about women's availability to care have been challenged since the 1990s as education and employment opportunities for girls improved and marriage became more risky. As N. Folbre, a feminist economist, explained:

> As long as male individualism is counterbalanced by female altruism, as long as rational economic man is taken care of by irrational altruistic woman, families play a particularly important (and unfair) role. But when women gain the freedom to act more like men, pursuing their rational self-interest, the price of caring labour goes up.
>
> (*Who Pays for the Kids?*, Routledge, 1994, p. 119)

The rise in female employment has challenged the male breadwinner/female housewife model. The British post-war social security scheme was built around the centrality of *both* paid and unpaid work. Women, once married, had no obligation to undertake paid work, unlike their husbands and unmarried sisters. They belonged primarily in the home, engaged in unpaid work – i.e. care. Today, the model underpinning European welfare states is developing into the individual worker model. 'Work' means paid work, which takes priority over unpaid work. Women as well as men have an obligation to take it, thus becoming 'active' citizens and avoiding poverty.

By the beginning of the twenty-first century, Britain had a national childcare strategy with the objective of developing the formal childcare market so that mothers could take up paid employment outside the home while other paid workers (almost entirely female) cared for their children. The provision of both formal and informal social care of adults, especially of the growing number of frail elderly, is gradually becoming a policy issue across the EU as the retirement age for women, as well as for men, is being raised in order to reduce the cost of pensions. However, in Britain, formal services to enable older carers to stay in or return to paid work have yet to attract the additional resources that childcare services have received in recent years.

Distinctions between the formal labour market and the 'informal' care system remain. The childcare strategy only supports care in the formal sector: care provided within the family attracts no subsidy. While free half-time education has been expanded for all 3- and 4-year olds, child-care services for children must be paid for. Similarly, the government rejected recommendations of the Royal Commission on Long Term Care in 1999 that care of older people should be provided on the same basis as healthcare – i.e. free at the point of use. In England and Wales social care services attract charges. The Scottish experience of providing free personal care since 2001 shows that, contrary to official expectations, families do not care less, although many care differently.

Family Obligations

Finch and Mason's research on family obligations has looked at how the meaning of responsibility or obligation is understood and practised in families. They challenge the concept of 'fixed obligations' associated with a genealogical link and argue that 'in reality the responsibilities which people feel and acknowledge towards their relatives have more complex and more individual roots' (1995: 180). Obligations between spouses may be more fixed in character (we know less about obligations that cohabitees feel towards each other), but those between parents and adult children can be very variable. They argue for seeing responsibilities as commitments which are built up between specific individuals over time, perhaps over many years. This is done:

> through contact, shared activities and particularly through each giving the other help as it is needed. This process of reciprocity – accepting help and then giving something in return – is the engine which drives the process of developing commitments. Although people do not work with a simplistic balance sheet, reciprocal help given and received over time is a crucial factor in understanding how family relationships operate.
>
> (Ibid.: 54)

These commitments between the generations can survive divorce, although women are much more successful than men in maintaining relationships both with their children and with their former in-laws. This may have consequences for men's care in old age. Finch and Mason warn policy-makers against attempting to enforce obligations which are not consistent with the ways in which families practise and understand their obligations. For example, the failure of the Child Support Act, 1991, to ensure that absent fathers paid maintenance for their children is explained in part by the shift in the obligation to maintain children from the legitimate or social father to the biological father. This was contrary to deeply held beliefs about family responsibilities.

Collective Obligations

The relationship of state welfare policies to both the market and the family has always been the subject of debate. Some have argued that the development of market economies has damaged the family's capacity to support its members. More than fifty years ago, when many Western industrialized nations were debating the future of their state welfare systems, Alva Myrdal wrote, in an influential book: 'Changes in the economic structure of society weaken the family as an institution. Unproductive age groups have no assured place in the new economic order of individualistic money making in nationwide competitive markets' (*Nation and Family*, Kegan Paul, 1945, pp. 4–5). Social welfare provision, or what Myrdal calls 'collective devices', were therefore necessary to substitute for the security once provided by families. Titmuss, writing in the 1950s and 1960s, had a similar view of social welfare as a mechanism for compensating individuals and families who were damaged by economic growth. Those who benefited from a thriving and expanding economy had an obligation to share those benefits with the less fortunate. For him, state welfare policies were also mechanisms for extending altruism beyond the family:

> The ways in which society organises and structures its social institutions – and particularly its health and welfare systems – can encourage or discourage the altruism in man; such systems can foster integration or alienation, they can allow for 'the theme of the gift' – of generosity towards strangers to spread among and between social groups and generations.
>
> (1970: 225)

Titmuss studied blood donors in the NHS as an example of a willingness to give to strangers – moreover, strangers never encountered. He found that their willingness to give stemmed from a sense of obligation to a wider society and confidence in future unknown strangers, who in their turn would give their blood should others, including themselves, ever need it. (It is interesting that when, in the 1980s, the NHS sold blood products abroad, the willingness of some to donate their blood was reduced.)

Others have been rather more sceptical of developing what R. Pinker subsequently called 'the altruistic potentialities of ordinary citizens'. He concluded:

> The welfare institutions of a society symbolise an unstable compromise between compassion and indifference, between altruism and self-interest. If men were predominantly altruistic, compulsory forms of social service would not be necessary; and if men were exclusively self-regarding such compulsion would be impossible. The spirit of altruism, far from being a natural flowering of human nature, must be seen as the product of the rigorous discipline of injunction to self-denial and the repression of the grosser form of self-love.
>
> (Social Theory and Social Policy, Heinemann, 1971, p. 211)

William Beveridge, regarded as one of the principal architects of the British postwar welfare state, proposed a social insurance system based on a clear contract between employers, employees and the state. The risks of unemployment, sickness and old age were pooled. He embedded in his social insurance and social assistance schemes rules to ensure that men's obligations to take paid work in order to support their families, and women's obligations to provide domestic services for their husband and children, were carried over from earlier social security systems. In the last resort, prison faced men who refused work and failed to support their families. However, Beveridge too wanted to encourage altruism within the wider society. This he called 'a sense of Divine Vocation'. Unlike many social policy analysts at the time – or since – he noticed women's altruism: 'Serving, exhausting oneself without thought of personal reward – isn't that what most women do most of their lives in peace or war?' (Pillars of Society, Allen and Unwin, 1943, p. 38). Forty years later, Land and Rose (1985) found many social policies were still based on taken-for-granted assumptions about women's willingness and availability to care for other members of their families, so much so that it was only remarkable when it did not happen. Women's altruism within the family was therefore more accurately described as 'compulsory'.

Jose Harris, Beveridge's biographer, more recently urged historians to investigate 'if, for good or ill, particular welfare policies do encourage particular types of economic, moral or civic behaviour' (William Beveridge: A Biography, Oxford University Press, 1977). As 'choice' and 'competition' are increasingly used as mechanisms for allocating resources within twenty-first-century welfare states and the public are encouraged to think of themselves as 'consumers' rather than as 'citizens', this is an important question for social policy researchers. For example, a study of attitudes towards increasing choice in health services revealed concerns that the promotion of 'an individualistic choice agenda could override concern about lowering the thresholds of severity that justify medical attention. This, in turn, could reduce the degree of self-restraint exercised by some in the use of limited NHS resources' (R. Rosen et al., *Public Views on Choices in Health and Health Care*, King's Fund, 2005).

Self-Reliance and Self-Protection

The debates about social welfare in the UK during the 1980s and 1990s were dominated by those who believed that state welfare provision undermines both the efficient working of the economic market and obligations within the family. This was coupled with a view that only the poor need state welfare provision – the middle classes and the wealthy can look after themselves. In her first speech in the 1979 general election campaign, Margaret Thatcher said:

> [W]hat is the real driving force of society? It's the desire for the individual to do the best for himself and his family. People don't go out to work for the Chancellor of the Exchequer, they go out to work for their family, for their children, to help look after their parents . . . that's the way societies improve – by millions of people resolving that they'll give their children a better life than they had themselves, and there's just no substitute for this elemental human instinct.
> (Cited in W. Webster, *Not a Man to Match Her*, The Women's Press, 1990, p. 59)

Taxation was seen to be not only damaging to enterprise but also a way of 'buying your way out of your obligations to society', to use the words of a Home Secretary, and was therefore undesirable. Margaret Thatcher herself asserted that 'there is no such thing as society'. So, by definition, state welfare policies could neither foster, nor be fostered by, altruism and reciprocity beyond the family.

This view of society comprising self-seeking, individualistic people has been strengthened by the rise of sociobiology.

Eugenics, which underpinned the belief in the naturalness of inequalities and hierarchies in the first half of the twentieth century, was influential in the social policy debates of the time in Britain and the United States. Sociobiology is now providing a similar ideological basis for undermining the arguments for a universalistic welfare state. From the early 1970s, its proponents have been arguing that prime among the traits inherent in our nature is selfishness. Richard Dawkins claimed that everything organisms do is done out of self-interest. In the preface to his first best-selling book, *The Selfish Gene* (Oxford University Press, 1976) he wrote: 'We are survival machines – robot vehicles blindly programmed to preserve the selfish molecules known as genes.' Thus, he argued, 'at the gene level, altruism must be bad and selfishness good. . . . The gene is the basic unit of selfishness' (ibid.: 38). In this model women's greater commitment to child-rearing follows from the belief that women and men must adopt different strategies to maximize opportunities to spread their genes into future generations. Altruism is explained away. As a fellow sociobiologist at the time wrote:

> What passes for co-operation turns out to be a mixture of opportunism and exploitation. The impulses that lead one animal to sacrifice himself for another turn out to have their ultimate rationale in gaining advantage over a third, and acts for the good of the 'society' turn out to be performed for the detriment of the rest. . . . Scratch an 'altruist' and watch a 'hypocrite' bleed.
> (M. Ghiselin, *The Economy of Nature and the Evolution of Sex*, University of California Press, 1974, p. 247)

Sociobiology is now being challenged within the biological sciences, but genetic determinism and reductionism serve to turn attention away from the environmental and structural causes of inequalities, fail to recognize the interdependence of individuals within society or of societies across the globe and so support the view that a minimal welfare state is not only desirable but all that is possible.

By the beginning of the twenty-first century, the global dominance of neo-liberalism framed these debates. In their analysis of the changing relationship of individuals to each other and to the wider society, Beck and Beck-Gernsheim (2002) use the concept of 'individualization'. This is different from individualism and the concept of the self-sufficient individual embedded in neo-liberal economic theory. Individualization can be thought of as 'institutionalized individualism', which does not breed a 'me-first' society. On the contrary, those who want to have a life of their own have to be very sensitive to others' needs and wants as well as able to negotiate the terms of living together. Traditional family relationships and class divisions can no longer be taken for granted as they were earlier in the twentieth century. Beck and Beck-Gernsheim argue that 'in developed modernity . . . human mutuality and community rest no longer on solidly established traditions, but, rather, on a paradoxical collectivity of reciprocal individualization' (2002: xxi–xxii).

Emerging Issues

The emphasis on increasing economic activity rates for all adults is a shared goal across the EU and will inevitably bring unpaid work into sharper focus. In those countries where childcare and social care services have become a collective responsibility, demonstrating a public commitment to solidarity between the generations as well as between rich and poor, it is easier to reconcile paid work and care. This is not the case in the UK. A key objective of the welfare state in the UK continues to be 'to rebuild the system around work and security' (to quote a remark made by Tony Blair in 1998). At the same time, the assumption that 'it is family and friends, of course, who still take on most of the caring responsibilities' (Tony Blair, preface to the Green Paper on Health and Social Care, 2005) prevails. If this care is to be 'given willingly and not taken for granted', then it will become increasingly important to understand and nurture altruism and reciprocity both inside and outside the family. This in turn will require a more fundamental review of the obligations and rights of citizenship.

Guide to Further Sources

R. M. Titmuss's *The Gift Relationship* (Allen and Unwin, 1970) has remained an important contribution to the social policy literature on altruism and reciprocity and includes his empirical study of blood donors. H. Land and H. Rose, 'Compulsory altruism for some or an altruistic society for all?', in P. Bean, J. Ferris and D. Whynes (eds), *In Defence of Welfare* (Tavistock, 1985) exposes how women's altruism underpins social policies. J. Finch and J. Mason, *Negotiating Family Responsibilities* (Routledge, 1995) studies the processes by which family members meet – or not – the obligations between them.

D. Collard, *Altruism and the Economy* (Oxford University Press, 1978) discusses altruism and its relevance to economic and social analysis from an economist's point of view. N. Folbre, *The Invisible Heart* (The New Press, 2001) analyses the importance of the values of love, reciprocity and obligation which underpin our society and economy. J. O'Neill, *The Missing Child in Liberal Theory* (University of Toronto Press, 1994) argues for a renewal of the social contract between the generations and criticizes a political economy which emphasizes individualism and ignores social responsibility. M. Midgley, *Evolution as Religion* (Methuen, 1985) gives a philosopher's perspective on these concepts and provides an excellent critique of sociobiology. U. Beck and E. Beck-Gernsheim, *Individualization* (Sage, 2002) explores the meaning and consequences of individualism.

N. Gilbert, *Transformation of the Welfare State* (Oxford University Press, 2002) is a comparative study of welfare reform in European countries and the US in the context of a free market world. M. Daly and J. Lewis, 'The concept of social care and the analysis of contemporary welfare states', in *British Journal of Sociology*, 51/2 (2000): 281–98, provides a comprehensive overview of social care and its importance, located as it is in principle and practice at the intersection of state, market and family.

Part II

Key Perspectives

Chapter 8

Neo-Liberalism

Nick Ellison

Overview

- Neo-liberal ideas pose a significant challenge for supporters of extensive systems of public welfare because they believe these systems are expensive, inefficient and unnecessary.
- Neo-liberalism has its roots in classical liberal thinking and in the writings of Adam Smith in particular. Core ideas have changed little over time with the belief in individual freedom and the free market continuing to underpin neo-liberal ideals.
- Late twentieth-century neo-liberalism is closely associated with the work of Milton Friedman and Friedrich von Hayek, the latter refining ideas of 'negative liberty' and the role of the free market to challenge socialist and social democratic conceptions of 'social justice'.
- For neo-liberals, extensive public welfare systems need to be sharply cut back to eliminate bureaucratic waste, reduce taxation, allow greater choice through the private provision of goods and services and reduce welfare dependency.
- For all its apparent elegance, neo-liberal thinking contains critical flaws. For example, the conception of 'negative liberty' is unduly restricted and the faith in pure market solutions, particularly where welfare goods and services are concerned, may be misplaced.

The Neo-Liberal Challenge

Neo-liberal ideas are immensely challenging for those who believe that the state has a central role to play in the organization and delivery of 'welfare' in economically developed societies. Why? Because neo-liberals fundamentally question the need for the majority of publicly funded, state-delivered or state-regulated institutions that, taken together, comprise a 'welfare state'. As they developed from the 1960s onwards, the core beliefs and principles of neo-liberalism are best understood as a concerted attack on the comprehensive systems of social protection that emerged in Western Europe and the UK in the immediate post-war period, as well as on socialist and social democratic assumptions about the importance of social equality and social justice that underpinned them.

Two important arguments stand out. First, neo-liberals believe that nation-states were undermined economically during the post-war period (roughly 1945–80) because governments diverted resources away from productive, entrepreneurial firms and individuals operating in the free market to the systematic state-based protection of vulnerable sections of their populations. The high taxation required to sustain levels of welfare provision that went beyond a basic 'safety-net' for the worst off reduced both the scope for investment and also incentives to act entrepreneurially in the marketplace. Second, neo-liberals argue that, ironically, comprehensive social protection does not work anyway. For one thing, public money is wasted on vast welfare bureaucracies that appear keener to preserve their own budgets than to provide a good level and choice of services to those in need; for another, welfare recipients tend to become 'welfare-dependent' and so fail to act as responsible individuals earning in the marketplace, and looking after themselves and their families.

These claims about the damaging effects of state welfare will be examined in more detail below. It is worth noting here, however, that, whether or not neo-liberal ideas are considered valid, they force those who engage with them to think hard about their own values and beliefs. How 'responsible' should individuals be for their own welfare and well-being, for example? How far should the state intervene to support the lives of vulnerable individuals and groups? Rather differently, should the free market and the individual freedom on which neo-liberals claim it depends be regarded as the key organizing principles of human societies? A brief historical survey of classical liberalism and its contemporary – neo-liberal – variant will show how perennial these questions are and, indeed, how relevant they remain to modern social policy.

From Classical Liberalism to Neo-Liberalism: An Historical Survey

The roots of neo-liberalism lie in the particular understandings of the nature of the free market and individual freedom developed by liberal political economists in the late eighteenth and nineteenth centuries. Although writing in political, social and economic circumstances very different from his modern-day counterparts, Adam Smith (1723–90) is regarded as the founding figure of a political philosophy that considers the free market to be the main organizing feature of society and believes state intervention in market activities to be inherently destructive. Smith argued that the market could secure individual *and* social welfare, and, most importantly, human liberty. It could create these benefits, in his view, because, paradoxically, individuals' self-interested pursuit of wealth naturally leads to *collective* prosperity. Simply put, the selfish desire to prosper and make a profit is constrained by competition in the marketplace because free competition among producers inevitably leads to falling prices and thus a 'natural' balance between supply and demand. So long as this self-correcting mechanism is allowed to function relatively unhindered, prosperity would be assured. Indeed, the only justification for interference in the marketplace, so far as Smith was concerned, was precisely to preserve its freedom. A legal framework for market operations is important, for instance, as is the provision of certain public goods such as law and order and public health.

This basic set of beliefs was endorsed and extended by successive generations of liberal thinkers in the Victorian era – with one interesting twist. While Smith and early Victorian thinkers like David Ricardo were primarily concerned with the nature and role of the free market and the place of free individuals within it, their counterparts writing in the mid-to-late Victorian period took the further step of elevating this economic individualism into a political creed that stressed the virtues of individual responsibility, hard work and 'self-help'. As Heywood (2003: 53) has noted, Samuel Smiles's popular volume *Self-Help* (1859) 'begins by reiterating the well-tried maxim that "Heaven helps those who help themselves"'. This perspective was given greater philosophical expression by Herbert Spencer, who used Darwinian notions of the 'survival of the fittest' in the animal kingdom to justify inequalities of power, income and status in human societies.

Taken together, these ideals of individual liberty, the free market and the minimal state, with the added element of personal responsibility and self-help, make up the classical liberal legacy. Neo-liberals like Hayek and Friedman, writing in the postwar period, more or less reproduced these ideas in their own thinking – but enhanced particular aspects in their sustained attack on the failings of twentieth-century state collectivism embodied in the interventionist 'Keynesian welfare state'.

Neo-Liberalism in the Late Twentieth Century

Friedman is best known for his commitment to limited government and the conviction that individuals' natural initiative and drive can only be released if they are allowed to compete freely in the marketplace (see Friedman 1962). He was particularly critical of Keynesian economic policies designed to stimulate demand in periods of economic recession, because the government borrowing that this entailed only served to fuel inflation. Friedman argued that governments should restrict their activities to controlling the amount of money in the economy at any time – expanding or contracting money supply depending on the balance of inflationary and deflationary tendencies, but otherwise keeping taxes and spending low so as not to distort market outcomes.

Hayek's ideas pushed beyond economics into a developed neo-liberal political philosophy. The free market and minimal state were certainly cornerstones of this perspective, but Hayek also built on the ideal of human liberty proposed by Smith and others. In particular, he used a concept of 'negative freedom' to underpin an approach to politics and society that proved particularly influential for a generation of neo-liberal thinkers that emerged in the late 1970s and 1980s in the UK and USA. For Hayek (1960: 12), freedom meant 'independence of the arbitrary will of another'. Individuals were 'free' so long as they were not coerced into decisions or actions that they would not otherwise take. Indeed, like Smith, the only form of 'coercion' that Hayek would countenance was from a minimal state dedicated to ensuring, through an agreed impersonal legal framework, that private individuals could not arbitrarily limit others' actions and choices.

Box 8.1   Key principles

- *Human liberty*: the freedom of individuals to act as they choose, without interference from institutions or other individuals, providing only that their actions are consistent with the liberty of others
- *A competitive market economy*: kept as free as possible from state interference
- *Preservation of the rule of law*: a constitutional framework that limits state powers and institutionalizes rules of property, contract and tort
- *Minimal public provision*: applying only to those goods like public health that markets cannot efficiently provide
- *'Safety-net' security*: for older people and others unable to work in the marketplace

This understanding of liberty is 'negative' because it argues that individuals should be free *from* constraints – what each individual does with this freedom is a private matter. Taken together, Hayek believed that human liberty and the free market, working through a process of what he termed 'catallaxy', would create a natural, spontaneous socio-economic order more efficient and less coercive than the state-based, interventionist systems produced by socialist or Keynesian social democratic forms of governance. Any attempt to interfere with this natural order – however well meaning – would only increase the likelihood of coercion and so reduce liberty. Hayek (1960: 385) was especially critical of efforts to 'limit the effects of accident' through policies designed to produce greater 'social justice', arguing that policy-makers and others could not possibly possess the necessary levels of information to ensure a better distribution of justice than that achieved in the marketplace – indeed it was a 'conceit' even to try. It was this conviction that the organization of society should approximate as closely as possible to the natural order produced by the market that inspired the neo-liberal counter-attack against extensive state welfare systems in the 1970s and 1980s.

Neo-Liberalism and Welfare

For neo-liberals, 'welfare states', with their large, complex, public welfare bureaucracies, are inherently coercive. Coercion comes through monopolistic state provision of social services which has the effect

---

Box 8.2

Two concepts

- *Bureaucratic over-supply*: key public servants will devise budget-maximizing strategies to increase salaries, prestige and other resources as opposed to dispensing high-quality services to client populations.
- *State coercion*: state welfare services are monopolistic and therefore restrict choice. Users are forced to rely on state services and have no means of challenging their nature and quality.

Five remedies

- *Reduction of state welfare provision*: reduced state activity will allow private and voluntary organizations to enter the welfare marketplace, cutting the costs of public sector bureaucracy.
- *Greater choice of services*: new service-providers will allow welfare consumers greater choice of provision.
- *Negative income tax*: for those on low incomes, the state should subsidize earnings to ensure continued participation in the marketplace. NIT is a simple single 'payment' adjusted to cover basic needs.
- *Safety-net welfare*: individuals and their families should be encouraged to insure against risk. The worst off will need public support, but income should be provided at subsistence level and services delivered through voucher schemes where feasible.
- *Tax cuts*: savings from the closure of monopolistic state bureaucracies should be returned to individual earners through tax cuts.

of 'squeezing out' private and voluntary alternatives, thus limiting both consumer choice and the freedom of individuals to supply welfare goods and services. The fact that, with the exception of a wealthy minority, individuals in the UK have to obtain medical care from the state-run National Health Service and education from state comprehensive schools constrains choice and decision-making, according to neo-liberals, and thus restricts human liberty.

In addition to the problem of state coercion, neo-liberal thinkers like Seldon and Minford in the UK, and public choice economists such as Niskanen and Tullock in the US, have argued that civil servants have an interest in expanding the size of their budgets 'because their salaries and frills of office vary directly with the size of the budgets they administer' (Seldon 1987: 7). This tendency is compounded by politicians, who collude with budget maximization strategies because they believe that voters respond positively to public spending on key services. Unfortunately, according to neo-liberal thinkers, politicians are rather less keen on raising the taxes required to pay for these services, with the result that 'bureaucratic over-supply' inevitably leads to unmanageable public sector deficits and subsequent budget crises.

Taken together, monopolistic behaviour that crowds out alternative service-providers and civil servants' tendencies to protect their own budgets are perhaps the worst evils of state welfare, as neo-liberals see it. However, Seldon lists a number of other features which exacerbate the problem. For example, the high taxation required to fund extensive public welfare systems depresses incentives and therefore reduces risk-taking in the marketplace – and tax collecting is also costly. Again, owing to lack of competition, state-supplied services tend to neglect quality, while public sector employers and (unionized) employees can be resistant to change, thereby compromising innovation in terms of both choice and quality of

service. Finally, Seldon makes the point that the real losers in the welfare game are the poor. Low-income groups lack the resources to contest bureaucratic decisions and pay a higher proportion of their earnings in taxation to fund poor-quality services. Moreover, as Murray (1984) argues, lack of choice leads to welfare-dependency and failures of personal responsibility because families on low incomes are not encouraged to take active decisions about the goods and services they require, or to budget to meet their costs.

In view of the above, it is not surprising that neo-liberals have a very different conception of 'welfare' from that prevailing in many of the developed economies in the post-war period. As Minford (1991) makes clear, the waste associated with monopolistic provision and over-supply can be reduced through privatization strategies, which would widen individual choice and also encourage individuals to understand that many services should be paid for. In his view, the state should provide only a minimal 'safety-net' for the poorest. In terms of income for this group, a safety-net approach advocates a Negative Income Tax (NIT) to subsidize low wages and maintain incentives to work – this system replacing costly means-tested systems with effectively one 'payment' covering housing costs and other recognized needs associated with, for instance, family size. Elsewhere, health and education services would have to be 'paid for' by vouchers which could be exchanged at surgeries, hospitals and schools of choice. For Minford, there would be no extra help for vulnerable groups like retired people, who should have made provision for their old age by contributing to a pension plan during their working life, while – echoing Murray's views – the extent of support for single parents should be minimal because 'there is a trade-off . . . between alleviating distress and encouraging the conditions for more distress' (1991: 79). Finally, savings made from the drastic reduction of state welfare services would be handed to individual earners in the form of tax cuts – the idea being that potential consumers would be able to use a greater proportion of their earnings to buy services of their choice for themselves and their families.

Neo-Liberalism and Welfare: A Critique

Box 8.3   Four criticisms

Neo-liberals fail to:

- appreciate the potential of 'positive' freedom;
- distinguish between freedom and 'ability';
- appreciate that privately run institutions can also act coercively;
- understand that the socio-cultural dimensions of welfare are important.

Although neo-liberal arguments about the size, power and expense of state welfare systems are compelling, it is important to consider briefly some of the conceptual difficulties associated with this perspective. Four key points will suffice here – each of which fundamentally questions the core assumptions that underpin the neo-liberal approach. First, might it be that the definition of human liberty employed by Hayek and others is too narrow? It focuses exclusively on *individuals* and, as mentioned, is conceived negatively as 'freedom from' constraint. This understanding dismisses a 'positive' conception of liberty cast in terms of the 'freedom to', for example, make the most of one's potential, or for social groups – women or minority ethnic populations – to pursue collective benefits like equal opportunities, which are perceived as adding to their collective liberty. Second, as

Plant (1990) argues, neo-liberals do not distinguish between 'freedom' and 'ability'. For Plant, the free market distributes income and resources neither fairly nor equally, and those with less earning power and few other advantages, often through no fault of their own, have less *ability* to use their liberty than wealthier individuals. It is possible to argue, then, that absence of ability is an effective constraint on the freedom of the less fortunate.

Third, state institutions are not necessarily more or less coercive than their private sector counterparts. *Any* organization can act in a high-handed fashion and be insensitive to the needs of its 'customers' – and state welfare agencies are certainly no exception. Nevertheless, private sector service providers can also 'coerce' consumers by creating price cartels, thus restricting choice, or by providing 'selective information' about the benefits of their products. In each case, providers are able to circumvent the supposedly price-reducing environment of the competitive market. Arguably, too, state institutions can at least be called to account through the democratic process if service provision is unsatisfactory. Where neo-liberal objections about bureaucratic over-supply are concerned, critics would argue that executives and managers in the private sector appear no less successful at expanding salaries and budgets than their public sector counterparts.

Finally, on taxation and incentives, comparative analysis suggests that expectations about tax levels vary greatly in different countries. The US or the UK favour low taxation on the grounds that it stimulates entrepreneurial behaviour and encourages personal responsibility. Scandinavian countries, however, despite some adjustments in recent years, tax highly and provide comprehensive social services as a basic citizenship right. Significantly, high tax rates and an extensive welfare state do not appear to have reduced Swedish economic competitiveness or created high levels of welfare-dependency. Might it be that attitudes to taxation, incentives and responsibility have a socio-cultural dimension, which influences individuals' decision-making and the kind of rationality they deploy?

Emerging Issues: Neo-Liberalism in the Twenty-First Century

On one reading, neo-liberal thinking has had a clear impact on welfare systems in countries like the UK and the US. No UK government – the Conservative administrations of the 1980s and 1990s included – set out to implement a purely neo-liberal agenda, but key elements of neo-liberal thinking have undoubtedly influenced social and economic policy-makers over the past thirty or so years. Perhaps the key 'headline' is that New Labour governments have broadly accepted the free market as the principal system of resource allocation for the economy as a whole in a way that 'Old Labour' simply did not. Even though core goods and services like healthcare are not allocated strictly according to market principles, governments have increasingly mimicked market behaviour by creating 'internal markets' or 'quasi-markets' within publicly funded services. Increasingly, too, private companies provide certain services to the health and education sectors, while private funding for new schools and hospitals is channelled through Private–Public Partnerships and the Private Finance Initiative.

'Welfare' has certainly got tougher. Those in receipt of unemployment benefits have actively to seek work, and many single parents and disabled people are also being strongly 'encouraged' to find employment. Benefits themselves are less generous and more rigorously means-tested than they were in the heyday of the Keynesian welfare state – and these changes have contributed to an increasing sense that welfare is no longer about the *protection* of groups and individuals who are deemed vulnerable to market forces, but about the provision of (basic) opportunities for 'responsible individuals' to capitalize on as best they can.

And yet, to make too much of this shift towards markets and tough welfare, or to ascribe it *solely* to neo-liberal influence, would be to go too far. In the UK in recent years, the undoubted enthusiasm for elements of the neo-liberal agenda has gone hand in hand with demands that the inequalities of the marketplace be balanced by policies that enhance social inclusion and 'equity', if not 'equality' (see chapter 5). For all the faults and vagueness of 'third way' welfare, a concern with social justice persists – to the point, in fact, where neo-liberal calls for *pure* market solutions look increasingly dated. As to the role of neo-liberal ideas in the turn towards markets in the 1980s and 1990s, it is important not to overstate the case. Ideas *reflect*, as much as drive, economic, political and social change. Global economic competition, the changing nature of work and rising unemployment, the dramatic impact of the new information and communication technologies, and the increasing affluence of the majority of people in economically developed countries – each of these factors and many others affect prevailing understandings of the role and purposes of welfare, encouraging new thinking and forcing policy changes as government struggle with complexities and contingencies often beyond their control.

In many ways, then, the 'emerging issue' for neo-liberal thinking in the twenty-first century is much the same as it is for other nineteenth- and twentieth-century ideologies. With traditional divisions between state and market, public and private, losing their erstwhile significance in favour of more nuanced understandings of these relationships, and with a host of other challenges growing in importance, how successfully can neo-liberal solutions maintain relevance and credibility in this complex and rapidly changing world?

Guide to Further Sources

The Adam Smith Institute (ASI), The Centre for Policy Studies, and Civitas, three key neo-liberal think-tanks, run websites that provide a wealth of information about contemporary neo-liberal thinking, including current publications (<www.adamsmith.org>, <www.cps.org/uk>, <www.civitas.org.uk>). The ASI and Civitas also have interesting blogs carrying pithy views about current politics and news (<www.adamsmith.org/blog>, <www.civitas.org.uk/blog>).

The 'classic' economic case for the free market and limited government is made by M. Friedman, *Capitalism and Freedom* (Chicago University Press, 1962). For a more philosophical account of neo-liberal ideas, see F. Hayek, *The Constitution of Liberty* (Routledge, 1960). Essential reading for anyone wishing to understand the neo-liberal approach to state welfare is P. Minford, 'The role of the social services: a view from the New Right', in M. Loney, R. Bocock, J. Clarke, A. Cochrane, P. Graham and M. Wilson (eds), *The State or the Market: Politics and Welfare in Contemporary Britain* (Sage, 1991). A further and equally combative example from another devotee can be found in A. Seldon, *The New Economics*, Study Guide No 2 (Libertarian Alliance, 1987). See also Seldon's pamphlet, *Whither the Welfare State* (IEA, 1981). These approaches are echoed in the USA by C. Murray, *Losing Ground* (Basic Books, 1984) – a neo-liberal account of the failure of the US welfare system containing contentious remedies for welfare dependency.

The best short critique of the neo-liberal perspective is R. Plant, *Citizenship and Rights in Thatcher's Britain: Two Views, R. Plant and N. Barry* (IEA, 1990). A more developed account can be found in D. King, *The New Right* (Palgrave, 1987). For a general overview of liberal ideas, see A. Heywood, *Political Ideologies: An Introduction*, 3rd edn (Palgrave, 2003).

Chapter 9

The Conservative Tradition

Robert Pinker

Overview

- By the 1870s, the Conservatives were transforming themselves into a party of national unity and social reform. Disraeli's vision of a 'One Nation' Britain was underpinned by policies designed to steer a middle way between the extremes of liberal individualism and socialist collectivism.
- During the 1930s, a small but growing number of Conservative politicians came out in support of strengthening the role of central government in the fields of economic and social policy.
- After their 1952 election victory, the Conservatives extended the provisions of the welfare state and, in doing so, consolidated a cross-party policy consensus that was to survive into the 1970s.
- From 1979 onwards, this consensus fell apart as the Thatcher and Major governments – intent on rolling back the frontiers of the state – implemented new policies of privatization and welfare pluralism. The trend towards more centralization, however, gathered momentum and continued doing so after Labour's 1997 election victory.
- In 2006, the Conservatives – then in opposition – launched a programme of policy reappraisal and 'intellectual renewal'. Growth in the economy and the public sector, more equitable access to services and more local decision-taking were identified as preconditions for social well-being. Within these new parameters, the Conservatives began re-establishing themselves as a party of the centre ground.

Conservatism and the Enlightenment

Conservatism is as much an attitude of mind as the doctrine of a political party. It is a generic way of looking at the world, of conceptualizing society and responding to social change. True conservatives know in their hearts that all political and economic theories are subject to a law of diminishing marginal utility. They are as sceptical of the free play of market forces as they are of state regulation, which sets them apart from both neo-liberals on the one hand and socialists on the other. They look on compromise as the invisible hand that reconciles equally important but frequently conflicting imperatives.

The scholars of the Enlightenment laid the foundations of the modern social sciences and opened a new era in the application of scientific methods to the study of social problems. They challenged the traditional institutions of political and religious authority and delineated new kinds of relationship between the state, civil society and individuals in a spirit of optimism regarding the possibilities of social progress. The guiding tenets of the French Revolution – liberty, equality and fraternity – were inspired by some of the most powerful traditions of Enlightenment thought.

By the start of the nineteenth century, however, an intellectual reaction against Enlightenment thought was becoming more overt, widespread and influential. This development was inspired by a number of conservative thinkers who were opposed to the ideals and objectives of the French Revolution. There were also some early socialists who had supported many of the revolutionary ideals, but who were deeply disillusioned with the political, social and economic outcomes. Although these intellectual movements were separated by fundamental political differences, their leading thinkers shared a common belief in the virtues of an organic model of society and an aversion to what they saw as the rampant individualism of the new social orders which were emerging in Western Europe and North America.

The conservative approach to social welfare starts not from the formulation of abstract principles, but from the reality of established social institutions such as the family, community, class, religion and private property. Allied to these beliefs was a hostility towards the encroachment of the central government into local affairs and a natural suspicion of free market liberalism. Edmund Burke is generally considered to be the founding father of modern Conservatism, although for the greater part of his life he was a leading Whig politician. 'Politics', Burke argued, 'ought to be adjusted, not to human reasoning, but to human nature; of which the reason is but a part

and by no means the greatest part' (cited in O'Gorman 1986: 13). Certainly there was a place for reason in politics, but it should be exercised under the guidance of precedent and opinions that have stood the test of time. Burke thought that in political life, the arts of government and reform should not be taught a priori because abstract principles took insufficient account of the complexities of human nature and society. He described the sentiments which create the moral framework of a nation in developmental terms: 'To be attached to the subdivision, to love the little platoon we belong to in society, is the first principle (the germ, as it were) of public affections. It is the first link in the series by which we proceed towards a love to our country and to mankind' (cited in Gilmour 1978: 157).

From the early nineteenth century onwards, close normative affinities developed between the doctrines of political economy, utilitarianism and British liberal thought. By contrast, conservative political philosophy remained closely identified with an organic ideal of social organization. Romantic conservatives like Samuel Coleridge, Tory radicals like Richard Oastler and William Wilberforce and maverick populists like William Cobbett shared a common detestation of the theories propounded by Jeremy Bentham, David Ricardo and Thomas Malthus. They denounced the new Poor Law because they believed that its introduction would further undermine the traditional framework of obligations and entitlements on which British society had always been based.

Much of the subsequent history of Victorian conservatism can be seen as a gradual process of coming to terms with the realities of industrial and urban change and reconciling as far as possible the old values of order, hierarchy and paternalism with the new values of competition and possessive individualism. Under Robert Peel's administration, the Corn Laws were finally repealed and a long overdue start was made on fiscal and administrative reform. Benjamin Disraeli's vision of 'One Nation' sought to reaffirm the ideal of an organic model of society held together by traditional bonds of patriotic sentiment but strengthened by new solidaristic doctrines and objectives, including the extension of representative democracy through the enfranchisement of the respectable working class, a programme of popular welfare reforms and the inculcation of a sense of imperial mission in the British people.

The party that had once opposed the growth of empire became the party of empire, and the old values of patriotism became overlaid with a new doctrine of imperialism. In the 1890s, Joseph Chamberlain set out to make the Conservatives the leading party of social reform. In his Tariff Reform League he tried to link the objectives of imperial preference and social reform together in one programme. Chamberlain hoped that the revenue raised from tariffs on non-imperial imports could be used to finance a radical programme of free education and universal old age pensions. The League was founded in 1903 but it did not long survive the Liberal election victory of 1905.

Conservatism and Social Reform

By the end of the nineteenth century British conservatism had come to terms with market capitalism. Its own paternalist tradition of collectivism lived on, but it was now complemented by a defence of industrialism *and* a limited measure of state intervention in social welfare. It had become a tradition of thought that was as much opposed to liberal individualism as it was to socialist collectivism. Writing in 1947, the young Quintin Hogg, a leading Conservative thinker later to become Lord Hailsham, indicted liberalism as the 'body of doctrine aimed at reducing the authority of the state to a minimum'. It was, he went

on to argue, 'the Tory Party which took its stand in the nineteenth century against the principles of laissez-faire liberalism' and supported the idea of state regulation in some spheres of economic activity. Conservatism, he argued, stood for the ideals of economic democracy, the extension of property ownership and the diffusion of political power (Hogg 1947: 48–51).

Nevertheless, the Conservative Party spent most of the first two decades of the twentieth century in standing against the rise of liberal collectivism. It opposed most of the social reforms introduced by the Liberals from 1905 to the outbreak of the First World War. It should, however, be noted that when the Conservatives were in office during the inter-war years, they left the basic structure of these new provisions intact. In some sectors of social service they imposed cuts and in others they introduced new benefits, notably with regard to widows, orphans and old age pensions. It was a Conservative administration that replaced the Poor Law with Public Assistance in 1929 and opened the way for local authorities to develop their own hospital services. In many respects, the Conservatives were more successful than the Liberals in reconciling the conflicts between individualism and collectivism that beset both parties during the inter-war years.

It was, however, during this period that a minority of Conservative politicians began to campaign for more radical collectivist policies. In 1938, Harold Macmillan – then a young and dissident backbencher – published his classic exposition of the case for Tory collectivism. In *The Middle Way* he set out a powerful defence of both private enterprise and a corporatist-style economy managed on Keynesian lines. It commended a substantial degree of subsidy for state-owned public utilities, policies of full employment with minimum wage legislation and a major extension of the statutory social services. At the time, Macmillan and his supporters were largely ignored.

Like the neo-liberal Conservatives of the 1960s they had to wait for nearly two decades before their policy proposals were to be taken seriously and implemented.

During the Second World War, the Conservative Party was both collectivist and anti-collectivist in its approach to social reform. It committed itself to supporting policies of full employment, educational reform and the introduction of family allowances. It opposed some of the key proposals of the Beveridge Report and went on to suffer a humiliating electoral defeat in 1945 as a consequence. At the time of the 1945 general election, Quintin Hogg anticipated this defeat when he wrote an 'open letter' to his party. He asked his colleagues whether they were being progressive enough in their attitude to reform and he went on to argue that if the Conservatives continued to oppose the Beveridge plan they would end up not only 'dead but damned'.

In the event, the Conservatives were damned but not left for dead. During their years in opposition they began a radical reappraisal of their approach to social policy issues. Some of the younger Conservatives, notably Enoch Powell, Ian MacLeod and Angus Maude, were invited by the party to write a monograph on the future of the social services. Their proposals were published in 1950 under the title *One Nation*, and were endorsed at the party's annual conference of that year.

Although the *One Nation* group was critical of some aspects of the newly established post-war welfare state, notably with regard to what it considered to be its undue reliance on universalism, it recommended a higher rate of public sector home building, support for the National Health Service, the maintenance of full employment and closer cooperation with the trade unions.

Much has been written about the extent to which the years between 1951 and 1979 can be described as a period of post-war consensus between the major political parties regarding the future of the welfare state. When the Conservatives were returned to office in 1951, they did not dismantle the institutional framework of the post-war settlement. In many respects they extended it. Yet it was during this period that neo-liberal Conservative scholars and politicians started to mount their critique of collectivist welfare and to extend their influence throughout the rank and file as well as the top echelons of the Conservative Party.

Conservatism and the Challenge of Neo-Liberalism

When Edward Heath took office in 1970 he dallied briefly with some of the free market policies of the neo-liberal 'new right' but soon abandoned these approaches in the face of rising unemployment. After Margaret Thatcher became leader of the Conservative Party in 1976, the tide of influential opinion in the party turned sharply against all forms of collectivism and the neo-liberal theories of the 'new right' moved into their ascendancy.

The ensuing battle for the 'soul of the Conservative Party' is described in retrospect by Ian Gilmour, who was to become one of its first ministerial casualties. Only two years before Margaret Thatcher became Prime Minister in 1979, Gilmour felt able to claim that the Conservatives supported both private enterprise and private property, but that first and foremost it was a party of national unity. As such, it abjured all forms of ideology because all ideologies support particular class interests and, as such, were a threat to national unity. Up to that point, at least, it could be said that the ideals of an organic society and a unitary welfare state still enjoyed support in some sections of the party.

Margaret Thatcher was not, in this or any other meaning of the term, a traditional Conservative. She was intent on transforming and revitalizing a failing British economy by giving greater play to the role of competitive market forces and rolling back the economic and social frontiers of the state. Under her leadership, the Conservatives went on to win four successive general elections and remained in office from 1979 to 1997. She was succeeded by John Major as Prime Minister in 1990.

Simon Jenkins, in his book *Thatcher and Sons*, identifies two distinct stages in the unfolding of Conservative economic and social policies during this period. From 1979 to the mid-1980s, priority was given to cutting taxes, holding down public expenditure, privatizing industries, reforming employment and trade union laws and selling off council houses. Inflation was brought under control, the economy was made more competitive and the frontiers of the state were rolled back, despite the protests of One Nation traditionalist 'wets' within the party.

The second stage of the Thatcher revolution began after her third election victory in 1987. High priority was given to social policy reform. The National Health Service was reorganized into a network of internal markets, designed to raise standards of service efficiency, to make services providers more accountable to government and to optimize patient choice. In education, a National Curriculum was introduced along with a system of pupil attainment tests. Schools were allowed to opt out of local authority control and receive their budgets direct from central government, subject to support from a majority of the parents. The universities were placed under strict government control. Private landlords and Housing Associations were allowed to take over housing estates, subject to the agreement of a majority of their tenants. Rent controls in private housing were abolished. The introduction of a new poll tax in place of the old local rating system was deeply unpopular and eventually became one of the causes of Thatcher's fall from office.

These examples illustrate some of the ways in which the structure of the British welfare state was transformed, rather than rolled back, during the Thatcher years. The old corporatist ethos gave way to a new model of welfare pluralism in which closer cooperation between the public and the private sectors was encouraged. Most importantly, the long-term decline of the British economy was checked and put back on a growth trajectory.

The paradox at the heart of Thatcher's transformation of the British welfare state was that although the policies were directed towards libertarian and devolutionary ends, they had to be imposed from the top down by central government diktat. As is so often the case in democratic societies, the more radical policies become, the more vigorously they are opposed. In this respect, Thatcher considered the local authorities and most public sector professional workers to be part of the problem. She did not trust them and she set about marginalizing them.

For all these reasons, despite the introduction of internal markets, the NHS command structure was made more highly centralized than ever before. Under the new regime of the National Curriculum, all aspects of educational policy and classroom practice were made subject to continuous control and surveillance from the centre. In Jenkins's view, Thatcher 'centralised government, enforced Treasury discipline and regulated both public and private sectors to an unprecedented degree.' (2006: 4).

The Conservatives went on to win their fourth general election in 1992 under John Major's leadership. Thereafter, in social policy, priority was given to tackling the problem of long-term welfare dependency. At that time, there were more than a million lone parents of whom two-thirds were dependent on income support. The Child Support Agency was established and charged with the task of making absent fathers contribute towards the cost of maintaining their families. Unemployment benefit was replaced by a Jobseekers' Allowance. All applicants were required to demonstrate that they were actively seeking work or willing to undertake retraining. These 'welfare-to-work' initiatives were key elements in the government's ongoing efforts to check the rising level of social expenditure.

A broad consensus on social policy ends and means eventually emerged within the Conservative Party during the Thatcher and Major years of government – in marked contrast to the increasingly acrimonious debate about Europe. When Thatcher signed the Single European Act in 1986 she did so in the belief that the European Community, as it was then called, would develop into a loosely knit federation of free-trading sovereign states. It soon became clear that the other member states were intent on policies directed towards achieving tax harmonization, a common currency and eventual political union. She met this prospect with increasing hostility.

Margaret Thatcher left office a convinced Eurosceptic and left behind a party that was deeply divided over Europe. John Major strove unsuccessfully to hold the party together on this issue. When he signed the Maastricht Treaty in 1991, he opted Britain out of the corporatist Social Chapter and refused to make an unconditional commitment to eventual monetary union. This compromise did not placate his Eurosceptics. Thereafter, as he ruefully notes in his *Autobiography*, trench warfare split the party and continued to do so long after it lost the 1997 general election.

The New Labour government, under Tony Blair's leadership, signed the Social Chapter. Blair initially supported the plan for a new European Constitution, but after the French and the Dutch voted against it in 2006, he changed tack in favour of a larger Union run on free market rather than corporatist lines. For the first two years following its 1997 election victory, New Labour imposed strict budgetary restraints on public spending. Thereafter, social expenditure rose steadily although the gap between the richest and poorest grew wider. Most remarkably, the neo-liberal model of a mixed economy of welfare that New Labour had inherited from the Conservatives was left largely unchanged. If anything, it became more mixed as new public-private partnerships proliferated across the social services.

Similar trends became apparent across the broader spectrum of economic policy. Clause IV of the Labour Party's Constitution had been rewritten, to the chagrin of its own traditionalists. Far from renationalizing the economy, New Labour continued to privatize as much of the remaining public sector as possible. And most significantly, its centralized command structure was steadily strengthened and expanded by a plethora of new laws, regulations and directives. In summary, the ease with which New Labour took over the middle ground of British politics left the Conservatives in search of a new and distinctive political identity.

Emerging Issues

Between 1997 and 2005, the Conservatives lost three general elections with three different leaders. In the public mind, they remained associated with the least popular neo-liberal policies of the Thatcherite revolution. They were still perceived as a party divided over Europe. Their claims that taxes could be cut without lowering standards of social service provision were not taken seriously.

Shortly after David Cameron became Conservative Party leader in 2005, he launched a comprehensive programme of policy reappraisal and 'intellectual renewal'. Nine policy teams were appointed and, at the time of writing, they had published five 'interim' reports. Three of them were focused on social policy issues.

The Well-being of the Nation identified four 'core values' which the authors believed should inform and direct Conservative public policy-making. These values were described as the creation of new partnerships between government and the professions, upholding the principle of equitable access to public services, restoring the processes of local decision-making in policy implementation and sustaining the growth of the economy and the public sector as the necessary preconditions of general well-being. On all matters of accountability, central government should be the last port of call and turned to only when all local systems had manifestly failed.

The two interim reports on economic policy were more explicitly neo-liberal in the advice they offered. The authors of *Growth in Britain* argued strongly that cutting taxes on capital was an essential precondition of economic growth. The Tax Reform Commission's Report recommended a tranche of comprehensive tax cuts to the value of £21 billion. George Osborne's response, as the Party's Shadow Chancellor, was that he had no intention of endorsing any amount of unfunded tax cuts. At the 2006 party conference, Cameron made it equally clear that he was not disposed to 'flash up some pie-in-the-sky tax cuts just to show what we stand for'. He went on to promise that a new Conservative government would repeal the Human Rights Act. All three reports wanted to reverse the centralizing trends in British public policy that began during the Thatcher years and were given added momentum under New Labour.

The old post-war corporate consensus fell apart in the 1978 'winter of discontent'. Although the Thatcherite neo-liberal reforms of the 1980s successfully revitalized the British economy, they might well have foundered in a backlash of political protest as unemployment levels topped three million. As it happened, the statutory social services were not reformed on neo-liberal lines and a basic level of income support was maintained throughout these difficult years. New Labour, for its part, has not reverted to old-style corporatist economic policies.

The new consensus that has subsequently developed rests on the premise that economic growth is *the* precondition for the enhancement of social well-being. Governments need not 'tax and spend' in order to maintain decent standards of social service provision. Conversely, they cannot make swingeing tax cuts without lowering those standards.

These are the new parameters within which the Conservatives must re-establish themselves as a party of the centre ground. They have yet to explain how they will reconcile the principle of equitable access to public services at national levels with their commitment to extending the scope for decision-making at local levels. Nevertheless, there are already some indications that the party is beginning to reaffirm and reinterpret the values of traditional conservatism in its process of 'intellectual renewal'. It remains to be seen whether it can achieve a similar consensus on Europe.

Guide to Further Sources

Quintin Hogg's spirited presentation of *The Case for Conservatism* (Penguin Books, 1947) is still worth searching for online. Roger Scruton's *The Meaning of Conservatism* (Macmillan, 1984) explores its diverse philosophical qualities in comparison with those of liberalism, socialism and Marxism. Ian Gilmour's *Inside Right* (Quartet, 1978) contains useful chapters on key Conservative thinkers. Frank O'Gorman's *British Conservatism* (Longman, 1986) provides extracts from key texts and commentaries.

Part III of W. H. Greenleaf's second volume of *The British Political Tradition* (Routledge, 1988) explores the Conservative response to the rise of collectivist ideologies over the past 150 years. Harold Macmillan's *The Middle Way* (Macmillan, 1966) sets out a new agenda for modern conservatism as a social-democratic response to the problems of reforming capitalism and defeating socialism.

I. Gilmour's *Dancing with Dogma* (Simon and Schuster, 1992) offers a riveting account of the politics of change in the Conservative Party under Thatcher's leadership. Robert Blake's two volumes on *The Conservative Party from Peel to Thatcher* (Fontana, 1985) offer a definitive study of the development of the modern Conservative Party.

Two other recent publications are strongly recommended: John Charmley's engaging and perceptive *History of Conservative Politics, 1900–1996* (Macmillan, 1996) and Simon Jenkins's thought-provoking *Thatcher and Sons: A Revolution in Three Acts* (Alan Lane/Penguin Books, 2006).

Updates on new developments in Conservative Party policy can be accessed on <www.conservatives.com> by typing 'policy' into the search engine.

Chapter 10

Social Democracy

Robert M. Page

Overview

- In the modern era the term 'social democracy' has been used to describe parties, governments or states which have sought to exert collective control over capitalism on grounds of social justice.
- Although the terms 'social democracy' and 'democratic socialism' are often used interchangeably, the former tradition is more commonly associated with social reform rather than the radical transformation of society.
- Social democratic welfare states are characterized by a commitment to egalitarianism, the maintenance of full employment and a wide range of high-standard universal welfare services. Sweden is seen as an exemplar of such a welfare state.
- Modern social democratic parties such as New Labour have adopted a more positive approach to capitalism and have demonstrated a willingness to introduce welfare reforms which support, rather than challenge, market imperatives.
- Support for traditional forms of social democracy appears to be in decline.

Introduction

The political doctrine of social democracy has been closely associated with social policy and the welfare state from the mid-twentieth century. Indeed, social democratic societies have traditionally been seen as synonymous with progressive forms of state welfare.

This chapter will address five dimensions of social democracy. First, attention will be devoted to a brief examination of what is meant by the term 'social democracy'. Second, the British 'form' of social democracy – democratic socialism – will be considered. Third, the defining characteristics of a social democratic welfare state will be highlighted by looking at the case of Sweden. Fourth, attention will be focused on the modernized social democratic approach to social policy that New Labour has been pursuing in the UK. Fifth, the issue of whether social democracy can survive in the twenty-first century will be discussed.

What is Social Democracy?

The notion 'social democracy' defies concise classification. Historically, it has been associated with political movements seeking fundamental economic and social change along Marxist lines. In the more recent past, the term has been used to describe the modest reform programmes of post-1945 Western European political parties which were intended to humanize rather than abolish capitalism.

The commitment to non-violent change has been one discernible feature of social democracy since the end of the nineteenth century. The Social Democratic Party in Germany, for example, responded to Bernstein's thesis that the predicted immiserization of the working class under capitalism had not materialized by abandoning the revolutionary Marxist road to socialism in favour of a constitutional path to social reform. By the end of the First World War, a clear division had emerged between revolutionary communist parties and the more reform-minded social democratic parties.

Pragmatism could be said to be the second universal feature of social democracy. Idealistic policy objectives have been eschewed by social democrats in favour of more pragmatic or 'possibilist' agendas.

Other defining features of social democracy are less easy to identify. According to Gamble and Wright, social democracy 'is not a particular historical programme or political party or interest group, or even an unchanging set of values. As a political movement its only fixed point is its constant search to build and sustain political majorities for reforms of economic and social institutions which counter injustice and reduce inequality' (1999: 2). One of the problems with such broad definitions of social democracy is that they can encompass those governments which believe only modest intervention is necessary to constrain market 'failures' as well as those that believe the pursuit of social justice requires more extensive forms of state action.

Despite these definitional difficulties, it is evident that the term social democracy has, at the very least, tended to be associated with particular economic and social policies at particular points in time. In the second half of the twentieth century, for example, Western European social democracy was most commonly associated with Keynesian forms of economic interventionism, designed to secure full employment and economic growth, as well as redistributive forms of state welfare. Indeed, those European nations which actively pursued such policies, such as Sweden, came to be regarded as emblematic social democratic nations or regimes.

Democratic Socialism: The British Version of 'Social Democracy'?

Although the term social democracy is often used to refer to centre-left political parties in continental Europe, it is not as widely used in Britain, where the closely related doctrine of democratic socialism has achieved much greater prominence (see chapter 11). Democratic socialism in Britain has both 'ethical' and 'Fabian' roots. Ethical socialists believed that the operation of capitalism, underpinned as it was by a legal system which permitted wealthy property-owners to exploit and control the poor, was both unfair and immoral. To counter such exploitation, the ethical socialists supported collective action and social reform. The Fabian socialists also favoured greater degrees of collectivism and social reform. Although many Fabians shared the moral outrage of their ethical compatriots in relation to the dehumanizing impact of capitalism, they were equally, if not more, concerned with the inefficiency of the capitalist mode of production. Like the Marxists, the Fabians believed that capitalism was prone to crisis and that it would inevitably be superseded by a more efficient planned economy. Unlike the Marxists, however, the Fabians did not believe that the abolition of capitalism could only be achieved by means of violent revolution. They believed that once a reform-minded government had been elected, it would prove possible to use existing state institutions to bring about the economic and social transformation of society. The post-1945 Labour governments of Clement Attlee operated on this premise. Planning and nationalization were the chosen instruments in the economic sphere, while the creation of the welfare state was seen as a way of taming the Five Giants identified by William Beveridge.

This 'fundamental' form of democratic socialism was challenged by the influential Labour 'revisionist' Anthony Crosland in the mid-1950s. In his seminal text *The Future of Socialism* (1956), Crosland argued that post-war Britain could no longer be regarded as an 'unreconstructed capitalist society' (p. 57). He contended that capitalist power and control had been diluted by the steady advance of democracy, increasing degrees of state intervention, growing trade union influence and the emergence of a more autonomous, socially responsive managerial class. For Crosland, these developments meant that different *means* should now be employed to create an egalitarian society. Crucially, and controversially, Crosland believed that more extensive public ownership was not necessary for the creation of an egalitarian post-war society. Although he acknowledged that greater economic equality was still required, especially in the distribution of wealth, he believed that modern socialism should focus on social equality. High-standard healthcare and housing were accorded central significance in Crosland's 'strategy of equality', as was the development of socially inclusive comprehensive schooling.

For Crosland, growth-driven egalitarian forms of social expenditure of this kind would enhance the position of working-class citizens without alienating middle-class taxpayers, who would, in any event, derive some personal benefit from state welfare provision. Crosland believed that a democratic socialist society could best

be achieved by 'mechanical' rather than 'moral' means (see P. Clarke, *Liberals and Social Democrats*, Macmillan, 1978). Unlike moral reformers who seek to create an egalitarian social culture by persuading the better off that it is their duty to support their less advantaged neighbours, the mechanical reformer relies on carefully devised policies and programmes which produce egalitarian outcomes by stealth. Significantly, though, this mechanical strategy was dependent on sustained levels of economic growth. If growth could not be generated, the strategy of equality would fail, as indeed it did when Labour was in government between 1964 and 1970 and again from 1974 to 1979.

While some have viewed Labour's adoption of Crosland's 'revisionism' as a decisive shift from the transformative democratic socialist strategy pursued by Attlee to a more reformist social democratic approach, others contend that while the means have changed, the overall goals have remained the same.

It is often suggested that there was a social democratic consensus in Britain between 1945 and 1979. It is argued that during this period both Labour and the Conservatives were in accord over the need for high levels of employment, a mixed economy and a welfare state. Support for this thesis is based less on the existence or otherwise of an ideological accord between Labour and the Conservatives than on the degree of policy convergence when the respective parties were in government. While arguments about the pros and cons of this thesis continue, it is generally agreed that any such consensus came to an abrupt halt with the election of the first Thatcher government in 1979. Moreover, although certain post-1945 governments have pursued policy agendas in accordance with social democratic aims, few would suggest that the UK should be regarded as an example of a social democratic welfare state.

Social Democratic Welfare States

Given the elasticity of the concept of social democracy itself, one might expect to find an equally diverse range of social democratic welfare arrangements. Certainly, it is possible to tackle injustice or pursue greater equality by various configurations of public, private, voluntary and informal provision. From this perspective, the key determinant of a social democratic welfare state might be regarded as the achievement of 'socially progressive' outcomes rather than adherence to a particular principle (universalism), means (public provision) or form of governance (national rather than local). This would enable many countries to be classified as social democratic welfare states even though they have different histories, traditions and organizational arrangements. While this might prove acceptable to some, others find it more problematic. In his book *The Three Worlds of Welfare Capitalism* (Polity, 1990), Esping-Andersen argues, for example, that social democratic welfare regimes should be distinguished from both liberal and conservative regimes by their preference for decommodified, comprehensive, universal state welfare services provided on the basis of citizenship which marginalizes the role of private, voluntary or informal provision. Social democratic regimes of this kind have flourished in Scandinavia.

Sweden

Sweden has come to be regarded as an exemplar of a social democratic welfare state. This stems in part from the fact that the Social Democratic Party has been in power in its own right or in coalition almost continually since 1932 (the exceptions being 1976–82, 1991–4 and since 2006). In attempting to create a more egalitarian society, the Social Democrats did not pursue a class-based electoral strategy. Instead, they sought, successfully, to create a broader coalition of support. Per Albin Hansson, who led the Social Democrats from 1928 to 1946, coined the term 'The People's Home' to emphasize his party's message that the Social Democrats would govern the nation in an inclusive way so that the values of equality, selflessness and cooperation could take root. This was deemed to require the removal of class differences, the establishment of universal social services and industrial democracy. Although the Social Democrats were highly critical of the exploitative nature of capitalism, they believed it could be reformed through purposeful government action and by enlisting the cooperation of industrialists. Accordingly, they sought to exert social control over the market economy rather than resort to nationalization. This led one influential American journalist – Marquis Childs – to assert, in a book entitled *The Middle Way* (Yale University Press, 1936), that the Swedish Social Democrats were pursuing a path midway between the free market capitalism to be found in the United States and the centrally planned economy of the Soviet Union.

By the late 1930s the Social Democrats 'middle way' had begun to take shape. Under the Saltsjobaden Accord of 1938, employers and trade unionists entered into an agreement to work cooperatively so that economic productivity and worker prosperity could be enhanced without recourse to damaging industrial disputes. Although the government was not expected to be formally involved in these industrial agreements, it was required to create a macro-economic climate conducive to full employment and to support active labour market policies which enabled workers to move from declining industries to those that were prospering. The government was also expected to develop high-quality welfare services and to ensure that income was distributed in an equitable way.

In the period from the 1945 to the early 1970s, the key features of the Swedish social democratic welfare 'model' were put in place. Full employment, universal state welfare provision, industrial democracy, a solidaristic wage policy and an active labour market programme became defining features of Swedish society. The development of high-quality day-care facilities also enhanced gender equality by providing women with the opportunity to undertake paid work.

The post-1945 expansion of the Swedish welfare state came to a halt in the late 1970s and '80s as economic growth slowed in a period marked by inflationary wage settlements, a sharp increase in oil prices, growing unemployment and budget deficits. Attempts to revitalize the economy whilst maintaining full employment in the early 1980s resulted in some cutbacks in welfare expenditure. By the 1990s more stringent reforms were deemed necessary as Sweden struggled to cope with severe international financial pressures occasioned by its decision to deregulate its financial markets in the mid-1980s. Ongoing economic pressures of this kind led the Swedish Social Democrats to review their approach to the welfare state. This has resulted in more diverse welfare arrangements, including increased levels of non-state provision, internal markets and user charges. Such developments raise the question of whether these changes are compatible with the central 'tenets' of social democratic thought or, alternatively, its gradual abandonment? In exploring this question it is useful to look at an example of the New Labour government in the UK which has been following a self-professed modernized social democratic approach.

New Labour and Modernized Social Democratic Social Policy

According to both Tony Blair and the influential sociologist Anthony Giddens, New Labour's so-called 'Third Way' should be regarded as a modernized form of social democracy (see chapter 12). The need for such modernization is seen as inevitable in an era which has witnessed the demise of communism, the growth of global markets, changing family and work patterns and more diverse forms of personal and cultural identity. While New Labour upholds the values of equal worth, opportunity for all, rights and responsibilities and active communities, it maintains that a modern social democratic party should not be wedded to traditional means as it endeavours to create a fairer society. Although New Labour has reiterated its commitment to the welfare state, it believes that this does not necessitate any strict adherence to the policies pursued by the post-war governments of Attlee (1945–51), Wilson (1964–70 and 1974–6) or Callaghan (1976–9).

According to New Labour there are *seven* distinguishing features of a modern social democratic welfare state.

1 *Active rather than passive welfare system*. Crucially, this means that all those of working age not currently engaged in employment should be encouraged to return to work in order to avoid the debilitating effects of long-term dependency on state benefits.

2 *Diverse range of publicly funded providers*. It should no longer be assumed that publicly *funded* services should be publicly *provided*. Better outcomes might be achieved, and the public interest better served, by encouraging voluntary agencies, social enterprises or private firms to provide welfare services.

3 *Consumer focused*. A modern welfare state should focus on the needs and preferences of service users. It is contended that such users no longer want uniform and undifferentiated services. Rather, they require more bespoke forms of provision that better meet their needs and aspirations.

4 *Reduced commitment to universalism.* There is no longer deemed to be any automatic need to provide welfare services on a universal basis. A modern social democratic government should not defend the universal principle per se, but rather seek to provide services in ways (including selectivity) that best meet the expressed needs of self-interested consumers.

5 *Equality of opportunity rather than outcomes.* A modern welfare state should aim to extend the level of opportunity in society by tackling socially constructed barriers to individual advancement such as poor schooling or inadequate health provision. The removal of such barriers should drive social policy rather than the redistribution of resources from the better off to the poor.

6 *Fostering an active and responsible citizenry.* Individuals should be expected to take more responsibility for their own welfare and to take an active part in tackling need within their local community. New Labour lays great stress on the link between rights and responsibilities. Rather than seeing state support as an unconditional right, citizens should regard such provision as part of a 'gift' exchange. From this perspective, unemployed citizens should respond, for example, in a positive way to government attempts to help them find work by taking advantage of any work, educational or training opportunities that present themselves.

7 *Close monitoring of service standards.* Modern welfare services should be regularly monitored to ensure that service users are provided with the highest possible standard of provision. Unlike traditional social democrats, New Labour is more sceptical of the claim that welfare professionals, motivated by a public service ethic, can be relied upon to develop high-quality, cost-efficient services. Rigorous target-setting, audit and inspection are deemed necessary if a modern welfare state is to operate in an effective and efficient manner.

The abandonment of traditional social democratic welfarism?

New Labour's pursuit of a modern social democratic form of social policy has led some critics to question whether this amounts to the abandonment of the more traditional form of the doctrine. It can be argued that New Labour has jettisoned three key features of traditional social democracy.

First, the use of non-state providers and the incorporation of market terminology such as 'customers' and 'producers' is seen as undermining the non-commercial ethos of public services. Moreover, modern social democrats have been criticized for assuming that contemporary citizens only value the welfare state as discerning consumers rather than as citizens who derive satisfaction from knowing that such provision is freely available for all on the basis of need.

Second, New Labour's focus on removing opportunity barriers, rather than combating growing inequalities in income and wealth, is viewed as too easy a capitulation to market-driven patterns of distribution which are neither fair nor legitimate.

Third, New Labour's decision to link 'good' citizenship to labour market participation is deemed to be too radical a departure from traditional forms of social democracy as it can undermine the value accorded to unpaid caring and voluntary activity.

Emerging Issues: Can Social Democracy Survive?

The long-term future of social democracy has been questioned in recent years.

Although the electoral appeal of social democratic parties has become more volatile in recent decades, the fact that they are still able to attract significant degrees of popular support suggests that this doctrine continues to resonate with the public. What is less certain, though, is whether contemporary forms of social democracy have sufficient commonality with previous versions of this doctrine. Certainly, there are doubts as to whether it is possible for social democrats to embrace the global market, promote consumerism and diversity and yet still create a fairer society. It could be argued that some of the revisions adopted by contemporary 'social democratic' governments are merely tactical devices that will allow them to pursue more traditional policies when more favourable economic and social circumstances emerge. Alternatively, though, the growing reluctance of social democratic governments to support or initiate social policies which challenge market imperatives might be indicative of a growing realization that there is now limited popular support for any party that sets out to challenge the rule of the market in a post-communist age. From this perspective, it is harder to refute the claim that social democracy, or at least that variant based on universal welfare, strong economic regulation and redistribution, is now in terminal decline.

Guide to Further Sources

Donald Sassoon's *One Hundred Years of Socialism* (I. B. Tauris, 1996) provides a magisterial overview of the twists and turns of socialist and social democratic ideas and practice in Western Europe in the twentieth century. Anthony Crosland's revisionist text (*The Future of Socialism*, Jonathan Cape, 1956) which has been reissued by Constable (2006), has come to be regarded as one of the most significant statements of British post-war social democratic thought.

Timothy Tilton, *The Political Theory of Swedish Democracy: Through the Welfare State to Socialism* (Clarendon Oxford, 1991) and Sven Olsson, *Social Policy and Welfare State in Sweden*, 2nd edn (Arkiv, Lund, 1993) both have informative overviews of the development of Swedish social democracy and social welfare.

Anthony Giddens has published a number of influential texts about modernized social democracy in Britain in recent years, including *The Third Way: The Renewal of Social Democracy* (Polity, 1998), *The Third Way and Its Critics* (Polity, 2000), *Where Now for New Labour?* (Polity, 2002) and *Over to You Mr Brown* (Polity, 2007).

Stimulating essays about contemporary social democracy are to be found in edited collections by Andrew Gamble and Anthony Wright, *The New Social Democracy* (Blackwell, 1999) and Matt Browne and Patrick Diamond, *Rethinking Social Democracy* (Policy Network, 2003). The future prospects for social democracy are examined by Chris Pierson in *Hard Choices: Social Democracy in the 21st Century* (Polity, 2001) and Tony Fitzpatrick in *After the New Social Democracy: Social Welfare for the Twenty-First Century* (Manchester University Press, 2003).

English-language versions of the emerging policy agendas of West European social democratic parties can be accessed via the web. Two such sites are the Social Democratic Party of Germany, <www.spd.de/menu/1682660>, and the Swedish Social Democratic Party, <www.socialdemokraterna.se>. Policy Network is an international think-tank which seeks to debate and promote modernized forms of social democracy: <www.policy-network.net>.

Chapter 11

The Socialist Perspective

Hartley Dean

Overview

- The socialist perspective on social policy argues that capitalism as a social and economic system is inherently inimical to human well-being.
- It regards the welfare state as an ambiguous phenomenon that has benefited disadvantaged and working-class people, while also subjecting them to social control in the interests of capitalism.
- This perspective has nonetheless played a role in the development of social policy in capitalist societies.
- It has informed past attempts to establish 'communist' social and economic systems with different approaches to welfare provision.
- Furthermore, it represents an intellectually significant critique of particular relevance to our understanding of social inequality and the practical development of alternative social policies opposed to capitalism.

Introduction

There are many types of socialism, but the central concern of a socialist perspective on social policy is with the role of the state in either promoting or undermining human welfare. We shall discuss this perspective – first in terms of socialism as *critique*, and, second, in terms of socialism as *practice*. The socialist perspective reaches beyond mere social awareness: the 'social-ism', that may inform social conservatism, social liberalism or social democracy. What defines socialism is that it is, on the one hand, fundamentally critical of capitalism and, on the other, a call to political action. We shall also discuss whether socialism is – as some would claim – now dead.

Socialism as Critique

Elements of socialist thinking have been traced back to a variety of sources, from the Bible to the seventeenth-century Levellers. But socialism is best understood, like liberalism, as one of the principal 'meta-narratives' of the post-eighteenth-century Enlightenment era. While liberalism champions individual freedom, socialism champions social equality. Socialism emerged in Western Europe as a political critique of the capitalist economic system and its social consequences.

Essential tenets

Socialism as a creed is humanistic, collectivist (or, at the very least, cooperative) and egalitarian. Modern socialism articulated itself in opposition to industrial capitalism: its dehumanizing effects, its individualistic competitive ethos and the ways in which it exacerbated social inequality. Early social-ists were idealists and utopians and many drew upon religious authority or ethical argument for their beliefs, as indeed some do today. But the writings of Karl Marx (1818–83) offered a brand of 'scientific' socialism that crystallized its essential tenets. His central insight is that it is the ownership of the natural, physical, techno-logical and financial resources required for the maintenance of social life (the 'means of production') that determines the struc-ture of society itself. Marx's argument was that human history has been a story of struggles between dominant and oppressed classes. Under capitalism – the most recent stage in human history – the mass of humanity has become alienated from the means by which to produce what it needs to sustain its own existence. Capitalism, however, contains the seeds of its own destruction, because the oppressed class under capitalism (the working class) will in time be able to seize control of the state apparatus established by the dominant class (the property-owning capitalist class). Socialism, therefore, is the project by which workers' control will be exercised, leading in time to a classless or communist society in which human needs can be fully realized and properly satisfied. Marx did not offer a blueprint for a classless society. Nor was he a theorist of the welfare state, which did not exist in his lifetime. He offered an analy-sis of capitalism's unjust and contradictory nature and of the relations of social and economic power on which it was founded.

The capitalist welfare state did not emerge until the twentieth century. As we shall see, certain of its proponents and sup-porters subscribed to some kind of social-ism. From a socialist perspective, however, there are various ways in which we can interpret the role of the welfare state as it has in practice developed. We can distil these into three kinds of explanation: the instrumentalist, the structural-logical and the neo-Marxist. These explanations overlap in some respects and they all contend that the capitalist welfare state remains a capitalist institution rather than the outcome of a socialist transformation.

Instrumentalist critiques of the welfare state

Some critics would interpret literally a sug-gestion once made by Marx that the state behaves as the managing committee of the capitalist class. The welfare state in capital-ist countries ultimately serves the interests of the capitalist, not the working class. The key positions in government and adminis-tration are held by people from relatively privileged backgrounds or those who have an underlying allegiance to 'the establish-ment' and/or the status quo. The welfare state, by implication, is a conspiracy against the working class.

According to this kind of explanation, the shape and nature of the welfare state are deliberately contrived to accord with the economic requirements of capital. The welfare state has become both the hand-maiden of capitalism and its henchman. Through health and education policies, the state ensures an orderly supply of healthy and educated workers for industry and commerce, so reducing the costs of repro-ducing labour power. Through a range of social services, the state ensures that the costs of the weak and vulnerable do not fall on industry. At the same time, through social security and labour market policies the state manages those workers who are unemployed or temporarily unproductive. Whereas Marx had pointed to the funda-mental instability of capitalism, the welfare state has not hastened its demise, but smoothed over its contradictions and helped sustain it.

Structural-logical critiques of the welfare state

A different line of reasoning is that the functioning of the state under capitalism is not a cunning conspiracy so much as a consequence of capitalism's structural constraints or immanent logic. The state behaves like a managing committee only in a metaphorical sense. It is not necessarily a willing handmaiden or henchman. It has a degree of autonomy. And yet well-meaning reformers remain, in part at least, captive creatures of circumstance. In the last instance it is economic imperatives that determine the outcomes of social policy. This happens because, in order to survive, the state must acknowledge certain priorities over which it has no control. For example, it must maximize economic growth, protect profits and maintain social order. In liberal democracies, economics trumps politics. Presented in this way, this is a deterministic or functionalist argument.

A more abstract variation is that the essential *form* of the welfare state is derived from or mirrors the unequal relations of power that characterize capitalist market relations. So, just as capitalists obscure the exploitative nature of their relationship to labour through the legal fiction of the individual wage bargain, so the state obscures the disciplinary nature of its relationship to its citizens by making welfare goods and services appear as a form of 'social wage' or democratic settlement. Not only are social welfare reforms one-sided compromises driven by economic imperatives, but the beneficiaries of such reform are being ideologically manipulated in the interests of capital so they cannot see the true nature of their oppression. This gloomy scenario can be brightened up using the ideas of thinkers such as Antonio Gramsci (1891–1937), who argued that not everyone is hoodwinked by capitalist ideology, nor are they necessarily persuaded by the inevitability of capitalism's logic. Part of the socialist project has to do with whose ideological interpretations of the world will dominate. Drawing on this kind of insight, it has been suggested that state policy – including social policy – can be understood not as the inevitable outcome of capitalist structures, but as a distillation of the class forces in play within an enduring political struggle. Socialism can act as a counter-hegemonic force.

Neo-Marxist critiques

There is a group of academics who in the 1970s brought together elements of the above critiques to produce a distinctive overarching neo-Marxist critique. In a critical review Rudolf Klein (1993) dubbed this 'O'Goffe's tale'. The epithet captured the names of three of the most prominent contributors to the neo-Marxist critique: James O'Connor, Ian Gough and Claus Offe. The essence of O'Goffe's tale is that the welfare state has proved to be an ambiguous phenomenon, since it exhibits two kinds of contradiction.

First, while the welfare state has brought real benefits to the working class and the most disadvantaged members of capitalist society, it has also played a part in repressing or controlling them. The welfare state succeeded in increasing social consumption and living standards, but capital has benefited more than labour. State welfare enhanced the productivity of labour, while minimizing the adverse social consequences of the capitalist economic system. It regulated both the quantity and the quality of labour power. The development of social citizenship and its attendant rights and responsibilities played a necessary part in constituting the modern wage labourer and in according popular legitimacy to capitalism. It also subjected the working class to new forms of administrative scrutiny and normative control – through, for example, compulsory education and stringent social security regulations. Significantly, the welfare state has not succeeded in abolishing poverty.

The second kind of contradiction is that the stabilizing influence which the welfare state brought to capitalism would be fiscally and politically unsustainable. Capitalism could neither survive without having a welfare state, nor could it endure the costs and implications of having one. To an extent, this prophecy has been borne out, since many capitalist countries sought to 'roll back' their welfare states towards the end of the twentieth century and to shift the responsibility and costs of welfare provision from the public to the private sector, from the state to the individual or, in effect, from capital to labour. At the same time, many poorer countries have been persuaded in their pursuit of capitalist economic development to establish no more than limited state welfare provision.

Socialism as Practice

Socialism is concerned not only to critique capitalism and to question its fundamental ethos, but to challenge it politically. Anarchistic and libertarian socialists have envisioned a society in which human welfare would be achieved through mutuality and cooperation, without any kind of state intervention (because the state, axiomatically, is oppressive). However, we shall concern ourselves here with two strands within the socialist perspective that have sought practically to harness state power as a means of promoting human welfare: the gradualist and the revolutionary.

Gradualist socialism

The emergence of the capitalist welfare state is attributable, in part at least, to the effects of class struggle. Class agitation and the growth of the labour movement in capitalist societies were significant factors in the way in which – from the end of the nineteenth century onwards – state social welfare provision developed, although how

this played itself out differed between countries. Socialism is concerned with collective rather than individual agency and socialists played a key part in helping to mobilize the working-class movement. While some socialists had hoped this mobilization would lead to the revolutionary overthrow of capitalism, others calculated that a transition to socialism should be achieved progressively and/or by stealth. This, as the twentieth century progressed, was the position of Fabian socialists (a key intellectual influence within the British Labour Party) and of Social Democratic parties across Europe (especially in Scandinavia, where the most extensive capitalist welfare states have been developed).

Gradualist socialist politicians, such as Anthony Crosland, argued that the development of a mixed economy and the policies of a Labour government in the post-Second World War period were such that, by the 1960s, a country like Britain was no longer a capitalist society in the original sense. However, it can also be argued that social liberalism was probably a stronger force than gradualist socialism in the creation of the modern welfare state. 'Enlightened' capitalists were prepared not only to concede some of the demands advanced by organized labour, but to promote measures that would compensate for the foreseeable failures and correct the inherent instabilities of free market capitalism. The extension of state welfare, therefore, was implicated in the transition from industrial to post-industrial or 'advanced' capitalism in which both the state and the market play a role. Capitalism has changed and, by and large, Fabians and social democrats have become effectively resigned to improving this new form of capitalism, not overthrowing it and to the further amelioration by state intervention of the effects of market forces. There is a distinction to be made between the contemporary social democratic perspective discussed in the last chapter and the socialist perspective discussed in this one. The former seeks to reform and extend the capitalist welfare state as an end in itself; the latter in one way or another to supersede it.

Revolutionary socialism

Revolutionary socialism aims to overturn capitalism not by gradually transforming the state, but by taking command of it so that it may properly serve the interests of the working class and the oppressed. Marx's contention had been that if this were achieved, the state would in time 'wither away' as a truly classless society emerged. There were in the course of the twentieth century examples of socialist revolutions – most notably in Russia in 1917 and China in 1949. The societies that resulted were called 'communist' regimes, despite the fact that in none of them did the state wither away. On the contrary, what characterized such societies was a highly centralized and enduring form of state planning. The countries in which socialist revolutions occurred were not at the time fully industrialized capitalist countries, and revolution was pursued not so much by the organized working class as by vanguard activists. The programmes the activists adopted were informed by visions of human progress. The social and economic arrangements they wanted would be based not on the wastefulness of unfettered competition, but on rational planning and cooperation. The intention was to maximize human welfare.

Even supporters of the socialist perspective admit, however, that such examples of 'actually existing' socialism turned out to be a failure. Not only did 'communist' regimes never reach the stage when universal human welfare could be assured without state intervention, but in many instances the socialist project was cruelly stripped of its essential humanity. Initially, under the Soviet system, for example, citizens were guaranteed work with state enterprises that offered a range of social benefits as well as wages. Prices were subsidized. Housing,

education, healthcare and pensions were all provided. However, the standard and nature of welfare provision were such that they often failed to satisfy human need. There are three kinds of explanation for this. First, the ruthless idealism of the original revolutionary activists entailed a desire to reform not only society, but the human race itself: however beneficent in intent, it was 'top down' and authoritarian in nature. Worse still, such idealism was easily diluted, distorted or corrupted: for example, the Stalinist era that succeeded the Bolshevik revolutionary era became brutal and totalitarian. Finally, it may be argued that socialism should be an international project, since it is impossible to establish socialism in just one country or group of countries: in an interconnected world, dominated by capitalist modes of economic production and by global markets, systems such as that in the former Soviet Union can end up functioning not as state socialism, but as centrally regulated state capitalism. Alternatively, a small socialist country, such as Cuba with its impressive health and education systems, may suffer reduced living standards because its capitalist neighbours will not trade with it.

The Death of Socialism?

This leads to the suggestion that socialism is now dead: that the historic 'cold war' between socialism and capitalism has ended with a global victory for capitalism. Towards the end of the twentieth century, we witnessed the collapse of Soviet communism. 'Post-communist' countries are now attempting to transform themselves into capitalist welfare states. Even communist China is now adopting extensive market-based reforms. We have, supposedly, entered a postmodern age in which the meta-narratives of liberalism and socialism have been superseded (see chapter 15) and new approaches to social policy – such as the Third Way – are increasingly ascendant (see chapter 12).

There are two questions that the socialist perspective must now address. The first has to do with the nature of social class and the unfashionable notion of 'class struggle'; the second with the global nature of capitalism and the scope for anti-capitalist social policies.

Class versus identity?

The concept of class has been central to the socialist perspective. But as we pass from the industrial age to an information age, the nature of class structures in capitalist societies has been changing. And as we pass from the age of cultural modernity to an age of postmodernity, we have become preoccupied with issues of identity, not class.

Throughout the capitalist world the 'traditional' working class has been declining. Post-industrial capitalism no longer needs large numbers of manual workers. It is wrong, however, to suppose that socioeconomic class divisions have disappeared. It's just they have got more complicated. The division within industrial capitalist society, according to sociologists, was between a manual working class and a nonmanual middle class. With technological advances, the number of manual workers falls, while the nature of non-manual work radically changes. So the middle class grew, but became fragmented between routine clerical, administrative and retail workers on the one hand and skilled managerial and professional workers on the other. Sociologists now conceptualize the division within post-industrial capitalist society in terms of a distinction between the core and the periphery of the labour market: the core consisting of highly skilled, relatively privileged and secure workers; the periphery of low-skilled, relatively disadvantaged and insecure workers. As may be seen from chapter 17, capitalist societies are becoming ever more unequal as the gap between rich and poor increases. There is an incontrovertible and enduring association between people's socio-economic status and their life-chances. From a socialist perspective, conceptualizing the class divide requires some sophistication, but the concept is as meaningful as ever it was. Contemporary socialist theorists argue that, while there are those in capitalist societies who occupy anomalous or ambiguous class positions, there is still a fundamental distinction to be drawn between the many who sell their labour (whether it be manual, technical or intellectual) in order to live and the few who own or control a significant amount of capital.

If, despite this, the idea of class has lost salience, this is in part because a new politics of identity has tended to displace the old politics of class. The last third of the twentieth century witnessed the emergence of new social movements, which began to address issues hitherto neglected in class-based struggles over the distribution of power and resources. These movements addressed matters such as human rights, global poverty and ecological issues, but significantly they also included second-wave feminism, the black power and anti-racist movements and, for example, movements of disabled people, older people, gays and lesbians. The struggles these movements promoted were not about material redistribution, but 'parity of recognition' (Fraser 1997). They were concerned with social injustices arising from social divisions other than class. None of this necessarily precludes the possibility of alliances between movements and the combination of different struggles. Feminist socialism and eco-socialism, for example, now provide their own distinctive strands within the socialist perspective. What the socialist perspective emphasizes is the extent to which the social inequalities inherent to capitalism can exacerbate or fuel all kinds of oppression and injustice.

Emerging Issues

As an intellectual critique, the socialist perspective plainly is not dead. Nor is it necessarily dead in any practical sense. So long as anywhere in the world there is active resistance to capitalism, socialism is more than an atavistic curiosity. It is possible to point to recent instances of popular resistance – for example, against the poll tax in Britain and against welfare and labour law reform in France – though these were not directly fomented by socialist analyses. There have of late been remarkable electoral successes for left-wing presidential candidates in several Latin American countries, though this probably signals swings towards social democracy, rather than socialism. There have also been spectacular and violent 'anti-globalization' demonstrations mounted against the World Trade Organization and the G8 summits of rich nations, though in practice the anti-globalization movement represents an eclectic mixture of political groups, social movements and non-governmental bodies. Nonetheless, the emergence of such things as the Jubilee 2000 campaign for the reduction of 'third world' debt and the burgeoning of organizations like the World Social Forum would seem to signal the basis of what amounts to an *anti-capitalist* alliance. The essential contest, it has been suggested, is a struggle between 'those who want inclusive globalization based on co-operation and solidarity and those who want the market to make all the decisions' (George 2001: 1).

Writers like Alex Callinicos have envisioned a global campaign for an anti-capitalist manifesto – including distinctively socialist social policies. A transitional programme might incorporate such things as universal basic income, progressive and radically redistributive forms of taxation, widespread reductions of working hours and the defence of public services, none of which by themselves would be sufficient to achieve socialism, but which together amount to a fundamental challenge to capitalism. The central question raised by the socialist perspective on social policy is whether the short-term interests of capitalism are compatible with the long-term needs of humanity.

Guide to Further Sources

For an accessible general introduction, see Tony Benn's *Arguments for Socialism* (Penguin, 1980). The different types of socialism are described in Tony Wright's *Socialisms* (Routledge, 1996), though his attempts to cast social democratic and Third Way thinking as socialist require critical assessment.

Introductions to classic neo-Marxist thinkers may be found in V. George and R. Page (eds), *Modern Thinkers on Welfare* (Prentice Hall, 1995). But for a critique of the neo-Marxist approach, see Rudolf Klein's 'O'Goffe's tale', in C. Jones (ed.), *New Perspectives on the Welfare State in Europe* (Routledge, 1993). Ian Gough's *Global Capital, Human Needs and Social Policies* (Palgrave, 2000) is an important recent contribution. For a recent social policy text by revolutionary socialists, see I. Ferguson, M. Lavalette and G. Mooney, *Rethinking Welfare: A Critical Perspective* (Sage, 2002). And for a contrasting 'post-socialist' account, see Nancy Fraser's *Justice Interruptus: Critical Reflections on the Post-Socialist Condition* (Routledge, 1997).

A useful website is that of the World Social Forum, <www.worldsocialforum.org>, where, for example, Susan George's paper, 'Another world is possible', may be found (Library of Alternatives, 2001). Similarly, Alex Callinicos's *Anti-Capitalist Manifesto* (Polity, 2003) is interesting from a social policy perspective. Other websites of potential interest include <www.greensocialist.org.uk> and <www.redpepper.org.uk>.

Chapter 12

Third Way Perspectives

Martin Powell

Overview

- It is difficult to define the Third Way.
- The Third Way is best represented by the USA Clinton Democrat (1992–2000) and UK Blair New Labour (1997–2007) administrations.
- The Third Way can be examined in terms of discourse, values, policy goals and policy mechanisms.
- The Third Way in practice shows a wide variety of new policy goals and mechanisms, which increasingly seem to draw upon neo-liberalism.
- Some forms of Third Way policies are likely to continue into Gordon Brown's term of office as Prime Minister, and beyond.

Introduction

Unlike some of the political perspectives covered in the other chapters in this section, the Third Way has had a short history. There have been a number of previous 'third' or 'middle' ways associated with such diverse individuals as David Lloyd George (Liberal Prime Minister, 1916–22) and Harold Macmillan (Conservative Prime Minister, 1957–63; see chapter 9), and with movements as different as Swedish social democracy and Italian fascism. However, the current use of the term is generally associated with the writings of Anthony Giddens and the policies of the Democrat administrations of Bill Clinton in the USA (1992–2000) and of Tony Blair's New Labour government in the UK (1997–2007).

Giddens's book, *The Third Way*, has been very influential. It is an (academic) best-seller, and has been translated into many languages. Proponents of the Third Way claim that it is new and distinctive from both traditional social democracy and neo-liberalism, but stress that it is a renewed or modernized social democracy: a left-of-centre project (see chapter 10). In this sense, the Third Way is simply a convenient label that may be used interchangeably with 'new social democracy' or 'progressive governance'. Any search for a third way must begin with a trichotomous framework, differentiating the Third Way from the old left and the new right – although some critics find a dichotomy, arguing that the Third Way is essentially neo-liberalism. Blair and Giddens have also claimed that the Third Way represents a combination of the best features of the USA and continental Europe, bringing together American economic dynamism and European social inclusion.

There are continuing debates about the definition of the term, and whether a government can be termed 'third way'. Clinton and Blair both claimed this label for their administrations. Others have adopted a different label. For example, the German Social Democratic Party (SPD) under Gerhard Schroeder used the slogan 'Die Neue Mitte' (the new middle). Social Democratic and Labour parties in countries such as Belgium, Denmark and the Netherlands introduced different policies from 'old' social democracy. Like the British Labour Party, they generally claim that their values have not changed, but that economic and social changes mean that new policies must replace old policies that no longer work in today's world (see below).

For a few years around the turn of the century, third way left or left-of-centre governments were in power in many parts of Europe. However, the left then gradually lost control in a number of countries – including Germany and Sweden. The UK's Labour Party is a rare exception: a left-wing party that has remained in power over a long period; indeed, Tony Blair was the longest serving Labour Prime Minister in British history before handing over to Gordon Brown in the summer of 2007. During Blair's tenure as Prime Minister, New Labour made serious attempts to 'modernize' the welfare state (see especially Parts IV, V and VI).

This chapter aims to provide a brief introduction into these large and complex debates. The first section examines the dimensions of the Third Way, arguing that it is useful to unpack the concept with a focus on discourse, values, policy goals and policy mechanisms. The second part discusses the broad features of the Third Way in practice, concentrating on the social policies of New Labour in Britain (as chapter 35 shows, there are some differences between the administrations in London, Cardiff and Edinburgh), but also introducing examples from other countries.

The Essence of the Third Way

Much has been written about the Third Way, but its essence, or main 'dependent variable', remains unclear. Many critics dismiss it as vague and amorphous. This view has considerable validity, but does not apply solely to the Third Way. Despite much effort, similar attempts to pin down the essence of socialism and social democracy or democratic socialism have not resulted in a clear consensus (see chapters 10 and 11).

The problem in examining the Third Way is that the term is used in very different senses. A number of commentators have suggested broad characteristics or themes of the Third Way or 'new social democracy'. These include social inclusion, civil society, active government, investment in human and social capital, redistributing opportunities or assets rather than income, positive welfare, prevention, an active approach to employment, and rights and responsibilities. However, this conflates different elements such as means and ends. As a heuristic device, it is useful to distil these into separate discussions of discourse, values, policy goals and policy means or mechanisms.

The Third Way has generated a new discourse, or a new political language. Clinton and Blair share a number of key slogans or mantras, such as being 'tough on crime, tough on the causes of crime'; 'a hand-up, not a hand-out'; 'hard-working families that play by the rules'; and 'work is the best route out of poverty'. In addition to new phrases, there is a redefined language where old words have new meaning. For example, the Third Way vocabulary – or 'New-LabourSpeak' – includes terms such as 'full employment' and 'equality', but they have very different meanings from their traditional usage. The term 'welfare' itself is a good example of how discourse is central to 'winning the welfare debate': there have been some attempts to view 'welfare' in its more negative meaning, as held in the USA. Conversely, terms such as 'active' and 'modern' are regarded as unambiguously good.

The new discourse does not simply consist of new terms, but also emphasizes the relationship between them. The Third Way is a political discourse built out of elements from other political discourses to form, in Blair's term, political 'cross-dressing'. For example, 'enterprise' belongs to the right, while 'social justice' belongs to the left. The language of the Third Way is a rhetoric of reconciliation, such as 'economic dynamism as well as social justice', 'enterprise as well as fairness'. These terms are not deemed antagonistic: while neo-liberals pursue dynamism and enterprise and traditional social democrats justice and fairness, the Third Way delivers both. The more radical claim is of 'going beyond' or transcending such themes: it is not simply about managing the tension between the promotion of enterprise and the attack on poverty, but claiming that they are no longer in conflict. However, it does seem difficult to achieve a reconciliation of some terms, such as inclusion and responsibility. The carrot of inclusion can be dangled in front of all, but there must be some stick with which to beat the 'irresponsible'.

Some commentators have suggested a number of core values for the Third Way. These include CORA (community, opportunity, responsibility and accountability) and RIO (responsibility, inclusion, opportunity). However, the values of the Third Way remain problematic. This is mainly for two reasons.

First, adequate understanding of values require more than one-word treatments. Terms such as 'equality' are essentially contestable concepts, meaning different things to different people. It follows that values must be more clearly defined and linked with goals (see below).

Second, and linked, it is not clear whether the Third Way is concerned with 'old' values, new or redefined meanings of old values, or new values. The best-known accounts argue the first position. For example, Blair has claimed that the Third Way is concerned with the traditional values of social democracy. However, critics doubt whether Blair's values – equal worth, opportunity for all, responsibility and community – adequately summed up traditional socialism in Britain. Moreover, some terms have been redefined. For example, the old concern with equality of outcome and redistribution has been diluted. A few 'new' values also appear to have been smuggled in. Positive mentions of terms such as entrepreneurship were rarely part of the vocabulary of traditional social democracy.

Blair claimed that policies flow from values. In this sense, goals or objectives may be seen as a more specific operationalization of values. For example, equality is often referred to as a value, but this may result in very different policy objectives, such as equality of opportunity or equality of outcomes. It follows that advocates of equality might desire very different goals – for example, a reduction of inequalities of income, wealth, health status and educational qualifications – or merely that there must be an equal opportunity to enter a race with a large gap between rich prizes for the winners and nothing for the losers.

It is claimed that traditional values and goals must be achieved by new means. In some ways this has parallels with Croslandite revisionism (see chapter 10). Anthony Crosland separated the means and ends of socialism, suggesting that the Labour Party means of nationalization was not the best way of achieving the end of equality. Similarly the Third Way claims that new times call for new policies. The

Table 12.1 Dimensions of the Third Way in social policy

Dimension	Old Social Democracy	Third Way	Neo-liberalism
Discourse	Rights	Rights and responsibilities	Responsibilities
	Equity	Equity and efficiency	Efficiency
	Market failure	Market and state failure	State failure
Values	Equality	Inclusion	Inequality
	Security	Positive welfare	Insecurity
Policy goals	Equality of outcome	Minimum opportunities	Equality of opportunity
	Full employment	Employability	Low inflation
Policy means	Rights	Conditionality	Responsibilities
	State	Civil society/market	Market/civil society
	State finance and delivery	State/private finance and delivery	Private/state finance and delivery
	Security	Flexicurity	Insecurity
	Hierarchy	Network	Market
	High tax and spend	Pragmatic tax to invest	Low tax and spend
	High services and benefits	High services and low-ish benefits	Low services and benefits
	High cash redistribution	High asset redistribution	Low redistribution
	Universalism	Mainly universal services and mix of universal and selective benefits	Selectivity
	High wages	Minimum wages and tax credits	Low wages

world has changed and so the welfare state must change. However, new solutions will not be based on outdated, dogmatic ideology. There is a new emphasis on evidence-based policy-making. Research, experiments and trials will find the best ways of working that will be 'mainstreamed' throughout government. A key phrase of this new pragmatism is 'what works is what counts'. The Third Way is more receptive to solutions based on the market and civil society than to traditional social democracy. This results in a more eclectic policy mix. There are no 'textbook', ideological solutions, but each case will be examined on its merits, and what works in one area may not work in another.

Table 12.1 presents a necessarily rather stylized account of the Third Way, which has been distilled from a variety of sources. It does run the risk of some rewriting of history, caricaturing the old left, the new right and the Third Way, which has been a feature of both advocates and critics.

The Third Way in Practice

This section develops some of the themes of policy goals and means from table 12.1. While most of the examples are taken from the UK (more details on individual policy areas may be found in Part VI), a few from other countries are included.

New Labour emerged during the long period of opposition to the Conservative government of 1979–97. In opposition, it carefully studied the electoral success of Clinton's 'New Democrats' in the USA. Clinton's Third Way stressed the themes of work, conditionality and responsibility, and promised to 'end welfare as we know it'. The then Labour leader, John Smith, set up the Commission on Social Justice which flagged up many elements of the Third Way in its report of 1994. It rejected the approaches to social and economic policy of the *Levellers* (the old left) and the *Deregulators* (the new right) and advocated the middle way of an *Investor's* Britain. This approach features much of the discourse which was to become central to New Labour: economic efficiency and social justice are different sides of the same coin; redistributing opportunities rather than just redistributing income; transforming the welfare state from a safety-net in times of trouble to a springboard for economic opportunity; welfare should offer a hand-up not a hand-out; an active, preventive welfare state; paid work for a fair wage as the most secure and sustainable way out of poverty; and the balancing of rights and responsibilities. An investor's welfare state is proactive, emphasizing prevention and stressing causes rather than effects, attacking the causes of poverty rather than its symptoms, preventing poverty through education and training rather than simply compensating people in poverty.

New Labour has probably set itself more targets than any previous British government, and has established Public Service Agreements and Performance Assessment Frameworks throughout government departments. However, despite the claims of SMART (specific, measurable, accurate, relevant, timed) targets, many have turned out to be too vaguely defined and difficult to operate. In broad terms, New Labour set targets for increasing educational qualifications, reducing child poverty and health inequality but not, crucially for 'old Labour' critics, income equality. New Labour rejects a simple, fiscal equality to be achieved through the tax and benefit system. It claims instead to seek a more ambitious and dynamic redistribution of assets or endowments. In short, instead of compensating people for their poverty with transfer payments, it aims to improve opportunities by increasing poor people's levels of health and education. Critics who argue that New Labour's aims are all less radical than those of Old Labour are wide of the mark. Old Labour would be proud of the child poverty and health inequality targets. However, they are long-term goals, and there is no certainty that they will be met. There have been similar, but generally less marked, retreats from fiscal redistribution and equality of outcome in countries such as France, Germany and Sweden.

In terms of policy instruments, New Labour emphasizes conditional or contractarian welfare. Rights are not 'dutiless' but tend to be given to those who have fulfilled their obligations. The main obligations are connected with work, but others are concerned with housing or looking after the welfare of young children with the help of health professionals. At the extreme, this can be seen as a change from a patterned to a process-driven distribution: distribution does not depend simply on people's need, but also on their actions and behaviour. This fits with changes in other countries. The most extreme examples are found in the USA. Welfare is now time-limited, indicating that it is seen as a temporary 'hand-up' not a permanent 'hand-out'. This means that there is a large incentive to find work, even in low-paid 'McJobs'. In some states, single mothers on welfare are not given additional benefits for any subsequent children. Moreover, single mothers with young children are forced to find paid work. However, in many countries there are less extreme moves to conditionality through 'active labour market policies' that aim to move people from welfare to work.

Services are largely financed by the state, but may be delivered by private or voluntary bodies in a 'purchaser/provider split'. Rather than hierarchies or markets, coordination and collaboration through 'partnerships' or networks are stressed. New Labour has ended the old 'class war' with private education and health providers, and now wishes to work with them through agreements or 'concordats', in which, for example, NHS patients will be treated in private hospitals. The government encouraged new 'independent' (for-profit) centres to treat NHS patients, and allows patients to choose a private hospital under its 'choose and book' scheme. Moreover, many hospitals and schools have been built and run under a revamped Conservative Private Finance Initiative (PFI), which, when in opposition, Labour once termed 'privatization'.

This more pluralist provision is one way in which many countries can already be said to be on the Third Way. Britain tended to be exceptional, in that the state traditionally owned most of the country's hospitals as well as a relatively high percentage of its housing; elsewhere ownership of such facilities was more widespread. In some countries, basic state services are supplemented with a private or voluntary extension ladder (in the case of pensions, for example). The state expects people to provide more of their own resources towards contingencies such as old age, but in return the government will assist low-income savers and provide regulation of the financial market. Tax and service levels will be pragmatic rather than dogmatic. There is a general tendency to prioritize services such as health and education that can be preventive in nature and increase human capital over reactive, passive, 'relief' cash benefits. Redistribution will be 'for a purpose' and based more on endowments rather than in terms of transfer payments, although there has been some 'silent' or 'backdoor' fiscal redistribution, especially to families with children.

Work is central to the Third Way. Key policy goals are evident in such slogans as 'work for those who can; security for those who cannot' and 'making work pay'. Full employment is the aim, but this is to be achieved in terms of 'employability' through the 'supply-side' rather than by 'old'-style Keynesian demand management. Work is now more flexible, with an increase in part-time and temporary employment. All governments can do is to equip workers with the skills to meet new challenges and to add some element of security to this flexibility – resulting in 'flexicurity'.

The balance between security and flexibility varies. Countries such as the Netherlands appear to have stressed a genuine mix, while the UK and the USA seem to tend more towards the neo-liberal concept of a lightly regulated labour market. Similarly, the Third Way's work-centred social policy may have a different mix of carrots and sticks. On the one hand, it may emphasize carrots in the form of advice from case workers and investment in human capital. The thinking behind the slogan 'making work pay' includes a national minimum wage, in-work benefits of tax credits (or fiscal welfare) and making high-quality affordable childcare available to all. On the other hand, critics argue that the Third Way in the USA tended to 'starve the poor back into work' through low or time-limited benefits.

Debates about universalism versus selectivity will not be dogmatic. On the one hand, inclusion through universal services or civic welfare is stressed. On the other, there may be increasing selectivity in cash benefits such as targeting the poorest pensioners and new area-based policies.

Emerging Issues

Few European countries remain untouched by the Third Way. Indeed, it might be claimed that elements of the Third Way predate Blair and Clinton in that many European countries have long had a more pluralist (i.e. less statist) welfare system and Sweden has operated active labour market policies since the 1930s, but it is probably true to say that many policy elements (e.g. work obligations) have sharpened in many countries. It is more difficult to detect the ebb and flow of Third Way policies in many other European countries, as social democratic governments have come and gone, with only New Labour in the UK being continuously in power since 1997.

However, New Labour does appear to have changed its character over its period of office. While it has arguably moved more towards the left by (stealthily) introducing higher tax and spend policies, critics argue that it has moved more to the right in favouring the market, privatization, choice and consumerism. Since Tony Blair stepped down in 2007, there have been debates about whether Blairism (or the Third Way, progressive governance or 'Tonyism' – after both Blair and Giddens) will outlast Blair. Most commentators do not expect substantial deviation from existing policies either from Gordon Brown's Labour government or from a Conservative government were it to win the next general election. In other

words, there appear to be few emerging issues, but, rather, a broad continuation of the present course.

It is as yet difficult to judge the success of the Third Way either in principle or in practice. Part of the difficulty is due to the relatively short period in office of Third Way governments; but a greater part is perhaps associated with the diverse nature of the project. Defining the Third Way, and deciding which governments and policies have adhered to its ideology, remains problematic. Different commentators argue, variously, that there is a single third way, that there are different third ways, or that the Third Way is simply neo-liberalism. Similarly, it has been claimed both that the Third Way is largely confined to the USA and the UK and that most countries in Europe are Third Way.

However, on balance, it seems that, to some extent, a number of countries are pursuing policies that have some new and distinctive elements. Whether they are termed 'Third Way' or 'progressive governance', some new label may be required, as discourse, values, policy goals and policy means or mechanisms are not 'old' social democracy, or simply neo-liberalism. Administrations such as Clinton's Democrats and Blair's New Labour may appear to be more towards the neo-liberal end of the spectrum than countries such as Belgium, Denmark, Germany, the Netherlands and Sweden under social democratic or coalition governments. However, it is likely that elements such as 'active' and 'positive' welfare, consumerism, obligations and a more pluralist welfare state are here to stay, and it is very doubtful that there will be a return to the traditional social democratic welfare state.

Guide to Further Reading

As Third Way social policy represents work in progress, the most up-to-date details will be found in newspapers, biographies, autobiographies and diaries of politicians, and articles in academic journals. Proposals for new policies can be found from the think-tank broadly sympathetic to New Labour, the Institute of Public Policy Research (<www.ippr.org.uk>) and from the international Policy Network (<www.policy-network.net>).

Below is a selection of some of the existing books published on the topic. T. Blair, *The Third Way* (Fabian Society, 1998). This brief pamphlet gives the 'political' equivalent of A. Giddens's book, *The Third Way* (Polity, 1998), which was the influential original source written by the leading academic proponent of the Third Way. Giddens, *Europe in the Global Age* (Polity, 2007) restates and updates this, with chapter 4 ('From Negative to Positive Welfare') being of greatest relevance to social policy.

M. Powell (ed.), *Evaluating New Labour's Welfare Reforms* (Policy Press, 2002) examines New Labour's successes and failures in social policy in its first term. M. Powell and M. Hewitt, *Welfare State and Welfare Change* (Open University Press, 2002) takes a broader approach, examining the changes between New Labour's 'modern welfare state' and earlier social policies, and providing some explanation for these changes. J. Lewis and R. Surender (eds), *Welfare State Change: Towards a Third Way?* (Oxford University Press, 2004) explores the Third Way in the UK and internationally. G. Bonoli and M. Powell (eds), *Social Democratic Party Policies in Contemporary Europe* (Routledge, 2004) sets the UK in the wider European context.

Chapter 13

Feminist Perspectives

Jane Lewis

Overview

- Social policies may both underpin traditional gender roles and permit their transformation.
- It is important to consider the extent to which gender inequalities which manifest themselves in gender divisions persist, and are manifest in access to income and resources of all kinds and in the meaning of concepts crucial to the analysis of policies.
- The development of social policies is related to both family and labour market change, and at the household level to changes in both family form and in the nature of the contributions men and women make to families in respect of income and unpaid care work.
- Women's relationship to the welfare state tends to be more complicated than that of men: they are clients, paid and unpaid providers of welfare.
- Gender equality is not easy to conceptualize: same treatment (of individual women) to men, the recognition of (group) differences, and whether to emphasize equal outcomes or opportunities are again on the agenda with the setting up of the new Commission on Equality and Human Rights.

Feminist Approaches

Post-war writing on the welfare state made very little mention of women. Richard Titmuss's classic essay on the divisions of social welfare stressed the importance of occupational and fiscal welfare in addition to that provided by the state, but omitted analysis of provision by the voluntary sector and the family, both vital providers of welfare and both historically dominated by women providers. Yet the post-war settlement in respect of social provision made huge assumptions regarding the roles and behaviour of men and women in society. Policy-makers followed Beveridge in assuming that adult men would be fully employed, that women would be primarily homemakers and carers, and that marriages would be stable. However, the most significant post-war social trends have been the vast increases in married women's labour market participation, in the divorce rate and in the extra-marital birth rate, all of which have had a disproportionate effect on women.

The first post-war feminist analyses of social policies began to appear in the 1970s. Emanating mainly from socialist feminists, they tended to be critical of the post-war settlement. For example, Elizabeth Wilson's pioneering study of women and welfare published more than thirty years ago argued that 'social welfare policies amount to no less than the state organization of domestic life' (*Women and the Welfare State*, Tavistock, 1977, p. 9). This view was similar to that adopted by some Scandinavian feminists at the time and stressed the patriarchal nature of the post-war welfare state. The Scandinavians highlighted the way in which women had become the employees of the welfare state on a huge scale, but found themselves for the most part doing the same kind of jobs that they had traditionally done at home – for example, childcare. These jobs remained low paid and low status in the public sector – hence the charge that state patriarchy had replaced private patriarchy. In Britain, it was also stressed that many of the assumptions of the social security system, for example, were traditional. Thus if a woman drawing benefit cohabited with a man, it was assumed that he would be supporting her and her benefit was withdrawn. This early feminist analysis attacked the family as the main site of female oppression and also attacked the welfare state for upholding traditional ideas about the roles of men and women within the family.

More recent feminist analysis has focused less on whether state intervention is good or bad, and rather more on unpacking the complicated relationships between women and welfare systems, and the significance of gender in the analysis of social policies. For it is not possible to reach any easy conclusion as to the effects of social welfare policies on women. If we return briefly to the example of cohabiting women, we can see that, while state policies enforced traditional assumptions about a man's obligation to maintain as soon as he appeared in a household, social security benefits have nevertheless played a significant part in permitting non-traditional, lone mother households to exist autonomously, and have thus played a part in permitting the transformation of traditional family forms. To take a second example: the recent efforts of most Western welfare states to address the problems of balancing work and family have often made it easier for women to reconcile their responsibilities for paid and unpaid work, but such an approach has not necessarily resulted in a more gender equal division of work.

Later feminist analyses of social policy have stressed the extent to which gender – the social construction of masculinity and femininity – is important as a variable in the analysis of policies, particularly in respect of their outcomes, and as an explanatory tool in understanding social policies and welfare regimes. Feminist analysis has insisted that the whole fabric of society is gendered. Thus access to income and resources of all kinds – for example, education – is gendered, as are the concepts that are crucial to the study of social policy: need, inequality, dependence, citizenship. Once the persistence of gender divisions is understood, it becomes easier to appreciate the persistence of inequalities. For example, while the occupational structure has changed enormously over the past century, there are still men's jobs and women's jobs. A man's job may become a woman's job, as in the case of librarian or bank clerk, but the gender divisions remain and, with them, status and pay differentials.

However, it would be a mistake to think that it is possible to identify a single feminist approach to social policy. Feminists have differed both in their theoretical approaches and in the issues they have focused on. Since the early 1990s, there has been more emphasis on 'difference' and thus, for example, on the fact that the interests of women carers may be different from those of women being cared for, as will black women's interests differ from those of white women. In other words, the politics of contested need will be present between different groups of women as well as between women and men. This has made the definition of what constitutes gender equality difficult. Nevertheless, feminist social policy analysts have evolved their own questions and vocabulary and it is to these that we now turn.

Feminist Challenges

Feminists began by challenging mainstream sociological and economic literature that purported to explain women's position, particularly in the family and in employment, the central argument being over the reasons for gendered inequalities in society. Mainstream analysis considered these to be the product of a combination of biology and choice, which in turn rendered them inappropriate targets for social reform. Functional sociologists and neo-classical economists agreed that, given that women wanted children, biology and differential earning power made it rational for husbands and wives to maximize their utilities by husbands becoming the primary earners and wives the primary carers. If they did go out to work, women would therefore choose local part-time work that suited them. The traditional male breadwinner model was thus portrayed as the most efficient and as an essentially harmonious family form.

Feminist questioning of these models focused on both the family and the workplace. Rethinking the family involved, first, stressing that there was no such thing as *the* family, either in terms of a single family form or in terms of a single experience and understanding on the part of the different family members. As Jessie Bernard (*The Future of Marriage*, Penguin, 1976) noted a generation ago, there were in fact *two* marriages: his and hers. Male and female interpretations of their position could differ fundamentally. In regard to the economics of the family, Eleanor Rathbone (*The Disinherited Family*, Arnold, 1924) raised the

crucial question about the purpose of the wage as early as the 1920s. If the wage was and is a reward for individual effort and merit, how was and is it supposed to provide for dependent wives and children? Feminists have continued to ask awkward questions about the maintenance of family members. Social investigation and policy-makers assumed that money entering the family was shared equally between family members, but feminist investigation has shown unequivocally that this is not the case and that where conflict between the partners becomes violent, women often find themselves better off drawing benefits than relying on their male providers. Thus feminists have questioned both the harmonious working and the efficiency of the traditional male breadwinner family model.

They have also questioned whether women's role in reproduction is sufficient to explain their position in the labour force. Such a view minimizes the role played by discrimination. It also ignores conflicting evidence in terms of women's aspirations revealed by the post-1960s dramatic rise in female educational achievement, and the structural constraints experienced by women. Women may choose to have children, but mainstream models also assume that they must necessarily rear them. Questions as to who should care for and maintain children have therefore been central to the feminist analysis of social policies, in particular how far there should be collective provision for children in the form of cash (typically in modern welfare states in the form of child benefits) and care (via day care and nurseries and/or paid parental leaves), and how far individual mothers and fathers should assume responsibility for both cash and care.

Women and the Welfare State

Insofar as women have featured in the traditional texts on social policy and administration, they have tended to do so as clients of the welfare state. Feminist analysis has emphasized that women's position in relation to modern welfare states is far more complicated than this. In brief, they should be considered as clients, paid and unpaid providers, and agents.

Those who have charged that women have done disproportionately well out of the welfare state have pointed to the fact that they more often become clients, whether in terms of the number of visits they make to general practitioners, or the amount of benefit they draw, especially as lone mothers and elderly women. But women have also been the main providers of welfare. The vast majority of the increase in post-war employment for married women has been in the service of the welfare state (for example, as health workers and teachers), and women have always provided most of the informal, unpaid welfare within the family.

Women's position as both clients and providers is complicated and is directly related to the unequal gender division of paid and unpaid work in society. Analyses of entitlements to welfare, such as Gosta Esping-Andersen's (*The Three Worlds of Welfare Capitalism*, Polity, 1990), which examine the conditions under which people are permitted to withdraw from the labour market and thus depend on a strict distinction between work and non-work, cannot encompass the reality of women's existence. The woman who withdraws from the labour market often does so in order to care for children or a dependent adult. She therefore withdraws from paid work in order to engage in unpaid work. So women who are clients of the welfare state are quite likely also to be acting at the same time as unpaid providers of welfare. Similarly, analyses of welfare outcomes that do not take into account women's contribution as unpaid providers will inevitably overestimate what women take out of the system as opposed to what they put in.

Women's agency is also problematic. Seemingly, women have had little say in the making of modern welfare states. Recent historical literature has suggested that women may have had more influence when the mixed economy of welfare was tipped more firmly in favour of voluntary and family provision at the beginning of the twentieth century. Thus in the United States, for example, women's voluntary organizations lobbied successfully for mothers' pensions (an early form of child benefit), protective labour legislation for women workers and maternal and child welfare legislation. Theda Skocpol (*Protecting Soldiers and Mothers*, Harvard University Press, 1992) has suggested that at that time the United States set out on the road to becoming a 'maternalist' welfare state in contrast to the 'paternalism' of the European states, which were built up around the concept of social insurance and which in turn relied heavily on the male breadwinner model.

Certainly the relationship between social provision and women's political participation is difficult. T. H. Marshall's much cited idea (*Sociology at the Crossroads and Other Essays*, Heinemann, 1963) that states proceeded from the granting of civil rights in the eighteenth century, to the granting of political rights in the nineteenth and to social rights in the twentieth, breaks down completely when women are introduced into the analysis. Women in most Western countries were granted social protection before they were granted the vote, usually in the form of protective labour legislation, which was in turn often designed to reinforce the gender division of labour and to exclude women from certain kinds of employment. The major programmes of modern West European welfare states were legislated by men and, in the case of social insurance, working as it does through the labour market, primarily for men. However, women have historically played an important role in local politics and in local campaigns around welfare rights and tenant groups, for example. In addition, the fact that women played very little part in the establishment of the programmes of the modern welfare state does not mean that the development of social provision is unimportant in securing women's participation. In the Scandinavian countries, which are acknowledged to have developed the most generous citizenship-based welfare entitlements, women have also succeeded in gaining the greatest formal political representation in Parliament.

Welfare Challenges and Gender Equality

The settlement at the heart of the modern welfare state was that between capital and labour. But it is increasingly recognized that there was a second key settlement between men and women. The old labour contract was designed first and foremost for the regularly employed male breadwinner and provision had to be made for women. The gender settlement meant that those marginal to the labour market got cash cover via dependants' benefits. The labour/capital settlement can be characterized as security traded for dependence, and a similar set of arrangements can be said to have marked the gender settlement. The male breadwinner model was based on a set of assumptions about male and female contributions at the household level: men having the primary responsibility to earn and women to care for the young and the old. Thus this model made provision for the unpaid work of care, but at the price of inscribing female dependence on men.

The traditional male breadwinner model family that was built into the post-war settlement assumed regular and full male employment *and* stable families in which women would be provided for largely via their husbands' earnings and their husbands' social contributions. It could not survive family change in terms of, first, the changes in family form (high and stable divorce, fewer marriages, increased cohabitation and single motherhood) and, second, the changes in the contributions men and women make to households, particularly in the form of women's increased earnings.

Family change in all its dimensions is now recognized as an independent variable of the first importance, as Western societies struggle with low fertility, population ageing and the need to maximize adult labour market participation in order to stay competitive. It is this nexus of challenges that has brought work and family issues – which are key to the problem of gender equality – onto the political agenda. Governments in the twenty-first century have increasingly recognized the need, first, to address care issues, particularly as the numbers of frail elderly increase, and to encourage fertility so as to address population ageing and ensure that there are enough workers to pay the pensions of elderly people, and, second, to get all adults, male and female, into the labour market.

Historically, most welfare states were preoccupied with making provision for the risks that might befall the male breadwinner – unemployment, sickness, and poverty in old age – and through him, allowances were also made for wives and children as his dependants; while trade unions fought for a 'family wage' to enable the male worker to support his dependants. With labour market and family change such assumptions no longer make sense. This is why some have suggested that welfare states must make provision for *new social risks* in respect of the care and support of young and old dependants.

As women do more earning, should men be encouraged, cajoled or coerced into caring, or should care pass increasingly to third parties: to state- or market-provided institutional care, to employers, voluntary organizations or, perhaps, to migrant workers? Or should care perhaps stay in large measure the province of women in the family, meaning that they are employed only part time and/or receive monetary compensation for care? These questions also raise, in an acute form, issues in respect of the role of the state that are the bread and butter of social policy analysis in terms of the form of provision, and the level and type of finance, but that are also new, particularly insofar as they involve thinking about the politics and distribution of *time* – for work and for care – as well as *money*.

There has been substantial convergence in Western countries in terms of a shift away from policies based on the notion of a male breadwinner family, and towards policies based on the idea of an adult worker model family. However, it must be noted that in many West European countries, the UK included, women tend to be employed part time. They are therefore not fully individualized or economically autonomous, which raises the possibility that policies based on adult worker model assumptions may be as far removed from the social reality as the old model of dependence on a male breadwinner. The temptation for governments has been to intervene to help women to reconcile paid and unpaid work by investing in childcare services and 'parental' leaves (which in all EU member states are taken primarily by women), rather than undertaking the much harder task of seeking radically to change the male career pattern. Thus women's position may be improved without a significant progress towards gender equality.

Emerging Issues: Equality or Difference?

Feminist analysis of women's structural position in society and the particulars of their relationship to modern welfare regimes has shown why it is that equal opportunities legislation that focuses heavily on the public world of employment is bound to have at best only moderate success. The gendered divisions of paid and unpaid work and the gendered inequalities that result require a much more sophisticated policy package. Aiming to treat women in the same way as men will not do. On the other hand, acknowledging and recognizing female difference within social policies is likely to reinforce it, as was the case with post-war social security policy which, recognizing the degree to which married women were dependent on men, served to perpetuate it. Similarly, policies designed to help women to 'reconcile' responsibilities for paid and unpaid work without seeking to change men's behaviour reinforce the gendered division of work. However, governments face major problems if they try to prescribe change at the level of the household in advance of social attitudes.

Feminist analysis has shown that the problem of same or different treatment is a central one for modern social policies, but is also beginning to suggest ways of transcending this particular dichotomy. Equal opportunities policies at EU and member state levels have moved from an emphasis on same treatment (which tends to require that a comparison be made between the individual woman and a comparably situated man), through a focus on 'positive action' (which pays more attention to the discrimination experienced by women as a group), to 'mainstreaming'. Mainstreaming carries the idea that policies in pursuit of gender equality will no longer be confined to an equal opportunities 'ghetto', but will rather be integrated across all fields of policy-making. This has the potential to address disadvantage without denying difference. However, there is the danger that the aim of gender equality may be 'lost' or 'diluted' when it is no longer an exclusive policy focus.

The new institutional arrangements for pursuing equality in the UK bring together race and ethnicity, disability and gender (in a Commission for Equality and Human Rights). It remains to be seen how far the aim of eradicating different forms of inequality will take equal place, and how far the Commission will handle the problem of sameness and difference. There is some indication that the new body will interpret equality through the 'capabilities approach' developed by the Nobel Prize-winning economist Amartya Sen, with its emphasis on the importance of securing 'real agency freedom' for the individual. Feminist analysis has also begun to suggest that a way of transcending the sameness/difference dichotomy may lie in the promotion of policies that permit 'genuine' or 'real' choice for women and men in terms of the socially necessary activities, whether paid or unpaid, that they wish to perform.

Guide to Further Sources

There is now a range of texts that provide an introduction to feminist approaches to social policy. Fiona Williams, *Social Policy: a Critical Introduction* (Polity, 1989) provides an interesting introduction to feminist theory as it relates to social policy. Gillian Pascall, *Social Policy: a Feminist Analysis*, 2nd edn (Routledge, 1999) covers many of the substantive fields of social policy. Mary Daly and Katherine Rake, *Gender and the Welfare State* (Polity, 2003) is a more advanced text, which also draws on comparative material. Work that has served to gender crucial concepts and approaches to the study of social policy is also important, especially Ruth Lister, *Citizenship: Feminist Perspectives*, 2nd edn (Palgrave, 2003). Barbara Hobson, Jane Lewis and Birte Siim (eds), *Contested Concepts in Gender and Social Politics* (Edward Elgar, 2002) is an edited collection of key concepts that is also comparative.

Chapter 14

Green Perspectives

Michael Cahill

Overview

- The environmental damage produced by our economic system is all too plain to see in oil spills, greenhouse gases, loss of the rainforests, traffic pollution and many other consequences of the industrial way of life.
- Widespread loss of life is predicted in the coming decades as global warming leads to changed weather patterns. The human cost is already manifest across the globe, as drought, hurricanes and flooding have produced hundreds of thousands of 'environmental refugees'.
- Over the last quarter of the twentieth century concern for the environment has moved from the province of small, non-influential pressure groups to the agendas of the world's leading nations.
- There are many varieties of green thought, but they are all united in their belief that the environment should take priority in social and political discussion.
- Climate change is persuading governments around the world to take environmental issues much more seriously than they have in the past.

The Development of Environmentalism

Widespread interest in the environment can be traced back to the publication of the *Limits to Growth* report in 1972. The authors used various computer models to see how long the world's stocks of basic non-renewables would last given population increases and continuing economic growth. Also in the early 1970s, Friends of the Earth and Greenpeace were formed and began to popularize the environmental message with imaginative and persistent campaigning. Shortly afterwards, in 1973, an oil price hike by oil producers in the Middle East led to widespread energy-saving measures in the Western world, although this was not to endure. An environmental movement began to emerge with a growth in the membership of environmental pressure groups.

However, green political parties were in their infancy in the 1970s and did not gain electoral success until the 1980s, when, in Germany, Die Grünen gained seats in Parliament, took power in many local government areas and, by the late 1990s, was forming part of the national government. But it was not so much political parties or pressure groups which spread green ideas; rather, it was the impact of what was happening to nature. In the late 1980s, two extremely serious environmental problems were acknowledged: global warming and the discovery of holes in the ozone layer. In the 1990s, the quickening pace of environmental crisis – particularly the onset of climate change – pushed the issue of the environment onto the agenda of the leading industrial countries. This was symbolized by the attention given to the United Nations Earth Summit held in Rio de Janeiro in 1992, which committed the international community to a programme of sustainable development.

Greens are united in their recognition of the fact that there are natural and social limits to material progress. These have now been reached: the planet is over-populated, emissions from industrial and transport activity are damaging the biosphere, there is insufficient food to feed the population and species extinction proceeds apace. The green response is to call for a reduction in the burden of human activity on the planet which could have important implications for social policy. Just how this can be done is at the heart of green arguments and debate. Obviously it is of paramount importance that environmental policies do not themselves damage the welfare of the poorer sections of the population.

There are a great many ways to classify green thinking. A basic distinction can be made between 'light' and 'dark' green.

Dark greens see the survival of nature and the planet as all-important. Human activity, particularly in the past 200 years – i.e., since the emergence of industrialism – has despoiled the planet and threatens the existence of other life forms. This leads some greens to call for severe curbs on population. Dark greens believe that humans, in order to reduce their burden on the planet, need to reduce their consumption patterns. They are at one with supporters of animal rights in calling for an end to the second-class treatment of other sentient creatures on the planet. Rather than people

from the poor world looking to the rich West for a model, 'dark' greens would have the rich world try to imitate the poor world. Lifestyle change is key to this, with people adapting their way of life in order to reduce the damage they cause to planet earth. In reply to the charge that this is not terribly attractive to generations reared on consumer products, dark greens argue that if people were to reduce their consumerist lifestyle then they would gain immeasurably. Yet one cannot ignore the fact that many people do gain a sense of their own identity from material possessions. It is important to note that this is a message for the here and now. A sustainable way of life involves reducing one's impact on the environment straight away and not waiting for some future government to legislate. It can be seen that 'dark' greens integrate a set of ethical beliefs with their political and social views.

Light greens are reformists: they want to work with the grain of advanced industrial societies, and adopt a pragmatic approach. For them, the environmental problems of the world are neither too grave nor too large to be beyond the problem-solving capacity of science and technology. They believe that it is possible to have both continued economic growth and solutions to environmental problems. Many think that it is possible to use market mechanisms to correct the environmental imbalances which abound. Various techniques can be used to weigh the claims of the environment against other factors. Forms of cost-benefit analysis, assigning a monetary value to natural resources, can be used to decide on the degree of environmental protection required. Equally, it is possible for modern industry to clean up its act and, indeed, the production of technologies to do this will be a highly profitable investment. 'Light' green thinking is not a distinctive ideological position: it prioritizes green issues within existing modes of thinking about the world's political and economic problems.

It is frequently described as environmental (or ecological) modernization.

Varieties of Green Thought

Many writers dispute the claim that there can be a distinctive green ideology, arguing that many of its key propositions are taken from other traditions of political and social thought. Clearly this is an important and contentious issue, for its resolution will bear upon the viability or otherwise of separate green parties. Let us now summarize some of the positions whose adherents have added the prefix 'eco' to their belief, and notice that what they have in common is that they lay stress on certain aspects of their 'parent' ideology in order to reformulate it as a response to the environmental crisis.

Eco-socialism

Eco-socialism is really only as old as the green movement, although it has to be admitted that many of its decentralist arguments were anticipated by the early socialists 100 years ago. Eco-socialists link the damage done to the biosphere to the organization of economic life under capitalism. They are of the belief that a remodelling of this economic system will lead to a society where the profit imperative will not lead to ceaseless encroachment on nature. They do not believe that large-scale production processes must disappear, only that they should be planned and controlled to prevent pollution and waste. Clearly there is a real question-mark as to whether the international capitalist system would permit such a transformation to occur.

Eco-feminism

Eco-feminism regards the exploitation of nature as being historically linked to the exploitation and subordination of women. It attributes many of the environmental problems of our time to the triumph of 'male' values – ambition, struggle for control and independence – over 'feminine' values – nurturing, caring and tending. Naturally there is some considerable doubt as to whether these values can be seen as specifically male or female. All we can say with certainty is that, in the history of the modern world, one set of values has been more widespread among men than women, and vice versa. Eco-feminists argue that men must become more caring and nurturing and this should be reflected in the world of work, with unpaid, caring work being given a much higher priority by men. Women, for their part, need to take from masculinity the idea of being strong and assertive. In practical terms, this means sharing the care of children and domestic work. In paid work, eco-feminists would call for a retreat from a masculine ambience which devalues the emotional life – at the same time criticizing those feminisms which exalt individual autonomy and self-determination for women for seeing them as merely the female embodiment of consumer capitalism.

This critique becomes more pertinent as, in richer countries, women are increasingly gaining higher-status and better-paid employment, leaving caring work to be done by others. There is within eco-feminism a quasi-spiritual dimension exalting 'female' values, but there is also a more practically based eco-feminism in the poor world which points to the importance of women's resistance in some countries to the environmental destruction wrought by industrialism.

Green conservatism

Traditional conservatism in England emphasized the small community and the rural village, and was, in the first half of the nineteenth century, opposed to the industrial system and urban life. In some ways this made it akin to the programmes of dark greens today. The system of market liberalism has been a powerful force which, in moulding and expressing many people's desires for greater wealth, has released enormous energies which endanger the environment. There are many ways in which a politics of 'limits' and restraints on the use of economic and technological power would be close to the traditional conservative position.

The Welfare State

The welfare state divides green thinkers and reveals the different strands of thought which are present in green movements. Many greens are opposed to the welfare state. They are not against the goods that it delivers – free education, free healthcare, a national minimum wage – rather, they object to the fact that it is the *state* which delivers these services. However, for some greens this is tempered by the acknowledgement that inequalities in access to services and inequities in distribution are capable of being ameliorated by a state apparatus. Welfare states are large bureaucracies and, as such, have the capacity to control people's lives, a tendency that greens believe should be resisted. They argue that a decentralized welfare system would lead to less need for welfare, as citizens would be providing these services for themselves and each other. There is a high degree of emphasis on the advantages and positive benefits of mutuality – voluntary organizations of like-minded citizens providing services for themselves in their local community.

In discussing the future of the welfare state under a green regime, one must remain sensitive to the different green positions. Many argue that welfare does not have to be provided by the state at all; indeed, it would be more spontaneous and appropriate if it were *not* provided by the state, but rather by citizens themselves and their voluntary organizations. The neighbourhood and the voluntary organization, together with whatever form of local administration emerges from this collaboration, would attend to the welfare needs of the local population.

One of the key problems with this line of argument is that it downplays the role of social justice and disparities in income. Admittedly, structures of welfare can be oppressive, but they are also routine and accessible. This is an important consideration for the weak, vulnerable and isolated, who rely on the local welfare state for regular support and assistance. It might also be added that there are some who will find it difficult, whatever the society, to find ready acceptance and help – they might be mentally ill or they might have a disability of some kind – and state services, by employing professionals, aim to integrate such people into the community. The role of professionals is central to the discussion of the place of welfare in a green society. Many greens are unenthusiastic about using them, believing that they have usurped the caring and nurturing roles which individuals and communities ought to be undertaking themselves. Many greens feel that the use of professionals tends to render clients into passive consumers of welfare when they should instead be self-determining individuals.

Green Social Policies

Greens argue that paid work is overvalued and that this has had destructive consequences for both society and the individual. Greens were among the early proponents of a citizen's income (also known as basic income) which would be available to all. The intention here is that this would provide some recognition of the worth of unpaid work. There are many variations on the idea, but essentially this income would replace all National Insurance benefits, tax allowances and as many means-tested benefits as possible. For greens, such an income has the attraction that it can begin the process of revaluing unpaid work, since those who do unpaid caring work would receive the citizen's income in their own right. It fits in with the green idea that there should and could be more opportunities for local employment, such as workers' cooperatives, and removes some of the disadvantages associated with the low rates of pay often attached to such work. Equally, the income would be paid to those who do voluntary work.

Critics of such a scheme – especially the full-blown scheme outlined here – point out that it could bear very heavily on the taxpayers who have to fund it, although a crucial aspect, of course, is at what rate the income is paid. Some also argue that a citizen's income would be likely to diminish the incentive to work, although this is a problem common to all social security provision of a safety-net income and is not peculiar to a citizen's income. Another telling criticism is that it would require a great deal more centralized and bureaucratic state machinery than is currently seen as necessary in most accounts of a future green society.

Nevertheless, under such a green society the locality would be restored to its place as the centre of people's lives. And greens would go further in this direction because they believe that many tasks can be recognized through the spread of local exchange trading schemes (LETS). These – which already operate informally in some small communities – are token economies where people trade their skills with one another and are usually computed on the basis of so many hours worked. The tokens earned, however, remain a local currency and this ensures that the local community benefits from this activity. The advantages of LETS are obvious. They enable a deal of 'economic' activity to take place without the need for conventional employment. They enable those who are poor (that is, without cash income) to obtain goods and services outside of the cash economy.

At the national level, environmental modernizers argue for a taxation regime which moves away from taxes on individual income towards taxes on pollution. These eco-taxes would need to take many forms in order to deal with the various unsustainable activities prevalent in an advanced economy. For example, a resource depletion tax would try to ensure that a certain resource was only extracted to an agreed level. Pollution taxes could be levied on goods which have deleterious consequences for the environment in order to promote the sale of benign products. In like manner, these benign goods can be zero-rated for some taxes in order to encourage their consumption. Climate change has concentrated the minds of governments on the need to reduce carbon emissions. Various taxes have been proposed which would encourage a reduction in behaviour that produces carbon. Admittedly this is a 'big ask' given that the global economy is premised on the mobility of goods, people and capital.

Sustainable Development

Following the 1992 UN Earth Summit, which pledged the world's leading nations to a programme of sustainable development, the UK government committed itself to sustainable action across all policy sectors. Sustainable development was defined as development that meets the needs of the present without compromising the ability of future generations to meet their own needs.

The Labour government elected in 1997 linked sustainable development to issues of social policy. Its strategy, reiterated in *Securing the Future* (2005), gives sustainable development objectives across government and contains indicators upon which progress can be judged. These indicators are a mix of the social, economic and environmental; amongst many others, they include air pollution levels, populations of wild birds, river water quality, as well as unfit homes, crime levels and educational levels. The Labour government was committed to promoting economic growth as well as sustainable development, and some of its environmental critics feel that wherever there is a conflict between the two, it is usually the perceived needs of the economy which prevail. They cite the commitment to airport expansion when it has been clearly shown that air travel is a growing source of carbon emissions, and the expansion of a road-building programme which gives priorities to the car as opposed to the sustainable modes of walking and cycling.

Ever since someone coined the slogan 'think global, act local', the locality has been central to green and environmental thinking. The recognition that one's local environment is important has been seen in the Local Agenda 21 projects sponsored by local authorities throughout the UK following the 1992 Rio Summit, which now form part of the community strategy in local government. Even those people who have scarcely ever heard of the notion of 'sustainability' will be concerned about their local environment: the dog dirt on the pavement, graffiti, lack of safe play spaces for their children and so on. The future of Brazilian rainforests and holes in the ozone layer are certainly more remote and less easy to understand, but all sections of the population can relate to issues around their local community and will have views on what needs to be done.

Environmental Justice

There is accumulating evidence that poor people tend to suffer disproportionately from pollution. To give some examples: the bulk of vehicle exhaust pollution generated by commuter motorists driving in and out of urban centres affects those in low-income areas living adjacent to major roads; the major polluting factories tend to be sited close to low-income areas; children in social class 5 are five times more likely than children in social class 1 to be killed in road accidents. These are examples of environmental injustice, where poverty is compounded by a poor environment and a greater exposure to environmental hazards. When Hurricane Katrina hit the United States mainland in August 2005, leaving 1,836 dead in its wake, the majority of the residents of New Orleans and the other urban areas were able to flee by car. Those who were left behind, and who took refuge, for example, in the Superdome Football Stadium in New Orleans, were without access to personal transport and predominantly black. Too often, in addition, the poor do not enjoy the benefits which produce these environmental hazards: those on the lowest incomes are the least likely to own a car, for example. In a society where mobility is important for the maintenance of social networks, this can be a significant handicap. The focus of the UK government on social exclusion has revealed the ways in which those on low incomes are often coping with a poor environment and inferior facilities.

Emerging Issues

This chapter has outlined various green social policies which would be part of a future society where green values were dominant. In the shorter term, the emerging issues in the area of environment and social policy are likely to be debated within a light green or environmental discourse. The debates will, in all likelihood, concentrate on the following issues, amongst others:

- Governments will increasingly resort to environmental taxation. This could very easily make goods and services more expensive for those on the lowest incomes, so in dealing with climate change right through to road pricing, mechanisms will need to be put in place which will protect the poorest.
- If it is accepted that the standard of living and way of life enjoyed by the populations of rich world countries are not sustainable for the entire population of the planet, then those of us in the rich countries will have to live more simply and with much less use of energy. Sustainable consumption is likely to become a significant issue.
- As it is recognized that consumer societies are bad for the health of the planet, there will be an increasing focus on well-being and the quality of life.

Guide to Further Sources

There are a number of texts which explicitly examine the links between the environment and social policy. M. Huby, *Social Policy and the Environment* (Open University Press, 1998) is essential reading. M. Cahill, *The Environment and Social Policy* (Routledge, 2002) is an introductory text. For more extended discussion, see the essays in M. Cahill and T. Fitzpatrick (eds), *Environmental Issues and Social Welfare* (Blackwell, 2002) and T. Fitzpatrick and M. Cahill (eds), *Greening the Welfare State* (Palgrave, 2002).

There are some excellent introductions to green ideologies. A. Dobson, *Green Political Thought*, 3rd edn (Routledge, 2000) is a good starting point, in which issues of sustainability and policy implications are discussed. Equally useful is J. Barry, *Environment and Social Theory* (Routledge, 1999) which examines the various ways in which the environment is explored in social theory. For a text that covers green political thought, parties, pressure groups, social movements and environmental policy-making, see N. Carter, *The Politics of the Environment*, 2nd edn (Cambridge University Press, 2007).

Useful websites are: Local Exchange Trading Schemes: <www.letslinkuk.net> and Citizen's Income: <www.citizensincome.org>. The New Economics Foundation publishes a number of useful pamphlets, particularly on well-being, available at <www.neweconomics.org/gen/>. The UK government's sustainable development site is at <www.sustainable-development.gov.uk/>. The Sustainable Development Commission is a government-appointed 'watchdog', available at <www.sd-commission.org.uk/>.

Chapter 15

Postmodernist Perspectives

Tony Fitzpatrick

Overview

- Postmodernism describes a disillusionment with traditional social and political theories of society, one which clears away many of their premises and assumptions in order to make room for new approaches and ways of thinking.
- Post-structuralism shares this need to depart radically from previous philosophies, though it is more theoretically and methodologically precise, drawing attention to the instabilities of identity and the imprecisions of meaning.
- As postmodernism and post-structuralism have themselves become established features of the intellectual landscape, many have queried their importance or relevance; in some respects they appear distant from the 'bread-and-butter' issues of social policy, yet in others they articulate the changing social realities with which social policy must get to grips.
- Other social changes include increased attention to the concept of risk and the extent to which the avoidance, navigation or embracing of risk is central to contemporary notions of citizenship and well-being.
- And with class no longer as predominant as it used to be, some believe that we must look to a wider variety of social movements to understand the agents and engines of recent social developments.

Introduction

Postmodernism was *the* intellectual fashion of the 1980s and, like all fashions, it attracted zealous supporters and equally zealous critics. Yet postmodernism's legacy has somehow confounded both sides. It did not sweep away traditional schools of thought, as its supporters had anticipated, yet nor has it proved to be an empty, transitional fad, as its critics had hoped. This is because postmodernism's roots reach far back into the history of ideas, reinventing some old themes within new social, politi-

cal and cultural contexts. By the 1990s it had seeped so far into the humanities and social sciences that it could not have been drained away without damaging the geographies of contemporary debate. By the time it took an interest in postmodernism, the latter already nurtured the intellectual soil upon which social policy depended.

Theories of the Postmodern

The turn towards postmodernism was largely inspired by a disillusion with traditional forms of politics and social philosophy. The 'rediscovery' of Marxism in the 1960s inspired the left to believe that alternatives to consumer capitalism were both imaginable and achievable. By the 1970s, however, many activists and intellectuals had become disenchanted with Marxism and began to rethink the meaning of emancipation and progress.

Jean-François Lyotard contended that we can no longer cling to 'meta-narratives'. A meta-narrative is a system of thought that attempts to understand the social world within a single, all-encompassing critique. Marxism is one such 'grand narrative' in that it seeks to explain all aspects of society in terms of material production and class struggle. This is like trying to step beyond the social world and understand it from the outside. But Lyotard, like Wittgenstein before him, insisted that there is no 'outside' to which we can aspire; since we are enmeshed within language, there is no space beyond language that would enable us to map the world in its entirety. Therefore, knowledge must proceed from 'the inside', from within our language-using communities: knowledge is always contextualized and particular rather than absolute and universal. Lyotard defines postmodernism as an 'incredulity towards meta-narratives' and so a rejection of the view that emancipatory politics can be based upon a single system of thought.

> In contemporary society and culture – postindustrial society, postmodern culture – the question of legitimation of knowledge is formulated in different terms. The grand narrative has lost its credibility . . . regardless of whether it is a speculative narrative or a narrative of emancipation.
>
> (Jean-François Lyotard, *The Postmodern Condition*, Manchester University Press, 1984, p. 37)

Jean Baudrillard goes even further. Marxism may have been appropriate in an age of production, but we now live in societies of signs and codes. Indeed, so ubiquitous are these signs and codes that they no longer symbolically represent reality; instead, the philosophical distinction between reality and representation has collapsed into a 'hyperreality'. Whereas we could once distinguish between original objects and their copies, hyperreality implies that only copies exist and no originating source for those copies is identifiable. Ours, then, is an age of simulations that endlessly refer only to other simulations. The infinite circularity of these self-references is what Baudrillard calls the simulacra: everything is a reproduction of other reproductions. Society implodes in on itself and we cannot liberate ourselves from the simulacra: ideologies of progress are just another form of seduction to the system of codes.

These ideas came under considerable attack from other theorists. Jürgen Habermas alleges that postmodernism is a philosophical justification for social and political conservatism. For if progress is now taken to be impossible and undesirable, then this resembles a conservative defence of the status quo. Habermas charges postmodernist theorists with depending upon the very philosophical premises and assumptions that they claim to have dispelled.

However, there are some who, while not supporting postmodernism per se, insist that its emergence and popularity reveal something very important about recent social change. Fredric Jameson describes postmodernism as 'the cultural logic of late capitalism' in that it accurately describes the fragmentation and heterogeneity of contemporary life. This is because of developments within capitalist production and consumption. Our cultures are pervaded by surfaces, hybrids, repackaging, parody, pastiche and spectacle because this is now the most effective way of valuing, circulating and consuming commodities. Capitalism dominates by seeming not to dominate, by fragmenting both itself and the objects of domination. So Jameson is insisting that postmodernism *can* be utilized by those committed to a progressive politics of the left.

What, then, are the basic tenets of post-modernism? Postmodernists:

- reject universalism;
- believe truth to be contextual;
- reject foundationalism and essentialism;
- avoid binary distinctions;
- support identity politics;
- celebrate irony and difference.

Postmodernists reject the idea that certain values, judgements and propositions apply universally across space and time. For critics of postmodernism like Christopher Norris this leads inevitably to relativism, the idea that there are *no* universal standards of morality and truth. This, he argues, tempts postmodernists into intellectual absurdity, such as Baudrillard's claim in 1991 that the Gulf War had not happened.

However, as a defender of postmodernism, Richard Rorty argues that it is the futile search for absolute truth which creates relativism, so if we stop searching for that which is unobtainable then we can transcend the sterile distinction between universalism and relativism. This does not leave us unable to speak about truth; it means that truth is contextual, i.e. dependent upon the frame within which truth-claims are made. As Chantal Mouffe observes, ideas are rooted within particular traditions and there is no 'God's eye view' which is external to all traditions. Postmodernists define liberalism not as a universal doctrine but as a tradition that must engage equally with other traditions and perspectives. The world resembles a text and so we can only speak about it from within the text itself.

Postmodernists also reject foundationalism and essentialism. Foundationalism is the notion that knowledge and belief are based upon axioms and principles that are in no need of demonstration because they are self-evident – e.g. murder is immoral. Postmodernists argue that there are no such foundations, as we can never fully justify

any knowledge- or belief-claim. If the world is a text, then each 'word' within it depends upon an infinite number of others for its meaningfulness. Essentialism is the idea that objects have essences which, once identified, enable us to explain the object in question – e.g. human nature is essentially good. For postmodernists, though, all objects and their supposed essences are merely social constructs.

Postmodernists insist that we should avoid thinking in terms of binary distinctions, hierarchies and structures – e.g. nature versus culture. Postmodern feminists like Judith Butler argue that this way of thinking reflects masculinist assumptions about the world – that the world is divisible into parts which relate to one another in relations of higher and lower, superior and inferior. Postmodernist architecture is not organized around a centre: there are no edges and peripheries or, rather, *everywhere* is an edge *and* a periphery! Instead, postmodernists prefer to emphasize the importance of centreless flows, fluidities, networks and webs.

Postmodernism is often taken to prefer a form of identity politics based around culture and the self. Oppression and discrimination are not just about a lack of resources but also about a lack of recognition and status, about not being able to shape the norms which define and exclude you. Yet identity – of individuals, groups, societies – is never fixed but is in a state of indeterminate flux, being constantly renegotiated and redefined. Identity implies not only 'resemblance to' but also 'difference from'.

Finally, postmodernism embodies a playful, ironic stance: postmodernists often refuse to take anything too seriously, including postmodernism! Yet rather than being self-indulgent this playfulness is meant to be a celebration of diversity, hybridity, difference and pluralism. For Rorty, philosophy is not the 'mirror of nature' but a means of devising new vocabularies and descriptions.

Rather than debating which description is real, our job is to assist each other in endlessly deconstructing and reconstructing our understanding of the social world. Solidarity, rather than truth, is the proper object of inquiry.

Postmodernism and Social Policy

The initial reluctance of the social policy community to engage with these ideas is understandable. Postmodernism is too abstract for many researchers working in what is a highly empirical field, challenging some of its fondest assumptions. In order to defend those assumptions it is the *weaknesses* of the postmodern critique that social policy theorists have often chosen to highlight.

For instance, if social policy is concerned with welfare then we must be able to distinguish between higher and lower forms of well-being in making interpersonal, historical, cross-national and cross-cultural comparisons. Yet it is precisely these judgements that postmodernism might disallow. By embracing relativism, contextualism, antifoundationalism and anti-essentialism, postmodernists seem to undermine notions of truth and social progress and so undermine efforts to create greater freedom, equality and community. But if these notions should *not* be dismissed – as their enduring popularity might suggest – then perhaps we should reject postmodern ideas because their political and social consequences are likely to be damaging.

Take one example. Social policy is arguably based upon the view that there is such a thing as human nature consisting of certain basic needs. The job of welfare systems is to enable those needs to be fulfilled. But if human nature is a modernist fiction, as postmodernists claim, and if needs are constructed through language rather than being natural, then the rationale of state welfare may be undermined.

This is one of the reasons why some social policy commentators are very suspicious of postmodernism, accusing it of providing an intellectual justification of anti-welfare state politics.

Others, though, insist that postmodernism and social policy need not be so hostile. Traditionally, social policy has been concerned with class – i.e., income and occupation. Yet although our identities are undoubtedly constructed in terms of class relations, there may be other forms of relations and divisions that are also important: gender, ethnicity, sexuality, religion, disability, nationality, age. Therefore, social policy must take account of these additional categories and perhaps postmodernism might assist the subject in doing so. Yet this is where disagreement kicks in, for how should we weigh class against non-class divisions? For some, class is still of central importance and postmodernism therefore an unwelcome distraction. For others, there has to be a more equitable balancing of class and non-class relations. Nancy Fraser suggests that social justice requires both redistribution and recognition, not only material questions of distribution but also cultural questions of status and respect for different groups.

Another form of rapprochement between postmodern themes and social policy is outlined by Zygmunt Bauman. Bauman believes that we now live in a postmodern world, one which has been individualized, fragmented and, through the flows of globalization, speeded up. Yet in their rush to celebrate this, postmodernists themselves often neglect the role of deregulated, global capitalism in bringing that state of affairs about. Postmodern capitalism, says Bauman, empowers the wealthy by disempowering the poor. Collective systems of welfare – though also the victims of global capitalism – are the means by which we recognize our interdependency and reassert the importance of common values and needs:

One measures the carrying capacity of a bridge by the strength of its weakest pillar. The human quality of a society ought to be measured by the quality of life of its weakest members. . . . This is, I propose, the only measure the welfare state can afford, but also the only one it needs . . . this is also the sole measure which resolutely and unambiguously speaks in the welfare state's favour.

(Zygmunt Bauman, *The Individualized Society*, Polity, 2001, p. 79)

The influence of postmodernism may also extend to the delivery of services. Social policy has been characterized by a debate between universalists and selectivists, with the former resisting the means-testing advocated by the latter. A postmodern slant on this debate suggests the provision should be universal but that, within this framework, there must be a greater sensitivity to the particular needs and demands of certain groups. Social policy is about process as well as outcome, yet reforms repeatedly place the former within a consumerist, market-dominated discourse. A progressive postmodernism stresses the importance of non-market types of participative inclusion and discussion.

So although some believe postmodernism and social policy to be irreconcilable opposites, others think that both contribute to our understanding of self and society.

Post-structuralism

Post-structuralism agrees with postmodernism that we cannot transcend the traditions in which we are embedded. For post-structuralists, what we call reality is no more than a temporary effect of discourse and signification, with no stable reality beyond the play of language. Truth is therefore discursive, i.e. there is no such thing as 'Truth', merely a series of truth-claims that have to be understood in terms of the subjectivities expressing them. What we call truth is just another face of power

and there are no structures of reality lying beneath the social surface. Power has endless faces and there is no real one underpinning all the rest.

Michel Foucault focuses upon the conditions (the discourses) through which knowledge and ideas are generated. He sets out to understand discursive practices through a 'genealogical' approach which closely traces the history and operation of power within a number of institutional settings, e.g. prisons, asylums, clinics. For instance, in the nineteenth and twentieth centuries madness was medicalized, redefined as mental illnesses that require specialized treatment rather than imprisonment. Foucault analyses the extent to which medicalization is just another form of incarceration. The rest of us define ourselves as normal and reasonable through this categorization of madness as the 'other' of normality and rationality.

The judges of normality are present everywhere. We are in the society of the teacher-judge, the doctor-judge, the educator-judge, the 'social worker'-judge; it is on them that the universal reign of the normative is based; and each individual, wherever he may find himself, subjects to it his body, his gestures, his behaviour, his aptitudes, his achievements.

(Michel Foucault, *Discipline and Punish*, Penguin, 1991, p. 304)

So Foucault identifies the 'panopticon' as the essential metaphor for all modern forms of discipline and normalization. The panopticon was a design for a prison that would use the least number of prison officers to survey as many prisoners as possible. The prisoners would not know when they were being observed and so would need to act as if they were under constant surveillance. Using these ideas, we can understand welfare systems as discourses that internalize the disciplinary mechanisms of normative surveillance, constructing and monitoring the prison officers within all of us. To be a subject is to be constantly policing oneself. Post-structuralism does not offer manifestos for welfare reform. Instead, it is a kind of 'spring-cleaning' exercise, a way of undermining our commonly held assumptions.

Many within the social policy community reject these ideas, however. If universal accounts of the good or of welfare are impossible, then what reason do we have to prefer one truth-claim over another? What happens to the struggle for universal emancipation, progress and justice? Ironically, just as some Marxists interpret everyone as a representative of their class, so post-structuralists often treat agents merely as the embodied spaces of discourses flowing in and around them. I may believe in progress and rationality *as* a white, Western, middle-class male, but that does not mean I hold those beliefs *because* I am a white, Western, middle-class male. Perhaps truth is not simply another face of power.

Risk Society

There are other theorists who, while believing that modernity has changed, do not imagine that the modern period is over. Ulrich Beck argues that we have reached the beginning of a *second* modernity. The first modernity was an age of industrial progress and all political and social institutions were designed to generate 'goods' (welfare, economic growth) in a world that was taken to be stable, knowable and scientifically calculable. By contrast, the second modernity is a risk society characterized by the attempt to limit, manage and navigate a way through a series of 'bads' and hazards. For instance, nuclear and industrial pollution undermine the simple class hierarchies of the industrial order, affecting the ghettoes of the rich as well as those of the poor: '[R]isk societies are *not* exactly class societies; their risk positions cannot be understood as class positions, or

their conflicts as class conflicts' (Ulrich Beck, *Risk Society*, Sage, 1992, p. 36).

One implication is that whereas state welfare was once thought of as a protection against collective risks – e.g. through social insurance provision – the welfare state has now become a principal source of risk. Tony Giddens agrees with much of Beck's thesis and insists that welfare reform must be based upon a notion of 'positive welfare' in which people are equipped with the skills needed to find their way through the new social environments of insecurity, transforming risks-as-dangers into risks-as-opportunities.

The risk society idea has proved to be very influential, but has attracted many criticisms. Some reject the sociological assumptions upon which it is based. The contrast between the first and second modernities may be too crude, and the suggestion that class structures have become less important has been condemned as naïve. Also, Beck may neglect the extent to which risks have been produced politically by those opposed to welfare state capitalism.

Social Movements

Nevertheless, the idea that class is less salient now than in the past has also appeared in other schools of thought. Some have argued that society is best understood as consisting of social movements. A social movement is a process of collective action, a network of interrelated actors who share similar values, identities and objectives in a given socio-historical context.

Social movement theories emerged in the 1960s when those such as the civil rights, the feminist, the peace and the gay/lesbian movements arose to challenge specific forms of injustice. Those theories do not necessarily replace a class analysis but they certainly demand that class analyses be rethought.

In terms of social policy we can identify the 'new' social movements, listed above, partly as a product of the welfare state. With rising prosperity, increased educational opportunities and the growth of the public sector, new social movements emerge as traditional distributional conflicts begin to subside. For instance, as the middle class expands in size and influence, conflicts related to culture and lifestyle appear and lead to new conceptions of politics and social organization.

> When the unemployed youth of the suburbs say that they want someone to listen to them and understand them . . . they are expressing an idea that is as important as the workers' old demands for social rights. . . . The words and the life of every individual must be central to collective life; before he or she becomes a citizen who takes part in the life of the state or a worker who plays an economic role, the individual must be a personal Subject who can construct an individuated life. This is the road we have to take if society is to rediscover the integration it has lost, and it will not do so by calling for stricter discipline or appealing to the general interest.
>
> (Alain Touraine, *Can We Live Together?*, Polity, 2000, p. 263)

This means that new social movements may also bear implications for the welfare policies of the future. They offer new perspectives on what it means to be a citizen and a client of the welfare state. So as well as providing for basic needs and aiming at the goal of social justice, perhaps social policy should also try to fulfil other needs, ones that are less material in nature and related more to quality of life. This is the point that Fraser seems to be making (see above). Some, though, resist these ideas, arguing either that society should not be thought of in terms of social movements or that the existence of the latter should not distract us from the fundamental questions of distributive justice.

Emerging Issues

All the ideas reviewed above deal with three main themes that show no sign of dissipating in importance. First, whether we should describe ourselves as still living in a period of modernity. Second, whether class is the main organizing principle of contemporary society. Finally, how we should try to understand society and judge the best means of reforming it and its welfare institutions. Social policy debates in the twenty-first century continue to revolve around these themes and these new directions.

Guide to Further Sources

Useful websites include Shannon Weiss and Karla Wesley, *Postmodernism and Its Critics*, at <www.as.ua.edu/ant/Faculty/murphy/436/pomo.htm>; Martin Ryder, *Contemporary Philosophy, Critical Theory and Postmodern Thought*, at <http://carbon.cudenver.edu/~mryder/itc_data/postmodern.html>; Internet Modern History Sourcebook, at <www.fordham.edu/halsall/mod/modsbook56.html>.

H. Bertens and J. Natoli, *Postmodernism* (Blackwell, 2002) is a comprehensive survey of the key figures in postmodernism, also providing an effective introduction to contemporary social theory. J. Carter (ed.), *Postmodernity and the Fragmentation of Welfare* (Routledge, 1998) is a useful collection of essays reviewing the initial impact of postmodernism on social policy. P. Leonard, *Postmodern Welfare* (Sage, 1997) is a well-written and accessible book that provides an incisive overview of the relevant debates. J. Rodgers, *From a Welfare State to a Welfare Society* (Macmillan, 2000) is a wide-ranging analysis that places postmodernism within a broader theoretical and policy-related context. S. Sim (ed.), *The Routledge Companion to Postmodernism* (Routledge, 2001) is a comprehensive guide, with articles on philosophy, politics and culture, as well as some of the key figures of postmodernism. Finally, R. Strickland (ed.), *Growing Up Postmodern: Neoliberalism and the War on the Young* (Rowman & Littlefield Publishers, 2002) contains an interesting collection of chapters examining factors relating to the postmodern fetish for consumerism and how young people both succumb and resist.

Part III

Context

Chapter 16

Divisions and Difference

Sharon Wright

Overview

- The study of the social divisions of welfare is concerned with understanding fundamental and enduring differences between social groups in their experiences of welfare provision and the type of outcomes that they receive from it.
- Key divisions have been identified as existing between men and women, disabled and non-disabled people and between people of different socio-economic classes, ethnic groups, religions, nationalities, ages and sexualities.
- Social divisions can be complex and cross-cutting.
- Some social groups have distinct and identifiable welfare needs that are different from other categories of people. Researchers and campaigners have argued that such differences should be recognized formally and taken into account when social policies are designed and implemented.
- Social divisions are related to, but distinct from, social inequalities, social justice and issues of equity and equality.

Introduction

We are who we choose to be. This is the message conveyed by influential multi-billion dollar marketing ventures. In the twenty-first century, whole industries are directed at convincing us that we can buy the lifestyle of our choice. The implication is that what we buy can help us to be who we want to be – to have the body we want, the relationships we want, the job we want, the leisure activities or the home we want. If we don't like how we look or how we feel, then we can buy a product or a service to change it (if that doesn't work out, then there is always something to buy to make us feel better about the whole thing: shoes, chocolate or beer, maybe). Processes of individualization, mass consumption and the blurring of social boundaries can all contribute to give the impression that anyone can be anything. But, as social scientists, we are compelled to break the surface of these superficial impressions of contemporary society and probe more deeply. How much choice do we really have in determining our own prospects? Can we choose freely to be who we want to be or are our life experiences and life-chances already structured by forces beyond our individual control?

The starting point for our analysis of contemporary social relations is to observe that all individuals share aspects of their identities with other people. Shared characteristics can form the basis of group cohesion and a sense of inclusion. However, acknowledging that we belong to one group also involves highlighting that we are excluded from membership of certain other groups – for instance, as a white woman, I am neither a black woman nor a white man. This leads us to the main argument of this chapter – that there are differences between social groups and that these differences can be significant and consequential. For instance:

- You are more likely to experience poverty if you are a woman rather than a man.
- You could live up to ten years longer if you are a lawyer rather than a labourer.

These are examples of how experiences of well-being and life-chances can be related to differences between social groups. These social inequalities provide a radical challenge to the picture of contemporary society that was painted in the opening paragraph of this chapter. We do not live in a social world where anyone can be anything – far from it. We live in societies that are structured, stratified and deeply divided. Ultimately, recognizing that substantial, long-term divisions exist between different groups within society implies that these groups may have different interests and that these interests may be the source of conflict.

The study of the social divisions of welfare recognizes the importance of understanding the different needs and experiences of social groups and argues that where these differences are fundamental and enduring, a division exists in society. The 'big three' social divisions that have received greatest attention in academic literature are class, gender and 'race' or ethnicity. Chronologically, class was the first category to receive sustained attention from social scientists, in the late nineteenth

and early twentieth centuries. Much later, in the 1970s and 1980s, feminists and anti-racist writers became more prominent in identifying different social cleavages that had, until then, been largely ignored. This gave birth to a new field of academic attention, the study of new social movements. Furthermore, a number of other divisions have been identified and explored more recently: disability, age, nationality and sexuality.

This wider body of work is relevant for our discussion of social divisions in the sense that it sought to recognize and legitimize difference. For instance, it challenged the basic assumptions on which the welfare state had been built, such as the structure of families (the stereotypical lifelong marriage with 2.4 children no longer holds true). It became necessary to acknowledge that lifestyles, relationships, family formations and the role of men and women had changed dramatically since the post-war period. This led to an increased awareness of issues of difference and the need to recognize the ways in which underlying policy assumptions interact differently on particular groups in society. For instance, the conditions for receiving access to council housing were found to be inherently racist because of their weighting towards those who had been resident in particular geographical areas for longest. Similarly, taxation arrangements (such as the married man's tax allowance) and inheritance laws assumed that long-term relationships were heterosexual, meaning that gay men, lesbian women and bisexual people were excluded from financial benefits and discriminated against in terms of joint claims on property or assets. Thus, is it essential to recognize that policies which appear to be neutral can have differential impacts upon diverse categories of people. For example, welfare-to-work policies are presented as neutral in constructing paid work as the best way to provide for welfare needs. However, on closer inspection, we can see that compelling people who receive social security benefits to look for paid work may conflict with their other responsibilities, most significantly with caring roles. For example, in the UK, it is perfectly legitimate for a married woman to stay at home to bring up her own children. But, if the same woman was to split up from her husband, she would be required to discuss the possibility of paid employment before being allowed to claim social security benefits, so her role as a full-time mother might be open to challenge.

Understanding Difference and Divisions

The experience of social divisions is related to differences between social groups. As we have already seen, each of us shares aspects of our identity with other people. The relationship between different groups is complex and variable. Social differences can (but do not always) lead to social divisions. At some points, one aspect of our group identity might be more important than others. On a rainy Saturday afternoon, for instance, being Scottish may matter more to a row of rugby spectators, as they watch their national team play against England, than being male or female, or being working class or middle class. However, Scottish national identity may have become much less important by 9 o'clock the following Monday morning when the rugby fans go back to their usual activities. Gender is likely to have a big influence on whether or not they are at home looking after children. For those in paid work, gender and class are likely to be related to the type of job they do and the amount of money they get paid for it. Women, for instance, earn 17 per cent less than men per hour for full-time work (EOC, 2006). Even amongst graduates, men earn 15 per cent more than women within five years of leaving college (ibid.) This example

provides two insights. First, that it is impossible to make blanket assumptions about which aspects of group membership are most important to people's identities. Secondly, we can observe that people can belong to multiple groups and that social divisions may intersect or be cross-cutting. Ultimately, the differences between men and women or people of different classes, for instance, are of interest to us here because they are related to their command of personal and collective resources, such as wealth, status and power. Since these are the means by which they can protect themselves from risks such as poverty, they bear a direct relationship to their means of meeting welfare needs.

Membership of some social categories may be dynamic, fluid or transitional, while membership of other categories may be more fixed. Clearly, for each individual, membership of some social groups is more fixed than others – gender (for most people) remains the same throughout their lifetime, but everyone gets older, moving through different phases of childhood, youth, adulthood and older age. It is interesting to consider how these multiple, and perhaps conflicting, social identities are negotiated, reconciled or changed. Each of us can exercise a degree of choice over membership of some social groups. For example, although we cannot choose the gender we are born with, it is possible in some cases to change it. Similarly, we have no say as to the geographical place into which we are born, but we are able to move to another town or country; and we may choose to seek an alternative national citizenship. However, such identity and status markers are often so deeply embedded that we would never consider exercising this choice. On the other hand, we may experience a change that moves us against our will from one category to another – for example, a car accident could move us from being non-disabled to being disabled. So there is a complex relationship between the exercise of individual agency, or choice, and the impact of wider structural constraints. To answer one of the opening questions of this chapter, it seems that although individuals can exercise some choice in decisions about their lives, they often do so within very powerful constraints. The value of a social divisions approach is that we can begin to understand some of the major axes of these structures of opportunity and constraint.

A word of caution: there is a temptation to simplify the analysis of social divisions of welfare to a discussion of 'winners' and 'losers'. Perhaps in some ways it is inevitable that discussion of different social groups and their relative positions in relation to material and social resources will slip into the terrain of moral value judgements. However, it is important to recognize the roots and limitations of such an approach. In relation to understanding social divisions, using the winner/loser distinction does have the advantage that it allows us to demonstrate a series of processes of opportunity and constraint in education, the labour market and social policies that reward some activities (i.e. paid work) over others (i.e. unpaid care). On the other hand, speaking of 'winners' and 'losers' engages us in a value-based discussion that affords primacy to financial position within society. The problem with adopting such a stance is that not all human activities can be evaluated in economic or monetary terms. For instance, feeling loved is very important to personal well-being, but has very little to do with financial position or social status. Is it really adequate, for instance, to say that a lone mother who receives social security benefits has a 'worse' life than a wealthy male company director? We can certainly identify a gendered social division in their material circumstances. However, to say that the lone parent has lost out and the male executive has won is only useful up to a certain point. This position would mean that spending time bringing up children would have to be ranked below the genera-

tion of income through paid work. Indeed, this is precisely the value judgement that many governments around the world have adopted in their design of welfare-to-work policies. Such policies encourage or compel lone parents to look for (and preferably to engage in) paid work, leaving less time available for parenting their children, who will have to be looked after by someone else during working hours. So socioeconomic position is only one part of the picture and does not, in itself, tell us whether certain groups of people have a 'better' or 'worse' life.

We cannot, therefore, oversimplify the issue of social divisions. In terms of social policy analysis, we are interested in how social divisions affect well-being. Understanding divisions and difference is concerned with the role of the state and the market in creating, perpetuating, mediating or tempering the structures and processes that influence people's life experiences and life-chances. Since social policies are designed to intervene in areas of well-being (for instance health, income, housing or education), understanding how they impact differentially upon groups in divided societies is a crucially important task. Studies of the social divisions of welfare have shown, essentially, that the costs and benefits of a welfare state are shared out unevenly between different groups of people. That is, the financial support (e.g. social security for disabled people) and services (such as health services) offered by the welfare state, as well as the costs of maintaining it (through paying taxes or charges), impact differentially on particular groups of people. Often this literature is based on an explicit or implicit argument that certain groups in society benefit unfairly from past and present welfare arrangements, whilst others are disadvantaged. People from more affluent socio-economic groups, for instance, can be shown to benefit more from services such as healthcare, but may pay proportionally less in some types of tax than their less affluent counterparts (however, this is a complex issue, since the taxation burden and redistributive effects of welfare vary depending on how they are measured: see chapter 18).

The next section uses the example of class to provide a more in-depth illustration of some of the key issues involved in analysing social divisions. Class was chosen as a case study because it is one of the most fundamental divisions in contemporary society. Also, unlike many of the other categories of division and difference, class is not explicitly investigated in greater depth elsewhere in this book (for gender, see chapters 13 and 21; for 'race' and ethnicity, see chapters 20, 46 and 51; for age, see chapters 47, 48 and 49; for disability, see chapter 50; and for religion and nationality, see chapter 20).

Class: A Case Study of Divisions and Difference

Class presents an interesting example because, although it was the first social division to be recognized, it is now commonly misunderstood or overlooked. The work of classic theorists Karl Marx and Max Weber in the late nineteenth and early twentieth centuries, was extremely influential in recognizing deep divisions in societies. The main argument is that societies are stratified, or layered (like a wedding cake), with clear divisions between different social classes, which have largely separate and conflicting interests. Marx believed that the struggle between social classes would drive social change. Weber (although he accepted much of Marx's analysis) had a different view – that occupational classification would determine social status and life-chances. Although societies have changed significantly since this body of work was written, these approaches continue to have relevance in their recognition of class differences and, more particularly in Marx's

analysis, class interests and conflicts. This leads us to a view of individuals who are connected to wider society through processes that are political and exploitative.

Perhaps it is partly *because* of this long history of class analysis – and the socialist or communist associations that it conjures up – that it has become distinctly unfashionable to talk about class divisions in society. Some commentators have even gone so far as to announce the demise of class. Popular perceptions of class seem to be influenced by the life stories of high-profile personalities like David Beckham, J. K. Rowling or Alan Sugar. Each of these individuals, and many more like them, have tales to tell of building massive personal wealth from humble beginnings – playing football at school, writing in a café, or selling vegetables out of the back of a van. However, these extraordinary triumphs of personal talent over adversity, leading to multi-millionaire status, are exactly that: extraordinary and individual. The reason that they are so newsworthy is that they are exceptional. The vast majority of people living in Britain retain the social class that they were born into, much the same as they did a century ago. Where social mobility between classes does occur, it is generally at the boundaries between classes, rather than the extremes of rags to riches. Thus, it is possible to identify distinct social classes (see below for further detail on how this is done in practice) and it is evident that these classes are considerably cohesive. The next question to think about is: do the interests of different classes coincide or conflict? Furthermore, how do processes of inclusion and exclusion operate to reinforce positions of advantage and disadvantage? There are no easy answers to these questions, but it is worth considering, for instance, the ways in which class divisions are reproduced over generations through subtle processes of inclusion and exclusion. For example, during the transition from childhood to adulthood, young people

Table 16.1   UK National Statistics Standard Occupational Classification

1   Higher managerial and professional occupations
1.1   Large employers and higher managerial occupations
1.2   Higher professional occupations
2   Lower managerial and professional occupations
3   Intermediate occupations
4   Small employers and own account workers
5   Lower supervisory and technical occupations
6   Semi-routine occupations
7   Routine occupations
8   Never worked and long-term unemployed

Source: National Statistics 2007.

experience a series of opportunities and constraints as they make important life decisions like when to leave school, what sort of job to get and whether or not to go to university.

Class-based analysis also provides a fruitful basis for reflection on the welfare state. On the one hand, it is interesting to think about the role that class interests played in the development of state welfare. For instance, one explanation for increased state intervention in the early twentieth century and later in the establishment of the post-war welfare state, was that it was a response to 'pressure from below' – working-class people (who previously had not been voters) were demanding that their welfare needs be met. On the other hand, more than half a century later, we could ask questions about why the welfare state has not made more of a difference in addressing class-based inequalities in health, education or the eradication of poverty. Class is, therefore, very much alive as a major social division.

Socio-economic classification

The precise definition of class – and what it means to people – is the source of much debate and research. In the UK, socio-economic class has been defined and measured officially since 2001 using the Standard Occupational Classification system (see table 16.1). Previously, different ways of defining class were used (for instance, Social Class based on Occupation, formerly known as the Registrar General's Social Class Index, and Socio-economic Groups).

The current classification is based on occupation, taking into account the status and size of the organization, the type of occupation and the status of the job (for instance, routine or professional, lower supervisory or higher managerial). This is the classification that is used in official surveys to capture a sense of the social and economic position of UK residents.

Such classifications are both useful and problematic. It is important to have some system by which classes can be identified, otherwise class-based statistical analysis would be impossible (for instance, to measure the extent of social mobility or the differences in life expectancy between different classes). However, any classification is likely to be imprecise. It is difficult to design a single scheme that can take into account an amalgam of factors, such as power, status, authority, responsibility, level of skill or professional expertise, and relate these meaningfully to command of resources. Feminists have also criticized the traditional method of categorization of married women according to their husband's occupation.

One particular difficulty is presented for those who are not in paid employment. If socio-economic class is determined primarily by occupation, then how should people who do not have paid employment be categorized? The idea of a distinct class of non-workers can be traced back to Marx, who identified a group below labourers that he called the 'lumpenproletariat'. More recently, however, the analysis of this type of group has been heavily politicized in highly controversial debates about whether or not an 'underclass' exists. This issue is not, therefore, simply a mundane matter of statistical classification. The term 'underclass' was coined by an American academic, Charles Murray, who argued that a separate and dangerous group of poor people existed, whose behaviour presented a threat to the moral fabric of society. Murray's work has been discredited in a number of ways. The research methods that he used to reach his conclusion have been exposed as deeply flawed. Furthermore, his work has been interpreted as politically motivated and biased by right-wing values and beliefs about how other people behave. Most seriously, the idea of an underclass has been seen as offensive, particularly in relation to its racist undertones. Using the underclass label has, therefore, been viewed generally by sociologists as an unacceptable way of conceptualizing issues of class difference and poverty. Instead, many academics prefer to consider people who have very low incomes as 'living in poverty' or 'experiencing social exclusion' (see chapter 17). This has the advantage of moving the analysis away from only considering individual behaviour (or agency) to incorporating wider structural causes, such as worldwide economic recession, for understanding phenomena such as unemployment. We must also remember that 'non-workers' cannot be used as a definition for a class that is associated with poverty, since it would also include a range of people who do not have jobs but nonetheless have incomes or assets from other sources (such as rich land-owners).

Emerging Issues

Understanding how differences between social groups affect well-being is an essential part of understanding how societies operate and how social policies affect our everyday lives. There are major differences between individuals and groups of people in relation to their life-chances and life experiences. The first category to be identified by theorists was class. From the 1970s onwards, gender, 'race' and ethnicity were also identified as key divisions. More recently, growing attention has been paid to inequalities that relate to age, religion, sexuality, health and disability. Researchers and campaigners have argued that diversity needs to be recognized as legitimate in the design of social policies. Challenges remain for policymakers in balancing the recognition of diversity with the provision of fair policies that produce equitable outcomes. For students and analysts of social policies, social divisions are an important way in which major axes of inclusion and exclusion can be understood.

Guide to Further Sources

Fiona Williams, *Social Policy: a Critical Introduction* (Polity, 1989) is a classic text, which is still an essential read. Williams's approach is particularly interesting because she provides a critique of the inherent gender and racial assumptions embodied in welfare policies and also reflects on the limitations and biases of the academic study of social policy. For a broader sociological understanding of social divisions and differences, there are two indispensable introductory collections: G. Payne, *Social Divisions*, 2nd edn (Palgrave, 2006) and P. Braham and L. Janes, *Social Differences and Divisions* (Blackwell/Open University, 2002) both provide thought-provoking accounts from a series of different perspectives.

There is a range of excellent books that explore class, gender and ethnicity in greater detail. K. Roberts, *Class in Modern Britain* (Palgrave, 2001) provides a comprehensive overview of class, economic change and social mobility. Also be sure not to overlook R. Crompton, *Class and Stratification*, 2nd edn (Polity, 2001). Key reading in the field of ethnicity is D. Mason (ed.), *Explaining Ethnic Differences* (Policy Press, 2003). For a firm foundation in gender analysis, try N. Charles, *Gender in Modern Britain* (Oxford University Press, 2002).

Two useful web-based sources are: EOC (Equal Opportunities Commission), *Facts about Men and Women in Great Britain* (2006), available at <www.eoc.org.uk> and National Statistics, 'The National Statistics Socio-economic Classification' (2007) at <www.statistics.gov.uk/methods_quality/ns_sec/default.asp>.

Chapter 17

Poverty and Social Exclusion

Pete Alcock

Overview

- Poverty has always been a major concern for social policy researchers and policy-makers.
- Academics and policy-makers disagree about how to define and measure poverty.
- Definition and measurement has more recently been extended to include also the problem of social exclusion.
- Poverty and social exclusion are multi-dimensional problems; but evidence suggests that both grew in prominence in the 1980s.
- Academic and policy concern is increasingly focused on the global dimensions of poverty and exclusion.

Introduction

The problem of poverty has been a key concern of social policy throughout its development. Some of the earliest policy measures introduced in the UK were concerned with poverty, including in particular the Poor Laws, which can be traced back to the beginning of the seventeenth century and provided the core of social policy provision throughout the nineteenth and early twentieth centuries. Poverty has also always been a major focus for academic analysis and research. Some of the earliest social policy research in the UK, and indeed in the world, sought to define and to measure the extent of poverty in the late nineteenth century in London (in the work of Booth) and York (in the work of Rowntree).

Poverty has always been at the centre of social policy in part because it provides a bridge between academic debate and policy action. Starting with Booth and Rowntree, academics have been concerned to define and measure poverty not merely as an academic exercise, but also because of a belief that, if poverty did exist, then policy-makers would be obliged to do something about it. This is because poverty is a policy problem. As I have argued elsewhere (2006: 4–6) it is an *unacceptable* state of affairs, which requires some form of policy response. Debate about, and evidence of, poverty therefore 'drives' policy development. This is the main reason it has always been a core social policy issue, although this is a status which now extends to social exclusion too, as we shall see shortly.

There has also, however, been much debate, and disagreement, about exactly what poverty is and how we should seek to define and measure it. This is in large part, of course, because of its role as a policy driver. The different ways in which we define and measure poverty, and the differing extent of the problem that we therefore reveal, will lead to different demands for policy action, and different forms of policy response. The definition and measurement of poverty is bound up with the policy response to it. This again is what makes it such an interesting concept for social policy scholars; and over time, research on poverty has attracted some of the leading social policy scholars. Academics want to research social policy because they believe, or hope, that this will lead to policy action.

Defining Poverty

The question of how to define poverty is thus at the heart of policy debate and academic analysis; and it is a question to which there is no simple or agreed answer. Academics and policy-makers disagree about how to define poverty, in large part because they also disagree about what to do about it. This was captured most revealingly in a quotation from John Moore, Secretary of State for Social Security in the Thatcher government of the late 1980s, who sought to dismiss recent academic research which had suggested a growing problem of poverty in the country:

> The evidence of improving living standards over this century is dramatic, and it is incontrovertible. When the pressure groups say that one-third of the population is living in poverty, they cannot be saying that one-third of people are living below the draconian subsistence levels used by Booth and Rowntree.
>
> (Speech to Greater London Area CPC, 11 May 1989)

In the 1980s the Conservative government did not believe that specific policies were needed to combat poverty beyond the well-established provision of social security benefits; and their argument that, by the standards of poverty determined at the end of the nineteenth century few people in Britain were poor, meant that there was no need for further policy action.

After that, of course, the Labour government under Tony Blair took a different view, identifying child poverty in particular as a serious social problem and pledging to eradicate it by 2020 (see Walker, 1999). And this led the government to initiate a review by the Department for Work and Pensions (DWP) of the definition and measurement of child poverty, which resulted in the adoption of a new, threefold, definition of poverty (see Alcock, 2006: 79). This definition includes both absolute and relative dimensions; and the distinction between these different approaches to understanding poverty underpins the policy differences between Moore and Blair.

Absolute poverty is the idea that being in poverty means being without the essentials of life, and it is sometimes referred to as 'subsistence' poverty. It is often associated with the early research of Booth and Rowntree, who were concerned to identify a subsistence level based on the cost of necessities and then to measure the numbers of people with household incomes below this level, and hence unable to provide for themselves and their families. However, in practice, what is essential for life varies according to where and when one is living; and indeed, when Rowntree repeated his research later on in the twentieth century, he extended his list of essential items (see Alcock, 2006: ch. 5). Despite John Moore's assertion, most commentators do accept that the 'draconian' levels of the nineteenth century are not a valid basis for determining what it means to be poor more than 100 years later.

Relative poverty takes up this notion of changes in the determination of poverty levels over time and place. It has been associated in particular with the work of Peter Townsend, who in the 1950s and 1960s developed a new definition and measurement of poverty linking income to social security benefit levels, which showed that, despite general increases in affluence and improved social security protection, a significant proportion of the UK population did not have enough to achieve the living conditions 'customary' in society (Alcock, 2006: 64). According to this approach, as overall living standards rise so too does the notion of what it means to be poor, so that any definition of poverty will be relative to the average standard of living of all within society. This is sometimes taken to be some proportion of average income levels, which, as we shall see, has in practice become widely used as a poverty level in the UK and across many other developed countries.

Defining poverty by reference to average incomes is potentially a circular approach, however. It would suggest that however much incomes rise, a fixed proportion would always be poor; and it was just this illogical relativism that Moore was seeking to attack in 1989. What it means to be poor may change over time; but there must be more to the definition of poverty than simply the proportion of average income received.

Income is only an indirect measure of poverty in any event, of course. It is what we are able to buy with our incomes that determines our actual standard of living. This was recognized by Townsend, who sought to identify indicators which could be used to determine whether someone was going without essential items of living. It has since been taken further by a group of researchers led by David Gordon, who used a major social survey to identify those items which a majority of the population thought to be essential for modern life and then measured the numbers unable to afford most or all of these in a Poverty and Social Exclusion (PSE) survey carried out at the end of the last century (Pantazis et al., 2006). This includes both absolute (the notion of essential items) and relative (those considered necessary by contemporaries)

elements of the definition of poverty. This is the way in which most debate about the problem of poverty is now conducted (see Lister, 2004: ch. 1); and it is recognized specifically by the government in its measure of child poverty mentioned above and in other official assessments of policies on poverty and deprivation.

Deprivation and Exclusion

In developing his relative approach to poverty, Townsend was aware that maintaining a customary standard of living involved more than just having a sufficiently high income. He recognized that people's health, housing conditions and working conditions would also affect living standards, and yet these might be determined by factors beyond current income levels. Townsend discussed these other dimensions of deprivation in the report of his major research on poverty (*Poverty in the United Kingdom*, Penguin, 1979), and argued that it was this notion of deprivation, rather than simply income poverty, which better captured the problem of an inadequate standard of living in modern society.

In the mid-1980s, the contributors to a Child Poverty Action Group (CPAG) pamphlet (Golding, 1986) took up this broader approach and drew attention to an increasingly wide range of other aspects of modern life, which could lead to deprivation for those excluded from them. These included information and communication technology, banking and financial services, and leisure activities, all of which are now readily recognizable as essential elements of modern life. The CPAG book was called *Excluding the Poor* and it highlighted the notion of exclusion from social activities as an important element of the problem of poverty. It is not just what we *have*, but what we *do* (or do *not* do) which can be a problem in society; and it is this notion of social exclusion which has begun to accompany poverty as a broader conceptualization of this key driver of social policy in early twenty-first-century Britain.

In fact, the notion of social exclusion has to some extent been imported into the UK from continental Europe, in particular through Britain's membership of the EU. Some of these different European influences and their implications for the definition and measurement of poverty and social exclusion are discussed by the contributors to a collection edited by Graham Room in 1995, where it is suggested that it was French researchers in particular who were influential in getting EU politicians and policy-makers to accept this broader conception as a focus for EU action. This prompted one senior EU officer to say that, 'today the concept of social exclusion is taking over from poverty' (J.-P. Tricart, quoted in D. Robbins et al., *Third Report of EU Observatory on National Policies to Combat Social Exclusion*, EU, 1994, p. 12).

Social exclusion has become a central feature of UK academic and policy debate over the last decade or so too. In 1997 the publicly funded research centre, the Centre for the Analysis of Social Exclusion (CASE), was established at the LSE to explore the theoretical and empirical dimensions of the problem. Some of the early work of CASE is reported in Hills et al. (2002), where the researchers developed the idea of exclusion as non-participation in key social activities such as:

- *consumption* – purchasing of goods and services;
- *production* – participating in economically or socially valuable activity;
- *political engagement* – involvement in local or national decision-making;
- *social interaction* – with family, friends and communities.

These drew on and expanded the approach developed in the CPAG book back in the 1980s, and led the researchers to focus

their attention on a range of different ways of measuring social exclusion using both quantitative and qualitative approaches, which revealed that the experience of exclusion varied over time and place, with different people experiencing different dimensions of the problem at different times.

These broader and more varying dimensions of social exclusion have been a focus of EU policy intervention since the 1990s, with all countries committing themselves in Lisbon in 2000 to drawing up and reviewing National Action Plans to promote inclusion. In the UK this was led after 1998 by a special Social Exclusion Unit (SEU), established by the Prime Minister and reporting direct to the Cabinet Office. The SEU was never intended to combat all the different aspects of exclusion mentioned above. It aimed instead to concentrate on a small number of key policy priorities such as rough sleeping, school exclusion and teenage pregnancy. However, its work did have wide-ranging implications for policy across government, and beyond, as can be seen from the reports and other documents which can still be found on its website. In 2006 it was restructured to become a Task Force, and much of its work transferred to the Department for Communities and Local Government.

The work of the SEU was only one element of a broader range of strategies developed by the UK government since 1997 to combat social exclusion. These are now summarized and reviewed in an annual report called *Opportunity for All*, and available on the DWP website, which also includes a summary on annual progress against a list of fifty-nine different indicators of poverty and exclusion, including school attendance, infant mortality and fear of crime, as well as more traditional measures such as low income. From this it is clear that academic debate and policy practice in twenty-first-century Britain embrace a wide range of multiple dimensions of poverty and social exclusion. There is no longer just one driver of policy action on poverty; and consequently no longer just one measure of the problem either.

Measuring Poverty and Social Exclusion

The fifty-nine indicators listed in *Opportunity for All* provide a wide range of measures of poverty and social exclusion, which aim to respond to the multiple dimensions of the problem as it is now conceived by both academics and policy-makers. However, the complex and changing information that these measures provide, as revealed in the work of the CASE researchers (Hills et al., 2002), do not make it easy to understand to what extent poverty and social exclusion are a problem in modern society, or what policy action can, or should, do about it. The problem might indeed be a complex one; but there is sometimes a need for simple summary measures.

This is to some extent recognized by both academics and policy-makers; and in practice there are some simple (proxy) measures of poverty and social exclusion which are widely employed by researchers and politicians and which provide important evidence of the scale of the problem. Most important here are the data on income levels produced annually in the *Households Below Average Income* (HBAI) report, available on the DWP website. This uses a measure of poverty based on those households with an income below 60 per cent of median average income (that is, the midpoint in the income distribution). This is a widely quoted level: it is incorporated into the official definition of child poverty and is also adopted in many other developed countries, in particular across the EU.

On this measure, 11.4 million people were poor in the UK in 2004–5, a drop of 2.5 million since 1996–7 after Tony Blair's Labour government came to power. The figure includes 3.4 million children, a drop of 0.8 million, but not quite enough for the government to hit its first target of a 25 per cent reduction in child poverty in five years on its way to the 2020 target of removing it altogether. The HBAI figures also include information about the differing risk of poverty for different social groups, with lone parents shown to be at particular risk, and for different geographical regions, with Inner London having the highest levels of poverty. Other social dimensions of poverty, including the varying impact of ethnicity and disability, are summarized in the regular CPAG publication *Poverty: The Facts* (Flaherty et al., 2004) and can be followed on some of the websites listed at the end of this chapter.

The proportion of average incomes measure can also be used to track the changing extent of poverty and social exclusion over time. This has been done over a number of years by Hills, whose most recent analysis is reproduced here in Figure 17.1. The figure actually uses a 50 per cent of mean average income to determine poverty, rather than the 60 per cent median level referred to above. This is because the earlier data relied on employed only this measure (both are now used in practice); but both give broadly similar results across the population as a whole. BHC refers to the fact that income levels have been calculated before taking account of housing costs. These may have a significant impact on poverty levels, as suggested above, and the HBAI data also includes measures after housing costs have been accounted for, usually leading to evidence of higher levels of overall poverty.

Despite these inevitable complexities, however, what figure 17.1 reveals is that the overall level of poverty in the UK grew dramatically in the 1980s – just at the time when John Moore was denying that it was a problem. Since the 1990s there has been some decline in poverty levels, as suggested

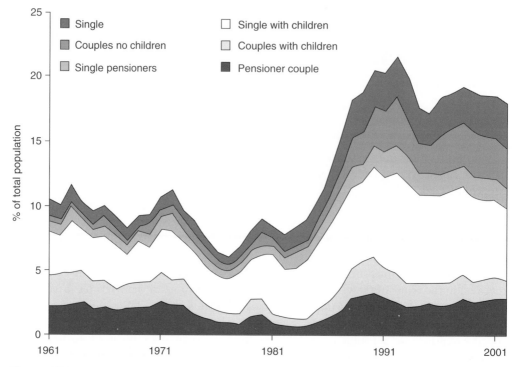

Figure 17.1 Population with below average income (BHC), 1961–2002/3
Source: Hills 2004: p. 48, fig. 3.1.

above, with some stabilization at the beginning of the new century. However, there has been no return to the much lower levels of poverty experienced in the 1960s and 1970s. This suggests that poverty and social exclusion are much more serious problems at the start of the twenty-first century than they were in the middle part of the twentieth.

Of course the explanations for these changes are complex, and Hills explores some of them in his book. Given the time it takes to calculate these statistics, there is also inevitably always some time lag in the availability of information on the latest trends. Nevertheless, these figures suggest that the government's target of eradicating child poverty within twenty years will be a demanding one, and will require policy changes that go some way beyond current initiatives such as the tax credits and benefit increases discussed in chapter 38. In moni-

toring achievements here, the government also tends to employ broader measures of poverty, including some element of exclusion from accepted customary standards as developed in the PSE survey – although the evidence from this suggests that on these measures, too, levels of poverty and social exclusion in the country remain high (see Pantazis et al., 2006).

Emerging Issues

The levels of poverty and social exclusion in the UK are high at the beginning of the new century. These compare unfavourably with some other EU nations such as France and the Netherlands; but other countries have higher levels, for instance Italy and Greece and, beyond Europe, Japan and the US. To a significant extent, poverty and social exclusion are major problems in all countries across the world. And this is much more serious when developing countries are taken into account, in particular those in Africa and the Indian subcontinent. Here, poverty and exclusion are much more pressing, with millions in Africa facing starvation and early death.

Poverty and social exclusion are therefore international – or rather global – problems. This was brought starkly into relief by the *Make Poverty History* campaign in 2005, which sought to put pressure on the developed nations to make commitments to relieve poverty in Africa and elsewhere. This did lead to some action to increase international aid for developing countries and to 'write-off' debts and trade deficits where these were preventing future economic development. Earlier than this, the 117 nations that attended a United Nations (UN) summit on social development in Copenhagen in 1995 committed the UN to a goal of eradicating global poverty through international action; and international agencies such as the UN Development Programme, the World Health Organization (WHO) and the World Bank have been instrumental in implementing a range of international programmes to combat poverty and promote economic development across the world.

There is an increasing recognition amongst leading politicians and policy-makers that poverty and social exclusion are global, and not just national, problems; and that concerted international action will be needed to address these – although the extent of the commitment and resources required, and the time taken to achieve significant results, may not be fully appreciated by many. The scale of this international challenge is also now being explored by academic researchers, notably by Townsend himself, who has written about the need to combat 'World Poverty' (Townsend and Gordon, 2002). The future policy climate for poverty and social exclusion is therefore increasingly likely to become an international one, within which national governments can only play a limited role.

Within the UK, the national problems of poverty and social exclusion are for the moment high on the political agenda, and this is true of the devolved administrations in Scotland and Wales too. Here the range of measures to promote inclusion and combat poverty has never been more extensive (see Alcock, 2006: Part IV). This is in large part because of the increasing recognition that the problem is a complex and multilayered one, which requires a wide range of policy responses. Poverty and social exclusion are therefore likely to continue to be major drivers for social policy in the twenty-first century, just as they have been since the seventeenth – although, as the conceptions of the problems broaden and deepen, so too does the challenge of combating them.

Guide to Further Sources

The most comprehensive general book on research and policy on poverty and social exclusion is P. Alcock, *Understanding Poverty*, 3rd edn (Palgrave, 2006). R. Lister, *Poverty* (Polity, 2004) provides a convincing explanation of why poverty is a problem and how we should respond to it, as does P. Spicker, *The Idea of Poverty* (Policy Press, 2007). The CPAG produces regularly updated summaries of the major statistical information on poverty, the most recent being J. Flaherty, J. Veit-Wilson and J. Dornan, *Poverty: the Facts*, 5th edn (CPAG, 2004). A longer-term overview of trends is provided by J. Hills, *Inequality and the State* (Oxford University Press, 2004).

R. Walker (ed.), *Ending Child Poverty* (Policy Press, 1999) is a collection of papers on the context for the child poverty pledge. Early discussion of the dimensions of social exclusion can be found in P. Golding (ed.), *Excluding the Poor* (CPAG, 1986); G. Room (ed.), *Beyond the Threshold* (Policy Press, 1995) contains papers from European commentators on social exclusion; and a summary of the more recent CASE research can be found in J. Hills, J. Le Grand and D. Piachaud (eds), *Understanding Social Exclusion* (Oxford University Press, 2002). The extensive findings of the 2000 PSE survey are now available in C. Pantazis, D. Gordon and R. Levitas (eds), *Poverty and Social Exclusion in Britain* (Policy Press, 2006). P. Townsend and D. Gordon (eds), *World Poverty* (Policy Press, 2002) contains contributions on the developing global context of poverty policy.

Government websites are important sources of official policy and research reports, in particular the Department for Work and Pensions, at <www.dwp.gov.uk>, and the Social Exclusion Task Force, at <www.socialexclusion.gov.uk>. An independent website with up-to-date statistics on poverty and social exclusion is maintained by the New Policy Institute and Joseph Rowntree Foundation (JRF) at <www.poverty.org.uk>. The JRF's own website, <www.jrf.org.uk>, contains copies of their many research reports in the area. The CPAG site, <www.cpag.org.uk>, includes information on campaigning activity, policy briefings and summaries of new statistics.

Chapter 18

The Distribution of Welfare

John Hills

Overview

- The distribution of resources is central to the provision of welfare through social policy, although distribution and redistribution take place through both state and private and voluntary transfers.
- There is a range of different rationales underpinning the redistribution of resources to promote welfare.
- There are different ways of measuring distribution and its benefits for different groups. How it is paid for – and who pays – is very important in this.
- Much of the redistributive effect of welfare is as a sort of 'savings bank', transferring resources between different stages of people's own lives.
- However, redistribution also plays a significant 'Robin Hood' role, benefiting poorer sections of society most, particularly once one allows for how it is paid for.

Introduction

Distribution is a central issue in the appraisal of social policies; for some, it is *the* central issue. Much of the justification advanced for social policy is in terms of distribution: 'without a National Health Service providing free medical care, the poor could not afford treatment'; or 'the primary aim of social security is preventing poverty'.

Most of this chapter is about the distributional effects of government spending on welfare services. However, redistribution and its measurement are not issues only for government. A major social policy development in the 1990s was the creation of the Child Support Agency to attempt to enforce payments by absent parents (generally fathers) to parents 'with care' (usually mothers). These payments were potentially important in terms of distribution, but they fell outside the 'welfare state'. In practice, the agency itself failed to deliver support to many mothers and it is being replaced after 2008 by a new Child Maintenance and Enforcement Commission which itself will have more autonomy and which will be run by an independent board not governed – or appointed – by the state.

Whether redistribution is occurring can depend on the point of analysis. Under private insurance for, say, burglaries, a large number of people make annual payments (insurance premiums) to an insurance company, but only a small number actually claim and receive payouts from the company. After the event (*ex post*) there is redistribution from the (fortunate) many to the (unfortunate) few. But, looking at the position in advance (*ex ante*), not knowing who is going to be burgled, all pay in a premium equalling their risk of being burgled, multiplied by the size of the payout if this happens (plus the insurance company's costs and profits). In 'actuarial' terms there is no redistribution – people have arranged a certain small loss (the premium) rather than the risk of a much larger loss (being burgled without insurance).

If you look at pension schemes over a single year, some people pay in contributions, while others receive pensions. On this 'snapshot' view, there is apparently a redistribution from the former to the latter. But with a longer time horizon, today's pensioners may simply get back what they paid in earlier. Redistribution is across their own life cycles, rather than between different people.

Assessing redistribution depends on the aims against which you want to measure services, and the picture obtained depends on decisions like the time period used. The next section discusses the first of these issues, the aims of welfare services. The subsequent sections discuss the conceptual issues raised in trying to measure distributional effects, illustrate some of the empirical findings on different bases and discuss their implications.

Aims of Welfare Services

As other chapters in this volume also show, there is little consensus on the aims of social policy, or on government intervention to provide or finance welfare services. For some, the primary aim of welfare services is redistribution from rich to poor. Whether the welfare state is successful therefore depends on which income groups benefit: do the rich use the NHS more than the poor, and are social security benefits 'targeted' on those with the lowest incomes?

For others, this is only a part of the welfare state's rationale. Depending on political perspective, other aims will be more important. Some of the main aims advanced and their implications for assessing distributional effects are as follows:

1 *Vertical redistribution.* If the aim is redistribution from rich to poor, the crucial question is which income groups benefit. Since welfare services do not come out of thin air, the important question relates to who are the *net gainers* and who the *net losers*, after taking account of who pays the taxes that finance welfare provision. Allowing for both benefits and taxes in understanding distribution has become even more important since the government started using 'tax credits' (which count as reduced tax liabilities) instead of some cash benefits in the late 1990s.

2 *Horizontal redistribution on the basis of needs.* For many, relative incomes are not the only reason for receiving services. The NHS is there for people with particular medical needs; it should achieve 'horizontal redistribution' between people with similar incomes, but different medical needs.

3 *Redistribution between different groups.* An aim might be redistribution between social groups defined other than by income; for instance, favouring particular groups to offset disadvantages elsewhere in the economy. Or the system might be intended to be non-discriminatory between groups. Either way, we may need to analyse distribution by dimensions such as social class, gender, ethnicity, age or age cohort (generation), rather than just income. An important issue in recent years has been the distribution of public spending between areas, particularly rich and

poor neighbourhoods (Bramley and Evans 2000).

4 *Insurance*. Much of the welfare state consists, in effect, of insurance against adversity. People 'pay in' through tax or national insurance contributions, and in return, if they are the ones who become ill or unemployed, the system is there to protect them. It does not make sense just to look at which individual happens to receive an expensive heart bypass operation this year and present him or her as the main 'gainer' from the system. All benefit, to the extent that they face the risk of needing such an operation. The system is best appraised in actuarial terms – that is, in terms of the extent someone would expect to benefit on average.

5 *Efficiency justifications*. An extensive literature discusses how universal, compulsory and possibly state-provided systems can be cheaper or more efficient than the market left to itself for some activities, particularly core welfare services like healthcare, unemployment insurance and education. Where this is the motivation for state provision, one might not expect to see any redistribution between income or other groups. Services might be appraised according to the 'benefit principle' – how much do people receive in relation to what they pay? – and the absence of net redistribution would not be a sign of failure.

6 *Life cycle distribution*. Most welfare services are unevenly spread over the life cycle. Education goes disproportionately to the young and healthcare and pensions to the old, while the taxes that finance them come mostly from the working generation. A snapshot picture of redistribution may be misleading – it would be better to compare how much people get out of the system over their whole lives, and how much they pay in.

7 *Compensating for 'family failure'*. Many parents do, of course, meet their children's needs, and many higher-earning husbands share their cash incomes equally with their lower-earning wives. But in some families this is not so – family members may not share equally in its income. Where policies are aimed at countering this kind of problem, it may not be enough to evaluate simply in terms of distribution between families; we may also need to look at distribution between individuals – that is, within families as well.

8 *External benefits*. Finally, some services may be justified by 'external' or 'spill-over' benefits beyond those to the direct beneficiary. Promoting the education of even the relatively affluent may be in society's interests, if this produces a more dynamic economy for all. Appraisal of who gains ought to take account of such benefits (although in practice this is hard).

The relative importance given to each aim thus affects not only the interpretation placed on particular findings, but also the appropriate kind of analysis.

Conceptual Issues

As will already be clear, there is no single measure of how welfare services are distributed. It depends on precisely what is measured, and apparently technical choices can make a great difference to the findings.

The counterfactual

To answer the question, 'how are welfare services distributed?', you have to add, 'compared to what?'. What is the 'counterfactual' situation with which you are comparing reality? A particular group may receive state medical services worth £1,000 per year. In one sense, this is the amount they benefit by. But if the medical services did not exist, what else would be different? Government spending might be lower, and hence so too would tax bills, including their own. The net benefit, allowing for taxes, might be much less than £1,000 per year.

Knock-on effects may go further. In an economy with lower taxes, many other things might be different. At the same time, without the NHS, people would make other arrangements: private medical insurance, for instance. The money paid for that would not be available for other spending, with further knock-on effects through the economy. Britain without the NHS would differ in all sorts of ways from Britain with it, and, strictly speaking, it is this hypothetical alternative country we ought to be using as a comparison in order to measure the impact of the NHS. In practice, this is very difficult – which limits the conclusiveness of most empirical studies.

Incidence

Closely related is the question of 'incidence': who *really* benefits from a service? Is it children who benefit from free education, or their parents who would otherwise have to pay school fees? Are tenants of subsidized housing the true beneficiaries of the subsidies, or can employers attract labour to the area at lower wages than they would otherwise have to pay? In each case, different assumptions about who really gains may be plausible and affect the findings.

Valuation

To look at the combined effects of different services, their values have to be added up in some way, most conveniently by putting a money value on them. But to do this requires a price for the services received. This is fine for cash benefits, but not for benefits which come as services 'in kind', like the NHS or education. To know how

much someone benefits from a service, you want to know how much it is worth *to that person* – but you cannot usually observe this. Most studies use the cost to the state of providing the service. But 'value' and 'cost' are not necessarily the same. It may cost a great deal to provide people with a particular service, but if offered the choice they might prefer a smaller cash sum to spend how they like: the cost is higher than its value to the recipients.

Distribution between which groups?

Comparing groups arranged according to some income measure is of obvious interest, but so may be looking at distribution between social classes, age groups, men and women or ethnic groups. A related issue is the 'unit of analysis': households, families or individuals? A larger unit makes some things easier: we do not have to worry about how income is shared within the family or household. But it may mask what we are interested in – for instance, distribution between men and women. It may also affect how we classify different beneficiaries. The official Office for National Statistics (ONS) results described below examine the distribution of welfare benefits between *households*. In this analysis, a family with four children 'scores' the same as a single pensioner living alone – the situation of six people is given the same weight as that of one person. Weighting each person equally may affect the picture.

Distribution of what?

The question of what is being distributed will depend on what, precisely, counts as the distribution. Is it, for instance, gross public spending, net public spending after allowing for taxes financing services, or gross public spending in relation to need? Each will give apparently conflicting answers. NHS spending may be concentrated on the poor, but this could simply be a reflection of their poor health. And, allowing for differences in sickness rates, the distribution of NHS care in relation to need may not, in fact, favour the poor after all.

Similarly, the gross benefits from a service may appear to be 'pro-rich'; that is, its absolute value to high-income households might exceed that to low-income households by, say, 50 per cent. But if the tax which pays for the service is twice as much for rich households, the *combination* of the service and the tax may still be *redistributive*, in that the poorer households are net gainers and the richer ones net losers.

Time period

In a single week, fewer people will receive a service than over a year. As services vary across the life cycle, a snapshot taken across a single year will differ from the picture taken across a whole lifetime. But available data relate to short time periods: there are no surveys tracking use of welfare services throughout people's whole lives. To answer questions about lifetime distribution requires hypothetical models – the results from which depend greatly on the assumptions fed into them.

Data problems

Finally, research in this area is based on sample surveys: whole population surveys like the Census do not ask questions about incomes and service use required. Even the sample surveys may not be very specific, asking, for instance, whether someone has visited a GP recently, but not how long the consultation lasted, whether any expensive tests were done and so on. Results assume that GP visits are worth the same to all patients. But this may gloss over the point at issue: if GPs spend longer on appointments with middle-class patients – and are more likely to send them for further treatment – the distribution of medical services

may be 'pro-rich', even if the number of GP consultations is constant between income groups.

Some Empirical Results

This section illustrates some of these issues by considering findings from recent empirical analysis, contrasting the gross distribution of welfare services with that of the taxes required to pay for them, and showing the differences which result from switching from a 'snapshot' to a 'lifetime' perspective.

Cross-sectional redistribution

Figure 18.1 shows official estimates of the average benefits in cash and kind from welfare services received by households in different income groups in 2004–5. Households are arranged in order of 'equivalent disposable income' (that is, income including cash benefits but after direct taxes like income tax, and allowing for the greater needs of bigger households). The poorest 'decile group' (tenth) is on the left, the richest on the right. On average, households with the bottom half of incomes received 2.4 times as much from cash benefits (including the child and working tax credits) as those with the top half. Means-tested benefits such as income support and housing benefit are most concentrated on the poorest, but even 'universal' benefits such as the retirement pension are worth more to lower- than to higher-income households.

The figure also shows estimates of the combined value of benefits in kind from the NHS, state education and housing subsidies. Sefton (2002) suggests that such figures can be qualified on various grounds, such as the omission of the benefits of higher education for students living away from home (which tends to understate benefits to high-income households), or the

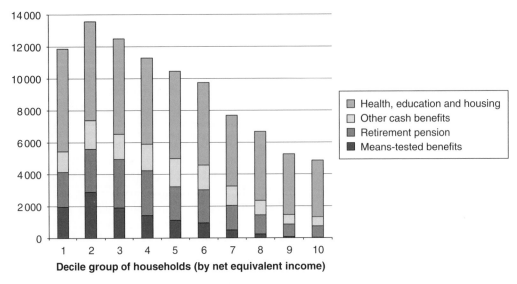

Figure 18.1   Welfare benefits by income group, 2004–5
Source: Jones 2006.

way in which housing subsidies are calculated (which tends to understate benefits to low-income households). Also, the assumption that people of the same age and gender use the health service equally is not necessarily correct: other characteristics affect service use too. However, even with adjustments for such issues, the general picture is similar: benefits in kind are less concentrated on the poor than are cash benefits, but households at the bottom of the distribution receive considerably more than those at the top. On the ONS's estimates, these benefits in kind were worth an average of £6,400 for the poorest tenth of households in 2004–5 but only £3,500 for the richest tenth. According to this, the absolute value of welfare benefits is greatest for lower-income households, and much lower than average for higher-income families. Taxation, by contrast, is greater in absolute terms for those with higher incomes (although it is not necessarily a greater proportion of income).

Most welfare spending is financed from general taxation, so it is hard to be precise about *which* taxes are paying for welfare:

for example, if state education were abolished, would it be income tax or VAT which would fall? Figure 18.2 compares the total of welfare benefits given in the previous figure with the ONS's estimates of the impact of national insurance contributions and an equal proportion (just over 80 per cent) of each other tax to cover the remainder of welfare spending. For the bottom six-tenths of the distribution, benefits are higher than taxes and the figures suggest a net gain; for those in the top four groups – particularly the top two-tenths – taxes are higher, suggesting a net loss.

These results suggest that on a cross-sectional basis, the combination of welfare services and, on plausible assumptions, their financing is significantly redistributive from high- to low-income groups (although they say nothing about the scale of such gains in relation to 'need', such as for medical care).

Life cycle redistribution

The picture looks rather different over a lifetime. As discussed above, actually

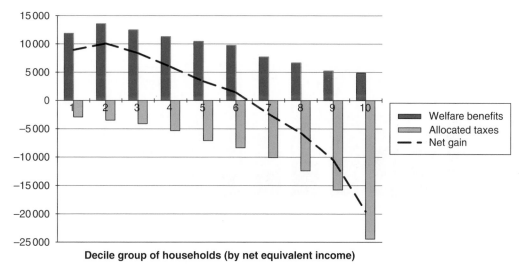

Figure 18.2 Benefits and allocated taxes by income group, 2004–5
Source: Jones 2006.

measuring 'lifetime' impacts of benefits and taxes is not straightforward. The findings in figure 18.3 are drawn from a computer simulation model of 4,000 hypothetical life histories (based on demographic and family patterns as they were in the late 1980s; see Falkingham and Hills 1995). The model builds up the effects of the tax and welfare systems on a wide range of individuals on the assumption that the systems remain in a 'steady state' (based on those of the early 1990s) for their whole lives. Its results therefore illustrate the lifetime effects of systems at one moment in time, not a forecast of the combined effects of different systems which may apply in future.

The top panel in figure 18.3 (a) gives a 'lifetime' analogue of the cross-sectional picture in figure 18.1. The bars show total lifetime benefits from social security, education and the NHS going to each group of model individuals, ordered by their average *lifetime* living standards, with the 'lifetime poorest' on the left. The 'lifetime poorest' receive somewhat more than the 'lifetime richest', but the striking feature is that the overall distribution of gross benefits is

much flatter than on an annual basis. Regardless of lifetime income, *gross* receipts look much the same, with each income group receiving an average lifetime total of around £200,000 (valued at 2001 prices).

Over their lives people both receive benefits and pay taxes. Those with higher lifetime incomes pay much more tax than those with low incomes. In effect, people finance some of the benefits they receive through their *own* lifetime tax payments. However, some people do not pay enough lifetime tax to pay for all of their benefits; they receive 'net lifetime benefits' from the system. These net lifetime benefits are paid for by others who pay more than enough tax to finance their own benefits; they pay 'net lifetime taxes' into the system.

The bars in the top panel of figure 18.3 are therefore divided between 'net' and 'self-financed' benefits, the latter being a rising proportion moving up through the income groups. The bars in the lower panel show where the net lifetime taxes are coming from. Net lifetime taxes also rise, moving up through the income groups. Finally, the line in the lower panel of figure

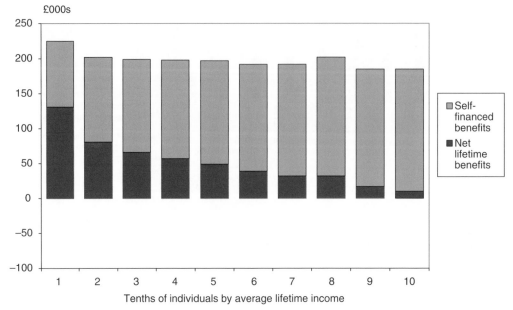

(a) Gross benefits in cash and kind

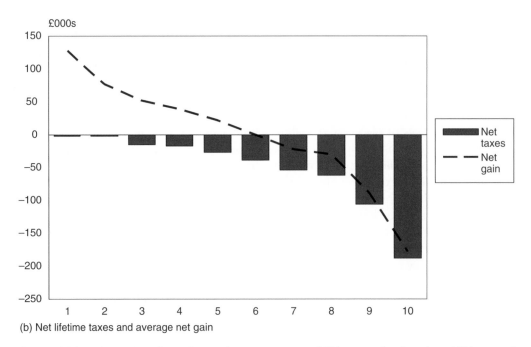

(b) Net lifetime taxes and average net gain

Figure 18.3   Lifetime benefits and taxes by income group (2001 prices, but based on 1991 tax and social security systems)

Source: Falkingham and Hills 1995: table 7.6.

18.3 (b) – analogous to that in figure 18.2 – shows the net gain or loss from the system to each lifetime income group as a whole. The bottom five groups are again net gainers on average; the sixth group breaks even; the top four groups are net losers.

Thus, even on a lifetime perspective, the system does appear to redistribute from 'lifetime rich' to 'lifetime poor' (and also, importantly, from men to women, when the results are analysed by gender). However, the diagram suggests that *most* benefits are self-financed over people's lifetimes, rather than being paid for by others (see also chapter 29). On these results, nearly three-quarters of what the welfare state does is like a 'savings bank', and only a quarter is 'Robin Hood' redistribution between different people (see Barr 2000 for more discussion of this role of the welfare state).

Emerging Issues

How welfare services are distributed has a major bearing on whether we judge them successful. But such judgements rest on a particular series of choices in the way in which distribution is analysed. Alternative ways of looking at the problem – including the kinds of results presented in the previous section – can give a very different impression, suggesting that it is highly unlikely that the poor would be better off and the rich worse off if welfare services were swept away. These remain fundamental issues for social policy, but ones where care is needed in how they are analysed, and in defining exactly what question is being answered by that analysis.

Guide to Further Sources

N. Barr, *The Welfare State as a Piggy Bank* (Oxford University Press, 2000) examines, from an economics perspective, the way in which the welfare state distributes income across the life cycle, including detailed discussion of pensions, medical insurance and student finance. G. Bramley and M. Evans, 'Getting the smaller picture', *Fiscal Studies* 21/2 (2000): 231–67, looks at where public spending goes on an area basis, comparing use of public services in rich and poor electoral wards in three English local authorities. It provides the kind of analysis needed to examine whether spending is (and can be) 'targeted' on poor areas. F. Jones, 'The effects of taxes and benefits on household income, 2004/05', *Economic Trends* 630 (May 2006) gives official estimates of the distributional effect of taxation and of a large part of public spending, including social security and welfare services; this is produced annually by ONS and is available on their website, <www.statistics.gov.uk/articles>.

J. Falkingham and J. Hills (eds), *The Dynamic of Welfare: the Welfare State and the Life Cycle* (Prentice Hall/Harvester Wheatsheaf, 1995) looks at the impact of the welfare state, taking a life cycle perspective and using a variety of approaches, including presenting results from a computer simulation model, LIFEMOD. J. Hills, *Inequality and the State* (Oxford University Press, 2004) discusses trends in inequality in Britain in recent decades, the factors that have driven them (including the impacts of tax and benefit policy of the kind discussed here), and public attitudes towards inequality, taxes and welfare spending.

T. Sefton, *Recent Changes in the Distribution of the Social Wage*, CASEpaper 62 (London School of Economics, 2002) (<http://sticerd.lse.ac.uk/case/publications/papers.asp>) looks in detail at the distribution of government spending on health, education, housing subsidies and personal social services. It looks in particular at how they changed between 1996/7 and 2000 (with earlier comparisons back to 1979), examining the extent to which changes in the 'social wage' have reinforced recent cash redistribution measures.

T. Sefton, 'Give and take: attitudes to redistribution', in A. Park, J. Curtice and K. Thomson (eds), *British Social Attitudes: The 22nd Report* (Sage, 2005) is a chapter of the report of the 2004 British Social Attitudes survey looking at people's views of how both welfare benefits and taxation should be distributed. It reveals an interesting contrast between declining support in Britain for 'explicit' redistribution from rich to poor, but continuing very strong support for principles of 'fairness' in taxation and social spending that implicitly have strong redistributive effects.

Chapter 19

Social Policy and Economic Policy

Colin Hay

Overview

- In most contemporary accounts economic and social policy are presented as antagonistic or oppositional – social policy is generally depicted as a drain on competitiveness and as bad for economic performance.
- In such accounts it is economic policy rather than social policy which is seen as the overriding imperative – where economic and social policy clash, it is economic policy which should dominate.
- Such a view represents a significant departure from the previous Keynesian orthodoxy in which social and economic policy choices were seen to be complementary – social policy was good for economic performance.
- The demise of the Keynesian orthodoxy and its replacement by a monetarist/new monetarist orthodoxy has been associated with a particular understanding of the constraints entailed by economic globalization.
- Ironically, there is considerable evidence that such constraints are exaggerated – with social policy being rather less corrosive of competitiveness than is often assumed and with regionalization rather than globalization being the more accurate description of the changing character of the UK economy.

Introduction

If there was ever a time when social policy choices could be made in the absence of economic policy constraints, that time has long since passed. To understand social policy choices today is to understand economic policy choices, for the two are now more intimately connected than ever before.

Behind this state of affairs lies a highly influential, though often implicit, view of the economic constraints which national policy-makers must now negotiate if their policy choices are not to compromise economic performance. In the logic of this new orthodoxy, social policy is more difficult to justify than once it was. For whatever the merits of the welfare state in its own terms, its effects are as much economic as social. Moreover, since the generosity of the welfare state is perhaps the greatest single determinant of the national burden of taxation, and since taxation might credibly be seen as a drain on competitiveness, an economic audit of the welfare state is unlikely to identify the need for increased expenditure. Or so one might think. In fact, as we shall see, the depiction of the welfare state (and the expenditure with which it is associated) as an unambiguous burden on competitiveness is overly simplistic. However superficially persuasive and, indeed, pervasive such a view might be, it captures little of the complexity of the relationship between social and economic policy that I seek to explore in this chapter.

The Changing Relationship between Economic and Social Policy: From Keynesianism to Monetarism and Beyond

As the Introduction perhaps already serves to indicate, a series of often taken-for-granted economic assumptions has served to shape decisively the contemporary debate on the future trajectory – and indeed the very viability – of the welfare state. Many of these assumptions are intimately connected to debates about competitiveness in an era of globalization. In order to have an opinion on the future of the welfare state, it seems, one has to have something to say about the consequences of economic globalization (see chapter 53). This makes social policy analysis a more difficult task than once it was, requiring students of social policy to take up positions on a range of issues which would once have been seen as solely the preserve of economics and political economy.

Yet while economic considerations have certainly come to dominate debates about appropriate social policy choices as never before, it would be wrong to see economic and social policy as having previously been unrelated. Social policy choices have always had economic implications, just as economic policy choices have always had implications for social policy. What has changed is the extent to which social and economic policy considerations are seen to

pull in opposite directions. Here it is instructive to consider briefly the changing relationship between these distinct but interdependent policy domains since the rapid growth of the welfare state in the early post-war years.

The first thing we might note is that the growth of the British welfare state in the 1940s was seen at the time, as it still is today, as an important part of the *solution* to the economic crises of the 1930s. Couched in economic terms, the problem was one of a lack of societal demand for the products of the process of mass production which new technologies had facilitated. Productivity gains associated with such technological innovations reduced the dependence of manufacturing processes on labour. The result was to make many workers redundant, quite literally, thereby reducing their potential to consume at precisely the point at which mass production became possible for the first time. Excess supply and insufficient demand produced both recession and previously unprecedented levels of unemployment.

Keynesian economics presented a ready solution. This came in the form of demand-management, a key part of which was a generous welfare state, free at the point of access to all. Through a series of transfer payments to the unemployed, the homeless, the sick and disabled, retirees and the like, the welfare state served to generalize levels of demand sufficient to ensure both high and stable growth rates throughout the early post-war years. In short, by putting money in the hands of the poor, it generated new demand for the developing consumer culture of the post-war years.

Such measures had a variety of other economic advantages. They were, as the economists put it, 'counter-cyclical', injecting demand when it was most needed. In recession, when unemployment was high, transfer payments would grow, since the number of those eligible to receive them would also grow. Conversely, when demand was high and unemployment low, the number of benefit recipients – and hence the total amount of demand injected into the economy – would fall. Furthermore, this was a very efficient way of injecting demand into the economy. For benefits were invariably targeted at the most needy, who were, in turn, the most likely to spend (rather than save) any additional income they received. In both respects, welfare spending was equilibrating for the economy, and the welfare state need only be mildly redistributive for it to have this effect. Social policy was, in short, good for economic performance; a healthy symbiotic relationship existed between the two.

What brought this happy coincidence of social and economic policy choices to an end? In a word, globalization – or at least this has become the pervasive view. Globalization presents a series of potential problems for the symbiotic relationship between economic and social policy described in the previous paragraphs, ushering in the need for monetary orthodoxy and fiscal discipline. First, demand-management becomes far more difficult to achieve domestically. In an open (or global) economy in the context of an international recession, the injection of demand into the domestic market through generous transfer payments may serve merely to create an influx of cheap foreign imports. Far from stabilizing the economy, this may compound its problems by generating a balance of trade deficit funded out of taxation receipts.

Yet, important though this is, it is not perhaps the principal problem. More significant still in contemporary accounts is the sheer cost of the welfare state and the drain on national competitiveness that this cost represents (or is seen to represent). The welfare state, especially if it is 'free at the point of access to all', is not free – indeed, it is extremely costly, and those costs are borne through taxation, both direct and indirect, personal and corporate. The problem is that in an integrated global economy, businesses not burdened by high levels of taxation enjoy a clear competitive advantage – all things being equal, they can produce and supply their goods to market for less. Whilst this was always true, its significance is far greater in an integrated world economy. For in such a context national businesses are pitted against international competition as never before – their success or failure is dependent on national competitiveness in a way that it was not previously.

A third factor is scarcely less significant in contemporary accounts. This relates not to the heightened competition between nationally based businesses to bring goods to market for less, but to the competition between nations to attract globally mobile business investment. In the early post-war years, so it is argued, national policy-makers did not have to deal with multi- and transnational corporations. Today they do. Such corporations are not bound to a host economy in the same way as a traditional business enterprise. Indeed, in many accounts they are presented as footloose and fancy-free, searching the globe for the best sites in which to make a productive investment. Such corporations do not have to put up with levels of taxation and other aspects of the regulatory environment of a given economy which displease them – they can up tools (quite literally) and relocate. Consequently, in order to retain high levels of investment, production and hence employment, national policy-makers must adjust their preferences to those of business. The welfare state and the high levels of taxation out of which it is funded are amongst the most obvious likely casualties.

Finally, and of at least equal significance, in a context in which financial markets are more integrated internationally, and concerted speculative attacks can more easily be unleashed upon rogue economies, policy-makers must seek above all to avoid the wrath of financial market actors. In particular, it is argued, they must be able to make credible commitments as to their capacity to control inflation and must commit themselves to avoid running up substantial budget deficits. If they are unable to do so, their currency is likely to suffer on the foreign exchange markets. In such a context, the capacity to control both inflation and debt becomes perhaps the key test of a government's economic credibility.

So what impact is this likely to have on contemporary social policy choices? The first impact is an indirect one. International competition, in the standard account, constrains economic policy choices and these, in turn, have implications for social policy. Keynesianism is no longer possible, since demand injected into an open economy may serve to suck in imports, and borrowing to stimulate demand invites speculative attacks on foreign exchange markets. What is required in its place is a dogged commitment to the control of inflation and levels of public debt – the defining features of a monetarist or new monetarist economic orthodoxy. Typically, as in Britain since 1997, these are achieved by a rules-bounded approach to economic policy. Here, responsibility for the control of inflation (through the setting of interest rates) is essentially subcontracted to a central bank now independent of government influence and mandated constitutionally to deliver a given inflation target. Yet this depoliticization of monetary policy is not deemed sufficient to ensure macro-economic 'prudence' since it leaves fiscal policy in the hands of elected officials. But here too rules come to the rescue – this time in the form of the Chancellor's 'golden fiscal rule' of no net borrowing over the business cycle. Such self-imposed monetary and fiscal policy discipline has clear implications for social policy. First, it ensures that in a context in which there is an inflationary shock (associated, for instance, with a steep rise in oil prices), interest rates will increase regardless of the consequences for domestic demand and levels of unemployment. As this suggests, higher levels of unemployment are accepted as a price worth paying for the control of inflation. Second, in this new economic paradigm the capacity of government to borrow in order to continue to satisfy welfare need in more difficult phases of the global business cycle is significantly eroded.

If these are the indirect consequences which follow from globalization in the new orthodoxy, then there is a series of more direct consequences too. First, since taxation is a burden on competitiveness, all aspects of social policy must be subject to stringent financial audit. Those elements which neither represent value for money nor contribute directly to competitiveness must be scaled back. Secondly, those benefits that the welfare state continues to provide must be justified principally in terms of their contribution to the efficient operation of the labour market – rather than in terms of their contribution to considerations of social justice. Thus, in place of traditional welfare programmes, we have 'welfare-to-work' schemes designed more to enhance the 'employability' of workers than to provide for their needs and those of their families.

This, then, is the new orthodoxy. But is such a view warranted and can it be reconciled with the available empirical evidence? Arguably not. In the sections that follow we look at the evidential basis for such claims, examining contemporary levels of welfare state expenditure, the extent to which recent decades have seen a systematic process of welfare retrenchment and, more briefly, the empirical case for and against the globalization thesis.

Why Should Social Policy Be Bad for Economic Performance?

As we have seen, the now conventional orthodoxy pits social policy against economic performance in a fairly unambiguous way. Yet there are good reasons for questioning the corrosiveness of the relationship between social and economic policy that this view reflects.

First, however persuasive it might appear to argue that (Keynesian) demand-management is rendered more difficult in a context in which social transfers may fuel imports, there are clear problems with such a thesis. For the point about social transfer payments is that they are targeted on those (like the unemployed) with the least disposable income. Welfare recipients are not only more likely to spend the transfer payments they receive; they are also more likely to do so by purchasing staple goods (milk, bread, meat, eggs), and these, in turn, are far more likely to be sourced from the domestic market. In other words, transfer payments are a far more effective means of stimulating domestic demand than almost any other tool of demand-management (such as reductions in general levels of taxation). As this suggests, they are relatively immune from the pressures of globalization. Moreover, transfer payments typically represent a redistribution of wealth from the most affluent to the poorest in society. Given that the former are more likely to save than spend any increase in disposable income arising from a reduction in taxation, and given that they are more likely to acquire cosmopolitan tastes sourced through imports, a scaling back of social transfer payments is likely to worsen the balance of trade figures. Even in an open or global economy, then, transfer payments are an effective means of demand stimulation. Furthermore, in a highly integrated economic space such as the EU, peaks and troughs in the economic cycle are likely to be shared – in other words, when Britain is in recession it is likely that France and Germany are in recession as well. Consequently, if a high proportion of Britain's trade is with other EU economies (and, as we shall see presently, it is), then the co-ordinated injection of demand into the EU economy is likely to be an effective means of restoring economic growth.

The depiction of the welfare state as a simple burden on competitiveness is no less problematic. It rests on a particular understanding of competitiveness – and a particularly limited understanding of competitiveness at that. This conception is exceptionally widespread; but that does not make it right. It assumes, quite simply, that competitiveness is to be gauged solely in terms of the cost for which a business or economy can supply a good to market. As a consequence, all forms of taxation and all regulatory restrictions are burdens on competitiveness since they increase the costs of a commodity. Couched in such terms it is not at all difficult to see how and why the welfare state might be seen as a burden on competitiveness.

But, a moment's further reflection reveals that cost is not the sole, nor arguably even the principal, determinant of consumer choice in contemporary markets. The quality, performance, technological sophistication and even the brand identity of the goods on offer are just as important – arguably, more so. Moreover, by and large economies characterized by the highest levels of social welfare expenditure tend to compete in markets which are less price-sensitive than quality-sensitive. As the Swedes would have it, consumers do not buy Saabs and Volvos because they are cheap. The point is that if we concede that there is more to competitiveness in international markets than cost minimization, then the competitive audit of the welfare state becomes far more complex than is conventionally assumed. High levels of societal welfare, though expensive in terms of taxation, may well be associated with a healthy and dedicated workforce, with cooperative rather than adversarial industrial relations, with long employment tenure, with high levels of skill (human capital), technology transfer and product innovation, and with

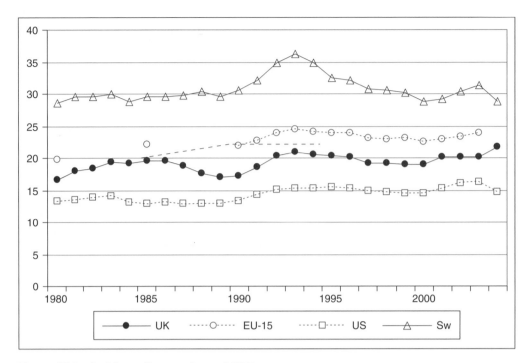

Figure 19.1   Social spending as a share of GDP
Source: OECD 2006, Social Expenditure Database (SOCX), available at <www.oecd.org/cls/social/expenditure>.

high domestic levels of consumer demand – all of which might be seen to correlate positively with economic performance.

This is a crucial point. For it suggests that the state's capacity to care for the welfare of its citizens may be less eroded by the pressures of international competition than we, or indeed it, have tended to assume. But that, of course, is ultimately an empirical question. To answer it we must turn to the evidence.

Welfare Retrenchment – Has It Happened?

Given the pervasiveness, in Britain as elsewhere, of the view that the welfare state is an increasing burden on competitiveness, one might be forgiven for expecting to see very clear evidence of welfare retrenchment in recent years. Yet such evidence is rather difficult to find.

Figure 19.1 displays public social spending (expressed as a share of national product) since the 1980s for the UK, Sweden, the US and the member states of the European Union. It shows that the long-term trend for social spending to rise that was established in the early post-war period has not been reversed in recent decades. Moreover, it shows that the UK is hardly the exception to the general rule either. Indeed, it is only Sweden that has witnessed a substantial recent erosion in social spending and arguably this owes far more to a sharp increase in unemployment and hence social transfer payments in the first half of the 1990s than it does to external factors.

Figure 19.2 looks at the UK case in a little more detail, showing the changing composition of public spending since the

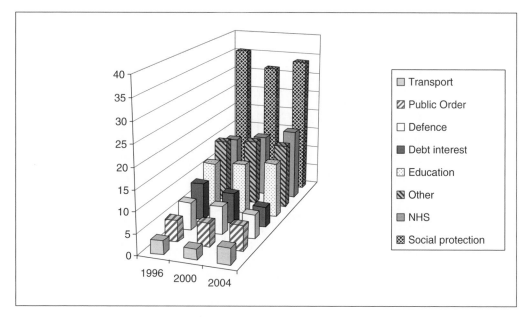

Figure 19.2 Composition of UK public spending, 1996–2004
Source: calculated from HM Treasury Website (<www.hm-treasury.gov.uk>).

mid-1990s. Social transfers and the public provision of both healthcare and education remain the largest single items of public expenditure. Moreover, taken together, the share of total public spending that they account for has grown consistently in recent years. Indeed, the only item of expenditure to have declined noticeably is the proportion of public spending going to service public debt. Had the first New Labour government not been so effective in reducing levels of national debt and had interest rates not been so low, public spending would have grown at a significantly higher rate since 1997.

Yet we should we wary of concluding from data such as this that there has been no process of welfare retrenchment in Britain in recent years. For this would be to assume that levels of need or demand for welfare have remained essentially static. This is far from being the case. A number of 'welfare-inflationary' factors might be identified. Most obvious here are demo-graphic change (an ageing population and an increase in the proportion of the population above or below working age), and the escalating unit costs of healthcare provision. If we attempt to control for such factors, we see fairly strong evidence of welfare retrenchment since the 1980s, despite rising levels of social spending. Whilst aggregate expenditure has risen in recent years, this has failed to keep pace with the rising demand.

If we look closely, then, we do see evidence of welfare retrenchment. But it is nonetheless the case that recent decades have witnessed the further growth of the welfare state; there is little evidence of this trend being reversed. This would seem to imply that the context in which social policy choices are made today is rather more favourable than is invariably assumed. It certainly invites us to look once again at the evidence of the pressures arising from international competition and the constraints upon welfare state expenditure

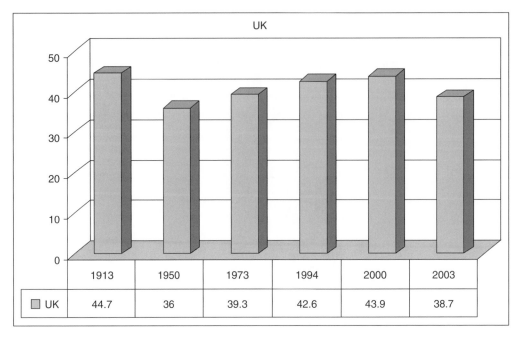

Figure 19.3 Ratio of merchandise trade to GDP, 1913–2003 (%)
Source: calculated from Hay 2006a: 264.

with which these are invariably associated. It is to these questions that we now turn directly.

Competitiveness and the Welfare State

The challenge to the new orthodoxy comes in two forms – a challenge to the notion that economies such as Britain have indeed experienced in recent years a process of globalization and a challenge to the notion that the welfare state today is an unambiguous burden on competitiveness. We consider each in turn.

Britain is certainly an open economy, the trade it engages in representing a significant proportion of its national product. Yet, surprising though it may seem, and as figure 19.3 shows, Britain is in fact a less open economy today than it was in 2000 or even 1913. The recent trend is, then, one in which the British economy has become more closed not more open.

But this is not the most significant piece of the evidential jigsaw. Figure 19.4 shows the share of Britain's total export trade destined for EU markets. This shows that, far from experiencing a globalization of its trading relations, Britain conducts an ever greater share of its trade with its nearest (European) neighbours. This is a story of European regional economic integration, not of globalization. This is a very important observation. For it suggests that Britain's economic performance is, if anything, less and less dependent on its *global* competitiveness, while being more and more dependent on its *regional* (European) competitiveness.

This is all very well, but it does little directly to challenge the pervasive argument that generous welfare states are an unsustainable drain on competitiveness in an ever more closely integrated regional

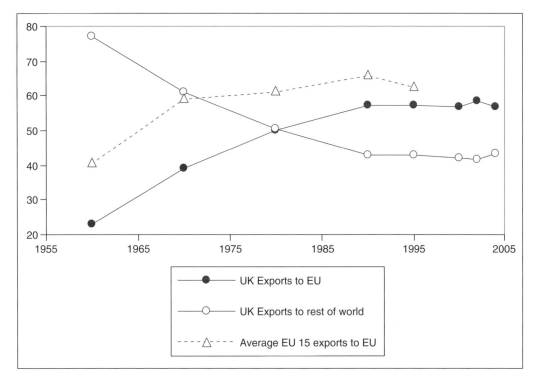

Figure 19.4   UK exports to the EU as a percentage of total exports, 1960–2004
Source: calculated from UK Trade Information Dataset (<www.ukintrastat.com>).

and/or global economy. Yet the evidence here is certainly no more easily reconciled with the orthodox view. Two points might here simply be noted.

First, as is widely noted, the most open economies in the world today are invariably those with the largest welfare states and most generous benefit entitlements. There is no direct evidence to show that welfare states are a burden on competitiveness.

Secondly, if we examine the investment behaviour of transnational and multinational corporations, something very interesting emerges. Foreign direct investors are not more likely to invest in low taxation economies than high taxation economies. A substantial and growing body of empirical evidence in fact shows that, after access and proximity to market are taken into account, educational attainment and skill levels are the most critical factors in determining the

attractiveness of an economy to mobile investors. Low wages, low levels of corporate taxation and the absence of labour market regulations are not positively correlated with investment. Investors, it would seem, are perfectly prepared to pay the price of the highly trained and educated workforce that many developed economies are capable of providing. This rather confirms the point made earlier that there is more to competitiveness than the ability to bring a good to market for less.

Emerging Issues

Social policy and economic policy are more closely interlinked than ever before, with economic policy choices invariably trumping and circumscribing social policy choices. This is due, in large part, to the prevailing orthodoxy which sees social policy and economic policy as increasingly oppositional in character.

Yet, as the preceding pages have sought to show, however influential such a vision is, it lacks evidential support. Contemporary welfare reform is, it seems, often informed by a perceived tension between welfare spending and economic competitiveness for which there is little evidence. Indeed, as we have seen, there is a very strong case for seeing the welfare state as crucial to competitive success of the most advanced economies in the world today, amongst them the British economy. High levels of welfare expenditure are simply not incompatible with an open and competitive economy. As this, in turn, suggests, the symbiotic relationship established between social and economic policy in the early post-war years has proved rather more resilient than we tend to assume.

Guide to Further Sources

I. Gough, 'Social welfare and competitiveness', in I. Gough, *Global Capital, Human Needs and Social Policies* (Palgrave, 2000) is a thorough and detailed exploration of the complex relationship between economic competitiveness and social welfare. J. Gray, *False Dawn: the Delusions of Global Capitalism* (Granta Books, 1998) is a clear statement of the prevailing orthodoxy which pits social policy against economic policy in an era of globalization. C. Hay, 'Managing economic interdependence: the political economy of New Labour', in P. Dunleavy, R. Heffernan, P. Cowley and C. Hay (eds), *Developments in British Politics 8* (Palgrave, 2006a) provides an account of New Labour's negotiation of international economic constraints. C. Hay, 'Globalization's impact on the state', in J. Ravenhill (ed.), *Global Political Economy* (Oxford University Press, 2006b) is a review of the empirical evidence on the extent of globalization and its impact on the policy-making autonomy of the state. D. Held, A. McGrew, D. Goldblatt and J. Perraton, *Global Transformations: Politics, Economics, Culture* (Polity, 1999) is a balanced and judicious survey of the literature on globalization. Finally, P. Hirst and G. Thompson, *Globalization in Question*, 2nd edn (Polity, 1999) is the most sustained and detailed critique of the globalization orthodoxy.

Chapter 20

Culture and Nationhood

Fiona Williams

Overview

- Notions of *nationhood* and *nationality* have been central to the development and practice of social policy, but notions of 'Britishness', and the meanings and conditions attached to British nationality, have changed over the past century.
- The welfare state emerged in the early twentieth century within the confines of the nation-state; eligibility to the social rights associated with welfare reforms was based in part on nationality. This contributed to processes of inclusion in and exclusion from citizenship.
- Social policies have been seen as important in the process of nation-building and the development of national unity, for example, following war, or social upheaval.
- Notions of Britishness have influenced the *cultural norms* underpinning welfare practices, often excluding or controlling those to be seen outside of, or a threat to, the nation – ethnic and religious minorities, single mothers, disabled people; but these too have been challenged over time.
- By the twenty-first century there were three main challenges to traditional notions of culture and nationhood in welfare: cultural diversity and debates about multi-culturalism; the development of supranational social policy, especially through the European Union; and migration.

Introduction

An examination of the relationship between social policy and notions of nationhood and nationality involves a critical understanding of the development of welfare in relation to the nation-state. In the case of British social policy it requires us to unpack the ideological and material dimensions of 'Britishness' in welfare policy and practice, and how these have changed over time as the meanings and conditions attached to British nationality and culture have themselves changed.

This chapter looks first at the historical context of the emergence and development of the welfare state in Britain, and at the centrality of notions of nationhood and nationality. It then examines some of the contemporary challenges to this history.

The Historical Context

The period from the 1870s to the 1920s was when most Western industrialized welfare states were established. It is commonly accepted that the context in which the first forms of state collectivism took place was the development of industrial capitalism, combined with a sharpening of class–capital relations; that is, an increasingly organized and enfranchised labour movement. It was also a period that saw the removal of women, children and older people from paid labour, creating a clearer demarcation between the public sphere of paid work and political life and the private sphere of domestic life (see chapter 13). However, in order to acknowledge the significance of *nation* we need to add a third important process that was taking place at this time. That was the growing significance given to national unity and national identity through the (imagined) homogeneous cultural, ethnic, racial and linguistic community of the nation-state. This was a period of an increasing 'nationalization' of society, when the boundaries of nationhood were being given greater economic, social, legal, political and ideological meaning. In other words, the introduction of social rights through social policy reforms took place within a context in which the boundaries of citizenship were becoming more circumscribed (for example, by nationality) and its constituency more complexly differentiated (by class, gender, disability, age and sexuality). The consolidation of national unity and the national ideal was achieved partly through state social reforms around the first forms of collectivism: education, public health, social insurance and, later, maternity provisions. At the same time, the rights and benefits attached to these provisions marked exclusion from, and inclusion in, the 'nation-welfare state'.

Some social policy writers have identified this relationship between nation and welfare as central to an analysis of social policy development as that between the state, the market and the family. Williams (1995; see also Lewis 1998) argues that, over the twentieth century, in different industrialized countries, a variety of welfare

settlements emerged from the state's attempt to consolidate changes in the social relations of power caught up in three interconnected spheres:

- *Work*: the organization and conditions of production.
- *Family*: the organization and conditions of social reproduction.
- *Nation*: the organization and conditions of the nation-state.

Citizenship and Nationality

One of the ways in which exclusion from citizenship operated was by making British nationality the condition of eligibility to social rights. So, for example, anyone who had not been both a resident and a British subject for twenty years was not eligible for a pension under the 1908 Pensions Act, and non-British residents who had been living in Britain for less than five years received a lower rate of benefit under the health insurance policies of the 1911 National Insurance Act, even though they paid full contributions. Just as significant was the fact that the context in which these Acts were passed was one which fed easily into the racialization of nationality; that is, that an assumed ethnic or racial difference marked out an individual as alien or non-British. The 1905 Aliens Act marked the introduction of the first immigration controls and, with it, the institutionalization of the 'no recourse to public funds' rule – that any person entering the country who could not support herself or himself without recourse to public funds or welfare provision, or who was homeless within the first twelve months, should be deported – a rule which still exists today and has been tightened up for refugees and asylum-seekers.

Campaigns at this time were aimed at Jewish refugees and were supported by all political parties and most labour organizations. They gave rise to and legitimated virulent anti-Semitism and imperialist chauvinism. Moral panic about foreigners provided a stepping-stone to link the politics of welfare and nationality to the practices of racism. It became common for people who were assumed to be 'aliens' (that is, who were not white, English-speaking and Christian) to be threatened with deportation if they applied, legitimately, for public funds, or for welfare agencies to be used to police illegal immigrants, or for racialized groups to be treated as scroungers irrespective of their social rights. For example, during growing unemployment in 1919, the Ministry of Labour sent secret instructions to labour exchange managers that black seamen who were eligible for the 'out-of-work-donation' – a relatively generous, non-contributory, non-means-tested benefit – should not be informed of their rights (Fryer 1984: 299). In these ways, the formalized condition of nationality was translated into the racialized conditions of eligibility and into a fear of 'aliens' as the bearers of inferior cultures and as welfare 'scroungers'. The use of welfare agencies as internal immigration controls and the perception of racialized groups as scroungers were carried in different ways into the postwar welfare state (see Williams 1989).

The subsequent history of Commonwealth migration to Britain from the 1950s presents an ironic twist in the relationship between citizenship, race, nationality and welfare. With the shortage of labour in the late 1940s, the recruitment of labour from the Commonwealth (especially the Caribbean and later the Indian subcontinent) was perceived by the government as a simple administrative solution because, by virtue of Britain's imperial model of citizenship, these colonized workers were already British citizens. However, as British citizens, they had access to more than work and residence rights: they had, formally at least, rights to welfare benefits and services. In effect, many of these were denied through the processes of direct or indirect racism.

For example, new migrant workers were unable to fulfil residency qualifications for low-cost public housing and were forced into the private sector and into further forms of discrimination. The very universalism of the welfare state depended upon a restricted notion of the norms of eligibility and need. At its heart was the image of the white male breadwinner family. Where black migrant workers and their families deviated from this norm, then cultural and material differences were cast in pathological terms. An example of this was the recruitment of Afro-Caribbean women to work in low-paid jobs with unsocial hours (often in the newly developing welfare services). This meant that children were left behind with relatives until it was possible to bring them over, or, if they did come, their mothers were faced with little provision for the children of working mothers. Either way, their actions challenged the dominant familial ideology of the day, which emphasized the role of women in the home as wives and mothers and warned against the disastrous consequences of mother–child separation. Because of the entrance conditions imposed upon them as migrant workers, Afro-Caribbean women were seen to be failing as mothers, especially by welfare professionals. Evidence that emerged by the 1980s showed that disproportionately higher numbers of black children had been taken into care.

Nation-Building, National Unity and Welfare

Nation-building has been one of the central aims of welfare state reforms, and at times this has been closely connected to the effects of war and the maintenance of the Empire. At the end of the nineteenth century, the poor health of recruits for the Boer War led to nutritional and health reforms for children. After the First World War, 'homes for heroes' was the slogan for the first major development of public housing. Richard Titmuss identified the Second World War as both the spur to post-war construction and the modern welfare state, and also as generating a solidaristic and egalitarian impulse and 'an enlargement of obligations – an extension of social discipline – to attend to the primary needs of all citizens' (Titmuss 1963: 84).

At times, however, nation-building operated over the twentieth century in ways which privileged some groups over others, and tried to generate national unity and the national interest to override emerging class or gender conflict. The influence of the eugenics movement on social policies between the two world wars is an example of this. Eugenics was the belief that heredity was the cause of most social problems, including physical and mental disabilities, 'feeblemindedness', pauperism, prostitution and alcoholism, and that these could be eradicated by policies aimed at encouraging the 'fit' to breed and discouraging the 'unfit'.

Two sets of social policies illustrate the complex ways in which improvements for the working class were cast in ways which superimposed the national interest over class or gender interests. Policies for the regulation and supervision of motherhood (e.g. school meals for the needy in 1906 and the Maternity and Child Welfare Act, 1918) established clinics and health visitors and were accompanied by the emergence of voluntary organizations working to promote child welfare and domestic hygiene. While these services met mothers' desperate needs, they also consolidated women's place in the home and served to tie women's role in the family to the development of 'race' and nation (see Davin 1978; Williams 1989). They aimed to increase the quality of the 'race' to maintain national efficiency and to prevent 'racial decay', and the quantity of the 'race' to defend the Empire. A propaganda film made in 1917 to mark National Baby Week started with the slogan: 'the

Race marches forward on the feet of the children'. Women, as bearers of children and reproducers of culture, formed a real and symbolic link between the racialized ideals of nationhood and nation-building by unifying the nation, populating it and servicing it.

Other policies, however, aimed to deter certain groups from breeding. The 1913 Mental Deficiency Act followed eugenic thinking by implementing the grading and segregating of 'mental defectives' – a category broad enough to encompass unmarried mothers, epileptics, people with mental health problems, petty criminals and people with physical, speech and hearing impairments. The more hapless of these groups were institutionalized in what were called 'colonies', away from both the outside world and the opposite sex.

These ideas about the role of welfare in sustaining Britain's imperial role and racial supremacy shifted after the Second World War. While there was an egalitarian impulse, as noted by Titmuss above, the universalism of the post-war welfare state had limitations as far as some social groups were concerned. Women (or, more particularly, white women) had a special duty, as the 1942 Beveridge Report extolled: '[H]ousewives as wives and mothers have vital work to do in ensuring the adequate continuance of the British race and British ideals in the world.' As the Empire began to fall away, the welfare state became central to the reconstruction of post-war Britain and brought a new order – of social justice and egalitarianism – that attempted to replace the old imperial ideal in sustaining national cohesion. If national unity and egalitarianism provided the impulse of the new welfare state, it was, ironically, migrant workers from the former colonies who helped to build and service it. Even more ironically, as we have seen, it was these workers and their families who, over the post-war period, found themselves excluded from these same institutions and began, in response, to challenge the boundaries of citizenship and the cultural norms of policies which had been cast in earlier decades.

Contemporary Shifts in Nation and Welfare

The post-war welfare state was central to national reconstruction. British culture and national unity were the rationale for state intervention. However, by the 1980s notions of national unity were used to justify *less* state intervention with more central state control. Emphasis was placed upon the traditional family as the transmitter of 'decent' British values and responsible for morality and discipline. The 1988 Education Act sought to reduce the impact of anti-discriminatory practice in favour of traditional morality and British cultural values. The Act also provided for parents to choose education for their children appropriate to their children's culture. While this could be seen as a shift towards the acknowledgement of cultural diversity, it also represented a form of cultural essentialism where cultures are seen as fixed and unchanging in both form and attachment. In addition, nationality and immigration laws were further tightened. The attempts by the New Right to reassert and protect the supremacy of British culture were, primarily, a form of defensive resistance to challenges to a sovereign, culturally homogeneous nation-state. These challenges included, from within Britain, the reality of a multiethnic population, greater visibility in the diversity in family forms and sexual partnerships, and pressure for devolution. Outside Britain, the breaking up and shifting of national boundaries, the growing significance of supranational political bodies, such as the European Union, the rise in transnational identities and movements, increases in migration and asylum-seeking across the globe, and economic and cultural globalization worked to undermine national identity and sovereignty.

Where the New Right sought to resist many of these changes, New Labour from 1997 attempted to accommodate and manage them, albeit in contradictory ways. New Labour in its early years emphasized the need to tolerate cultural diversity within civil society, yet it also strove to present an image of a 'one nation' Britain based upon 'strong families' and 'strong communities' and bound by a common set of moral values attached to the rights and responsibilities of citizenship. In this, nation and citizenship became connected through the responsibility of men and women to be in paid work, for paid work was seen as the defence against social exclusion, the passport to tax credits and benefits, as well as the basis for Britain's prosperity in the global economy.

However, the report of the MacPherson Inquiry in 1999, set up by New Labour, challenged this consensual image by revealing the extent of institutional racism in the police force. It recommended anti-racist strategies and monitoring, not only within the police force, but also in all public institutions (Race Relations Amendment Act 2001). At the same time, however, New Labour's practice in relation to asylum-seekers contradicted this anti-discriminatory commitment. The 1999 Immigration and Asylum Act eroded the rights of asylum-seekers by withdrawing their eligibility to social security assistance and a work permit. A new 'racialized subject' was reborn: claims of 'bogus asylum-seekers' from both media and government gave substance to the idea of Britain as part of an emerging 'Fortress Europe', rather than the possibility for some sort of 'post-national citizenship'.

On the other hand, a dynamic yet cautionary vision of 'Britishness' was provided by the Parekh Report: *The Future of Multi-Ethnic Britain* (Parekh 2000). It talked of a 'community of communities', of finding ways of nurturing, not simply tolerating, diversity 'whilst fostering a common sense of belonging'. The report was vilified by the media for what was seen as an attack on Britishness, and few of its recommendations saw the light of day. Yet, within months, these overlapping issues of belonging, identity and racism were vividly demonstrated in disturbances in northern towns following provocation by the fascist National Front Party. The riots drew attention to the experiences of young Asian people to racial harassment, segregation and lack of employment and training opportunities. While recognizing this, the then Home Secretary, David Blunkett, called for minority ethnic groups to take greater responsibility to become integrated into 'British norms' and assume a 'British identity', proposing also a requirement on migrants to pass an English-speaking test of citizenship. This was subsequently introduced in 2004, extended in 2005 to testing would-be citizens' knowledge of life in the UK, and further extended in 2007 to those applying to reside long-term in the UK, even when retaining their own national citizenship.

These moves represented a new stage of policies and debates about identity, culture and belonging, with asylum-seekers, refugees and migrants (see chapter 51), and British religious minorities, especially Muslims, as the focus of concern. They contain two main elements: one concerns integration and cohesion. Examples are the citizenship tests described above, the setting up of a government commission on *Integration and Community Cohesion* in 2006, and the introduction of citizenship in the school curriculum, one part of which focuses on inclusion and diversity. While some of these measures were welcomed, there have been criticisms. A report from the National Institute for Adult Continuing Education in 2006 said demand for English language classes far outstripped demand. In addition, by presenting integration as the responsibility of the migrant or minority

community, these measures detract from the need to tackle racism in the majority community, or the inequalities in housing and employment that give rise to segregated communities.

The second element is a challenge to multiculturalism and cultural diversity and an espousal of core 'British' values. This has emerged from the political left, as well as the right. In 2004, David Goodhardt, a liberal intellectual, wrote an influential essay which argued that as cultural diversity grows, then the solidarity born of a common culture is eroded; and when solidarity declines, then the moral consensus on which a welfare state depends becomes impossible to sustain. In fact, there is little evidence to show a consistent correlation across societies between high cultural diversity and low welfare expenditure (Banting and Kymlicka 2007). Nonetheless, the dangers of multiculturalism have informed debates about faith schools and cultural practices. A national debate about the right of Muslim women, girls and teachers to wear the *niqab* or full headscarf was instigated by Jack Straw, a Cabinet minister, who argued that it was a barrier to communication and integration. Two court cases in 2006 ruled against the rights of a pupil and a teacher to wear the full headscarf at school. These developments were, partly the consequence of a growing Islamophobia following terrorist attacks in the USA, Madrid and London, and part of a trend in Europe of reverting to an assimilationist approach (where different cultures assimilate into the dominant culture) and away from cultural pluralism (which seeks to recognize the diversity of cultures). What is new is the focus upon religion as the basis for un/acceptable cultural practices.

Emerging Issues

EU enlargement in 2004 and 2007 to include Central and Eastern European and

Baltic states has put one of the aims of the EU – the free movement of labour – to the test. In 2007 a points test was introduced to restrict entrance to only the most skilled workers from the poorer regions of the EU. However, this is likely to increase illegal immigration and unregulated cheap labour. This, along with Islamophobia, will provide possibilities by right-wing groups for the political exploitation of racism. For government this points to one of the most compelling issues for twenty-first-century societies: how to strengthen the bonds of solidarity in culturally diverse societies. Currently, progress on this has been limited. Challenging religious fundamentalism by discrediting multiculturalism suffers from the problem of identifying as 'problems' the very groups society seeks to integrate, and removing access to rights by migrants and asylum-seekers (see chapter 51) only reinforces such groups as second-class citizens. The articulation of common and inclusive 'British' values needs to avoid falling back on the cultural supremacy inherited from imperialism and to challenge the racism that has been its inheritance.

Guide to Further Sources

To pursue this subject, you need to go beyond the discipline of social policy to work on nation-states, nationality and 'race'. However, work which does look at the historical significance of nation both in itself and in relation to family and work in the development of the modern welfare state is F. Williams, *Social Policy: A Critical Introduction. Issues of Race, Gender and Class* (Polity, 1989), and 'Race/ethnicity, gender and class in welfare states: a framework for comparative analysis', *International Studies in Gender, State and Society* 2/2 (1995): 127–59. An interesting set of case studies on the relationship between nation and welfare is to be found in G. Lewis (ed.), *Forming Nation, Framing Welfare (*Routledge, 1998). There is also the classic essay on the relationship between war and welfare in R. Titmuss, *Essays on 'the Welfare State'* (Unwin University Books, 1963).

Detailed historical work can be found in A. Davin, 'Imperialism and motherhood', *History Workshop Journal* 5 (1978): 9–65; P. Fryer, *Staying Power: the History of Black People in Britain* (Pluto Press, 1984); and W. R. Brubaker, 'Immigration, citizenship and the nation-state in France and Germany: a comparative historical analysis', *International Sociology* 5/4 (1990): 379–407. The three titles are self-explanatory; these works cover the historical background to the issues raised in this chapter. For contemporary issues on Britishness, see B. Parekh, *The Report of the Commission on the Future of Multi-ethnic Britain* (Runnymede Trust, 2000), and compare it with David Goodhardt's essay against multiculturalism, 'Too Diverse?', *Prospect Magazine* 95 (2004): 49–56, and contrast that with K. Banting and W. Kymlicka, *Multiculturalism and the Welfare State* (Oxford University Press, 2007). For an analysis of the shift away from multiculturalism in Europe, including Britain, and of issues such as the 'headscarf' debate, see R. Lister and F. Williams, et al., *Gendering Citizenship in Europe* (The Policy Press, 2007).

Chapter 21

Social Policy and Family Policy

Jane Millar

Overview

- There have been significant changes in patterns of family formation and dissolution, and so in family structures, in the UK in the past half-century. There have also been changes in employment patterns, with most mothers, especially those with older children, now in paid employment.
- Family values and norms about the 'right thing to do' have become more complex and dependent on context. But this does not imply a lack of commitment to family, although these commitments are subject to reflection and negotiation.
- Family policy can be defined in relation to policy goals, to areas of activity and to institutional structures. The key areas of activity include the regulation of family behaviour, cash and tax transfers for families, and the provision of services.
- In the UK family policy has become more explicit in recent years, and in particular there has been substantial development of policies to support parents in employment and in parenting, and a focus on the needs of children as investments for the future.
- Other countries are also facing similar issues and challenges, and family policy is at the heart of important debates about the future direction for the welfare state.

Introduction

Families are very much at the centre of contemporary political and policy debate in Britain. All political parties claim to have policies that support families and sustain family life; media attention on issues such as working mothers, divorce and teenage motherhood is intense; and academic interest in the relationship between family and state has made this a growing area of research and publication. Family policy can

be defined in a very broad way in that almost every action that government does or does not take – whether it be in the fields of social security, taxation, health, education, housing, employment, transport or whatever – has an impact on families and on family life. But family policy can also be defined in a much tighter way, as those policies that directly target families and which are intended to have an impact on the circumstances and functioning of families.

This chapter covers two main topics. Family change, it is often argued, has upset

Table 21.1   Family formation and family structure in Britain over 30 years

	Early/mid-1970s	Early/mid-2000s
Percentage children born outside marriage	8	43
Percentage single women cohabiting	8 (1979)	31
Median age at first marriage for women/men	21/24	29/31
Number of abortions, women aged 15–44	160,000	186,000
Fertility rate (live births per 1,000 women)	84	59
Number of divorces	79,000	155,000
Divorce rate per 1,000 married population	5.9	13.0
Percentage families headed by lone parents	8	24
Percentage one-person households	18	29
Average household size	3.1	2.3
Percentage of population aged under 16	25	19
Percentage of population aged over 65	13	16

Sources: *Population Trends 105* (2001); *Social Trends 36* (2006).

the assumptions on which the welfare state was built and created new needs or new social risks that require different policy responses. The first section summarizes key trends in UK family formation and structure, and discusses government responses to these. The second section discusses definitions of family policy and outlines some key current policy developments and debates. The main focus here is on families with dependent children.

Family Change and Social Policy

Much social policy is concerned with families and family life, and in the making of policy certain assumptions must be made about families and family roles. It has often been argued, for example, that the provisions of the post-war British welfare state rested on a very clear model of family life, in which men were full-time workers and women were full-time carers. Families were assumed to be stable and long-lasting, and the family roles of men and women were seen as being quite distinct.

It is debatable how far real families ever conformed to this idealized model, even in the 1950s, a decade in which family structures were unusually stable and homogeneous. Families today, however, are much more volatile and heterogeneous. Although the 1960s are often characterized as the 'permissive decade', it was really in the 1970s that patterns of family life in Britain began to change very rapidly. The 1969 Divorce Reform Act, implemented in 1971, made divorce possible for a much wider range of people. Cohabitation also began to rise at that time, as did rates of extra-marital births. Table 21.1 summarizes some key trends in family formation and structure over the past thirty or so years. As can be seen, there have been some very significant changes over this period. Many more children are born outside marriage, more couples are cohabiting, first marriage is later, abortion is more common, women have fewer children and there is a higher risk of divorce. As a consequence, there are more lone-parent families, more people live alone and the average household size is smaller. The population is also growing older, with a lower percentage aged under 16 and a higher percentage aged over 65. This also includes more of the very elderly, with more people now aged 85 and above.

Table 21.2 Mothers, part-time and full-time employment, UK 2005 (%)

	All	Youngest child aged		
		0–4	5–10	11–15
Married/cohabiting				
Full-time work	30	22	29	39
Part-time work	42	39	47	42
Lone parent				
Full-time work	26	14	25	46
Part-time work	29	21	34	29

Source: Labour Force Survey, Office for National Statistics, <http://www.statistics.gov.uk/cci/nugget.asp?id=1655>.

Employment patterns have also changed over this time period. In the early 1970s just about half of married mothers were employed, usually women with older children, since mothers at that period typically spent several years out of the labour market to provide full-time care for their husbands and children. As table 21.2 shows, by the mid-2000s, almost three-quarters of married mothers are employed, and even among those with pre-school age children six in ten are employed. Employment rates are lower for lone mothers than for married mothers, but have been rising more rapidly in recent years, and may well reach similar levels to married mothers over the next few years. The government has set a target of an employment rate of 70 per cent for lone mothers by 2010. Many employed mothers, both married and lone, are in part-time jobs. Most women who work part time say that they prefer to do so, as it makes combining work and care easier, but part-time work does tend to be restricted to certain parts of the labour market and to be lower paid. Nevertheless, the earnings that women contribute to family income are increasingly important in maintaining living standards and preventing family poverty. The income gap between no-earner, one-earner and two-earner families is a key factor in widening economic inequality.

These family and employment trends have been characterized as the decline of the 'male breadwinner' family that was, as noted above, at the centre of the twentieth-century welfare state (see box 21.1 for discussion of the new 'adult-worker' model). The family type of married couple with the man at work and the women at home now accounts for less than a quarter of all families with children. It is important, however, to recognize that family situations change over time. Families form, break up and reform, and people move in and out of work. Thus, although the male-breadwinner family is a minority at any one time, it is still an important stage in the family 'life course' for many people. This is also true, for example, of lone parenthood. The women (and less commonly, men) who become lone parents do not usually stay lone parents for ever – many remarry or set up home with new partners and even if they do not, their children grow up and leave home. Lone-parenthood can therefore be characterized as a stage in the family life course, rather than as a fixed and separate family type.

The extent to which family relationships and values and norms about family life have also changed alongside changes in family structure has been the subject of much debate in the sociological literature.

Box 21.1 Changing assumptions about the family: from male breadwinner to adult worker

Assumptions about how families are, and what families should do, are an essential element underpinning welfare states. Lewis and Giullari (2005) argue that the assumption of a 'male breadwinner model' of the family, that was characteristic of the welfare state in the twentieth century, is in the process of being replaced by an assumption of an individualized 'adult worker' model. Under this new model, all adults have the duty and responsibility to engage in paid employment. That being so, more care work must be taken out of the family and 'commodified' – that is, provided in the public and formal arena, either by governments or in the private market.

This 'de-familialization strategy', as they call it, assumes that care can be readily moved into the public arena. But Lewis and Giullari argue that this is not the case: 'The problem is that care cannot be fully de-familialized or commodified, because it is passive as well as active, because it is emotional and relational, because the pressure for women to care is stronger than it is for men and is a part of gendered identity formation, and because the fragmentation that has resulted from welfare state restructuring has increased the need for family and informal care' (ibid.: 87). They go on to discuss what a 'genuine choice' between work and care for both women and men might mean for policy, and argue that it would involve a much more radical transformation of the welfare state (see also this volume, chapter 13).

It is sometimes argued that family commitments have become weakened because people are now more 'individualized' and motivated by their own personal goals and aspirations. As people focus more on their individual needs and self-actualization, they become less committed to sustaining family ties. In *Rethinking Families* (2005), Williams summarizes findings from a research programme which explored issues of personal relationships, intimacy, family values and obligations, and love and care in family and friendship networks. A key conclusion from this research is that, while the 'new conditions' of more fluid and complex family structures and work/care patterns 'have changed the shape of commitments they have not undermined commitment itself' (p. 83). Families are very important to people, but family obligations are negotiated rather than fixed, family

values are complex and there is no simple consensus about what is the 'right thing to do'. Thus it can no longer be assumed that all families are broadly the same, with the same sorts of needs and resources. Nor can it be assumed that everyone shares the same values about family life.

The issue of whether and how governments should respond to family change is also an issue of debate and controversy. Some people see the welfare state as having weakened and undermined the family and call upon government to turn the clock back and restore 'traditional' family structures and roles. Others are more pragmatic and argue that policy should reflect these changes and seek to ensure that people are not disadvantaged as a consequence. There is no clear consensus about these issues across or even within political parties, and in practice policy responses to family change have tended to be incoherent or even contradictory.

Defining Family Policy

As already pointed out, there is no simple way to define family policy. Some definitions include everything that affects families, whether intended or not. Others include only those policies directly targeted on families, with particular goals in mind. Hantrais, for example, offers a definition that focuses on policy goals: '[F]amilies policies, in the plural, can be characterised as policies that identify families as the deliberate target of specific actions, and where the measures initiated are designed to have an impact on family resources, and ultimately, on family structure' (2004: 132). However, as discussed above, there are very different political and ideological views as to the role of government in relation to the family. Hantrais herself goes on to note that many governments do not explicitly identify the family as a target for policy, nor seek to influence family structure. And as Smart (2005: 554) has argued, we should not necessarily seek consistency or clarity of policy goals in relation to family life. There is no consensus or mandate for 'a crisp set of rules and obligations' to govern family life, and attempts by governments to define such rules can quickly run up against different values (see also chapter 7 in this volume).

It may be more useful, therefore, to define family policy in relation to areas of activity. This is usually taken to encompass three main areas:

1   *The legal regulation of family behaviour*: laws relating to marriage and divorce, to sexual behaviour, to contraception and abortion, to parental rights and duties, to child protection.
2   *Policies to support family income*: tax allowances, family and child benefits,

parental leaves and benefits, enforcement of child support.
3   *The provision of services for families*: childcare provisions, subsidized housing, social services, community care.

We can also consider family policy in relation to the institutional framework for policy delivery. Establishing a government department to deal specifically with family matters is one way of doing this, but this is relatively rare. But, as family policy has become more high profile in many countries, there have been moves to provide clearer lines of political responsibility and accountability for provision.

This is the case in the UK, for example, where family policy has changed radically in recent years. Millar and Ridge (2002), reviewing the Labour government's family policy since 1997, argue that there have been significant changes in the nature of family policy. They illustrate this with reference to four main policy areas – childcare (the introduction of a 'national childcare strategy'), child poverty (the pledge to end child poverty within twenty years), lone parents and employment (the target of 70 per cent employment rates for lone parents within a decade) and measures to help parents reconcile employment and family life (parental leave and improved maternity leave and pay). They conclude that family policy in Britain has become more explicit, with new goals and new sorts of measures and provisions (see also chapter 48). Similarly, Williams argues that the UK now has an 'explicit, universal and child-centred family policy' (2005: 289). Her review of Labour's family policy identifies four key themes underpinning policy. First, there is a strong focus on supporting 'hard-working families', encouraging and supporting parental employment. Second, policy is child-centred, especially aimed at investing in children as future citizens (see box 21.2). Third, there is a stress on the importance of parental responsibilities and concern to

Box 21.2 Family policy and the social investment state

Family policy is at the centre of ideas about the 'social investment state'. In contrast to the redistributive focus of the twentieth-century welfare state, the social investment state would focus on investment in social and human capital, in enabling people to develop and use their full potential. This means investment in parenthood (to support people to become parents), in parents themselves (to enable them to bring up the next generation) and investment in children (as citizens of the future who need the skills for the future knowledge-based economies).

Such an approach focuses policy attention on the needs of children, but, as Lister (2003) points out, the focus is very much on children as the 'citizen-*worker* of the future' rather than on the experience of childhood now. Thus, the 'quality of their childhood risks being overshadowed by a preoccupation with their development as future citizen-workers' (ibid.: 437). Lister also raises other concerns about the social investment model, including the lack of concern with issues of current poverty and inequality, the way in which the rights of citizenship are so closely linked to paid employment, and the way that gender inequalities tend to be reduced to issues of work/life balance for mothers (see also chapter 48).

raise and support parenting skills. Finally, there is some acknowledgement of diversity, with rights for same-sex couples, for example.

Family policy has thus become more explicit in the UK over the past decade. This is also true in many other countries too, as they face similar social and economic changes, including more diverse family structures, rises in women's employment and population ageing. Hantrais (2004) provides an overview of family policies in Europe, covering the European Union twenty-five member states and highlighting the range of policy approaches and policy measures that have been introduced in recent years.

Emerging Issues

Family policy is at the heart of important debates about the future direction for the welfare state. This involves both normative issues about policy goals and in particular

about the role of the state in relation to the family and how far governments should intervene in family life. For example, the increased focus on 'parenting' includes positive support and extra resources, but is also about sanctions and social control. Parenting classes, anti-social behaviour orders, and measures that tie access to benefits and services to particular actions or behaviour show how social care and social control become intertwined. Sanctions may also come up in other ways. The current approach to achieving a 70 per cent employment rate for lone parents, for example, is largely based on the voluntary participation of lone parents, and requirements to seek paid employment are still relatively weak by comparison with many other countries. This may change, especially if employment rates do not rise sufficiently or quickly enough.

There will also be ongoing debate about the level and type of support, in cash and on kind, for families with children and about how the needs of families can and should be balanced against the needs of other groups, such as elderly people or single people of working age. The focus on eliminating child poverty in the UK has meant extra resources targeted towards children over the past decade. This pledge may not continue in the future, especially if – as is likely – the child poverty target proves difficult to achieve. Here too the policy concern may become more focused on how to change the behaviour of people in poverty rather than the redistribution of income.

Debates about the future of welfare in the context of an ageing population are also strongly focused on family policy, or more specifically on the issue of increasing employment rates among all adults, in order to maintain economic viability. The 'adult worker model' and the 'social investment state' raise substantial and difficult questions about gender roles and gender equality, and about how caring roles and responsibilities can be met in the future. The next edition of this book will probably need several chapters on family policy, as these issues become even more important than they are now.

Guide to Further Sources

The article by J. Lewis and S. Giullari, 'The adult worker model: family, gender equality and care: the search for new policy principles and the possibilities and problems of a capabilities approach', *Economy and Society* 34/1, (2005): 76–104, argues that the adult worker model is becoming increasingly central to policy, with potentially adverse consequences for women. It explores the gendered implications of this and stresses the importance of valuing and sharing care work.

R. Lister, 'Investing in the citizen-workers of the future: transformations in citizenship and the state under New Labour', *Social Policy & Administration* 37/5 (2003): 427–43, explores the way in which children are becoming increasingly central to policy in the UK, especially as workers of the future.

C. Smart, 'Texture of family life: further thoughts on commitment and change', *Journal of Social Policy* 34/4 (2005): 541–56, uses the example of the attitudes of grandparents to divorce to explore the ways values are formed and change in the light of personal experience. F. Williams, *Rethinking Families* (Calouste Gulbenkian Foundation, 2004) provides an overview of key family changes and discusses research findings about 'how people balance work, care, and commitments to family and friends'. In 'New Labour's family policy', in M. Powell, L. Bauld and K.Clarke (eds), *Social Policy Review* 17 (Policy Press, 2005), pp. 289–302, she reviews key policy developments and the values underpinning these.

J. Millar and T. Ridge, 'Parents, children and New Labour: developing family policy', in M. Powell (ed.), *Evaluating New Labour's Welfare Reforms* (Policy Press, 2002), pp. 85–106, reviews policy in respect of children, lone mothers and parental employment.

L. Hantrais, *Family Policy Matters: Responding to Family Change in Europe* (Policy Press, 2004) provides an overview of debates and policies in the EU and the twenty-five member states.

The Office for National Statistics gives access to social trends, population trends, etc. and to various data sets that can be used to create tables and charts. The website is at <http://www.statistics.gov.uk/>.

Chapter 22

The Political Process

John Hudson

Overview

- The making of social policies is an inherently political act.
- The UK has a strong and relatively centralized government.
- Some theorists suggest the state is losing power through a process of 'hollowing out'.
- Delivering policy change is not easy. Incremental, rather than radical, change tends to be the norm.

Introduction

All social policies emerge from a political process of one kind or another. Indeed, the making of social policies is an inherently political activity that often entails lengthy debate about complex moral issues on which it is difficult for groups of people with different values to reach agreement. There is also a sense in which social policies create winners and losers: those who directly benefit from policy decisions and those who do not – perhaps by being granted or denied access to a service or ending up with more or less money in their pocket. Consequently, debates about social policy often involve groups competing against each other in order to ensure their interests are at the forefront of policy decisions. In democratic societies, different groups and interests make their claims heard through the political process. Understanding how and when the political process allows voices to be heard – and where and

when there are failings in the process – helps us a great deal in understanding why particular policies exist and how far they might be open to change in the future.

Westminster and Whitehall

In the United Kingdom, policy is theoretically made in Parliament at Westminster. Members of Parliament vote on proposed laws in the House of Commons and those that gain the backing of a majority of MPs come into force, providing that the House of Lords does not use its rather limited constitutional powers to block those proposals. Technically, the Queen must also approve new laws, but in practice her role in the process is merely ceremonial.

However, this is a rather simplified interpretation of the reality. MPs are members of political parties and will ordinarily follow a party line during votes in the House of Commons. Indeed, each party employs whips, whose job it is to persuade reluctant MPs to vote as their party leaders expect them to, and although there are usually some rebels who will disobey the whips' instructions, they are generally a small minority. Tightly disciplined parties play a hugely important role in the UK's political system, because the party with the largest number of MPs in the House of Commons forms the government, its leader becomes the Prime Minister and its senior spokespersons become the senior ministers that form (with the Prime Minister) the Cabinet. Usually, the governing party has more than half of the MPs in the House of Commons (a 'governing majority'), because the UK's voting system is designed to produce a clear winning party at general elections. What this means in practice is that the governing party effectively controls the Commons and, consequently, is the dominant force in the UK political system. This, in turn, means that the laws passed by Parliament are, for the most part, those that are proposed by the government of the day. Though individual MPs have some limited opportunities for trying to persuade Parliament to turn their own ideas into laws, few so-called 'Private Member's Bills' actually become laws.

Yet, it would be wrong to underestimate the importance of Parliament in the political process. Though the government usually has the upper hand in the relationship between the two, Parliament plays an important role in scrutinizing the government and calling it to account. In addition to the role it plays in debating proposed laws, Parliament is also empowered to examine government decisions on a *post hoc* basis, and it has a powerful system of select committees that can investigate areas of policy that they feel are of concern. These committees can call on ministers and civil servants to explain decisions they have taken, and a critical report from a select committee can cause real headaches for the government. Similarly, all government min-

isters have regularly to answer questions in Parliament, and the weekly Prime Minister's Questions (PMQs) provide a valuable opportunity for the opposition political parties to place their concerns on record and to probe for answers in areas of political controversy. Ultimately, it is also true to say that a government – and, especially, a Prime Minister – that loses the support of MPs is likely to lose power. Indeed, the Labour Prime Minister Jim Callaghan had to call a General Election in 1979 (which his party lost) after losing a vote of confidence in the House of Commons, and his successor as Prime Minister, Margaret Thatcher, resigned as Prime Minister in 1990 after losing the support of her own MPs. In short, the UK government's power both emanates from and can be constrained by the Westminster Parliament.

However, while Parliament forms the focal point of the UK political system, in practice the majority of the government's decisions are made well away from the public environment of Westminster. The government has considerable executive powers that arise from its day-to-day management of public services and hundreds of decisions are made on a daily basis by ministers and civil servants working in government departments in Whitehall. It is impossible for Parliament to debate each of these decisions in detail ahead of their taking place, not least because many concern specialized matters that cannot be easily grasped without considerable prior knowledge of the salient issues. Indeed, the complexity of the issues in hand can be a problem for government ministers too and many will rely heavily on the advice of civil servants when making decisions. Though civil servants are employed to guide and advise government ministers, some political scientists have suggested that the civil servants themselves are the real masters of the political system: their detailed knowledge of issues and of the workings of the political system can give them the upper hand in their dealings with government ministers. In part, this is simply a result of the longevity of their respective roles: senior civil servants will typically have spent several decades working inside government, but it is rare for a minister to stay in the same post for more than a couple of years. However, there are those who suggest that the culture of the civil service propagates a conservative set of values and acts to constrain governments by advising ministers against sweeping changes and delaying or even blocking radical proposals. Perhaps because of this, recent years have seen ministers draw on the advice of an increasing number of political advisers who are not constrained by the civil service's rules and traditions.

Beyond Westminster and Whitehall

While Westminster and Whitehall provide the hub of the UK political system – and act as the focal point for the media's coverage of politics – political scientists have long recognized that any meaningful analysis of the political process needs to look beyond the formal institutions of central government. Indeed, some have critiqued this focus on the 'Westminster model' and urged us to adopt a much broader perspective that encompasses governmental and non-governmental groups found elsewhere in the political system.

From a social policy perspective, consideration of formal governmental bodies outside Westminster is essential, for they play a huge role in the making and delivery of social policy. At the local level, elected councils (sometimes known as local authorities) are responsible for administering many key areas of social policy and have some (limited) powers that allow them to tailor services to local needs or wishes. For instance, social care provision (see chapter 44) is managed by local authorities and the level of spending and quality of service

varies somewhat from place to place. Likewise, Scotland, Wales, Northern Ireland and London have devolved assemblies or parliaments that give them a greater degree of control over certain areas of policy: the Scottish Parliament, for instance, has responsibility for many of the key areas of the welfare state in Scotland and there are important differences in the nature of healthcare and education policy between Scotland and England as a consequence (see chapter 35). The EU also plays an important role in areas such as employment policy (see chapter 36) and some other supranational organization such as the IMF, OECD and World Bank can influence the detail of policy too (see chapter 37). Domestically, some fields of policy are heavily influenced by small unelected bodies – often made up of experts in the field – that may advise government on policy or even have responsibility for the delivery of some areas of policy. These bodies are often called quangos – quasi-autonomous non-governmental organizations – and there are more than 800 of them in the UK, dealing with a diverse range of issues that include the arts (e.g. the Arts Council for England), workplace safety (the Health and Safety Executive) and fertility treatments (the Human Fertilization and Embryology Authority). Taken together, all these different layers of government play a considerable role in the political process and can restrict the power of the national government. Indeed, some political scientists have talked of a 'hollowing out of the state' occurring as more power is exercised by bodies outside Westminster.

On a similar note, some political scientists have suggested that the government's power is also constrained by strong 'policy networks' in each field of social policy. These networks are not formal organizations – they have no official leaders, offices, contact points and so on; instead, the term 'policy network' is a metaphor used by political scientists to describe the manner in which government is loosely connected to a whole series of outside organizations and interests which it typically needs to negotiate with when introducing policies. So, for instance, when making changes to healthcare policy, the government will regularly consult the leaders of the medical profession for their views, not least because organizations such as the British Medical Association (BMA – a body which represents doctors) can make life very difficult for the government if they openly challenge proposed healthcare policies. Trade unions, major businesses and pressure groups regularly use their power to influence government decisions and, although they are not elected by the people, they speak to government with considerable authority.

On top of all this, government is necessarily constrained by public opinion. General elections that determine the number of MPs in each party must take place at least every five years and the need to retain sufficient popularity to win a further term of office is often a key driver of policy decisions. Regular elections to other branches of government (local authorities, the European Parliament and so on) take place between general elections and can place pressure on unpopular governments to adopt a different course of action if their party performs badly. Governments often undertake regular opinion polling to gauge the popularity of key policy proposals too, and MPs play a crucial role in feeding back the views of their constituents. We might add too that the media plays a considerable role in both communicating and shaping public opinion. Some have suggested that the owners of high circulation newspapers place pressure on governments to adopt policies that are favourable to their political bias; certainly, it seems to be the case that carrying the endorsement of widely read newspapers such as the *Sun* or *Daily Mail* could help a political party to secure victory in a tightly contested general election.

The Power of Government: Political Institutions

Despite the power of policy networks and of Parliament, the UK government has considerable control over the policy-making process. Indeed, the UK's constitution is designed to produce strong governments and the party that wins the general election can usually expect to spend four or five years in power with considerable control over Parliament. The government is undoubtedly the most powerful player in the UK political process, even though its power is constrained in a significant way by national and international organizations and by public opinion.

Yet, while it may seem somewhat obvious to state that the government is the most powerful player in the political process, it would be wrong to assume that the way in which the UK political system is organized is typical. Indeed, when compared to other democracies around the world, it may seem to offer an unusually strong concentration of power in the hands of the Prime Minister and the national government he or she leads. We do not have space here to offer a systematic comparison of the UK with other nations, but a few important points are worth highlighting.

First, we should stress that the UK is a classic example of a 'parliamentary system' of government in which the party with the largest representation in parliament forms the government and its leader becomes the nation's political leader. While many nations follow a similar approach (e.g. Australia and Sweden), many others do not. In the USA, for example, there is a presidential system of government in which the leader (i.e. the President) is elected directly by the people rather than being merely the leader of the biggest party in parliament. Indeed, a feature of such systems is that the separate election of parliament and the president can create political gridlock if different political parties control the different elements of the political system. In fact, this is precisely the situation that faced George Bush for the final two years of his presidency of the USA. In such instances, the leader's political power is seriously restricted.

In a similar vein, the organization of parliaments varies between nations too. In the UK, the House of Commons is by far the most important part of Parliament, not least because the House of Lords is an unelected body and so has little democratic legitimacy. In some countries, however, the different houses of parliament have more-or-less equal powers, particularly if (as is usual) both are elected. In such cases, it is possible for the two houses to be controlled by different sets of political parties, again making it more difficult for the government to pass controversial laws that their opponents disagree with. These various systems reflect different principles of democratic government: some place an emphasis on separating powers between different bodies in order to deliver strong checks and balances that prevent one part of the political system dominating, while others place an emphasis on delivering strong governments that can act relatively unhindered after winning popular backing in an election.

In this context, the voting system also plays a crucial role in shaping the power of a government. In the UK, a first-past-the-post voting system exists: each party puts up candidates in local constituencies (there are around 650 in the UK) and the candidate receiving the most votes in a constituency becomes the MP for that area. This system is designed to produce clear winners in locally rooted contests and to elect a named representative for each constituency in the country. However, some claim that such an approach produces inequities at the national level, because the final number of seats each party has in the House of Commons is not determined by the total number of votes they received throughout

the country as a whole. Indeed, in the UK it is theoretically possible for a party to receive millions of votes, yet finish second in each constituency contest and so have no MPs at all. In many other countries (e.g. New Zealand and Sweden) such a situation could not arise, because they employ a proportional representation (PR) voting system in which MPs are distributed between parties on the basis of their share of the national vote. In such circumstances, it is unusual for a party to have more than half the total number of MPs. Indeed, PR voting systems often allow many smaller parties to gain a foothold in parliament and one important consequence of this is that single party governments are rare. Instead, two or more parties often work together in a coalition government and some argue that this requires a more consensual approach to politics and policy-making than is found in the UK.

Finally, it is worth adding that a broad distinction can be drawn between political systems where power is concentrated in the hands of a strong national (or 'central') government (so called 'unitary states') and those where strong regional level governments counteract the power of the central government (known as federalism). The UK, broadly speaking, is a unitary state, but many other nations – such as Germany and the USA – are based on federalism. A federal system constrains the power of the central government, not least because the regional states are often given responsibility for delivering many key aspects of social policy. In the USA, for instance, some of the most important parts of the welfare state vary in nature across the nation because the different regions of the USA are free to determine the rules of key social security and health programmes.

The nature of these political institutions matters enormously, because the political system not only acts as a forum for political debate, it also influences the distribution of political power, or, in a phrase commonly used in political science, the political process 'mobilizes bias'. In other words, the political system empowers some interests at the expense of others. The UK system deliberately concentrates power in the hands of the government: it is a relatively centralized system that places relatively few checks on the power of the Prime Minister. Many view this as an undesirable state of affairs and, as we note below, there is an ongoing debate about the desirability of constitutional reforms.

The Power of Government: Policy Change

Although the UK government certainly has much power, this does not mean that it can change social policy however it desires. Indeed, one of the major themes of political science is the very real difficulty governments can face in trying to deliver policy change. It is often observed that policy change tends to be incremental rather than radical – i.e., it proceeds via small steps. This can be a source of real frustration for politicians: Tony Blair, for instance, famously bemoaned the 'forces of conservatism' that held back his attempts to reform public services. In part, the generally incremental nature of policy change is a consequence of the issues discussed above: opposition political parties, policy networks, public opinion, the civil service and the media can all act to put a brake on change.

However, there is a more general issue about the nature of social policy and the political process that is worth noting here. Many policy analysts have suggested that the social policy agenda of any given government is very heavily shaped by the social policies it inherits from its predecessors. So, for instance, any UK government's health policy will start from the fact that there is a large, well-established, government-funded National Health Service that is free

at the point of use for all citizens of the country. By contrast, health policy in the USA is fundamentally shaped by the fact that there is no comprehensive public healthcare service and that private health insurance plays the dominant role in the supply of health services to much of the population. Existing policy heavily shapes our expectations, our interests and even our values. In other words, policy thinking rarely starts from a blank sheet, but instead is necessarily based on a response to previous policy decisions. Or, to use the terminology of political science, we can often observe very strong 'policy feedback'.

Some political scientists have argued that the influence of past decisions on future decisions results in social policies showing strong signs of 'path dependency'. By this they mean that different countries are often locked into quite different policy pathways that they find it hard to break out of: to take the healthcare example from above, the differences between the UK and USA healthcare systems have persisted for more than fifty years, despite governments in each country trying to introduce radical reforms. One way of visualizing this is to compare policy development to the climbing of a tree: two people may start out at the bottom of the same tree, but as they take different routes through its branches they end up at quite different points and, moreover, the further they continue to climb up the branch they have chosen, the further apart they become. Some policy analysts have suggested that this path dependency can be observed across entire welfare states, with different countries having very different systems that remain largely in place even when governments change. So, for instance, the USA has long had a rather minimal welfare state, while Sweden has long had a relatively extensive one; these differences have persisted for decades and survived the election of governments of quite different political persuasions.

Emerging Issues

The UK's political system does not change quickly or easily. Indeed, its key institutions have shown remarkable persistence over the last two or three hundred years. However, there are undoubtedly some interesting challenges that lie ahead and there is a possibility that some significant changes to the UK political process will take place in the coming years. Chief amongst these is the issue of the future of the UK itself. Devolution of power to Scotland has raised some complex questions about whether there is a need for an English Parliament and also prompted some renewed calls for Scotland to seek independence. Relations between the EU and its member states are also at something of a turning point, with ongoing debates about the need for a constitution that more clearly defines the role and scope of the EU unresolved at the time of writing. There is also an ongoing debate about the structure of local government in the UK, with many advocating a strengthening of its role and extension of its powers. Equally, there are voices calling for a more regional approach to government, though the rejection by voters of proposals for a regional assembly in the north-east of England may have killed off this agenda for the time being. At Westminster, there have long been calls for the House of Lords to be reformed in order to make it more democratic, and change is likely to continue on this front, with proposals for reform being debated at the time of writing. The smaller political parties have for a long time been campaigning for the voting system to be made more proportional, but the bigger parties have so far resisted pressures to introduce changes.

Guide to Further Sources

There are many comprehensive textbooks that provide an introduction to the workings of the UK's political system: B. Jones, et al., *Politics UK: Fifth Edition* (Longman, 2006) is one of the best. A useful long-running text that offers a cross-national comparison of political systems is R. Hague and R. Harrop, *Comparative Government and Politics: Sixth Edition* (Palgrave, 2004).

Many useful textbooks look more specifically at how social policies are made. C. Bochel and H. Bochel, *The UK Social Policy Process* (Palgrave, 2003) offers an overview of the process in the UK. F. Hudson and S. Lowe, *Understanding the Policy Process: Analysing Welfare Policy and Practice* (Policy Press, 2004) offers an introduction to many of the key theories, as does M. Hill, *The Public Policy Process* (Pearson, 2004).

Claims that the UK government has been 'hollowed out' and that 'policy networks' constrain government have been made in a number of texts, but the most pertinent is R. Rhodes, *Understanding Governance* (Open University Press, 1997). A sophisticated body of work examining the impact of institutions on social policy known as 'historical institutionalism' contains many interesting, but often complex, ideas, including those about 'path dependency'; Hudson and Lowe (see above) provide an introduction. Those wishing to go a stage further in this area might find P. Pierson (ed.), *The New Politics of the Welfare State* (Oxford University Press, 2001) an interesting read.

Chapter 23

Evidence and Evaluation

Stephen Harrison and Ruth McDonald

Overview

- Social programmes aim to change some aspect of the social world, such as improve health, reduce crime or poverty, or increase literacy. This chapter deals with how such programmes may be evaluated and the role played by evidence and micro-economic analysis in the process.
- Key concepts in programme evaluation are: inputs, processes, output, outcomes/effectiveness, efficiency, cost-effectiveness and equity.
- Recent government interest in programme evaluation has been paralleled by the growth of various 'evidence-based' policy movements.
- Contemporary academic approaches to evaluation have followed several broad trends in relation to the use of evidence. Researchers influenced by approaches originating in medical research generally give priority to quantitative evidence from experimental research designs that employ randomized 'intervention' and 'control' groups. In contrast, practitioners of 'theory-driven' evaluation prefer research designs based on explicit theories about how the programme is expected to produce desired effects. Despite the high profile of these approaches, a wider range of quantitative and qualitative approaches continues to be used to evaluate social policies and programmes.
- Economic evaluation assumes that resources are scarce and that policy-makers must choose between competing candidates for investment. It is concerned not only with effectiveness but also with the question of whether the benefits of a policy or programme exceed the costs.

Introduction

To evaluate something is literally to assign a value to it. In this very broad sense, social policies are being evaluated all the time; for example, an opposition politician alleges that the Home Office is not 'fit for purpose', or the BBC's *Today* programme on Radio 4 doubts whether government targets for eradication from hospitals of the bacterium MRSA will be met. Moreover, there is a long tradition of the use of evidence in the formulation of social policies, including Lind's discovery in the eighteenth century that citrus fruits prevented the disease of scurvy, Chadwick's work on urban sanitary conditions in the mid-nineteenth century, and Booth and Rowntree's careful documentation of poverty at the end of the nineteenth century. This chapter, however, deals with research that uses evidence to investigate the effect of specific social policies. Such evaluations are often carried out by university academics, by in-house researchers in welfare organizations or by freelance consultancies, and systematically investigate some aspect of social policy, drawing on empirical evidence, either collected as part of the evaluation itself and/or available from published sources. In practice, such evaluations are usually concerned with social programmes – that is, specific interventions ostensibly aimed at changing some aspect of the social world, such as improving health, reducing crime or poverty, or increasing literacy. It is the evaluation of such programmes that is the subject of this chapter.

We begin with an overview of key concepts, followed by an elaboration of two topics, the problem of attributing cause and effect to social programmes, and microeconomic analysis as an approach to evaluation. Given the great variety of social programmes found in contemporary society, it is inevitable that much of our account is quite abstract, though we have illustrated some of our points with simple examples.

The Key Concepts

Programme inputs can be measured in either (or both) material terms (such as staff, buildings, equipment and consumables) or financial terms. These distinctions are important both because they lead to different approaches to evaluation and because it is not always possible immediately to translate financial resources into desired material resources, such as skilled staff. Processes are the programme itself, that is, what is done to the people whom it targets: criminals are imprisoned, cancer patients receive drugs and/or radiation therapy, school children are subjected to a 'literacy hour'. In practice, evaluations are

concerned with rather narrower groups than described above. Hence we might wish to investigate the effect of a particular drug on patients at a particular stage of progression of a particular type of cancer. Or we might wish to know whether a particular regime in young offender institutions reduces the rate of re-offending within a specified time period. Programme outputs are a measurement of the number of people who have been through a programme or some aspect of it, such as patients discharged from hospital, young offenders discharged from prison or pupils leaving school.

Programme outcomes (or effectiveness) are the effects that the programme has had on individuals who have been through it. Evaluators may start with a reasonably clear idea of the outcomes espoused by programme 'owners' (such as government departments or local administrative agencies). Where this is the case, such expected outcomes will be included in the evaluation, though evaluators might wish to operationalize them into measurable terms. They often face a trade-off here; the more narrowly conceptualized the outcome measure, the more easily and cheaply data can usually be collected, but the less it may reflect the whole of what is hoped for from the programme. Moreover, social programmes are likely to have a range of effects, rather than a single effect, and some of these may be unintended and undesired. For instance, measures intended to 'name and shame' poor performers might lead to concealment of problems or faking of performance data. Furthermore, the distinction between output and outcome is not always self-evident. For instance, an evaluator of a higher education programme must decide whether the number of successful graduates is an outcome, or only an output relating to a different outcome such as the number of persons able to fill vacancies with specified skill requirements. Some evaluations also make a distinction between outcome and programme impact. This is particularly important where evaluation is conducted in contexts which might not be typical of where the programme might be 'rolled out' if deemed successful. Thus a pilot study conducted with particularly committed or enthusiastic staff or in an elite institution (such as a teaching hospital) might not be generalizable to more ordinary settings. A programme might therefore be effective without demonstrating a broader impact.

Other evaluation concepts can be derived from the above, most importantly efficiency and cost-effectiveness. The productive efficiency (sometimes termed 'X-efficiency') of a programme is the ratio between its inputs and output. The higher this ratio, the less efficient the programme – and vice versa. We noted above that inputs might be measured in material or financial terms, and either may be used in such measurements. Thus 'unit' cost per prison inmate day, number of hospital patients discharged per bed per annum, and average caseload per social worker are all examples of efficiency measures. It is important to notice that efficiency improvements in a programme do not necessarily save money overall. If the average length of hospital stay falls, we can expect unit cost per case to fall. But if this results in the newly released beds being occupied by additional patients, total costs of running the hospital may well increase, as the additional patients will need additional drugs, operations and so on. (Productive efficiency differs from allocative efficiency, which we do not discuss here.)

The cost-effectiveness of a programme is its costs, expressed in money terms, per unit of outcome. For the purpose of such calculations, outcomes may be expressed in 'natural' units such as lives saved, job applicants placed or crimes prevented, or 'artificially' in terms of 'utilities' (see below) that provide a lowest common denominator, thereby allowing the comparison of different programmes with different outcomes.

Finally, equity is often presented as a desirable outcome for social programmes and its inclusion in evaluations may be important. Individuals are treated equitably if they are treated in accordance with their needs. According to this criterion, persons with identical needs should be treated identically ('horizontal' equity) and persons with different needs should be treated proportionately differently ('vertical' equity). The calculation of equity can be difficult as it requires both a means of assessing 'need' and (given that it is rarely feasible to assess equity for each individual recipient of a programme) a decision as to what social groups should be compared. Thus, evaluators may have to decide how far they are interested in (say) equity between ethnic groups as opposed to (say) equity between different geographical areas or different socio-economic groups.

Approaches to Research Design and Evidence

Although US governments have a longer history of programme evaluation, UK governments have shown considerable interest in the last twenty years. One of the earliest policy areas to generate such interest, and one which has lent its philosophy to other policy areas, is healthcare. The so-called 'evidence-based medicine' movement, imported from Canada in the early 1990s, focuses on the use of research to assess whether specific medical 'interventions', such as drugs or surgical procedures, are effective in terms of treating specified illnesses. The underlying philosophy of this approach to evaluation is that research designs must seek to deal both with biased results that otherwise might arise from the effects of unknown factors that affect the results of the intervention (so-called 'confounders') and the possibility that doctors are more likely to give new treatments to patients whom they judge likely to benefit, leaving older treatments or inactive treatment ('placebos') for patients judged less likely to benefit from the intervention being evaluated. Such 'selection bias' might of course give a very misleading impression of the effectiveness of the new treatment, suggesting that it would work for a larger proportion of patients than would actually be the case. Evaluation researchers in this tradition therefore emphasize a number of features of research design.

First, experimental designs are preferred. In such designs, the intervention group receives the treatment prescribed by the programme, whilst one or more control groups receive either no treatment, or a placebo, or perhaps an older intervention than the one being evaluated. Second, such researchers prefer the research subjects (patients, in the case of medical research) if practicable to be randomly allocated between intervention and controlled groups. (Such designs are often termed 'randomized controlled trials' or 'randomized field trials'.) Third, it is preferred that, where practicable, both the research subjects and the members of staff implementing the programme are unaware of which individuals are in the intervention or control groups. Such 'blinding' is often feasible in drug trials, but impossible to effect in studies where it is perfectly obvious which intervention is being received. Fourth, this research tradition prefers the systematic aggregation of findings from a multiplicity of trials, using special quantitative techniques of 'meta-analysis', in order to produce evaluation findings that are held to be both valid and generalizable.

These preferences have been systematized by medical researchers into a so-called 'hierarchy of evidence', which claims to judge the quality of evaluation research by means of the designs of the studies. These highly rigorous approaches are not beyond criticism, in particular because the studies are often conducted in highly untypical settings that may not be generalizable to the policy area more widely, and because studies of complex or social interventions (such as hospital 'stroke units') often fail to specify the intervention in any detail. However, they have found their way into official UK health policy, for instance in the criteria for recommending treatments used by the National Institute for Health and Clinical Excellence (NICE) and have also influenced evaluation researchers from other policy sectors, especially criminologists interested in the outcomes of various policies for crime reduction or reduction of re-offending. The websites of the Cochrane Collaboration (healthcare) and the Campbell Collaboration (other policy sectors) provide a forum for research of this kind.

A second tradition of evaluation research that has achieved prominence partly as a result of its explicit opposition to the above approach is the theory-driven approach, often influenced by various 'critical realist' philosophies. Rather than focusing primarily on the relationship of inputs to outcomes in the manner of experimental designs described above, such approaches seek to utilize research designs based on explicit theories about the processes by which the programme is supposed to achieve its objectives. To take a well-known example, a theory-driven approach might investigate whether and how closed-circuit television (CCTV) cameras are supposed to reduce crime. Several theories are available. CCTV might identify offenders, leading to conviction and imprisonment. Alternatively, the known presence of CCTV might deter offenders. Yet again, the presence of CCTV might make the general public feel safer and therefore more likely to frequent areas covered by it, leading to more informal surveillance and greater difficulty for criminals to operate unobserved. (There are several additional theories about how CCTV might 'work'.) An evaluation study based on such explicit theorizing would seek to collect data (often qualitative and quantitative) to shed light not just on whether CCTV was associated with reduction in crime, but on how that effect was achieved. Such evaluations are often also concerned with unsought consequences of programmes, for instance whether the presence of CCTV might simply 'displace' criminal activity to places not covered by cameras. Theory-driven evaluations are often very concerned to identify the contexts in which programmes are effective and ineffective. For instance, does the effectiveness of CCTV differ according to whether the local pattern of crime represents the activity of a relatively few, highly active offenders, or whether there is a much larger number of opportunistic thieves?

The experimental and theory-driven traditions described above are perhaps the highest-profile approaches to social policy evaluation in the UK, to some extent because their proponents have conducted high-profile debates about their relative merits. However, it is likely that a high proportion of evaluation research falls into neither category, simply utilizing more general quantitative and qualitative social scientific research methods. Not all quantitative approaches to evaluation utilize experimental methods, sometimes because they are simply impractical, perhaps for ethical reasons, or because a study is based on retrospective data. Such observational (or econometric) approaches generally apply complex statistical techniques to establish relationships between large-scale retrospective data (which may have been originally collected for routine official administrative purposes) whilst adjusting statistically for possible confounding variables. (The term 'observational' here may be confusing; it does not imply that the researchers actually observe the phenomena that they are studying, but rather that the data represent what has occurred naturally in the real world, as opposed to the situations created by researchers working in the experimental tradition.)

Qualitative approaches, including in-depth interviews, non-participant observation and documentary analysis, may be particularly favoured by evaluators who wish to obtain a deep ethnographic understanding of some policy field, rather than narrowly to assess the impact of a particular programme. Such researchers may wish to understand how social categories (such as 'high-risk offenders' or 'frequent attenders' at GP surgery or possessors of 'poor parenting skills') are created by the operation of social policies. They may wish to understand how the identities adopted by programme staff and/or recipients affect the programme's operation or outcomes. Or they may wish to understand the broader social and/or organizational culture in which social policies are enacted. Finally, it should be recognized that a great deal of evaluation of social programmes occurs within the organizations that deliver them. Such practitioner, or joint practitioner/ service user research may be quite small-scale, informal and never published, but may yet provide learning that impacts on practice within the organization. A particular form of this approach is action research, based on the manner in which individual service professionals are assumed to learn. Action research is thus based on a cycle of enquiry, intervention and evaluation carried out collaboratively by groups within the organization rather than by external evaluators. It might therefore be said to sacrifice wider generalizability of findings in return for context specificity and participants' commitment to act on its results.

Economic Evaluation

Economic enquiry proceeds from the perspective that societal resources are scarce. The notion of opportunity cost ('what are the benefits we forgo from the next best alternative, by spending money in this way?') underpins economic evaluation.

There are three main types of economic evaluation and the method chosen depends on the circumstances. Economic evaluation is comparative and so examines costs and benefits in relation to some alternative (this may be an alternative programme or policy or it may be the status quo).

Cost-Effectiveness Analysis (CEA) is used where a policy's intended effects are measured in terms of 'natural units' (lives saved, crimes prevented). It calculates the costs and benefits of an intervention or policy and compares this with an alternative (competing intervention or status quo) to assess cost-effectiveness. The results of CEA are often expressed as incremental cost-effectiveness ratio such as incremental cost per crime prevented. The term 'incremental' indicates that what is being measured is the change in costs and benefits, compared with an alternative intervention.

Cost-Utility Analysis (CUA) addresses the limitations arising from CEA's use of 'natural' units of outcome that cannot allow for the wider comparisons that (say) a government might wish to make. For example, if we compare the cost per life year saved with the cost per crime avoided, or with the cost per cancer detected, we are not comparing like with like. Although the costs are expressed using a common metric (money) the outcomes/outputs are not. CUA attempts to overcome this problem by expressing outcomes using a common scale, a number of which have been devised, including the Quality Adjusted Life Year (QALY). Whilst this may be a good idea in theory, in practice it is no easy task to devise a common scale which captures programme effects for different types of interventions and outcomes equally well. Further problems relate to the weighting to be given to different dimensions and the selection of groups to make the assessment; should teachers, children or parents assess the utility derived by children from a literacy hour?

CEA and CUA provide answers to policy questions insofar as they assess the extent of benefits generated from investment. In cases where costs and benefits of a policy are lower than the comparator, then the decision is an easy one. Here the policy 'dominates' and decision-makers should adopt it since it will save money and increase benefits. However, for many, if not most, policies being evaluated, costs are higher, but benefits are also higher. The result is that the evaluation concludes for example that the incremental cost per crime prevented is £x or that the incremental cost per QALY is £y. This 'answer' raises further questions, the most important of which is 'does £y per QALY' represent a cost-effective use of resources? The policy-maker then has to make a value judgement about whether to invest and what the cut-off point is beyond which a policy or programme does not represent a cost-effective use of resources.

Cost-Benefit Analysis (CBA): whereas all methods of economic evaluation can quantify inputs in monetary terms, they differ with regard to the measurement of outputs and/or outcomes. As we have seen, CEA focuses on single-dimensional, 'natural units' and CUA seeks to capture the multi-dimensional nature of programme or policy impacts using utility measurement scales. The former are an attempt to capture an objective measure of impact, the latter use subjective evaluation of individuals, although these are aggregated on a common scale to calculate overall utility for groups of people. CBA is very different from these two approaches in that outcomes are measured on the same scale as inputs and all are measured in monetary terms. The approach is to add up all the costs and all the benefits and subtract the costs from the benefits. If costs exceed benefits then the programme should not be undertaken, but if benefits exceed the costs the programme should be implemented. Advantages of CBA include the fact that it does not leave the decision-maker with more questions, since it provides a clear answer on whether a policy should be implemented and it uses a common metric which allows for comparison across very different types of policy (it can address allocative as well as productive efficiency). However attributing monetary values to non-market goods (such as human lives) is problematic. Proponents point out that other methods also require decision-makers to do this, but in a manner that is less transparent. Refusal to fund (say) a medical programme which costs £35,000 per life year saved implicitly places a value on life.

Emerging Issues

Methods of evaluation are wide-ranging. The results of evaluations may provide a systematic and/or transparent source of information, but the fact that designing and conducting evaluations requires value judgements raises questions about the extent to which they can ever provide an 'objective' view. The issue of whose values should be used in the process is also an important one if evaluations are to command legitimacy. It is rare for governments simply to act on the results of research, since the research may suggest conclusions that are at odds with prevailing political values and priorities. Moreover, research may not accord with the prevailing public view.

Some areas of contemporary UK social policy, especially the NHS, have sought to institutionalize and legitimize value judgements through new regulatory organizations such as NICE. Experience to date with very public disputes over the availability of drugs for breast cancer, dementia and the prevention of blindness suggests that such evaluations do not necessarily command public or political assent.

Guide to Further Sources

H. T. O. Davies, S. Nutley and P. C. Smith (eds), *What Works? Evidence-Based Policy and Practice in Public Services* (Policy Press, 2000) provides a wide-ranging review of theories and methods, along with substantive descriptions of evaluations in several fields of public policy.

A substantial and wide-ranging textbook is C. H. Weiss, *Evaluation: Methods for Studying Programs and Policies*, 2nd edn (Prentice Hall, 1998); D. T. Campbell and J. C. Stanley, *Experimental and Quasi-Experimental Designs for Research* (Rand McNally, 1966) is the classic text on its topic.

The web pages of Cochrane Collaboration (<www.cochrane.org>) and the Campbell Collaboration (<www.campbellcollaboration.org>) provide extensive material about the experimental approach to evaluation. R. D. Pawson and N. Tilley, *Realistic Evaluation* (Sage, 1997) is a clearly written and high-profile explanation and justification of the 'theory-driven' approach. I. F. Shaw, *Qualitative Evaluation: Introducing Qualitative Methods* (Sage, 1999) contains a wide-ranging discussion of qualitative approaches to evaluation.

E. Hart and M. Bond, *Action Research for Health and Social Care: a Guide to Practice* (Open University Press, 1995) presents a comprehensive discussion of action research philosophy and methods, along with several substantial case studies.

Also worth looking at is M. F. Drummond, M. J. Sculpher, G. W. Torrance, B. J. O'Brien and G. L. Stoddart, *Methods for the Economic Evaluation of Health Care Programmes*, 3rd edn (Oxford University Press, 2005).

Part IV

Welfare Production and Provision

Chapter 24

State Welfare

Catherine Bochel

Overview

- State welfare is highly complex and takes a number of forms.
- There are major debates around the extent to which the state should be involved in welfare and the balance of provision between the public, and other sectors.
- There are also major debates about the relationships between individuals and the state with regard to welfare.

Defining the State

The modern state is complex and made up of diverse elements. It also relates to a greater and lesser extent to other widely used concepts, such as 'country', 'nation' and 'government'. As a result, it is difficult to define in simple terms. There are many different views and conceptions of 'the state': for example, some have seen it as providing protection and security; for some, the term 'state' has connotations of secrecy and control; and for others it is the power of the state and the ways in which this is exercised which are of greatest importance. Clearly, views of the state are many and varied, and although they may contribute to our understanding of the state and its relationships with other entities, the requirements of space and concision demand a more focused approach here. Suffice it to say, therefore, that one of the most important reasons for studying the state is that it has enormous influence over our lives, and thus the relationships between the state and society and the state and individuals form a key underlying dimension to much of the discussion within this chapter.

The state and the mixed economy of welfare

Given that the term 'welfare state' appears to imply that the bulk of welfare is provided by the state, an impression perhaps reinforced by the fact that services used by much of the population, such as healthcare and education, are widely associated with the public sector, it is perhaps unsurprising that there is a popular belief that the state is the dominant institution in the provision of welfare services. However, this is no longer the case, if indeed it ever was. In the early twenty-first century, welfare services are funded and provided by a variety of different organizations across the private, public, not-for-profit and informal sectors. In reality, therefore, there is a plurality of providers, including in areas such as healthcare and education, and even more so in relation to services such as childcare, housing and pensions. This is often referred to as 'the mixed economy of welfare'. Indeed, one of the key debates over the past three decades has been about the relative sizes and roles of the different sectors, and the role of the state in the funding and provision of welfare services.

The balance of responsibility for service provision has changed over time, and we can see, for example, a shift from a growth in public provision after the inception of the welfare state to a greater role for other sectors in the 1980s and 1990s. In recent years, there has, arguably, been some degree of political consensus on the state as a large-scale funder of many welfare services, but with provision frequently undertaken by or in partnership with organizations from other sectors.

Analysing the state

Although there are many approaches to describing and analysing the state, one is to view it as a sovereign institution – it exercises legitimate power and is recognized as doing so by other states (although even here the growth of supranational organizations, such as the European Union, raises questions about the degree of sovereignty) – the government of which comprises a range of institutions through which laws and policies are developed and implemented.

There is also a range of different views of the state that can be used to help us understand the way in which state power is exercised (see chapter 22). For example, in liberal democracies, pluralist theory suggests that power is widely distributed and that many groups and organizations are able to influence policy. In contrast, other perspectives, such as those from elite and Marxist approaches, suggest that power is more restricted.

Given the difficulties of defining and analysing the state, and the particular focus

of this chapter, it is perhaps appropriate to concentrate on the functions of 'government' in respect of state welfare. In the United Kingdom, the main institutions of government are:

- Central government: the Westminster Parliament, the Prime Minister, the Cabinet and government departments. Within these departments there are divisions between, for example, the Treasury, which is responsible for managing public expenditure, and 'spending departments', such as those responsible for services like education and training, healthcare, pensions and social security. It is also possible to make further distinctions, between, for example, departments which largely play a policy-making role, setting direction and frameworks for services that are delivered by other organizations, such as local government, and those that are more involved in the direct delivery of services, such as healthcare through the NHS, the state pension and other benefits. To further complicate the situation, particularly during Gordon Brown's tenure as Chancellor of the Exchequer, the Treasury, which previously had seen its role as taking an overview of government income and expenditure, played a more proactive role in a range of initiatives which had significant impacts on social welfare.
- The Scottish Parliament, the National Assembly for Wales and the Northern Ireland Assembly, each of which is able to exercise differing levels of power over welfare policy and provision within their jurisdictions (see chapter 35).
- Local government, one of the responsibilities of which is to oversee the management and delivery of a range of services and responsibilities as delegated by central government, such as the bulk of primary and secondary education, parts of social care, and some elements of social housing (see chapter 34).

- A wide range of agencies at each tier of government variously referred to as quasi-autonomous non-governmental organizations (quangos), non-departmental public bodies (NDPBs) and Next Step agencies and extra-governmental organizations (EGOs). These are effectively organizations that perform some of the functions of government but at arm's-length from the departments to which they are responsible. Whilst these are frequently susceptible to reorganization and renaming by governments, examples from the early 2000s include Regional Development Agencies, Local Strategic Partnerships, the Learning and Skills Council, the Housing Corporation, the Commission for Equality and Human Rights, the Food Standards Agency, the Independent Police Complaints Commission and the Identity and Passport Service.

State Involvement in Welfare

It is also possible to analyse the state in terms of the functions that it performs, such as defence, the collection of taxation, the delivery of services and regulation. As is apparent from the discussion above, and through the variety of other chapters in this book that deal with or touch upon aspects of state welfare, state involvement in welfare happens in different ways. Among the most important are:

- Policy-making and the passage of legislation: the state plays an important role in formulating policy in many areas, in central government, the devolved administrations and local government, with the two higher tiers also being able, in some circumstances, to direct local authorities or other agencies to implement their policies. State institutions, legislation and policies also provide the framework within which all services are delivered.

- Funding: central government funds the great bulk of state welfare. It does this in a variety of ways: as a direct provider of services, such as the NHS; indirectly through local government, 'arm's-length' agencies, or private or not-for-profit providers, whether this is through grants or contracts for service provision; and through direct financial assistance to individuals, as is the case with the state pension, child benefit or income support. In addition, the state also provides fiscal support for some people through tax relief, tax credits and other forms of support such as free or subsidized prescriptions.

- Delivery: as is apparent from the two preceding points, the state plays a major role in the direct delivery of services, such as the NHS, state education and large areas of social care, although again responsibility for some services is channelled through local government.

- Enabling: from the 1980s the state has arguably developed its role in enabling or overseeing service delivery by other organizations, including the private and not-for-profit sectors, rather than in the provision of services itself.

- Regulation and direction: recent years have also seen a much greater awareness of the regulatory role of the state, and this has been very apparent in relation to social policy (see chapter 32). Examples of regulatory bodies in the early 2000s include the Commission for Social Care Inspection, which is responsible for registering, inspecting and reporting on the provision of social care in England; the Healthcare Commission, which inspects both NHS and independent healthcare provision in England and which has some oversight in Wales; the Office for Standards in Education (Ofsted) which again has responsibility in England; and the Financial Services Authority, responsible for regulating the financial services industry throughout the UK.

- Partnership and collaboration: this has become increasingly important in the delivery of welfare services, and across all tiers of government there has been a shift in emphasis to bringing a range of organizations from different sectors together to respond to issues and to deliver services in a way that is intended to be more flexible and comprehensive than would be achieved through agencies working alone or in competition with each other.

Given the variety of roles that the state plays in relation to social policy, and the existence of a mixed economy of welfare, it is unsurprising that it is possible to identify a whole range of different permutations of state involvement. For example, education can be privately delivered and funded, delivered and funded by a mix of both private and public funding or solely publicly funded and delivered. In the case of private healthcare, it is not funded or delivered by the state, but elements of it are regulated by the state, and in some cases the state will itself purchase private provision for public patients. These examples can be repeated across the variety of welfare services and provision. Clearly, therefore, there is enormous complexity in the mixed economy of welfare.

The range of the discussion above, together with the numbers and types of bodies noted, serves to provide some indication of the complexity of the role of the state in relation to the production and delivery of welfare. As the state has grown and changed, so too have its functions. There is now considerable debate as to what the role of the state should be. For example, some argue that the number of roles and functions of the state are now so great that it has reached the point where it can no longer undertake all of them successfully, and that it is necessary to get a

range of other organizations involved, for example in relation to service delivery and administration. Some believe that a large state apparatus is inefficient, bureaucratic, unresponsive to the needs of its citizens, and reduces freedom and choice. Others argue that the state should retain much of its role but that it needs to be more efficient and effective in fulfilling it. And yet others argue that there is scope for further expansion of the role of the state in social policy, particularly in relation to reducing inequalities. All these arguments are reflected not only here, but in other chapters in this book and in wider debates in society.

The Changing Role of the State

From the mid-nineteenth century, there was a gradual spread of state involvement in welfare through the introduction of public health and environmental reforms. A significant extension of the state's role came when a series of reforms to welfare were introduced by the Liberal governments of 1906–14, which in many respects provided the foundations for the development of a welfare state. Following the Second World War, fundamental changes to state welfare were introduced by the Labour government of 1945–50, following a blueprint set out in the Beveridge Report of 1942 (see also chapter 1). The period from 1945 to the 1970s is often portrayed as being one of political consensus on key issues, stemming from a combination of the economic philosophy of Keynes, and the social policy of Beveridge, enshrining the ideas of the mixed economy and the welfare state. In reality, it may have been more of a consensus on means, rather than ends, but nevertheless, this period saw a steady growth in the role of the state in welfare provision underlining a shift from an anti-statist position to one of welfare collectivism.

However, from 1979 the Conservatives, led by Margaret Thatcher and then John

Major and influenced by new right thinking, pursued a strategy of reducing the role of the state in welfare. From 1979 there was an emphasis on 'managerialism', in the belief that the introduction of private sector business methods into the public sector could make it more efficient; and from 1988, a range of different policy instruments, often termed 'the new public management', was used. These included the greater use of markets, ranging from privatization (for example, sales of council houses), through compulsory competitive tendering (such as cleaning services in hospitals), to the introduction of market-type mechanisms into the provision of public services (for example in health and education); the development of a view of the state as an enabler rather than a provider of welfare services, with greater provision by the private and voluntary sectors and by individuals themselves; and the devolution of non-essential functions, such as policy implementation and service delivery, previously undertaken by central and local government to organizations such as quangos, non-departmental bodies and Next Step agencies. Such developments served, over time, to make the organization and delivery of services much more fragmented and complex, while there was little agreement among commentators about their success or their social impacts.

While the changes under the Conservatives may, in general, be seen as relating to views that favour a more minimal state and in particular a lesser role for the state in the provision of welfare, under the New Labour governments from 1997 the pattern was rather less clear, and it is possible to identify a number of sometimes overlapping, or even contradictory, strands to the relationship between the state and welfare:

- An emphasis on 'what works', with the efficient and effective delivery of public services being viewed as paramount, regardless of the sector to which the providing agencies belong. However, some have seen this approach as enabling the private sector, in particular, to enter new areas of state welfare, resulting in what is effectively a form of privatization.

- An emphasis on partnership, including across the sectors, with 'partnership' being seen as a way of utilizing the perceived strengths of the private and not-for-profit sectors for social ends, whilst at the same time recognizing the complexity of contemporary society.

- The development of an 'enabling state' – with the role of central and local government frequently being seen as an enabler of services, rather than as a direct provider.

- Following on from this, greater use of non-statutory agencies as service deliverers.

- Increased use of a variety of mechanisms for regulation, audit and inspection of welfare services and providers, to some extent associated with the greater degree of complexity and the changing role of the state arising out of the developments outlined above.

- The development of different conceptions of the appropriate role for the state in relation to welfare, such as the encouragement of an 'active welfare state' in which citizens' rights are matched by responsibilities (for example, the state has a responsibility to help people, including getting people back into work, whilst individuals have obligations to help themselves and, for example, to take work if it is available).

- Increased public expenditure in some areas of state provision, notably social protection, education and the NHS. At the same time expenditure on housing has, in contrast, remained fairly static.

- Increased use of indirect 'fiscal welfare', particularly through the expansion of tax credits aimed at lower-income groups, including the use of those associated with incentives to individuals to find and remain in work.

- To some extent, a greater diversity of approaches across the constituent components of the UK, with, for example, the decision of the Scottish Executive in 2000 to provide personal care free for older people, and the decision of the Welsh Assembly to abolish prescription charges from April 2007 (see chapter 35).

The range and diversity of developments under New Labour have fed into debates about and attempts to redefine the relationship between individuals and the state, some of which have been variously interpreted, for example, as influenced by new right or traditional social democratic thinking. At the same time, particularly under the leadership of David Cameron, the Conservative Party has sought to distance itself from some aspects of the Thatcher era, and has accepted that there is, in some areas of social policy at least, a significant role for the state. However, while there may, on the face of it, appear to be a greater degree of political consensus on the state and welfare than for some time, it is equally clear that the debates on this will continue into the future.

Emerging Issues

There is a range of issues that are likely to continue to impact on the development of state welfare in the future. Those discussed below are currently some of the most important, but as with the nature of social policy these may change over time.

Individuals' relationships with the state

The relationships between individuals and the state have been central to the development of social policy over the past three decades. The new right's influence on the Conservative governments during the 1980s and 1990s was reflected in attempts to reduce the role and size of the state and an emphasis upon individuals providing for themselves and their families. While there has been an echo of this in some areas of social policy under New Labour, an emphasis on individuals' rights and responsibilities has been a key dimension of the approach to state welfare since 1997. As noted above, there appears to have been the development of something of a political consensus around this, together with the acceptance of a role for the state in assisting this and in supporting those who are unable to help themselves. Among the concepts associated with these debates in recent years have been 'self-provisioning', the 'active welfare state' and 'personalized welfare'.

The size and role of the state

As is evident from this and other chapters, there is a debate about the extent to which the state should be involved in welfare and the balance of provision between the various sectors. What appears clear is that the mixed economy of welfare is set to continue to be a central feature of social policy, but the form and extent of the role that is appropriate for different sectors remain contentious.

Citizen involvement in welfare

Conservative and Labour governments have sought to encourage citizen participation in welfare services through a variety of mechanisms and exercises ranging from market-like approaches to consultation and in some instances greater empowerment in decision-making. Pressures for such change include notions of individual choice, which may also be seen as a spur to efficiency and effectiveness for providers, concerns over the rights and responsibilities of individuals, and a belief that if you involve individuals in decision-making then you are more likely to end up with solutions that people feel meet their needs.

The complexity of state welfare

Relationships between central government and the variety of providers, including arm's length agencies and local government, have become more complex, at least in part as a result of the fragmentary systems of welfare provision. The challenges associated with establishing a clear overview of what is happening, and in exercising control over those responsible for policy implementation, mean that accountability and regulation are therefore likely to remain key issues.

Multi-level governance

Developments such as devolution in Scotland and Wales have enabled the Scottish Parliament and Welsh Assembly to develop their own welfare measures, which may differ significantly from those put in place by the Westminster Parliament. At the same time, the role of the European Union in relation to social policy has developed somewhat, although many areas of welfare provision remain the clear responsibilities of individual states.

The scope of the nation state

Finally, there is a range of wider factors which may influence state welfare, such as globalization and supranational governance (see chapters 37 and 53). The potential impacts of these have been widely debated, but for now it is sufficient to say that the forms and development of state welfare and the extent to which these allow control by national governments over the development of state welfare are highly contested areas.

Guide to Further Sources

A more detailed understanding of historical developments can be gained from R. Lowe, *Welfare State in Britain Since 1945* (Palgrave Macmillan, 2004) which gives a comprehensive account of the development of the welfare state, and B. Lund, *Understanding State Welfare: Social Justice or Social Exclusion?* (Sage, 2002), which considers the evolution of state welfare in the context of various theories. C. Pierson and F. G. Castle, *The Welfare State Reader* (Blackwell, 2000) considers a wide range of different perspectives, debates and challenges to the welfare state.

C. Bochel and H. Bochel, *The UK Social Policy Process* (Policy Press, 2004) covers a range of perspectives on government and J. Newman, *Modernising Governance: New Labour, Policy and Society* (Sage, 2001) considers the politics and policies of New Labour.

M. Powell (ed.), *Understanding the Mixed Economy of Welfare* (Policy Press, 2007) offers an up-to-date account of welfare pluralism, while C. Pierson, *Beyond the Welfare State? The New Political Economy of Welfare* (Cambridge University Press, 2007) provides a comprehensive guide to the issues of welfare reform.

Useful web sources providing information on services and policies include: <www.cabinetoffice.gov.uk> (the Cabinet Office) and <www.dwp.gov.uk> (the Department for Work and Pensions).

Chapter 25

Commercial Welfare

Christopher Holden

Overview

- There are many different kinds of for-profit companies that are involved in the delivery of welfare services.
- The extent and type of state welfare activity largely determines the scope for commercial welfare.
- Recent reforms in advanced welfare states have led to a 'blurring of the boundaries' between the public and private sectors, often involving 'quasi-markets' and government purchasing of services from private providers.
- The more the provision of welfare services relies on markets and private providers, the more important regulation of these becomes in the pursuit of social policy goals.

Introduction

Commercial welfare services have always been an important feature of welfare provision. This chapter begins by discussing the nature of commercial welfare, and outlines some of the different types of for-profit firms involved in it. It then moves on to look at how government reforms in countries like Britain have increased the involvement of such firms in recent decades. Finally, it examines important emerging issues, including regulation and how the role of the state may change as private provision of welfare increases.

Markets and Businesses in Welfare

Commercial welfare involves the sale and purchase of welfare services and products in markets of one kind or another. The sellers of these services are usually aiming to make a profit, although not-for-profit providers such as voluntary organizations (or provident associations, which are also technically non-profit-making) may also be involved in welfare markets. Even these types of providers, however, must usually try to maximize their income if they are to remain competitive. The consumers of these services are individuals, although the payers may be the individuals themselves (or their families), insurance companies (with the contributions to the insurance plan paid by the individuals or their employers), or state agencies. In principle, services necessary for the satisfaction of human welfare needs may be sold and bought in markets in the same way that any household item may be. There are two key reasons, however, why welfare services should be distinguished from other goods and services.

The first is that welfare services are by definition so important for the meeting of basic human needs that governments often decide they should take action to ensure that all their citizens have access to at least a certain minimum level of these. If governments did not take such action, many of their citizens would not be able to afford to meet their basic needs, leading to huge inequalities. In countries like Britain during the course of the twentieth century, this government action often took the form of direct provision by state agencies, as well as state funding and regulation of them. Direct state provision was widely seen as the best way of ensuring that services would be provided to the degree and standard that the government thought necessary. In health services, for example, private provision was pushed to the margins by the creation of the National Health Service (NHS) in Britain, which was (and is) paid for out of general taxation and free to citizens at the point of use. However, as we will see, governments have increasingly begun to question the idea that the state itself should be the provider of welfare services if the needs of their citizens are to be met.

The second key reason why welfare services should be distinguished from other goods and services is that the market often does not provide them efficiently. There are many reasons why this is the case (see chapters 6 and 30). Deciding what kind of healthcare you need, or what kind of school you should send your children to, is not the same as choosing a new television, and you are much more dependent on the knowledge of professionals. Therefore, even if markets and private providers are to play a role in the delivery of welfare services, these need to be carefully regulated to ensure that they help to meet the goals of social policy.

So government provision of welfare services (at least in advanced welfare states)

has often helped to restrict the extent to which private firms have been able to make profits by selling those services, even though most other goods and services are provided through markets. In most countries, commercial provision of welfare services such as health and social care, education, pensions and other financial products, and of course housing, has always continued to exist wherever firms can make a profit. However, the extent of the development of the welfare state in any given country, and the type of that welfare state, has tended to be the largest factor determining the scope for private provision. The less state provision there has been, the more scope there has been for private provision. Nevertheless, in many countries (including Britain) there have always been a number of private firms that have benefited from payments by the state to provide services on behalf of the government and, as we shall see, the number of such firms has been growing considerably as a result of government policies. Furthermore, firms that produce goods such as medicines that are crucial for the delivery of welfare services have also benefited hugely from state funding.

Where state provision or funding of services is low, the size and shape of the market is largely determined by the degree of effective demand, i.e. how much people are willing and can afford to pay for services. Since people will not necessarily have the money to pay 'out of pocket' for support when they need it, this tends to encourage the development of commercial insurance schemes. In countries like Britain, with, for example, tax-funded public health services, these have tended to be taken out by those whose employers pay for health or other insurance as a non-wage benefit, or those who are relatively better off and can afford to pay, for instance, to be treated more quickly or in more pleasant surroundings than those provided by the public system.

Box 25.1   Types of for-profit welfare firms

The first, and most important type of firm for social policy, are the firms that directly provide welfare services to the public. There is a wide range of such firms, from those that provide healthcare, including hospital, diagnostic, dental, optical or pharmacy services, to those that provide education at school, further or higher levels. Other such firms provide adult and child social care, as well as training, employment, housing or prison services. Secondly, there are firms that produce goods that are indispensable to the delivery of welfare services, such as medicines and educational materials. These kinds of firms have been somewhat neglected in the study of social policy, but their behaviour often has important implications for welfare outcomes. Thirdly, there are firms that supply services to the organizations (both public and private) that directly provide welfare services. For example, all hospitals, whether they are run by state agencies or by private firms, rely on companies that distribute medicines to them, clean their premises and provide catering services to their patients and staff. Firms in this category may also provide consultancy or management services to direct providers by, for example, taking over the management of a state-owned school or hospital where the existing management has been deemed to have failed. Fourthly, there are firms that provide insurance or financial services such as health and disability insurance, private pensions and mortgages. Fifthly, there are firms that are involved in the design, building and maintenance of the premises from which welfare services are provided, such as hospitals and schools, as well as prisons and the construction of houses. This type of firm has become much more important in Britain in recent years as a consequence of the Private Finance Initiative (PFI). There are also a number of different firms that, whatever their business, provide some form of occupational welfare services to their own employees.

There are in fact a large number of different types of for-profit firms involved in some way in the delivery of welfare services (see box 25.1). Any of these companies may be entirely privately owned by one or two individuals or by a small number of investors, or they may be 'public' in the sense of being listed on the stock exchange so that people may buy shares in them. They range from small individual owners of care homes to huge multinational corporations (MNCs). Currently, the most multinational firms are those that produce welfare-related goods such as pharmaceuticals (rather than services), but as the provision of welfare services by private firms increases, these firms too are likely to become more multinational, and international trade in welfare services between countries is likely to increase. Such developments will need careful study if the goals of social policy are to be safeguarded and advanced. As well as firms performing the different roles in the production of welfare described in box 25.1, a variety of firms whose core business activities may have little or nothing to do with the direct provision of welfare may also exert influence on social policy. For example, firms may participate less directly in the management of state welfare services through various types of boards or sponsorship deals, as is the case with academy schools. Firms might also take political action, such as lobbying politicians about social policy issues, in order to protect or advance their interests (if, for instance, they thought the minimum wage was too high).

We can see, then, that there has always been a huge range of different firms that are involved in some way in the delivery of welfare services, often deriving a large portion of their income from the government by selling goods or services as inputs to state providers, as well as selling these goods and services directly to the public for private payment. The most important type of private companies for the meeting of social policy goals consists of the direct providers of services. In Britain, the most rapid growth in the involvement of private firms in welfare delivery in recent years has been among these very providers, such as for-profit health services providers, and this will be discussed further in the next section.

Government Policy and Welfare Markets

We have said that the extent and type of government welfare activity is the most important factor determining the scope for commercial welfare. Paying attention to the *type* of government activity is particularly important, because it is not simply a case of the presence or absence of such activity. The government may choose to pay private sector companies to provide welfare services, or mandate other organizations to administer services, rather than provide them itself. Government-mandated social insurance schemes are one example of this. So, for example, many European countries have social health insurance schemes, whereby citizens (or their employers on behalf of them) pay into independent funds, which are regulated by the government and which pay for their healthcare when they need it. The governments in these countries usually pay contributions for those who

can't afford to do so for themselves, so that everyone has access to a minimum level of healthcare. This set-up often means that citizens can choose to access the services of private healthcare providers as well as public ones, and have their bills paid by the social insurance fund. In this way, private providers make their money not simply from private payments (either private insurance or out-of-pocket), but from payments by government-mandated insurance funds. Government activity in the pursuit of social policy goals may therefore support rather than undermine commercial providers, depending on the form it takes.

In the United States, where the welfare state is much less extensive than in most other economically advanced countries, but where many citizens can afford to pay for their needs, commercial welfare is more developed than in any other country (see chapter 55). There is therefore a huge market in health and other services, with large chains of for-profit hospitals, for example. Inequalities in access to welfare services are consequently also much greater than in most other economically advanced countries, since not everyone can afford to pay for the services they need. Even here, however, the government provides some support for its poorest citizens, with a government-funded health insurance service called Medicaid for the poor and a similar scheme called Medicare for older people. People making use of Medicaid or Medicare are just as likely to be treated by private providers as anyone else, but the provider will claim back the cost of the service from the government scheme. Because these providers are motivated primarily by the pursuit of profit, this sometimes leads to problems such as fraudulent claims by private providers for people they haven't actually treated.

As already discussed, in countries like Britain, where services such as healthcare have mainly been provided by the state since the end of World War Two, there has been less opportunity for commercial welfare. However, since the 1980s, that has begun to change as a result of reforms to the way welfare services are organized. Britain has been a leader in such reforms, first under the Thatcher and Major Conservative governments and then under New Labour, setting out a path that some other advanced welfare states have followed. The role of commercial welfare providers has increased as a result of two main changes. First, there has been a relative shift towards individuals taking responsibility for their own needs, so that people cannot rely on the state for their pension, for example, but must make their own provision through occupational or private pension schemes. Secondly, there has been a relative shift towards the state paying private companies to provide services that it used to provide itself.

This second change has involved the introduction of 'quasi-markets' into welfare services that were previously provided almost exclusively by state agencies. Reforms to the NHS are a good example of how these changes have provided more opportunities for private providers. Thatcher adhered strongly to a pro-market neo-liberal ideology, but she realized that public support for the NHS meant that she couldn't simply privatize it in the straightforward sense of just getting rid of the NHS and leaving people to buy health services in an open market without government support. She therefore introduced an 'internal market' into the NHS, whereby the purchase of services was separated from their provision. This involved hospitals and other services (the providers) being reorganized into independent trusts, which would then provide services under contract to health authorities and 'fund-holding' GPs (the purchasers). At this point there was very little purchasing of services from the private sector, but NHS trusts were expected to behave more like independent businesses 'selling' their services to the purchasers, hence the term 'internal market'.

However, the purchaser–provider split was also introduced into social care services like residential and nursing care for older people, with local authority social service departments as the purchasers and a 'mixed economy' of private, voluntary and state agencies as the providers. Here the market was not 'internal', but involved external for-profit providers, who soon dominated the provision of social care. Large multinational corporations moved into this new market alongside smaller private providers, making most of their profits providing care services under contract to local authorities. The purchaser–provider split was thought by Thatcher to allow more choice for service users and to be more efficient than the old state-provided services, even though it involved extra costs in administering contracts.

This new 'mixed economy of care' eventually became the model for public services adopted by New Labour governments, even though in opposition they had opposed the internal market in the NHS. Once in office, New Labour soon embarked on a new programme of reform within the NHS, in which new organizations based on groups of GPs, called Primary Care Trusts (PCTs), would be the purchasers and independent NHS trusts (including new 'foundation trusts') would compete with for-profit providers to treat NHS patients. Overseas healthcare corporations were invited by the government to set up 'diagnostic and treatment centres' as part of a policy to contract out to the private sector up to 15 per cent of the elective procedures paid for by the NHS.

The increasing involvement of commercial firms in welfare has also included new ways of commissioning welfare facilities such as schools and hospitals, through schemes such as the Private Finance Initiative (PFI). PFI involves for-profit consortiums financing and maintaining, as well as building, such facilities. It has been controversial because it means that these are then owned by the consortium for a period of 20–30 years, with welfare agencies such as NHS trusts locked into inflexible long-term leases which may not be cost-effective.

Bringing the private sector into the heart of the welfare state in these ways has led to a 'blurring of the boundaries' between the public and private sectors. The process begun under Thatcher's neo-liberal Conservative governments was much extended by New Labour, which professed a more pragmatic approach to the delivery of public services, summed up in the phrase 'what counts is what works'. New Labour's 'Third Way' ideas claimed to combine the best of the market and the private sector with the best of state action, in order to provide services in new and more effective ways. In practice, however, this pragmatic approach often seemed to lapse into a presumption that the private sector usually does things more effectively than the public sector, leading to a view that where services can be contracted out to the private sector, they should be.

Emerging Issues

This turn towards the private sector in Britain has both led and reflected a more general drift among policy-makers across the developed world towards the view that the state should 'row less and steer more'. In other words, the pursuance of social policy goals does not necessarily require the state to directly provide services; rather, it is the role of the government to ensure that these goals are met through whatever means seem necessary. In this view, therefore, it may be better for the government to pay for other agencies and organizations to provide the services, including for-profit companies, or simply to oblige its citizens to make adequate provision for themselves, by paying into pension funds, for example. However, it is not enough for the government to fund the services, or to make sure that citizens pay for themselves; where companies are providing services primarily in the pursuit of profit, the government needs to think carefully about two things if it is to 'steer' services effectively.

First, where the government funds private sector provision, it needs to think about the kinds of behaviour that are encouraged by the payment system. Any kind of payment system creates its own incentives to behave in a certain way. For-profit providers, voluntary organizations and autonomous public agencies such as foundation hospital trusts will all tend to act in ways that maximize their income, even if other goals are also important to them. Markets, including the 'quasi-markets' created by governments, are premised upon this very fact. So the government needs to design its payment system very carefully in order to try to incentivize companies to act in the optimum way. It also needs to specify its contracts with providers very clearly so that they know what is expected of them.

Secondly, the government needs to make sure that it regulates providers properly. This means that the government must create a set of rules within which all providers must operate, monitor adherence to these rules and apply sanctions where they are not adhered to. Different types of regulatory 'instruments' may be needed in order to ensure that different policy goals are met (see chapter 32). For example, governments usually want to ensure that certain minimum standards are met in the delivery of services; i.e., they want to ensure that quality goals are met. In a hierarchically organized service that is directly provided by a state agency, they can do this at least partly through the agency's internal management structure. However, where services are provided by independent providers, they need to set up special regulatory agencies, such as the Commission for Healthcare Audit and Inspection or the Commission for Social Care Inspection, whose job it is to monitor the quality of services, and take effective action where standards are not met. This means that they must specify clearly what the standards are that are expected to be met, how they will be monitored, and what action may be taken towards those organizations that fail to meet them.

However, perhaps the biggest concern about the use of markets in welfare is their impact upon equity. The principle of equity is at the heart of the welfare state, and markets may have profound implications for both equitable access to services and for equitable outcomes. Markets are based upon competition and responsiveness to incentives rather than, for example, the encouragement of a public service ethos, and will therefore tend to change the nature of the welfare system. Careful thought therefore needs to be given to what the goals of social policy should be, and what are the most appropriate means to achieve them.

These issues of equity, quality and regulation are of the utmost importance given that governments are likely to continue to allow or encourage commercial welfare provision to expand. In the context of an increasingly liberalized and integrated world economy, welfare markets themselves are likely to become increasingly internationalized, with an ever greater movement across national borders of welfare firms, practitioners and service users. Such developments have the potential to enhance the sharing of knowledge and skills between countries, but also make regulation of services even more difficult and have potentially even greater implications for equity, both within countries and between them.

Guide to Further Sources

Further insight into and debates on the issues raised in this chapter can be found in M. Powell (ed.), *Understanding the Mixed Economy of Welfare* (Policy Press, 2007); K. Farnsworth and C. Holden, 'The business-social policy nexus: corporate power and corporate inputs into social policy', *Journal of Social Policy* 35/3 (2006): 473–94; C. Holden, 'The internationalization of corporate healthcare: extent and emerging trends', *Competition & Change* 9/2 (2000): 185–203; K. Farnsworth, *Corporate Power and Social Policy in a Global Economy: British Welfare Under the Influence* (Policy Press, 2004); M. May and E. Brunsdon, 'Commercial and occupational welfare', in R. M. Page and R. Silburn (eds), *British Welfare in the Twentieth Century* (Macmillan, 1999).

Chapter 26

Occupational Welfare

Margaret May

Overview

- Occupational welfare is a key, but neglected, component of the UK's welfare mix.
- It is best defined as the 'non-wage' elements of the reward packages provided by employers that enhance employee well-being.
- Provision has been reshaped and grown in significance over the last decade.
- Shifts in provision reflect the changing calculations of employers and other stakeholders, particularly the state.
- It has significant consequences for public welfare, labour market behaviour and social equity.

Introduction

As other chapters show, welfare services can be provided by one's family and a range of governmental and non-statutory agencies. In meeting life events or other needs, many individuals also benefit from the support provided by their employers as part of their remuneration. Though sometimes dismissively termed 'fringe benefits', such provision can substantially enhance recipients' disposable income, standard of living and opportunity structures. Signifying this, careers advisers frequently counsel graduates to apply for posts offering benefits as well as appropriate salaries. For employers, too, such support is far from peripheral, often amounting to a third or more of basic pay costs.

Employer investment of this kind has long been a feature of the welfare com-plex in many countries. In some, notably America and Japan, it is a crucial element of the 'welfare mix'. Until recently, enterprise-based welfare was also central to Chinese and Eastern European provision (see chapter 56). Elsewhere in Europe, collectively negotiated employee benefits form a significant dimension of the welfare order. Whatever the setting, moreover, workplace welfare is widely promoted by the state, directly through legislation and indirectly through fiscal and other measures.

In the UK, however, apart from pensions, it has attracted little attention from policy analysts. In part, this reflects the limitations of official data and difficulties in accessing organizational information. But it is also a product of the widespread subsumption of employer provision within an undifferentiated notion of 'private' or 'market' welfare. Equally critically, workplace regulation and its place in regime theorization (see chapter 52) has not been integral to policy analysis but left to the discourses of economics, employee relations and human resource management (HRM). Hence this chapter, whilst framed by social policy concerns, draws on a wider literature. It outlines the definitional issues faced in studying occupational provision, recent developments in the UK and the policy issues raised by this form of welfare.

What is 'Occupational Welfare'?

Discussion of occupational provision within social policy stems from Titmuss's concept of the 'social division of welfare' (see chapter 1). Writing in the 1950s, he highlighted the extent to which the growth of state services had been mirrored by the spread of what he termed 'occupational welfare'. Though differing in inception, he argued the two were functionally equivalent and, from an individual's standpoint, met the same needs.

This notion of the correspondence between state and employer-sponsored welfare remains the starting point for research. Recent analysts vary, however, in their views of the constituents of occupational welfare and, in operationalizing it, distinguish between:

- a narrow definition – focusing solely on welfare arrangements voluntarily provided by employers; and
- a broader definition – embracing mandatory as well as voluntary schemes.

Some draw a further distinction, arguing that policy analysis should be confined to interventions with a clear social orientation. In practice, such demarcations are difficult to sustain. Whatever the derivation, workplace, like statutory services, have manifold, often overlapping, functions and welfare implications. Mandatory pro-

grammes often originate in measures developed by some employers for social as well as business ends. In requiring others to follow suit, obligatory and voluntary provision often operate symbiotically. Employers, for instance, may 'top up' statutory minima, secure powers to offer more generous schemes, or institute other services. Governments, in turn, may underwrite such developments through fiscal or other levers and press employers to expand into new areas.

Hence this chapter adopts a broad-based conception. In this, it is in line with current HRM analysis and practice. Here, occupational welfare is viewed as the above-base and incentive pay elements of the reward packages provided by employers that enhance employee well-being. This approach captures the scope and diversity of the services dispensed by employers and the many past and current incarnations of voluntary, mandatory and state-backed provision. It also allows for the role of employers' social protection contributions and increasingly important but less tangible time-based benefits such as holidays and leave arrangements.

The Main Forms of Occupational Welfare

Accordingly occupational welfare can be categorized along nine dimensions based on the type of support offered. The full range is discussed elsewhere, but table 26.1 provides an indication of the support that employees might benefit from. In considering these, a number of cross-cutting variables should be noted. First, spouses or partners and children may be included, though this varies with the form of provision and from employer to employer. Secondly, there are marked differences in modes of service delivery. Some organizations rely on in-house provision, others on external suppliers or combinations of both.

Table 26.1 The main forms of voluntary and mandatory occupational welfare

Type of Provision	Examples
Social security	Statutory social security contributions
	Mandatory and above-mandatory pay substitutes (e.g. sickness and redundancy payments, paid maternity, paternity and adoption leave)
	Voluntary pay substitutes (e.g. maternity and childcare grants, life, critical illness, disability and personal accident insurance, death in service and occupational pensions)
	Voluntary pay supplements (e.g. professional indemnity insurance, interest-free loans; affinity benefits)
Social care	Mandatory and above-mandatory leave arrangements (e.g. for parents, carers, civic duties,)
	Voluntary support services (e.g. counselling; pre-school, school-age and adult care, work–life balance and pre-/post-retirement services; lifestyle benefits)
Healthcare	Mandatory and above-mandatory health and safety measures
	Voluntary 'illness services' (e.g. private medical insurance and cash plans)
	Voluntary rehabilitation services (e.g. for individuals with ongoing health problems, returning to or re-entering employment)
	Voluntary 'wellness', 'well-being' and 'healthy ageing' services (e.g. screening, diagnostic and referral services; health education and promotion)
Education and training	Mandatory and above-mandatory health and safety and young workers' training
	Employer-provided training
	Employer support (e.g., for professional/personal development, children's education)
Housing	Employer-provided accommodation
	Voluntary financial assistance (e.g. with mortgage/rent, relocation, insurance)
Transport	Company cars
	Voluntary assistance (e.g. with car purchase/lease, other forms of commuting; driving lessons; tax; fuel; insurance)
Leisure	Organizational recreational facilities
	Voluntary support (e.g. for club/other membership, attendance at sports/other events)
Concierge services	Voluntary provision (e.g. information and referral services; cafeterias; meal allowances/vouchers; domestic services)
Community participation	Voluntary support for employees' community activities (e.g. school governorships; committee work; fund-raising; mentoring; secondments; leave)

Most fundamentally, they diverge radically in terms of the range, mix and service type offered and the ways these alter over time.

Ascertaining the extent and role of workplace welfare is, consequently, a complex task. Nevertheless, recent surveys generate similar profiles of the patterning of provision since the 1990s. First, employers' overall welfare responsibilities and the role of HRM staff as agents of the state grew as Labour incrementally extended or introduced mandatory schemes and used other incentives to persuade employers to widen their offerings. Concurrently, organizations launched a welter of new initiatives and revamped or curtailed others. Secondly, different types of provision were then reshaped along different lines with varying consequences for employees.

The most far-reaching changes were in occupational social security, for employers the most expensive and for employees the most valuable form of support. Most publicized were the restructuring of occupational pensions and the initiation of mandatory employee savings. Stimulated by tax concessions and contracting-out arrangements, the former had evolved into a crucial 'second pillar' supplementing Britain's minimalist state pension system. By the 1980s around half the workforce had such cover, mostly in the form of defined benefit (DB) final salary plans.

Maintaining them as part of a broader rebalancing of public and private pensions was integral to Labour's welfare agenda. But plummeting equity markets in the early 2000s, combined with tighter regulation, tax changes and concerns over rising longevity, led many firms to switch new employees to defined contribution (DC) money purchase or other low-cost schemes. This entailed a significant transfer of investment risk to employees at the accumulation and claimant stage. Public sector employers too were forced to adjust their historically more generous arrangements. Union pressure meant change was subject to protracted negotiation. But the general trend was to replace DB with cheaper though less risky career average plans.

To sustain occupational provision as part of its wider pension reforms in 2007, Labour proposed all employees be automatically enrolled from 2012 in a national system of personal accounts (PAs) or an approved occupational plan providing equal or better benefits. Tax-supported, but largely funded by compulsory employer and employee contributions, PAs are targeted at moderate to low-income earners without access to workplace pensions and intended to complement not compete with existing schemes.

Whether this will be the case or not is unclear. But in Labour's schema, occupational pensions remain a key welfare fixture, with employer and government-led provision operating in tandem along lines characteristic of other benefits. With fiscal assistance for small companies, over three-fifths of workplaces, for example, offered above-statutory occupational sick pay. Provision of above-mandatory redundancy pay also spread, with many organizations adding outplacement services to their benefit packages.

As crucially during the 1990s, leading employers widened their benefit portfolio to include a range of support schemes for parents and carers. Building on these initiatives, and in line with EU strategy, Labour gradually increased maternity leave and pay, introduced paid and unpaid paternity leave, as well as provisions for new parents to share leave. Despite substantial increases in employers' national insurance contributions, the universalization of these benefits spurred many to boost their offerings or add new benefits. Of these, the most common were supplements to pay in the form of affinity, discount and voucher schemes, provision of which burgeoned from the late 1990s.

A similar pattern of organizational and government-driven change characterized workplace care. One major development was the spread of employer-initiated counselling, advice and referral services. Filling a major gap in state welfare, these ranged from help with relationship, care and legal issues to financial and debt management. Giving employers some protection against stress-related litigation, they also encompassed work-related concerns. To offset pension changes, and filling another gap, some employers also developed retirement planning services. Numerous others initiated holiday, work–life balance, child- and eldercare measures.

Labour left much of this development to employers. But it required that all employers provide certain services and time-based benefits. Statutory holiday entitlements were progressively increased and emergency and flexible working request rights for carers and parents of young and disabled children instituted. Promotional, benchmarking and funding instruments were also deployed to persuade organizations to implement above-statutory and work–life balance services.

In developing counselling and care schemes, many, particularly leading-edge employers, redesigned their occupational health systems on more proactive lines and launched a plethora of 'wellness' and 'wellbeing' programmes. Training in a range of organizations was similarly reshaped. Some large firms established corporate universities, others accreditation for work-based learning, and there was a steady rise in staff development more generally. Concomitantly, employers increased support for employees' community activities, launched new concierge products and reoriented their leisure and transport services. Some also revamped accommodation support, notably by offering mortgage assistance rather than pensions.

In these areas too, Labour fostered employer action. The mechanisms used,

though, were promotional or fiscal, most visibly in workplace health and training. In contrast to northern and continental Europe, both were traditionally viewed as primarily an organizational responsibility. In furthering employer action, Labour sought to incorporate them more directly within a wider public strategy. Its public health agenda centred on organizations pledging more proactive services with the workplace as a key site for delivering preventative care. Its skills, 'train to gain' and lifelong learning policy similarly engaged employers in an assortment of partnership schemes (see chapter 42). Under the 2007 skills pledge, employers were expected to offer Level 2 training to all their staff by 2010 with the likelihood of statutory training in the event of non-delivery. To spur take-up, training was state-funded. But as with employee welfare tax subventions generally the fiscal transfers involved were far from transparent.

Variations in Occupational Welfare

The picture that emerges is thus of a substantial rise in occupational welfare propelled by the mandating of discretionary and a government-supported reshaping of voluntary provision. The latter, however, was far from uniform. In very general terms employer outlay varied according to:

- Organizational size: welfare systems were commoner in large entities, which also dispensed more generous schemes.
- Sector: public sector organizations were more munificent than commercial or voluntary organizations in the level and range of provision.
- Industry: companies operating in financial, professional and other 'knowledge' industries, capital-intensive manufacturing and high-end retailing invested more heavily in welfare programmes than those trading in other markets.

- Employment status: some benefits and services were provided for all or most employees, others confined to senior staff who were also often entitled to more comprehensive benefits.

This segmentation meant workplace welfare also varied along other dimensions. The concentration of women in the 'five Cs', in smaller firms and lower tiers of employment meant they were often excluded from or accessed a narrow range of benefits. Similar differentials pertained to members of ethnic minority groups. Despite equal opportunities legislation, coverage of some services, particularly training, varied enormously between full- and (mainly female) part-timers.

None of these disparities was new. But they were complicated by other factors, particularly the extent to which provision was contingent on employee contributions and the spread during the 2000s of flexible 'cafeteria' benefit and salary sacrifice systems. Though analogous to 'personalized' services and co-payments in public welfare, they added to the fragmented, amorphous nature of voluntary provision and the many variations in employer sourced, co-funded and tax-subsidized schemes.

Accounting for Occupational Welfare

For policy analysts the patterning of employer-sponsored welfare presents major conundrums regarding its genesis, distribution and the role of state-backed provision. Its roots clearly lie in a multitude of organization-specific considerations, as do fluctuations in the perceived value of different benefits. But recent study highlights a number of broad imperatives shaping the strategies of the main stakeholders in workplace welfare.

Governmental Calculations

Traditionally, governmental endorsement of occupational welfare has been attributed to five main factors. Irrespective of their political complexion, successive post-war governments viewed it as a means of meeting gaps in state provision whilst simultaneously containing and masking public expenditure through fiscal subsidies for employer schemes. In the case of pensions and other contributory schemes, it also helped finance government borrowing and corporate investment. But whereas Labour's stance was often ambivalent, Conservative administrations, particularly in the 1980s and 1990s, saw occupational schemes as a means of minimizing public welfare.

Labour's espousal of occupational welfare has been little discussed, but is an important element of its bid to modernize Britain's welfare system and economy. In part, the governments' interventions were driven by EU directives and the requirements of the EU Employment Strategy. But they were also structured by Labour's belief in conjoining social justice with economic efficiency through the construction of an enabling, opportunitizing, market-oriented welfare system. With paid work seen as the solvent of social exclusion, maximizing labour market participation lay at the core of its agenda. It was also essential to fund public services and support an ageing population. Boosting employment, however, was contingent on developing working practices supportive of parents, carers and employee well-being generally. They were also central to Labour's bid to plug Britain's long-standing productivity gap and meet the challenges of globalization. In its view, in order to compete in world markets Britain had to move away from high-volume production towards specialist trading in less imitable, added value knowledge-based products and services. Co-relatedly, to manage the requisite flexible, discretionary and relational labour, employers needed high-commitment HRM practices.

Public service reform was equally contingent on inculcating high-performance working. Hence, in promoting workplace welfare as part of its wider agenda, the government enjoined state agencies to lead by example. In this, it reverted to the post-war notion discarded in the 1980s and 1990s of public bodies' role as 'model' employers and disseminators of 'best practice'. Such thinking partly accounts for the long-standing differences in public and private sector occupational provision. It also underlies that in the voluntary sector. In both instances, however, it reflects competitive pressures from other employers and their varying calculations.

Employer calculations

Historically, one impulse was the notion of social stewardship, upheld by some leading Victorian and Edwardian employers and subsequently by the 'industrial welfare' movement in Britain and 'welfare capitalist' lobbies in America and Japan. These advocated occupational services to forestall state welfare. But they also propagated an enduring 'mutual gain' conception of responsible employers supporting their staff, with both profiting from consequentially high productivity. Similar thinking often underlies recent moves placing occupational provision under an organization's CSR banner.

The genuine welfare concerns prompting these developments should not be discounted. But most studies highlight the strategic and operational grounds for workplace welfare. As a corporate citizenship function, it secures the social legitimacy necessary to generate customer trust and a strong brand image. It is also, as radical analyses emphasize, a powerful tool in the management and control of the labour process. From these perspectives it was initially deployed to pre-empt unionization and minimize resistance to new modes of production, functions which arguably continue to underpin contemporary developments.

Where unions were recognized, however, they played a major role in the gestation and spread of workplace benefits, integrating them into their membership drives and collective bargaining as a means of plugging gaps in statutory welfare, income-enhancement or offsetting low pay rises and changes in work practices. Despite the steep fall in private sector unionization since the 1980s, union pressure remains a key element sustaining both employer provision and differences between workplaces. Benefit bargaining also remains significant in the heavily unionized public sector, contributing to the more extensive schemes offered to state employees. In this respect collective agreements as in Europe play a key but often overlooked role in the UK's welfare mix.

But for large employers particularly, occupational welfare has long served other labour management purposes. As a recruitment tool, it functions to attract high-calibre staff, especially in shortage areas and tight labour markets. In terms of retention, reward and performance management, it is a means of binding staff to an organization, sustaining internal labour markets and firm-specific skills and boosting productivity. As importantly, workplace schemes facilitate restructuring, enlisting support for technological and other change and cushioning redundancy. They also contribute to employers' human capital, reputation and risk-management strategies, countering the 'survivor syndrome' and compensating for flatter career structures. Welfare initiatives uphold these strategies directly and symbolically in other ways, by enhancing job satisfaction, minimizing absenteeism and maintaining employee motivation and well-being. Most critically, they contribute to a culture and polyvalent resource base that is difficult to replicate.

Recent economic developments have given added resonance to the role of occupational schemes in managing change and meeting the needs of increasingly diverse workforces. In these respects there is a correspondence, widely endorsed by HRM advisers and the benefits industry, between Labour's concerns and those of many employers. But their salience differs according to variations in capital, product and labour markets, technology and organizational size. Put simply, firms in markets characterized by intense, margin-based competition, with price- rather than quality-sensitive customers, or those in low-technology, labour-intensive sectors face very different pressures from those in high-technology, capital-intensive industries that are dependent on employees' expertise. The economics of production also varies with shareholder expectations and organizational size. But though 'knowledge' and related industries grew over the last decade, there was also a large-scale rise in routine, lower-level work in the service and care sectors, much of it undertaken by women and members of different ethnic minorities. The majority of employees, moreover, continued to work for small rather than large entities with their very different computations.

Emerging Issues

In the context of this 'hour-glass economy', the place of occupational provision and its interplay with taxation in Britain's welfare mix are likely to become more central in policy analysis. Though employees have gained significant new occupational welfare rights and many employer initiatives are workforce-wide, there are major intra- and inter-organizational differences in voluntary provision. Unlike state services, entitlement is determined not by social risk, need or issues of equity and social inclusion, but by employment status and HRM concerns.

The prime beneficiaries are those in the upper echelons of large organizations who also gain most from fiscal relief. Occupational provision reinforces the dispersion of disposable income and social divisions generated by a bifurcated economy. With employees in insecure, minimum or low-wage jobs least likely to access key benefits, particularly training, it also cements social immobility.

For some observers, the way forward lies in further mandation and fiscal support. Increased parental leave is under discussion and there is bipartisan support for flexible working request rights for all parents. Similar rights for all employees are being mooted, statutory training for all employees is under discussion within the government and the EU, as are proposals to strengthen occupational health and social care. However, there is also widespread opposition to mandation. From a neo-liberal stance, workplace welfare is a matter of employer judgement, and one that carries dangers of restricting employees' freedom to determine their welfare needs and services. Regulation distorts labour market behaviour, increases employers' costs and reduces their competitiveness in world markets. Whilst advocating an enabling platform Labour's policy-formers also oppose measures threatening personal incentives and wealth creation.

From other perspectives there is concern that, as potentially with pensions changes, mandation will foster new forms of differentiation. While common employee rights are necessary, social policy goals are best met through cutting tax relief for occupational benefits and investing in egalitarian state welfare to generate a flourishing economy. These issues are at the heart of social policy. With concern over class as well as other forms of inequality moving up the agenda of the OECD and EU, as well as in the UK, they are likely to frame debate over occupational welfare cross-nationally and in Britain.

Guide to Further Sources

The issues raised in this chapter are explored more fully in E. Brunsdon and M. May, 'Occupational welfare', in M. Powell (ed.), *Understanding the Mixed economy of Welfare* (Policy Press, 2007); M. May and E. Brunsdon, 'Commercial and occupational welfare', in R. M. Page and R. Silburn (eds), *British Social Welfare in the Twentieth Century* (Macmillan, 1999) and K. Farnsworth, *Corporate Power and Social policy in a Global Economy* (Policy Press, 2004).

Current developments can be tracked through the various studies conducted by Income Data Services, Industrial relations Service and <www.cipd.co.uk> (the Chartered Institute of Personnel Development website).

Chapter 27

Voluntary Welfare

Jeremy Kendall

Overview

- 'Voluntary welfare' is nurtured and delivered through a plethora of organizations situated between the market and the state.
- The scope, scale, structure and diversity of these organizations have increasingly been recognized and captured in empirical work, and through increasingly sophisticated theoretical accounts.
- Deepening interest in 'social capital' has latterly reinforced the existing trend to attend to the role of associations in social, political and economic life.
- Volunteering is increasingly understood as involving a wide and rich range of motivations and social structures.
- The increasing proximity of many of these organizations to the state has generated an increasingly animated debate.

Introduction

'Voluntary welfare' – meaning the contribution of organizations between the market and the state to social well-being – embraces an extraordinarily diverse range of activities. Many of these allow needs to be met in society that would otherwise go unrecognized and unmet. From pre-school playgroups, hospices and Age Concern groups well known in many local areas, to Barnardo's and the Child Poverty Action Group on the national stage, and CAFOD and Oxfam internationally, the scope and scale of this 'sector' are remarkable in Britain. The groups which populate it are often legally recognized as 'charities', although many organizations the public believe are charitable do not fall into this category, and others – such as independent schools and some exclusive hospitals – which the public believe are not, do fall into it. The legal position of 'charities' was changed with the implementation of the Charities Act 2006, which in part aimed to rectify some of this confusion by aligning the definition in law more closely to public perceptions and expectations. This was by a combination of widening the definition, on the one hand, and, on the other, making demonstrable public benefit a requirement for all registered charities for the first time.

Many other countries with long track records of liberal democracy also have their own rich traditions of voluntarism, although the form and shape they take varies dramatically from country to country. But increasing policy recognition of these groups in the UK has now reached such a level that they may be considered 'mainstream'. The key drivers for this development include policy-makers' beliefs that voluntary organizations can be more responsive, cost-effective or responsible than the alternatives, can exhibit greater sensitivity to the needs of socially excluded constituencies, and seem to be central in helping to generate social capital and foster social enterprise. Some of these beliefs are well based on evidence and argument, and others less so. This is all against the backdrop of a loss of faith in market and state solutions – the voluntary welfare sector is increasingly promoted as a necessary additional ingredient for supposedly exhausted narrow models of 'statism' for the political left, and 'market dogma' for the right. In this sense, the sector partly finds support for what it is not, as well as reflecting what it can demonstrably achieve.

Since the 1980s, the study of the voluntary sector, in relation to public welfare services and beyond, has taken shape as a recognizable multidisciplinary field of studies in its own right. At national and international levels, it now has university-based and other research centres, scholarly associations with significant and engaged memberships and widely read dedicated journals, which serve as vehicles for dissemination alongside other generalized social science media. It also has a very broadly delineated but increasingly well-mapped and anatomized subject matter – with comparative, international research a particularly challenging and vibrant element of this. It involves the application of styles of argument and analytic techniques honed in the traditional social science disciplines, so its embrace includes sociology, economics, political science and social psychology. But it also offers a space for creative new ways of blending approaches from within and across these disciplines, as well as

hosting and interacting with established interdisciplinary bodies of thought. We could think of its relationship with 'social policy' in this way, as well as its connections with 'public administration', 'policy analysis' and 'local government studies', for example.

Definitions and Types

An attempt to capture the diversity and variety which characterizes this terrain has been made with the label 'a loose and baggy monster'. Its fluidity and fuzziness have led some commentators to argue that talk of a 'sector' is unhelpful or even dangerous. Especially in the continental European discourse, some prefer metaphors such as 'space' or 'field', or represent the subject matter as part of (organized) civil society. Others (including this author) persist in using 'sector' pragmatically as a good enough form of working shorthand, while explicitly attending to diversity and fluidity as potential subjects of analysis rather than prior assumptions.

If one pragmatically accepts the 'sector' construct, how might this be defined? The definition of the sector is not only contested; it is *essentially* contested. There is no 'one size fits all' formula, but the appropriate formulation depends on the specific purpose of the analyst, against the backdrop of their values and priorities. For example, Marxists would tend to deny the possibility of a durably independent sector flourishing in actual existing capitalist systems. Another route is neo-elitist, also adopting an anti- or post-positivist epistemology, but now accepting the existence of the sector – albeit with roots as a project of 'construction' pursued in the interests of the powerful. That is, as a political construct flowing from the agendas of special interests, politicians and allied researchers. However, if we subscribe to a liberal, positivist worldview – involving the claim that there is an organizational terrain 'out there' which can be scientifically 'discovered' – a 'structural operational' definition seems to work well for cartographic purposes. This defines into the 'non-profit sector' *formally organized* entities which are *constitutionally/legally separate* from the state, bound *not to distribute surpluses* ('profits') to owners, and demonstrably benefiting from some degree of *voluntarism* (uncoerced giving) of money ('donations') or time ('volunteering').

Once we have identified our terrain in this way, it can then be useful to differentiate organizations within it in a number of ways, for heuristic or hypothesis generation and testing purposes. 'Types' can be distinguished according to their social functions – such as service provision, advocacy, innovation, 'community-building' (or 'community development') and value expressive roles. Other taxonomies refer to how leading actors' or constitutional instruments' values, norms and motivations compare – usually aligned to some normative view that some such are good/progressive/constructive/healthy – while others are not. Contrasts can also be made in terms of resource base (financial or human resource size and other measures of scale); and of governance/control rights distribution.

Also much used now is the policy field distinction (analogous to the idea of 'industries' in economic life, now tailored to the areas of salience for these groups). For British social policy purposes, this makes a good deal of analytic sense. We are usually interested in distinguishing, in decreasing order of economic (but not necessarily social) significance: education and research (only if maintained voluntary schools and universities are treated as in scope, despite their systemic proximity to the state), social care, development and housing, and health. Some writers would also include religion. The developmental trajectory of sector roles and relations has demonstrably varied

significantly from field to field. This is a reflection of variations in the policy legacies, ideologies and politically constrained national and sub-national government capacities which prevail in each case. The way 'mainstreaming' under current conditions concretely takes shape – and ultimately whether or not it helps or hinders the sector, and with what consequences – can similarly be expected to vary along these lines (cf. Kendall 2003, comparing the policy trajectories in social housing, care and support for older people, and environmental action).

Finally, distinguishing associations according to whether or not they evidence significant trust-building, interpersonal, face-to-face interaction was long a common practice in sociological accounts. But it is now increasingly widespread in interdisciplinary circles in the context of renewed interest in the sector as a vehicle for 'civic renewal' or social capital investment (see below). Thus 'secondary associations' – with demonstrably active memberships and apparently vibrant cultures of participation, reciprocity and networking – are seen as more conducive to economic and political success than 'tertiary associations' – that is, passive, 'armchair' or 'cheque book' membership-based associations (family and friendship circles being the 'primary' form of association).

Overall, the single formulation which probably has most currency in social policy 'on the ground' in Britain, cutting across these swathes, is probably still simply 'the voluntary sector'. But the interested student of policy also needs to be acquainted with the three overlapping official formulations of the central state and the most powerful regulatory arm thereof: the Charity Commission (see the Commission's website; also see the definitions of, and explanation for 'third sector' and 'social enterprise', as currently favoured, on the OTS, and Charity and Third Sector Finance Unit websites).

Theorizing the Third Sector

So far we have acknowledged the relevance of two epistemic traditions, the positivist 'discoverers' and the political 'constructors', as well as the (distinct) Marxist line of argument. As governments have become ever more preoccupied with 'performance' measurement, it is pertinent to note that the former broad distinction has also appeared in the analysis of 'effectiveness' and 'performance'. Positivist and social constructionist tools have both been used for evaluative purposes in relation to this sector in social policy fields. But most effort in the past two decades has probably gone into attempting to answer two further fundamental questions. First, why do we need a third sector at all in developed market economies? Second, what difference does the third sector make not only in terms of productivity in economic life, but also political performance? This is where 'social capital' has recently come to the fore.

A leading role in the field has been taken by economic theory – first as inspiration, and then as whipping boy. Arguably, indeed, this territory initially achieved critical mass as a significant autonomous multidisciplinary specialist area of knowledge (rather than as low-profile niches within disciplines), in large part thanks to the sharp analytic thinking of American economists in the 1970s and 1980s. Burton A. Weisbrod was one notable pioneer, suggesting that these organizations could be seen as a response to the inabilities of both markets and states to provide 'collective goods' (services where benefits cannot be limited purely to paying customers, and in which one person's consumption does not completely exclude that of other people). Up until that point, the mainstream assumption in orthodox economics was that the 'market failure' associated with the provision of public goods traduced a role for the state. Henry Hansmann was a second

leading instigator, with a theory of 'contract failure' pointing out how these organizations seemed to be providing under conditions of 'asymmetric information' where donors or users could not, for reasons of distance or vulnerability, surmise output quality. It was deemed they could be protected from exploitation by the non-distribution constraint – since there were no shareholders waiting in the wings, eager to profiteer at funders' and users' expense. Finally, Estelle James shifted attention from the demand to the supply side, pointing to the role of ideological (including religious and political) entrepreneurs in starting and sustaining such organizations. These insights have generated a debate within economics, with wide-ranging elaborations and syntheses, primarily in the US, but also used to frame analysis of the sector's policy and social roles in Britain.

Reacting against (catalysed by) the initial 'economistic' lines of reasoning, further, more socio-political models have been developed. The criticisms levelled have included these models' ahistorical character (not a 'problem' in fact for most economists, who tend to privilege predictive power over realism), their claimed failure to recognize patterns of cooperation (rather than substitution) as between sectors, their tendency to represent sectoral divisions of labour as reflecting free(ish), efficient choice and a stable demand, and their claimed tendency to privilege analysis of the 'service provision' function over others. Better, these critics argue, to see sector outcomes as reflecting some combination of macropolitical power; and/or to acknowledge the part played by needs rather than wants, and bring in normatively/duty-bound actors rather than sovereign consumers at the micro-level.

Prominent here has been Evers's welfare mix approach, bringing in non-instrumental rationalities, and emphasizing the tensions at stake between market-driven, state-driven and community-driven logics, and also Salamon and Anheier's social origins framework, borrowing conceptually from Esping-Andersen's welfare regime theory (see chapter 52). This is more institutionally specific than Evers's account, and has been applied empirically. It is an attempt to account for how the strategizing of elite political groups at key moments of welfare system design has formatively advantaged, or conversely marginalized, the third sector vis-à-vis the directly owned and controlled state.

Social Capital

Overlaying the approaches outlined above, 'social capital' now also exerts a powerful new influence on thinking in this field. This idea is not only concerned with delivering welfare services, but also with more general ties, habits, relationships and interactions in communities: these function better, it is claimed, when involving trust, reciprocity, stability and respect. So, it also clearly relates closely to the 'functions' of 'community-building' or 'community development' suggested earlier, with much longer pedigrees in the British context. What is new about contemporary community-oriented arguments is that relations of trust and norms of reciprocity are presented as not just socially constructive, but as economically and politically instrumental. The word 'capital' underlines economic value – while, at the same time, keeping in play the imagery of citizenship and public minded-ness. Robert Putnam's work is key here. The voluntary welfare sector, in particular those parts which are 'secondary' (see above) and/or involve volunteers, is now highlighted as a school for fostering civic skills, an arena for rebuilding decayed 'community' values, even 'renewing' democracy itself – while simultaneously strengthening economic performance. No wonder it appeals! But can we really have our cake and eat it? The argument is inten-

sifying, and the evidence base growing, with vibrant rounds of claim and counter-claim. This will run and run.

Voluntarism and Voluntary Welfare

Voluntarism – taken here to mean action not directly constrained by state coercion or market imperatives, and outside the informal sector (see chapter 28) – is an explicit ingredient in some of the theories encountered above, and implicit in others. Arguably, it should be placed centre-stage in any attempt to understand the relation-ship between this sector and policy. This is neither self-evident nor circular: two of the three current official policy definitions – 'third sector' and 'social enterprise' – don't in principle demand the presence of this as an active ingredient. (The 'charity' case does, since the default legal assumption is that those with ultimate governance control – 'trustees' – should not be paid.)

As state engagement with the sector has grown and public funds have flowed, espe-cially into larger organizations, private donations have dwindled in relative terms to become a fairly limited form of support. Despite much talk of a 'giving age' under-stood in terms of finance – with politicians, the National Council for Voluntary Orga-nizations (NCVO) and others looking jeal-ously across the Atlantic – in Britain as elsewhere in Europe, the main way volun-tarism is manifested is through unpaid labour. And while the global hours put in by paid workers were demonstrably similar to those of volunteers in the mid-1990s (the last year for which comparative data was available) in terms of numbers of people involved, the latter still vastly outnumber the former. (Most paid workers, even in the voluntary sector, are full time; most volun-tary workers contribute less than half a day per week.) Moreover, in the key policy field of social care (see chapter 44), even in 'full-time equivalent' terms, volunteering has remained more important than paid work in the sector – and across all sectors here, there are still many more volunteers than paid employees.

So, why do people volunteer? In Titmuss's time (see chapter 1), we would have alluded to the centrality of altruism fostered by market subordination, to be contrasted with the self-interest thought to characterize paid work (prototypical of markets). But the understanding of volunteering has come on in leaps and bounds, and a much more complex and variegated picture is now in evidence – although it is still arguably possible to discern broad distinctions between apparently more publicly and more privately oriented underpinnings. Recognized motivations for volunteerism which mix altruism and self-interest include deliberate or incidental 'social capital' building, investment in human capital (with advantages for the individual and society in terms of training and experience useful across working life), 'intrinsic' satisfaction from the act of volunteering and the associated processes of relationship-building with others, 'extrinsic' satisfaction from the results of volunteering, and the relatedly psychic benefits, or gains in self-esteem and respect.

Obviously, pro-volunteering state policies and funding programmes may directly or indirectly help or hinder organizations' capacity to recruit and retain volunteers. But there are numerous other ways in which social policy connects with volunteering. For example, formal education policy and other educative experiences are relevant, because socialization experiences seem to impact on people's basic disposition to volunteer. Attitudes towards volunteering – and the character of opportunities to get involved – seem to be systematically related to ethnicity, gender and social class, while the nature of paid work and domestic sphere commitments also seem to shape individuals' willingness and ability to get involved in volunteering.

Emerging Issues

Under New Labour, voluntary welfare gained a new significance, with plaudits much in evidence under both Blair's and Brown's premierships. All the other mainstream parties are equally keen to be seen to endorse these organizations for the reasons mentioned in the introduction. Recent and ongoing policy reviews confirm this in the case of the Conservatives, currently in opposition.

An ever-higher public policy profile – and the greater state proximity it is bringing – raises a range of concerns about autonomy, identity and social functioning. Marxist writers (and some influenced by the Foucauldian tradition), as well as those on the right in principle hostile to state intervention in all its forms (see chapter 8) tend to read this trend deterministically or fatalistically. For them, this trend does, or will, necessarily lead to these organizations' 'incorporation', 'co-option' or 'subordination'. However, those working from other analytic perspectives are more open to evolving evidence and argument, and consider the issue of how state and third sector can and do co-evolve as an empirical question.

As stressed before, there are necessarily severe limits to generalization here because of the sector's diversity in terms of, inter alia, size, substantive policy field, ideologies, level of engagement with the state, etc. However, we can perhaps highlight two key questions which commentators on policy in the years ahead will need to keep at the forefront of their analysis.

First, how do evolving, inherited and new third sector policies play out in practice – at the level of front-line implementation – from the perspective of the relevant organizations, and their stakeholders – not least, users/beneficiaries and volunteers? Rhetorical acknowledgement has reached, or is close to, saturation point; what matters now is the extent to which claims of policy supportiveness are followed through into concrete practice. Are assertions that these organizations and those involved with them will be given room to breathe – and even flourish as their relations with government get closer – being respected? The research to date is mixed on this point – especially in relation to the fractious financial dimension of transactions – and a very close eye will need to be kept on how the process pans out in the years ahead.

Second, are any relevant policies – including front-line practices – evolving in a balanced way? Are institutions and relations taking shape which respect the range of functions and diversity of roles we have identified? Perhaps the key challenge is to ensure that the drive to increase the sector's role in public service delivery does not undermine its functioning in other dimensions – including social change-oriented campaigning, and community development contributions.

Guide to Further Sources

A stimulating but demanding comparative consideration of the issues addressed in this chapter is provided by H. K. Anheier, *Nonprofit Organizations: Theory, Management, Policy* (Routledge, 2005). D. Billis and H. Glennerster, 'Human services and the voluntary sector: towards a theory of comparative advantage', *Journal of Social Policy*, 27/1 (1998): 79–98, is an interesting attempt to draw upon economic and organization theory to interpret the role of the sector. A. Evers and J.-L. Laville (eds), *The Third Sector in Europe* (Edward Elgar, 2003) offers a wide-ranging, rich and intriguing – although sometimes polemically anti-American – overview of current issues. J. Kendall, *The Voluntary Sector: Comparative Perspectives in the UK* (Routledge, 2003) provides the most systematic and up-to-date critical account. W. W. Powell (ed.), *The Nonprofit Sector: A Research Handbook*, 1st edn (Yale University Press, 1987) and W. W. Powell and R. Steinberg (eds), *The Nonprofit Sector: A Research Handbook*, 2nd edn (Yale University Press, 2006) are widely regarded as the 'bibles' of research on nonprofits in the US.

Anyone interested in social capital needs to read the work of R. Putnam. Moving from the sub-national, to the national and international are *Making Democracy Work* (Princeton University Press, 1993), *Bowling Alone* (Schuster & Schuster, 2000) and an edited collection, *Democracies in Flux* (Oxford University Press, 2002), which includes influential chapters by P. A. Hall on the UK and T. Skocpol on the US. D. Scott, 'The role of the voluntary and community sectors', in J. Baldock and N. Manning (eds), *Social Policy*, 2nd edn (Oxford University Press, 2007) offers a strong synopsis, and is recommended as complementary reading to this chapter.

Useful web sources include: <http://www.cabinetoffice.gov.uk/third_sector/index.asp> (the Cabinet Office for the Third Sector site); <www.ncvo-vol.org.uk> (run by the National Council for Voluntary Organizations, the main coordinating and infrastructure agency for information and policy development within the English voluntary sector); <www.vssn.org.uk> (Voluntary Sector Studies Network: the primary UK academic and research association); <http://www.hm-treasury.gov.uk/documents/public_spending_and_services/third_sector/pss_thirdsector_index.cfm> (HM Treasury Charity and Third Sector Finance Unit site, arguably as significant as the Cabinet Office site since the Treasury ultimately controls public expenditure).

Chapter 28

Informal Care

Caroline Glendinning and Hilary Arksey

Overview

- Informal or unpaid carers provide the majority of physical, emotional and practical support to sick, disabled or older people.
- Care-giving can have negative impacts on carers' physical health and emotional well-being.
- Carers can find it difficult to combine paid work with caring, but giving up employment, or reducing the number of hours worked, can have negative impacts on finances and future work prospects.
- Evidence suggests that the effectiveness of government policies to support carers has been of limited value.
- The future supply of informal carers may not be adequate to support an ageing population.

What Is Informal Care?

'Informal care' describes the extra help given to ill, disabled and older people by friends and relatives, as distinct from that given as part of a formal paid job such as nursing, care assistant, home help or support worker. Informal care refers to care provided in addition to the normal support that family members give each other as a matter of course. Carers of disabled or older people have different experiences and needs to people with childcare responsibilities. For example, people undertaking care of the elderly tend to be older than those bringing up children and at different stages in their employment career and life cycle. They may not live in the same house as the person they are looking after. Informal care is less predictable than childcare; the care recipient's condition may fluctuate or deteriorate over time and care commitments are therefore likely to increase rather than decrease, unlike the demands of caring for children. Reflecting these differences, social policies tend to treat informal care differently from childcare. As the population ages, the support provided by informal carers is increasingly important – indeed, informal carers are the main source of help for older people in all developed societies. A 2007 report estimated that the value of the support provided by carers in the UK was £87 billion a year – more than the annual total spend on the NHS, which stood at £82 billion in 2006–7.

Informal care can involve:

- personal or physical care – help with bathing, toileting, feeding, getting in and out of bed, moving around inside or outside the house;
- other practical help – shopping, cooking, cleaning, paying bills;
- keeping someone company or making sure they avoid danger.

Carers: Who Are They?

The 2001 Census asked everyone for the first time whether they cared for someone who was sick, disabled or elderly. Across England and Wales, there were about 5.2 million carers (one in ten of the population); about 175,000 of these were under the age of 18. Two-thirds (68 per cent) cared for up to 19 hours per week; 11 per cent for 20–49 hours per week and 21 per cent for 50 or more hours per week.

Compared to people giving only practical help, carers providing personal care are more likely to be close relatives, to live in the same household as the person they support and to have sole responsibility for providing support. Carers also offer considerable levels of support and encouragement to relatives and close friends with mental health problems, as well as helping them to deal with officials, managing finances and supervising medication.

Although it is people in their 50s who are most likely to be providing care, as the population ages, the number of older informal carers is increasing. Across the UK there are 1.5 million carers aged 60-plus; of these, almost 350,000 are 75 and over and more than 8,000 are aged 90-plus.

Traditionally, caring has been thought of as a female responsibility; overall, women are slightly more likely than men to be carers. But, as they get older, men are more likely than women to become carers and the amount of care they provide also increases. At age 85 and above, more than half of male carers and almost half of female carers provide more than fifty hours of care each week.

Many carers also have paid work; about one in eight adults working full-time are also carers, as are 17 per cent of part-time working adults. Female carers are more likely than male carers to work part time. Not surprisingly, the likelihood of carers working fewer hours or not at all increases with the number of hours spent on caring. The incidence of caring is highest among unemployed or economically inactive adults, of whom 21 per cent are also carers. However, it is not clear how far people give up paid work because of care commitments or become carers because they are already economically inactive.

The poorer health of people from minority ethnic communities suggests that there is likely to be a greater demand for informal care among these communities. In addition, difficulties in accessing appropriate health and social services may increase the demands on ethnic minority carers, who are also more likely to experience poverty, poor housing, lack of information and social isolation.

Partly reflecting the unequal distribution of ill-health and disability, Wales has a higher proportion (11.7 per cent) of carers than any English region. Within England, the north-east has the highest proportion of carers (11 per cent) and London has the lowest (8.5 per cent). There is a steady turnover of carers: each year a third of co-resident carers and 40 per cent of carers living in a different household become carers of others, and similar proportions stop caring.

The Consequences of Caring

Without adequate support, caring can damage carers' health, particularly their mental health and well-being. Many, particularly older, carers are not in good health themselves. The risks of bad health increase with the intensity (amount of time each week) and duration (length of time) given to caring. Nevertheless, many carers also report emotional rewards from being able to help someone they feel very close to.

Carers who give up paid work, reduce their hours of work or are prevented from following career opportunities lose out financially compared with non-carers. Their earnings are likely to be lower than average, particularly if they spend twenty or more hours a week caring. Caring often involves extra costs (for example on transport, laundry, extra heating, special food or equipment), so savings can be depleted. Social security benefits for carers do not make up for loss of earnings. Breaks in employment or low earnings are also likely to reduce carers' pension entitlements and increase the risk of poverty in their own old age, particularly for women.

There is evidence that carers experience many of the factors that contribute to social exclusion, including isolation, difficulty in obtaining help for their own health problems and difficulties in obtaining other services to help care. Indeed, an older or disabled person who has an informal carer is likely to be assessed as being less at risk, and therefore less likely to receive services, than someone living at home.

that academic researchers have generated to support its arguments. The Princess Royal Trust for Carers, founded in 1991, is another UK organization for carers which aims to influence policy, for example by representing carers on select government steering groups. Both organizations provide information and advice for carers through their websites and through local carers' groups and centres.

The UK is relatively unusual in providing a social security benefit directly to carers who have to give up employment in order to care. In 1975 the Invalid Carer's Allowance (now Carer's Allowance) was introduced for full-time carers who have only minimal income from other sources. Although the allowance is very low, carers do have direct entitlement to it, in contrast to some other countries such as Germany, where carers risk being financially dependent on the person they care for.

Since 1995, a series of initiatives has been introduced to provide carers with access to services (see box 28.1); responsibility for implementing these policies rests with local authorities. The 1995 Carers (Recognition and Services) Act gave some carers entitlement to an assessment of their circumstances and the needs arising from their care-giving role. This entitlement depended on the person receiving care also

Policies to Support Carers

The UK has a more extensive range of policies for carers than most other countries. Carers' issues rose on the policy agenda through the vigorous and effective campaigning of carers' organizations. Following its merger in 1986 with the National Council for Carers and their Elderly Dependants, the Carers National Association (now known as Carers UK) has developed into a highly successful campaigning organization, frequently using the knowledge

---

Box 28.1 Policy landmarks for carers

1995 Carers (Recognition and Services) Act
1999 National Strategy for Carers
2000 Carers and Disabled Children Act
2004 Carers (Equal Opportunities) Act
2007 New package of support and services for carers

receiving an assessment; moreover, carers had no entitlement to services in their own right. Subsequent policies have extended carers' rights to both assessments and services.

The 1999 National Strategy for Carers emphasized carers' needs for information, encouraged the establishment of local centres to provide advice and support and introduced the Carers Special Grant, which comprised £140 million over three years to enable local authorities to develop innovative and flexible respite care services to give carers a break. This funding has since continued, although in 2004 the ring-fencing was removed.

Under the 2000 Carers and Disabled Children Act, carers' rights to an assessment of their needs were strengthened and, for the first time, carers could receive services in their own right, or a cash direct payment instead to arrange their own services.

The 2004 Carers (Equal Opportunities) Act (which came into effect in April 2005) had even wider ambitions. When assessing carers' needs, local authorities have to consider their aspirations to participate in paid work, education, training or leisure, and must provide appropriate information, advice and support.

Further improvements in help for carers were announced in the 2006 White Paper *Our Health, Our Care, Our Say: A New Direction for Community Services*, which the following year were translated into a £33 million package of support and services. The majority of the money (£25 million) was for local authorities to provide emergency support services for carers. Again, this reflects the successful campaigning of Carers UK, which first drew attention to the difficulties experienced by carers in finding someone else to take over their responsibilities in a crisis such as sudden illness. The remainder was split between a national advice and information service to enable carers to access much needed infor-

mation about their rights and entitlements (£3 million), and an 'Expert Carers' programme which aims to provide training for carers to enable them to manage their own, and the health of those they are looking after, better (£5 million).

Meanwhile, the flexible working regulations included in the 2002 Employment Act gave parents of children under age 6 (18 if they are disabled), the right to request flexible working arrangements from their employer. In April 2007 this right was extended to at least some carers of adults and older people who live with the person they are caring for. Flexibility over the time and place of work and the ability to take time off in emergencies are essential for many carers to remain in paid work. However, there are no measures that compensate carers for any earnings they may lose as a result of taking time off, or that entitle carers to a period of paid leave to care for a terminally ill relative, as in Canada and Sweden.

How Adequate Are These Policies?

The Carer's Allowance remains one of the lowest benefits in the UK social security system. It provides only token replacement of the incomes lost when carers have to give up paid employment and, because of its stringent eligibility criteria, it does not encourage carers to combine work and care. Carers who spend long periods out of work altogether risk poverty in their own old age as only their minimum pension entitlement is protected.

The 1995 Carers (Recognition and Services) Act made only a limited impact. The number of carers' assessments was low, carers were often unaware that an assessment had taken place and few received written results of the assessment. Although the 1999 National Strategy was broadly welcomed, it was criticized for failing to address the poverty experienced by many carers, and also for a lack of coherence and possible conflicts between the different policy strands; for example, the government is keen that carers continue to care but at the same time it is (even more) keen that they take part in paid work. A further criticism was that the strategy did not address adequately the complex nature of care-giving relationships, or take account of the perspectives of care recipients.

Assessment practice and the provision of information to carers did not appear to improve significantly following the 2000 Carers and Disabled Children Act either. One study found that across ten local authorities, only a handful of carers were receiving support in their own right, such as taxi fares to attend carer support groups or evening classes, driving lessons or holidays.

Carers can also receive cash direct payments as well as services. These offer more flexibility, so that carers can, for example, buy substitute care in order to continue shift-working; this would not have been possible with traditional services. However, the number of carers receiving direct payments remains low and there are major variations between local authorities in the numbers receiving direct payments.

Key Issues and Debates

There are major questions about the adequacy and appropriateness of current policies to support carers. While the UK remains ahead of many countries in this respect, carers nevertheless remain at high risk of stress, poor health, social isolation and poverty in both the shorter and longer terms. For a number of reasons, these problems are not easy to resolve.

Who should be supported: disabled and older people or informal carers?

Opinion is divided as to who should be the primary target of policy – carers or disabled

and older people themselves? The National Strategy for Carers stated that 'helping carers is one of the best ways of helping the people they care for'. Practitioners and policy-makers may assume that the needs and interests of carers and the people they support are the same and can therefore be addressed by the same policies and services. However, as public awareness of carers has increased, organizations of disabled people have argued that this overlooks *their* rights for choice, control and self-determination. Indeed, disabled people have argued that the very terms 'care' and 'carer' imply dependency, that they are a 'burden' and are less able to make choices for themselves. Moreover, a policy focus on carers has been criticized for failing to recognize the reciprocity that underpins many care-giving relationships; many disabled adults and older people also care for others at the same time as needing support with their own personal and daily activities.

Research shows that providing services for disabled and older people is the most effective way of supporting carers, because it reduces the pressures on family and friends. At the same time, replacing some of the help provided by informal carers with formal services does not necessarily reduce the support provided by relatives and friends, though it may change the nature of that support. In Scotland, increases in funding for formal services for older people have enabled carers to concentrate on providing social support, such as keeping relatives company and taking them out, rather than having to undertake mundane tasks and intrusive intimate care; extra services for the older person also helped carers to sustain care-giving for longer.

Models of informal care in policy and practice

Traditionally, health and social care services have prioritized disabled and older people rather than the carers who look after them and this has led to carers occupying an ambiguous position. It has been suggested that social and healthcare professionals respond to carers according to one of four different models. The 'carer as resource' model treats carers instrumentally, as a taken-for-granted resource. The central focus is on the care recipient, and promoting carers' well-being is only important if it sustains care-giving. Carers' well-being receives slightly more attention in the 'carer as co-worker' model. Although the main focus of attention continues to lie with the person being looked after, carers' interests and well-being are encompassed within this model, albeit primarily on an instrumental basis. In the third model, carers are conceptualized as 'co-clients'; in other words they are seen as people with needs in their own right. Carers' interests and well-being are valued outcomes of policy and practice, and to that end services are provided aimed at making the caring situation easier for carers to manage. In the fourth, 'superseded carer' model, the need for support from an informal carer is dispensed with altogether by providing services that meet all the disabled person's support needs. Potentially, both the care recipient and the carer achieve independence.

Researchers argue that current policies are primarily based on the 'carer as resource' model, with some elements of the 'carer as co-client' model. Until the conceptual model underpinning policy shifts, it is likely that carers will continue to experience negative outcomes in their health, employment and finances.

Emerging Issues

Future demand for and supply of informal care

Population ageing is a global phenomenon; most countries in the Western world are experiencing decreasing fertility and increasing longevity, which has led to a shift in the age structures of populations. There are uncertainties about future disability trends, but there is some evidence to suggest that increasing life expectancies will see an increase in the length of time people spend with light and moderate disabilities, but not severe disabilities. Technology developments and changing patterns of healthcare will also increase the numbers of people needing extra support to live at home. Governments worldwide are concerned about whether in future the supply of informal care will keep pace with rising demand. However a number of factors affect the future supply of informal care:

- Population ageing also affects carers themselves; whether older people are able to support their partners and spouses will depend upon their own state of health.
- Adult children are less likely to live with their elderly parents than in previous generations. Although there is no evidence that they are less likely to care, they are less likely to be able to provide intensive personal care from a distance.
- Changing attitudes may lead potential carers to want to avoid the restrictions of care-giving.
- Disabled and older people may also expect greater choice and control over who supports them, with, therefore, the option of receiving help from informal carers or formal services.

Given the future demand for informal care and the willingness of many to provide that care for people they are close to, informal care will continue to provide a significant input. However, based on current patterns, the future supply of informal care is likely to fall short of increases in demand. Modelling projections of likely demands for long-term care services in England for people aged 65 years and above suggest that spouse carers are likely to become increasingly important, which raises issues about their support needs given that spouse carers are often elderly and in poor health themselves.

Competing priorities: care-giving versus employment

A growing area of debate – in many countries as well as the UK – is how to resolve the tensions between demands for informal care and the demands of the labour market. The peak age for beginning caring is 45–64 years; many carers (including women) are therefore in paid work when older relatives begin to need substantial help.

The National Strategy for Carers suggested that carers should be able to give up work to care altogether if that is their wish. However, those who decide to stop work do not currently receive adequate income maintenance benefits, adequate protection of their future pension entitlements, or targeted help to return to work once caring commitments cease. The 2004 Carers (Equal Opportunities) Act requires practitioners to consider carers' wishes relating to training and paid work when conducting assessments. There is still a long way to go, though, before social services practitioners recognize that it is legitimate for carers to take part in paid work and are able to offer appropriate services that are acceptable to both the carer and the person needing support.

Guide to Further Sources

Summaries of the 2001 Census data can be found in L. Buckner and S. Yeandle, *We Care – Do You?* (Carers UK, 2005). K. Stalker (ed.), *Reconceptualising Work with 'Carers': New Directions for Policy and Practice* (Jessica Kingsley, 2003) summarizes key debates on carers, including caring relationships, diversity, carers' participation and legal and quality issues. M. Howard, *Paying the Price. Carers, Poverty and Social Exclusion* (Child Poverty Action Group, 2001) examines policies and financial support for carers, from the perspective of carers themselves.

T. Shakespeare, 'The social relations of care', in G. Lewis, S. Gewirtz and J. Clarke (eds), *Rethinking Social Policy* (Sage, 2000) challenges assumptions about 'care', 'dependency' and 'independence'.

L. Pickard, R. Wittenberg, A. Comas-Herrera, B. Davies and R. Darton, 'Relying on Informal Care in the New Century? Informal Care for Elderly People in England in 2031', *Ageing and Society* 20 (2000): 745–72, analyses factors affecting future demand for, and supply of, informal care. L. Pickard, 'Carer break or carer-blind? Policies for informal carers in the UK', *Social Policy and Administration* 35/4 (2001): 441–58, compares policies aimed at supporting informal carers with those aimed at supporting older people themselves.

J. Twigg and K. Atkin, *Carers Perceived: Policy and Practice in Informal Care* (Open University Press, 1994) uses evidence from carers and health and social care professionals to explore the reality of how service providers respond to carers and sets out four conceptual models of the relationship between informal carers and services.

The best starter websites are: <www.direct.gov.uk/carers> (a government site aimed at health and social care professionals who work with carers) and <www.carersuk.org> (the website of Carers UK which contains information about and for carers, including benefits, services and help for carers in employment and details of current campaigns relating to carers. It also hosts the pages of Employers for Carers – a source of examples of good practice for employers who want to support the carers in their workforce).

Chapter 29

Paying for Welfare

Howard Glennerster

Overview

- Some of the reasons why we have come to pay for many of the most important things in life through some kind of collective state funding lie in the economic theory of market failure.
- Another reason lies in the spread of our needs through the life cycle. Many arise when our claims on income are weak. The welfare state is, in large part, a savings bank that works when private banks cannot.
- How we pay for these services publicly or privately matters not just in terms of how the burden falls on rich and poor, but in taxation's impact on efficiency in the wider economy. How welfare institutions are funded also affects their own efficiency.
- Many welfare services are paid for privately both in cash and in time spent by carers.
- The scale and variety of funding mechanisms are described.
- Governments are using new ways to respond to the challenge of an ageing population, rising expectations of service standards and growing reluctance to pay through taxation.

Who Pays Matters

None of the ideals discussed elsewhere in this volume is attainable unless the means to achieve them are paid for by someone. Meeting socially defined needs, through some kind of welfare state, or providing for the care and education of those in one's own family, costs money. Who pays and how are of central importance to voters and to families.

If we have a generous set of public services and yet we pay for them through heavy taxes on the poor, we are not helping, but crippling them. If the way we tax people or means-test them is a big disincentive to work or save, that too is inefficient. If you, as a graduate of social policy, go to work in a human service agency, the first thing you will become aware of is its budget limit and the resources you have available to do a decent professional task. How do schools get their cash, or hospitals or social service organizations? Your working life will not make much sense unless you can answer these questions.

What Are We Paying For?

Other contributors to this volume have discussed what social policy means in general terms. For our purposes, we define it as the allocation of scarce resources necessary to human existence and well-being. We are not concerned with the economics of video recorders – at least not yet! Of course, the notion of exactly what is a basic necessity changes over time and between societies. The dilemmas about paying for the costs of such needs are, however, universal.

In this chapter we are concerned with the costs of ensuring that no one falls below an acceptable minimum standard of living, that citizens have an adequate diet, shelter, education and healthcare. We are concerned to ensure that those who can no longer look after themselves because of old age or infirmity are adequately cared for. How we pay for those ideals is one of the central political and economic debates of our time.

Market failure

There is no intrinsic reason why any of these services should not be purchased by individuals for themselves, if they have the money. All are purchased privately by the rich. Many economists argue that the state should confine itself to giving poor people enough money to exist and should cease to provide such services itself. That case was made in a highly influential book many years ago by Milton Friedman (1962).

There are, however, some basic characteristics of many human needs and the services that meet them that mean that they are not well suited to individual purchases in the marketplace. We cannot buy clean air in bottles and consume it as a private product. If the air is clean, it will be enjoyed by the whole population of our own and other countries. This 'non-excludability' is characteristic of what economists call a 'public' or 'social' good. Where goods and services are like this, we say that markets fail. (For a simplified account of market failure, as it applies to social policy, see Glennerster 2003.)

Nevertheless, such public goods are not free. We pay for the cost of clean air regulations in the price of goods produced in factories that have to install filters and burn smokeless fuels. A recent government report in the UK estimated the costs of taking action to limit climate change *and* the costs of doing nothing (HM Treasury 2006).

While some aspects of social policy concern the production of public goods such as clean air, others do not. We may be able to buy medical care or education, for example, but may make inefficient choices as private consumers since the information we need to choose efficiently is not readily available. There is an imbalance of information between seller and buyer. Economists call this a problem of information failure.

Furthermore, the thing we may want to buy might be so far in the distance that we find it difficult to take it seriously; worrying about future care in an old persons' home is a good example. How many of us are exercised about that? Pensions are another, slightly different, example. People put off taking action even if they know that theoretically they should take out a private pension. This kind of market failure, studied in the new behavioural economics, is discussed in the report of the recent UK Pensions Commission (First Report 2004).

Market failure, information failure and 'behavioural' failure between them explain why, in most of the world, many human services are provided and paid for, not through ordinary private markets but through collective means of funding – taxes, insurance contributions and the like or through compelling private action. Requiring or strongly encouraging membership of a private pension scheme is an example of the latter. None of this, notice, is logic-driven by the motive of being nice to poor people. This argument for state intervention is that it is more efficient in these special cases.

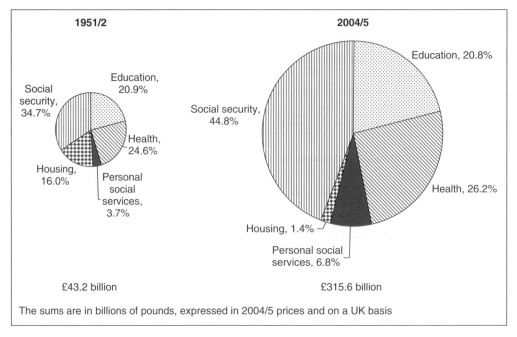

Figure 29.1   The size of the welfare state, 1951/2 and 2004/5
Source: Glennerster 2007.

Savings bank

We collectively pay for such services for another reason too. Many things we need, such as education for our children, a new home for the family, healthcare and pensions, cannot be financed very readily at exactly the time we want them. When we are ill, we have little, or possibly no, income to pay high healthcare costs. Education and housing are very expensive and demand payment early in a family's existence, before it has had time to amass sufficient savings. Only if the family has rich parents, a secure inheritance or a secure asset like a house will banks lend it the money to pay the bills now and repay later. So the market may make it possible for some families to borrow now to pay later for expensive necessities, but will not do so for most people and certainly not for the poor. This is called a 'capital market failure'. This is particularly important in the case of education. An able student with poor parents will not be able

to get a bank loan. Her human capital will not be developed to its full extent in the absence of a loan and this too is inefficient as well as unjust. This is the case for the state to make such a loan.

Part of what social policy is doing, therefore, is to shift the time at which people pay for the services they need from periods when they cannot pay to times when they can. Social policy is acting like a lifetime savings bank (Falkingham and Hills 1995).

How much does the government spend?

There is another way of looking at the question of what we are paying for. The total social policy budget funded by taxation is spent in ways that can be seen in figure 29.1. Pensions and other social security payments constitute 45 per cent of the total. The share taken by social security was much lower over fifty years ago when there was less unemployment and fewer old people. Then housing was a more important cost to the state. Now most people are buying their own houses. Education and health take a fifth and over a quarter of the total cost respectively of publicly funded welfare services.

Who Pays?

Despite the natural focus on public tax-financed social services in this volume, many of the human services included in social policy's remit are paid for directly out of individuals' own earnings or by private borrowing or insurance policies. In addition to this form of private welfare, firms may provide their employees with pension schemes or healthcare. Titmuss (1970) called this occupational welfare. A study by the Centre for the Analysis of Social Exclusion (CASE) at the London School of Economics calculated how much of the total costs of welfare were paid for in these different ways (Burchardt, Hills and Propper 1999; updated in Smithies 2005). It was the first time since Titmuss's early work that the national accounts had been recalculated to cover this range of funding sources. It turns out that 40 per cent of the nation's income is spent on the broad purposes of providing human services – the long-term care of dependent elderly, health, education, pensions and housing. Even this does not cover items not included in the nation's accounts: the care provided by family for its own members, which is discussed in chapter 28.

Of the total 'welfare activity' defined above, roughly 70 per cent is funded by the state out of taxation. That figure varies enormously between services. Roughly 70 per cent of the costs of housing are paid directly by individuals, but only 20 per cent of education and 15 per cent of health costs. This leaves a very large sum – £332 billion in 2005/6 – to be paid out of taxes. This is equivalent to 28 per cent of the country's total of incomes or Gross Domes-

tic Product (GDP). More than a quarter of everyone's income has to be taxed away to pay for these services or cash benefits.

Unusually among advanced industrialized countries, the UK relies overwhelmingly on taxes raised by the national government to pay for its social services. Less than 5 per cent of government revenue is funded by taxes raised by local government – the council tax. Health and social security are directly provided by central government agencies in one form or another. But housing, education and personal social services are not, and there has to be a complex system of grants that re-channels the taxes raised by central government to pay local council to provide them. In addition, government may tax some individuals less heavily to encourage a particular form of saving for retirement, house purchase or giving to charity. Economists call these flows tax *expenditures*.

Who Decides?

Her Majesty's Treasury is the central government department responsible for advising the Cabinet as to how much the economy can afford to spend on public programmes and it masterminds the complex round of negotiations between the spending departments that determine how much is to be available to, for example, the health service or universities in the next year. In 1997, Gordon Brown, then Labour Chancellor, changed the timing of these negotiations from an annual spending round to a biennial one, and more recently to a three-year cycle. Major decisions about which service gets what are taken as part of this Comprehensive Spending Review. These decisions, approved by Cabinet and Parliament, determine how much the NHS, universities, schools and local authorities will receive.

Local councils now get a grant which must be spent on schools and a general or untied grant which they can spend on any of their services. They also receive small specific grants which are tied to particular smaller services. What they are permitted to raise additionally from the council tax is heavily constrained by government rules. That tax is based on the value of property owned in the area. The basis of local taxation has always been politically controversial, never more so than the poll tax when Margaret Thatcher was Prime Minister. The whole basis of local finance was reviewed in 2007 by the Lyons Inquiry in England and the Burt Committee in Scotland.

Central government also allocates money to local health authorities and does so on the basis of a population-based formula which gives an area more money if it has more elderly or ill or poor people, because they use health services more. Once these local agencies receive their money, they then allocate it to increasingly autonomous units such as schools or hospital trusts. Schools compete for students and are paid for each one they attract. Hospital trusts compete for patients and are paid for those they treat. Social services departments pay their own old people's homes or voluntary agencies or profit agencies to provide services for the old or the disabled. Since 1997, there has been a very big shift in the funding of these latter services. In the past, most services for older people were provided by employees of local councils often working in residential care homes owned by the council. Now these homes are more often owned by private agencies. Places in these homes or services provided in people's own homes are bought from private providers. Private agencies also provide care to old people in their own homes but are funded by local councils (see chapters 24, 25, 34).

Required or Encouraged Behaviour

Governments can seek to encourage private individuals to act in ways that provide for their own welfare – to buy a house or save for their own pension. They have traditionally done so by giving tax relief to those who take out mortgages – no longer the case in the UK – or they reduce taxes for those who invest in a private pension. The government has proposed the introduction of another kind of incentive to get people to save for their retirement. Young people are often reluctant to take the initiative and save for retirement because the investment decisions are complex and retirement seems a long way away. However, evidence from other countries suggests that if employees are automatically opted into a private pension scheme, and if employers are required to add to those contributions, and government supplements them, then most people will not take steps to opt out. That, at least, is the hope that lies behind the government's latest pension plans (see chapter 26).

Vouchers and Quasi-Vouchers

So far we have described the way grants are allocated to local authorities and then onto bodies like schools and hospitals. Some economists argue that these institutions would be more likely to work efficiently if users had some sanction over them – the chance to choose another provider. There are pros and cons to this case (Le Grand 2003; Burgess, Propper and Wilson 2005). It is important to recognize that giving state schools, or hospitals, money on the basis of the number of children or patients they attract is already a form of voucher – a 'quasi-voucher' system.

Giving

Individuals give large sums of money and time to voluntary organizations, and statutory ones too, helping to visit old people or run youth clubs. Giving cash attracts tax relief, but giving time does not. In his classic study of blood-doning, Titmuss (1970) showed how giving blood to the National Blood Transfusion Service without compensation was not only a tangible example of individuals contributing to a larger social whole and enriching that society in the process, but also turned out to be a more efficient process because donors had no incentive to lie about their medical history. If blood donors were paid for their contribution, there would be more risk of infected blood entering the system, and people would have more of an incentive to lie about their medical history.

Feminist writers (see chapters 13, 28) have made us much more aware of the scale of giving that takes place within the family when women, and to a lesser extent men, undertake caring tasks. The personal social services budget would need to double if we were to pay women for these duties.

Rationing

We have seen that the Treasury essentially sets the limits to public spending on the social services – under political direction of course. The result is that the supply of these services is fixed by political decisions. Yet these services are free, or at least partly free. Prices cannot rise to levels that will equate demand with supply. The result is that service providers have to take some action to set priorities and ration care. As is also discussed in chapter 18, this may take the form of rules and entitlement to benefit, or judgements made by professional staff working to fixed budgets. The budgets they get may be the result of an explicit priority decision that a particular part of the service receive a given sum for that year, but exactly which patient or class of patient gets the service will usually depend on judgements made by professional staff in the front line. Rationing of scarce social policy resources thus takes

place in a whole range of decisions, which descend from fairly explicit judgements made by Cabinet about what each service will receive through more explicit allocations on a formula basis to areas and, indeed, to institutions like schools. But these are followed by front-line and less explicit judgements about which child in a class or which social work client gets most of the worker's attention. This is discussed more fully in Glennerster 2003.

Emerging Issues

The number of people over the traditional retirement age is rising faster than the number of families of working age. People are spending a growing proportion of their adult lives in retirement. The cost of providing health and social care for the over-70s and especially the over-80s is much higher than for younger age groups and the costs will fall increasingly on those of working age. This could add more than 5 per cent of GDP to the cost of the welfare state without any improvement in standards. The Pensions Commission (2005) recommended that the length of working life should rise in line with life expectancy so that the percentage of our lives we spend in retirement should remain constant. The UK government is in the process of implementing that recommendation, which is in line with policies in some other European nations – Sweden and Germany, for example. The costs of the health and social care systems will also rise sharply as they serve older people.

As demands for better services grow and the age structure of the population means costs rise, so the electorate is growing increasingly reluctant to pay substantially more in tax. The very small degree of local funding in the UK compared to other countries will come under scrutiny, as will the form of that local taxation. Proposals for change are under discussion.

The growing use of private and not-for-profit providers as the delivery agents for tax-funded welfare services is controversial and will continue to be hotly debated. In higher education, those who benefit will be increasingly expected to contribute to the costs of an education that makes them significantly better off. This is happening in England and it has long been the case in Australia. The model is attracting interest in other parts of Europe – but it is equally controversial.

The dilemmas facing families where elderly relatives need care and the family cannot provide it will grow. How far should the state provide that care free of charge and how far should families contribute to, or people be required to save for, their own old age? This is going to be a growing debate.

Guide to Further Sources

T. Burchardt, J. Hills and C. Propper, *Private Welfare and Public Policy* (Joseph Rowntree Foundation, 1999) covers some of the key issues addressed in this chapter in more detail, especially the complex ways in which public and private funding and provision interact. For an update, see R. Smithies, *Public and Private Welfare Activity in the United Kingdom, 1979–1999*, CASE paper no. 93 (LSE/CASE, 2005).

The Burt Inquiry 2006 and papers undertaken for it contain a useful history of local government finance in Scotland as well as an analysis and recommendations for change; available at: <www.lyonsinquiry.org.uk>. J. Falkingham and J. Hills, *The Dynamics of Welfare* (Harvester Wheatsheaf, 1995) shows how and why the welfare state redistributes income through the lifetime. M. Friedman, *Capitalism and Freedom* (University of Chicago Press, 1962), a very influential book, makes the case for minimal government intervention, vouchers and student loans. H. Glennerster, *Understanding the Finance of Welfare. What Welfare Costs and How to Pay for It* (Policy Press, 2003) covers all aspects of the finance of social policy and theories of rationing.

J. Le Grand, *Motivation, Agency and Public Policy: Of Knights and Knaves, Pawns and Queens* (Oxford University Press, 2003) sets out the case for giving consumers the power of choice between schools and providers of medical care as a way of encouraging better standards of service. The evidence is debated by S. Burgess, C. Propper and D. Wilson, *Choice: Will more Choice Improve Outcomes in Education and Healthcare? The Evidence from Economic Research* (The Centre for Market and Public Organisation, 2005). R. M. T. Titmuss, *The Gift Relationship* (Allen & Unwin, 1970) offers a different view, presenting the donation of blood as a parable for the virtues of giving in modern societies.

A stimulating review of the issues facing local government can be found in the report of the Lyons Inquiry (2007) and accompanying evidence and research papers <www.localgovernmentfinancereview.org>. Other major issues are covered in the Pensions Commission (First Report), *Pensions: Challenges and Choices,* The Stationery Office, 2004), Pensions Commission (Second Report), *A New Pensions Settlement for the Twenty-First Century* (The Stationery Office, 2005) and HM Treasury, *Stern Review: The Economics of Climate Change* (Cambridge University Press, 2006; also at: <stern.review@hm-treasury.gov.uk>). The Treasury website (<www.hm-treasury.gov.uk>) is also useful for giving up-to-date figures on public spending, the economy and taxation.

Chapter 30

Citizenship and Access to Welfare

Ruth Lister

Overview

- The principles governing access to welfare are, in part, an attempt to ration resources.
- A key criterion for assessing these principles is the extent to which they ensure that needs are met.
- Need may be interpreted in broad or narrow ways, drawing on principles of universal citizenship or selectivity.
- Access to welfare depends on residence status and is mediated through rights (conditional or unconditional) or discretion.
- Proposals to enhance welfare include substantive reforms to widen access and procedural or process reforms, designed to ensure respectful treatment of users, the securing and enforcement of rights and user-involvement in the development of welfare.

Introduction

Definitions of social policy tend to centre on human welfare and on the societal institutions designed to promote it. A critical question both for social policy and for individuals and groups is how resources, limited by economic and political constraints, are allocated so as best to promote welfare and meet human needs. In other words, social policy is partly about how resources are rationed. This chapter discusses the key competing principles which govern this rationing process and thereby the rules determining the access of individuals and groups to welfare, with particular reference to citizenship.

It begins by introducing some of the principal concepts upon which the chapter will draw, within the framework of different approaches to meeting need. The second section focuses more explicitly on the key principles governing access to welfare and their implications, drawing mainly on social security benefits as illustration. These principles are set out in diagrammatic form in figure 30.1. The chapter concludes by exploring some of the ways in which welfare might be enhanced through the promotion of citizenship and welfare rights.

Different Approaches to Meeting Need

A primary criterion for assessing the different principles governing access to welfare is whether the rules derived from them are

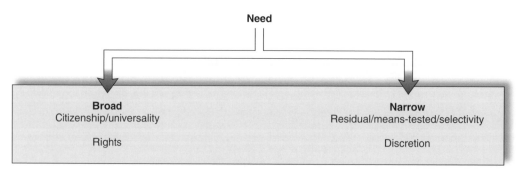

Figure 30.1   Access to welfare: interpretations of need

successful in ensuring that people's needs are met. The concept of need was discussed in chapter 4; it is by no means straightforward when applied to the question of access to welfare.

On the one hand it is invoked to justify an approach to social welfare which is *rights*-based and which is founded on the principle of *social citizenship*. As is further discussed in chapter 5, in this formulation the principle of need is counterposed to that of the market. The principle of social citizenship overrides (at least in theory, even if not always in practice) that of the market, in that it is argued that every member of society has a right to be able to participate fully in that society. This right has to be underwritten by the state so as to ensure that people are not totally reliant on the labour market to meet their needs. Social rights are necessary to enable people to exercise their political and legal rights. For example, without a home, it is very difficult to get on the electoral register, never mind receive a polling card. And although in theory we are all equal before the law, in practice some are more equal than others, so that without assistance from, for instance, the Community Legal Service, access to the law for those people living in poverty is effectively blocked. Nor, arguably, can people be expected to fulfil their responsibilities to the wider community as citizens if that wider community is

not prepared to ensure that their needs are met.

The principle of citizenship is also about equality of status. Consequently, those subscribing to it argue that everyone should have access to the same set of rights, the principle of universality, instead of dividing off people in poverty from the rest of society through the application of selective mechanisms, such as means-testing, which promote residual welfare.

Yet proponents of such selective mechanisms also appeal to the concept of need to justify their position. When resources are limited, the argument goes, they should be targeted upon those who really need them. Targeting can take various forms including, for instance, according to age. However, the most common mechanism, particularly in social security schemes, is means- or income-testing, whereby assistance is limited to those whose resources fall below a certain level (see chapter 38). The use of discretion, whereby officials or professionals decide what an applicant needs and what she can have instead of the applicant being able to claim on the basis of predetermined rights, is another approach, more common in the provision of services such as housing and community care. This individualized approach, it is contended, is more likely to ensure that the individual's 'true' needs will be met than one based on rigid rules. The disadvantages of such selective approaches are explored below.

In practice, the distinction between rights and discretion in meeting needs is not as clear-cut as this discussion might imply. On the one hand, officials often have to exercise judgement or discretion in applying the rules governing rights; on the other, discretion is frequently exercised on the basis of (non-legally binding) guidelines set down by central or local government. Nevertheless, as the basis for organizing access to welfare they represent two very different approaches. Together with the citizenship versus residual welfare models (discussed in chapter 52), these distinctions have implications for the welfare achieved by individuals and social groups, which are explored in the next section.

Access to Welfare

Immigration and residence status

First, we need to take a step back and consider what, for newcomers to a country, is the first gateway to access to welfare: rules which include or exclude people on the basis of their immigration or residence status. As chapter 51 also shows, one way in which nation-states can limit the resources devoted to welfare is to limit the access of non-nationals both through restrictive immigration and asylum laws and through circumscribing access to welfare for those immigrants and asylum-seekers allowed into the country. Here citizenship is being used as a tool of exclusion rather than inclusion, overriding rather than underpinning the basic principle of meeting need.

Many Western countries are now using both immigration and welfare laws to exclude 'outsiders' from their welfare benefits and services. Behind the ramparts of 'Fortress Europe', tougher laws have been enacted to exclude immigrants and asylum-seekers. In the UK, access to welfare has been tied more tightly to immigration or residence status, thereby making it more difficult for immigrants and asylum-seekers to receive financial or housing assistance from the state. This then may have consequences for minority ethnic group 'insiders', who might be subjected to greater scrutiny when claiming welfare; some can be deterred from claiming altogether for fear that their own immigration status might be jeopardized or to avoid racist practices.

Discretion

The potential for racist or other prejudiced attitudes leading to discriminatory decision-making by those controlling access to welfare is one of the chief arguments against the discretionary approach. Its roots lie in charity, where access to welfare was as likely to be governed by considerations of merit or desert as much as by need. It was partly in reaction to this that a number of rights to welfare were enshrined in the post-war welfare state. Nevertheless, discretion continued to play a role.

In the British social security system, the extent of this role in the safety-net social assistance scheme was a major focus of debate in the 1960s and 1970s. Much of the criticism of the scheme was directed to its continued heavy reliance on discretion, which was seen as acting as a rationing system which put too much power in the hands of individual officials, leaving claimants uncertain as to what they might get and without any rights to back up a claim for help. Gradually, the scope of discretion was reduced, but one of the most controversial aspects of the reform of social security in the mid-1980s was its revival in the form of the social fund – a cash-limited fund paying out mainly loans to meet one-off needs such as furniture and bedding. Discretion was reintroduced explicitly as a rationing mechanism to reduce expenditure on such one-off payments. The social fund is an example of how discretion can be managed on the basis of detailed official guidelines, without giving claimants themselves clear rights. More recently, the scope for discretion in some rights-based programmes has been widening again (see chapter 38).

Discretion plays a more prominent role in the social assistance schemes of many other European countries and in the UK in the service sector. Even if a right to a service exists, it is harder to specify how that right should be met by the statutory authorities, and professional interpretations of need come to the fore, again in the context of the rationing of limited resources. Thus, for example, the right to healthcare, enshrined in the British National Health Service, does not constitute a right to any treatment a user might demand; her right to treatment will be interpreted according to health professionals' assessment of her need.

In the field of community care, local authorities have a duty to assess the needs of disabled people, but they can then exercise their discretion as to whether and how they meet any needs that may have been identified. The exact boundaries between discretion and rights are, however, rather hazy here, as, in a few cases, the legislation has been used to require a local authority to provide a service once a need has been established. The problem is that, as long as local authorities' own resources are so limited, the temptation will be not to identify the need in the first place, so that discretion again comes into play as a rationing device. The same applies to the duty on local authorities introduced subsequently to meet the separately assessed needs of carers. The power that the discretionary approach gives to professionals has been challenged by the disabled people's movement, a development addressed in chapter 33. Instead of having to rely on professional assessments of their needs, some disabled people are framing their demands in the language of citizenship rights.

Rights

The advantage of the rights-based approach to welfare is that it gives greater power to users by providing them with (more or less) clear, enforceable entitlements. Provided she meets the criteria of entitlement, the claimant can refer to legal rules in support of her claim. Not all rights claims are, however, rooted in the principle of citizenship. As figure 30.2 indicates, rights too can be selective and the citizenship principle itself can be interpreted to embrace both unconditional and conditional forms of welfare.

Residual Selectivity

The case for selective means-tested welfare – that it targets help on those in greatest need – has long been the subject of controversy. (It should be noted here that, in the UK, some means-tested benefits have been transformed into tax credits, going further up the income scale than traditional means-tested benefits.) Critics point to the significant numbers of people who fail to claim the means-tested benefits for which they are eligible. The reasons are varied, but include the sheer complexity of the benefits and the claiming process. Minority ethnic groups are particularly likely to under-claim. Similarly, there is evidence that, as local authorities apply charges and means-tests to more services, some people prefer to do without.

Means-tests are also criticized for trapping people in poverty, as an increase in income reduces their benefit, and for penalizing savings. They do not necessarily provide people with genuine security, as changes in circumstances, which have been shown to be common among low-income working families, can affect entitlement.

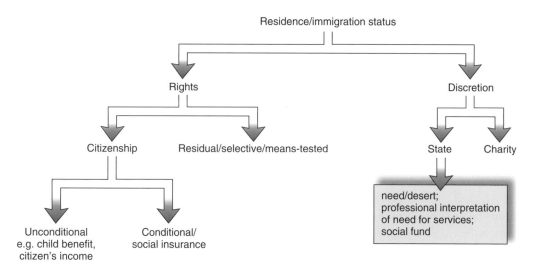

Figure 30.2 Principles of access to welfare

They also tend to disadvantage women in couples and to reinforce their economic dependence on male partners. Entitlement is normally calculated on the basis of a couple's joint income. This means that where, as is frequently the case, income is not shared fairly within a family, means-tests may be failing to target help on women within families who need it, with potential consequences for the welfare of children. Moreover, because of the strict rules limiting earnings while one is claiming social assistance, it is not generally worthwhile for the partners of unemployed claimants to undertake paid work.

Claiming a means-tested benefit all too often means admitting to the label of poverty, which can still be experienced as stigmatizing. One of the dangers of a residual welfare system, it is argued, is that benefits and services confined to 'the poor' can all too easily become poor benefits and services, as the rest of society no longer has an interest in ensuring their adequacy and quality. The United States is cited as an example. Thus, when access to welfare is confined to 'the poor' or nearly poor, it contravenes the principle of common citizenship.

Citizenship: Conditional and Unconditional

In the British social security system, social insurance is often held up as exemplifying the principle of common citizenship. Here, access to welfare depends primarily on having paid contributions of a specified value while in work and, for some groups, various work-related activities. However, it is, some would maintain, a conditional and limited form of citizenship which is promoted by the current social insurance scheme. Instead of overriding the market as a mechanism for distributing income, it mirrors market principles by confining entitlement to those with an adequate labour market record and, through additional earnings-related pensions, perpetuating (albeit in modified form) inequalities in earning power. Because the rules governing access to social insurance are based on male employment patterns, women, in particular, are the losers. A diminishing number of women are excluded from the system altogether because their earnings are too low to bring them into the social insurance system. Immigrants too are disadvantaged.

The conditional nature of the social insurance (and social assistance) system is being intensified through increasingly tough and extensive rules enforcing the obligation to seek and take work, which is promoted as the best form of welfare. In addition, in certain circumstances entitlement to benefit is being made conditional on other forms of behaviour; for example, entitlement to (a much enhanced) maternity grant is now conditional on attendance at child health check-ups and the possibility of reducing housing benefit as punishment for persistent anti-social behaviour has been mooted. Such policies reflect a central tenet of New Labour's 'Third Way' philosophy: that with rights and opportunities come responsibilities. The whole issue of the proper balance between rights and obligations has thus become an increasingly central one in debates about welfare.

Totally universal, unconditional, citizenship benefits are rare. The closest approximation in the British social security system is child benefit, which is paid for virtually every child in the country. There are a number of other benefits which are paid to people in specific categories, such as carers and disabled people, without either a contribution or a means-test. However, where paid as an income-replacement benefit in the form of carer's allowance, it is less generous than its contributory equivalent.

The social security systems of different countries combine the principles of access to welfare in different combinations, although generally with one predominating. Thus, for instance, as noted in chapter 52, the citizenship approach is associated with Scandinavia, the residual with the United States and the conditional social insurance with Germany. The UK, more than most, is a hybrid, but with an increased tilt towards a more residual model, which has led to a backlash across the political spectrum against means-testing, particularly of pensions. New Labour's principle

of 'progressive universalism' – basic universal support combined with additional help for those who need it most – exemplifies this hybridity in some areas of income maintenance. The citizenship principle does still operate in the National Health Service. However, as discussed above, it is difficult to operationalize in specific terms what is a generalized right to healthcare, free at the point of use. Moreover, it is an increasingly consumerist model of citizenship which dominates.

Emerging Issues

The weaknesses in current welfare arrangements have prompted a range of proposals for improvement. These can be divided into substantive and procedural or process reforms.

Substantive reforms

One area of substantive reform proposals aims at shifting the balance of social security entitlement from residual to citizenship-based principles of access. One example is the recasting of social insurance so that it excludes fewer people and, in particular, better reflects women's employment patterns. Another is the idea of a basic or citizen's income under which every individual would receive a tax-free benefit without any conditions attached. Access would be on the basis of citizenship rights alone. More narrowly, the replacement of the social fund with a system of clear rights to extra help, underpinned by a discretionary fall-back system, would enhance claimants' rights without losing the advantages of an element of discretion in the meeting of unusual needs.

The development of substantive rights to services is more difficult. One approach has been to suggest, as a first step, a framework of broad constitutional rights, partly building on the existing European Social Charter of the Council of Europe. This would provide rights to services at a generalized level, expressed as duties pertaining to government. Specific legislation would then need to develop more specific enforceable rights within such a framework.

Procedural or process reforms

It is easier to envisage how procedural reforms might improve access to welfare services. The Conservative government under John Major adopted such an approach in its Citizen's Charter. However, this was criticized as representing the principles of consumerism rather than citizenship, as the individual citizen's *qua* customer's rights were limited to the provision of information, the expression of choice and compensation claims for public services failing to meet Charter standards.

A more citizenship-oriented notion of procedural rights has been suggested by the Institute for Public Policy Research. Procedural rights to welfare focus on the processes through which substantive rights can be secured, on how people are treated (with dignity and respect) and the manner in which decisions are taken. An important element of procedural rights is enforceability. To access and enforce rights, people must have information about them and often need advice and assistance in negotiating with welfare institutions and taking cases to tribunals or, less frequently, the courts. Access to such information, advice and advocacy has itself been referred to as a right of citizenship by the National Consumer Council. This right is promoted by a range of agencies, such as law and advice centres and local authority and voluntary sector welfare rights specialists.

This right is also promoted by self-help groups, where users help each other without having to rely on professionals. The prin-

ciple of citizenship is taken still further in the growing demands for user or citizen involvement in service development (see chapter 32). The case is made on the grounds that welfare will be enhanced both by the greater democratic accountability of welfare institutions and by the empowerment of users. Thus, in incorporating a more dynamic and active conception of citizenship, which treats people as active agents rather than as simply passive recipients of rights, the principle of citizenship is promoted in terms of both outcomes and process. The principle of user involvement is now recognized in community care law, although in practice it still has some way to go to avoid criticisms of tokenism.

Whereas initially user involvement was developed at the level of local service delivery, more recently there have been demands for its extension to national policy-making. For example, the independent Commission on Poverty, Participation and Power, half of whose members had direct experience of poverty, called for greater involvement of people in poverty in decision-making that affects their lives, at both local and national level. Increasingly, it is being argued that the opportunity to participate in decision-making about welfare should be treated as a right.

This chapter has emphasized the importance of the principles which govern access to welfare resources, highlighting the processes of rationing involved and the ways in which different principles affect marginalized groups such as women, members of minority ethnic communities and disabled people. In considering approaches to the enhancement of welfare, it has focused on those which promote citizenship as opposed to residual selectivity. It has also underlined the significance of issues of process: procedural rights which assist people in claiming and enforcing substantive rights to welfare as citizens treated with respect and user involvement in the development of welfare.

Guide to Further Sources

A discussion of many of the ideas raised in this chapter can be found in H. Dean, *Welfare Rights and Social Policy* (Pearson Education, 2002), which offers a critical exploration of welfare rights, social citizenship and social legislation in historical and comparative context. P. Dwyer has written a couple of useful introductions to social citizenship. The first, *Welfare Rights and Responsibilities. Contesting Social Citizenship* (Policy Press, 2002), provides a discussion of the principles of social citizenship, which also includes the views of welfare users in relation to health, social security and housing. The second, *Understanding Social Citizenship* (Policy Press, 2004), relates social citizenship to welfare rights, puts it in historical context and considers issues of difference. Chapter 4 of T. Fitzpatrick, *Welfare Theory: An Introduction* (Palgrave, 2001) also covers key issues pertaining to social citizenship. For a more detailed exploration of principles of access to social security, see Robert Walker, *Social Security and Welfare* (Open University Press, 2005) and a number of chapters in J. Millar, *Understanding Social Security* (Policy Press, 2003).

Part V

Welfare Governance

Chapter 31

Managing and Delivering Welfare

John Clarke

Overview

- Delivering welfare is not simply a technical matter of choosing the most efficient delivery mechanisms.
- The design and control of welfare delivery is a political and contentious process.
- Reconciling conflicting political, economic and system control objectives produces complex and sometimes contradictory solutions.
- Processes designed to control dispersed welfare systems may produce unintended and contradictory effects.

Introduction

The delivery of welfare benefits and services is often discussed as a technical matter: choosing the most efficient and effective means of delivery is above, or below, politics. Since the late twentieth century, the processes of designing and coordinating systems of welfare delivery have become increasingly politicized. I use 'political' here in two senses: the first meaning relates to party politics (so there has been much controversy between political parties about how to reform welfare systems); the second sense refers to wider conflicts about the forms of power, authority and social relationships that are involved in the provision and use of welfare. In what follows, then, I will be focusing on the sometimes tense and contradictory relations between political ideals that shape the purposes of welfare; the organizational means that governments

use for the delivery of welfare; and concerns about the costs and consequences of welfare. Such contradictory pressures meet in the policies, processes and practices of delivering welfare and become the focus of debates about how to manage welfare.

Activating Individuals: 'Independence, Well-being, Choice'

The quotation in the above heading is taken from a government Green Paper about adult social care, published in 2005. It captures the ethos of the changing relationship between the state, welfare and individuals emerging in the twenty-first century. Most welfare benefits and services (in the UK and elsewhere) have been reformed in ways that aim to 'activate' individuals, making them autonomous and self-sufficient people, taking responsibility for themselves and their families. This commitment to activated individuals can take very different forms. In some cases, it involves the expectation that individuals can – and, indeed, should – be employed. Earning a wage is seen to reduce dependency, reduce public spending, give people a sense of self-worth, provide a role model for future generations and allow people to 'contribute to society'. In many instances, welfare systems have been redesigned in ways that make benefits more conditional and service processes more 'personalized' or 'individualized', for example, requiring individuals to attend assessment or evaluation interviews, or offering personal advisers to support individuals in job search or re-skilling.

Such changes reflect a drive towards 'personalizing provision', aiming to provide 'tailor-made' services adapted to the individual's circumstances, needs and wants. For example, in social care in the UK there has been a growing emphasis on enabling service users to choose or design the package of care that they receive, or on the transfer money in the form of 'direct payments' or 'individual budgets' to enable service users to exercise choices more directly (see chapters 30 and 33). In education, the principle of school choice (more accurately, the right to express a preference) has been granted to parents since the 1980s; while the reform of higher education aimed to extend the same consumerist logic of choice to students selecting institutions and subjects. In healthcare in the UK, there has been an increasing drive towards a conception of 'patient choice' as a central focus of system reform.

These models of activation and choice have attracted considerable controversy. Activation, for example, risks making welfare benefits and services more conditional, more restricted and less of a 'universal' right (although activation policies and practices vary substantially between countries). Choice policies have been challenged for making welfare services more unequal;

for fragmenting and disorganizing such systems; and for promoting an individualistic, or consumerist, version of citizenship. Whether the public see themselves as consumers or customers in their interactions with public services is another focus of controversy.

Such reform principles also create distinctive design and delivery problems. In particular, policies that promise 'personalization' require systems that can track and adapt to individuals and their changing circumstances or needs. They require the skills and capacities of 'case workers' to support and develop individuals (rather than merely assessing eligibility for benefits). They imply systems with 'spare capacity' in order to enable people to make choices. 'School choice' often involves parents not getting their 'first choice' school; while 'patient choice' will also be dependent on both system capacity, and the capacity of particular ('popular') hospitals to take on more patients. Such design issues bump into other design imperatives in uncomfortable ways.

Being Careful: Risks, Resources and Regulation

Not surprisingly, the activation of autonomous or independent individuals is not the only concern of welfare policy: questions of risk and issues of cost/resources are recurrent governmental worries. They have also had to find ways of exercising control and supervision over increasingly fragmented or dispersed welfare systems (regulation). Risk has become a concern for such diverse aspects of welfare systems as the role of private investment in creating welfare institutions (which bear the risk of twenty-five-year contracts for buildings and services in Public-Private Partnerships); the calculations of risk in relation to retirement pensions (and how such risks should be shared between the individual, the government and private financial institutions); and the assessment of risk associated with those who need social care (the risk that they may be a danger to themselves or others).

In all these contexts, there are conflicts both about what sorts of risks are tolerable and about who should bear the cost or the responsibility for them. In most settings, both public and private bodies may tend towards being 'risk averse', trying to minimize risks or, at least, their responsibility for risks. So, private corporations engaging in public–private partnerships in such fields as health and education have tried to win contracts that minimize their risk of low returns on investment by tying their public partners into long-term guarantees. Equally, social care assessments of the risks associated with people being supported as 'independent' may be driven by concerns to manage and control risks, and thus insist that some form of institutional care or other scrutiny is needed to 'safeguard' either the individual or the community. The goal of independence is offset against the risks of autonomy. Risk – and its management – have become critical issues for welfare delivery, but they do not necessarily sit easily alongside other desired goals.

The second governmental obsession about welfare delivery has been the persistent anxiety to contain or drive down costs – to make welfare systems more economical and more efficient. Despite increased levels of public spending on welfare benefits and services in many countries including the UK, the concern with efficiency has been a constant theme, manifested in many different ways. Many finance ministries make public spending plans on the basis of anticipated annual 'efficiency savings' being made (typically taking 2–3 per cent of service budgets each year). Funding for some services has been divided between basic block allocations and a proportion of public funds held back to be claimed through 'competitive bidding' from service-providing organizations. At the same time,

government departments, service systems and individual organizations have developed more elaborate financial control and reporting systems to track the flow of money, and link it more visibly to organizational outcomes (in the name of 'transparency').

The search for efficiency leads governments to explore alternative means of producing and delivering welfare. Such concerns were central to the dismantling of large professional bureaucracies of the post-war welfare state. Breaking up bureaucracies, introducing market mechanisms and expanding the provider roles of non-statutory agencies were all explored as ways of increasing the efficiency of welfare provision in other chapters (25–29). Finally, the concern with resources frequently translates into public discussions of welfare costs and who should bear them. So, for example, the UK has seen different policies (in England, Wales and Scotland) about who should pay for the residential care needed by older people (should it be predominantly private or public resources?). Discussions of 'co-payment' have also emerged around other welfare services (such as health and education), built around a conception that public funds might pay for a 'basic' universal service, but users should pay for what they need (or want?) beyond the basic level of provision.

The obsession with resources encounters the desire to build autonomy and choice into publicly provided services. If spare capacity is needed to make choice in services possible, then such spare capacity is also 'wasteful' and inefficient. In social care, it has meant the expansion of both means-testing and eligibility criteria processes to manage the growing demand for adult social care: those benefiting from publicly funded provision must be financially eligible and meet the needs thresholds (set by local authority social services or social work departments). And, as we saw above, they are also likely to be subject to risk assessments. Such processes combine 'personalization' (tailoring services more to the individual) and 'targeting' (concentrating on the most needy, the poorest or the most vulnerable) in complicated ways (that may also be expensive to administer).

The combined effect of different sorts of reform has been to create more complex welfare systems – often described as fragmented or dispersed systems. There are many reasons for this: the creation of welfare markets and mixed economies; the desire to have diverse or plural providers; the commitment to devolution and decentralization; the search for dynamic and flexible forms of organization; and the drive towards personalization and choice. In the following section we will explore some of these dynamics in more detail, but here it is important to note how such fragmented or dispersed systems also create new problems of control for governments. Rather than being the direct provider of services, governments have found themselves trying to find ways of managing complex systems at 'arm's length': a movement from provision to regulation. Two particular models of regulating welfare systems have proved particularly popular with governments: the first is the contract; the second is the audit.

The contract model has offered governments an organizational and symbolic device for welfare reform. The contract is a means of specifying cost-outcome elements of service delivery, such that a contractor undertakes to deliver x thousand services for x million pounds, within specified time, place and (sometimes) quality limits. The contract has been the building block for Public–Private Partnerships, for dividing government or local government departments (the 'purchaser-provider' split) and for organizing internal and external markets. Sometimes described as principal–agent theory (in which the principal purchases the activity of the agent to execute an agreed objective), the contract model

has been central to the workings of the dispersed welfare system in the UK. But the contract model is more than just a technical device for managing the interactions of different organizations (or parts of organizations). It also carries the image of 'being business-like' into the world of public services, making the provision of welfare services appear subject to the same principles as the 'private sector' or the 'market'. This imagery has been further extended into using the contract as a metaphor for the relationships between welfare services and their users. So parents and pupils are expected to agree to 'school contracts' (covering attendance, homework, behaviour and demeanour, for example). Social care users (whether adults or children) may be expected to sign up to contracts in which they agree to manage their own or their children's behaviour (in return for services, or as a way of avoiding less punitive interventions). Whether such documents constitute recognizable contracts (extracted as they are under forms of duress or threat), the language of the contract is powerfully appealing. Indeed, as this chapter was being written, the then Prime Minister (Tony Blair) was announcing a new 'social contract' between citizens and government (in which citizens would 'sign up' to their responsibilities before they could legitimately access welfare services).

Dispersed or fragmented structures of welfare provision have also been associated with the rise of regulatory processes concerned with the performance evaluation: the growth of 'audit'. Here, audit refers to a diverse set of processes and practices that are about evaluation, inspection, performance measurement and scrutiny, as well as the narrow financial or accounting sense of audit (see too chapter 32). The proliferation of such processes has been a distinctive feature of government attempts to control dispersed systems of provision 'at arm's length'. Such processes are associated with various perverse effects, of which three are worth noting here. The first concerns the effect of such evaluative processes on organizational behaviour. Following the axiom that 'what gets measured is what gets done', organizations tend to orient their efforts towards the targets, outputs or results that measure 'success'. Non-measured goals and activities tend to receive less attention and fewer resources. This might be significant if the setting of targets and measures is less than perfect as a framework of evaluating performance. The second concerns the costs of such audit or evaluation processes, since they consume resources (finance, time and effort) that might otherwise be spent on other activities, including service provision. Thirdly, such processes induce 'games-playing' as organizations try to manage their performance in ways that make them look successful. This last point underlines the ways in which evaluation systems both reflect – and exacerbate – 'low trust' between governments and public service providers. Intense scrutiny demonstrates governmental low trust, and encourages evasive behaviour in turn. Organizations know that in comparative/competitive systems of evaluation (league tables, star ratings) looking successful is important for gaining resources, attracting 'customers' and gaining some 'competitive advantage'. These issues point towards the next section, since comparative/competitive evaluation fits the logic of marketizing approaches to welfare provision.

Coordinating Complexity: Mixed Economies, Markets and Management

Since the 1980s, UK governments have sought to reform and modernize welfare provision through new organizing principles. These might be summarized as follows: mixed economies (or plural providers) are better that state monopolies; the market is a more efficient mechanism of coordination than state bureaucracies; and more and

better management can improve services in terms of both cost and quality. At times, these have been tempered by other principles – for example, there has been some enthusiasm for collaboration and partnership models – but these have tended to be added onto the underlying logics, rather than replacing them. In each of the three principles, the idea of the citizen as a consumer or customer plays a central legitimating role.

The 'mixed economy' refers to a combination of multiple providers of services, in principle drawn from different sectors: the public sector, the private (or commercial, or 'for profit') sector and the voluntary (or 'not-for-profit', or third) sector. Each sector is seen to bring different values, orientation and capabilities to the process of providing welfare: the private sector adds the entrepreneurial dynamism of the market (innovation, flexibility, customer-centredness); the voluntary sector adds a commitment to being 'close to users' and an ethical commitment; while the (necessarily reduced) public sector is governed by a 'public service ethos' and 'professional values'. The mixed economy thus creates diverse forms of provision that (in theory) 'fit' with a diverse society, enabling people to be served by organizations and in ways that match their circumstances and needs. However, since the mixed economies tend to be local (even if some of the organizations involved are national or even transnational), the match between differentiated populations and the diversity of services cannot be guaranteed. We should also note that there are different mixed economies of welfare, related to types of welfare service: social care is not the same as healthcare, which is not the same as education or housing. Mixed economies are differentiated by sector, service and locality. The creation (and maintenance) of mixed economies involves public spending to encourage 'new providers' to take the place of older public sector organizations. Mixed economies also tend to be organized through contractual models, in which the types, levels, quality and costs of services are specified.

The shift from states to markets has been a very widespread, though not universal, tendency. States continue to play critical roles as funders, designers and regulators of welfare provision, and even engage in some direct provision of benefits and services. However, the market principle has been widely adopted, although it can take different forms (see chapter 25). In some cases, governments have stood aside in order to allow market dynamics to act: most notably in financial services such as pensions (setting consumers free to choose). Such marketizing changes have not been wholly successful, and even the USA withdrew from Republican plans to turn pension funds into individual stock market portfolios. Secondly, the market model has been the dominant form of mixed economies – with national or local government departments inviting bids from would-be providers (with the expectation that market dynamics will drive down cost and drive up quality). Thirdly, service systems have been reconstructed around 'internal markets', in which purchasers and providers (or principals and agents) are distinguished and the provision of services is subject to a sort of contractual arrangement. The expectation is that mimicking markets in this way will gain some of the advantages associated with market discipline and market dynamics. Sometimes, such internal markets involve direct customers making choices (partly true in higher education; and the model for patient choice in UK healthcare); sometimes they involve 'proxy customers' (such as GPs or social workers) acting on behalf of the service user.

In these marketizing processes, boundaries have become blurred, for example, between internal and external markets, and between public and private sectors. For example, partnerships that span public and private sectors, or the creation of new 'hybrid' types of organization (such as Local Improvement Financial Trusts in primary healthcare) that do not belong to either the public or private sector produce a blurring. But it is also true that many of the markets created in these processes do not resemble the textbook image of the market very closely. Public–Private Partnerships, for example, involve very long-term contracting (up to 25 years), with guaranteed returns on investment, and contracting with a limited number of 'preferred' partners. Similarly, images of consumer choice provide much of the rhetoric of service reform, but choice in welfare services is highly constrained by the 'small print' (and by the separation of choice and payment). So, 'parental choice' in secondary education means the right to 'express a school preference', with no guarantees that you will get your choice, and creates system dynamics that induce 'successful' schools to find ways of selecting parents and pupils (what economists call 'cream-skimming').

At the heart of all of these processes of delivering welfare is the idea of management. More and better management, it is believed, can reconcile the competing objectives of welfare policy, and can ensure that they are pursued efficiently and that welfare services will be delivered through 'well-managed organizations'. In this view, managers are vital because of what they bring (a distinctive set of skills, talents and orientations to the efficient and effective accomplishment of organizational goals). They are also defined by who they are not: unlike staff or professional groups, they are not motivated by narrow or sectional interests (they have the service or organization's interests at heart); unlike politicians, they are not motivated by ideology or political commitments (they plan and direct rationally); unlike public service bureaucrats, they are not tied to the rule book (being able to bring about organizational transformations); and unlike service users, they are not driven by immediate needs (they can take an overview). Managers have come to occupy the central place in coordinating all of the complexity of systems of welfare delivery. In the twenty-first century, they are increasingly expected to provide 'leadership' (inspiring staff to greater achievements) alongside their capacities to 'be business-like'. Not everyone believes this view of management and managers.

Emerging Issues

The tensions between competing principles for the organization of welfare intersect with the problems of organizing and coordinating welfare in dispersed systems. Dispersal sets in play dynamics that are unsettling – an oscillation between centralization and decentralization (the concern to exercise tight control versus the wish to get decisions made 'close to the customer'). Each drive to decentralize tends to create anxiety about control at the centre (over

policy, funding, targets, evaluation and so on). The decentralization of service delivery to local or neighbourhood level often coexists with plans to create larger administrative units (in policing and healthcare, for example). There are also dynamic tensions between dispersal and integration – governments oscillate between the desire to see diverse and multiple providers and the wish to rationalize and reintegrate some services into what might be called 'digital era' bureaucracies (since new technologies enable new forms of integration).

The mixture of tensions about policy objectives and the dynamics of dispersed delivery systems means that 'managing and delivering welfare' is unlikely to form a stable or settled system. Policy conflicts, the politics of system design, pressures to decentralize and control, new processes of exercising control, and new models of managing ensure that organizing welfare delivery will be not become a 'merely technical' matter.

Guide to Further Sources

J. Clarke and J. Newman, *The Managerial State* (Sage, 1997) examines the role and consequences of managerialism in the restructuring of the British welfare state. N. Flynn, *Public Sector Management*, 4th edn (Sage, 2007) is a lucid – and regularly updated – introduction to the conditions and problems of managing in the public sector.

J. Clarke, J. Newman, N. Smith, E. Vidler and L. Westmarland, *Creating Citizen-Consumers: Changing Publics and Changing Public Services* (Sage, 2007) explores the move to treating the public as 'consumers' of public services (health, policing and social care). B. Hvinden and H. Johansson (eds), *Citizenship in Nordic Welfare States* (Routledge, 2007)) explores some of the politics, policies and implications of activating citizens.

C. Miller, *The Production of Welfare* (Palgrave Macmillan, 2003) provides a thoughtful account of the production and distribution of welfare with particular attention to organizational processes. J. Newman (ed.), *Remaking Governance: Peoples, Politics and the Public Sphere* (Policy Press, 2005) contains essays examining changing configurations of the public realm. R. Paton, *Managing and Measuring Social Enterprises* (Sage, 2003) provides a thoughtful analysis of some of the possibilities and problems of measuring organizational performance.

Useful web sources include <www.policyhub.gov.uk>, a government site aimed to promote strategic thinking and improve policy-making and delivery across government, and the National Audit Office site, <www.nao.gov.uk>. The NAO scrutinizes public spending on behalf of Parliament, audits the accounts of central government departments and agencies, and a wide range of other public bodies, and reports to Parliament on the economy, efficiency and effectiveness with which they have used public money. See also the Scottish Public Services Ombudsman site, at <www.spso.org.uk>, which provides a 'one-stop-shop' for individuals making complaints about organizations providing public services in Scotland. The SPSO deals with complaints about councils, housing associations, the NHS, the Scottish Executive and its agencies and departments, colleges and universities and most Scottish public authorities.

Chapter 32

Accountability for Welfare

Janet Newman

Overview

- 'Accountability' designates a set of values and institutions concerning the relationship between public services and the citizens or users they serve.
- The notion of 'accountability' is a key feature of recent attempts to modernize state welfare.
- The notion of 'accountability' has been extended to encompass communities and users as well as other stakeholders.

Introduction

'Accountability' designates a set of values and institutions concerning the relationship between public services and the citizens or users they serve. Along with 'responsibility', 'transparency', 'responsiveness' and a host of other terms, accountability lies at the heart of a series of restructurings of the British state. It is associated with many of the shifts denoted by the rise of the 'new public management' (NPM) – the extension of audit and inspection, the focus on performance management and measurement, the separation between 'principals' and 'agents' in the delivery of public services, and so on. Such developments have given rise to a set of technologies and practices that affect how managers, professionals and staff experience their everyday working lives in a context of heightened risk, more complex working relationships and increased emphasis on personal responsibility and accountability. But accountability is also undergoing shifts in meaning as

a result of the emphasis, in the early part of the twenty-first century, on strengthening accountability to local communities (through new forms of neighbourhood governance) and to service users (through an emphasis on widening both voice and choice in the service relationship). This chapter attempts to clarify this crowded field, unpacking the concept and setting out a number of different definitions and focuses of analysis. It then traces changing notions of accountability and explores the implications of the shift of emphasis towards accountability to citizens, service users and communities. It ends by setting out some key questions and issues.

Unpacking 'Accountability'

Definitions are problematic since accountability is a concept with highly normative overtones – everyone talks about it as a positive thing, yet the concept carries widely different meanings and values. It can denote something as narrow as auditors 'checking

Box 32.1   Dimensions of accountability

Accountability *of whom*? – where does responsibility lie?
Possibilities include:

- Politicians – e.g. the relevant minister
- Designated senior officials – e.g. 'accounting officers' in the Civil Service
- Local managers – e.g. the chief executives of local authorities or hospital trusts
- Individual workers – e.g. individual doctors, social workers

Accountability *for what*? – what criteria are used in making judgements?
Possibilities include:

- Probity of expenditure
- Upholding professional standards
- Value for money
- Organizational performance
- Delivery of policy goals

Accountability *to whom*?
Possibilities include:

- Upwards (to line manager, chief executive and elected representatives)
- Downwards (to local communities, citizens or service users)
- Lateral (to peers, partners or colleagues)
- Outwards (to customers making choices through the marketplace)
- Inwards (to one's own sense of probity and ethics)

Accountability *through what means* – how are people to be held to account? What sanctions may be exercised?
Possibilities include:

- Reporting (e.g. 'rendering an account' through annual reports)
- Audit (e.g. examination of accounts, and/or of statistical measures of performance)
- Inspection (e.g. visits by Ofsted or the SSI)
- Democratic processes (e.g. elections)

the books' to ensure financial probity to something as broad as the evaluation of the outputs of an organization and the value for money of the services it delivers. It can be highly personal – the holding to account of an individual by managers, politicians or the public, or perhaps the 'whistle-blowing' on the part of an individual when they are witness to malpractice. But it can also refer to how organizations and groups balance their responsibilities to multiple stakeholders in complex systems, such as network-based projects or partnership bodies. In an attempt to pin down a rather elusive and slippery concept, the literature has become littered with typologies of accountability. Some writers focus on analytical distinctions within the concept itself, setting out different dimensions of accountability (see box 32.1).

Box 32.2 Accountability and governance

- *Governance through hierarchy.* This is based on the traditional image of the welfare state, with services delivered through large bureaucratic organization with long chains of command and formal rules and procedures. Accountability here is based on checking that administrative and financial responsibilities have been properly exercised. The challenge, however, is that there is little accountability for what was actually delivered.
- *Governance through markets.* This was the dominant model that emerged during the 1980s and 1990s and influenced a range of reforms based on the separation of purchasers and providers and the delivery of services through contract. Notions of accountability to consumers became much stronger in this period, with league tables, inspections and performance audits used to hold managers to account for the performance of their organizations. The challenge here concerns the difficulty of viewing public services as individual, rather than collective goods. There is little emphasis in this model on delivering effective outcomes for the communities and citizens as a whole.
- *Governance through networks.* Here accountability operates through influence and reciprocal relationships between actors in networks. This is a model that underpins the idea of professional accountability to one's peers. But it has become more important with the growth of partnership working and the increasing emphasis on delivering policy outcomes by working across traditional professional and organizational boundaries. The challenge here is that networks are diffuse and complex, with many reporting lines and relationships cutting across each other. The complexity of the emerging relationships produces a lack of transparency that makes it difficult for government, service users or citizens to hold actors to account.

Each of these different dimensions of accountability is the source of contested views. For example, there is a long debate about where responsibility and accountability properly reside. Should it be the minister, rendering an account to Parliament and thus to the people, or does he or she have so little direct control over particular decisions made during the service delivery process that responsibility should lie with the local chief executive or service manager? The tension between self-regulation and external scrutiny or intervention often lies at the heart of disputes about the accountability of public officials and public services, as well as debates about the control of the press, financial institutions, charities and political parties. There is also much debate about how to get the balance right between upward lines of accountability and those that emphasize accountability to users and communities. We can identify three different sets of assumptions about how public services should be delivered, each of which is based on a particular model of governance and raises particular accountability challenges (see box 32.2).

Such typologies are always simpler than the phenomena they seek to categorize. Accountability is, in practice, a multilayered and complex set of processes linking institutional rules with personal norms and values. It invokes ideas of morality and ethics as well as economy and efficiency. There is a need, then, to study how managers and staff make sense of and 'perform' accountability in complex regimes of governance.

Changing Notions of Accountability

Notions of accountability have long roots. Rulers, politicians, administrators and leaders have always had to render an account to those who appointed them or on whom their legitimacy depends, and they are held to account for infringements of the norms and rules of behaviour in the office they hold. Here, accountability is associated with the *person*. The penalties for infringements have varied from losing one's head, to losing one's office, to suffering a loss of credibility and reputation. The notion of financial accountability grew alongside the growth of institutions and laws protecting commercial trading. Both forms of accountability – personal and financial – became institutionalized in the welfare state and public services. Personal accountability was enshrined in the idea of professional self-regulation and in the general ethos of public probity and public service expected of public sector workers. Financial accountability was institutionalized in the processes of financial audit and regulated by bodies such as the National Audit Office and Audit Commission. The probity of public expenditure was the overriding concern.

During the 1980s and 1990s, public and welfare services went through profound transformations with the growth of managerialism and markets (see chapters 24 and 31). The separation of 'principals' and 'agents' involved in the development of market mechanisms and the contracting out of services, as well as the reshaping of organizations into a series of 'business units', were viewed as sharpening account-

ability and producing enhanced efficiency. These managerial reforms were accompanied by, and indeed partly delivered through, changes in the focus, scope and power of audit bodies. Their focus shifted beyond the traditional emphasis on the probity of public expenditure to whether public resources were being used in a way that gave value for money, as measured by the 3 'E's of economy, efficiency and effectiveness. The Audit Commission, responsible for auditing local authorities and health authorities in England and Wales, expanded its work to encompass questions of organizational design and management processes. It also produced a number of reports setting out good practice models for a range of activities from partnership working to the conduct of political business in local authorities.

This expansion was accompanied by a shift from the narrow focus on financial accountability towards what Pollitt et al. (1999) term 'performance' accountability. This was situated in the shift towards an increasingly dispersed and fragmented array of service delivery organizations that were hard to control from the centre (see chapter 31). Performance audit emerged in the context of the search for ways of addressing both giving autonomy – devolving power to local managers – and exercising some form of control. Audit, in this period, became much more than a question of 'checking the books' and ensuring that organizations had adequate systems of financial management. It became concerned with assessing internal organizational arrangements and the organizational outputs that resulted from them, assessed in terms of their 'value for money'. At the same time, it might be argued, notions of personal accountability – based on professional self-regulation and a commitment to public service values – became eroded as workers experienced traumatic shifts in their working lives and as the trust that had traditionally been placed in them, by both government and the wider public, was eroded. The further increase in regulation, inspection and audit can be viewed as filling the resulting trust vacuum.

New Labour's modernization programme was underpinned by a further extension of audit and inspection as successive governments sought to reform those parts of the public sector where, in their view, 'producer dominance' had survived the market and managerial reforms of the 1980s and early 1990s. There was a continued focus on organizational efficiency and performance alongside an attempt to sharpen accountability to users and local stakeholders. There was also a marked enlargement of the role of government as a regulator of services, setter of standards and guarantor of quality. A strengthened 'scrutiny' role within local government marked an attempt to modernize political management arrangements; and more attention was paid to the governance arrangements of organizations given increased autonomy by, for example, awarding them trust status.

Labour extended the regulatory role of government through its use of performance targets, standards, audit, inspection and quality assurance schemes, all backed by additional powers for government to impose mandatory measures on organizations deemed to be performing poorly. The role of the Audit Commission continued to expand, and new quasi-governmental bodies concerned with audit and inspection proliferated. Agencies concerned with the regulation of workforces developed alongside those involved in inspecting services (not least because of a few high-profile examples of bad practice leading to the death of elderly patients, of children in hospital, or young people in care). There was a considerable amount of 'churn' in health and social care as new bodies displaced existing institutions, alongside mergers and changes of name and function. Arrangements also differ in England, Scotland,

Wales and Northern Ireland (see chapter 35). The result is a crowded field that forms an additional tier in a complex system of governance.

This proliferation forms part of the 'audit explosion' that Power (2003) and others have critiqued. Audit may influence the behaviour of managers and staff in deleterious ways, leading to 'game-playing' as managers attempt to hit targets by distorting service priorities in key periods, or by shunting 'difficult' (and thus expensive) cases to other organizations or sectors. The tightening of organizational accountability and audit may be highly damaging to the effectiveness of the system as a whole. The transaction costs associated with inspection and audit may be extremely high, with complex organizations having to respond to multiple inspection agencies in ways that draw attention and resources away from front-line services. And the climate of performance compliance, accompanied by a perceived lack of trust and constant threat of failure, may have a deleterious effect on motivation and morale of staff, and change their orientation to their work. As Christensen and Laegreid (2002) argue (writing about NPM across Europe, not just in the UK), the pursuit of accountability can exact a price through the decline of a sense of responsibility which more detailed performance indicators will not rectify. Instead, the solution may lie in embracing a responsibility model.

Such difficulties have received greater recognition in recent years, with high-profile examples of data-manipulation hitting the headlines and with concerns about the process and consequences of audit and inspection being more widely acknowledged. This produced a shift to a 'partnership' discourse (with some audit and inspection bodies espousing a more enabling approach). It also came to influence the type and extent of auditing and inspection processes, with high-performing organizations becoming subject to a 'light touch' system that relied more on self-regulation than internal inspection, while poorly performing organizations remained subject to intensive external scrutiny coupled with the threat of the removal of powers. However, ranking systems lost some credibility after the abandonment of the start system for hospitals in 2005. This was linked to the difficulty of capturing internal differences and complexity in a simple fourfold classification, reported examples of data-manipulation to achieve targets and repeated challenges around the robustness of the rankings. Yet audit and inspection, and the ranking systems that they produce, continue to be a key instrument of governance. This is in part because of a new rationale of providing information to the public and to service users to help guide their 'choices' of provider and drive up performance 'from below' through consumer pressure.

Representing the People: Accountability to Citizens and Users

Labour's approach to modernization was associated not only with attempts to sharpen upward accountability but also to make agencies and service providers more accountable to local users and citizens (see chapters 33 and 34). As noted, a key theme in the market reforms of the 1980s and early 1990s had been the development of a consumer orientation in public services, with attempts to enhance the accountability of provider organizations direct to users and consumers. While consumers tended in practice to have little power to exercise choice of service provider or to influence the pattern of service delivery, a host of initiatives – from league tables to quality assurance schemes – flourished in the name of the customer. Public service providers began to engage in more direct forms of communication with users, including satisfaction surveys, complaints schemes and

various forms of consultation exercises. Through the 1990s there was also a developing interest in involving citizens in decision-making through various forms of public participation and involvement: citizens' juries, citizens' panels, local area forums, tenant management groups and a host of community-involvement strategies linked to urban renewal and regeneration programmes.

Labour built on these developments. The modernization agenda gave a high profile to public participation, and local authorities, police services, health services and a range of other public bodies developed new forms of engagement with citizens and service users. The centrality of public participation was linked to at least two sets of policy goals. First, the rhetoric of public participation was peppered with notions such as 'reconnecting' citizens and government, or of building an 'active' or 'responsible' citizenry. Such goals reflected dismay about the declining participation in formal elections and about the prevailing cynicism about the political process. The second set of political goals was more closely linked to the Labour government's drive to improve the performance of public services by creating challenges to 'producer power' from below. Consumerism and choice became key themes in Labour's third term, with limited choice of provider being introduced in health, an extension of choice in schooling and an emphasis on enabling choice through an extension of individual budgets in social care. Proposals for neighbourhood governance also attempted to strengthen accountability 'from below', with local communities being given powers to require the re-tendering of some local services considered to be of poor quality.

This emphasis on the accountability of public service providers directly to their users and communities offers a form of accountability that is both more direct (i.e. not mediated by long hierarchies upward to an eventual body of elected representatives) and more differentiated (i.e. capable of ensuring that different interests and identities have some form of presence in the process of public participation). However, the increasing emphasis on public participation, consumerism and neighbourhood governance sits uncomfortably with the traditional institutions of representative democracy and with the dominant patterns of upward, hierarchical patterns of accountability. Such tensions are exacerbated by the way in which the concept of accountability has been narrowed to a focus on accountability for organizational performance against government goals, targets and standards. This is an essentially managerial form of accountability – and one that may do little to redress the declining trust and confidence of the public in the government that is accountable to it.

Emerging Issues

Accountability is a *relational* concept: it rests on a range of assumptions about the relationship between the state and the public at large, between service providers and service users, between professionals and clients and between central government and local managers. As a relational concept it invokes questions of trust, doubt, expectations, motivations and morale that are not easily incorporated into the economic discourses of performance management and audit. For example:

- Does enhanced scrutiny improve performance? Or, by perhaps inducing compliance on the part of staff in ways that may damage the commitment they bring to working in public services, might it reduce their capacity and willingness to go beyond what is strictly required of them?
- Does emphasizing accountability to service users by extending choice raise

their satisfaction with the services they receive? Or might an emphasis on performance league tables coupled with a discourse of choice raise their expectations to a level that can never be satisfied?

Such questions are difficult to research and there is little objective evidence available, making notions of accountability, performance and choice the subject of conflicting normative standpoints. This matters, not least because of the ways in which notions of accountability are being stretched to incorporate notions of the personal responsibility of service users and citizens. Such notions are central to the twenty-first-century modernization of welfare states. They open up questions about how individual citizens and service users may be held to account where they infringe norms of behaviour, perhaps causing nuisance to their neighbours, failing to care for children in ways that are socially approved, or failing to take proper responsibility for their own health or financial security. Might new social policy measures (conditional access to treatment, punishment through 'anti-social behaviour' orders, and so on) produce instrumental forms of compliance – or perhaps herald a new form of accountability to, and responsibility towards, a wider collective entity (the community, the family or the wider public)?

Accountability is also a concept that involves conflicts over the proper *distribution of power* in a democratic society. Public bodies, from Parliament to the police, from democratically elected institutions to the whole range of non- or quasi-governmental bodies, have the capacity to make decisions over the use and allocation of resources. The increasing emphasis on private and not-for-profit bodies in the delivery of services raises particularly sharp concerns about where accountability lies and how far public bodies can hold them to account. The disputes around how, and to whom, service organizations should be accountable are therefore disputes about *power* – the limits of autonomy, the extent to which responsibility is delegated, the power of the state to inspect and to intervene where it judges that performance falls below a desired standard. At stake in the process of accountability, then, are struggles over power, over the boundaries of trust, over the meaning of democracy and over the conception of the 'public' in whose name accountability is exercised.

Guide to Further Sources

M. Bovens, *The Quest for Responsibility, Accountability and Citizenship in Complex Organisations* (Cambridge University Press, 1998) and 'Public accountability', in E. Ferlie, L. Lynn and C. Pollitt (eds), *The Oxford Handbook of Public Management* (Oxford University Press, 2007) provide an authoritative and theoretically sophisticated discussion linking notions of 'active' accountability on the part of individuals to more institutionally based conceptions. An analysis of the 'performance-evaluation' nexus in public services and how far this resolves questions of public can be found in J. Clarke, 'Performing for the Public: doubt, desire and the evaluation of public services', in P. Du Gay (ed.), *The Values of Bureaucracy* (Oxford University Press, 2004) whilst C. Pollitt et al. *Performance or Compliance? Performance Audit and Public Management in Five Countries* (Oxford University Press, 1999) provides a comparative study of the role of 'Supreme Audit Institutions', situating the audit process in the trajectories of managerial reform in each nation.

Critiques from differing perspectives can be found in M. Power, *The Audit Society* (Oxford University Press, 1997); M. Power, 'Evaluating the audit explosion', *Law and Society* 25/3 (2003): 185–202; J. Rouse and G. Smith, 'Evaluating New Labour's accountability reforms', in M. Powell (ed.), *Evaluating New Labour's Welfare Reforms* (Policy Press, 2002); T. Christensen and P. Laegreid, 'New Public Management – undermining political control?', in T. Christensen and P. Laegreid (eds), *The New Public Management: The Transformation of Ideas and Practice* (Ashgate, 2002); J. Newman, 'Constructing accountability: network governance and managerial agency', *Public Policy and Administration* 19/4 (2004): 17–33; M. Strathern (ed.), *Audit Cultures: Anthropological Studies in Accountability, Ethics and the Academy* (Routledge, 2000); M. Barnes, J. Newman and H. Sullivan, *Power, Participation and Political Renewal* (Policy Press, 2007); J. Clarke et al., *Creating Citizen-Consumers: Changing Publics, Changing Public Services* (Sage, 2007); and J. Newman, *Modernising Governance: New Labour, Policy and Society* (Sage, 2001).

Chapter 33

Welfare Users and Social Policy

Peter Beresford

Overview

- The role and involvement of welfare service users has traditionally been neglected in social policy, but with a new policy emphasis on them and the emergence of their own social movements, this now needs to be addressed.
- While the identity 'service user' has been contested, people are increasingly organizing around it and this raises major issues for ensuring that participation is truly inclusive, reflects diversity and does not mirror broader exclusions.
- Competing ideological approaches to user involvement have developed and need to be distinguished.
- Service users identify a range of key areas for involvement.
- Service users are concerned that interest in involvement may be short-lived. Two key issues are needed to challenge this. First, the evaluation of involvement and, second, the resourcing of a network of user-led organizations to provide a basis for sustainability.

Introduction

A key concern of recent UK social policy has been to develop a changed relationship with welfare users. The political new right sought to transform understandings of this relationship from one of support to one of dependence, often cast as inappropriate dependence. In the early 1990s, John Major's Conservative government emphasized the role of welfare user as consumer/citizen, with its 'citizen's charters' and public service 'hotlines' (see chapter 30). New Labour's Third Way stressed the service user's role as partner, participant and co-constructor of welfare. These developments have all had influence and equiva-

lents internationally, in other European countries and beyond, as well as borrowing from other approaches, particularly North American ones. Yet so far, social policy texts have had relatively little to say about welfare users. They have paid little (in some cases no) attention to their perspectives and discourses. In some cases, these discourses are far advanced, for example in the case of the disabled people's movement. There is now a range of movements associated with welfare service users, including those of older people, mental health service users/survivors, people with learning difficulties and people living with HIV/AIDS.

Some of these movements have long histories. There are also strong traditions of citizens' and community organizations, as well as organizations of poor and unemployed people. Yet if we take a range of widely used social policy textbooks, we find that discussion of and references to service users, their movements and critiques are generally very limited, if not non-existent. At the same time, over the last twenty or so years, there has been a growing awareness of the need to explore social divisions and issues of diversity in social policy and many texts now seek to do this, notably addressing issues of gender, ethnicity and sexuality. Yet this enquiry has barely developed in relation to welfare service users.

The Preoccupation with Welfare Supply

On the other hand, the social policy literature has paid considerable attention to shifts in the *supply* of welfare provision. This has been true from the emergence of 'welfare pluralism' in the early 1970s to the pressure for a shift to market supply under the political new right and the remix of state and private supply and funding under New Labour. All have figured centrally in social policy writings and, indeed, textbooks. It could be argued that the history of social policy, particularly UK social policy, since the 1970s, has significantly been recorded in terms of changes in service supply and the ideologies attached to these changes. The focus has been very much on welfare *supply*, but not welfare demand. Alcock has made a similar point, arguing that attention paid to the development, and the study, of social policy has concentrated predominantly on the structure and the funding of welfare provision rather than on the access to and use of the services themselves. The focus has thus been rather more on the *producers* than on the consumers of welfare (Alcock, *Social Policy in Britain*, 2nd edn, Palgrave Macmillan, 2003).

This focus can be seen to coincide with and follow from the interests and philosophies of the two dominant approaches to social policy which have most influenced recent Western understandings. These are Fabian and new right social policy (see chapters 1 and 8). Neither has prioritized the inclusion of welfare users or their perspectives. Fabianism has frequently been characterized as paternalistic in approach, while new right welfare has been more concerned with reducing state welfare interventions and regulating welfare users than engaging them. The discipline of social policy has largely followed their lead and ignored welfare service users.

The Importance of Including Welfare Users

However, this situation has now significantly changed, for at least two reasons. The first of these is the emergence of the welfare service user movements already referred to. Since the 1970s these have grown in scale and significance. They have pressed for user involvement in public policy, developed their own critiques and theories and exerted an influence on culture, legislation, policy and practice. This has particularly been true of the disabled people's movement, whose 'social model of disability' and philosophy of 'independent living' have increasingly been incorporated into disability and other social policies as well as influencing the understanding of countless disabled people.

Secondly, New Labour social policy approaches prioritize, even if only rhetorically, the inclusion and involvement of public, patient and service user. There are now legislative and other requirements for such participation, partnership and 'empowerment'. Ideas like 'putting the patient at the centre of the NHS' and policies like 'individualized budgets' and direct payments, which put welfare service users in control of funding streams to provide personal and other support, are now being advanced by government as key models for future social policy (see too chapter 31).

The involvement and perspectives of welfare service users have thus become central concerns in social policy. The discipline of social policy now even more clearly needs to address them. This is not to say that it needs to signal its support for, or agreement with, such developments. Rather, they are now explicitly part of its province – to explore, analyse, critique and offer insights on.

There are both practical and philosophical arguments for addressing and including service users and their perspectives. Clearly, they are now emerging as a key policy focus. But it is also difficult to see how a full and unprejudiced picture of social policy can be constructed without engaging both their views and their analyses. Service users have increasingly argued that disregarding their perspectives or seeing them merely as a data source, is a political or ideological decision that raises its own ethical problems, since it implicitly devalues what service users themselves have to say.

Who Is a Welfare Service User?

The question of *who* is a welfare service user is one that sometimes seems to have been advanced as an obstacle in the way of exploring and developing this discussion. In fact, it is one of those many issues which needs to be addressed as part of taking it forward. The problem that is raised is how a group of welfare users can be delineated when *anyone* can be on the receiving end of social policy – since most of us go to state schools, use the National Health Service and so on. Service users and their organizations counter this argument that 'we are all (or can all become) service users' by making clear that, in reality, some people are in different, more difficult or complex relationship with social policy services. They include in this people with learning difficulties, mental health service users, frail older people and people with

physical and sensory impairments who may have long-term and ongoing contact with specialist services, may be segregated in separate provision, institutionalized, stigmatized and in some cases have their rights restricted by law. They highlight high rates of unemployment, poverty and social isolation in these groups.

Also, while circumstances, like, for example, experiencing mental health problems, may be seen as temporary, they can have enduring personal and social consequences – for example, limiting people's eligibility to secure insurance or adopt children. Thus, while being a welfare service user may be a complex status and not demarcate an homogeneous group, for some people it can become a key identity in how they are treated, affecting their life-chances and quality of life. Many different circumstances may be included in the category 'welfare user' – for example, being poor, homeless, a child or young person in state care, unemployed, a lone parent, in the penal system, chronically sick or having a life-limiting illness or condition. These situations cannot necessarily be treated as the equivalent of going into hospital for a routine surgical procedure, or choosing a state school for your child. While some social policy commentators privately argue that talking about 'welfare service users' creates an artificial and arbitrary 'them and us' situation in relation to social policy, service users argue that the term reflects a reality for many people. Groups at the heavy end have historically been disempowered and disadvantaged and have had little involvement in the construction of social policy either as a public policy or as an academic discipline. They seek to challenge the status quo.

Decoding Meanings of User Involvement

Once welfare service users' perspectives and potential role in social policy are acknowledged (while recognizing the complex, shifting and permeable nature of their identities and status), the issue is raised of how these are to be included in social policy. All service user movements have placed an emphasis on speaking and acting for themselves. They have stressed the importance of being able to offer their own views, ideas and analyses, rather than these being mediated and interpreted by others. What this effectively means is that to engage with service user perspectives means directly *involving* service users. Participation or 'user involvement' has become a central concern of service users and been increasingly emphasized in government policy and provision. Thus social policy as both discipline and activity needs to involve welfare service users. However, current interest in welfare users' involvement should not be allowed to obscure very different and competing understandings and ideologies of involvement which have been emerging. Government, service system and service users use the same terminology, but do not necessarily mean the same thing. There are currently at least two key different (if overlapping) approaches to, or models of user involvement. These may be described as:

1 The managerialist/consumerist approach, whose focus is the service system and whose concern is to gain public, patient and service user input to inform services and provision. This is the predominant model of user involvement in welfare, health and social care and has underpinned both state and service system discussions and developments in user involvement.

2 The democratic approach, whose concern is much more clearly with people's *lives* and improving their lives; where people as patients, public and service users highlight the need to have more say over the services they use to get the best out of them and to have

more say and control over their lives in general. This approach to user involvement has been developed by service users and their organizations. While it has been influential among them and has contributed to change, it nonetheless tends to represent a counter discourse rather than the dominant one.

These two approaches are concerned with and promise different things. The managerialist/consumerist approach is essentially concerned with information-gathering – with making it possible for 'consumer views' to be heard. It connects with ideological commitments of government encouraging the private sector to play a much larger role in both the financing and provision of public services (see too chapters 25 and 31). It links with both the rhetoric and values of the market. There is no suggestion of any redistribution of power to service users. Because of this, service users often interpret it as tokenistic and a 'tick-box exercise'. However, increasing the effective say and control of service users is the goal at the heart of the democratic approach to involvement. Its liberatory purpose is key for service users.

Individuals and organizations will need to be clear about these distinctions when they make decisions about the kind of user involvement that they want to offer or that they wish to engage with. This is true at all levels, from central government and local services, to specific projects and initiatives and indeed the operation of professional organizations like the Social Policy Association. Problems frequently arise from the failure to do so. Each of these approaches to involvement raises major issues for governance. Strengthening the market may mean more consultations and information-gathering exercises, but it does not necessarily mean more power, accountability or effective involvement for service users. Critics of this shift to the market see it as potentially weakening rather than strengthening such citizen involvement. The democratic approach to involvement advanced by service users can be seen to constitute a form of participatory democracy. Given that in the UK and other Western societies, we live in self-proclaimed representative democracies, major issues are raised about whether and how these two approaches to democracy can be reconciled.

An Inclusive Approach to Involvement

We have seen how, once the project of engaging and involving service users is addressed, issues are raised by the conceptual complexity of the category 'welfare user'. But another set of issues is also raised in practice about *which* service users are being engaged and involved. Concerns are frequently expressed, particularly by policy-makers and service-providers, that only a limited and 'unrepresentative' range of service users become involved. These are frequently seen as a narrow group of 'activists', characterized as 'the usual suspects'. Service user organizations, like Shaping Our Lives, the national independent user-controlled organization and network, are no less concerned that as wide a range of service user can be involved as possible. This means addressing issues of diversity along lines of sexuality, gender, culture, class, ethnicity, age and so on. But it also means working to engage groups that face particular exclusions and marginalization in society. This notably includes groups of people like those who do not communicate verbally, frail older people, refugees and asylum-seekers, homeless people and those in institutions.

Barriers can be overcome, but experience indicates that to do so, it is essential to put in place carefully worked out policies and practices for access and support, so that it is possible for as wide a range of people who wish it to be involved on as equal terms as possible. This means going much further than ensuring physical access, for example, for wheelchair users, important though this is. It also means addressing communication, cultural and intellectual access, ensuring that supports, structures and processes are developed which maximize the opportunities for the widest range of welfare users to become involved and which support and encourage their informed and active involvement. In this way, groups facing the most serious difficulties, including, for example, people with life-limiting illnesses and conditions, who may be very ill and have restricted time and energy, can be involved effectively, helpfully and ethically. Addressing these issues not only has cost and resource implications; it also means that *how* things are done will be different. Effective broad-based user involvement cannot just be grafted on to existing ways of working; it has far-reaching implications for both the process and the orientation of activities.

Key Areas for Involvement

In the late 1980s and early 1990s, when user involvement began to be embodied in government legislation, the emphasis was on user involvement in planning services and in individual 'comment and complaints' procedures. Many service users found these two areas of focus difficult to relate to. Planning services was something far removed from their lives. Complaining meant things had already gone wrong and many people were reluctant to complain about service providers on whom they were dependent. Since then, service users have identified other fruitful areas in which to get involved. These include user involvement in quality improvement, occupational practice, developing user-controlled support, research and in professional education and training.

User involvement in improving quality

There has recently been considerable political and policy emphasis on improving quality and developing quality and performance indicators and standards in health and welfare services. Ideas have mainly come from policy-makers, practitioners and managers. They have tended to be bureaucratic and managerialist in inspiration and approach. We know that patients' and service users' concerns and priorities are not necessarily the same as those of service system professionals; quality and performance can mean very different things to the two. Pressure has developed for service users to be involved in both the development of quality standards and outcome measures and in evaluating and interpreting them. The work of Shaping Our Lives on developing 'user defined outcome' measures has signified the beginnings of this process.

User involvement in occupational and professional practice

All service users by definition connect with practice and practitioners. Occupational *practice* is a key, but often neglected, domain for user involvement. Such involvement can transform occupational practice into a joint project between service user and worker, where the former plays an active role in structuring and shaping practice in accordance with their rights and needs. In this way, practice – based on service users' views and preferences – becomes a systematic process of discussion and negotiation, which is what the best practice has always been. This represents the most direct (and perhaps the most effective) expression of user involvement. It also offers an effective route to user involvement in planning and management, through the systematic collection, collation and analysis of the individual views, ideas, knowledge and experience of service users.

Developing user-controlled services and support

A key but often overlooked area in which health and social care service users have taken forward involvement has been in the development of their own support arrangements and services. The best known of these are the direct payment schemes which disabled people pioneered and which are now embodied in legislation. Growing out of the independent living movement, which is committed to disabled people having the support they need to live their lives on as equal terms as possible to non-disabled people and based on a social model of disability, direct payments put service users in charge of the 'package of support' they need. Government is now prioritizing new systems of individualized support which put together different welfare funding streams under the control of the individual service user. Service users have also developed their own collective user-controlled services. While these have often been restricted by inadequate and insecure funding, the evidence is that they are particularly valued by service users more generally.

User involvement in research

There is now increasing interest in and requirements for service users to be actively involved in research. This makes it possible for evidence-based policy and provision – on which there is increasing emphasis – to include service users' experiential knowledge as well as other knowledge sources which have traditionally been given greater credibility. Service users have also developed their own emancipatory research approaches, which challenge positivist research values of neutrality and objectivity and which prioritize research as a means of bringing about change as well as generating knowledge. Through such user involvement research, service users are developing their own discourses as well as their own investigations and critiques of existing and alternative policy and provision.

User involvement in education and training

Service users argue that one of the most effective ways of changing practice and service cultures is through involving themselves in occupational education and training. This has led to the widespread development of 'user trainers' and training for user trainers. Service user organizations have pressed for their involvement in all aspects and stages of professional education and training, from providing direct input to being involved in developing course curricula, providing course materials and, indeed, selecting, evaluating and assessing courses and students. The new social work qualification introduced in 2003 requires the involvement of service users in all stages and aspects of the degree.

This also raises major issues for professional organizations like the Social Policy Association. Service user movements argue: 'Nothing about us without us.' This has implications for the SPA's own involvement of welfare service users in the discipline and its own activities, including educational initiatives, discussions, publications and other outputs, research, conferences and events, as well as its management and in the development of the social policy workforce.

Emerging Issues

There are two further issues to which insufficient attention has as yet been paid. These are the evaluation and sustainability of service user involvement.

Evaluating involvement

While there have been growing pressures and requirements for user involvement in social policy, and strong philosophical and ethical arguments have been advanced for it, questions remain about whether and how it actually leads to the improvement of policy, practice and research. For example, what kind of involvement is most helpful in given circumstances? How is it most usefully implemented? As yet, little systematic evaluation has been undertaken and evidence of the efficacy of involvement is limited. If user involvement is to progress as policy and practice, it is essential that it is subjected to systematic and rigorous monitoring and evaluation to maximize the lessons for good practice. Service users and their organizations need to be centrally involved in such evaluation.

Sustaining involvement

There are strong fears among welfare users that interest in their involvement may be short-lived and that user involvement could be a temporary blip in essentially paternalistic and regulatory approaches to social policy. They see the development of a network of securely and adequately funded local user-controlled organizations and a shift away from support for traditional large charitable organizations for service users as key to sustaining user involvement. The Prime Minister's Strategy Unit recommended the establishment of such a network of service user-led organizations and this is seen as key to the effective involvement of service users for the future.

Guide to Further Sources

The many issues raised in this chapter can be explored through the following sources, the titles of which are indicative of the concerns and debates addressed: C. Barnes and G. Mercer, *Independent Futures: Creating User-Led Services in a*

Disabling Society (BASW/Policy Press, 2006); M. Barnes, J. Newman and H. Sullivan, *Power, Participation And Political Renewal: Case Studies in Public Participation* (Policy Press, 2007); P. Beresford, 'Service users, social policy and the future of welfare', in L. Budd, J. Charlesworth and R. Paton (eds), *Making Policy Happen* (Routledge, 2004), pp. 141–51; F. Branfield and P. Beresford et al., *Making User Involvement Work: Supporting Service User Networking and Knowledge* (Joseph Rowntree Foundation, 2006); PMSU (Prime Minister's Strategy Unit), *Improving The Life Chances Of Disabled People, Final Report* (Cabinet Office, 2005). Shaping Our Lives, *Shaping Our Lives – From Outset to Outcome: What People Think of the Social Care Services They Use* (Joseph Rowntree Foundation, 2003); and M. Turner and P. Beresford, *User Controlled Research: Its Meanings And Potential* (Involve, 2005).

Useful websites include: <www.shapingourlives.org.uk> (Shaping Our Lives, the national user network); <www.jrf.org.uk> (the Joseph Rowntree Foundation site – a major source of information on social policy research and development); <www.invo.org.uk> (Involve: promoting public involvement in NHS, public health and social care research) and the Disability Archive UK at <www.leeds. ac.uk/disability-studies/archiveuk>.

Chapter 34

Local and Regional Government and Governance and Social Policy

Guy Daly and Howard Davis

Overview

- The analysis of local provision involves the study of both local government and local governance.
- Both are a key element of social policy formation and provision.
- Local government structures are subject to constant reorganization and there is continuous tension between central and local concerns.
- The development of local governance is best considered in terms of four main phases, the latest involving the introduction of new partnership systems and pressures for civic renewal and engagement.
- These are presenting new challenges and questions about the configuration of local governance.

Introduction

The 'local', however the term is defined, has in the past helped shape social policy and provision – and continues to do so today. As explored elsewhere in this text, social policy may be defined in a traditional Beveridgean manner, with a focus on welfare services such as healthcare, education, housing, personal social services and care, income maintenance and employment; or it could be given a more expansive definition, which also encompasses leisure, transport and the environment; or it could include more recent constructions which focus on community safety and social inclusion. Whichever approach is used, local government and local governance are key parts of social policy and provision. These

different terms – local government and local governance – are generally used to distinguish between the elected local councils, on the one hand, and the wider range of local public service bodies, on the other.

Although Britain has a more centralized set of government and governance arrangements than many of its fellow European Union member states, the state at the centre directs and works alongside local, regional and devolved (Scotland, Wales and Northern Ireland) policy-making and implementation structures (see chapter 36). Indeed, when one compares UK governmental structures with other European states, one notes that local government is constitutionally weaker within the UK and, at the same time, the units of local government are relatively large but have relatively fewer councillors per head. What this means is, first, that in the UK, local government's influence tends to emanate from the scale and nature of its operations rather than through constitutional strength and, second, that UK local government is liable to, and has experienced, constant reorganization and changes to its responsibilities.

This chapter sets out to describe how the local state has played, and continues to play, a part in constructing and delivering social policy. As we will see below, the development of local government and local governance has enabled local arrangements for the provision of welfare to develop, arguably over four stages: up to the post-war welfare state settlement, the period of post-war consensus between 1945 and the mid- to late 1970s, the break-up of that consensus and the dominance of new right thinking and policy-making and, latterly, the period of New Labour and beyond.

The Development of Local Government and Local Governance

History is often an important influence on the way that things are done and the structures and institutions that are in place. The government and governance of local communities is no exception. This history can be traced back for centuries. Present-day local government, however, really begins in the nineteenth century and has, in many ways, a strong connection with the progress of the Industrial Revolution. In particular, as urbanization and industrialization increased, the need for a wider range of services became more apparent.

Sanitation, elementary education, public health, law and order, and physical infrastructure were vital in building successful businesses and economies. In what might be seen as a period of enlightened self-interest by the local 'great and good', local public bodies increasingly took over service

provision from private and charitable organizations.

Key dates include the 1835 Municipal Corporations Act, the 1834 Poor Law Amendment Act, the Local Government Acts of 1888, 1894 and 1929 – and parallel legislation for London, Scotland, Wales and Ireland. By the time of the Second World War, local councils in urban areas were responsible for, and running, most local public services – literally from cradle to grave. In rural areas this was less the case and local public services were far less developed.

Local governance within the post-Second World War consensus

The period from 1945 up until the election of the Thatcher Conservative government in 1979 is often described as a period of consensus across the major political parties and this is arguably as true for local governance and local government as it is for other social policy arenas. The period was one in which local government was a major partner in building the welfare state, reflected in a significant growth in local authorities' expenditure between 1945 and 1979. Local councils had key responsibilities for providing:

- social housing – provided through local authority council housing departments;
- education – in which local authorities were responsible for overseeing and providing state education at primary, secondary and tertiary levels as well as parts of higher education provision with the establishments of technical colleges and polytechnics;
- personal social services and social care for children and older people;
- community-based healthcare until 1974;
- public health;
- public protection – police and fire services, ambulances (until 1974), consumer protection.

Local governance and the new right

However, during the 1970s the consensual period of expansion and belief in state provision, including through local government, started to be questioned. The period of Conservative control between 1979 and 1997 signalled the definitive break with the post-war consensus. Indeed, it can be argued that local government was one of the prime sites for the new right reforms in social policy. The Thatcher and Major governments' approach to local government can be typified by period as follows:

- the early 1980s – focusing on controlling total and individual local authorities' expenditure;
- the mid-1980s – restructuring with the abolition of the Greater London Council (GLC) and the metropolitan county councils, and shifts of responsibilities away from elected local government into government appointed local bodies ('quangos');
- the mid- to late 1980s – challenging local authorities' role as the direct providers of services through privatization and the encouragement of local authorities to be enablers of services rather than direct providers;
- the early 1990s – new managerialist approaches, for example with the promotion of citizen's charters, league tables, inspection and audit.

All of local government's main services were affected, including:

- education – the centralization of control including the weakening of local education authorities, the implementation of the national curriculum, local management of schools and the independence of further and higher education;
- housing – the 'Right to Buy' scheme which encouraged tenants to buy their council homes at a discount, the trans-

fer of whole estates through the creation of Housing Action Trusts and, in the 1990s, the first examples of large-scale stock transfer schemes;
- social care – the promotion of local authority social services departments as enablers of residential and domiciliary care;
- the introduction of competitive pressures into many services through compulsory competitive tendering (CCT) and the purchaser/provider split;
- the creation of Urban Development Corporations – for example in Bristol, Liverpool, Birmingham and London Docklands, which took over key urban regeneration responsibilities from local government in parts of these cities.

All in all, the Thatcher and Major periods of government have been depicted as a time when the local state was 'hollowed out' with the privatization of certain local authority responsibilities, increased central pressure on those services that remained and the shift of some responsibilities to local quangos. Even so, the period of 1979–97 was not one of passive acquiescence by local government. On the contrary, perhaps in part as a response to the politics of the new right, this period saw the emergence of what has been described as the 'urban left' in local government. In a number of cities – for example, Liverpool, Sheffield, parts of London and in the Greater London Council itself – Labour-controlled councils adopted radical left agendas in most areas, such as transport, housing, policing, education, jobs and services generally, multiculturalism, positive action for disabled persons' groups and lesbian and gay groups. Local government was often the site of political dispute between the new right and the left, epitomized by the fights over the introduction of the 'poll tax'.

However, although the Conservative power base in local government had been virtually wiped out by the time New Labour came to power in 1997, much of the urban left's agenda had been defeated by Conservative central government legislation. Paradoxically, much of the urban left agenda (for example, rights for disadvantaged groups) has subsequently been absorbed into mainstream social policy. What this also shows is the continual tension between central government and local governance bodies. On the one hand, the centre (Parliament) may wish for a universal policy and yet, because, for example, inequalities are not spatially uniform, at the local level particular solutions may be required to meet specific concerns.

Local and regional governance and New Labour

The New Labour administration of 1997 arrived with a huge agenda for change. Many in local government and other public services were pleased to see a change of government. They felt battered, undervalued and under severe pressure after eighteen years of Conservative rule. Labour moved quickly to use the language and rhetoric of partnership between national and local government. It also soon repealed one of the most hated aspects of Conservative local government legislation – the obligation to subject local public services to open competition with the private sector (known as CCT) – and replaced it with a new duty of continuous improvement.

However, it soon became apparent that, like its Conservative predecessor, Labour also had its doubts about local government. There was to be no return to old (pre-Conservative government) ways of working. There was to be no simple undoing of Conservative legislation affecting local government and local public services, and the Blair administration quickly identified what it saw as a number of problems with local government as it stood.

It saw localities as lacking a clear sense of direction with a lack of coherence and

cohesion in delivering local services. The quality of local services was seen as too variable with too many councils allegedly failing to deliver acceptable standards of service. Furthermore, responding to low voter turnout at local elections and to the perceived atmosphere of 'sleaze' surrounding the public sector in the closing years of the Conservative period of government from 1979 to 1997, Labour also saw the need for a new democratic legitimacy and a new ethical framework.

The government wished to see recognized local leaders and strong leadership with clear accountability and revitalized local democracy. There should be continuously improving quality services for all – with clear service standards. Well-performing councils were to be rewarded with increased flexibilities. The energies of local people and organizations would be harnessed, working in partnership with local councils to develop a shared vision for the whole community.

While many aspects of the government's aspirations were widely shared, its solutions were, however, not always so warmly embraced. Among the more controversial aspects have been the requirements on councils to streamline their decision-making arrangements – leading to the separation of executive and representative roles among councillors. This led to the creation of local authority Cabinets and Executives and the concentration of executive powers in fewer hands, something that many in local government regretted. A small number of authorities moved to having directly elected Executive Mayors.

Legislation also gave central government new powers to act on service failures by local government and introduced the concept of inspection to all local government services. The investment in inspection undoubtedly increased the focus on service improvement and unlocked some long-standing problems in a number of authorities. However, the inspection process came at some cost – a matter of increasing concern to local councils as the regime rolled out and on. There were also arguably diminishing returns. This led in time to moves towards more proportionate and risk-based approaches to inspection, though the controversy about the respective costs and value of inspection continues (see chapter 32).

The agenda, then, has been two-pronged. On the one hand, there has been a considerable investment in key services along with an emphasis by central government on the important role of local government. However, at the same time, the government also emphasized and enacted major programmes of reform in order to bring about its vision of a revitalized local government.

Challenging the performance management of authorities and services has been key to New Labour's approach. Central government has sought to embed a culture of continuous improvement and innovation across the whole range of local public services. The period since 1997 might therefore be characterized as one of continuous revolution, in which change management has been key. As such, the government and governance of local communities remain faced with major challenges and change in just about everything done at the local level. Key to this are:

- an emphasis on community leadership rather than direct service delivery;
- increased engagement of, and responsiveness to, local communities and service users;
- an emphasis on performance management and increased efficiency in the use of resources;
- an emphasis on impacts and results;
- pragmatism rather than ideology as to the best ways forward.

In addition, Labour has created regional structures alongside the devolved adminis-trations in Scotland, Wales and Northern Ireland. In England, Regional Development Agencies and indirectly elected Regional Assemblies have been established to oversee spatial, planning and regeneration matters. London is the only area in England to have a directly elected regional administration. Elected Regional Assemblies for the rest of England have been mooted but not established, though there was a referendum in the north-east of England in November 2004, where the electorate rejected the proposal by a margin of four to one, arguably demonstrating that the issue has gained little popular ground.

In part because of the emphasis by New Labour on 'what works is what counts', local government and governance continue to be conducted within a mixed and changing structural and organizational context. We now move on to describe local government structures.

Local and Regional Government Structures

Most of the UK population is served by so-called 'unitary' local government structures. This is where there is just one authority for the particular area providing all or most local government services in that area. These authorities come in a variety of guises and with a variety of titles, but all are responsible for the spectrum of local government services – from street cleaning to lifelong learning, from trading standards to social care.

An exception to this general rule exists in those parts of England outside the main urban areas – the English shires. In these areas, a two-tier local government system exists, comprising a county council and a number of district councils. Here, the county council is responsible for those services thought to need a larger scale for their operation, such as lifelong learning, social care and strategic planning. The district councils, on the other hand, have responsibility for most local environmental services (such as refuse collection and street cleaning), together with housing, leisure services and local development control. However, the two tiers are increasingly working closely together and beginning moves towards a 'virtual unitary' structure where, although the two tiers of local government continue to exist, they may share services and seek to offer seamless service delivery to the public.

All the councils mentioned above are directly elected by local electors, whether they are in a unitary or a two-tier setting. There are, though, some differences in electoral arrangements between different types of council.

In London, in addition to the London local authorities (the London boroughs), there exists a directly elected regional authority – the Greater London Authority (GLA) – comprising an Assembly and a Mayor for London. The GLA is responsible for key London-wide functions, such as public protection (police and fire), transport and economic development. Outside London, the rest of England has appointed Regional Assemblies (that is, they are not currently directly elected bodies) and Regional Development Agencies (RDAs), which oversee spatial and regeneration strategies for their respective regions. Regional Assemblies have four main strategic responsibilities: planning, housing, advocacy and policy development, and scrutiny of the RDAs. The RDAs are mainly responsible for economic regeneration. Scotland, Wales and Northern Ireland have their own directly elected devolved Parliament or Assembly (see chapter 35).

One other tier of directly elected government that needs to be mentioned is the parish. Parish, town or community councils are a key link in the chain of local representation. They do not exist in all areas – most notably having been absent from the main urban areas – though this is beginning

to change. They also, for the most part, have powers rather than duties – acting as the voice of villages, small towns and neighbourhoods and making that voice heard to other tiers of government as the occasion demands. They have few service delivery responsibilities.

Some important local services are not provided by elected local government at all. Key amongst them are health services, which are the responsibility of the various arms and agencies of the National Health Service, and policing, which generally comes under a local police authority or police board. In addition, the Regional Assemblies and RDAs mentioned above are responsible for policy in relation to spatial and regeneration strategies.

In order to overcome the fragmentation of local public services between local government and other bodies, there has, since the 1997 general election, been an increasing emphasis on partnership working. In England, for example, Local Strategic Partnerships (LSP) have been established in all local authority areas. The aim of the partnerships is to bring together all the key local public service bodies – councils, police, health, etc. – to agree key common objectives and priorities for all the local public services in that area. Typically, these include a number of objectives seeking to make their communities healthier, cleaner, greener and safer – with better education and employment prospects. The term 'local governance' is today used to refer to these wider local public service provision and partnership arrangements – distinguishing them from the elected local government (council) structures described earlier. An example of such an LSP – that for Coventry – is provided in box 34.1.

Emerging Issues

As we have seen from the discussions above, local government and local and regional

Box 34.1 Local Strategic Partnerships – Case study: Coventry Partnership

The Coventry Partnership is the local name for Coventry's Local Strategic Partnership (LSP). The Partnership is made up of senior people from Coventry's key public, private, community and voluntary organizations.

The aim of the Partnership:
'To bring together the resources, energy and creativity of key organizations, groups, communities and people in a single group to work to meet the economic, social and environmental needs of the City of Coventry and the health and well-being of its people.'

What is its purpose:

- to improve mainstream services to produce better outcomes in the most deprived areas and contribute to sustainable development;
- to work together to provide better local and city-wide services, particularly focusing on less well-off areas of the city;
- to build on these successful activities and integrate them into their main services so that they become more responsive and address the real needs of local people.

The objectives of the Partnership are:

- to set the overall strategic vision for the City of Coventry and to secure partnership commitment and action to delivering the vision;
- to implement and further develop Coventry's Community Plan or Strategy;
- to develop and deliver the Neighbourhood Renewal Strategy for Coventry to meet local needs and priorities and narrow the gap between the most disadvantaged communities and the rest of the city;
- to work with statutory bodies in developing and implementing public service agreements to improve public service;
- to bring about the strategic alignment and integration of plans, partnerships and initiatives within Coventry.

The Community plan features eight main themes that Coventry people have said matter most to them:

- jobs and our local economy;
- health and well-being;
- environment;
- community safety;
- equalities and communities;
- learning and training;
- housing;
- transport.

Source: <http://www.coventrypartnership.com>

governance remain important for the shaping and delivery of social policy. From the Industrial Revolution onwards, as well as during the period of establishing the post-war welfare state, through the period of new right and more recent New Labour governments, local governance has been required to coordinate and deliver social policy.

However, issues remain around the need for local and regional governance arrangements to engage more effectively with social policy agendas, including local inequalities and local needs, as we move into the 2010s. We are therefore likely to see continued debate over:

- increased civic engagement and civic renewal, for example through greater participation of citizens in local decision-making;

- more devolution to local bodies;
- the wish for increased democratization of local and regional governance structures;
- the effectiveness of stronger leadership structures via a single elected leader or mayor.

Even so, local government is likely to remain key to the production and coordination of local plans to improve the health, education, economic prosperity, housing, environment, safety and security of their communities. Local Strategic Partnerships will remain key to this coordination. Indeed, it is arguable that without local government to lead on these initiatives, local and regional governance would be even more complicated, disjointed and fragmented than it is today.

Guide to Further Sources

A useful overview of the management and governance of public services can be found in T. Bovaird and E. Loffler (eds), *Public Management and Governance* (Routledge, 2003). B. Denters and L. E. Rose, *Comparing Local Governance: Trends and Developments* (Palgrave, 2005) is a good introductory text that compares local governance in the UK with a number of other European countries, the USA, Australia and New Zealand. The debates over partnership can be followed in C. Glendinning, M. Powell and K. Rummery (eds), *Partnerships, New Labour and the Governance of Welfare* (Policy Press, 2002).

R. A. W. Rhodes, *Beyond Westminster and Whitehall: Sub-Central Governments of Britain* (Unwin Hyman, 1988) remains a key text on the nature of the relationships between central government and local governance structures. J. Stewart, *The Nature of British Local Government* Macmillan, 2000) is a good source for capturing the traditions and historical underpinnings of British local government. G. Stoker and D. Wilson (eds), *British Local Government into the 21st Century* (Palgrave Macmillan, 2004) provides an analysis of key developments in local governance in the UK in the opening years of the twenty-first century. D. Wilson and C. Game (eds), *Local Government in the United Kingdom*, 4th edn (Palgrave, 2006) also offers a good general introduction to the subject.

Useful websites include <www.lga.gov.uk> (the Local Government Association site – there are equivalents for Scotland, Wales and Northern Ireland) and <www.direct.gov.uk> (a gateway portal for all public services and government departments).

Chapter 35

Social Policy and Devolution

Richard Parry

Overview

- The United Kingdom is a unitary, London-centred state that has made a political adjustment to the wishes of Scotland, Wales and Northern Ireland by devolving powers over many areas of social policy.
- England still dominates in both scale and thinking, and retains control over the tax-benefit system.
- The organization of the welfare state within the devolved nations is more coherent than in England.
- The devolved nations have made some interesting policy initiatives, generally in the direction of a more universalist and less privatized welfare state.
- The current arrangements are politically and financially unstable.

Introduction

The United Kingdom is a strongly unitary state and lacks a clear concept of regional differences in social policy in terms of formation, implementation and content. The main source of difference is the status of Scotland, Wales and Northern Ireland within the United Kingdom, enjoying nationhood but not statehood and, since 1999, having their own devolved elected administrations with extensive powers over social policy. This chapter seeks to provide a guide to the range and type of nation-specific social policy legislation; the powers and responsibilities of the devolved systems and their separate social policy agencies in the three nations; and the major policy initiatives at sub-national level.

The Problem of English Dominance

The starting point is the dominance of England in the United Kingdom. It accounts for 85 per cent of the population and London, its capital, is the centre of political, governmental, cultural and media activity. This centralization, so taken for granted in Britain, is not inevitable. In the United States, the levels of unemployment and health benefits vary among the states. In Germany all of education is run at the *Land* level and social care services vary according to municipality. Italy, Spain and to some extent France have been developing regional government in recent years. There is a general uniformity of social security benefits in these countries, but the systems have a less concentrated administration than does Britain's. Only Britain carries through the concept of uniformity and standardization so far (in particular in the uniformity of benefit rates). Britain has a lesser sense of federal political structure, with a uniform structure of subnational government, than any country of comparable size.

Scotland, Wales and Northern Ireland have long had distinct historical traditions and political profiles. Scotland was independent until 1707 and the Act of Union preserved its legal system, Presbyterian Church and local government. It had stronger traditions in education and medicine than did England, and became a United Kingdom leader in these fields. Wales was never a defined independent state, but its linguistic and religious pattern was clearly different. Pressure from the Scottish and Welsh Labour Parties led to a political commitment by Labour in 1997 to transfer the powers of the Scottish Office to a Scottish Parliament able to pass primary legislation in those areas, and of the Welsh Office to a National Assembly for Wales, administering and financing them within a framework of Westminster legislation. Both were elected under a system that included a minority of regional seats allocated from party lists to make the overall seat distribution as proportional as possible. Referendums in September 1997 approved the proposals by a strong majority in Scotland (74 per cent) but a bare 50 per cent in Wales. Scotland also voted 63 per cent to give its Parliament limited powers to raise income tax, but this has not so far been used. Elections were held in May 1999 and the new administrations assumed their powers on 1 July 1999. Labour fell short of overall majorities and (in Scotland from the start and in Wales from October 2000) formed a coalition government with the Liberal Democrats. After the 2003 elections, Labour was just able to form a majority administration in Wales on its own. After the 2007 elections, in Scotland the pro-independence Scottish National Party edged just ahead of Labour in seats and votes and formed a minority administration; in Wales, Labour lost relatively more ground, but after unsuccessful attempts by the other parties to negotiate an alternative coalition, it returned as a minority administration.

Ireland had a separate Parliament until 1801, then united with Great Britain, but split in 1922 into an independent country (later the Republic of Ireland) and the six counties of Northern Ireland, which remained in the United Kingdom but were given a local Parliament. This was suspended in 1972, but the peace process led to the Belfast, or Good Friday, agreement of April 1998 that specified a law-making assembly and an Executive with members of all political parties. The Executive ran, with interruptions, from December 1999 to October 2002, when it was suspended and direct rule from Westminster reinstated. Political talks in 2006 (the St Andrews Agreement) paved the way for elections in March 2007 that reinforced the position of formerly 'extremist' parties in each community, the Democratic Unionists and Sínn Fein, and in an historic compromise they agreed to work together in the Executive, which was reactivated in May 2007.

Devolution does not mean that social policy is no longer debated at the UK level. If separate systems at sub-national level are less good than the norm, they will not be politically attractive, and if they are better and more expensive, national governments may not be happy to finance them. Politically, the need for separate political management of Scotland, Wales and Northern Ireland is now decisively conceded, but with Westminster still the fiscal underwriter of devolution, there is a tension in United Kingdom social policy between tolerating differences on grounds of diversity and choice, and resisting them on grounds of uniform citizen rights without 'postcode lotteries'.

Nation-Specific Social Policy Legislation

The legislative framework for social policy is generally the same for social security throughout the United Kingdom (Northern Ireland has different original legislation but has had strict parity of structure and rates, and devolution has not altered this). Pre-devolution, education and housing legislation were largely the same in England and Wales but different in Scotland and Northern Ireland (especially in the structure of school examinations in Scotland and denominational education in Northern Ireland). These latter two nations also had a distinct tradition in health. Scotland temporarily converged with the English norm after it was included in the Conservative Party's internal market legislation in 1991, but later returned to a centrally run uniform structure, merging NHS Trusts into Health Boards in 2004. In Wales, NHS local management has been aligned to local government boundaries. Both nations have resisted the English approach of Foundation Trust Hospitals and the use of privately contracted services has been less (see table 35.1 for a comparison of structures).

Since devolution, the Scottish Parliament is free to legislate in non-reserved areas, and in addition the Sewel Convention allows it to ask Westminster to make changes in statutes in devolved areas as part of UK legislation (used most notably in the 2004 law to institute civil partnerships). The most significant Scottish Parliament social policy legislation includes the 2001 Housing (Scotland) Act which created a single kind of social tenancy and new policies on homelessness, the 2002 Community Care and Health (Scotland) Act to set a framework for non-means-tested personal care, the 2003 Mental Health (Care and Treatment) (Scotland) Act to implement a careful reform of mental health policy after review by the Millan Commit-

tee in 2001 and the 2004 Anti-Social Behaviour Act (Scotland), seen as taking a tougher attitude to youth crime issues. Perhaps the most eye-catching initiative was the ban on smoking in public places in March 2006, over a year ahead of the rest of the UK.

The National Assembly for Wales does not have full powers to make primary legislation, and its policy discretion is within a legislative framework set by the Westminster Parliament. The first Wales-only post-devolution act was one to establish a Children's Commissioner for Wales, but there were then major Wales-only provisions in education and health legislation and the scope of the Assembly via secondary legislation in practice widened. The 2006 Government of Wales Act introduced the concept of an 'Assembly Measure' in devolved areas, edging closer to full law-making on the Scottish model and allowing this to be achieved after a further referendum.

The Operation of the Devolved Administration

The Scottish and Welsh administrations (which call themselves the Scottish Government – until 2007 this was the Scottish Executive – and the Welsh Assembly Government) are descendants of the 'joined-up' former Scottish and Welsh Offices. Scotland has non-statutory departments – in social policy areas, education, health and justice and communities serving Cabinet secretaries for health and well-being, education and lifelong learning, and justice. Wales has groups serving ministers for education, health and social justice; since April 2006 the main central delivery agencies (Education and Learning Wales, Welsh Development Agency, and the Qualifications, Curriculum and Assessment Authority for Wales) have been absorbed into the Assembly government civil service. In

Northern Ireland, social policy depart-ments, which have statutory existence as part of the power-sharing between parties, are Education, Employment and Learning (including post-16 education), Health, Social Services and Public Safety, and Social Development (including housing and social security).

The role of committees of elected members is an essential part of the systems, as part of a general philosophy of openness and participation. All three have perma-nent committees in the subject-area of each minister that combine the functions of leg-islative scrutiny and policy investigation. In Scotland, the committees have the power to initiate legislation; there is also a Public Petitions Committee to consider petitions from citizens on an issue or grievance, which has sometimes led to the investiga-tion of a local health problem by a single member. In Wales, the assembly and admin-istration were initially a single legal and corporate entity; assembly clerks were civil servants and ministers sat on committees, but in May 2007 a Westminster-style sepa-ration took effect.

In Northern Ireland, concurrent mem-bership of local authorities by many Assem-bly members, and the running of most social policy through province-wide central government bodies, means that the Assem-bly's work has been much more issue- and locality-based than external impressions of political divisions might suggest. Northern Ireland's previous devolved government until 1972 maintained religiously discrimi-natory features in education and housing while seeking parity with mainland stan-dards in health and social security. Later policies emphasized equal opportunities (with explicit legislation against religious discrimination, and Catholic schools now funded equally) and left a relatively benign and well-resourced climate for social policy, with minimal direct political input. The economic and security context of policy left politicians disinclined to attack the welfare

state, and the Northern Ireland Assembly was slow to pass any distinctive social policy legislation. School education retains selectivity on academic grounds in a way not found in the rest of the United Kingdom: a review of post-primary education in 2001 recommended that it should be ended, and direct rule ministers reaffirmed the plan to implement this in 2008.

The residual Whitehall arms remain. The Northern Ireland Office still has responsibility for police, prisons and crimi-nal justice. but these are intended for devo-lution to the Assembly at a later stage. The Wales Office has had a role in facilitating Welsh legislation within the UK govern-ment's programme, but the Scotland Office has no such function and its official role of monitoring Scottish interests in the UK Cabinet system is of dubious necessity. Where liaison is really important, the Scottish government deals directly with the Whitehall department.

The administration of social policy in the four nations of the United Kingdom is summarized in table 35.1. Local govern-ment in the three nations is much more neatly organized than it is in England. In 1996, local government in Scotland and Wales was reorganized from two-tier (regions or counties and districts, the pattern in much of England) to single-tier (32 and 22 authorities). Northern Ireland has had 26 districts since 1973, but with all the important social functions administered by appointed bodies (Education and Librar-ies Boards, Health and Social Services Boards – uniquely in the United Kingdom uniting health and social work – and the Northern Ireland Housing Executive). Other functions – roads, water, social secu-rity – are administered by agencies of the Northern Ireland Civil Service. Plans in November 2005 called for the reduction of the number of local authorities from 26 to 7 (with Belfast unchanged) and single Northern Ireland authorities for health and education.

Table 35.1 Who runs United Kingdom social policy

Health	Scottish Executive Health Department	Welsh Assembly Government NHS Directorate	Department of Health and Public Safety	Department of Health
	14 Health Boards	22 local health groups	4 Health and Social Services Boards	NHS Executive and 10 Strategic Health Authorities
			15 Health and Social Services Trusts	56 Foundation Trust hospitals
				118 acute/specialist trusts
				296 Primary Care Trusts
Education	Scottish Executive Education Department/ Enterprise and Lifelong Learning Department	Welsh Assembly Government (Education Group) 22 local authorities	Department of Education/ Department of Employment and Learning	Department for Education and Skills
	32 local authorities	Education and Learning Wales (within Welsh Assembly Government)	5 Education and Library Boards	Local authorities Higher Education Funding Council for England
	Scottish Funding Council (further and higher education)			Further Education Funding Council
Housing	Communities Scotland (agency within Scottish Executive Development Department)	Housing for Wales (*Tai Cymru*) (within Welsh Assembly Government)	Department of Social Development Northern Ireland Housing Executive	Local authorities Housing Corporation
	32 local authorities	22 local authorities	Housing associations	Housing associations
	Registered Social Landlords (including housing associations)	Housing associations		
Training	Scottish Enterprise, Highlands & Islands Enterprise	Education and Learning Wales (within Welsh Assembly Government)	Training and Employment Agency (within Department of Employment and Learning)	Learning and Skills Council
	22 areas of the local enterprise network			25 Sector Skills councils

Source: compiled mainly from Departmental Reports, Cm 6800-20 (HMSO 2006).

Table 35.2 Spending per head on social policy, 2005–6 (£)

Index: UK = 100	Total social	Social protection	Health	Education and training	Housing and community amenities
Northern Ireland	122	121	111	125	295
Scotland	113	112	119	108	186
Wales	106	112	100	100	86
London	109	100	113	116	165
North-east	112	114	111	108	101
North-west	107	114	107	102	108
Yorkshire & Humberside	100	99	103	101	85
West Midlands	98	101	96	100	72
South-west	93	96	94	89	46
East Midlands	91	92	90	96	61
East	86	88	87	84	41
South-east	87	86	88	90	65
(UK average	5,615	2,813	1,481	1,166	155)

Source: calculated from HM Treasury, *Public Expenditure Statistical Analyses 2005–6*, Cm 6811 (2006), table 7.11.

Needs and Resources at Sub-National Level

The UK's social policy has been underwritten by an implicit north-west to south-east gradient – Scotland, Wales, Northern Ireland and northern England were seen as relatively deprived and so could claim additional resources to deal with their problems. These differentials have narrowed, though since devolution Scotland has weakened relatively on unemployment and incomes, an issue in the debate over independence. Parts of Scotland and Wales have qualified for help from European Union Structural Funds because of the decline in smokestack industries like coal and steel, urban multiple deprivation or rural deprivation (see chapter 36). An opportunistic redrawing of the map in 1999 allowed West Wales and the Valleys to join Northern Ireland in qualifying for 'Objective 1' status in 2000 because of their low income

per head. The reduced money on offer from 2007 to 2013 is spread more thinly between 'competitiveness' and 'convergence' programmes, the latter including West Wales and the Valleys. But because house prices are lower and public sector health and education better serviced, the non-English nations may feel better off and rank high in subjective quality-of-life indices.

This provides the backdrop to the position on relative public spending (table 35.2). Figures for 2005–6 reveal that Northern Ireland and Scotland receive more social expenditure per head than does any region of England, 22 and 13 per cent more than the average, but that Wales (6 per cent more) is behind London and the north-east. The differentials have converged since devolution started. Housing differentials stand out: over 25 per cent of Scottish dwellings are still owned by social landlords against under 20 per cent in England and Wales, but general rent subsidies have been nearly eliminated in recent years and public housing expenditure is small. More important is Scotland's advantage in health and education, which is more structural in nature and does raise issues for expenditure management. A Needs Assessment Study in 1979 confirmed that provision to Scotland ran ahead of need, and there has been post-devolution pressure for a new exercise.

The formula (the Barnett formula) used for apportioning expenditure to the nations remains after devolution: put simply, the budget changes year-by-year in step with changes in corresponding English expenditure and is transferred as a block to the devolved administrations which can alter priorities within the block without reference to the Treasury. This avoids constant haggling over items and is meant to converge expenditure over time, because new money is apportioned on a population basis rather than on historic shares. In practice, the differentials are moving only slowly and they are no longer underwritten by palpable economic disadvantage.

Flexible Initiatives at Sub-National Level

An important justification for devolution is that it allows for flexibility and experimentation within the UK. Centralization of policy change, with its massive reorganizations (health, education, local government structure and finance) proceeding in one step throughout the country, risks the centralization of error to which England is prone.

Devolution has enabled Wales to match some of Scotland's long-standing capacity to innovate and experiment in social policy. In 1968 the Scottish system of children's hearings (non-judicial disposals of the cases of children in trouble) defined, in contrast to England, the policy area as social work rather than law and order. Scottish school examinations remain quite different, with

broadly based Highers rather than more specialized A-levels. From 1998, the 'Higher Still' proposals integrated post-16 academic and vocational qualifications. The Welsh language is promoted in Welsh schools more than ever before, even in nearly exclusively English-speaking areas, and post-devolution Wales has moved further towards a distinctive educational policy through the abolition of school tests for 7-year olds, the elimination of league tables for school examination results and work on a 'Welsh baccalaureate' to replace A-levels (piloted from 2003 in a looser form).

Since devolution, policy initiatives have tended to greater generosity in Scotland and Wales. The main developments are that Scotland has abolished student tuition fees and partially reinstated loans; Wales made prescriptions and check-ups free for the under-25s and over-60s, prior to abolishing them entirely, and introduced a 'learning grant' to provide variable financial support to students in both higher and further education, with a system of 'learning pathways'. Scotland, and to a lesser extent Wales, is moving towards non-means-tested personal care for the elderly in assessed need in response to the 1999 Royal Commission on Long-Term Care for the Elderly. Scotland's policy attracted much attention, but caps on the allowable fees and the need for local authority assessment of needs make it less free and universal than it might seem. All these were pursued under pressure from the Liberal Democrats and many Labour ministers were uncomfortable at moving in different policy directions from New Labour in London.

On the administrative side, much depends on the scale of the problems and the personal interest of ministers and officials. Wales had pioneered deinstitutionalization in the mental health area. The speed and nature of response to drug addiction and AIDS in Scotland has been facilitated by local responsibility. Housing has national bodies (Communities Scotland, formerly Scottish Homes, and Tai Cymru) able to mobilize housing associations and now absorbed into the civil service. Industrial development and training has had a much stronger and better-resourced administrative impetus in the territories than in England. The distinctiveness of policy in the territories should not be exaggerated, but the existence of their administrative apparatus both before and after devolution is a clear advantage when compared to the English regions.

Emerging Issues

Devolution has brought into focus two long-standing themes: the uniformity of social security rules (and of Treasury-based policies like the New Deal and tax credits) that make it hard to run devolved anti-poverty policies, and the ability of the three non-English nations to do things their own way, with relative Westminster indifference. Paradoxically, devolution policies that were meant to leave the territories to take local decisions have highlighted the occasions where the logic of their policy-making differs from that of the UK government. Before devolution, the relatively kind treatment of Scotland and Northern Ireland (but less so of Wales) on policy and expenditure was one of the political assumptions of the United Kingdom: now, it is coming under closer scrutiny, especially in some English regions where devolution opened up a potential sense of unfair dealing in relation to the non-English parts of the UK. Four issues have emerged that are likely to be taken further in the years ahead:

1   *Nostalgia for universalism*: the devolved administrations have resisted the targeting and differentiation now found in UK policy. In Wales, free prescription charges became an emblematic policy and were achieved for all in April 2007.

Scotland has pursued a more limited route on matters like free eyesight check-ups. Universalist thinking is evident in personal care for the elderly and, to a lesser extent, student support.

2   *Divergence in policy unrelated to local circumstances*, especially in health service organization (all matters except the framework of professional pay and conditions and the principle of non-charging of patients) and the 'lifelong learning' area (skills training, higher and further education in terms of provision, financing and charging – see chapters 40 and 42).

3   *Creative whole-system thinking*: the Scottish Executive's Futures Project appraised a wide range of political and social variables in their Strategic Audit of 2006, many of them not under the control of the executive or of government at all. The Scottish Parliament's Futures Forum has been the vehicle for a wider research effort, including a report on 'positive ageing'. The Welsh Assembly Government's joining-up agenda has been the most systematic in the UK, with the Beecham report 'Beyond Boundaries' in July 2006 and the WAG response, 'Making the Connections: Delivering Beyond Boundaries', in November 2006. Equality provisions (gender, ethnicity, religious community, language) have been taken forward in all three devolved nations with a valuable thinking-through from first principles.

4   *The risk of political instability*: the current devolution settlement seeks to respond in a non-uniform way to political pressures around the United Kingdom without any overall concept of multilevel government. After the north-east of England's 78 per cent 'no' vote to a regional assembly in 2004, devolution in England is stalled. A chronic problem is the so-called 'West Lothian question' – 59 MPs from

Scotland sit at Westminster (reduced from 72 in 2005) and can vote on England-only legislation in devolved fields. The Barnett formula is more than 25 years old and makes the devolved administrations vulnerable to changes in social policy expenditure in the Treasury's spending reviews. So far, there has not been full fiscal responsibility on them to fix tax levels in accordance with their spending decisions. The principal parties opposed to Labour in Scotland and Wales (the Scottish National Party, a single-party minority government since May 200, and Plaid Cymru – the Party of Wales) are to the left of Labour on social policy but favour full self-government for their nations. The initial excitement around devolution died down after 2001 as the UK-led international agenda gained political salience. Protection of the welfare state and exploration of further potential for self-government became the main themes of the 2007 devolved elections, and the outcome – two minority governments after an inability to negotiate majority coalition programmes – put into question whether the 1999 arrangements were in practice the stable settlement that their proponents had claimed.

Guide to Further Sources

Keeping up with post-devolution developments is not always easy: the best work is that of the Constitution Unit, which publishes quarterly monitoring reports on each of the devolved nations and the English regions: available at <www.ucl.ac.uk/constitution-unit> and with annual volumes from 2000 to 2005, most recently A. Trench (ed.) *The Dynamics of Devolution: The State of the Nations* (Imprint Academic, 2005).

A good summary is in J. Adams and K. Schmueker (eds), *Devolution in Practice 2006: Public Policy Differences Within the UK* (Institute for Public Policy Research, 2005). A pioneering comparative study is S. Greer, *Territorial Politics and Health Policy* (Manchester University Press, 2005). Research promoted by the ERRC Devolution and Constitutional Change Programme (2000–6) is summarized at <www.devolution.ac.uk>.

Journals like the quarterly *Scottish Affairs* and the annual *Contemporary Wales* are very useful. There is a wealth of statistical data in *Regional Trends*, published annually by The Stationery Office for the Office for National Statistics.

Publications of the devolved administrations are available on their websites: <scotland.gov.uk> and <wales.gov.uk> and <nics.gov.uk>. In Scotland, parliamentary reports are available at <scottish.parliament.uk> and Northern Ireland Assembly debates and reports are available at <ni-assembly.gov.uk>.

Chapter 36

Social Policy and the European Union

Linda Hantrais

Overview

- Social policy was a concern for the founder member states of the European Economic Community only insofar as it served to underpin economic development.
- Enlargement of the European Union brought increasing diversity of welfare systems, making harmonization difficult to achieve.
- The Union's institutions have progressively extended their authority, and EU intervention in national social affairs has become pervasive.
- The open method of coordination has been widely applied to social policy at EU level as a more viable alternative to hard law.
- While the Union has not been fully recognized as a legitimate supranational actor in the social policy field, the competence of member states has been eroded.

Introduction

The United Kingdom was not one of the six founding member states of the European Economic Community (EEC), established in 1957 with the signing of the Treaty of Rome. Following accession in 1973, the British government opposed Community action in the social policy area, and the UK was the only member state not to sign the 1989 Community Charter of the Fundamental Social Rights of Workers. Its opposition led to the Chapter on Social Affairs being relegated to a Protocol and Agreement on Social Policy, which were appended to the Maastricht Treaty on European Union when it came into force in 1993. The British government also sought to impede

the progress of legislation on workers' rights, including proposals for improving part-time working conditions, reducing working hours and introducing parental leave, on the grounds that they would impinge on national sovereignty and adversely affect employment. The election of the New Labour government in 1997 marked a turning point in the country's relations with social Europe. The UK signed up to the Agreement on Social Policy, which meant that the social chapter could be incorporated into the Treaty of Amsterdam in the same year, thus lending social policy a stronger legal base. Employment moved up the European agenda, and its priority was endorsed by both the Treaty and the Luxembourg Summit, also held in 1997, when the first employment guidelines were adopted. At the turn of the twenty-first century, as the Union enlarged to the East, a European social model was emerging, embodying citizenship rights and the core values that all member states were committed to pursue.

This chapter looks at the way in which the social policy remit of the European Union (EU) has evolved both prior to and since British membership. The European social policy formation and implementation processes are examined in an overview of the main policy-making bodies, the instruments available to them and the areas of intervention where they have been most active. The chapter goes on to identify some of the key debates surrounding the European social dimension, before commenting briefly on the linkages between national and European institutions engaged in social policy formation.

Developing the Union's Social Policy Remit

Although, as its name implied, the EEC was essentially an economic community, from the outset it acquired a social policy remit. Articles 117–28 of the Treaty of Rome, which dealt with social policy, advocated close cooperation between member states, particularly in matters relating to training, employment, working conditions, social security and collective bargaining. They also stated the need to observe the equal pay principle and make provision for the harmonization of social security measures to accommodate migrant workers. Specific arrangements were to be made for operating a European Social Fund (ESF) to assist in the employment and re-employment of workers and encourage geographical and occupational mobility.

In the post-war context of rapid economic growth, the underlying objectives of European social policy were to avoid any distortion of competition and promote free movement of labour within the Community. Since the welfare systems of the founder member states (Belgium, France, Federal Republic of Germany, Italy, Luxembourg, Netherlands) were based largely on the insurance principle, which depended on contributions from employers and employees, it was feared that unfair competition might arise if some countries levied higher social charges on employment, leading to social dumping as companies relocated to areas with lower labour costs. The expectation was that the functioning of the common market, in conjunction with the Treaty's rules preventing unfair competition, would automatically result in social development, so that the Community would not need to interfere directly with redistributive benefits. By the mid-1970s, economic growth was slowing down following the oil crises, and the belief in automatic social harmonization was called into question. A more active approach to social reform was therefore required. A 1974 resolution from the Council of Ministers on a social action programme proposed that the Community should work to develop common objectives for national social policies but without seeking to standardize solutions to social problems and without removing responsibility for social policy from member states.

Despite attempts to give a higher profile to social policy in the 1980s, the principle of subsidiarity, observed in the social action programme, set the tone for social legislation in subsequent years. The 1980s were marked by pressures to develop a 'social space', which the Commission President, Jacques Delors, saw as the natural complement to the completion of the internal market. Delors advocated social dialogue between trade unions and employers (the social partners) as a means of reaching agreement over objectives and establishing a minimum platform of guaranteed social (implying workers' employment-related) rights, to be applied by individual member states with a view to stimulating convergence.

The problem of agreeing even a minimum level of protection for workers was apparent in the negotiations leading up to the Community Charter of the Fundamental Social Rights of Workers, which did not have force of law and was couched in non-specific terms. The action programmes for implementing the Charter continued to recognize the importance of observing national diversity, and the Maastricht Treaty formalized the principle of subsidiarity, meaning that the Union is empowered to act only if its aims can be more effectively achieved at European than at national level. Since decisions about social policy frequently concern individuals or families, it can be argued that they are best taken at a local level remote from European institutions. Accordingly, opportunities for concerted action among nations are minimal.

EC membership has taken place in five successive waves, each making harmonization, or even convergence, of social policy provisions more difficult to achieve. The social protection systems of the six original EEC member states can be considered as variants of what has come to be known as the Bismarckian or continental model of welfare, based on the employment-insurance principle. The member states (Denmark, Ireland, United Kingdom) that joined the Community in the 1970s subscribed to social protection systems funded from taxation and aimed at universal flat-rate coverage. The southern states (Greece, Portugal, Spain) that became members in the early 1980s had less developed welfare systems, whereas the Nordic states (Finland, Sweden) that joined in 1995 shared features with Denmark, and Austria was closer to the German pattern. The two island states (Cyprus, Malta) and ten post-Soviet states (Bulgaria, Czech Republic, Estonia, Hungary, Latvia, Lithuania, Poland, Romania, Slovakia, Slovenia) that acceded to the Union in 2004 and 2007 brought yet further variants of welfare systems. The goal of harmonizing social protection seemed to be more pressing with the move towards the Single European Market (SEM) and economic and monetary union (EMU), and evidence could be found to suggest that some convergence occurred in the 1990s as a result of the common trend towards retrenchment of welfare, made necessary by economic recession, the shift towards mixed systems of welfare and progress towards EMU. However, attempts at European level to harmonize so many disparate welfare systems were progressively abandoned.

Social Policy-Making Processes in the EU

Despite the relatively limited social policy remit in the founding treaty, after fifty years of operation, the Union has developed what can be described as a multi-tiered system of governance. The Union's decision-making, legislative and implementation procedures depend upon a number of institutions, with their own functions and operating mechanisms, but often competing with one another. The Nice Treaty adopted at the European Council meeting in December 2000 and the resulting Convention charged with drafting an EU Constitution set out to revise these decision-making procedures in preparation for enlargement.

The Council of Ministers remains the main governing body representing national interests and responsible for taking decisions on laws to be applied across the Union. All the heads of government meet twice a year to determine policy directions. The presidency of the Council rotates between member states every six months, providing the opportunity for national governments to set the policy agenda, with each member state having a fixed number of votes. The Nice Treaty proposed a re-weighting of votes to ensure that the influence of the smaller countries would not become disproportionate to their size. The Single European Act (SEA) of 1986 had introduced qualified majority voting (QMV) in the areas of health and safety at work, working conditions, information and consultation of workers, equality between men and women and the integration of persons excluded from the labour market, with the aim of facilitating the passage of contentious legislation. QMV was extended to active employment measures when they were introduced into the Amsterdam Treaty, and provision was made in the Nice Treaty to apply QMV to anti-discrimination measures, mobility and specific action supporting economic and social cohesion.

The Commission formally initiates, implements and monitors European legislation. Commissioners are political appointees but are expected to act independently of national interests. Since 2005, each member state has one Commissioner. The directorates-general (DGs) are responsible for preparing proposals and working documents for consideration by the Council of Ministers and, therefore, play an important part in setting the Union's policy agenda. For example, the 1995 White Paper on European Social Policy, drafted by the DG for Employment and Social Affairs, established a framework for EU action through to the twenty-first century. The Nice Treaty reinforced this role by providing for the Commission to establish a Social Protection Committee to monitor the social situation, promote exchange of information and prepare reports and opinions.

The European Court of Justice (ECJ), which sits in Luxembourg, is the Union's legal voice and the guardian of treaties and implementing legislation. Its judges are appointed by the governments of member states for six-year terms of office. Its main tasks are to ensure that legal instruments adopted at European and national levels are compatible with European law. Through its interpretation of legislation, it has built up a substantial and influential body of case law in the social area. The Amsterdam Treaty extended the ECJ's jurisdiction further by giving it powers to ensure that the article on fundamental rights is observed by EU institutions. The Charter of Fundamental Rights of the European Union, finalized at the Nice summit in 2000, provides a clear statement of the rights of all European citizens, thereby reinforcing the role of the ECJ.

The European Parliament is directly elected by citizens of member states. It has budgetary and supervisory powers. Although it cannot initiate bills, it can decline to take up a position on a Commission proposal and require the Commission to answer its questions. MEPs form political rather than national blocks. Their powers were increased by the SEA, and then by the Amsterdam Treaty, which extended Parliament's involvement in decision-making in the social policy area. The Nice Treaty applied the codecision procedure to the same social areas as for QMV.

The Union's legal sources include primary legislation in the form of treaties and secondary legislation ranging from regulations, directives and decisions, which are its most binding instruments, to recommendations, resolutions and opinions, which are advisory, or communications and memoranda, which are used to signal initial thinking on an issue. Relatively few regulations have been introduced in the social field, with the exception of freedom of movement of workers and the Structural Funds. Directives, which lay down objectives for legislation but leave individual states to select the most suitable form of implementation, have been used to considerable effect in the areas of equal treatment and health and safety at work. Recommendations have played an important role in developing a framework for concerted action and convergence in the social policy field.

The open method of coordination (OMC) was formally introduced as a method of intervention at the Lisbon Summit in 2000. It offers a soft-law alternative designed to encourage cooperation, the exchange of best practice and agreement on common targets and guidelines for member states, supported in the case of employment and social exclusion by national action plans. It relies on regular monitoring of progress to meet the targets set, allowing member states to compare their efforts and learn from the experience of others.

The Union has established a broad array of multilayered and fragmented policy-making institutions and instruments, which are often in competition with national systems. European policy-making is, therefore, subject to a complex process of negotiation and compromise, involving vested interests and trade-offs. While the progress of the social dimension has undoubtedly been slowed down by internal wrangling, the Union has gradually extended its area of competence and authority.

EU Social Policy Intervention

The Commission's objective of removing barriers to the free movement of labour has served to justify policies for coordinating social protection systems, mutual recognition of qualifications, the improvement of living and working conditions and directives on equality of access to social benefits and measures to combat poverty. From the 1970s, Community programmes were initiated in these areas, and the Commission also set up networks and observatories to stimulate action and monitor progress in the social field.

Rather than seeking to change national systems, action in the area of education and training focused initially on comparing the content and level of qualifications across the Community in an attempt to reach agreement over transferability from one member state to another. General directives were issued on the mutual recognition of the equivalence of diplomas. From the mid-1970s, action programmes were initiated at European level to develop vocational training, encourage mobility among students and young workers and stimulate cooperation between education and industry. By the early 2000s, the Commission was advocating investment in human resources through quality education and lifelong learning as important components in the European social model and European identity.

Several articles in the EEC Treaty were devoted to the improvement of living and working conditions as a means of equalizing opportunities and promoting mobility. Particular attention was paid to health and safety at work, resulting in a large body of binding legislation. The introduction of QMV meant that the health and safety banner could be used to initiate directives designed not only to ensure the protection of workers against dangerous products and other industrial hazards, but also to control the organization of working time, protect pregnant women and take forward wider issues concerning public health.

In line with the priority given to employment policy and working conditions at European level, the Commission has instigated legislation and set up action programmes to protect women as workers, including directives requiring equal pay for work of equal value, equal treatment and employment-related social insurance rights. Increasingly, attention has been paid to measures designed to help reconcile occupational and family life. Legislation in this area was, for many years, opposed by some member states – notably Denmark and the UK – which were wary of the possible impact on employment practices and equal opportunities. The British opt-in to the social chapter in 1997 resulted in the UK signing up to the parental leave directive, which meant that the directive on part-time work could finally be adopted. Gender mainstreaming was introduced to deal with persistent inequalities in all areas of activity.

In the 1970s, the impact of economic recession, rising unemployment and demographic ageing moved onto the policy agenda, while the prospect of greater freedom of movement heightened concern about welfare tourism and the exporting of poverty from one member state to another, as unemployed workers and their families sought to move to states with more generous provision. The Commission, therefore, funded a series of action programmes to combat poverty and social exclusion, and the Structural Funds were deployed to underpin regional policy by tackling the sources of economic disparities. The employment guidelines, introduced by the Amsterdam Treaty, served as a major plank in the Union's strategy to combat exclusion from the labour market by improving employability through active policy measures.

In a context where greater life expectancy has been accompanied by heavy demands on pension provision, health and care services, member states have become increasingly concerned, individually and collectively, about the effects of population ageing on social protection systems. The Commission has monitored provision for older and disabled people, particularly with regard to maintenance and caring, arrangements for transferring the rights of mobile workers and pensioners and the overall impact of policy on living standards. Communications published in 1999 and 2006 proposed strategies for strengthening solidarity and equity between the generations.

Despite the considerable body of legislation on freedom of movement, information about intra-European mobility suggests that migration between member states has remained relatively low, although enlargement to the East initially provoked an unprecedented westwards wave of internal migration from Central and East European countries. Progressively, more attention has been paid to the problems arising from third country migration and the challenges it poses not only for coordinating national policies but also for issues concerning refugees and asylum-seekers. This progression was recognized when the right to equality of opportunity and treatment, without distinction of race, colour, ethnicity, national origin, culture or religion, was written into the Treaty of Amsterdam, and all discrimination on these grounds was outlawed in the Union's Charter of Fundamental Rights.

While doubts may be expressed about the coherence of the Union's social policy remit, these examples illustrate how the Union's institutions have developed a wide-ranging competence in social affairs, with the result that they have become a major, if disputed, social policy actor.

Key Issues in European Social Policy Analyses

In the early 2000s, the Commission still formally recognized that member states should remain responsible for their own systems of social protection, but, as in the original Treaty of Rome, it continued to advocate closer cooperation with a view to identifying possible common objectives and solutions. The debates of the 1970s and 1980s over fundamental issues, such as whether or not the Community should have a social dimension, seemed to have lost their salience in the face of pressing socio-demographic problems requiring common responses.

Although EU member states have generally failed to agree about the extent of the involvement of the Union in the social policy area or the form it should take, they did seem able to reach a broad consensus about the major social problems they were confronting in the early 2000s. Demographic trends in combination with technological and structural change, the impact of further enlargement and the extension of the Union's sphere of influence were creating new pressures on welfare systems. Member states were jointly seeking ways of dealing with persistently high levels of unemployment, shortages of skilled labour, long-term dependency of older people and the changing structure of households and gender relations, while struggling to contain the costs of providing high-quality services.

These trends were calling into question the principles on which national social security systems were founded. EU member states were concerned to ensure the financial viability and sustainability of social protection systems, while safeguarding employment and avoiding the development of a dependency culture. Population ageing had raised questions about the conditions governing retirement age and pension rights, while also exacerbating the problems of making provision for health and social care. Different mixes of solutions were being tried: greater targeting of benefits, the tightening of eligibility criteria and emphasis on active measures to move people off benefits and into work, the introduction of new social insurance schemes to cover long-term care and the privatization of services. By the early 2000s, the Commission had identified as a major challenge the need to modernize social protection systems in response to socio-economic change and enlargement, while at the same time consolidating the European social model and reinforcing intergenerational solidarity.

Emerging Issues: Sharing European and National Competence

Despite the blocking tactics of some member states, a considerable body of legislation and practice – *acquis communautaire* – has been put in place, requiring compliance from national governments and constraining their domain of action. However, the changes brought about by the SEA, Maastricht, Amsterdam and Nice Treaties, the British opt-in to the social chapter and the shift towards less binding forms of legislation in the social field have tended to result in standards being set that can realistically be achieved by the least advanced countries – the lowest common denominator – and have left individual member states with greater discretion in policy implementation.

The illustrations used in this chapter of the Union's social policy competence suggest that the policy-making process is dependent upon the ability of a plurality of national and supranational actors to cooperate in setting objectives, initiating, enacting and implementing legislation. The sharing of responsibility distinguishes European structures from those of most international organizations. As in federal states, the Union has to steer a difficult path in acting for the greater good of its member states, which is itself not easy to identify, while not encroaching too far into national sovereignty or infringing the principle of subsidiarity. A delicate balance has to be struck in accommodating the interests of the different tiers of the Union's institutions, some of which are protecting and promoting national causes (Council of Ministers and Parliament, national governments), while others are expected to act independently of governments (Commission and ECJ). Consequently, the Union has still not secured full legitimacy as a supranational authority in the social policy field, whereas the competence of member states has undoubtedly been eroded.

Guide to Further Sources

The development of the social dimension of the Union, its role in setting a European-wide social policy agenda and the impact of its policies at national level are analysed by L. Hantrais, *Social Policy in the European Union*, 3rd edn (Palgrave and St Martin's Press, 2007). M. Ferrera, *The Boundaries of Welfare: European Integration and the New Spatial Politics of Social Protection* (Oxford University Press, 2005) examines how European integration has redrawn the boundaries of national welfare states from a comparative public policy perspective. P. Pestieau, *The Welfare State in the European Union: Economic and Social Perspectives* (Oxford University Press, 2006) analyses the performance of the welfare state in terms of the debate between equity and effficiency. The edited collection, G. De Búrca, *EU Law and the Welfare State: In Search of Solidarity* (Oxford University Press, 2005) explores the ways in which EU law impinges on national welfare systems and the resulting tensions it produces.

Regular updates on demographic trends, the social situation, social protection and employment are available at: <www:europa.eu.int/comm/employment_socialindex_en.htm> (the Directorate General for Employment, Social Affairs and Equal Opportunities website).

Chapter 37

Social Policy and Supranational Governance

Nicola Yeates

Overview

- International governmental and non-governmental organizations constitute an increasingly crucial element in understanding social policy-making and provision.
- International organizations are involved in the financing, regulation and provision of welfare and influence policy formation in diverse ways.
- Debates over social policy reform at global level are caught up in wider discussions about whether to reform or radically change the structure of global governance.
- Global social policy focuses attention on these transnational dimensions of social provision and governance and raises new questions about the study of social policy.

From (Inter)national Social Policy to Global Social Policy

As is discussed elsewhere in this volume, there is a growing debate about the extent to which globalization processes are implicated in current changes in national welfare systems (see chapters 53 and 54). A further dimension of this is the emergence of global social policy as a field of study and an activity that transcends, or cuts across, nation-states (see chapter 1). The distinctive focus of global social policy lies with the transnational dimensions of social policy and welfare provision, in particular on:

- the extent to which social policy issues are increasingly being perceived to be global in scope and cause;

- the emergence of transnational forms of collective action, including the development of supranational organizations and multilateral modes of governance; and
- how these modes of governance and policy-making are shaping the development of social policy and the social outcomes of policy.

Global policy analysts – and advisers – thus challenge the prevailing assumption that the nation-state is the only (or best) socio-spatial category for perceiving and understanding welfare arrangements. They emphasize that social policy is now a central issue in global politics, and that global and national social politics are deeply intertwined.

Box 37.1   Examples of global groupings of IGOs and INGOs

IGOs	*INGOs*
Global	
World Bank	World Economic Forum
International Monetary Fund	World Social Forum
United Nations	World Water Forum
UN agencies, e.g. International Labour Organization, World Health Organization, Unicef	International Confederation of Free Trade Unions
	International Planned Parenthood Federation
World Trade Organization	
Organization for Economic Cooperation and Development	Oxfam, War on Want
	International Pharmaceutical Industries Association
G8, G77, G24 etc	
Regional	
European Union	European Services Forum
North American Free Trade Agreement (NAFTA)	European Trade Union Confederation
	European Social Forum
ASEAN (Association of South East Asian Nations)	Asian Social Forum
	African Social Forum
South Asian Area for Regional Cooperation (SAARC)	
Mercado Común del Sur (Southern Core Common Market) (Mercosur)	
Caribbean Community and Common Market (CARICOM)	
Southern African Development Community (SADC)	

International Organizations

International cooperation and action in matters of social policy are by no means a recent phenomenon, but over the course of the last century this cooperation expanded and intensified. A multiplicity of international organizations (IOs) are now involved in a wide range of international agreements, treaties, regulations and accords. These IOs include both international *governmental* organizations (IGOs) and international *non-governmental* organizations (INGOs). IGOs are essentially international forums through which sovereign governments enter into collaborative political and legal relationships, while INGOs are entities through which voluntary, charitable, trade union, professional associations, industry organizations and business groups collaborate. Some of these organizations operate on a worldwide scale, others do so on a world-regional scale. Box 37.1 provides some illustrative examples of these different groupings.

Box 37.2 Examples of social governance at national, world-regional and global levels

	National	*EU*	*Global*
Economic stability	Central banks	European Central Bank in Eurozone	IMF / Bank for International settlements
Revenue	Taxation	Customs revenues, plus member state donations (note discussion of tax harmonization)	Mix of UN appeals, ad hoc global funds, multilateral overseas development assistance
Redistribution	Tax and income transfers policy	Structural funds Common Agricultural Policy	Ad hoc humanitarian relief, special global funds, debt relief, differential pricing of drugs
Regulation	State laws and directives	EU laws, regulations and directives, including Social Charter	UN conventions WTO trade law Voluntary corporate codes of conduct
Citizenship rights	Court redress Consumer charters Tripartite governance	Court redress Tripartite governance	UN Commission for Human Rights but no legal redress

Source: adapted from Deacon et al. 2003.

At whatever scale they operate, IOs vary considerably in terms of resources (see box 37.2). A number of INGOs command significant budgets and are better staffed than some IGOs (compare, for example, the WTO's 630 staff with Oxfam's 2,800 staff). Some IGOs have no independent legal force or permanent secretariat; others have the force of international law behind them (WTO, EU, UN) and/or substantial bureaucracies (ILO, WB, EU, UN). Many may be little more than political alliances or 'clubs' comprising a minority of the world's governments without a permanent secretariat (G8, G24, G77).

IOs' Involvement in Social Policy

IOs are playing an increasingly significant role in policy formation and implementation. Of all such formations, the EU has the most extensive social policy programme (see chapter 36), but substantial and routine co-operation exists in a variety of domains bearing on individual and communal welfare:

- trade, fiscal, investment and macro-economic policy;
- the environment;
- employment and livelihoods;

Box 37.3 Examples of IO involvement in welfare provision, finance and regulation

	Provision	*Finance*	*Regulation*
Global	Humanitarian relief, population programmes, social development projects, special global (health, social) funds delivered through IGOs and INGOs	Revenue raised from appeals, donations and ODA channelled into ad hoc humanitarian relief, special global funds, debt relief and differential pricing (drugs)	International labour and social standards through ILO, OECD conventions; human rights through UN; social, health and education in international trade law, economic forums
Regional (EU)	Human resources/ social funds, regional development funds	Revenues raised from customs and government donations distributed through agricultural and structural funds	Labour and social standards through regulations, directives and agreements

Source: adapted from Deacon et al. 2003.

- migration and asylum;
- social security and pensions;
- education and training;
- health and social care;
- housing;
- food and water security;
- fertility and population control;
- humanitarian and development aid.

IGOs

The involvement of IGOs in the regulation, financing and provision of welfare services is substantial (see box 37.3). There have been important attempts at regulation through international level standard-setting by the UN and its agencies, such as the ILO and WHO. These organizations have also experimented with international financing for welfare services (e.g. ILO's Global Social Trust), as has the World Bank (through its development loans programmes). The WTO is an important actor in global social policy as a result of its role in implementing international trade treaties, such as the GATS (General Agreement on Trade in Services), TRIPS (trade-related intellectual property) and TRIMS (trade-related investment measures).

INGOs

INGOs are involved in all parts of the global policy-making process, in agenda- and norm-setting, and in policy formation and implementation. Some enjoy official consultative status, working, for instance, through various UN and World Bank NGO Committees. They have also been encouraged to mobilize transnationally, aided by EU and UN funding. Equally critically, NGOs play a key role in delivering many IGOs' programmes, including humanitarian aid. Their local presence offers a link to areas and groups that IGOs lack and a means of filling gaps in provision for poor, rural and conflict-ridden communities where political and economic conditions do not attract for-profit providers.

This growing participation of NGOs in global policy formation and implementation is often seen as signifying the emergence of a 'global civil society' and the democratization and socialization of global politics. For some, though, it is consistent with the global neo-liberalism which equates voluntary action with such values as self-interest, hard work, flexibility, freedom of choice, private property and distrust of state bureaucracy. Also, many INGOs are associations of industrial, commercial and for-profit organizations. From this perspective, IGOs' encouragement of civil society participation in social policy simply involves INGOs in residualizing social policies, albeit dressed up in the language of social development, participation, and empowerment.

The Impact of IOs on Social Policy

It is, however, difficult to ascertain the influence of either IGOs or INGOs on national social policies. One reason for this is the multi-dimensional nature of this influ-

ence and its multiple manifestations. Recent studies therefore tend to distinguish between different kinds of influences and channels that impact on social policy, for example:

- Many IGOs provide a forum for mutual education, analysis and debate. While this may not directly or immediately produce formal agreements or common policy agendas, it promotes shared analyses, beliefs and concerns that inform policy discussion and provide a platform for future collaboration.
- International social standards – as defined in the UN's human rights charters, the ILO's Labour Conventions or the WHO's Health Conventions, for example – provide a global socio-legal framework for national social policies.
- Market integration processes generate a need for and may direct social policy regulatory reform. For example, the creation of a Common Market in Western Europe and Latin America involved labour and social security measures to promote labour mobility.
- Economic integration impacts on the quality of social provision. The creation of regional or global markets in welfare services may undermine cross-class social solidarity, while free movement of capital may trigger a competitive devaluation of public welfare schemes ('social dumping').

Studies of IO influence on social policy also ask what makes some organizations successful in some contexts rather than others. These emphasize how national governments often seem to freely 'pick and mix' among a range of proposals offered to them; at other times they may be steered to accepting certain recommendations through the provision of financial aid or other inducements and benefits. Recognizing these issues, recent studies therefore tend to emphasize the subtle and less subtle ways in which IGOs try to influence national policy reforms and their mixed successes in achieving their goals.

In sum, IOs do more than form part of the social policy backcloth or context: they actively participate in the political and policy processes and set (or attempt to influence the setting of) the terms of international trade, aid and development policies; the allocation and use of aid, development and social funds; and social standards and norms.

IOs also oversee, and are sometimes directly involved in, the implementation of social policies and programmes. Through these activities these actors shape the distribution of resources worldwide, frame social policy debate in national and global spheres of governance, and influence the nature of social provision in national contexts.

Asking questions about the ways in which IOs are involved in the making of social policy disrupts the national focus of attention. This carries through to the concepts we work with (see above). In the following section we look at how social policy concepts can be applied to the analysis of global policy interventions.

Social Policy Concepts in a Global Context

Equality, rights and justice

In transposing the concepts of equality, rights and justice from the interpersonal or intergroup level to the global one, global social policy analysts analyse the extent to which the world is a 'fair' place. They often do so by examining international datasets on poverty and social inequality to gauge the extent to which the social welfare needs of the world's population are being met and how resources are distributed worldwide.

They also analyse the differences in the extent to which citizenship rights are differentially embodied and guaranteed by global formations. Here, we could contrast European arrangements with the lack of progress at the level of global institutions. The Council of Europe provides European citizens with the right to equal treatment before the Court of Human Rights in Strasbourg; the UN identifies similar rights through the International Covenant on Economic, Social and Cultural Rights and the Declaration of Human Rights, but it has no mechanism for their legal enforcement nor does it allow individual rights of petition. A further issue is the hierarchy of economic and social rights: some international treaties (e.g. WTO's GATS, North America's NAFTA) have established certain enforceable economic (trade and investment) rights for businesses while eschewing protective social and labour rights for citizens.

A question arising from the application of the citizenship concept to the global context concerns the extent to which social rights are inherent rights that attach to all human beings irrespective of the cultural and economic context. 'Cosmopolitans' argue that some or all of the presently defined labour standards defined by the ILO Philadelphia Declaration (1944) are universal rights. 'Nationalists' advocate a kind of global relativism, arguing that it is for individual countries and communities to decide what constitutes an appropriate set of rights and what mix of rights carries corresponding social obligations.

Efficiency, equity and choice

In a global context, debates about efficiency, equity and choice become a discussion about whether global production and trade should be subject to social rules.

'Free' trade advocates argue that international trade is the best way of improving individual and communal welfare, as globally competitive countries, businesses and labour forces will attract more investment and opportunities. Critics, however, point to how global competition often involves the super-exploitation of vulnerable labour forces in poorer countries, and how rich countries like the UK and US maintain international trade barriers while demanding that developing countries remove theirs. They argue that free trade policies encourage countries to engage in competitive social deregulation to attract foreign investment or prevent capital flight overseas, measures which produce inefficient, sub-optimal social and economic outcomes.

Some advocates of 'free trade' policies are beginning to appreciate the benefits of certain kinds of social regulations, if only to avoid the worst economic effects of political and consumer activism against products made involving exploited labour. But attempts to establish coherent global social regulations have seen limited success. One unsuccessful attempt in the late 1990s was the 'social clause', which proposed making market access conditional upon governments meeting 'core' labour standards. This was opposed on the grounds that 'free' trade will 'lift all boats' and that it is a form of protectionism by the Global North against the Global South. Recent regulatory measures have shown a tendency towards voluntarism: the OECD Guidelines for Multinational Enterprises set out principles for socially oriented business practices, but MNCs' observance of them is strictly voluntary. And although voluntary codes of corporate conduct have proliferated, outside monitoring of their implementation rests upon the efforts of individual NGOs.

A further issue concerns the effects of 'free trade' policies and international trade treaties on the quality of public health and welfare services. There are concerns that international trade law (GATS) may prevent governments from financing comprehensive public services and providing adequate consumer protection for commercial products since doing so could breach the requirement for regulatory measures to be 'least trade restrictive' and not to 'distort' the market.

Altruism, reciprocity and obligation

Applications of the ideas of altruism, reciprocity and social obligation to the global sphere can be found in many of the policies and programmes of IOs and international agreements. The IMF and World Bank embody these ideas insofar as they provide finance for socio-economic development projects in 'developing' countries; the UNHCR has overall responsibility for the care of refugees worldwide. The specification of a target of 0.7 per cent of national GDP that countries should allocate for Overseas Development Assistance (ODA), debt relief packages for low-income highly indebted countries and the Millennium Development Goals (MDGs) are further examples of recent moves to globalize a sense of social solidarity. Other experiments in the international financing of social goods exist, such as the ILO's Global Social Trust in the field of social security. In the health field, examples include international agreements on the differential pricing of drugs and ethical codes of conduct to regulate the international recruitment of medical personnel (nurses) from certain developing countries by rich countries in the Global North.

Alongside IGOs are the efforts of philanthropic and charitable (including faith-based) groups. Northern Foundations (Ford, Volkswagen, Soros, Gates) are involved in funding global programmes of social research and social provision. Many of the recently created global funds and programmes, such as GAVI (the global vaccinations programme) and the GFATM (Global fund to Fight AIDS, Tuberculosis and Malaria), involve private sector financing. Many of UNICEF's activities and campaigns are funded by charitable and commercial support (through its Save the Children appeals).

One question is whether these apparent expressions of altruism, obligation and humanitarianism are little more than disguised self-interest on the part of those providing the finance. International loans and other kinds of aid often provide good economic returns to the lenders. The granting of economic aid to poorer countries, for example, may involve them purchasing the goods and services of businesses based in the lending countries. Many Western aid and development organizations make use of international humanitarian aid to conflict and disaster zones, sometimes competing with local NGOs for those funds.

Global Social Reform

For many analysts and activists, addressing the weaknesses of IOs is an indispensable part of social policy reform campaigns. One problem with IGOs in particular is that they do not possess state-like powers. There is no centralized international mechanism to negotiate and enforce treaty obligations worldwide and there is no coherent means for legal redress by aggrieved citizens. There is no central bank. IGOs do not have independent revenue-raising powers and depend on donations from governments and philanthropists. The IMF comes closest to a nascent international state insofar as it carries out a number of state functions, such as the allocation of funds and the regulation of some aspects of international finance, but it lacks the political resources and coercive capacity of states.

A reformed UN system is sometimes regarded as the best means for developing a more coherent and effective global social policy. UN reform could involve various democratization reforms to it, providing it with an independent source of funding (perhaps out of global taxes), and a lead role in working with the new groups of countries, the IMF, World Bank, WTO and regional groupings to plan in an accountable way for equitable global social development. Others argue that entirely new global institutions are needed rather than just the reform of old ones. Most agree that such reform would also necessarily involve addressing power imbalances within these organizations and the lack of effective representation by poorer and developing countries. While some analysts look forward to the reinvention of global governmental institutions, others seek an enhanced role for world-regional associations of nations through which to deliver social policy more attuned to the needs of the region concerned.

Others are sceptical about the extent to which supranational institutions (whether on a global or world-regional scale, new or reformed) can ever be reformed in the interests of social development and instead seek their dismantlement altogether. These kinds of argument are often advanced in the context of 'de-globalization' initiatives, especially by advocates of localization and self-reliance policies that promote the viability of smaller-scale, localized and diversified economies. This alternative social vision involves inventing (or returning to) forms of economic and social organization that are hooked into, but not dominated by outside forces.

Emerging Issues

Social policy is a vibrant and challenging area of global politics. Over the coming years, debate about what role international organizations can play in the realization of global social justice will remain at the fore-ground of political and policy debate. Issues that will feature in these debates are as follows:

- whether the reliance on commercial solutions and philanthropy to global social and policy 'solutions' is one that is 'fit for purpose';
- whether voluntary corporate codes of conduct are any longer an adequate approach to raising social and labour standards;

- what impacts the tendency towards the use of public-private partnerships in global social policy have on the development of public services provision;
- how the intellectual property regime impacts on attempts to solve global public health and bio-security problems;
- how adequate social provision and protections can be extended to and secured for the greatest number of people worldwide, including those who move across the borders of nation-states.

Guide to Further Sources

There are two texts of primary relevance to this area. The first and most comprehensive is N. Yeates (ed.), *Understanding Global Social Policy* (Policy Press, 2008). The second is B. Deacon, *Global Social Policy and Governance* (Sage, 2007). Deacon provides a good overview of global governance reform, but for treatment of the social policy dimensions of regionalism, see N. Yeates and B. Deacon, *Globalism, Regionalism and Social Policy*, UNU-CRIS Working Paper 0-2006/6 (2006); available at <www.cris.unu.edu/admin/documents/20060418154630.O-2006-6.pdf>.

The journal *Global Social Policy* publishes full-length and shorter articles on a wide range of policy issues, together with a digest of recent developments.

For more about the social policy impact of supranational organizations, see K. Armingeon and M. Beyeler, *The OECD and European Welfare States* (Edward Elgar, 2004); P. Willetts (ed.), *The Conscience of the World* (Hurst, 2004); T. Weiss and L. Gordenker (eds), *NGOs, the UN and Global Governance* (Lynne Rienner, 1996); J. O'Brien et al., *Contesting Global Governance* (Cambridge University Press, 2000) and P. Stubbs, 'International non-state actors and social development', in B. Deacon et al., *Global Social Governance* (STAKES, 2003), pp. 130–61. For further discussion of the de-globalization/localization agendas, see J. Mander and E. Goldsmith (eds), *The Case Against the Global Economy and for a Turn Toward the Local* (Sierra Club Books, 1997) and C. Hines, *Localization: A Global Manifesto* (Earthscan, 2000).

There are extensive online resources covering issues of global social policy: <www.globalwelfare.net>, developed by the SPA's ICSP group, is a principal gateway into these resources. It provides a range of resources including an extensive set of links to research and activist organizations' websites.

Part VI

Welfare Services

Chapter 38

Income Maintenance and Social Security

Stephen McKay and Karen Rowlingson

Overview

- Social security represents just under one-third of all government spending – about the same as spending on education and health combined. The largest group of benefit recipients are children, 13 million of whom receive Child Benefit, through their parents. Pensioners come next, with 12 million receiving the State Retirement Pension.
- Definitions of social security vary from the broad, encompassing all methods of securing an income, to the narrow, focusing on state systems of income maintenance.
- Social security systems vary in their aims. The British system focuses on alleviating poverty, hence considerable reliance on means-tested provision. Continental European systems focus more on insurance-based systems and redistribution from rich to poor.
- State benefits are typically divided into: *contributory benefits*, such as the State Retirement Pension; *means-tested benefits/tax credits*, such as Income Support; and *contingent or categorical benefits*, such as Child Benefit.
- There has been an emphasis from both Conservative and Labour governments in Britain on individual responsibility rather than state provision. This is evident in recent reforms of pensions, disability benefits and child support.

Introduction

The incomes of individuals and families come from several sources – from the private sector through wages/salaries, support from other family members and often from the state in the form of cash benefits. The discussion of social security takes this as its starting point, sometimes looking broadly at the range of income sources, usually looking more narrowly at the role the state plays in maintaining incomes. Different welfare states play very different roles in income maintenance, from minimalist schemes existing only for the poor (if then), to comprehensive systems covering an extensive range of risks to income security, and involving significant redistribution.

The Importance of Social Security

This chapter provides an overview of social security in Britain. Most people spend much

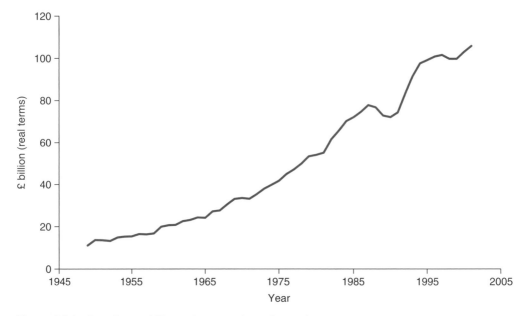

Figure 38.1   Spending on UK social security (in real terms)

of their lives either receiving or paying for social security – often both at the same time. However, the system is far from simple and most of us understand very little about what it aims to do, how it operates and its effects. A number of facts illustrate the importance of the social security system in Britain:

- Government spending on social security benefits and tax credits in the UK in 2005–6 was around £140 billion per year – just under one-third of all government spending and about the same as health and education spending combined. This represents about £2,300 each year for every woman, man and child in the country.
- Some 70 per cent of British households receive at least one social security benefit, with 13 per cent of working age households receiving a key out-of-work benefit.
- One in six dependent children live in households receiving an income-related benefit (such as the main safety-net benefit, Income Support), which is regarded

by many as an income insufficient for 'normal' participation in society.

The benefits responsible for the greatest spending are the Retirement Pension, Income Support/Pension Credit, Housing Benefit, Child Benefit, Disability Living, Allowance and Incapacity Benefit. Social security benefits are paid mostly from general taxes and from specific contributions for social security – which we know as National Insurance.

Since the Second World War, spending on social security has risen continuously (see figure 38.1). These figures have been adjusted for inflation, and hence show the 'real' growth in total spending in this area. There has been a tenfold increase over the period, with only occasional dips generally associated with times of falling unemployment.

What is 'Social Security'?

Social security clearly plays a central role in people's lives. But what is meant by social security? There is no universally accepted neat definition, and it may be defined in a number of ways.

Starting with the very widest definition, it is sometimes used to refer to all the ways people organize their lives in order to ensure access to an adequate income. This wide concept includes securing income from all sources such as earnings from employers and self-employment, financial help from charities, money from a family member and cash benefits from the state. If we take the widest definition, then the private sector is the foremost provider of income maintenance as earnings from employment and profits from self-employment are the chief source of income for most people of working age, and pensions in retirement are often based on such earnings.

A slightly narrower definition of social security would include all types of financial support, except those provided by the market system. In this way, reliance on the immediate or extended family would still be classed as helping to achieve social security. However, it is increasingly usual to adopt an even narrower definition, and to regard social security as those sources of immediate financial support provided by the state.

This debate about definition is, of course, important across the range of services studied within social policy. The study of health is broader than the activities of the National Health Service, for example, and the provision of care extends well beyond the social services.

The definition of social security as the system of cash benefits paid by the government to different individuals appears to be fairly simple and unproblematic. But it is inadequate not least because some 'benefits' are not paid for by the state, or need not be. For example, statutory sick pay used to be paid by government, but, while it remains a legal entitlement, it is now mostly a cost met by employers. There are also occupational schemes for sickness, widowhood

and retirement that are similar to state benefits, and which have a similar function, but which are organized by employers. One could also envisage the government finding ways to 'privatize' what are currently state benefits, or instigating new compulsory private provision, perhaps for pensions. So, both voluntary employer schemes and some programmes mandated by government may also be classed as social security – neither of which neatly fit the above definition.

Another rather grey area is the distinction between cash benefits, systems of tax allowances and, increasingly, 'tax credits', which are the responsibility of Her Majesty's Revenue and Customs (HMRC, formerly the Inland Revenue). Tax credits have become an increasingly important part of the 'social security' system. The government generally prefers to see them as standing apart from social security benefits – in particular, that they are designed for workers, rather than those not in work. There are, however, good reasons for seeing tax credits as very similar to social security benefits, as there are important areas where tax credits and benefits perform similar roles.

For the reasons mentioned above, it is difficult to give a precise definition of social security, and different people/organizations will prefer different definitions. In this chapter, we take a fairly pragmatic approach, focusing on state systems of income maintenance – largely benefits (administered by the Department for Work and Pensions) and tax credits (administered by HMRC).

The Aims of Social Security

Having defined social security we now ask what are the aims of the system? The answer is complex. Like elsewhere, the system in Britain has evolved over time and so is not what would be designed if policymakers were now starting from scratch.

> **Box 38.1   Possible aims of social security**
>
> - ensuring against the risks of particular events in life, such as retirement, unemployment and sickness;
> - relieving poverty or low income;
> - redistributing resources across people's life-cycles, especially from working age to retirement;
> - redistributing resources from rich to poor;
> - 'compensating' for some types of extra cost (such as children, disability);
> - providing financial support when 'traditional' families break down.

Furthermore, different parts of the system have different aims and so it is not possible to identify a single or even main aim. With these reservations in mind, box 38.1 lists some of the possible objectives of social security.

Within these general aims, the British social security system has been designed to achieve the following:

- to maintain incentives for self-provision (through earning and saving);
- to keep take-up of benefits high;
- to counter possible fraud;
- to ensure that administrative costs are low.

The aims of the British system have traditionally been more limited than those of systems in Europe, if wider than in some parts of the rest of the English-speaking world. The importance of relieving poverty in the British system explains the considerable reliance on means-testing in Britain. Receipt of means-tested benefits depends on a person or family having resources (typically income, and often savings) below a certain level in order to receive benefits. Means-testing is also common in America, New Zealand and Australia but much less common elsewhere, especially in continental Europe where social security tends to be less centralized and more concerned with income maintenance and compensation.

An Overview of the Current System

The social security system today is a highly complex organism which has evolved over time and which very few people understand in all its detail. For every possible generalization about the system there are myriad caveats which need to be made. It is therefore difficult to give a brief overview without over-simplifying the system and, as a result, possibly giving misleading information. Nevertheless, this chapter attempts to provide such an overview. There are various ways of classifying the different benefits in the UK system. For example, benefits can be categorized by means of two distinctions: universal versus means-tested; contributory versus non-contributory. If we use the rules of entitlement as our yardstick, social security can be divided into three main components: contributory benefits (benefits which rely upon having paid contributions), means-tested benefits and tax credits (benefits which depend upon income) and contingent benefits (benefits which depend upon your position or category), as follows.

Contributory benefits

The main root for the current social security system lies in the Beveridge Report published in the early 1940s, although insurance-based and other benefits had been introduced well before this time. At the heart of the Beveridge approach – of contributory benefits or 'social insurance' – is the idea that people face a range of risks that might lead to severe reductions in living standards. These include the risk of unemployment, or being incapacitated and unable to work, or retiring, or losing the main income-earner in a family. Some risks are rather uncommon, and relatively unrelated to economic circumstances, such as widowhood. Other risks, such as retirement, are much more widespread and predictable.

The main issues that arise with social insurance include:

• Why should the state provide this service, rather than private insurance? What relationship should there then be between state and private insurance?
• What risks should be covered?
• On what basis should contributions be made, or be deemed to be made?

Entitlement to social insurance benefits is based on having paid National Insurance contributions, and being in a risk covered by these benefits (such as unemployment or retirement). These benefits are individualized in that the earnings of a partner do not generally affect entitlement. The main benefit in this group is the State Retirement Pension. Other benefits are the contributory parts of Incapacity Benefit and the contribution-based Jobseeker's Allowance (JSA).

Means-tested benefits/tax credits

Entitlement to means-tested benefits depends on the level of 'family' resources, particularly income and savings. The four main examples in the British system are Income Support/Pension Credit, Working Tax Credit, Housing Benefit and Council Tax Benefit.

The system of benefits based on means-testing, particularly for those on low incomes, is sometimes known as 'social assistance'. In Britain, social assistance is almost synonymous with Income Support (and its equivalent for older people, Pension Credit), and income-based JSA for unemployed people. These benefits are paid to those whose income and savings are below defined levels, taking into account the size and type of family.

Countries differ a great deal in the extent of this type of provision. In Australia and New Zealand, almost all benefits include an element of 'means-testing'. This does not mean that only the poorest may receive benefits – in some instances the aim is to exclude the richest rather than to include only the poorest. Child tax credit plays a similar role in the UK, with most families with children now entitled to it. In much of Northern Europe, social assistance plays a much smaller role, picking up those not covered by the main social insurance system. In addition they are often administered locally, with local organizations having some discretion about the precise rules of entitlement.

Additional conditions are often attached to receiving social assistance. People of working age, without sole responsibility for caring for children or disabled adults, must be able to work, available for work and actively seeking work. In past times, they may have had to enter a workhouse to qualify.

Contingent benefits

These are sometimes referred to as categorical benefits or as non-means-tested and non-contributory. Entitlement depends on the existence of certain circumstances (or contingencies) such as having a child (Child Benefit) or being disabled (Disability Living Allowance, Severe Disablement Allowance).

In the British social security system, some benefits effectively recognize that certain groups of people face extra costs which the

Table 38.1 The benefits with the most recipients, 2005/2006

Winter Fuel Payments	>11.5 million
Retirement Pension	11.6 million
Child Benefit	7.4 million families receiving Child Benefit for 13.1 million children
Council Tax Benefit	5 million
Housing Benefit	4 million
Income Support/Pension Credit	4.9 million
Disability Living Allowance	2.8 million
Incapacity Benefit	1.7 million

state will share. The clearest example is benefits for dependent children and Child Benefit. There is no test of contributions, and the family's level of income is not taken into consideration (at the present time). There are, however, certain tests of residence that must be satisfied. Disability benefits provide another example, where some elements are purely contingent and reflect neither means nor previous contributions.

It is worth emphasizing that this division into three groups is something of a simplification of differences between benefits. Means-tested benefits do not just depend on financial resources; they tend also to rely on some combination of being in a particular situation or a particular family type. For example, able-bodied single people may only claim Income Support if they meet conditions relating to being unemployed. And it is possible for certain sources of income to affect contributory benefits, for example Jobseeker's Allowance and Incapacity Benefit (both contribution-based) can be reduced if a person receives income from a personal or occupational pension.

Who Receives Social Security Benefits and Tax Credits?

According to government figures, Winter Fuel Payments and the Retirement Pension are the 'benefits' with the largest number of recipients – both with more than 11 million

recipients in 2006. Child Benefit comes next, with 7.4 million families, followed by the key means-tested benefits. Disability benefits of various kinds also have very large numbers of recipients (see table 38.1).

Alongside benefits for different groups, there are also benefits to help people meet specific extra costs of living. Housing Benefit helps people pay their rent if they are on a low income. The cost of this benefit has increased dramatically since the 1980s because there has been a deliberate policy shift from subsidizing 'bricks and mortar' (in terms of low council rents) to subsidizing individuals (by raising rents and paying benefit to those on low incomes). While low-paid renters can receive help, those with mortgages are mostly denied assistance with their housing costs. Those on low incomes can also receive help with their council tax. The other major benefit to help meet extra costs of daily living is the Social Fund. This is another distinctive feature of the British system, although social workers in some other countries can give out money to people in need. The Social Fund is a much-criticized part of the system, particularly as claimants are mostly given loans rather than grants.

How Social Security is Delivered

In 2001, the Department of Social Security merged with parts of the Department for

Employment and Skills to become the Department for Work and Pensions (DWP). This reinforced an increasing emphasis on 'work as the best form of welfare'. The new department increasingly differentiates those above and below working age as well as those in paid work and those not. All those claiming benefits who are of working age but not in paid work are given a 'work-first' interview, when issues about employment are discussed prior to a claim for financial support being dealt with.

Jobcentre Plus is the agency providing benefit and job-search services, while the Pension Service deals with pensions and older people. The Disability and Carers Service provides compensation for disabled people and their carers. In a bid to cut administrative costs, the DWP increased the number of its contact centres from fewer than ten in 1998 to around 80 in 2004, and was operating 62 in November 2005.

The DWP is also currently responsible for the Child Support Agency, though this is due to be abolished according to current plans. The new 'tax credits' are the responsibility of HMRC. Local authorities remain responsible for Housing Benefit and Council Tax Benefit. The DWP employs 120,000 staff, one-quarter of the Civil Service, in more than 2,000 locations.

In July 2004 Gordon Brown, then Chancellor of the Exchequer, outlined plans to cut more than 104,000 civil service jobs across the UK when he set out his three-year spending plans. Almost a third of these cuts (30,000) were expected to be made from the DWP and its various agencies. About half of these cuts had been made by the summer of July 2006 when the department was criticized by a Parliamentary Select Committee for an 'appalling' level of service.

Benefit Levels, Poverty and Adequacy

Since the early 1980s, expenditure on benefits has risen in both absolute and real terms. But increasing expenditure on benefits has not generally been fuelled by rises in the real levels of benefit, and indeed there is widespread evidence that benefit levels are not adequate to meet people's basic requirements. Beveridge initially aimed to set benefits at subsistence levels according to budget studies in the 1930s, but there is disagreement about whether he achieved this. Price inflation means that benefit levels have to be raised every year ('uprated'), otherwise they are worth less in real terms. There is some evidence that both the initial levels of benefits and the uprating to prices in the 1940s were not set correctly. In more recent years, some benefits have been frozen and others have been linked to price inflation rather than to wage inflation (if it was higher). This means that benefit recipients have become increasingly worse off, relative to workers. Moreover, since the early 1980s more benefits have been brought within the scope of income tax, such as the State Retirement Pension, JSA and Incapacity Benefit, and this has affected the relative generosity of these benefits.

Benefits in Cash and in Kind

In most cases, the aims of social security are achieved by paying cash benefits. However, this need not be the case. Benefits could be provided 'in-kind', through providing either services or vouchers that may only be spent on certain types of good. In the USA, an important method of providing for poor families is through the Food Stamps Program. This gives out vouchers that must be exchanged for food. In Britain, receiving Income Support and some other benefits carries with it the right to some services at no charge, such as dental treatment, eye examinations and legal aid ('passported benefits').

The British system developed along two lines: the national social security system generally provided cash benefits to cover needs such as for food, clothes and money for bills, whereas other needs, particularly the need for social care, were covered by local social services departments which provided in-kind services.

Emerging Issues

Since the early 1980s, there has been an increasing emphasis from all governments on individual responsibility rather than state provision. This trend looks set to continue with a number of important reforms on the horizon. For example, the 2006 Pension Bill, based on some of the recommendations of the independent Turner Commission, requires people to work for longer before claiming the State Retirement Pension (which will be linked to rises in earnings and therefore be more generous, eventually). Individual saving will also be encouraged through the introduction of new personal accounts. As far as disability benefits are concerned, the Incapacity Benefit is due to be scrapped in favour of a new Employment and Support Allowance where, again, individuals will be expected to secure their incomes through the labour market where at all possible rather than through the state. And the Child Support Agency is also due to be abolished with the expectation that individuals will be expected to make their own arrangements where possible.

The British system continues, therefore, to tread a neo-liberal path towards minimal state support in favour of income maintenance through the labour market and individual savings. However, this approach appears doomed to fail to meet Tony Blair's pledge to eradicate child poverty by 2020. It seems certain that either this pledge will be broken or a radical new approach will have to be taken.

Guide to Further Sources

There is a general lack of good, up-to-date textbooks on social security. It is best to start with J. Millar (ed.), *Understanding Social Security* (Policy Press, 2003). This edited collection covers the key benefit groups and general issues in relation to social security. Its focus is the UK and it provides a user-friendly introduction to the main issues. R. Walker, *Social Security and Welfare: Concepts and Comparisons* (Open University Press, 2005) is aimed at those who already have a general understanding of the key issues. It focuses on the objectives and outcomes of social security systems through cross-national comparisons. Another useful introductory textbook (sadly out of print) is S. McKay and K. Rowlingson, *Social Security in Britain* (Macmillan, 1999).

Those wanting to keep up to date should read the journal *Benefits*; details are online at: <https://www.policypress.org.uk/journals/benefits/>. The Department for Work and Pensions publishes regular research reports, and press releases, at <www.dwp.gov.uk>. Figures on tax credits may be found at <www.hmrc.gov.uk>. The Institute for Fiscal Studies (<www.ifs.org.uk>) produces timely commentaries on reform, from an economic perspective.

Chapter 39

Employment

Alan Deacon

Overview

- Unemployment has fallen sharply since the mid-1990s and by 2005 had reached a thirty-year low.
- It is not clear how far the New Deal programmes have contributed to this decline, but it is likely that they have had a small but positive effect.
- There has not been a comparable decline in the number of people who are neither in work nor registered as unemployed – the so-called economically inactive.
- Employment polices are now increasingly targeted at this group, especially lone parents with dependent children and disabled people.
- This widening of the scope of employment policy has been sharply criticized on the grounds that it devalues unpaid work such as caring.

Introduction

Employment policies occupy a central but controversial place in debates about the future of welfare. For millions of people, paid employment is not only their major – or sole – source of income, it is also the basis of their social standing and of their self-esteem. Those without such work are at greater risk of poverty and are more likely to experience ill-health. Moreover, their children are less likely to do well at school and to obtain secure, well-paid jobs. Unemployment is also linked to a range of other social problems. Whatever the precise patterns of causality, it is undeniable that communities in which unemployment is high are also disproportionately affected by crime, family breakdown and anti-social

behaviour. For governments, high rates of employment boost tax revenues, reduce spending on social security benefits and make it easier to fund other social policies and to meet the anticipated costs of an ageing population.

Britain's New Labour government consistently declared its ambition to 'rebuild the welfare state around work' (DSS 1998: 23). In 1998 a Green Paper on welfare reform promised that a 'comprehensive welfare-to-work programme' would 'break the mould of the old passive benefit system' and would form the basis of a new contract between government and those claimants who were capable of work. 'It is the Government's responsibility to promote work opportunities and to help people take advantage of them. It is the responsibility of those who can take them up to do so' (ibid.: 31). This approach has subsequently been extended to groups that had not previously been expected to seek paid work, most notably lone parents and people with disabilities. This widening of the scope of employment policies, however, has been fiercely resisted by some critics, on the grounds that such an emphasis on paid employment must devalue caring and other forms of unpaid work.

The purpose of this chapter is to provide a brief introduction to these policy developments and debates. Before doing so, however, it outlines recent trends in the labour market, and looks at the operation to date of New Labour's welfare-to-work programmes.

Trends in Employment, Unemployment and Economic Inactivity

The first point to make is that Britain has one of the highest employment rates in the world. Over 70 per cent of working-age men and women were in paid work in 2005, compared to 66 per cent in Germany, 63 per cent in France and 58 per cent in Italy (DWP 2007: 18). Britain's employment rate has risen by two percentage points since 1997, and by four percentage points since 1993.

It is not surprising, then, to find that the rate of unemployment in Britain has fallen sharply since the early 1990s. The number of people claiming unemployment benefit, for example, had fallen to a thirty-year low of less than one million by 2004, and the number in receipt of benefit for more than a year had dropped by 75 per cent to fewer than 130,000. This figure was less than one-tenth the total of long-term claimants in 1986 (DWP 2006a: 16). If a broader measure of the number of people who are available for work is adopted, then the figures are higher, but the downward trend remains (Brewer and Shephard 2005).

The decline in unemployment, however, is far from the end of the story. In recent years, more attention has come to be paid to the numbers of people who are economically inactive. This term refers to those who are neither in paid work nor looking for it. An increase in such 'inactivity' is not necessarily a problem; full-time students, for example, are counted as inactive. In reality, the major cause of inactivity amongst men is long-term sickness or disability and amongst women it is withdrawal from the labour market to care for family or home. In both of these cases, inactivity gives rise to the same vulnerability to poverty and disadvantage as does unemployment, and policy-makers and commentators have increasingly used the terms 'the workless' or 'the jobless' to cover both those who are unemployed and those who are inactive. The overall rate of economic inactivity has not changed significantly since 1997 – or indeed since 1979 – and so the number of people living in 'workless' households has not fallen by anything like so much as the number unemployed. One commonly cited statistic, for example, is that over 15 per cent of children live in workless households.

New Labour's Welfare-to-Work Programmes

The greater attention now paid to worklessness rather than unemployment has been reflected in an important shift in emphasis within the government's welfare-to-work programmes.

Broadly speaking, 'welfare-to-work' programmes have three interrelated objectives:

• To increase the job opportunities available to welfare claimants. This can be done through the payment of subsidies to employers who take people directly off the unemployment register, through job creation schemes that provide temporary work for various groups amongst the unemployed, and through training and work experience schemes.

- To inform claimants of the opportunities created and to improve their motivation and skills. This can be done through an expansion of personal counselling and advice services along with educational and training initiatives.
- To give claimants a greater financial incentive to take advantage of these opportunities. This can be done by enhancing the benefits paid to those in work – most importantly tax credits – and/or by imposing stiffer sanctions on those who fail to participate in the programmes.

It was back in November 1995 that the Labour Party, then in opposition, announced plans for what was to become the first of six New Deal programmes. This first programme was targeted at young people (aged 18–24 years) who had been on benefit for 6 months. They were to be required to take one of four options: full-time education, a job in the private sector for which the employer would receive a subsidy of £60 a week, work with a voluntary agency, or a placement on an environmental taskforce. The original programme is now known as the New Deal for Young People (NDYP). It later included a self-employment option and what came to be termed the 'gateway': a period of intensive advice and preparation prior to any job placement. This is intended to make participants more attractive to employers, and also to make it less likely that those who are already 'job ready' will be drawn onto the programme.

From the outset, however, the most striking feature of the NDYP was that it was compulsory. Anyone who failed to take any of the options would face benefits sanctions. In the words of Gordon Brown, then Shadow Chancellor, 'simply remaining unemployed and on benefit' would no longer be condoned. This message has since become so familiar that it is easy to forget that the introduction of compulsion marked a radical shift in Labour policy. Critics argued that it was both unfair and counterproductive to make individuals' entitlement to benefits conditional upon their participation in these programmes. It was unfair, they said, because such conditionality implied that it was the claimants' own fault that they were unemployed, and that claimants only had to be prodded into action in order for them to find a job. It was counterproductive, they said, because in order to be effective such programmes needed to work with enthusiastic volunteers and not uncooperative conscripts. Against these criticisms, supporters of compulsion have argued that because the effect of prolonged joblessness is to de-motivate claimants, it is reasonable to 'prompt, support and require' them to take steps which are to their long-term benefit but which they would not otherwise take (DWP 2007: 78). More broadly, however, New Labour has consistently justified conditionality on the grounds that it expresses and enforces the mutual obligations of government and claimant. In January 2006 another Green Paper reaffirmed that, as 'support is increased, so will the level of conditionality for claimants' (DWP 2006a: 6).

The same arguments have been used to justify compulsion in a similar but smaller programme, the New Deal for 25 Plus. This is targeted at older claimants who have been receiving benefits for eighteen of the previous twenty-one months. Much more significant, however, is the way in which elements of compulsion have been introduced into New Deals which provide for people who are not required to register for work as a condition of receiving benefit. The New Deal for Lone Parents (NDLP), for example, is a voluntary programme targeted at lone parents in receipt of income support benefits. From April 2001, however, new claimants were required to attend a work-focused interview at which a personal adviser sets out the support they would be given to find work and the in-work benefits and help with childcare that would be available should they take a job. These interviews are now mandatory at quarterly, six-monthly or yearly intervals, depending on the age of the youngest child.

Similarly, the New Deal for Disabled People (NDDP) remains a voluntary programme, but new claimants to incapacity benefits are required to attend work-focused interviews. The central feature of the NDDP itself is the intensive support provided by a personal adviser both during job search and for the first six months after starting work.

The effectiveness of the New Deals to date is a matter of fierce dispute. The numbers participating in the NDYP, for example, peaked at 140,000 in 1999, but then fell steadily to fewer than 70,000 in 2005 (Brewer and Shephard 2005: 7). Over the years, around 40 per cent of participants have moved into jobs lasting at least thirteen weeks. Not surprisingly, the government and its advisers point to this as evidence of success. The report by David Freud, for example, declared that, by 'any measure, these programmes have been a success'. The NDYP, he said, 'has got over 700,000 people into work' and 'the equivalent figure for the New Deal for 25 Plus is around 280,000' (DWP 2007: 23). The Institute for Fiscal Studies (IFS), however, dismissed such statements as containing 'no meaningful information' about the effectiveness of the New Deals. 'This is because many individuals who enter the programme would have found jobs anyway, even if the New Deal programme had not existed' (Brewer and Shephard 2005: 8). The IFS estimates that NDYP increased the probability of a participant finding a job by around five percentage points – the equivalent of around 17,000 young people a year leaving benefits when they would not otherwise have done so. This makes the gross cost per job very high, and both the Con-

servative and Liberal Democrats proposed to scrap the programme had they won the 2005 election.

The effectiveness of the NDLP is even harder to assess. The numbers on the scheme have risen substantially, and with more than 70,000 participants in 2005 it had overtaken the NDYP. It is also notable that the employment rate of lone parents rose from 45 per cent to 56 per cent between 1997 and 2005. That said, it is still the case that only around 10 per cent of lone parents on income support are choosing to go on NDLP. Evaluations suggest that around a quarter of NDLP participants move off income support because of the programme (Hills and Stewart 2005: 38). The NDDP is also a large programme, but it is not considered to have had a significant impact upon the activity rates of disabled people (ibid.: 41).

Taken altogether, then, the New Deals have probably had a 'positive but small' effect, and if account is taken of the benefits that claimants would have received anyway, they probably represent value for money (Brewer and Shephard 2005: 12). Moreover, most assessments agree that the personal advisers have proved to be a valuable innovation, and much appreciated by the great majority of claimants. By the end of New Labour's second term, however, there was something of a consensus amongst policy-makers and commentators that the New Deals were running out of steam, and that a new initiative was needed (Hills and Stewart 2005: 45).

New Ambitions for Employment Policy

In a Green Paper published in January 2006 the government announced that it had set itself the aim of 'an employment rate equivalent to 80 per cent of the working age population' (DWP 2006a: 18). In order to achieve it would have to:

- reduce the numbers receiving incapacity benefits by one million;
- increase the number of older people (55–64 years) in work by one million;
- increase the number of lone parents in work by 300,000 – raising the employment rate for this group to 70 per cent.

This is an ambitious target – only Iceland currently has an employment rate of 80 per cent. New Labour is attempting to redraw the boundary between those who are and those who are not expected to work. The Green Paper, for example, spoke of challenging 'the assumptions that people with health conditions and disabilities, women with dependent children, and older people cannot work or do not want to work' (DWP 2006: 19).

There are two main reasons why the government is so keen to raise the employment rate. The first is that the more people there are in work, the easier it will be to support the growing number of pensioners. Indeed, by the time this edition of *The Student's Companion* is published, the number of people over state pension age will have exceeded the number of children for the first time (DWP 2006a: 20). The second reason is simply that the government is convinced that work is good for people, and often cites evidence that children in working households are less likely to be disadvantaged at school or in later life (DWP 2007: 30). Above all, New Labour believes that reducing worklessness is the key to tackling child poverty. A child living with a workless lone parent, for example, is five times more likely to be poor than one living with a single parent in work. Similarly, the risk of poverty for a child in a couple household is 61 per cent if no adult works, 14 per cent if one adult works and 1 per cent if both adults work (DWP 2007: 81).

This does not mean, of course, that the government's strategy will go unchallenged.

Two aspects in particular are open to criticism. First, the government proposes to give a much bigger role to the private and voluntary sector in delivery of employment programmes, effectively paying them by results. Second, it is increasing still further the degree of conditionality in the benefits system. A new Employment and Support Allowance will place new obligations upon disabled people who are judged to be capable of some work, and, early in 2007, the government seemed likely to accept a recommendation that lone parents should be required to take at least a part-time job when their youngest child was 12 years old. This latter proposal was justified by the much greater availability of childcare and by the fact that such requirements exist in most other comparable countries. Against this, it will be argued that not all parents have access to suitable childcare, and that in any case lone parents should retain the right to decide to be a full-time parent as long as they feel that this is the best interests of their dependent children. Critics have also emphasized that although workless families are more vulnerable to poverty, having someone in work does not guarantee that a household will not be poor. New Labour introduced a national minimum wage in April 1999, and this was subsequently increased more quickly than the rise in average wages (Brewer and Shephard 2005: 7). It has not, however, had a significant impact upon wage inequalities, and in 2006 half of all poor children were living in households in which at least one adult was working (<www.poverty.org.uk>).

Emerging Issues

The arguments about how far lone parents should be expected to seek paid work, and the role that employment policies can play in reducing poverty, are both part of a much broader debate about the implications of New Labour's attempts to promote and expand paid employment. On a practical level, a society in which paid work is a near-universal expectation of non-disabled adults will require a radical change in the expectations and practices of households, government and employers. People will need to be able to work far more flexibly in order to balance their commitments. They will also need far more in-work support if they are to manage the inevitable crises and to reconcile the conflicting demands upon their time and attention. It is no coincidence, for example, that one lone parent in ten leaves his or her job in any one year – double the rate of other parents (DWP 2006b: 40). More generally, about two and a half million people – or 12 per cent of the total workforce – already combine paid work and care, and it is estimated that each one saved the government around £10,000 a year in 2004. Moreover, the ageing population means that the number of carers is expected to increase by 50 per cent in the next thirty years. At the very least, then, there is a clear tension between polices which aim to maximize the number of people in work, and policies designed to support carers (Arskey and Kemp 2006).

This in turn raises still more profound questions about whether paid work is indeed the only, or even the primary, way in which citizens can contribute to the common good. Is it reasonable to equate financial self-sufficiency with independence, as government documents often seem to do? The Freud Report, for example, talks of the 'difficult heritage' of 'passive labour market policies', contrasts 'welfare dependence' with 'robust self-reliance', and calls for welfare reform to 'generate clear signals around independence' (DWP 2007: 46). Others would argue that such statements reflect too narrow an understanding of the meaning of self-reliance (Young 2002). They would call instead for employment policies that begin with the recognition that everyone is dependent upon others at some point in their life, and which attempt to strike a more even balance between work and care.

Guide to Further Sources

H. Arksey and P. Kemp, 'Carers and employment in a work-focused welfare state', in C. Glendinning and P. Kemp (eds), *Cash and Care: Policy Challenges in the Welfare State* (Policy Press, 2006) explores the tension between the aims of increasing employment levels and of supporting carers. The best source of statistics and information on the numbers and circumstances of carers is <www.carersuk.org.uk>.

M. Brewer and A. Shephard, *Employment and the Labour Market* (Institute for Fiscal Studies, 2005) reviews the operation of welfare-to-work programmes in New Labour's first two terms. The IFS regularly publishes evaluations and assessments of the individual programmes (<www.ifs.org.uk>).

An early statement of New Labour's aims in welfare reform and of the 'mutual obligations' of government and claimants can be found in: Department of Social Security, *A New Contract for Welfare* Cm 3805 (HMSO, 1998). Department of Work and Pensions, *A New Deal for Welfare: Empowering People to Work*, Cm 6730 (HMSO, 2006a) comprises the Green Paper which outlines how and why New Labour is aiming to raise the employment rates of lone parents, disabled people, and older people.

I. M. Young, 'Autonomy, welfare reform and meaningful work', in E. F. Kittay and E. K. Feder (eds), *The Subject of Care: Feminist Perspectives on Dependency*

(Rowman and Littlefield, 2002), pp. 40–59, is a powerful critique of the assumption that personal autonomy is dependent upon financial self-sufficiency, or that all paid work is necessarily meaningful.

The report to the DWP by Lisa Harker, which calls for a 'New Deal for Parents', is to be found in: Department of Work and Pensions, *Delivering on Child Poverty: What Would It Take?* Cm 6951 (HMSO, 2006b). This offers much greater support to parents irrespective of the benefits they are receiving and is likely to shape future thinking on welfare-to-work in conjunction with the Freud Report, published as: Department of Work and Pensions, *Reducing Dependency, Increasing Opportunity: Options for the Future of Welfare to Work* (Corporate Document Services, 2007). The Report makes the case for both enhanced support and greater conditionality for lone parents and people with disabilities. The implementation of this strategy can be followed through <www.jobcentreplus.gov.uk/JCP/Customers/New_Deal>. Statistics on the labour market can be accessed most readily through the links at <www.statistics.gov.uk/instantfigs/asp>.

R. Dickens, P. Gregg and J. Wadsworth, *The Labour Market Under New Labour* (Palgrave Macmillan, 2003) is a collection of essays on the major developments in the labour market in recent years, while J. Hills and K. Stewart, *A More Equal Society?* (Policy Press, 2005) is an authoritative analysis of New Labour's reforms to 2005.

An insider account of the history of the employment services between 1945 and 1997 can be found in D. Price, *Office of Hope* (Policy Studies Institute, 2000). This provides a balanced assessment of the continuities and differences between Thatcherism and the early years of New Labour.

Chapter 40

Healthcare

Rob Baggott

Overview

- Healthcare issues are prominent in most industrial societies. Healthcare absorbs a large proportion of taxpayers' money and attracts considerable media attention.
- Although the medical profession remains powerful within the healthcare system, the perspectives of patients, users and carers are increasingly acknowledged.
- Three main models of healthcare funding exist – tax-based, state insurance and private insurance. The UK is mainly a tax-based system. Large sums of money have been committed to the NHS in recent years, but financial problems and inequities in funding remain.
- There is increasing plurality in service provision, encouraging the private sector into the NHS 'market'.
- Renewed efforts have been made to encourage partnership working between the NHS, local government, voluntary groups and the private sector.

The Importance of Health and Healthcare

In modern societies, the state accepts a high degree of responsibility for the health of its citizens. This is reflected in the high level of public expenditure on health services in most industrialized countries. Around three-quarters of health expenditure in such countries is provided by the public sector. The state also takes steps to protect and promote the health of the public. This involves regulating health risks and allocating resources to services that affect health, such as housing, income support, educa-

tion, regeneration – even transport. Indeed, governments are increasingly concerned about the health effects of people's socio-economic circumstances, environment and lifestyles (see HM Government/Department of Health 2004).

Healthcare is not like most other goods or services. Supply tends to create its own demand. Hence a technological breakthrough – such as a new breast cancer drug – generates demand from people who believe it will save their lives, even if this turns out to be misplaced. It is difficult to be a rational economic actor when you are ill. Moreover, people lack the specialized, technical knowledge needed to purchase healthcare appropriately. Indeed, even where privately funded healthcare is substantial, as in the USA, access to services is regulated by gatekeepers such as insurance companies, professionals and healthcare management organizations. Furthermore, a healthcare market based on private purchasing power tends to discriminate against the very people that need treatment. Poorer people, people with disabilities, children and elderly people have the greatest health needs. Yet they are also the least likely to afford private health insurance (and their premiums tend to be higher as they are regarded as high risk by insurers) or to pay directly for care services.

Many believe that healthcare underpins social solidarity and citizenship, and should be regarded as a basic human right. Although economic and social inequalities are tolerated, there is an enduring sentiment that good health should be available to all and that people's health should not be determined by their socio-economic circumstances or where they live. Indeed, while poverty and bad housing have often struggled to get on the political agenda in the UK, variations in life expectancy between different parts of the country and the so-called 'postcode lottery' of healthcare have, in contrast, continued to attract media attention.

Health issues are prominent in most industrial societies. Health services absorb a large amount of taxpayers' money and are major employers (the NHS is the third largest employer in the world). Health issues are often highly emotionally charged, attract considerable media attention and are the subject of single-issue pressure group campaigns. Moreover, the policy arena is inhabited by powerful interest groups, such as the medical profession and the drugs industry, which are highly skilled in influencing the political agenda. In addition, health issues are a major concern for voters and provide a focus for party political debates.

What is Health? What is Healthcare?

Health can be seen in a negative way, as the absence of disease (Aggleton, 1990). This is associated with the traditional 'biomedical' approach to health, which is dominated by a desire to identify the symptoms of disease and, through scientific enquiry, establish its causes and appropriate courses of treatment. The positive approach to health takes a broader view and is encapsulated in the definition produced by the World Health Organization in 1946: 'a state of complete physical, mental and social well-being and not merely the absence of disease or infirmity.' This approach focuses on the promotion of health and well-being in a wider sense.

Generally, the term 'healthcare' refers to goods or services that meet the health or medical needs of an individual or community. However, there are difficulties in defining this in practice. Indeed, there are often disputes over whether a particular service should be regarded as healthcare (the responsibility of the NHS, and mostly free at point of delivery) or social care (the responsibility of local authorities). Healthcare can be divided into primary, secondary and tertiary care. Primary care is provided by GPs and other professionals (community nurses, health visitors) in practices, clinics and community-settings (including the patient's home). Around 90 per cent of contacts between the public and the health services take place in primary care settings. Primary care includes activities such as preventive services (immunization, screening, health promotion), care (such as changing dressings and monitoring health) and treatment (prescribing and administering drugs, and even minor surgery). Secondary care refers to the range of acute and specialist services provided by hospitals. Highly specialized services – known as tertiary services – deal with complex conditions referred by other hospitals and specialists.

Sometimes services are concentrated in specialist hospitals (mental hospitals, children's hospitals), but the trend has been to run services through general hospitals dealing with a wide range of health problems.

Despite these distinctions, the boundary is shifting. Healthcare is increasingly provided in community settings and this is expected to increase in the future (HM Government/Department of Health 2006). Similarly, the differences between prevention and treatment services are expected to blur. Increasingly, disease prevention and health promotion are expected to be part of all services, not just those geared to health education, immunization, screening and early detection of illness.

Healthcare is often defined by the boundaries of professional work. Hence the close association of primary care with the work of the GP and other community-based health professions (such as community nurses, for example). The health professions, particularly the medical profession, are traditionally very powerful. They have shaped services to reflect their own expertise and interests. As a result, services have developed in a paternalistic way. However, there are countervailing forces. A substantial amount of care is provided by volunteers and informal carers. There are around seven million carers in Britain. People engage in self-help and self-medication (for example, buying medicines over the counter) and chronically ill people with long-term conditions increasingly self-manage their illnesses. Indeed, people with conditions such as asthma, arthritis and diabetes are increasingly acknowledged to be 'expert patients', managing their health with appropriate input from professionals. More generally, there is a greater emphasis today on the perspectives of patients, users and carers, their choices and their views. The professions increasingly see the patient as a partner in the process of healthcare. Nonetheless, they remain powerful within the healthcare system and can exert influence in subtle ways, such as the control of information and definition of values and ideas about health and healthcare.

Funding Health Services

There are three main issues:

- Can we raise sufficient funds for healthcare?
- What is the best way of raising this money?
- How should these funds be allocated within the health services?

The question of how much should be spent on healthcare is tricky. The extent to which the public will adopt healthy lifestyles is one key factor that will help determine the level of funding needed in the future (Wanless 2002). The growing elderly population is likely to increase pressures on health budgets, though no one really knows by how much. It is possible that tomorrow's elderly population may be fitter and healthier than today and might not require as much healthcare as some predict. Another factor is technology. In the future, microtechnology, nanotechnology and genetic therapies could lead to interventions for conditions currently difficult or impossible to treat. As noted above, supply tends to create its own demand in healthcare. This tends to increase costs, but not always. For example, the use of 'keyhole' surgery is now routine. Because such techniques are less traumatic for the patient, they have facilitated the growth of day surgery, contributing to a reduction in average in-patient costs.

In the UK, the government has committed huge resources to the NHS in recent years. Having had one of the most miserly healthcare systems in the industrialized world, the UK is now committed to spend sums that will place it around the European average for healthcare expenditure. Yet despite the large increase in NHS funding, many parts of the service face financial difficulty. This has led some to consider alternative ways of funding the NHS.

In essence there are three main models of healthcare funding: tax-based systems, state insurance systems and systems based on private insurance. The UK falls into the first category, most funding coming from general taxation (with a contribution from the national insurance scheme). However, there are co-payments for some NHS services – such as prescription charges. Over a tenth of the UK population have private health insurance. Moreover, many people pay directly for some healthcare services (such as alternative therapies, over-the-counter medicines, physiotherapy and even surgery). Additional healthcare funding is generated by the National Lottery and from other charitable sources.

The allocation of funding within the NHS is also an important issue. Historically, budgets were allocated to health authorities on the basis of previous allocations adjusted for inflation. Following criticism that this system did not reflect differences in the health needs of health authorities, new formulae were devised, which have since been revised. The current approach is to give local health authorities (known as Primary Care Trusts) a budget to commission health services for local people. Their budgets are in turn determined by a formula which reflects needs (such as the age of the population, deprivation and so on). Despite these changes, considerable inequalities remain in access to treatment between different local areas and between different socio-economic groups.

Organization, Planning and Commissioning

The NHS is often described as a typical monolithic state bureaucracy. However, since the creation of the service in 1948, there has always been considerable diversity. In this context, it must be acknowledged that the recent devolution of powers to Northern Ireland, Scotland and Wales has encouraged further diversity. NHS Scotland, for example, has abolished trusts, while NHS Wales has pioneered integrated local health authorities that focus strongly on health promotion. Scotland has introduced free long-term care for the elderly, while Wales intends to introduce free prescriptions for all. There are also important variations in how health services are managed and regulated. In addition, there are differences in policy, with Wales and Scotland less keen than England to extend private healthcare provision and deploy market forces within the NHS.

In England, the NHS is overseen by the Department of Health and the Strategic Health Authorities (SHAs). Within each SHA area, Primary Care Trusts (PCTs) are responsible for arranging and providing primary care services. They also commission services from NHS trusts (which provide a range of hospital and specialist services), specialist trusts (providing ambulance and mental health services, for example), care trusts (which provide health and social care to particular groups, such as elderly people or those with learning disabilities) and new Foundation Trusts (discussed further below).

PCTs also commission services from the private and voluntary (or 'independent') sectors. Indeed, one of the key buzzwords in the NHS today is 'plurality'. Government has been keen to encourage competition between the NHS and the independent sector. It established new independent sector treatment centres (ISTCs) to deliver non-urgent surgical care, paid for by the NHS. These will be expanded further and will absorb an increasing share of the NHS budget. It should be noted that commercial interests now play a much larger role in the NHS. As well as managing and delivering health services on its behalf, they have been involved in building new hospital and primary care facilities and providing support services.

Like its Conservative predecessors, the Blair governments placed their faith in market forces. The governments of Thatcher and Major presided over the introduction of an internal market within the NHS. This involved the identification of purchasers (GP fund-holders and health authorities) and providers (NHS trusts), who would negotiate contracts to deliver specific care. Financial flows were expected to follow these contracts, but in the end the government intervened in the market because of adverse side-effects (notably inequalities, inefficiencies and the political consequences of hospital closures). Initially, the Blair government abolished this market, only later to revive the idea. A new regime – Payment by Results – rewards hospitals and other service providers for the treatment they provide. GPs have more powers to run budgets, though not with the same level of freedom as under the previous fund-holding system. And patients are given more choice over where they are treated, including private providers as well as NHS hospitals.

Management and Regulation

Recent governments have sought to strengthen NHS management. This has involved identifying individuals with a clear remit for achieving aims and objectives (general managers and chairs of health authorities), tougher performance targets (such as reducing waiting times, reducing hospital infection rates) and new performance assessment systems.

At the same time, NHS organizations have been required to improve the ways in which they manage services. New health authority structures, introduced in the 1990s and modelled on corporate boards, were retained by New Labour. More

recently, amid much controversy, the Blair government created Foundation Trusts. These new organizations, while remaining part of the NHS, were promised greater autonomy, particularly in financial matters, in organizing and managing their activities and in setting their priorities. They were also expected to be more accountable to the local community. However, the autonomy and local accountability of Foundation Trusts may have been exaggerated. The amount of public participation in Foundation Trusts is low and managers have retained significant power over key decisions. Moreover, the trusts are regulated by a national body which sets the terms for their establishment and can intervene if they fail to comply. Furthermore, Foundation Trusts must comply with NHS standards as well as some national agreements (such as those on pay and conditions).

Despite the government's rhetoric about decentralizing health services and giving more autonomy to local people and local NHS bodies, there has been substantial centralization of the NHS. Since 1997 a number of new regulatory bodies have been established. These include the Healthcare Commission, which sets standards of care and management in England, inspects NHS organizations, and produces performance ratings. It also undertakes investigations of serious service failures. Others include the National Patient Safety Agency, which seeks to prevent 'adverse incidents' in healthcare (such as administering the wrong drug, for example), and the National Institute for Health and Clinical Excellence (known as NICE), which issues guidance to the NHS in England and Wales on whether or not treatments (particularly drug therapies) are cost-effective and should be adopted.

The regulation of professionals has also been strengthened. Following a series of scandals – including Harold Shipman (a GP who murdered many of his patients) and the Bristol Royal Infirmary case (involving poor standards of surgery in children with heart problems) – the government reformed the system of regulation for healthcare professions and, in particular, doctors. A new body was established (the Council for Healthcare Regulatory Excellence) to oversee the systems of professional self-regulation. The doctors' regulatory body, the General Medical Council (GMC), was reformed, by increasing the representation of lay people on its ruling body and extending its powers to suspend doctors suspected of bad practice. A further development is a system of revalidation, where all doctors will have to prove that they remain competent to practice, alongside a new system for investigating complaints against them.

Partnerships

Effective healthcare often depends heavily on other services run by others – such as social care, which falls under the responsibilities of local government. The relationship between the NHS and local government has been poor. Apart from some local areas, where relationships have traditionally been good, health and social care systems have been poorly coordinated. This has arisen from financial, organizational and cultural differences between the NHS and local government.

Many efforts have been made to address this problematic relationship. These have included joint planning and financial arrangements. More recently, a statutory duty of partnership was imposed on the NHS and local government to force cooperation. Other changes include the introduction of 'pooled budgets' between the NHS and local councils and a closer alignment of local authority boundaries with PCTs. For specific client groups receiving health and social care, care trusts have been created in some local areas. These arrangements, which in effect merge health and social care functions within a single body, are relatively rare.

Government has redoubled efforts to improve joint working on health matters more generally through more joint appointments of key posts (such as the local Director of Public Health), the creation of integrated teams of staff from the NHS and local authorities, integrated planning and common systems of performance assessment (see HM Government/Department of Health 2006). As part of efforts to create more 'joined-up' government, local area agreements (LAAs) have been introduced. These, along with stronger partnerships at local level (in the form of local strategic partnerships which include organizations such as the NHS, local government, other statutory bodies and the voluntary and private sectors), are entrusted with achieving clearer and consistent priorities for each local area.

Partnerships are also a way of improving public health. Local authority responsibilities for public health have been strengthened in recent years and councils now have powers to improve community well-being (which includes health). Building on previous and current partnership arrangements (such as Health Action Zones, which targeted health inequalities, and Sure Start, which aims to help families with children aged 4 years and under), the NHS will be expected to work much more closely with local authorities and other partners to address key public health issues such as smoking, alcohol misuse, obesity, sexual health and health inequalities.

Emerging Issues

All major industrialized democracies face similar problems in health policy and most are engaged in reforming their healthcare systems. The NHS is no exception. In the future, when undertaking reform, four key issues must be addressed.

First, healthcare systems must satisfy demands for health services, while controlling costs. Increasingly, the focus will be on improving the cost-effectiveness of services, by concentrating on interventions of proven effectiveness, using cost-saving and quality-enhancing technologies (including information technologies), limiting entitlement to those who can gain benefit and by clearer specification of health service priorities. This will also require better data on outcomes and costs, and improved utilization of this information by decision-makers, including clinicians.

Second, healthcare systems need to respond more effectively to the choices and views of service users and the wider public. It is acknowledged that health services should no longer be delivered in a paternalistic way. Service planners, managers and professionals must be more responsive to the preferences of the public and individuals. Even, so, greater voice and choice must be introduced carefully into the NHS. Not all people have the same capacity and resources to make choices or participate in decision-making. It is important that the extension of voice and choice does not lead to greater inequalities.

Third, the modern health service includes many stakeholders. The potential for fragmentation is real and must be avoided. It is important that pluralism in health services does not undermine the fundamental ethos of the healthcare system. More specifically, the presence of a larger number of organizations delivering services under the banner of the NHS provides a substantial challenge for regulators.

Finally, health must not be seen as purely the responsibility of the healthcare system. It is important to strengthen the contribution of other agencies (such as other government departments, local government and the voluntary sector) and to build effective partnerships geared to health improvement. Individual responsibility for health is also important. It is also necessary to acknowledge the influences of others on health, such as the media and business corporations (for example, the food and drink industry). Above all, the socio-economic and environmental factors that shape health status must be fully acknowledged and addressed.

Guide to Further Sources

For a general overview of health and healthcare issues, see R. Baggott, *Health and Healthcare in Britain* (Palgrave, 2004). The politics of healthcare is covered by R. Klein's *New Politics of the NHS* (Longman, 2005), C. Ham's *Health Policy in Britain* (Palgrave, 2004) and R. Baggott's *Understanding Health Policy* (Policy Press, 2007).

A number of books focus on the history and development of the NHS, including J. Allsop's *Health Policy and the NHS: Towards 2000* (Longman, 1995) and C. Webster's official history of the NHS, *The Health Services Since the War*, vols I and II (HMSO, 1988 and 1996).

P. Aggleton discusses the meaning of health in *Health* (Routledge, 1990). The rise of patient power is considered by C. Hogg in *Patients, Power and Politics* (Sage, 1999) and by R. Baggott, J. Allsop and K. Jones in *Speaking for Patients and Carers* (Basingstoke: Palgrave, 2004). *Public Health: Policy and Politics* by Rob Baggott (Basingstoke: Palgrave, 2000) gives a thorough account of public health issues. S. Peckham and M. Exworthy outline primary care in *Primary Care in the UK* (Palgrave, 2003). Rationing is discussed by C. Newdick in *Who Should we Treat?* (Oxford University Press, 2005) while A. Pollock's *NHS Plc* (Verso, 2004) explores the role of the private health sector in the UK.

The following official reports and policy documents are useful: D. Wanless, *Securing Our Future Health* (HM Treasury, 2002); Department of Health, *The NHS Plan* (The Stationery Office, 2000); HM Government/Department of Health, *Choosing Health: Making Healthy Choices Easier* (The Stationery Office, 2004); and HM Government/Department of Health, *Our Health Our Care, Our Say* (The Stationery Office, 2006).

Finally, some useful websites: The King's Fund (an independent health think-tank) at: <www.kingsfund.org.uk>; the Department of Health at <www.dh.gov.uk>; the Healthcare Commission (the regulatory body for healthcare standards) at <www.healthcarecommission.org.uk>; and the House of Commons Health Select Committee (which reports on health issues) at <www.publications.parliament. uk/pa/cm/cmhealth.htm>.

Chapter 41

Education in Schools

Anne West

Overview

- The school systems in the UK have differing legislative frameworks and policies. School structures, funding, curriculum and assessment vary.
- Choice, diversity and market-oriented policies remain significant in England, but not in the rest of the UK.
- A major focus of policy across the UK under Labour or Labour-led coalitions since 1997 has been to reduce achievement gaps between children from different social groups.
- Approaches to address the varying outcomes of young people from different social groups include an entitlement to part-time pre-school education for 3- and 4-year olds; a focus on the personalization of learning; and an education maintenance allowance for young people aged 16–19 from low-income families to encourage participation in post-compulsory education.

Introduction

The importance of education, particularly in terms of increasing human capital and economic competitiveness, is acknowledged at national and supranational levels. Education also plays a crucial role in terms of cognitive and skill development and personal and social development. It is significant for society more broadly given its role in socialization, fostering social justice and enhancing social cohesion. This multiplicity of purposes and its compulsory nature means that politicians and policy-makers have given education a high priority.

This chapter is concerned with schooling in the UK. It focuses on England, but refer-ence is made to other countries and in particular to Scotland. The first section presents a brief historical context and an overview of current school systems in the UK. The second section focuses on two current issues: choice, diversity and market-oriented policies; and reducing the achievement gap between different groups of pupils. The final section concludes with and highlights some emerging issues.

Schooling in the UK: Past and Present

Different trajectories in educational provision have been followed in the countries of the UK, but the churches have historically played an important role. In England and Wales, the Elementary Education Act of 1870 aimed to provide schools in order to fill the gaps in existing provision made by the church. Subsequently, the 1902 Education Act established local education authorities together with a system of secondary education. With the 1918 Education Act, fees for elementary schools were abolished and education became compulsory until the age of 14. In Northern Ireland, the school system, which developed along denominational grounds, goes back to the 1830s. In Scotland, legislation dating to the seventeenth century and before had established a parochial school system. This was extended from the 1830s until the 1872 Education (Scotland) Act created a Board of Education and education became the responsibility of local elected bodies with funding coming from the local property tax. Although fees were charged initially, free primary education was introduced in 1890, and in 1901, education became compulsory until the age of 14.

In England and Wales, the 1944 Education Act set up a universal system of free, compulsory schooling from 5 to 15 years (raised to 16 in 1972). State-funded schooling continued to be provided by local authority and church schools. The 1944 Education Act did not prescribe the structure of secondary education, but enabled the implementation of a 'tripartite' system, comprising grammar schools, technical schools and 'secondary modern' schools for the remainder. The 1947 Education Act (Northern Ireland) was similar to the 1944 Act.

Following the introduction of a selective system in England, concerns emerged, as the main beneficiaries of grammar schools were the middle classes. During the 1960s, there was a policy shift, and in 1965 the Labour government requested local education authorities to submit plans for the introduction of comprehensive education.

A broadly comprehensive ('all ability') system of education was eventually introduced across much of England. In Scotland, there was also a change from selective to comprehensive schools (Eurydice 2006). Northern Ireland, however, retained a selective system until recently.

Major changes in education policy took place under Conservative administrations between 1979 and 1997. Parental choice of school had a high political profile. In England and Wales, the 1980 Education Act enabled parents to express a preference for the school of their choice for their child; similar legislation was enacted in Northern Ireland. In Scotland, following the 1981 Education (Scotland) Act, parents had the right to nominate a school they wished their child to attend (make a 'placing request'), if they wanted him or her to attend a school other than the local school.

Subsequently, school diversity emerged, at least in theory, as a key policy issue in England, Wales and Scotland. Following the 1988 Education Reform Act in England and Wales, and the 1989 Self-Governing Schools etc. (Scotland) Act, schools could opt out of local authority control. They were then funded by the government and had more autonomy than previously. The majority of schools that opted out were in England – very few were in Wales and even fewer in Scotland.

In England, there was further diversification, with fifteen independent city technology schools being set up: their capital funds were intended to be met by private sector sponsors, with revenue costs being met by the government. In the early 1990s, the specialist schools programme was set up; this involved secondary schools obtaining sponsorship from the private or voluntary sector and submitting a bid to specialize in prescribed subjects (whilst still following the national curriculum). If successful, additional government capital and revenue funding followed (see below).

In England and Wales, the 1988 Education Reform Act introduced formula funding, whereby individual school budgets were determined predominantly on the basis of the number of pupils on roll (a quasi-voucher system – see chapter 30). Official school 'league tables' of public examination results were also published. Incentives were thus created for schools to maximize their income and their pupils' examination results via the newly created quasi-market (Le Grand and Bartlett 1993). Underpinning the reforms was the view that parents would choose the 'best' schools for their child, based on the information available – in particular, examination results – and that the ensuing competition between schools would result in educational standards increasing. Concerns were, however, raised about the crude nature of the published examination results. Because of the link between socio-economic background and attainment, schools with more advantaged intakes in general obtain higher results than those with less advantaged intakes. However, in terms of school quality, what is important is the value added by the school over and above social background factors. There were also concerns raised about 'cream-skimming' by certain schools, in the main church and grant-maintained schools (with control over admissions), selecting pupils likely to do well academically and enhance the school's league table position (see West 2007).

these schools by those from poorer backgrounds.

The state-maintained school systems in the UK vary. England and Wales have a similar legislative framework and that for Northern Ireland is also broadly similar. In Scotland, the legislative context is different, and some changes have also taken place since devolution (see chapter 35).

Compulsory education begins at the age of 5 except in Northern Ireland, when it begins at 4. Secondary school starts at 11 except in Scotland, when it starts at 12. Across the UK, compulsory education ends at 16. Post-compulsory secondary education for 16–19-year olds is provided in schools, sixth form colleges and further education colleges.

Across the UK, primary schools cater for children of all abilities. However, at secondary level, systems and structures differ. In Scotland and Wales, there is a comprehensive system. In England, the system is broadly comprehensive, although around 5 per cent of secondary schools are fully academically selective grammar schools. Further, a significant minority of nominally comprehensive schools, predominantly those that control their own admissions, use a variety of different methods that are to some degree selective (e.g., selecting a proportion of pupils on the basis of aptitude/ability in a subject area); and virtually all religious schools give priority to children on the basis of their religion (see West 2007). In Northern Ireland, a selective system is being replaced (see Eurydice 2005).

Private and State-Maintained Schools

In the UK, the vast majority of pupils of compulsory school age are educated in state-maintained schools, although fewer in England (93 per cent) than in the other countries of the UK. The remainder are in private schools, many of which charge high fees, thereby restricting access to

Curriculum and Assessment

The 1988 Education Reform Act introduced a national curriculum and programme of assessment in England and Wales, as did the 1989 Education Reform (Northern Ireland) Order. In Scotland,

England, Wales and Northern Ireland

- GCSE examinations (or pre-vocational equivalent) taken in individual subjects by most pupils (16 years);
- GCE Advanced Subsidiary levels (17 years);
- GCE Advanced levels may be taken (18 years); generally required for entry to higher education;
- Wales: Welsh Baccalaureate (or Welsh Bac) includes qualifications such as AS and A levels and a 'core' of key skills of varying types.

Scotland

- Scottish Certificate of Education examinations Standard Grade (16 years);
- Higher Grade examinations (17 years);
- Higher Grade/Advanced Higher Grade examinations (18 years) (generally required for entry to higher education).

there are non-statutory curriculum guidelines for pupils aged from 5 to 14 and there is a non-statutory testing programme; however, in order to evaluate overall pupil attainment, there is an annual survey of a sample of pupils known as the Scottish Survey of Achievement.

At the end of compulsory and post-compulsory secondary schooling there are public examinations across the UK; these vary between countries (see box 41.1) (see also chapter 42). In England, school and

college achievement and attainment tables ('league tables') are published by the Department for Education and Skills (DfES; now the Department for Children, Schools and Families) and in the press. At the secondary level, the key indicator is the percentage of pupils obtaining five or more GCSE passes (or equivalent) at grades A* to C (i.e. high grades); this is significant, as this level of achievement is generally needed for progression to academic courses post-16 – General Certificate of Education (GCE) Advanced (A) level – which are normally needed for entry to higher education.

School Management, Governance and Inspection

Local management of schools was introduced in England and Wales following the 1988 Education Reform Act (it was also introduced in Northern Ireland). Schools became responsible for deciding how the school budget from their local authority (which is determined largely on the basis of pupil numbers) should be spent. In Scotland, local authorities decide on the level of support to be given to schools. Most local authorities distribute their agreed budgets to schools on a formula basis, with pupil roll being the main determinant measure used. Individual schools are responsible for managing their own day-to-day expenditure via devolved school management, but, unlike in England, the school's 'normal complement' of staff is paid by the local authority (Eurydice 2006).

School governing bodies in England, Wales and Northern Ireland include parents and representatives of the school and local community; they have a largely strategic role, including managing the school's budget. In Scotland, following the 2006 Scottish Schools (Parental Involvement) Act, parent councils replaced school boards,

---

Box 41.2   School inspection

England: Office for Standards in
    Education (Ofsted)
Wales: Estyn (HM's Chief Inspector
    of Education and Training)
Scotland: HM   Inspectorate   of
    Education
Northern Ireland: Education and
    Training Inspectorate

---

which had some similarities with school
governing bodies; these are responsible for
helping to improve the quality of education
and to develop children's potential. Inspection bodies in each country have responsibility for ensuring that schools are providing
an acceptable quality of education (see box
41.2).

Current Issues

Two current issues are of particular interest
from a policy perspective. The first is that
of choice, diversity and market-oriented
reforms, which in England are seen as a
way of raising overall educational standards. The second issue relates to reducing
the achievement gap between different
groups of pupils.

Choice, Diversity and Market-oriented Policies

Grant-maintained schools were abolished
by the Labour government. In England and
Wales, following the 1998 School Standards and Framework Act, their status
changed, in the main to foundation schools,
although some became voluntary schools.

In Scotland, the 2000 Standards in
Scotland's Schools etc. Act abolished self-
governing status. Other aspects of policy in
relation to choice and diversity have
diverged, particularly since devolution. The
divergence is clearest when England and
Scotland are compared.

In England, market-oriented reforms
have continued under Labour. Official
'league tables' continue to be published
and, significantly, there has been an increase
in school diversity. The specialist schools
programme was relaunched and expanded;
the focus has changed insofar as schools
must have partner schools and a community focus. A small number of new faith
schools have also become part of the state-
maintained system. Independent 'acade-
mies' have been introduced with the aim of
improving the quality of education in disadvantaged areas; these are run by private
or voluntary sector sponsors, which contribute around 10 per cent of capital costs
to the school (the remainder is paid by the
government, as is the revenue funding).
They are similar in some ways to city technology colleges, but the financial contribution by sponsors is lower. Academy
sponsors control the school governing
body and the national curriculum does
not need to be followed. Diversity and
choice are also a key part of the 2006 Education and Inspections Act, which places a
duty on local authorities to promote
diversity and choice in their provision of
schools.

Legislation has sought to allay concerns
about cream-skimming by schools; the
1998 School Standards and Framework
Act and the 2006 Education and Inspections Act, along with a strong code of practice, can be seen as an attempt to regulate
what was a largely unregulated admissions
system.

Whilst league tables and school diversity
remain high on the political agenda in
England, the situation in the other countries of the UK is different. No official

Box 41.3 Comprehensive schools in Scotland

'Our comprehensive system is right for Scotland and it performs in the top class on the world stage. The comprehensive schools we want to see are rich, colourful and diverse, offering choice for pupils and with ambition for themselves and for every one of their pupils. No one in Scotland should be required to select a school to get the first rate education they deserve and are entitled to. Choice between schools in Scotland is no substitute for the universal excellence we seek and Scotland's communities demand' (Scottish Executive 2004: 1).

league tables are now published in Wales, Scotland or Northern Ireland. Moreover, in the case of Scotland, the 2000 Standards in Scotland's Schools etc. Act gave greater powers to local authorities in relation to refusing 'placing requests'. Significantly, there are no policies in place to increase parental choice of schools (see box 41.3).

There are only limited data available comparing educational outcomes across the UK, and none over time. However, the results of the Programme for International Student Assessment (PISA) (Organization of Economic Co-operation and Development, OECD 2001) in 2000 revealed that the outcomes were broadly similar for England and Scotland, suggesting that the different education systems perform similarly even though their policies in relation to school choice and diversity differ.

Reducing the achievement gap

A major area of concern across the UK relates to differences in the levels of achieve-

ment of children from different social groups. The 2006 Budget Statement by HM Treasury noted: 'Closing gaps in attainment and ensuring that all children reach their potential is a long-term challenge, but one that is essential if the UK is to prosper in an increasingly competitive global economy' (HM Treasury 2006: 145).

The association between poverty and low educational achievement is an important and persistent concern across the UK. In England, for example, pupils from low-income families perform less well, on average, in public examinations than do others: according to DfES figures in 2006, 20 per cent of children eligible for free school meals obtained five or more GCSE examination passes (including English and mathematics) at grades A* to C, compared with 48 per cent of those not eligible. Fewer children from lower socio-economic backgrounds continue in education and training beyond the age of 16 (see West and Pennell 2003).

There are also differences in terms of the achievement of girls and boys: these are also apparent outside the UK. In 2000, in PISA, girls outperformed boys in reading literacy in every participating country (OECD 2001). In mathematical literacy, boys performed better in some countries but not in others, and in the UK there were no statistically significant differences. In all OECD countries, males were more likely to be amongst the lowest-performing pupils; the low levels of achievement for some groups of boys are a significant challenge for education policy.

The evidence relating to the educational performance of children from different ethnic groups, most of whom live in England, is complex. High proportions of pupils of Chinese and Indian origin gain high grade GCSE passes, followed by pupils of white British, Bangladeshi, Pakistani, black African and black Caribbean origin. The overall differences are likely to be associated, at least to some extent, with disadvantage. Other groups of children also fare poorly, in particular those with special educational needs and those in care, a particularly vulnerable group.

The question arises as to how these achievement gaps are to be reduced. Policies are being directed to address this issue, and include targeting resources on disadvantaged schools/areas via specific initiatives and increasing the focus given to the teaching of literacy and numeracy. In addition, three major UK-wide initiatives are related to this overall aim: the National Childcare Strategy, the personalization of learning and the education maintenance allowance.

The National Childcare Strategy (1998) is aimed at improving access to good quality, affordable childcare for parents who wish to work outside the home. The focus has been on strengthening early years *education* provision (Lewis 2003). There are benefits of high-quality pre-school educational provision to a range of cognitive outcomes (Sylva et al. 2004). According to HM Treasury's Pre-Budget Report (2004) *Choice for Parents: The Best Start for Children*: 'Availability of childcare plays an important role in tackling disadvantage and child poverty, and supporting social mobility and equality of opportunity' (p. 4). Pre-school provision comprises an entitlement to free part-time nursery education for 3- and 4-year olds. The details and implementation vary between the countries of the UK, although voluntary and private providers have had a key role to play in the expansion of pre-school provision.

Personalization is seen by the government as being an important factor in relation to addressing socio-economic gaps in achievement (HM Treasury 2006). In England, it is seen as a key factor in tackling achievement gaps between different pupils from different social and ethnic groups. According to the White Paper, *Higher Standards, Better Schools for All*

(2005, Cm 6677): 'It means a tailored education for every child and young person, that gives them strength in the basics, stretches their aspirations, and builds their life chances. It will create opportunity for every child, regardless of their background' (p. 50).

Personalization in the Scottish context is defined differently in *A Curriculum for Excellence* (Scottish Executive 2004) where the stated aim is for the curriculum to 'respond to individual needs and support particular aptitudes and talents' (p. 14).

The education maintenance allowance began across the UK in 2004 and aims to encourage young people from low-income families to continue in full-time education beyond the age of 16. This is designed to increase levels of participation in education and training for young people between 16 and 19, where the UK fares poorly in relation to its international competitors (see also chapter 43).

Emerging Issues

Policy in relation to schools varies between the countries of the UK. However, there are common objectives in relation to increasing human capital and economic competitiveness, by improving overall attainment, and to reducing achievement gaps. The means by which these are to be achieved differ. In England, choice, diversity and increased competition are seen as being of key importance in terms of raising standards; in other countries of the UK this is not the case. In relation to seeking to reduce achievement gaps, major initiatives have been introduced under the Labour government across the UK, in particular, an entitlement to part-time pre-school education, the personalization of learning and the education maintenance allowance.

In terms of emerging issues, an area where policy is likely to develop further is in relation to the linkages between education and children's services as a result of, for example, the English Green Paper, *Every Child Matters* (2003, Cm 5860) and the delivery of integrated children's services by Scottish schools. Another issue relates to the role of parents in their children's formal education. The 2006 Scottish Schools (Parental Involvement) Act promotes the involvement of parents in schools with a view to improving the quality of education.

In England, the 2006 Education and Inspections Act makes specific reference to increasing opportunities for parental choice and requires local authorities to consider representations from parents about school provision in their area. The ensuing policies are likely to reinforce further, albeit in different ways, the important function that families – specifically in this case parents – have to play in their children's learning and education.

Guide to Further Sources

The Department for Education and Skills (DfES) publishes statistics relating to education and commissioned research on its website: <http://www.dfes.gov.uk>.

HM Treasury, Budget Statement (HM Treasury, 2006): the annual budget statement provides details of government policy priorities and associated public investment.

J. Le Grand and W. Bartlett (eds), *Quasi-Markets and Social Policy* (Macmillan, 1993) discusses quasi-markets in different policy areas including schools.

A. West, 'Schools, financing and educational standards', in J. Hills, J. Le Grand and D. Piachaud (eds), *Making Social Policy Work: Essays in Honour of Howard Glennerster* (Policy Press, 2007) examines the extent to which the Labour government has met its objectives in relation to expenditure and educational standards.

Findings from a key evaluation of pre-school education in England are presented in K. Sylva, E. Melhuish, P. Sammons, I. Siraj-Blatchford and B. Taggart, *The Effective Provision of Pre-School Education (EPPE) Project: Effective Pre-School Education, Final Report 1997–2004* (London: DfES, 2004); also available at: <http://www.dfes.gov.uk/research/programmeofresearch/projectinformation.cfm?projected=13144&resultspage=1>. Pre-school provision in England is also examined in A. West, 'The pre-school education market in England from 1997: quality, availability, affordability and equity', *Oxford Review of Education* 32/3 (2006): 283–301.

J. Lewis, 'Developing early years childcare in England, 1997–2002: the choices for (working) mothers', *Social Policy and Administration* 37/3 (2003): 219–38: this examines the National Childcare Strategy and discusses tensions between the social investment approach to childcare and the desire to promote mothers' employment.

Scottish Executive, *Ambitious, Excellent Schools: Our Agenda For Action* (2004) sets out the reform agenda for Scotland's schools and *A Curriculum for Excellence* (2004) is central to this agenda.

The concept of underachievement is examined in A. West and H. Pennell, *Underachievement in Schools* (RoutledgeFalmer, 2003), which also explores the achievement of different groups of children.

Eurydice is part of the European Community Action Programme in the Field of Education and Lifelong Learning: <http://www.eurydice.org/portal/page/portal/

Eurydice>; Eurybase is an information database on education systems in Europe, which is available via the Eurydice portal: <http://www.eurydice.org/portal/page/portal/Eurydice/DB_Eurybase_Home>. By clicking onto individual countries, detailed information on education systems can be found, including the following: Eurydice, *The Education System in England, Wales and Northern Ireland 2004/05* (2005); Eurydice, *The Education System in Scotland 2005/06* (2006). Eurydice and Eurybase are useful sources of information about the education systems in Europe on a country-by-country basis.

Organization for Economic Co-operation and Development (OECD), *Knowledge and Skills for Life, First Results from the OECD Programme for International Student Assessment (PISA) 2000* (OECD, 2001): this presents the 2000 PISA results for reading, mathematical and scientific literacy.

Chapter 42

Lifelong Learning and Training

Claire Callender

Overview

- Lifelong learning is an idea informing education and training policies; current policies have been prompted largely by globalization and changes in the labour market.
- Labour's post-compulsory education policies have both social and economic objectives, but the needs of the economy and market principles are prioritized.
- Labour's policies focus on improving the qualification and skill levels of the existing and future workforce by encouraging greater participation in post-compulsory education and expanding provision, especially for young people.
- Labour has used numerous policy levers to bring about these changes, including higher public spending and more output or target-related funding, new structures and arm's length agencies, changes to the curriculum and qualifications framework, and new relationships between providers, including employers and learners.
- Participation in post-compulsory education remains unequal, with those from disadvantaged backgrounds in greatest need but missing out.

Introduction

This chapter begins with an explanation of what lifelong learning is, who provides it, and why it came about. Next, it explores the ideas informing the Labour government's lifelong learning policies. The chapter then discusses Labour's post-compulsory education policies in England and the issues underpinning them, dividing them into those aimed at improving the qualifications and skills of the future workforce and those aimed at the current workforce. It concludes by highlighting some emerging issues.

What is Lifelong Learning?

Since Labour came to power in 1997, lifelong learning has dominated thinking about education and training for those aged over 16. At the heart of lifelong learning is the idea that learning should take place at all stages in a person's life – from the cradle to the grave – and that the learning should be embedded in people's lives. So it can take place anywhere – in schools, further education colleges, universities, at work or at home, or in the community.

Lifelong learning requires a system which gives everyone opportunities to learn at all levels, as and when they need to rather than because they have reached a certain age. These opportunities need to cater for people with university degrees and those without any qualifications; for those in highly skilled jobs wanting professional development and people in unskilled jobs or without a job experiencing difficulties reading and writing; and for people who have retired or just want to learn something new. This is a very different way of thinking about education and training, which in the past had been restricted to formal learning in specialized educational institutions, aimed mostly at school leavers and young people at the start of their working life.

Unlike many areas of social policy, lifelong learning is not targeted at one particular identifiable group, such as 'the poor' or 'the sick' – anyone can benefit from it. The different people affected by lifelong learning and the diverse methods involved mean there is no single policy covering all aspects of the process. Instead, there is a collection of policies and strategies, often aimed at a particular group, which together contribute to the overall goal of lifelong learning. It is, therefore, an idea that informs and underpins education and training policies: it captures an approach to a set of policies.

The policies most associated with lifelong learning focus on the period after the end of compulsory schooling at age 16. This stage of education is called post-compulsory education and training, and it can be delivered by a wide variety of providers. These include the state – in schools, sixth form colleges, further education colleges, and higher education institutions – the private and voluntary sector, and employers.

Unlike compulsory education, post-compulsory education and training are both non-statutory. Individuals, rather than the state, take responsibility for their own education and training, except for the unemployed where the state often intervenes, for example through training programmes

for the long-term unemployed. However, the most extensive post-compulsory education remains funded primarily by central government and takes place in further education colleges and higher education institutions. Employers too have a key role in providing and paying for training and there is also a growing private market in adult learning, as, increasingly, learners pay for, or contribute towards, their own costs.

There are no comprehensive statistics on the total number of people involved in post-secondary education. According to the Department for Education and Skills (DfES), in the UK in 2004–5 there were 5 million students and learners in further education colleges compared to 2.2 million in 1990–1. Four-fifths of them were aged over 19 and a similar proportion studied part time. There were a further 2.5 million higher education students taking undergraduate and postgraduate courses, compared to 1.1 million in 1990–1. In addition, in early 2006, more than 5 million people of working age (i.e. males aged 16–64 and women aged 16–59) were involved in some job-related training.

Why did Lifelong Learning Come About?

The late 1980s and 1990s saw a radical rethink about post-compulsory education and training and the emergence of the term 'lifelong learning' on the policy agenda. Why did this happen? The key drivers were globalization and changes in the labour market. Together they help us understand why lifelong learning policies were introduced, and the nature of these policies.

Globalization (see chapter 53) has had a profound effect on Britain's economic and social policies, including education. One result is that Britain has shifted towards what is called a 'knowledge economy' or 'knowledge society', based on high skills and specialist knowledge work. Thus, skills and knowledge are critical in Britain's ability to compete in the global economy and to drive economic growth.

Globalization, increasing competition and rapid scientific and technological advances are also leading to changes in the workplace – how work is organized and the nature of everyone's jobs. Few people today can expect to stay in the same job for life. Instead, they are likely to have more discontinuous and less secure work patterns over their lifetime.

These developments affect the qualifications, skills and competencies that workers need in order to perform their jobs, to keep them and to get new jobs. So training can no longer be confined to one point in our working life, typically after leaving school. Instead, many people will need to acquire new or different skills at various points in their lives, and often this will have to be fitted in around existing family and work commitments.

Labour's Ideology of Lifelong Learning

Tony Blair's Labour government believed that Britain's success in a 'knowledge economy' must be built on a very different foundation from the past. Success depends, first, on the creation and generation of technological improvement and innovation and, secondly, on a well-educated, highly skilled and adaptable or flexible labour force. This has profound implications for Britain's education and training system.

Labour's approach to post-compulsory education reform has to be understood as a response to these changes, and to policies introduced by the previous Conservative government and as a desire to reshape policy in line with its own particular philosophy and practices. What is distinctive about Labour's approach is that both economic prosperity and social inclusion and

justice are positioned as key goals of social policy, especially in post-compulsory education.

According to this way of thinking, skills are the key lever to improving workplace productivity. The most common measures of skills are qualifications. For a successful knowledge economy, people need qualifications, and with good qualifications, individuals can get well-paid and satisfying, secure jobs. It is via the education system, especially post-compulsory education, that individuals can acquire the qualifications required for a good job and reap the wider social and personal benefits of learning. Education, therefore, is recognized as the key route for increasing social mobility and social justice, while employment is a means of promoting social inclusion and tackling poverty.

In most of Labour's post-compulsory education policies, we can see evidence of economic and social goals and the bringing together of market principles and a social democratic emphasis upon equality of opportunity. The economic imperative of lifelong learning has dominated nearly all post-compulsory policies; indeed, most policy interest has been preoccupied with a narrow agenda of developing a more productive and efficient workforce. Tony Blair's comment – that 'education is the best economic policy we have' – captures this stance. Therefore, there is considerable discrepancy between the rhetoric around lifelong learning and the reality of Labour's policies in this area.

Another feature of Labour's lifelong learning policies, under the banner of their wider public sector 'modernization' agenda, is the ideology of the market and the introduction of quasi-markets, first promoted by the previous Conservative government. Competition between educational providers and institutions is the leading logic behind Labour's thinking. The aim is to stimulate more competition between institutions to increase efficiency, drive up quality and to give learners greater choice. Policy instruments such as performance indicators or targets, league tables, more stringent inspection regimes and mechanisms for assuring accountability have reinforced this, especially in further education, which has been particularly affected by lifelong learning policy developments.

Labour's Education and Training Policies

Labour believes that to secure economic growth it has to improve the qualifications and skill levels of all workers. The overall objective of the party's education and training policies is to boost the supply of such workers by encouraging higher levels of participation in post-compulsory education. Labour sees both the expansion of post-compulsory education and its key role in providing vocational and professional education for the existing and future workforce as central to this ambition. Some commentators, however, question the assumptions underpinning these policies, their emphasis on qualifications, whether qualifications are the best proxy for skills and how this undervalues informal incrementally gained knowledge (Wolf et al., 2006).

Since 1997, the Labour government has taken post-16 education more seriously than previous governments. It has allocated significantly more money, established new structures and 'arm's length' agencies that regulate, fund and organize education and training, such as the Learning and Skills Council – which was the first public body ever to have a statutory duty to encourage participation in learning – and created the first national strategy for skills.

However, it has been criticized for the plethora of policies and initiatives, some complementary, some overlapping, some competing. The number of centrally led and top-down interventions is consider-

able. To achieve improvement, the government has used the levers of funding (providers and learners), targets, the curriculum and qualifications, and relationships – including the influence of employers.

Labour's post-compulsory education policies can be broadly divided into those aimed at improving the qualifications and skills of the future workforce and those aimed at raising the skill levels of the current workforce.

Improving the Qualifications and Skills of the Future Workforce

14–19-year olds

Participation in education and training after the end of compulsory schooling has concerned policy-makers for decades. Low rates of participation post-16 are a significant weakness in the UK's education and training system, compared with other international competitors. According to the DfES, 73 per cent of 16-year olds and 58 per cent of 17-year olds were in post-compulsory education in schools, sixth form colleges or further education colleges in 2004–5.

Labour's 14–19 policies attempt to redress the failures of compulsory schooling (see chapter 48). Their key goal is to encourage more young people to stay in, or go back into, education and training so they have the qualifications and skills to progress in learning or the labour market. Those who leave education at 16 or 17 without good qualifications have far less chance of finding rewarding employment, or, indeed, any employment. They come disproportionately from disadvantaged backgrounds. These early leavers are a constant reminder of the inequalities in our learning system.

The Labour government has concentrated on reducing the number of the most excluded – those not in education, employment or training - and more recently those in jobs without training. The 2005 White Paper *14–19 Education and Skills* (Cm 6476) focuses on strategies to improve take-up, retention, progression and attainment. Labour has selectively reformed the curriculum and introduced new qualifications and apprenticeship schemes. However, this has not ended the long-standing divide between highly valued academic qualifications and the lower-status vocational (i.e. work-orientated) qualifications. The government rejected calls from numerous quarters for a more unified approach to qualifications, which would have involved the abolition of A levels. It has, however, provided more incentives and support, such as careers advice and information on learning opportunities (e.g. Connexions and learndirect), and introduced financial support for learners aged 16–19 through a means-tested grant called Educational Maintenance Allowances. But overall, these policies have had a limited effect on post-16 participation rates and qualifications.

Higher education

The government sees higher education (HE) playing a major role in meeting the needs of the labour market, especially the growing demand for highly skilled workers. Again, it has focused on increasing HE participation.

Labour's HE polices have concentrated on undergraduates, rather than postgraduates. They were shaped initially by the National Committee of Inquiry into Higher Education, chaired by Ron Dearing. The Committee, established under the previous Conservative government, reported in July 1997 shortly after Labour came into office. As the report's title – *Higher Education in the Learning Society* – suggests, the contribution of HE to lifelong learning was central. Amongst its many recommenda-

tions about the future purpose, size and funding of HE, the report argued for increasing and widening participation in HE, at the same time questioning who should pay for it. Both these issues, along with concerns about research, have dominated the HE policy agenda since 1997. They were also at the forefront of the government's vision of HE captured in the 2003 White Paper *The Future of Higher Education* (Cm 5753).

Labour's desire to increase and widen access and participation in HE is symbolized by their pledge to raise participation from around 43 per cent to 50 per cent of 18–30-year olds by 2010. The government wants more people to go to university, but it does not want just more of the same sort of people going. It seeks to change the inequalities in access and participation because young people from unskilled backgrounds are more than five times less likely to enter HE than those from professional backgrounds. So policies have focused on encouraging more under-represented groups to enter HE, especially young people from disadvantaged families.

The government has succeeded in increasing HE participation, but not in widening participation. The absolute number of university students has risen, especially since the expansion of HE in the late 1980s and early 1990s. But commentators question whether it is possible to reach the 50 per cent target, and whether it is even desirable. However, there has been little change in the proportion of working-class students going to university, so inequalities prevail.

The expansion of HE and the under-investment in HE under the Conservative government were key issues facing the Dearing Committee. It questioned who should pay for HE and contribute to its costs, and considered the balance of contributions from the state, individual students, students' families and employers. The Committee's arguments were based on market principles – those who benefit from HE should pay towards its costs. It recognized that society benefits and should pay the greatest share. But students, once they graduate, also benefit in terms of better employment prospects and enhanced earnings, so they too should contribute towards the costs of their education.

This 'cost-sharing' agenda has informed the key reforms of student funding and financial assistance, and has shifted more of the costs of HE away from the state onto individual students. The changes embodied in the 2004 Higher Education Act have radically transformed the HE landscape, heralding the marketization of HE, and greater competition. The introduction of variable tuition fees in 2006 has enabled universities to charge full-time undergraduates up to £3,000 for tuition. All students, irrespective of their family's income, have to pay tuition fees; an optional student loan, to be repaid after graduation, is available to help them do this. At the same time, student grants were reintroduced following their abolition in the 1998 Teaching and Higher Education Act. HE institutions are expected to contribute to student financial support via bursaries from the income received from tuition fees.

Improving the Qualifications and Skills of the Existing Workforce

Individuals with limited skills or poor basic education are economically marginalized, finding it difficult to get work or well-paid secure jobs. Thus, another thrust of government policy has been the first ever national 'skills strategy', focusing on adults with low-level or no qualifications. The aim is to increase the demand for learning by adults and to raise their qualifications to improve their employment prospects, including the unemployed, to move them from welfare into work. In addition, given demographic changes – the ageing population and the declining number of young people – existing workers will need to update their skills or learn new skills to meet the changing requirements of the labour market.

Skills strategy

The 2003 White Paper *21st Century Skills – Realising Our Potential: Individuals, Employers, Nation* (Cm 5810) established the skills strategy. It outlined the principles for allocating government funding for adult training, prioritizing those most in need. It identified exactly which groups of adults (aged 19+) are eligible for free learning, what type of learning should be free and who has to pay tuition fees. For the first time, an entitlement to free learning for all adults to gain a Level 2 qualification (equivalent to five GCSEs A*–C) was introduced for those without such a qualification. Later, this entitlement was raised to Level 3 (two A levels, or the equivalent) for 19–25-year olds by the 2006 White Paper *Further Education: Raising Skills, Improving Life Chances* (Cm 6768). To drive this policy, tough targets were introduced, based on the proportion gaining a Level 2 or 3 qualification. Backing up this entitlement was a financial incentive – a means-tested grant for those studying full time to help with living costs – and more help through advice, guidance and information services.

One consequence of this strategy was the disappearance of courses not delivering these priority qualifications, thereby threatening the goal of lifelong learning. Another has been the large numbers of adult learners paying tuition fees for the first time, or paying higher fees, because they fall outside the government's priority groups. So again, we see a social agenda alongside the marketization of provision, which means that more learners are having to shoulder a larger share of the costs of learning as the state's contribution falls.

'Skills for Life'

In 1998, Labour commissioned Claus Moser to investigate the issues and opportunities for improving basic skills – literacy, numeracy and English language competence. The Committee's report, *A Fresh Start – Improving Literacy and Numeracy*, found 7 million adults in the England had literacy and numeracy needs. 'Skills for Life', as this became known as, had been one of the top three priorities in the Labour Party 1997 manifesto, and was, subsequently, a significant driver of policy and practice in further education. As with other areas of government intervention in post-compulsory education, improvement focused on determining agreed levels and standards of competence delivered through a new national curriculum and measured by a raft of new qualifications, and reducing barriers to learning while improving the quality of teaching. One target group is the unemployed and other Jobcentre Plus clients.

Employers

The Labour government, like governments before them, has had limited success in persuading more employers to invest in training and train more of their workforce, especially small and medium-sized employers. Around 14 per cent of working-age people receive job-related training in any one month, which most often lasts less than one week. People with high levels of qualifications are far more likely than those with low or no qualifications to receive training. So work-based training is least common among those who need it most. These figures show the continuing inequalities in access to lifelong learning. They also suggest that continuing education and training does not succeed in making up for skills gaps emerging after compulsory schooling, but tend instead to reinforce disparities resulting from school education.

Through wide-ranging initiatives (e.g. 'Train to Gain'), the Labour government attempted to put employers in the driving seat, often by shifting training costs from employers onto the public purse. Policies introduced in its third term (e.g. National Employer Training Programme), and the recommendations of the Leitch Review (HMT, 2006), have given employers even more say, encouraging them to be more specific about their workplace skill needs. But, do employers know what they need? Moreover, these demand-led initiatives are voluntary. No UK government, yet, has introduced legislation to make it mandatory for employers to provide and pay for the training of their workforce.

Emerging Issues

While compulsory education is seen as failing to deliver the skilled workforce the economy needs, and as the demographic changes hit, governments will continue to use the post-compulsory sector as a means of redress. They are likely to introduce further reforms, including recommendations from the Leitch Review such as raising the school leaving age to 18, and more employer involvement in skills training. Other future issues include whether the current level of post-compulsory education funding is sustainable in the longer term and whether there will be increasing marketization and privatization in this sector, for instance, with the lifting of the £3,000 cap on HE tuition fees. Questions about the roles and responsibilities of individuals, the state and the private sector, including employers, in post-compulsory education provision and funding will continue well into the future.

Guide to Further Sources

L. Archer, M. Hutchings and A. Ross, *Higher Education and Social Class: Issues of Exclusion and Inclusion* (RoutledgeFalmer, 2003) explores issues around social class and widening participation and considers why it is that working-class groups are under-represented.

The *Oxford Review of Education* 30/1(2004) is a special themed edition on all aspects of post-compulsory education. R. Taylor, 'Lifelong learning and the labour governments 1997–2004', *Oxford Review of Education* 31/1 (2005): 101–18, explores New Labour's ideological perspective on lifelong learning and their lifelong learning policies.

An article that questions the assumptions underpinning the government's skills strategy and its reliance on targets and qualifications and whether these policy tools have been successful in meeting the government's objectives, is A. Wolf, A. Jenkins and A. Vignoles, 'Certifying the workforce: economic imperative or failed social policy?' *Journal of Education Policy* 21/5 (2006): 535–65. The Leitch Review of Skills, *Prosperity For All in the Global Economy – World Class Skills* (HMSO, 2006) is a useful review of the UK's long-term skill needs and how to achieve them.

The rise of lifelong learning across Europe, and the variety of policy trends, is examined by A. Green, 'The many faces of lifelong learning: recent educational policy trends', *Europe Journal of Education Policy* 17/6 (2002): 611–26.

Useful websites include *Education Guardian*, which has articles on current issues in post-compulsory education, at <http://education.guardian.co.uk>, and the Department of Education and Skills website, which includes sections on all aspects of post-compulsory education policies, plus government reports, statistics and research reports, at <http://www.dfes.gov.uk/>.

Chapter 43

Housing

Alan Murie

Overview

- Housing policy has played an important part in the modern welfare state but has involved a variety of approaches and there has never been comprehensive or monopoly provision of state housing.
- The growth of public housing between 1919 and 1979 meant that it formed a significant and highly desirable element in housing provision.
- As it grew, public housing changed and became more of a service of last resort and privatization involved further change and decline.
- Expanding home-ownership has been a consistent aim of government and has become the single most important element, but problems of access and affordability continue to be important.
- Policies to house homeless people and other key groups, and to regenerate and create sustainable neighbourhoods, remain important additional preoccupations of policy.

Introduction

Housing plays a central part in debates about social problems and social policy. Images of affluence, deprivation, status, segregation, stigmatization, social exclusion and community integration are all associated with where people live and so with their housing. At the same time, housing forms the focus for family life, it is the place for homemaking and it can represent a significant source and store of wealth.

Housing provision involves the market, state and voluntary sector and processes of production, exchange, ownership and control. Unlike some areas of social policy, housing has never been a state monopoly, but responses to housing problems have involved a significant role for the state. Council housing was critical for the improvement of housing conditions during the twentieth century and has had a major impact on British cities and towns.

The Historical Legacy

Accounts of the development of modern housing policy in the UK refer to the problems of nineteenth-century industrialization and reforms designed to control threats to the health of the whole population. (The detailed differences in the history of housing policy and in legislation relating to England, Scotland, Wales and Northern Ireland are not referred to in this chapter, which seeks to provide an overview that broadly applies across all territories.) Public health measures introduced in a market dominated by private landlordism had an impact upon the poor quality of the built environment but also made private investment in housing less attractive than in other sectors of the economy. The attempts to meet housing needs through philanthropic effort were insufficient and, before the outbreak of the First World War, there were proposals to introduce subsidies to enable local authorities to build affordable housing for working-class families. The effects of the First World War, including rent controls introduced to prevent exploitation of the wartime situation, and the post-war pledge to provide homes fit for heroes to live in, added to the case for a new policy.

The key development in housing policy was the introduction, in 1919, of Exchequer subsidies for council housing. Over the next sixty years, local authorities had an expanding and critical role in the provision of housing. Over the same period, the private rented sector declined and private provision switched towards individual home-ownership – more rapidly for some regions and more affluent households.

The Second World War halted housing construction. This, together with damage to property resulting from air raids, left a serious housing problem. Nonetheless, housing was not reorganized to the same extent as the rest of the welfare state in the immediate post-war period. There was no National Housing Service and local authorities remained the key providers of state housing in a system still dominated by private ownership. Housing, as a result, has often been regarded as a neglected service and the wobbly pillar of the welfare state. However, a stronger planning system and new towns programme, along with the retention of rent control affecting the private rented sector, meant that housing was more thoroughly managed by the state after 1945. Local authorities and new towns also received more generous subsidies and built housing on an unprecedented scale.

Between 1919 and 1979, council housing and owner occupation grew alongside one another. Governments consistently encouraged home-ownership and largely neglected private renting. The modernization of housing tenure throughout this period led to a significant improvement in house conditions. New building, slum clearance and improvement of older dwellings, combined with changes in household composition and affluence, reduced overcrowding, sharing and dwelling unfitness. The long-term decline of private renting was speeded by the reintroduction of rent control in 1939 and by subsequent slum clearance. Furthermore, as more affluent groups (influenced by a favourable financial environment) moved into home-ownership, and as a high-quality, subsidized council rented sector developed, the rent levels that people were able and prepared to pay for housing not subject to rent control were insufficient to make investment in private rented housing attractive.

From the 1970s onwards, policy was influenced by the view that the housing problem was largely solved. The agenda was less about housing supply and quality and more focused on aspirations for ownership. This focus fitted the competition between the political parties to be seen as the champion of home-ownership. Following the election of a new Conservative government in 1979, the introduction of the 'Right to Buy' policy resulted in more than 2 million dwellings being sold to sitting tenants out of a total of 6.5 million. Government's view of council housing had shifted. Significant new building by local authorities was no longer favoured. Deregulation of private renting, as well as of building societies and changes in housing finance, completed the shift from a managed to a market-based housing system. After 1988, housing associations became the preferred vehicles for the more limited volume of new social rented housing being built. The council housing stock declined in size as a result of the 'Right to Buy' and transfer of stock to housing associations. Some local authorities transferred the whole of their housing stock to housing associations and were left with a strategic or enabling role in housing, replacing their role as direct provider.

Both the sale of council housing and the shift to housing associations, whose borrowing was not counted as public expenditure, fitted concerns to reduce taxation and public expenditure. Public expenditure on the formal housing programme was cut and privatization of council housing generated cash receipts and was the single most significant part of the government's privatization programme after 1979.

By the end of the 1990s, housing policy had reached a low point. There was no longer a major programme of direct intervention to build high-quality housing for general household needs or for lower-income households, and the governance of housing was increasingly fragmented. The emphasis in policy had shifted towards dismantling the legacy of state intervention, relying on the private market to make provision and providing means-tested social security support to enable people to meet housing costs.

Tenure Changes

A nation of private tenants has become a nation of home-owners, with a transitional period in between with a more mixed tenure structure (table 43.1). These national figures obscure enormous local differences, with some localities dominated by public provision and others by home-ownership.

As tenures have grown or declined, so their characteristics have changed. The private rented sector became dilapidated, housing a residual population of elderly long-term tenants and a more mixed, transient population. The home-ownership sector and the council housing sector, which both developed in the 1920s catering for young families, have changed and diverged. The home-ownership sector continues to house the most affluent sections of the population, but now also houses very poor households, including the elderly and

Table 43.1   Housing tenure in the UK, 1914–2001 (percentages of all dwellings)

	Public rented	Owner-occupied	Private rented[a]
1914	<1	10	90
1945	12	26	62
1951	18	29	53
1961	27	43	31
1971	31	50	19
1981	30	56	13
1991	21	66	13
2001	15	69	12

[a] Including housing associations. Following the introduction of a new financial regime in 1988, housing associations have been regarded as part of the private sector. In 2001 they provided 6.5 per cent of the dwelling stock.
Sources: Mullins and Murie 2006; *Housing and Construction Statistics*.

households experiencing unemployment or other crises. It is also marked by enormous differences in value and desirability – from luxurious rural and suburban mansions to inner-city and ill-maintained housing.

The council and housing association sectors are referred to together as a social rented sector, reflecting a clearer role in housing those with various social, and not just housing, needs. This sector now caters more exclusively for low-income groups than in the past. However, tenants are no longer predominantly families with children, but include elderly persons, young lone parent households and those with long-term illnesses and disabilities. This pattern of change has been referred to as 'residualization' – the tendency for the poorest sections of the population to become more concentrated in social rented housing and especially in the least attractive parts of it. Tenure and social change, the exercise of choice, rationing of access and allocation of council housing have tended to leave those with least bargaining power in the least desirable housing.

The home-ownership sector in the post-war years has generally been associated with accumulation. Except for a period after 1990, when house prices fell in real terms and a considerable number of households were left with negative equity (the value of their property had fallen and was not sufficient to cover the outstanding mortgage), owner-occupiers have generally experienced rising property prices and an increase in wealth – in contrast to tenants with no equity stake in their property.

Homelessness

A key element of the debate about housing policy has always related to those who are not in housing or are in inadequate housing. In Britain, the term 'homelessness' is usually associated with a legislative category which does not include all of those who are inadequately housed and, in that sense, are without an adequate home. At the same time, it includes more than simply those who are without a roof over their heads. Research on homelessness in Britain has always identified the key role of the housing market in determining homelessness and the risks faced by ordinary families of becoming homeless because of the operation of that market.

The statistics which relate to the legislative category 'homeless' showed a considerable fluctuation after the late 1970s. It is generally accepted that this is associated with changes in the housing market and shortages of both social rented housing and affordable private rented housing. At the same time, the pattern has been exacerbated by demographic trends, changes in the benefit system, changes in institutional care and changes in employment. Homeless households are less likely to be 'ordinary' families than was the case in the past and instead include a wider mix of age groups and household types as well as households with multiple problems. More recent action to address the situation has reduced the level of official homelessness and targeted rough sleeping with some success.

Housing in the Welfare State

Tenure restructuring has been associated with changes in housing finance, taxation and subsidy. Rent control represented a form of subsidy to private tenants, protecting them from market prices. Subsidized council housing involved a redistributive transfer in favour of the council tenant. The various fiscal and other supports for home-ownership involved transfers to home-owners. Mortgage interest tax relief involved very large sums of money, especially in periods of high house prices and high interest rates. In general, these benefited better-off households paying higher rates of tax and with larger mortgages. Only in the

1990s did changes in the system of tax relief and its eventual withdrawal moderate this regressive pattern, although regressive tax relief for capital gains remained.

The social division of welfare in relation to housing has not benefited only affluent groups. The pattern of benefit in kind, which council tenants received in the form of subsidized high-quality housing, formed a significant part of the redistributive structure of the welfare state. Through the 1980s, the financing of council housing changed, rents increased and the system of finance shifted from the general Exchequer subsidy system, which originated in 1919 and applied to the tenure as a whole, towards individual means-tested housing benefit. Assistance with housing costs in the council housing, housing association and private rented sectors is now provided through the social security system. Council tenants as a group no longer receive subsidy. Indeed, their rents are such as to enable a cross-subsidy towards those who are on housing benefit. The poorest tenants are subsidized by fellow tenants.

After 1979, many of the more affluent tenants bought their council dwellings under the 'Right to Buy' policy. The cohort of tenants who benefited initially from subsidized rents and moved to the best council and new town homes were double beneficiaries when they were able to buy with very substantial discounts on market value prices and, in turn, to benefit from asset appreciation. Some owner-occupiers who are on income support also qualify for social security assistance. Housing finance remains partitioned, with different arrangements for different tenures, and a unified system of housing finance that is tenure-neutral has not been developed.

Regeneration and Management

Council housing, when it was built, represented high-standard, desirable housing which was in high demand. This was particularly true as most of it was traditionally built, consisting of houses with gardens. In some cases, estates had a poor reputation and in some phases, especially associated with slum clearance, housing quality was not as high and the reputation of areas was damaged from the outset. The short-lived period in which multi-storey flats were favoured as a result of government subsidy structures and the enthusiasm of professionals in local government also left an undesirable legacy in many areas. These parts of the council housing stock have increasingly become places of last resort. Difficult to let, difficult to manage and difficult to live in, these estates have been subject to important policy initiatives: local management, involving tenants in the management of areas, increased investment in dwellings, services and infrastructure. These interventions have generally had at least a short-lived positive effect, but do not solve problems of deprivation, segregation and stigmatization.

As social inequality increased in the UK, so the pressures on neighbourhoods with less attractive or less high-demand housing became greater. These are areas of mixed tenure and private sector housing as well as areas of social rented housing. Local economic and demographic changes have meant that there has been a change in the demand for the least attractive housing, whatever its tenure. Regeneration and management initiatives in these areas have been overwhelmed by changes in the economy and housing finance. The poverty trap and rising unemployment have made it more difficult for lower-income households to change their circumstances.

The response to this situation shifted from management initiatives towards more holistic local regeneration policies with a strong emphasis on employment, education and training. Housing and neighbourhood problems have become inextricably bound up with problems in the economy: the problems of lower-income households are not related just to housing, but are also related to limited access to jobs and other services; and housing activity is a significant part of economic activity and has a major role in regeneration.

The Contemporary Housing Situation

In the mid-1970s, it was widely argued that housing problems had been generally solved and what remained were specific, local problems which needed targeted interventions; but, generally, housing could be left to the market. By the mid-1990s it was difficult to retain this view, as homelessness and deprived council estates figured prominently in general images of social malaise. Social segregation and differentiation in cities was more striking than in the past and there were increasing problems of racial segregation, urban crime and patterns of inequality that were dysfunctional socially and economically. New problems in the owner-occupied sector were associated with older and low-income households and those affected by family or employment crises or by over-extended borrowing and high interest rates.

Where the UK had been a nation of tenants in 1900, it had become a nation of home-owners by 2000. But the reliance on the private market brought its own problems – shortages of supply and affordability. Although higher employment and incomes and low and stable interest rates made home-ownership less risky, private building did not expand to fill the gap left when local authority and new town housebuilding activity was almost eliminated. At the same time, deregulation of the private rented sector and demand for buy-to-let investment coming from households which already owned property contributed to rising prices. The deregulation of private renting and changes in the housing association sector have resulted in higher rents and

fewer rights for tenants. Rooflessness and rough sleeping in British cities remained more evident than before the 1980s. Nevertheless, rising employment through the 1990s and the portability of housing benefit meant that some groups had more choice – especially within the rented sector. Choices between tenures exist for some households, but for others there is no choice between dwellings, let alone tenures. While the housing situation has improved for the majority of households, problems within the sector have changed. Problems associated with changing demand and the quality of housing are evident in all tenures and are concentrated in some regions and submarkets.

The challenge for government was to reconstruct housing policy in a different social, economic and political context. Global issues and the competitiveness of economies prohibited the level of public sector borrowing or taxation that would be required to go back to large-scale public investment. The option favoured by successive governments was to transfer the ownership of public housing to new organizations (local housing companies with some local authority involvement) outside the public sector and public expenditure definitions. A ten-year programme of stock transfer was a cornerstone of the new Labour government's approach in England after 1997 and along with the continued operation of the 'Right to Buy' symbolized the continuity of policy between Labour and Conservative governments. However, there was a programme to raise the standard of all social rented housing (to a new 'Decent Homes standard') by 2010, and new strategies to address social exclusion and to achieve neighbourhood renewal.

The most systematic attempt to reorientate policy came later – in England the Communities Plan in 2003 (*Sustainable Communities: Building for the Future*, ODPM) and the Barker Review in 2004 (*Review of Housing Supply, Delivering Sta-*

bility: *Securing our Future Housing Needs'* *Final Report – Recommendations*, HMSO). The Communities Plan sought to reverse the legacy of decades of neglect and under-investment and make a step change to tackle the challenges of a rapidly changing population, the needs of the economy, serious housing shortages and the impact of housing abandonment. It involved a regionalization of housing policy and emphasized a sustainable approach to housing and planning – long-term approaches to stabilize communities and remove the need for periodic injections of funding to the same areas for the same problems. It acknowledged the need to develop different policies in places with different markets. In the Midlands and the North this included Housing Market Renewal Areas forming the flagship investment policy. In the south and east of England, continuing housing shortages, difficulties in labour force recruitment and retention and heightened affordability problems meant a more generous public expenditure package targeted upon new growth areas and key workers.

The Barker Review's remit was to consider the weak responsiveness of the 'new build' housing market in the face of rising house prices and to address the Treasury's concern that this had undesirable economic consequences. Rising house prices driving up the 'affordability threshold' generated high demands for public subsidy towards new affordable homes and resulted in the inability of high-price areas to attract workers on ordinary salaries. In addition, the leakage of equity into consumer spending created difficulties in controlling the money supply and had implications for the setting of interest rates and for inflation. The government accepted the review's recommendations to change the planning system and for additional funds to deliver additional social housing.

Emerging Issues

Housing after 2003 became more prominent in public policy than it had been for decades. Its role was not just related to social policy: the provision of shelter for citizens impacts on other parts of the welfare state relating to incomes, employment, health, social order and the family. It was also about economic policy: the role of cities in the global economy and the importance of housing, neighbourhoods and housing costs for the competitiveness of cities and the UK economy. The importance of home-ownership was evident also in its significance for the distribution of wealth; and asset-ownership was increasingly important for social policy, providing a resource in older age or funding for residential care and other services that the state no longer supported effectively. The private housing market remained the key to meeting the need for housing. But housing was too important for the government to stand and watch without intervening and so it has remained active, seeking to meet needs, moderate house price inflation and increase social rented housing provision in order to bring stability to the housing market. From the wobbly pillar of the post-war welfare state, housing seems likely to be the bedrock of the new asset-based, competitive welfare state.

Guide to Further Sources

Housing policy issues are discussed in the journals *Inside Housing* and *Roof*, which provide facts and figures and short critical articles. The academic journals in the field include *Housing Studies, Urban Studies, Journal of Housing and the Built Environment* and *European Journal of Housing Policy*.

D. Mullins and A. Murie, *Housing Policy in Britain* (Macmillan, 2006) is an introduction to housing policy in the UK, referring to historical developments, principal tenures and key housing policy issues. Another book that deals with the relationship between government and housing is P. Malpass, *Housing and the Welfare State: The Development of Housing Policy in Britain* (Palgrave Macmillan, 2005). An introduction to the history of housing and the social context for changes can be found in J. Burnett, *A Social History of Housing 1815–1985*, 2nd edn (David and Charles, 1985).

K. Gibb, M. Munro and M. Satsangi, *Housing Finance in the UK: An Introduction*, 2nd edn (Macmillan, 1999) provides a description of key aspects of housing finance, and C. Jones and A. Murie, *The Right to Buy* (Blackwell, 2006) outlines the origins, details and consequences of the sale of council housing in the UK.

A general outline of housing issues can be found in G. Bramley, M. Munro and H. Pawson, *Key Issues in Housing* (Palgrave Macmillan, 2004).

Up-to-date statistics are on the websites of government departments: the Department for Communities and Local Government, the Northern Ireland Office, the Scottish Executive and the Welsh Assembly.

Chapter 44

Social Care

Jon Glasby

Overview

- The origins of current social care practice in nineteenth-century philanthropy and in different understandings of the causes of and the best way to respond to poverty.
- The scope and scale of current social care.
- The creation of generic Social Services Departments (SSDs), the shift to a pur-chaser–provider split, and the break-up of traditional SSDs into new children's services and adults' services.
- The relationship between social care and other services such as healthcare and education.
- Emerging issues and priorities such as investing in longer-term prevention and the advent of direct payments and individual budgets.

Background and Introduction

In 1942, William Beveridge's report, *Social Insurance and Allied Services*, set out a blueprint for post-war welfare services. One of the most quoted sections of the report is Beveridge's description of 'five giants' or social problems which future ser-vices should seek to tackle: Want, Disease, Ignorance, Idleness and Squalor. While these are couched in very 1940s language, they nevertheless map across to current social issues and even to some current gov-ernment departments and functions (see table 44.1). Thus, as an example, a 1940s 'giant' such as 'want' becomes poverty or social exclusion, and has traditionally fallen under the remit of the social security system. Although other contributions to this book cover these various different services (see chapters 38 to 43), a key gap in table 44.1 is social care and social work. Is social care responding to a sixth giant that Beveridge failed to identify? Is it the glue that holds the other five together? Or is it a crisis service that works with people who fall through the gaps in other services? As dis-cussed below, it is arguably this failure to know exactly where social care and social work fit into the current system that is con-tributing to something of a crisis of confi-dence and identity in the profession.

Current Social Care

Crucial to an understanding of social care is the distinction between several key terms

Table 44.1 UK welfare services

Beveridge's giants/social problems	Government response/service
Want	Social security
Disease	NHS
Ignorance	Education and lifelong learning
Squalor	Housing and regeneration
Idleness	Employment and leisure

which are often used interchangeably. 'Social care' is an overall description for a range of services and workers who seek to work with both adults and children who are facing difficult changes in their lives. While this is a very broad description, the focus has tended to be on providing practical assistance and support for a range of specific service user groups, including children at risk of abuse, frail older people, people with mental health problems, people with learning difficulties and disabled people. By the early twenty-first century there were some 1.6 million people using social care services, with some 1.4 million people working in the social care workforce. While this is more than the entire NHS workforce, social care staff are employed by some 30,000 public, private and voluntary agencies. Social services also spend over £14 billion per year, with 30 per cent of people using social care services funding their own care.

In contrast, 'social worker' is the name for trained professionals (the social care equivalent of doctors, nurses or teachers), who are now degree-trained, registered with the national General Social Care Council and governed by various codes of professional conduct. Following the community reforms of 1990 (see below for further discussion), social workers are typically responsible for assessing the needs of individuals, and arranging services to meet those needs from a range of social care providers from across the public, private and voluntary sectors. Many have been tra-

ditionally employed in local authority 'Social Services Departments', although these have since been split into new children's and adults' services (see below for further discussion). Of the 1.4 million social care workforce, around 60,000 people are qualified social workers.

The History and Evolution of Social Care

While the history of social care is long and convoluted, a particular contribution has been made by a series of nineteenth-century voluntary organizations and philanthropists. Prior to this, much social support had been provided (as is still the case today) by families and local communities. In Tudor times, much of the support available was religious in nature and delivered via the monasteries. Following the dissolution of the monasteries and stimulated by rapid urbanization and industrialization, a number of more formal services began to develop via the now notorious Poor Law. While this included outdoor relief (payments to people in financial need), the main source of 'support' was typically the workhouse, with conditions deliberately made as harsh as possible so as to ensure that only the most needy applied for state help (an approach known as 'the workhouse test' and the principle of 'less eligibility'). Over time, workhouses became increasingly focused on different groups of people, with different approaches emerging for the able-bodied poor (often seen as lazy and capable of supporting themselves) and for frail older people, people with mental health problems and people with learning difficulties (who were increasingly seen as not to blame for their plight and hence deserving of assistance).

During the latter part of the nineteenth century, two prominent voluntary organizations were important in developing new approaches to the alleviation of poverty and in pioneering many of the approaches that later became associated with modern social work:

1 Founded in response to a proliferation of almsgiving following the depression of the late 1860s, the Charity Organization Society (COS) sought to adopt principles of 'scientific charity' – assessing those in need and providing charitable support only to those deemed deserving (with those deemed undeserving left to rely on the Poor Law and the workhouse). In this way, COS hoped to coordinate the provision of financial support and to give individuals an incentive to be self-sufficient (guarding against the danger that generous support would only encourage the feckless and thriftless). In many ways, similar notions underpin current debates about whether or not to give to people begging on the street – does this support those in need or does it encourage people to be dependent on this form of assistance?
2 Founded in 1884 with the creation of Toynbee Hall in Whitechapel, the Settlement Movement had considerable overlaps with COS (and the same individuals were often involved in both movements), but increasingly diverged over time. Settlement houses were essentially colonies of educated people living in poor areas of large cities, with the dual purpose of using the education and privilege of 'settlers' to help the poor, but also of getting to know the poor as

friends and as neighbours and hence understanding more about the nature of poverty. Over time, it became increasingly apparent to many settlers that poverty was not the result of individual failings, but the product of wider social forces, and a number of settlers (for example, Clement Attlee and William Beveridge) made significant contributions to the advent of a welfare state.

In many ways, these different perspectives continue to influence current practice, with social work approaches such as care management (see below for further discussion) continuing to focus on the assessment of individual need to ascertain entitlement to support, and community development and neighbourhood renewal focusing much more on community empowerment and on the individual in a broader social context. Both movements were also very influential in the development of early social work, with both COS and the Settlement Movement working with leading universities to help found early social work courses and provide placements and practical experience for students.

Following the Second World War, an increasing amount of social work activity came to be subsumed within two local government departments: specialist children's departments and health and welfare departments. These were later combined into generic social services departments (SSDs) following the landmark Seebohm report of 1968. By bringing together a range of adult and children's social care services, Seebohm argued, there was scope to create a more comprehensive and coordinated approach, to attract greater resources and to plan ahead to identify and meet the needs of a local area more effectively. SSDs were soon boosted by a growing national infrastructure, including a more unified and higher-profile system of social work education (advocated in various reports by Eileen Younghusband) and the creation of a new

National Institute of Social Work Training (which was later subsumed into a new Social Care Institute for Excellence).

In many ways, this system was to remain intact until the late 1980s, when a review of community care services by Sir Roy Griffiths (managing director of Sainsbury's supermarket) lead to the passage of the 1990 NHS and Community Care Act. Henceforth, social workers were to be 'care managers', responsible for assessing individual need and arranging care packages from a combination of public, private and voluntary services in order to meet this need. Consistent with the ideological commitments of the then Conservative government, these changes changed social workers into 'purchasers' rather than providers, and much of the new funding that accompanied the changes was to be spent in the independent (and often private) sector.

Since 1997, much of this ethos has remained, but with a growing emphasis on modernization (often portrayed as a 'third way' between the market-based ideology of the new right and the public sector values of Labour). Unfortunately, such a concept tends to be better at defining what a 'third way' is not (i.e. not the market and not the state), and the result has arguably been a wide range of different policies and approaches which can often seem rather eclectic in nature. However, central to much recent policy has been an emphasis on:

- Greater *choice and control* (with people who use services having more say over what they receive and how money is spent on their behalf). Perhaps the clearest example of this is the increasing role played by direct payments, whereby social care service users can receive the cash equivalent of directly provided services with which to purchase their own care and/or hire their own staff (shifting from being passive recipients of services to being their own care managers).

- Greater *partnership working* (with health and social care in particular becoming increasingly interrelated over time). In 2000, this led to the announcement of a new form of organization – the Care Trust – which was seen as a vehicle with which to integrate health and social care fully. While this model has not proved popular in practice, more recent policy has tended to allow more local discretion as to the best way forward (whilst being clear that doing nothing is not an option).

- A stronger emphasis on *citizenship* and *social inclusion* (with a growing tendency – slow at first – to look beyond traditional health and social care to more universal services, and various attempts to tackle discrimination and promote human rights). An example here is the emphasis in the learning disability White Paper, *Valuing People*, on four overarching principles (rights, inclusion, choice and independence), viewing social care and health in terms of what they can contribute to the lives of people with learning disabilities rather than as an end in themselves.

In structural terms, the key change under New Labour has been the abolition of generic social services departments, and their replacement with new integrated services for children and for adults. Thus, new Directors of Children's Services are now responsible for both education and children's social care, and often bring together wider partners via Children's Trusts. Similarly, Directors of Adult Social Services are charged with developing partnerships with NHS colleagues and broader services, and often oversee both adult social care and other services (such as housing or adult education). In recognition of such changes, many social services departments are splitting into a Directorate of Children's Services and various configurations of adult care (termed 'Social Care and Health',

'Social Inclusion and Health', 'Social Care and Housing', 'Adults and Communities', etc). Similar changes are also taking place elsewhere in the system, with policy increasingly diverging between the Department of Health and the Department for Education and Skills, and with an increasing split in the inspection system, in workforce development and in professional organizations. In many ways, this takes social care back to pre-Seebohm days (without necessarily stating why the need for generic SSDs which Seebohm placed at the heart of his vision for social care is now no longer relevant).

Emerging Issues

Always something of a crisis service for those in need, social care and social work have had a chequered history. While there has always been a need to support the most vulnerable in society, there has always been uncertainty over the best way to do this, from the different notions of poverty underpinning the voluntary action of the nineteenth century, to the different visions of Beveridge, Seebohm, Griffiths and New Labour. With increasing financial and demographic pressures, however, previous approaches are increasingly strained, and considerable uncertainty remains as to how best to refocus services towards a more preventative approach, secure added value through more effective inter-agency working and place the people who use services at the centre of decision-making. Whatever happens, history suggests that the imperative to support those most in need in society – be they adults or children – is unlikely to go away, and that some form of social support – whatever it is called and wherever it sits – seems as essential now as ever.

In the early twenty-first century, social care faces a series of challenges as it seeks to respond to a combination of social, economic and demographic changes. First and foremost, an ageing population, medical advances and changes in the availability of family support mean that there are more and more very frail older people in need of support, and a growing number of younger people with very profound and complex physical impairments and learning disabilities. With the national financial context looking increasingly tight, fundamental change may be required to meet new demands, and a range of government policies emphasize the need to move from a system of crisis support to one based much more around prevention and promoting well-being. Quite how to do this in practice (and how to invest in long-term prevention while also continuing to meet the needs of those in crisis) remains unresolved.

Allied to this, many public services are becoming more focused on the issue of outcomes, asking increasingly difficult questions about the extent to which current activity adds value or achieves anything different for service users. This is a hard concept in several public services, where the emphasis has traditionally been on issues of input, process and output (that is, focusing on what we do in social care, not on whether any of it makes any practical difference). In principle at least, an outcomes-based approach to inspection and performance management could lead to some searching questions about the contribution of social care and to a move away from notions of equality of input (treating everyone the same) to equality of outcome (working with different groups differently to achieve similar outcomes).

Also linked is the growing central role of partnership, with social care, health, education and other local services increasingly asked to work together to meet the needs of people with complex, cross-cutting needs. For all that this seems like common sense, working with multiple partners and reconciling different priorities and cultures is extremely labour-intensive, and questions remain as to the best way of developing effective inter-agency partnerships, the cost of partnership working and the extent to which new relationships are seen to add value to existing single agency approaches. At the same time, structural changes in children's and in adults' services have arguably left social care feeling very fragile and vulnerable, with a risk of being dominated by larger, better-resourced and more publicly popular services (such as the NHS or education). Of course, whether the partnership agenda is a threat or an opportunity depends on your point of view, and this can equally be seen as a chance to take what is important about social care values and principles and mainstream them.

Finally, the initial concept of direct payments has been developed by the more recent advent of individual budgets. Under this system, service users are assessed (or, indeed, self-assess), and are immediately given an indication of the amount of money to which someone with their level of need might be entitled. They can then choose how this is spent – whether in the public, private or voluntary sector, via direct services or direct payments, or via some sort of combination of any of the above options. In principle this is a bold and radical change to current practice and to the current balance of power, and could herald one of the most profound changes in social care since the advent of the Charity Organization Society. Whether this promise can be achieved remains one of the key questions as this edition of *The Student's Companion* goes to press, and a key area to watch in future.

Guide to Further Sources

The Department of Health (<www.dh.gov.uk>) is the central department responsible for health and social care policy. The General Social Care Council (<www.gscc.org.uk>) is responsible for regulating the social care workforce. The Social Care Institute for Excellence (<www.scie.org.uk>) is tasked with identifying what works in social care and disseminating good practice. SCIE's Social Care Online is a large (and free) database of relevant research and other publications.

Community Care is the standard trade publication, with up-to-date news, views, research and policy analysis.

For recent social care history, see R. Means and R. Smith, *From Poor Law to Community Care* (Macmillan, 1998) and R. Means, H. Morbey and R. Smith, *From Community Care to Market Care? The Development of Welfare Services for Older People* (Policy Press, 2002).

For specific service user groups, see M. Murphy, *Developing Collaborative Relationships in Interagency Child Protection Work* (Russell House, 2004), a practical introduction with examples from current practice; M. Lymberry, *Social Work with Older People: Context, Policy and Practice* (Sage, 2005), an introduction to key policy and practice dilemmas, with a helpful consideration of links between social care and health; R. Means, S. Richards and R. Smith, *Community Care: Policy and Practice*, 3rd edn (Palgrave Macmillan, 2003), a regularly updated textbook and one of the best introductions available to community care services for a range of adult service user groups; M. Oliver and B. Sapey, *Social Work With Disabled People*, 3rd edn (Palgrave, 2006), which is a classic textbook critiquing traditional social work practice; and A. Rogers and D. Pilgrim, *Mental Health Policy in Britain*, 2nd edn (Palgrave, 2001), one of the main introductory books on mental health services.

For direct payments, see J. Leese and J. Bornat (eds), *Developments in Direct Payments* (Policy Press, 2006).

Chapter 45

Criminal Justice

Tim Newburn

Overview

- Traditionally, criminal justice and penal policy have not been much studied by social policy scholars; this is now changing markedly.
- The main institutions of our 'modern' system of criminal justice came into being during the nineteenth and early twentieth centuries.
- A profound shift in emphasis away from welfare and rehabilitation occurred in the last three decades of the twentieth century.
- The dominant features of contemporary criminal justice have been punitiveness, politicization and populism.
- The late twentieth century saw a remarkable growth in the use of imprisonment and other forms of penal surveillance.

Introduction

In the main, scholars of social and public policy have tended to ignore the area of criminal justice. Compared with, say, health, education, welfare and culture, criminal justice has been relatively invisible. And yet, as Max Weber identified, the creation and maintenance of systems for protecting against the breakdown of internal social order is generally thought to be among the key characteristics and functions that define the modern nation-state. The period since the Second World War has seen a substantial increase in crime (though with a more recent down-turn) and a growing sense that this is one of the more pressing political and policy issues of the times.

The last two centuries or so have seen the progressive rationalization and bureaucratization of criminal justice and penal processes. From localized, community-based systems of policing and punishment, there have developed huge state-managed apparatuses and vast bodies of laws, rules and regulations, aimed at controlling crime.

The Criminal Justice System

The first thing to note is that there is no single system of criminal justice in the United Kingdom. There are three distinctive systems: in England and Wales, in Scotland, and in Northern Ireland. My focus here is primarily upon England and

Wales. The criminal justice system is made up of the following major agencies and organizations:

- *The Police*: forty-three constabularies in England and Wales (a further eight regional forces in Scotland, together with a single Police Service of Northern Ireland).
- *Crown Prosecution Service* (CPS): established in 1985 and currently administered in forty-two areas, contiguously with police force areas.
- Criminal Defence Service: providing legal support for those accused of crimes in criminal courts.
- *Magistrates' Courts and the Crown Court*: the vast majority of cases (generally the less serious) are heard in magistrates' courts, whereas the more serious are heard in the Crown Court in front of judge and jury.
- *Probation Service*: now a national service, though prior to 2000 it was divided up into local areas (police, CPS, etc). It is now in the process of being incorporated into the National Offender Management Service (NOMS).
- *Prisons*: there are currently just fewer than 150 prisons run by the Prison Service which is an executive agency linked to the Ministry of Justice (eventually to be wrapped up into NOMS with the Probation Service).
- *Youth Justice Board*: a non-departmental public body linked to the Ministry of Justice, with responsibility for oversight of youth offending teams and for commissioning places in prison for young offenders.
- *Youth Offending Teams*: formerly juvenile justice teams, these are multi-agency bodies responsible for the supervision of young offenders serving community sentences.
- *Crime and Disorder Reduction Partnerships*: established by the Crime and Disorder Act 1998, these are multi-agency partnerships involving representation from police, local authorities, probation, health, etc., and are tasked with monitoring local crime problems, and publishing and overseeing plans for local crime reduction.

Patterns of Crime

Broadly speaking there are two main methods used for measuring and tracking trends in crime. One is taken from data collected routinely by law-enforcement agencies concerning crimes reported by the public or otherwise coming to the attention of the authorities. In Britain, such data are collected by the police and are generally referred to as 'recorded crime statistics'. The second main method of crime measurement uses survey methods to elicit information from a representative sample of the population about their experiences of crime – primarily as victims wherever this is the case – usually over the previous twelve months. In England and Wales, this is the British Crime Survey (BCS), first undertaken in 1981 and which has run intermittently since then but is now an annual survey.

Both sources of data have their shortcomings. Recorded crime statistics can tell us little about those 'crimes' that are never reported to the police – estimated to be at least one half of all offences. By contrast, the BCS doesn't cover all crimes (those against under-16-year olds for example, corporate and organized crime and 'victimless' crimes such as drugs possession). It is generally advisable to consult and compare both sources when attempting to understand and track levels and trends in crime.

It is widely believed that we live in times of unprecedented levels of crime. Whether such beliefs are accurate rather depends on the time frame being referred to. It is certainly the case compared with, say, the 1940s, 1950s or 1960s that current levels

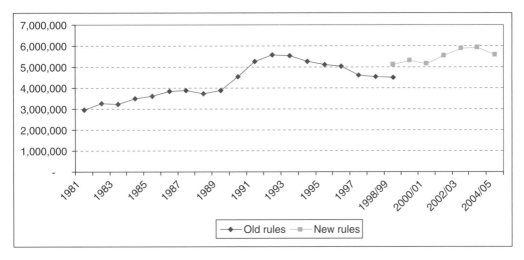

Figure 45.1   Overall recorded crime rate, England and Wales, 1981–2005
Source: Walker et al. 2006.

of crime are very high. However, if we take a longer historical perspective, then there is rather reliable evidence to suggest that previous eras were characterized by very high levels of crime and disorder, even by contemporary standards. Indeed, looked at one way, there was a reasonably substantial increase in crime during the inter-war years – crime increased by more than one-fifth between 1934 and 1938, for example. With the advent of war in 1939, there were concerns that a crime wave would result and, indeed, there was a substantial rise in indictable offences, an even more significant trend given that many of those most likely to be involved in criminal activity, young males, were abroad fighting the war. Most crime at this time was property-related and rises in violent crime were much shallower than those for theft and burglary.

It was in the mid-1950s that crime began to increase markedly, with recorded crime rising by almost 75 per cent between 1955 and 1960. Why might this be so? Well, one important point to note first is that this period saw a very substantial increase in the availability of mass-market consumer goods, many of which were portable. Second, changes in the labour market saw a substantial increase in the proportion of women going out to work, with the consequence that houses were left empty for considerably longer periods than had previously been the case. Third, it is also likely that the police became more assiduous in their recording of crime during this period. As can be seen from figure 45.1, crime continued to rise fairly markedly and consistently from that period on, all the way through to the mid-1990s, from when it began to fall.

Figure 45.1 shows levels of recorded crime from 1981 to 2005. Police-recorded crime data show crime rising relatively steadily during the 1980s and then increasing markedly from towards the end of the decade until 1992. From that point, recorded crime rates declined until 1998/9 when new 'counting rules' (ways in which the police record crime) were introduced. As the gap between the two sets of 1998/9 figures illustrates, the new counting rules produced an immediate increase in the number of offences recorded and, thereafter, appear to show crime increasing again

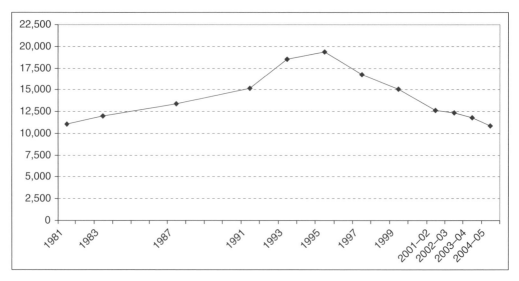

Figure 45.2   All crime (British Crime Survey) 1981–2004/05
Source: Walker et al. 2006.

until 2002/03, whereupon there is a further slight decline.

Data drawn from the various British Crime Surveys in many ways match the general trend visible from police-recorded statistics in the 1980s and early 1990s, though they depart quite significantly in the period since the late 1990s. BCS data, like police-recorded crime, show crime rising into the 1990s – in this case to 1995 – and then falling. By contrast with police-recorded crime, the downturn measured by the BCS continues for the whole of the decade since 1995. Indeed, according to the BCS, crime fell overall by 44 per cent during that decade and by 35 per cent since 1997. By 2005, crime was down slightly below the level recorded in the first BCS in 1981 (see figure 45.2).

A Brief History of Criminal Justice

Though the death penalty was the focus of the penal system in medieval times, and levels of capital punishment were high, executions underwent something of a brief boom in the second half of the seventeenth century. Much of the eighteenth century was characterized by a search for viable secondary punishments. Transportation (whereby prisoners were taken by boat to serve their sentences in penal colonies, mainly in America and Australia) was the other major form of judicial punishment in Britain and by the 1760s transportation to the colonies accounted for at least 70 per cent of all sentences at the Central Criminal Court in London. From this point on, however, transportation declined and the use of imprisonment began to grow.

The system of punishment in Victorian Britain differed quite significantly from that of the late eighteenth century. The use of the death penalty declined markedly throughout the 1800s, public ceremonies of execution ceased in 1868 and corporal punishment of adults was rare by the second half of the century. Put simply, imprisonment moved from being merely a repository for those awaiting trial, sentence or death, as had been the case in the sixteenth and seventeenth centuries, to a method of punishment that was inflicted on an increasingly wide range of offenders during the course of the eighteenth and nineteenth centuries. Although in Victorian Britain the formal priority of the prison system remained 'the repression of crime' through deterrence, nevertheless a growing emphasis on the reform and rehabilitation of offenders was growing.

In the pre-industrial era, 'policing' was a community-based, less formal set of activities. In the UK the establishment of formal policing was preceded by community-based systems such as the 'hue and cry' in which local citizens took responsibility for raising the alarm and for chasing down the offender. Nineteenth-century England was characterized by increasing concerns about crime. By the mid- to late nineteenth century, crime and disorder was perceived to pose a threat to social stability and it was around this time (in 1829 in London) that what we now understand as 'the police' emerged.

The nineteenth and early twentieth centuries saw the creation of all the fundamental institutions of the modern criminal justice system: the prison, the police, the courts and related systems of criminal prosecution, probation and, in due course, an increasingly complex array of non-custodial penalties (fines, probation, community service, etc.). Towards the end of the nineteenth century, separate systems for dealing with juvenile offenders also emerged. The first half of the twentieth century saw the consolidation and reform of the modern criminal justice system. This period drew to an end around the middle of the century and was the era in which the 'solidarity project' – in which the state was the guarantor of full citizenship and security for all – was increasingly eclipsed by market forces. Recent decades have seen the emergence of a rapidly expanding mixed economy in many areas of criminal justice and, crucially, what also to many appears to be a decisive shift in what are believed to be the purposes and ambitions of our criminal justice and penal policies.

The Aims of Punishment

In pre-industrial/colonial times, much punishment was public in character and, as such, was designed to shame, to bring forth expressions of guilt, remorse and repentance. Loss of freedom – through imprisonment – was far from a common response to criminal infractions and was not assumed, as yet, to be an effective method for stimulating reform. By the middle of the nineteenth century this had all changed and in the UK a major public debate about the prison system was under way. The system, it was suggested, was failing in its objective of deterring criminals, while simultaneously being too harsh. What emerged was a new system of punishment in which, although *deterrence* remained an important goal of criminal justice policy, reform and *rehabilitation* lay at its heart. The range of sanctions available to criminal courts expanded markedly, probation and other forms of training became established, and a range of new institutions became established or consolidated, many of which were conceived as direct alternatives to imprisonment.

The penal-welfare strategies that developed in the late nineteenth century reached their high point a little after the mid-twentieth century. However, there has been a radical restructuring and reorientation since that period. At the heart of this shift has been a decline of faith in the welfare and rehabilitative functions of criminal justice and the gradual rise to dominance of a set of discourses and practices that are more punitive, more politicized and more populist. By the late 1970s there was a clear loss of faith in the power of the state to reform and, through reform, to reduce crime.

Criminal justice policy in this period was caught up in the battle between two competing versions of the role of the state. The first emphasized welfare and civil rights, and the reduction of social inequalities. The other railed against 'big government' and sought to limit state intervention in citizens' lives in most areas – with the exception of criminal justice. In this second model the state has a much diminished role in managing and protecting social welfare, something increasingly left to the market, but has an increasingly enhanced role in the management of social order. Indeed, for commentators such as Charles Murray, rising crime and disorder were precisely a product of welfare dependency.

As a consequence, effective criminal justice and penal policy 'came to be viewed as a matter of imposing more controls, increasing disincentives, and, if necessary, segregating the dangerous sector of the population' (Garland 2001:102). Since the mid-1980s, such punitiveness has become the standard political position on crime and order for politicians of all hues. Thus, the other great change in this field concerns the politicization of criminal justice.

Criminal Justice and Penal Politics

Crime is now a staple of political discourse and of electoral politics. Although this may not feel surprising it is, in fact, a relatively new political phenomenon. Until the early 1970s in the UK, for example, criminal justice policy barely featured in major elections and certainly was far from the 'wedge issue' it has often been since.

In the criminal justice arena, politicians' concern with how they are likely to be perceived has had a profound effect on policy-making in recent times. Crucially, as numerous commentators have noted, by the 1990s the old divisions between 'conservative' and 'liberal' political positions on crime had disappeared, and had been replaced by what appeared to be a straightforward 'tough on crime' message. The past two decades have seen a progressively intensifying battle by the major political parties to be seen as the party of law and order. A 'tough on crime' stance has come to be associated with electoral success and its opposite, being 'soft on crime', with electoral failure.

The lengthy political dominance of conservatism during the 1980s in the UK led to vociferous debates within the British Labour Party over the possible sources of electoral success in what were clearly changed times. The party sought to dump its various 'hostages to fortune' (Downes and Morgan 2007) not least of which was its previously more liberal policies on crime control. New Labour embraced so-called 'Third Way' politics. In the criminal justice arena, this meant attempting to modify the old-fashioned liberal penal-welfarism that the party had largely clung to throughout the 1980s and into the 1990s by adding into the mix what was by now considered the *sine qua non* of successful electoral politics: a healthy dose of punitive rhetoric and the promise of similarly punitive policies. This mixture has never been more successfully captured than in Tony Blair's 1993 sound-bite, 'tough on crime and tough on the causes of crime'.

Contemporary Penal Policy

The clearest change in penal policy can be seen in relation to the use of imprisonment. Figure 45.3 shows the prison population in England and Wales for the past century or so. Standing at approximately 20,000 at the turn of the twentieth century, the prison population declined from the First World War through to the Second World War and then began to rise. It reached its turn-of-the-century levels again by the late 1950s and by the early 1980s reached an historic high in the low 40,000s. The population was reaching 50,000 by the end of the decade, at which point various strategies

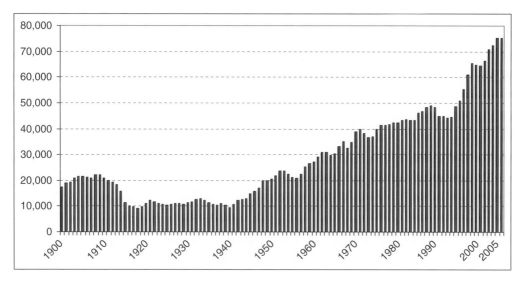

Figure 45.3 Prison population, England and Wales, 1900–2005
Source: Newburn 2007.

were employed, successfully, to begin to reduce the numbers incarcerated. At roughly the point that crime reached its peak in England and Wales, the prison population once again began to rise, and to do so markedly more quickly than at any point since the Second World War.

The reasons for the expanding prison population are complex. There are three main possibilities: an increase in the numbers being caught and sentenced, an increase in the seriousness of the crimes being prosecuted and an increase in sentence severity. There is little or no evidence that the changes reflect an increase in the numbers of offenders being caught or convicted – these have remained relatively stable. Indeed, there does not appear to have been any substantial increase in the seriousness overall of the offences before the courts.

Rather, the greatest change seems to have been in the severity of the sentences being passed by the courts. The proportion of offenders found guilty of an indictable offence (one that can only be tried in a Crown Court) receiving a custodial sen-

tence rose from 15 per cent in 1991 to 25 per cent in 2001 (Newburn 2007). Similarly, whereas a first-time domestic burglar had a 27 per cent chance of receiving a prison sentence in 1995, this had risen to 48 per cent by 2000. In addition, average sentence lengths for such offenders had risen from 16 to 18 months and, indeed, sentence lengths generally have been on the increase. It is not just in the area of the use of imprisonment that sentence severity has increased. Community penalties also appear to have been subject to similar processes. First, an increasing proportion of offences are subject to community penalties rather than fines or discharges. Second, the absence of previous convictions has been having a diminishing effect on the likely imposition of probation, community service, etc. and, third, the length of orders such as these has been increasing steadily.

If punitiveness is one of the defining features of recent criminal justice policy, then a further trait that can be identified, and one that is shared with other areas of public policy, is *managerialism*. There has been a progressive shift away from a simple concern with policy outputs and a move towards policy outcomes. As part of this, an enormous architecture of performance management has been created, visible in probation, prisons and policing. The 1998 Crime and Disorder Act brought in a raft of changes in youth justice, three of which have been central to recent Labour administrations' emphasis on outcomes. It introduced an overriding aim for the youth justice system, created the Youth Justice Board (YJB), a non-departmental public body responsible for monitoring performance, and created multi-agency Youth Offending Teams responsible for working with young offenders subject to penalties other than imprisonment. Similarly, though in a different area, the Act also introduced multi-agency Crime and Disorder (Reduction) Partnerships. These bodies have a responsibility to conduct local crime audits and publish plans for local crime reduction, against which their performance is assessed. Finally in this regard, there have been successive changes to policing – including a relatively recent (unsuccessful) proposal to reduce the number of forces substantially – which, again, have sought to increase government control over the management and delivery of criminal justice services.

As well as a range of measures to increase the severity of the penalties attaching to criminal offending, Labour governments since 1997 have invested considerable energy on what has come to be termed 'anti-social behaviour'. Anti-social behaviour orders (ASBOs) were introduced in the 1998 Crime and Disorder Act, though initially there was considerable reluctance in most parts of the country to use them. They have remained a centrepiece of the government's criminal justice policy and the Prime Minister and successive Home Secretaries repeatedly kick-started the initiative. A dedicated unit was created within the Home Office in 2003 to promote local activism, and considerable further legislation (the 2000 Criminal Justice and Court Services

Act, the 2001 Criminal Justice and Police Act, the 2002 Police Reform Act and, in particular, the 2003 Anti-Social Behaviour Act) has added a raft of additional powers which the authorities have been encouraged to use vigorously. The number of orders imposed nationally had only reached about 300 per year by 2001 but by the end of 2005 the rate had risen close to 3,000. ASBOs have proved controversial for a number of reasons, not least that they are civil orders that can result in criminal convictions if those subject to them fail to comply with their conditions. Side by side with the increasing use of formal criminal sanctions such as community and custodial penalties, there has been a considerable spread of this new form of contractualized social control with consequent dangers of drawing yet more people into the criminal justice system.

Emerging Issues

As I write, the situation is parlous. There aren't enough prisons to hold the record number of prisoners. The various agencies that are linked to the Home Office and the Ministry of Justice, and which deal with immigration, asylum and prisoners on parole, can't seem to keep track of all those prisoners that are released but who should be subject to deportation and related proceedings. And commentators on all sides of the political divide are unhappy with the current direction of the government's penal policy (it is either seen as being chaotic and too weak, or overly-intrusive and too tough).

Historically, the position of Home Secretary has always been a difficult one. Arguably, it is now more difficult than at any time in the past. This is not because the problems are that much more intractable. It is that, as a result of the penal politics of the last decade and a half, the job has become much more visible. Successive Home Secretaries have become increasingly preoccupied with tabloid headlines and the consequence has been that Home Affairs has become an everyday tabloid matter. While sympathy for Home Secretaries will almost certainly be in short supply, there are enormously serious issues at stake here. We now have more than 80,000 people in our prisons where a little over a decade ago it was 50,000 (and that was a record). The numbers subject to other forms of surveillance – from tagging to ASBOs – increase all the time. And, although crime has been dropping fairly consistently for a decade, the majority of the public think it has been on the increase. Tough political rhetoric encourages such mistaken beliefs and only further ratchets up the pressure on a creaking criminal justice system.

Guide to Further Sources

There are numerous very helpful sources of information on the web. The Home Office research website contains a huge amount of material, including criminal statistics, data from the British Crime Survey and scores of research publications: <http://www.homeoffice.gov.uk/rds/pubsintro1.html>. The International Centre for Prison Studies runs a website that contains lots of useful data on trends in the use of imprisonment around the world: <http://www.kcl.ac.uk/depsta/rel/icps/home.html>. The British Society of Criminology has an improving website containing information about its activities and about British criminology generally: <http://www.britsoccrim.org/>. Useful summaries of this data can be found in three published sources: D. Downes and R. Morgan, 'No turning back: the politics of law and order into the millennium', in M. Maguire, R. Morgan and R. Reiner (eds), *Oxford Handbook of Criminology*, 4th edn (Oxford University Press, 2007); T. Newburn, 'Tough on crime: penal policy in England and Wales', in M. Tonry and A. Doob (eds), *Crime and Justice*, vol. 36 (University of Chicago Press, 2007); and A. Walker, C. Kershaw and S. Nicholas, *Crime in England and Wales 2005/06* (Home Office, 2006).

The most influential book in recent years in the area is D. Garland, *The Culture of Control* (Oxford University Press, 2001), which explores the changing nature of crime and penal policy and culture in America and Britain.

A weighty, but definitive, tome is M. Maguire, R. Morgan and R. Reiner (eds), *Oxford Handbook of Criminology*, 4th edn (Oxford University Press, 2007). This is an edited textbook with contributions from many leading criminologists covering their particular areas of expertise. An introductory textbook, which covers the bulk of criminological topics and is aimed at the new undergraduate student is T. Newburn, *Criminology* (Willan, 2007).

A provocative, thoughtful and persuasive book in which the reasons for the changing nature of crime control in contemporary Britain are explored is R. Reiner, *Law and Order: An Honest Citizen's Guide to Crime Control* (Polity, 2007).

Part VII

Services for Particular Groups

Chapter 46

'Race' and Social Welfare

Lucinda Platt

Overview

- Around 8 per cent of the UK population is from a minority ethnic group, according to the 2001 Census classification.
- There is great diversity in history and current experience between the UK's minority groups.
- Nevertheless, all non-white minorities have typically faced racism and exclusion from services, as a result of racialized conceptions of belonging, rights and citizenship.
- Race relations policies developed in tandem with immigration controls to set the incorporation of minorities in contrast to the exclusion of non-citizens. In doing so, however, they presented ethnic minorities as being inherently problematic.
- The UK's minority groups show great diversity in outcomes across policy areas, though they share the experience of disadvantage relative to their skills and experience.
- Contemporary policy faces challenges in responding to the complexity and cross-cutting nature of issues of 'race' in relation to social welfare.

Introduction

As the 2000 Runnymede Report, *The Future of Multiethnic Britain*, pointed out, the UK has traditionally been a country of immigration and the population of the UK is multiethnic. As well as the different nationalities – English, Scots, Welsh and Irish – associated with the different countries of the UK, in 2001 around 8 per cent of the population belonged to a non-white minority ethnic group. The classification and policy consideration of British minorities has typically focused on non-white minorities; and racism within society and

within service provision was previously regarded as the primary challenge for policy development and delivery. However, diversity within the minority population is now widely acknowledged, as well as the particular needs of certain white minority populations and sub-populations; and there is consequent demand for responses which go beyond a unifying anti-racism and recognize the complex role of different histories and backgrounds in determining people's needs for and access to social welfare.

Issues of 'race' and ethnicity cross-cut areas of social welfare and thus have a bearing on many of the chapters in this book that treat distinct policy areas. But they are also the objects of policy. This chapter treats the development of 'race relations' policy and the way it articulates with conceptions of citizenship and citizen rights, before going on to discuss the ways in which issues of race and ethnicity have shaped both social policy needs and policy responses, using examples from housing and employment. It begins, however, with a consideration of the language of 'race' and ethnicity.

Concepts and Terminology

The language of 'race' is both emotive and contested. While it is recognized that races do not exist in any meaningful biological sense, the terminology of 'race' is embedded within both popular discourse and policy and people act as if the notion of race had meaning, including through racism. Racism is behaviour that uses physical markers of difference such as skin colour as the basis of assumed inferiority and as a justification for less favourable treatment, whether through verbal or physical abuse (racial harassment), through denying employment or by obstructing access to opportunities or services.

In Britain and Europe, the language of ethnicity has generally replaced that of race, as it is not, like race, explicitly tied to the erroneous belief in the existence of distinct racial groups. However, the two terms continue to be tied together to allow a discussion of racism in relation to ethnic difference. Ethnicity is a self-conscious and claimed identity that is shared with others on the basis of belief in common descent, and may be linked to country of origin, language, religion or customs; it may also be shaped by contact with others and experiences of colonization or migration. Insofar as ethnicity is self-consciously claimed, it is part of an individual's identity. However, its salience as an aspect of identity will tend

to vary with context, as will the particular ethnicity stressed. A person might feel their dominant ethnicity as Welsh or as British or as 'white' depending on the situation. Identification with a particular ethnicity will also be affected by the perceptions of others and their use of ethnic categories to situate an individual.

It is common when speaking of ethnicity or ethnic groups to specify that the objects of discussion are 'minority' ethnic groups. This use is intended to indicate not simply that the concern is with those groups that make up a small proportion of the population, but also to indicate the system of power relations which gives them a less-powerful status and which can be associated with the 'minority' status of children. The dual meanings of minority are important for policy, in that it is the relative powerlessness and marginalization associated with being from a minority ethnic group that is the central issue, rather than the small numbers. Such powerlessness will itself be mediated by other sources of advantage or disadvantage such as class or gender.

The Development of Race Relations Policy

Race relations policy developed as part of an approach to citizenship that constructed external exclusion as being the price to pay for internal harmony. Conversely, the development of race relations policy was seen as a means of justifying the introduction of increasingly stringent restrictions on those who were, nominally at least, British citizens, but had been resident in former colonial countries. Thus, somewhat paradoxically, the UK was foremost in Europe in the development of anti-discrimination legislation, while also imposing greater restrictions on entry to those who wished to immigrate.

At the same time, this association between 'good race relations' and immigration control was premised on a racialization of belonging: it was only non-white immigration that was identified as problematic. And the formulation of 'internally inclusive but externally exclusive' contributed to the construction of resident minorities as the source of pressure on public services, rather than recognizing the failure of social policy to respond appropriately to competition over resources.

Two early Race Relations Acts, in 1965 and 1968, were followed by a much more wide-reaching one in 1976, modelled on the Sex Discrimination Act of the previous year. The 1976 Race Relations Act outlawed direct discrimination, indirect discrimination (where a requirement or restriction disadvantaged a member of one group more than another and could not be justified on other grounds) and victimization (where complaining about discrimination resulted in less favourable treatment). It covered employment, education and the provision of services. It also established the Commission for Racial Equality (CRE). Under the Act, it was unlawful to discriminate against anyone on grounds of race, colour, nationality or ethnic or national origin. Nevertheless, the impact of this Act was limited to those cases where individuals brought complaints to Tribunal. It was unable to recognize or tackle structural elements to disadvantage; and while the CRE could investigate institutions where systematic discrimination seemed to be occurring (for example, school exclusions or housing allocations), it could not enforce recommendations.

The 1976 Act remained the primary race relations legislation until 2000. Following the conclusions of the Macpherson Inquiry into the racist murder of a black teenager and its findings of 'institutional racism', an overhaul of race relations legislation was considered necessary. This included a more proactive approach to institutional procedures and practices. The 2000 Race Relations (Amendment) Act increased the power of the CRE in that its recommendations became enforceable. The 2000 Act also put greater onus on public services to scrutinize their own practices and policies for potential discriminatory effects through the publication of Race Equality Impact Assessments. In 2007, the CRE and its powers were incorporated into the Equality and Human Rights Commission.

A concern with institutional practice and rights of citizens to fair treatment has been ongoing. But in recent years it has been accompanied by a parallel policy focus which emphasizes the responsibility of individuals to 'earn' their citizenship rights. A series of disturbances in northern English towns in the summer of 2001 resulted in an investigation led by Ted Cantle which stressed the importance of 'community cohesion' and argued that different sections of the population were leading 'parallel lives'. Rather than, as Scarman's report on the Brixton disturbances of 1981 had done, recognizing disadvantage and structural constraints as critical, Cantle's report identified lack of community leadership and separation of ethnic groups. The concept of 'community cohesion' was taken up as an injunction for minorities to integrate, and received further emphasis following the July 2005 London bombings. While the focus in this latter response was on religious affiliation, or, rather, the intersection between ethnicity and faith, it again questioned whether certain sectors of the population truly 'belonged' and sought demonstrations of assimilation to posited British values and standards. In this newer model, then, citizenship is constructed as a contingent rather than an absolute right.

However, it is not just the policies that are targeted on minority groups and on the promotion of race relations that shape the experience and outcomes of those of different ethnicities. Unique histories of groups both in relation to their settlement in the

UK and their subsequent experiences have resulted in particular relationships with policy and particular social needs, even as they have also been created through the operation of policies and opportunities. The next sections of this chapter consider how these histories have had consequences for minority groups using housing and employment as two examples. Exploration of social security, education and health policy would similarly enable consideration of the diversity of ethnic groups' experience and the role of policy, and suggestions for readings on these are included at the end of the chapter. The discussion is intended to illustrate the legacy of both individual and policy histories across generations, and the diversity of experience, which offers a challenge to mono-causal accounts or simple interventions.

Minority Histories and Social Welfare

The 2001 Census specified a range of options for its ethnic group question. As well as a white Irish category in Great Britain, a number of 'other' options and 'mixed' categories, which enabled people to acknowledge mixed parentage or identification, the minority groups were Indian (1.8 per cent of the population of Great Britain), Pakistani (1.3 per cent), Bangladeshi (0.5 per cent), Black Caribbean (1 per cent), Black African (0.8 per cent) and Chinese (0.4 per cent). Each of these minority ethnic groups has distinctive migration and settlement patterns and subsequent experiences of employment, housing and social security. Their pre-migration backgrounds and histories also influenced the educational qualifications and resources they brought with them or could call on, which could have long-run effects down the generations.

While there were members of these minority groups present in the UK in the first half of the twentieth century and before, the main period of immigration was in the post-war period, when Britain was facing acute employment shortages and had opened its borders to subjects from (former) colonies. Minority settlement tended to be in areas of high employment, but also high levels of housing competition. Jobs were often those that were the least desirable and the most precarious, leaving the employees susceptible to being laid off in times of recession or cut-back. Areas of settlement also reflected industries in which the different groups found, or could create, a particular niche at the time of arrival. Thus Caribbean men tended to work in the construction industries, settling in both London and the Midlands, while many Caribbean women were recruited to the new National Health Service. In 2001, over 60 per cent of Caribbeans lived in London. Pakistanis, whose period of migration peaked in 1961, tended to settle in the northern industrial towns and the Midlands and worked in the textile industries, which suffered a complete decline, as well as in the motor industries, where the decline was later and longer-run. Some Indians from the migration of the 1950s also worked in the Midlands textile plants, but they also settled in London, finding work in the service and health sectors. In 2001, 40 per cent of Indians lived in London and a further 30 per cent in the West and East Midlands, in particular in Leicester. The East African Asians, who typically define themselves as ethnically Indian, deprived of residence in Kenya and Uganda in 1967 and 1972 respectively, came as families, and though they had often lost their assets, they brought with them business skills, which they utilized in small business ventures. With these skills and with fluent English, they were very differently situated from the Vietnamese refugees (largely ethnically Chinese) who arrived in Britain as part of the settlement process from Hong Kong and who often lacked English, transferable qualifications and connections whereby to establish themselves.

The introduction of immigration controls in 1962 (after the Nationality Act of 1948 had granted entry to anyone with a British passport), also set up systems of sponsorship and chain migration. Chinese chain migration, for example, focused around catering and led to relatively dispersed patterns of settlement. Conversely, Bangladeshi chain migration, following on from a later period of primary immigration (in the 1970s and 1980s) focused around the catering and food industries, in which more than half of Bangladeshis work, and is associated with high local residential concentrations in parts of London (where over 50 per cent of Bangladeshis lived in 2001) and the West Midlands. Black Africans are a heterogenous group of relatively recent immigrants with their origins in a range of different countries and with different reasons for migration – asylum, education and employment. They often have high levels of qualifications, which are not reflected in the employment they achieve, and settle overwhelmingly in London (nearly 80 per cent lived in London in 2001), often finding work in the low-paid service sector.

Housing

These different histories, along with the practices, skills and resources that minority groups brought with them and subsequently developed, have resulted in very different housing and employment careers and in very different patterns of calls on state support. In areas where was a high demand for employment and where minorities settled in the immediate post-war period, there was also likely to be fierce competition for housing. In a significant early study of interethnic relations, the sociologist John Rex revealed how housing – demand, perception and processes of urban change –

could shape both groups' wider experiences and race relations overall (Rex and Moore 1967). Housing that was available to post-war immigrants was generally that which had been designated for clearance, but local authorities, reluctant to re-house what they deemed as a 'stranger' population, would often take the decision not to clear the properties. The net result was that the visible immigrant populations tended to be focused in small areas of run-down housing in the poorest parts of cities. One solution to housing pressure followed by some communities was to use pooled resources to buy cheap housing both to live in themselves and to let out to other migrants. Such 'investments' meant that Pakistanis had relatively high levels of owner occupation up to the 1990s, but at the same time it led to further problems, such as damp, lack of amenities and overcrowding. Additionally, owner occupation could tie individuals and families to a particular location even after the jobs were gone.

Access to local authority housing was initially limited by residence requirements, sometimes of five years, and investigations into allocations policies in a number of local authority areas showed that allocations systematically disadvantaged minority group members and contributed to concentrations of particular groups on certain estates. Thus, for example, where Caribbeans succeeded in accessing local authority housing stock, through fulfilling the residence requirements relatively early on, it was often the least desirable housing, which had further ramifications for its value following the introduction of 'right to buy' legislation in 1980 (see chapter 43). With their later period of primary migration and the tendency to settle in London, Bangladeshis were heavily dependent on local authority housing with around half of them in such accommodation. Larger average family sizes, the restricted availability of housing, and the nature of allocations policies often meant that Bangladeshis would end up in relatively poor-quality social housing; and they are still more likely to face difficulties than others in local authority housing.

Indians, like the Pakistanis, had high rates of owner occupation from early on, but for them this has been sustained, as the group as a whole has become more successful. This group is now able to select more easily where to live – for example, in more comfortable areas and where there are community resources. In this way, it can be seen that housing can serve to create a community for those who are successful. For those who are not, poor housing and residential concentration can be seen as a consequence of constraints: the failure of policy and the facts of material disadvantage.

Housing experience, then, was intimately tied up with initial patterns of settlement and of housing policies which both wittingly and unwittingly – according to a number of investigations – served to disadvantage those from minority ethnic groups. The effect of earlier policies can also have long-term effects both in terms of housing position and overall health and welfare and also in relation to opportunities for adjustment to processes of deindustrialization, through, for example, possibilities of geographic mobility and options to realize capital tied up in property.

Employment

Both settlement and housing careers have implications for the current employment status of minority ethnic groups. While it has been argued that minority groups responded relatively well to deindustrialization, it is nevertheless the case that the fate of industries to which they had been recruited had important impacts on both unemployment rates and subsequent work histories and the sorts of skills and experience they had at their disposal. Resources available to different groups from communities as well as from family have also played an important role. The demise of the textile industries had a particular impact on Pakistani employment and saw many moving into taxi-driving and chauffeuring. Self-employment is often regarded as evidence of entrepreneurialism and a positive choice, but for minority groups, research suggests that much self-employment is perforce rather than chosen because of difficulties in accessing employment, and represents work that is neither highly valued nor well rewarded. Similarly the food and catering industries in which a majority of Bangladeshis are employed are typically very poorly rewarded (and physically demanding), even if they offer an ongoing source of employment.

On the other hand, one in twenty of men of Indian ethnic origin are doctors, and the average pay for this group is high, which can facilitate opportunities for other members of the family or community, as well as for those who attain such highly qualified positions. Caribbean women (and increasingly Black African women) retain a relatively high concentration in public sector and specifically health service employment, which offers higher security and better pay than much private sector work. By contrast, Caribbean men face relatively high rates of unemployment.

All minority groups, and both men and women, face higher rates of unemployment than the average, and this is often accompanied by higher rates of economic inactivity, which may, arguably, represent discouragement, as well as higher rates of ill-health and the demands of bringing up a family (see figure 46.1). These absolute differences in employment chances are of concern to policy and were explicitly recognized in a Public Services Agreement target to close the employment gap between the majority and minorities, and the establishment of a cross-departmental Ethnic

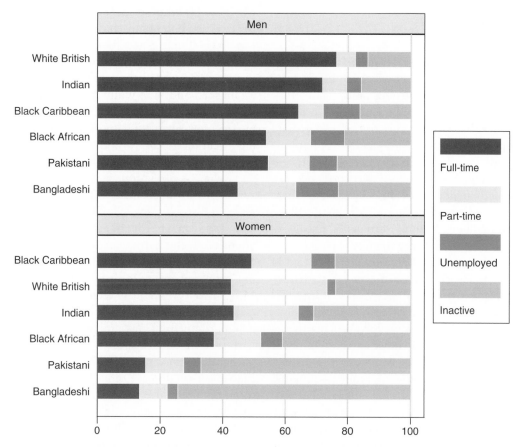

Figure 46.1 Distribution of types of economic activity and economic inactivity by ethnic group, ranked by proportions economically active
Source: Labour Force Survey, pooled quarters 2002–5. Person weights applied.

Minority Employment Task Force to pursue that target.

Analysis has shown that the absolute differences in employment chances are partly susceptible to explanation in terms of differences in qualifications, age, experience, sector of employment, rates of illness and region of residence. However, there typically remains what Anthony Heath has called an 'ethnic penalty' (Heath and McMahon 1997: 91). That is, there is a deficit in employment chances and in levels of pay that is associated with belonging to a particular ethnic group and which cannot be explained by known characteristics.

Some of this is attributable to discrimination by employers.

Policy is, therefore, invoking a range of strategies to address the employment target, including educational policy and skills development, making work pay, tackling discrimination, provision of appropriate childcare, addressing ill-health and utilizing policies focusing on neighbourhoods and deprived areas. The work of the taskforce thus reveals how interconnected are issues of 'race' and social welfare, and that simplistic understandings of causes and appropriate interventions to resolve particular disadvantages are not adequate to the task.

Emerging Issues

As noted, and demonstrated in this chapter, there is broad acceptance both of diversity among minority groups and that differences between groups can be as great as differences between minorities in aggregate and the majority. This clearly has implications for both policy development and delivery, and has been incorporated into much policy thinking. However, there remains a tendency to talk of 'BME' (Black and Minority Ethnic) groups as an aggregate source of policy interest. Treatment of minorities as a whole can also be found in policy levers such as the target to reduce the employment gap between majority and minorities. Sensitivity to difference is thus partial and can obscure the particular needs or the needs of the most vulnerable.

A further emergent issue is the distinctive position of 'new' migrants, compared to the more established minority groups that have received the majority of both research interest and policy attention up to the present (see also chapter 51). These include substantial numbers of white minorities, including those from Europe and particularly since the expansion of the EU in 2004, who are beginning to be recognized as potentially having distinctive experiences that place them neither with the majority white population nor within the paradigms used to consider the more established and 'non-white' minorities.

Moreover, diversity within groups is also recognized as being important. Increasing attention is paid to faith as the marker of difference between groups of individuals. Religious affiliation, it is argued, is or can be the most salient element of identity and can also be a source of discrimination and disadvantage. Such arguments bring attention to the particular disadvantage of Muslims; and there has been a corresponding development of policy concern with Muslims. However, it is recognized that it is the intersection of faith and ethnicity that is important. Religious affiliation is racialized in that Muslims are identified with particular minority ethnic groups; and centres of worship are often highly specific to an ethnic group: for example, churches that cater predominantly for particular Black African groups. Thus, religious affiliation may be an important element of experience to be aware of and for service delivery to be sensitive to, but it does not subsume ethnic difference.

Guide to Further Sources

The distributions and experience of minority ethnic groups in the UK is effectively summarized in ONS's *Social Focus on Ethnicity and Religion* (Palgrave, 2006), which draws largely on the 2001 Census data. There is an extensive literature on ethnicity and housing, of which P. Somerville and A. Steele (eds), *'Race', Housing and Social Exclusion* (Jessica Kingsley, 2002) is a recent example.

For an overview of employment research and its relation to poverty, see L. Platt, *Poverty and Ethnicity in the UK* (Policy Press, 2007). Social security policy is treated in L. Platt, 'Social security in a multiethnic society', in J. Millar (ed.), *Understanding Social Security: Issues for Policy and Practice* (Policy Press, 2003), pp. 255–76; and health and ethnicity are treated in J. Y. Nazroo, *Ethnicity, Class and Health* (PSI, 2001) and W. I. U. Ahmad, *'Race' and Health in Contemporary Britain* (Open University Press, 1993).

D. Gillborn and H. S. Mirza, *Educational Inequality: Mapping Race, Class and Gender – A Synthesis of Research Evidence* (Ofsted, 2000) provides a good overview of schooling; while H. Goulbourne, *Race Relations in Britain Since 1945*

(Macmillan, 1998) is a clear and direct account of the development of race relations policy.

Other works referred to or drawn on in the discussion are B. Parekh, *The Future of Multiethnic Britain*, The Parekh Report (The Runnymede Trust/Profile Books, 2000); W. Macpherson, *The Stephen Lawrence Inquiry: Report of an Inquiry* (The Stationery Office, 1999); T. Modood and R. Berthoud, *Ethnic Minorities in Britain: Diversity and Disadvantage* (PSI, 1997); *Community Cohesion: A Report of the Independent Review Team*, chaired by Ted Cantle (Home Office, 2001); J. Rex and R. Moore, *Race, Community and Conflict: A Study of Sparkbrook* (Oxford University Press, 1967); A. Heath and D. McMahon, 'Educational and occupational attainments: the impact of ethnic origins', in V. Karn (ed.), *Ethnicity in the 1991 Census: Volume Four: Employment Education and Housing among the Ethnic Minority Populations of Britain* (HMSO, 1997), pp. 91–3.

For the work of the Ethnic Minority Employment Task Force, see <http://www.emetaskforce.gov.uk/>. Other useful websites: the Commission for Equality and Human Rights: <http://www.cehr.org.uk/>; and the Runnymede Trust: <www.runnymedetrust.org>.

Chapter 47

Children

Tess Ridge

Overview

- Children are key recipients of welfare services across a wide range of policy areas, and their lives are considerably shaped by the type and quality of welfare services available.
- Modern childhood is undergoing considerable social and economic change and children of the twenty-first century live increasingly complex lives in a range of diverse family settings.
- Child welfare policies change over time, and depend on fluid and changing assumptions about the needs and rights of children, the needs and rights of parents and the role of the state in children's lives.
- There is increasing recognition in policy that children are social actors and bearers of rights. There is also a trend towards 'social investment policies' which focus on children as 'citizen workers' of the future.
- The chapter examines two major policy strategies developed for children, the 'Every Child Matters' agenda and 'Opportunity for All' – the government's anti-poverty agenda for children. Both represent a radical shift in the state's approach to children and bring children, as subjects of policy, in from the margins and right to the centre of government policies and services.

Introduction

In the UK in 2005 there were just over 12 million children under the age of 16 and they represented about 19 per cent of the population. The majority of these children were living in a family setting with their welfare needs being met by a range of informal and formal provision. Social policies for children need to be understood within the context of this informal/formal welfare mix. Children are often the target of policies and they are also important consumers

of welfare. They are key recipients of welfare services across a range of policy areas including education, health, housing and the environment, childcare, social services and financial support through the social security and tax system.

Children rely very heavily on welfare services for their present and future well-being, and their lives are affected by policies at local, national and transnational levels. Undoubtedly, in areas such as education, childcare and health these can have clear implications for children's well-being, but in other areas too, for example the environment and transport, policies can have an intended or unintended impact on children's lives. The way in which children are treated in the policy system is also dependent on how childhood is perceived at any one time. This chapter will examine how changing conditions of childhood may affect policies, and highlight some of the key debates and developments in this area.

Changing Conditions of Childhood

To understand how policy can affect children's lives, it is first important to recognize that childhood, as we know it, is a relatively modern social construction, which changes over time. In the twenty-first century, childhood in the UK is undergoing a period of considerable social and economic change. These changes will impact on the way that policies are developed. Prout (in Hallett and Prout 2003) highlights five significant social changes that have taken place since the last quarter of the twentieth century. First, declining birth rates and increasingly ageing populations: here the implications for policy are still unclear but may mean a shift of resources away from children towards older people. Second, increasing diversity in life circumstances and economic circumstances between children following social and demographic changes: this has resulted in growing income inequalities between children. Third, the impact of globalization as children are exposed to global flows of people, products, information and images; this is also linked to 'transnational childhoods' as children move between households across national boundaries. Fourth, the trend towards increasing institutional control over children's lives, resulting in longer periods spent in institutional settings such as schools and childcare. And, fifth, the emergence of children's voices in decision-making. This is explored further below in relation to children's rights.

Demographic and social changes in the last half of the twentieth century have also wrought considerable transformation in family formation and structure. Trends towards reduced fertility and later child-bearing have led to an overall reduction in the number of children being born in economically developed Western societies. Increasing instability in family life has led to a growth in cohabitation and rising rates of family dissolution, and this in turn has resulted in great diversity and complexity in family forms. As a consequence, children's lives are increasingly multifaceted and they can live in a variety of family settings. Whilst the majority of children still live with both their biological parents (married or cohabiting), one in four dependent children live in lone-parent families. These changes mean that 'children of the twenty-first century have a higher probability of experiencing parental separation, lone parenting, step families, visiting families, half-siblings and being an only child than children of any previous period of time' (Mayhew, in Bradshaw and Mayhew 2005: 34). Clearly, it is difficult for the state to provide effective universal or targeted policies for children who are living increasingly diverse and complex lives.

Children, Family and Social Policy

Like childhood, child welfare policies have also changed over time, and depend on fluid and changing assumptions about the needs and rights of children, the needs and rights of parents and the role of the state in children's lives. They are also affected by the political economy of welfare and different perceptions and ideologies of childhood that prevail at the time. A key example of the fluid nature of child welfare is provided by Fox-Harding's (1997) analysis of historical and contemporary childcare law and policy. She identifies four different value perspectives which have influenced

Table 47.1 Value perspectives in childcare policy

Laissez–faire and patriarchy	Limited state intervention in family relationships and family as a private sphere
State paternalism and child protection	State intervention in family life, a duty for the state to act and protect children. Overriding parents' wishes if deemed necessary
Defence of family and parents' rights	Services and financial support provided for families
Children's rights	Child should be treated as independent subject with rights

Source: Fox-Harding 1997.

policy provision for children at different times in the twentieth century (see table 47.1). Each of these perspectives means that children may be treated very differently in the provision of welfare, the formulation of social policies, and child protection.

The state's value position in relation to childhood and family life has been an important factor when it comes to shaping policies. Historically, children's needs and interests have remained hidden within the private sphere of the family and as a result they have tended to be invisible in the policy process. Their interests have been mainly served by social policies which are directed at the interests of the family. This 'familialization' of children has meant that policies which directly respond to children's needs are unlikely to be developed. This is apparent, for example, in the provision of childcare. Childcare in the UK has rarely been provided from the starting point of what is best for children, but rather as an important service for families, and in particular as a means to encourage mothers back into the labour market. This does not mean that childcare provided in this way is necessarily bad for children, but a system that developed from the perspective of children's needs and best interests – rather than those of their parents – may look very different from the childcare arrangements that we have today.

The assumption that children's best interests are consonant with their family's best interests is problematic and as a result, their needs and concerns are always in danger of being subsumed by the needs and interests of the family and of the state (see Hendrik 2005). There are also considerable 'tensions and contradictions' in the relationship between the state and the family and this reflects an ongoing debate between the rights and responsibilities of parents for their children and the obligations of the state to provide services for children and intervene in their lives when they are deemed to be at risk. Underpinning these tensions lies the fundamental issue of whether children are seen as a private good or whether society has a legitimate collective interest in ensuring their well-being.

Children's Rights

The issue of children's rights is also an important one for social policy. There is increasing recognition in policy that children are social actors and bearers of rights, as part of a new trend towards including the voices of service users in policy. Underpinning much of the movement towards children's rights has been a series of UK legislative acts – such as The Children Acts of 1989 and 2004 – and wider international conventions – such as the United

Nations Convention on the Rights of the Child (UNCRC). However, despite these advances there are still considerable areas of tension within policy regarding the rights of children. For example, although the government has reacted positively in terms of policy to the move to eradicate child poverty in line with the Articles 26 and 27 of the UN Convention on the Rights of the Child, marginalized children, such as children of asylum-seekers, tend to have far less attention paid to their welfare rights. There are also contradictions within policy; for example, as we have seen, children are increasingly included in policy formulation through consultation, but in education, a key policy area for children, they are unlikely to have a say in either policy or provision. In education in particular, the needs of children may be overshadowed by the perceived needs of the state, reflecting the perception of children as future adults, and education as a key policy medium for investment in children.

Children as a 'Social Investment'

Although children's needs have historically been hidden within the family, the position of children and families in welfare policy is changing. Ruth Lister argues that 'we are witnessing a genuine, unprecedented attempt to shift the social priorities of the state and nation to investing in children' (in Hendrik 2005: 455). This signals a profound shift in the position of children and families in the welfare mix as the state moves towards the development of a 'social investment state'. The 'social investment state' entails a movement away from traditional welfare policies towards policies built on investment in social and human capital. In this welfare strategy, children are central to future economic success; they are the 'citizen-workers of the future' (ibid.). In the 'social investment state' children are valued for the adults they will become and policies are explicitly targeted towards ensuring that their potential is developed to ensure the economic prosperity of the country in the future in order to maintain national economic prosperity in a competitive global market.

The development of social investment policies has, in many ways, been beneficial to children's interests in the UK. As Lister has highlighted, increased investment in policies to eradicate child poverty, develop a National Child Care Strategy and provide children's services such as Sure Start and Children's Centres, represents an improvement in state support and services for children. However, despite such improvements, there is a tension between policies that focus on children as future adults and the quality of life that they experience in childhood. This highlights a key debate about whether children are treated in policy as 'beings' (children in childhood) or as 'becomings' (future adults and citizen workers). Prout sums up this position: '[O]n its own a focus on futurity is unbalanced and needs to be accompanied by a concern for the present well-being of children, for their participation in social life and for their opportunities for self-realisation' (in Hendrik 2005: 464).

Two Policy Strategies

We now turn to examine two major policy strategies developed for children, the 'Every Child Matters' agenda and 'Opportunity for All', the government's anti-poverty agenda for children. Each of these policy developments reflects some of the tensions outlined above and involves policy-making across a wide range of welfare providers including education, health, social security and personal social services. They are both important policies for children and have the potential to make a significant impact on the lives of children in the future.

Every child matters

In 2004, following consultation, the government published *Every Child Matters: Change for Children* (2004), which represented a radical reform in children's services. The 'Every Child Matters' agenda was developed following a wide-ranging review of services for children, young people and families which included consultation with children and young people. It represents a radical shift in the state's approach to children, bringing them, as subjects of policy, in from the margins and right to the centre of government policies and services.

In *Every Child Matters* the government set out five key aims for children whatever their background or their circumstances (see table 47.2). These aims are considered central to the government's programme of change for children's services. To ensure their successful outcome, the Children Act 2004 set out a new framework of services and support for children and their families. These included a new Minister for Children, Young People and Families, who is based in the Department for Education and Skills and who has overarching responsibility for children, young people and families' policy and the Every Child Matters programme. A Children's Commissioner for England was also appointed in 2005, although the devolved authorities had already led the way with the creation of Children's Commissioners in Wales (2001), Northern Ireland (2003) and Scotland (2004). Children's Commissioners have responsibility for promoting the views and interests of all children and young people at a national level within a rights-based framework informed by the United Nations Convention on the Rights of the Child (UNCRC).

A further key element of the Every Child Matters agenda was the development of multidisciplinary services for children by integrating frontline services and focusing them around actual needs. This meant a radical reorganization of statutory children's services. Organizations involved with providing services to children – including hospitals, schools, police and voluntary groups – work together in teams to share information about children, protect them from harm and support them to achieve the five positive outcomes. Each Local Authority has a Children's Trust, an integrated partnership with statutory and voluntary service providers. Children's Trusts have a duty to involve children and young people in the policy process and the development of services that affect them. This marks a significant reform in service provision for children, and recognizes the need for children to have a voice in policy and services that affect them. However, Every Child Matters is not without tensions and contradictions. Integrated working is difficult to get right and research evidence shows that there is a need for considerable trust, cooperation and agreed terms of reference for integrated teams to work. The policy is also underpinned by a social investment approach which focuses on the child as a future adult. The role of schools is also changing. Extended Schools, which provide after-school care, reflect a welfare-to-work agenda, but are concerned more with parents' needs for childcare than with the needs of children per se. Increased acknowledgement of children's rights reflects the intention to involve children and young people in policy and service development. However, these are not fully developed and the location of the Minister for Children, and the new Ministry for Children, Young People and Families within the Department for Education and Skills highlights the centrality of education to the Every Child Matters agenda.

'Opportunity for all'

A key element of the Outcomes Framework is economic well-being, and this highlights an important area of social policy for

Table 47.2 *'Every Child Matters', the outcomes framework*

Being healthy	Physically healthy Mentally and emotionally healthy Sexually healthy Healthy lifestyles Choose not to take illegal drugs *Parents, carers and families promote healthy choices*
Staying safe	Safe from maltreatment, neglect, violence and sexual exploitation Safe from accidental injury and death Safe from bullying and discrimination Safe from crime and anti-social behaviour in and out of school Have security, stability and are cared for *Parents, carers and families provide safe homes and stability*
Enjoying and achieving	Ready for school Attend and enjoy school Achieve stretching national educational standards at primary school Achieve personal and social development and enjoy recreation Achieve stretching national educational standards at secondary school
Making a positive contribution	Engage in decision-making and support the community and environment Engage in law-abiding and positive behaviour in and out of school Develop positive relationships and choose not to bully and discriminate Develop self-confidence and successfully deal with significant life changes and challenges Develop enterprising behaviour
Economic well-being	Engage in further education, employment or training on leaving school Ready for employment Live in decent homes and sustainable communities Access to transport and material goods Live in households free from low income

Source: *Every Child Matters: Change for Children* (2004).

children. The UK has one of the worst rates of child poverty in the developed world, with nearly four million children living below the poverty line at the turn of the century. Children are particularly vulnerable to poverty, and fiscal support for them and their families through the tax and social security system plays a vital role in their protecting, especially for children who live in lone-parent households or where there is unemployment or long-term sickness and disability. The level of support provided by the state can be crucial in securing the economic well-being of children.

In 1999, faced with a child poverty rate of nearly four million, the Labour government pledged to eradicate child poverty within a 20-year period. To do so, it developed a major programme of welfare reform called 'Opportunity for All'. This includes initiatives across a wide range of social policy areas, including health, education, housing, social security and social care. Underpinning these policy responses are strong elements of 'social investment' and concern about the future prospects of low-income children. The policies include specific support for children through the education system, especially addressing literacy and numeracy, which can be seen as key elements in relation to social investment. Other education policies include Sure Start, an important initiative in early years care for disadvantaged children, and the Educational Maintenance Allowance (EMA) for older children (see chapter 42). Support for low-income parents came mainly through welfare-to-work policies, and the introduction of the minimum wage and childcare initiatives. There is also increased fiscal support through social security and the tax credits system, especially for children of low-income working parents. The government has committed itself to annual poverty audit reports which cover specific and measurable indicators relating to the well-being of children (see the Department for Work and Pensions website).

Despite the government's commitment to eradicating child poverty through its 'Opportunity for All' programme, there are tensions within the policy process. Critics of the policy point to the welfare-to-work agenda that underpins much of the policy. For example, policies that encourage mothers, especially lone mothers, into employment will have an impact on children's lives. The intention is that children will experience increased financial security; however, the balance of work and care within families is affected, and as a result so too are children's experiences of childcare and after-school care, as well as the length and quality of time that they are able to spend with their mothers. It has also proved very difficult to reduce the levels of child poverty, with some arguing that greater redistribution of income from rich to poor will be necessary to lift poorer families out of poverty. These are very sensitive policy issues that cut right to the heart of the child/parent/state welfare triangle. Income support policies for children reflect the tensions between the duties and responsibilities of parents and the duties and responsibilities of the state for ensuring children's well-being.

Emerging Issues

Childhood is undergoing considerable transformation, as social, demographic and economic changes impact upon the everyday lives of children and their families. Moves towards multidisciplinary services and the inclusion of the voices of children in the policy process are hard to achieve meaningfully. There are considerable tensions inherent in the 'Every Child Matters' agenda, and integrated working is difficult to get right. The role of Extended Schools is focused on welfare-to-work needs. Therefore the delivery of social care in schools may be problematic for children as they become more intensively scrutinized, institutionalized and contained within a school setting. Poverty is likely to remain a severe problem for many children and the adequate provision of benefits and state support for families in employment and – most critically – out of employment will be a key issue. The interests of children have slowly come in from the margins of policy, but formulating adequate and effective social polices still presents a considerable challenge for governments as they seek to reconcile the often divergent needs of the state, families and children.

Guide to Further Sources

A key text that introduces child policy issues is H. Hendrik, *Child Welfare and Social Policy, An Essential Reader* (Policy Press, 2005). Lorraine Fox-Harding, *Perspectives in Childcare* (Longman, 1997) is an older text, but provides a valuable insight into policy approaches to child welfare. C. Hallett and A. Prout (eds), *Hearing the Voices of Children* (RoutledgeFalmer, 2003) draws on the new social studies of childhood; it is a sociological approach but is focused on social policy and, in particular, on the emergence of children's voices in policy domains.

For a statistical insight into children's lives in the UK and an illumination of key trends in child welfare, read J. Bradshaw and E. Mayhew (eds), *The Well-being of Children in the United Kingdom* (Save the Children, 2005).

Government websites are valuable sources of policy documents and research. Two in particular are useful for following up the progress of policies mentioned in this chapter. The Department for Education and Skills has a children and families section which has details about Sure Start and Every Child Matters, and information from the Minister for Children, Young People and Families: <http://www.dfes.gov.uk/childrenandfamilies>. For annual reports and further information about 'Opportunity for All', see the Department of Work and Pensions website at <http://www.dwp.gov.uk/ofa/>. Further information about child poverty can be found on the Child Poverty Action Group (CPAG) website which also has a regular update on child poverty statistics: <http://www.cpag.org.uk>. On a wider stage the UNICEF website carries information about the UN Convention on the Rights of the Child and many other issues that affect children: <http://www.unicef.org>.

Chapter 48

Young People

Bob Coles

Overview

- This chapter starts with a brief discussion about what we mean by 'youth' and 'young people'.
- Youth policy in Britain emerged in three main phases. The first covers the arrival of youth policy in the period 1997–2000, mainly under the influence of the Social Exclusion Unit. This saw the first Minister for Young People.
- The second period of youth policy in Britain (2000–5) saw the birth, life and 'demise' of the 'Connexions Strategy' described at the end of 1999 by the Prime Minister as 'our front-line policy for young people'. Yet by 2005 no one spoke of this 'strategy' at all. We examine why.
- During the (overlapping) third period, youth policy became submerged in policy for 'children-and-young people' under the predominant discourses of the 2003 Green Paper *Every Child Matters* and further enmeshed following a 2005 Green Paper *Youth Matters*.
- The chapter concludes with a discussion of the implications of this.

Introduction

It is perhaps significant that writing this chapter for the third edition of *The Student's Companion* has required as significant a revision as was necessary for the second edition; such has been the pace of change in the development of youth policy in Britain in the last ten years.

Perspectives on Youth and Youth Transitions

'Youth' is often described as an interstitial phase in the life course between childhood and adulthood, and 'young people' as those at this phase in the life course. Different social sciences emphasize different aspects of this. The term 'adolescence' is often used in psychology describing biological and psychological aspects of physical, emotional and sexual maturation associated with the teenage years. Sociologists have more often defined youth as associated with institutional transitions, three of which predominate. The first involves completing education and entering the labour market – the school-to-work transition. The second involves attaining (relative) independence of families of origin (including partnering and family formations) – the domestic transition. The third involves moving from the parental home, sometimes initially involving temporary transitional accommodation, but eventually achieving a 'home' independent of parents – the housing transition. Political scientists and others have focused on the ways in which different rights and responsibilities accrue to young people during their teenage years. Indeed some analysts have talked about youth citizenship as being distinctive from the full citizenship of adults. As an applied social science, social policy draws on all these perspectives in order to provide a critical appreciation of how, to what degree, and in what ways the needs of young people are met.

The Polarization of Youth Transitions

The 'youth transition model' has proved especially useful in helping understand the 're-structuration' of youth that occurred in the last quarter of the twentieth century and continued into the twenty-first. It helps highlight the ways in which 'traditional transitions' have been replaced by 'extended' and 'fractured' transitions. 'Traditional transitions', commonplace until the mid-1970s, involve young people leaving school at the minimum school leaving age and almost immediately and unproblematically obtaining employment. As young people worked in their late teenage years, they continued to live in the parental home, they saved, formed partnerships, got engaged, then married and, on marriage, moved to their own home and started a family – usually in that order. In the twenty-first century, although significant numbers of young people still attempt some of the major transitions in their teenage years, traditional transitions have largely been replaced by 'extended transitions'. These involve longer periods spent in post-16 and higher education, longer periods of family dependency, later parenting (the average age of a woman having her first child is now over 26), more complex partnering

(often including cohabitation) and more complex and extended periods living in 'transitional housing'.

'Fractured transitions' refer to young people leaving school without securing a job or training, or leaving home without attaining a stable home of their own, and so experiencing various forms of youth homelessness. 'Fractured transitions' often involve drop-out from families as well as drop-out from education, training or employment. The longer periods of family dependency assumed by extended transitions occur at the very time when many family relationships may be brittle and some families are unable to cope with the tensions involved. By the age of 16 only around a half of young people are living with both biological parents, many have experienced the divorce or separation of their parents and significant numbers live with step-parents. 'Fractured' school-to-work transitions are also associated both with previous experiences of disadvantage (either in education, family life or both) and with other transition experiences – such as becoming a teenage parent, leaving home (often for negative reasons such as family disputes), or being involved in crime, drug misuse and/or the criminal justice system. This involves what the government since 1997 has referred to as 'social exclusion'.

The Emergence of Youth Policy in the UK, 1997–2001

Before the first New Labour Government in 1997, it could easily be argued that Britain did not have a youth policy. Previous governments took the view that youth-related issues were best dealt with by the great departments of state, such as Education, Health, the Home Office, etc. Some academics had argued passionately for the development of more coherence, illustrating how failure to coordinate policy left the different departments of state pulling in completely contradictory directions. Education policy had presided over a staggering increase of permanent exclusions from school by 450 per cent between 1990 and 1997, and exclusion from school was known to be strongly connected with involvement in youth crime. The withdrawal of benefits for 16–18-year olds in 1988 was intended to drive young people into training or post-16 education, but it led instead to 160,000 young people doing nothing, creating another path into youth crime, drug misuse and teenage pregnancy and thereby causing further problems for the Home Office and the Department of Health. Youth crime and drop-out were also known to be hugely expensive to the Exchequer as well as damaging to young people's welfare.

The chief instigator of youth policy in the early years of the first Blair government was the Social Exclusion Unit (SEU), set up shortly after the 1997 general election. The Unit was part of the Cabinet Office, fulfilled tasks set for it by the Prime Minister and reported directly to him. It was used to address issues around 'social exclusion' – recognized as a complex, multifaceted syndrome of disadvantage, the responsibilities for which spanned different government departments. 'Joined-up problems' were increasingly recognized as requiring 'joined-up solutions' and greater cooperation between government departments. Before the end of the century, the SEU had produced five major reports, all on predominantly youth-related issues:

- truancy and school exclusion;
- rough sleeping (including youth homelessness);
- poor neighbourhoods;
- teenage pregnancy; and
- 16–18-year olds not in education, employment or training (NEET).

Not all these reports can be described in detail here, but the third and fifth reports were to change the landscape of youth policy in Britain. The third report was on spatial clusters of disadvantage in poor neighbourhoods and the challenges faced by neighbourhood renewal. Because the topic was so huge and complex, after the report, eighteen Policy Action Teams (PATs) were set up further to develop policy in more detail. One of these (PAT 12) focused on young people. The report contained a chart showing that Britain was alone in Europe in not having a Minister, a Ministry, a parliamentary committee or indeed any vehicle for cross-ministerial discussion of youth matters. As a consequence, there was a mixture of duplication of effort in some communities, and deserts of no provision in others, with projects emanating from eight government departments, six units and ten other agencies. PAT 12 produced a radical new vision for the better coordination of youth policy across government. This involved a Minister for Young People, a Children and Young People's Unit (CYPU), to further develop and coordinate policy, and a high-powered Cross-Departmental Ministerial Group. Britain finally had its mechanisms for national youth policy coordination and the processes for consultation with children and young people on its further development began.

The Connexions Strategy, 1999–2005

The fifth report from the SEU *Bridging the Gap*, published in 1999, concerned young people aged 16–18 who were not in any form of education, employment or training (NEET). The report confirmed that being disengaged at the ages of 16 and 17 was a good predictor of later unemployment and also closely linked to educational disaffection and disadvantage prior to the age of 16. It was also correlated with an involvement in crime, misuse of drugs and teenage pregnancy. Other groups which predominated amongst those that were NEET included care leavers, young carers, young people with mental health problems and young people with disabilities and special educational needs. So, although responsibilities for NEET fell squarely within the DfES, many of the issues connected with NEET remained the responsibility of other departments such as the Department of Health or the Home Office. The SEU report, together with a government White Paper on Education, *Learning to Succeed*, suggested the development of a new multi-professional service to help give guidance, advice and support for young people between the ages of 13 and 19 – a Connexions Strategy with, at its heart, a new Connexions Service. Although there was no service badged as 'Connexions' in Scotland, Wales or Northern Ireland, similar multi-agency working was developed in these countries too.

The Connexions Service aimed to offer a universal service to all young people and a targeted service offering intensive and sensitive support to a minority of young people facing complex problems. One of the biggest challenges facing the new service was to provide both through a national network of Personal Advisers (PAs). The Connexions Strategy remit was much broader than that of the old careers services, which it absorbed or replaced. It aimed to provide (through a Connexions Partnership Board) the coordination of support and services across a range of different agencies. This included health agencies (including the drug prevention and advisory service, and teenage pregnancy and motherhood), education (including educational welfare and the youth service as well as schools and colleges), social services (including leaving care teams), youth justice (including the police and youth offending teams), housing departments and the voluntary sector (including youth homelessness projects). The Connexions Strategy anticipated it would deal with three tiers of

need. Most young people would only require information, advice or guidance on their education and learning, careers or personal development. Others, at risk of disengaging, needed in-depth support and guidance and help to assess their needs, to develop and support action plans and to monitor progress. A smaller group needed specialist assessment and support which may require services being 'brokered' from other specialist services. Connexions PAs were also expected to act as 'advocates' for young people, ensuring that appropriate services and benefits were obtained, playing the role of a 'powerful friend' where agencies were failing to comply with their duties and responsibilities. Front-line workers were called Personal Advisers no matter what role they played.

The majority of PAs provided careers education and guidance in the same way they had done before, and schools and colleges saw little change, except perhaps that PAs were spread even more thinly – each PA may have 800 young people to serve. PAs addressing more complex need often came from a different professional background – for example, youth work or work in the voluntary sector. Indeed, many retained their original base. Yet other PAs operated within specialist teams working with young offenders, care leavers or young people with special educational needs or disabilities.

Although the Connexions Strategy was intended to be *the* joined-up strategy for work with young people, in practice, until 2005 'joined-up' patterns of support were also being promoted independently by other government departments and agencies. Two deserve special mention. Addressing the extent, the expense and the ineffectiveness of responses to youth crime has been on the policy agenda for some time, after a critical report by the Audit Commission in 1996 – *Misspent Youth*. In opposition, the Labour Party spent a great deal of effort planning its proposals for change, many of which were contained in the 1997 White Paper, *No More Excuses*. The reforms of the youth justice system which followed the 1999 Crime and Disorder Act saw the creation of multi-agency youth offending teams (YOTs) in all local authorities, drawing together police, probation, social services and others in a concerted attempt to address and reduce youth crime. The Act also introduced a whole range of new orders (see chapter 45). The monitoring of all issues concerning offending behaviour and the criminal justice system for 10–17-year olds was made the responsibility of the Youth Justice Board, a quasi-autonomous national agency funded by the Home Office.

Young people leaving care (usually at around the age of 16 before 2001) were hugely over-represented amongst some 'youth problem' groups. The care system was the subject of a thorough and far-reaching review commissioned by the conservative government in June 1996 and resulting in the Utting Report in 1997. The government response proposed new forms of inspection, quality assurance and standards of care under a Quality Protects initiative. Arrangements for young people leaving care were reviewed in a Green Paper, which formed the basis of the 2000 Children (Leaving Care) Act, implemented in October 2001. One of the issues being addressed was that, although the majority of young people not in care experienced extended youth transitions and longer periods of family dependency, care leavers were moved to forms of independent living as early as the age of 16. This was both unsettling and often resulted in disastrous consequences. But, although there were some marginal improvements following the 2000 Act, progress was slow. Finally a further Green Paper, *Care Matters*, was published late in 2006, this time emanating from the DfES where the new Minister for Children, Young People and Families, appointed in 2005, was made responsible for all policy areas concerning children and young people – finally joined up in one place. The Minister was, however, invariably referred to as the Minister for Children, early signs that youth issues may become marginalized.

Everybody Matters (But Some More Than Others)

In September 2003, the government published a Green Paper (*Every Child Matters*) which was to have immense significance for policy development on children and young people. Although it was ostensibly a follow-through of an enquiry into child abuse, it signalled a reconfiguration of the structures of policy at both national, local authority and community levels. Following the consultation on the Green Paper, the 2004 Children Act also heralded the appointment of a Children's Commissioner for England to act as an independent champion for children, although, when appointed, in practice he used his position to comment on the conditions and services offered to vulnerable groups such as young asylum-seekers, and failures adequately to respond to the needs of children and young people, such as those with mental health problems. The Act further widened the responsibilities of the Minister to deal with youth issues previously dealt with by the DoH (teenage pregnancy, the looked-after children system, and family law, but interestingly *not* youth offending). At a local authority level, the Act required local authorities to have a single Director of Children's Services accountable for education *and* social services and the integration of services, and the commissioning of services, through Children's Trusts, which also have charge of the commissioning of Connexions and Youth Offending Teams. At a community level, a range of services for children and young people were to be co-located in Sure Start Children's Centres and Full Service Extended Schools. The Green Paper also announced a new Young People's Fund to promote activities for young people out of school.

Given this new constellation of structures for children, it was clear that some reconfiguration of the Connexions Strategy would have to occur. And during the summer of 2004 the DfES held three (separate) inquiries, which prefaced a Youth Green Paper (*Youth Matters*). One involved a 'top-to-bottom' review of careers education and guidance. Many careers companies felt threatened and marginalized by Connexions where the universal service of guidance for the majority of pupils in schools and colleges received less priority than targeted services for those at risk of disengaging. Schools too thought the service they received had declined and, in that they were embracing a wider 'full service' role for the welfare of pupils, thought the autonomy they were given here could be extended to information and guidance too. The second inquiry concerned a review of 'activities' for young people: 'things to do; places to go' became a mantra which recognized the need to address decades of decline and neglect in youth work. The youth service had been 'transformed' (in theory) by reviews in the late 1990s, but on the ground many youth workers found themselves starved of resources, limping from year to year on short-term contracts, constantly juggling their priorities in search of policy fads with funding opportunities. The DfES Five Year Plan in 2004 had promised a 'youth offer' and this was an opportunity to put some content around what this might involve. Finally, a third group examined services and support for vulnerable young people. The very existence of this group suggested that, despite favourable reviews by august bodies such as the National Audit Office, the bold ambitions of the Connexions Strategy were deemed to be failing. Indeed, no one talked about a Connexions Strategy any more,

only a service, and the Minister for Children went on record suggesting that the days of the Connexions Service may be numbered.

Why it was deemed a failure remains a mystery. Most evidence was positive about its achievements, especially in supporting vulnerable young people, although recognizing that there were areas where improvements could be made. To be sure, there remained confusion about the various roles and responsibilities of front-line workers, the PAs. Cross-referral between the universal and targeted services was poor in many partnerships. Joint working had not been smooth and straightforward and was a basis for conflict as well as cooperation. Conflict also often had to be resolved by front-line workers who sometimes felt exposed and unsupported by managers and/or clear protocols on joint working. Information-sharing was neither widespread nor reliable. Perhaps Connexions had not fulfilled all its ambitions, but, as the National Audit Commission pointed out, it had only been allowed to recruit around a half the number of PAs initially estimated to be needed to carry out its task.

Two major research projects examining Connexions (including one commissioned by the DfES itself) held a dissemination conference early in 2005 and, because there was unanimity amongst the delegates about what *not* to do with Connexions, they sent a communiqué to the DfES warning of the dangers of allowing schools to opt out and recommending that the reconfiguration of Connexions should build on its achievements rather than start again from scratch. After all, the problems it faced would have to be dealt with by whatever service was to succeed it. Yet, despite paying lip-service to 'evidence-based practice', Connexions was significantly weakened by the proposals in the Green Paper *Youth Matters*, especially through the failure to ring-fence its funding within the monies now to be distributed through Children's Trusts. What was most surprising was that a 'strategy' pronounced by the Prime Minister as 'the front-line policy for young people' could be allowed to wither and become marginalized by a junior minister after such a short time, and against the weight of evidence of its success.

Emerging Issues

The consultation process on the Green Paper *Youth Matters* was a sham. The questions were garbled and inappropriate, evidence was again marginalized and ignored, and the proposals in *Youth Matters: Next Steps* were 'carry on, regardless'. Many of the broad proposals were very similar to those in the Connexions Strategy albeit with broader provisions that encompassed, for instance, leisure services. Here, the government advocated the laudable aim of engaging young people in shaping local services. Yet, despite clear opposition to the means through which it proposed this should be done (via Youth Opportunity cards), the government declared its intention to go ahead with a series of pilot schemes anyway. A similar plastic card scheme (Connexions cards) had proved an expensive and disastrous failure, with a market penetration of only around 4 per cent. The government did,

however, promise to introduce legislation to make it a clear 'duty' of local authorities to ensure that young people had access to a wide range of positive activities. Volunteering was also encouraged, with a mix of public and private funds administered by the Russell Commission Implementation Body to promote schemes locally. Despite active lobbying for an expansion of careers education and guidance (CEG) into a more comprehensive all-age service, CEG was instead broadened to 'information, advice and guidance' (IAG), with promises of a mixed media service (including new technologies such as the internet and help-lines), quality standards, and opt-out permissive powers for schools. On targeted support for vulnerable young people, the government promised multi-agency working, a lead professional, a common assessment framework and new patterns of information-sharing. In all this, there was a deathly silence about Personal Advisers and Connexions workers. Its 'failures' were due to be reinvented all over again. Only its brand name remained.

This is a sad story of government reforms proceeding despite evidence and letting an important policy for young people 'accidentally fall' in the reconfiguration of policy for children. It went from being 'our front-line policy' to little more than a badge, reminiscent of the last verse of a children's song: 'Ten green bottles in five short years'.

Guide to Further Sources

Good social policy ought to think comparatively. H. Bradley and J. van Hoof (eds), *Young People in Europe: Labour Markets and Citizenship* (Policy Press, 2005) is a good start, on labour markets.

L. Catan, *Becoming Adult* (Trust for the Centre for Adolescence, 2004) summarizes the largest recent youth research programme funded by the ESRC; B. Coles and C. Lloyd, *Snakes and Ladders* (Joseph Rowntree Foundation, 2007) summarizes the seven-year youth research programme funded by JRF.

The second edition of A. Furlong and F. Cartmel, *Young People and Social Change* (Open University Press, 2006) is a rewritten version of a very influential text. For a biannual compilation of useful statistics on young people, look at J. Coleman and J. Schofield, *Key Data on Adolescence 2005*, 5th edn (Trust for the Centre for Adolescence, 2005).

S. Henderson et al., *Inventing Adulthoods: A Biographical Approach to Youth Transitions* (Sage, 2006) provides a theoretical 'breakthrough' that explores the interface between biography and structure – just add in the social policy condiment yourself (to taste).

Reporting on a specific study conducted in the north-east is R. MacDonald and J. Marsh, *Disconnected Youth. Growing Up in Britain's Poor Neighbourhoods* (Palgrave, 2005), but this does contain excellent reviews of debates around young people, the underclass and social exclusion.

The Green Paper proposing fundamental reform to youth policy, DfES, *Youth Matters*, Cm 6629 (HMSO, 2005), can be found at <http://www.everychildmatters.gov.uk/_files/Youth%20Matters.pdf>. This is a key policy document – if fundamentally flawed.

DfES, *Youth Matters: Next Steps* (HMSO, 2005), at <http://www.dfes.gov.uk/publications/youth/pdf/Next%20Steps.pdf> proposes, in effect: 'carry on regardless – ignore the evidence and the feedback – document'.

Chapter 49

Older People

Alan Walker and Tony Maltby

Overview

- The very meaning and nature of later life, old age and 'retirement' is changing in this new century.
- Older people have been a major focus of social policy since the early part of the twentieth century.
- The UK is an ageing society as a result of falling fertility rates and increasing longevity.
- Older people do not conform to the caricature of passive burdens.
- It is likely that in future the government will be responsible for provision of a more generous non-means-tested flat rate basic pension, with the earnings-related element being provided through a private sector or state-run savings scheme.

Introduction

Older people have always been a major focus for social policy and, because the UK is an ageing society, their importance to the subject is increasing further. In 2005 the government produced a comprehensive strategy for social policy on old age in *Opportunity Age* (DWP, 2005). In common with other Western societies, Britain is a country in which ageism and age discrimination are widespread, direct and indirect. These have not received, until very recently, the same sustained attention as those arising from sex and 'race' discrimination. At the time of writing, the 2006 Employment Equality (Age) legislation has just been implemented. It covers all ages yet will have a big effect upon the social policy of later life. Therefore, in this brief overview of key social policy issues affecting older people, we will focus on age discrimination, particularly its impact on the labour market. The two other key issues dealt with here are pensions and social care.

Who Are 'Older People'?

Before the advent of public pension systems, workers relied on the benevolence of their employers to provide occupational pensions and, in the late nineteenth century, it was common for people to work until their health failed rather than there being a fixed retirement age. The first state pension was introduced in 1908, with a pension age of 70, reduced to 65 in 1925, and in 1940, the pension age for women was cut to 60.

Table 49.1 Age groups as a proportion of total UK population (percentages)

Ages	2000	2011	2021	2031	2041	2051	2061	2071
0–14	18.2	17.0	16.5	16.0	15.4	15.3	15.1	14.9
15–29	19.0	19.8	18.1	17.2	17.2	16.8	16.4	16.4
30–44	22.5	20.3	19.8	19.6	18.3	18.3	18.3	17.8
45–59	19.3	19.9	20.0	17.9	19.0	18.0	17.7	17.9
60–74	13.4	15.0	16.1	17.6	16.1	16.6	17.0	16.2
75 & over	7.6	8.0	9.5	11.6	13.9	15.0	15.4	16.7
Persons (1,000s)	59,835	61,892	64,727	67,013	68,353	69,252	69,858	70,481
All ages	100.0	100.0	100.0	100.0	100.0	100.0	100.0	100.0

Source: Government Actuary Department mid-2004-based principal projections.

Following the recommendations of the Beveridge Report, the different pension ages (65 for men and 60 for women) were maintained. In the November 1993 Budget, the government announced that the state pension age was to be equalized at 65 and it would be phased in over ten years commencing in 2010. Thus, for much of the post-war period, old age in Britain has been defined statistically as those over the state pension ages – or those aged 65 and over. However, in an attempt to disassociate old age with receipt of a state pension and the pejorative correlation with dependency, from 1997 onwards much of the policy literature has used the age of 50 as the 'start' of old age. This chapter adopts the same definition.

Table 49.1 shows the proportion of the total population made up by different age groups, and the projected expansion in the numbers of older people. The two most important socio-demographic factors underlying population ageing are falling fertility rates and increasing longevity. At the turn of the twentieth century, those aged 65 and over comprised just 4.7 per cent of the population and those aged 80 and over a tiny 0.3 per cent. Presently, there are some 9.65 million people over 65 (comprising 16 per cent of the population) and nearly 2.7 million over 80, represent-ing just over 4 per cent of the population. Projections indicate these will rise so that the proportion of those over 80 will comprise 5.5 per cent in 2020 and 9 per cent in 2041 of the total population. Projections indicate that, by 2031, those aged 50–59 will comprise 28.6 per cent of the population and those aged over 85, 7.9 per cent.

At successively older ages, the proportion of women increasingly outstrips that of men – a result of the higher death rates among men. In 2005, 49 per cent of those aged 0–24 were women, for the 25–64 age group it was 50 per cent, for the 65–74 group 53 per cent, for the 75–84 group 59 per cent and for those aged 85 and over it was 70 per cent. Female life expectancy (at birth) exceeds the male rate by 4.4 years and, although male life expectancy is projected to improve over the next forty-five years, so will women's. Yet the gap is projected to narrow. By the year 2040, the differential will be 3.5 years (82.4 years for men and 85.9 years for women). The majority of men aged 75 and over are married (62 per cent) whereas the majority of older women are widowed, reaching 79 per cent for those aged over 85. Among black and minority ethnic groups the proportion of older people currently is much smaller than that of the white population – only 3.5 per cent aged 50 and over in 2001.

Table 49.2 Labour force participation rates of older men and women in Britain, 1951–2002

	1951	1961	1971	1981	1985	1990	1995	2000	2002
Men									
55–59	95.0	97.1	95.3	89.4	82.0	81.0	73.7	74.8	76.1
60–64	87.7	91.0	86.6	69.3	54.4	54.4	50.1	50.3	50.8
65+	31.1	25.0	23.5	10.3	8.2	8.6	8.2	7.9	8.0
Women									
55–59	29.1	39.2	50.9	53.4	52.1	54.9	55.7	57.6	59.6
60–64	14.1	19.7	28.8	23.3	18.9	22.7	25.0	25.9	28.5
65+	4.1	4.6	6.3	3.7	3.0	3.3	3.2	3.4	3.5

Sources: 1951–71, Census of Population for England and Wales and for Scotland; 1975–2002, Department of Employment, Gazette (various); UK Labour Force Survey.

Of course, population ageing is a positive sign of social and economic development, and this includes the role of social policy in combating many of the diseases that cut short people's lives in previous centuries. However, the growing numbers of older people have not always been viewed in such a positive light. What is overlooked is that 'old age' was defined (or in sociological terms 'socially constructed') in precise age categories by social policy (i.e. pension policy) and, therefore, it can be redefined as circumstances change. Thus older people themselves do not readily conform to their caricature as passive burdens; the majority remain active, often making important contributions within families (for example, to childcare), and reject discriminatory labels such as 'the elderly' in favour of more active ones such as older people or senior citizens (Walker and Maltby 1996).

Age Discrimination in the Labour Market

One of the main sources of exclusion is the labour market. Mindful of the decline in the numbers of young people entering employment and the cost of pensions, the government is currently running campaigns to try to persuade employers to recruit or retain older workers through the New Deal 50+, 'Pathways to Work' and other similar programmes. As table 49.2 shows, historically only a minority of men, in particular, were 'retiring' in the conventional sense of leaving work on or close to their sixty-fifth birthday. The majority left employment at earlier ages and reached the statutory pension age in a variety of non-employed statuses, such as unemployment, long-term sickness or disability and early retirement. The main factors explaining this growth of early exit among British men are demand-related. For many older workers, the loss of a job in their fifties or even late forties meant that they never re-entered employment.

The dramatic growth of early retirement since the mid-1970s has contributed to a redefinition of older people into two groups instead of one. The 'third age' covers those aged 50–74 and the 'fourth age' comprises those aged 75 and over. This distinction is sometimes used to imply that the former 'young old' are active while the latter 'old old' are passive, but this is grossly misleading. More recently, this trend towards early exit is being reversed (see table 49.3),

Table 49.3 Percentage of each age group in employment Great Britain (spring)

	1999	2002	2003	2004	2005	2006
Men						
16–24	63.2	63.0	61.4	62.3	60.0	57.6
25–49	87.8	88.2	88.4	88.4	88.3	88.4
50–65	68.6	69.9	71.8	71.9	72.4	72.8
65+	7.6	7.5	8.6	8.6	9.0	9.6
Women						
16–24	58.9	59.6	58.1	58.5	56.8	56.6
25–49	73.3	74.2	74.4	74.4	75.1	75.1
50–60	63.1	65.6	67.6	67.9	68.4	68.4
60+	8.1	9.0	8.9	9.9	10.5	11.1

Source: Labour Force Survey.

partially as a result of the Labour government's policy approach but more especially the result of recent economic growth. Even so, 1.3 million people over 50 are claiming incapacity benefits whilst vacancies remain unfilled.

Research to date has shown that people aged 50–60 face considerable discrimination from employers. For example, age restrictions in job advertisements are a common barrier to employment. Employers often restrict access to training programmes to workers under the age of 50. Yet when employers are asked to rank the most important factors discouraging the recruitment of older workers, 'lack of appropriate skills' comes top. There is, it seems, a sort of self-fulfilling prophecy at work here. Many employers have been shown to hold stereotypical attitudes towards older workers; for example, that they are hard to train, are too cautious, cannot adapt to new technology and are inflexible. Such prejudices are not supported by research evidence, but they continue to exert a powerful influence over the life-chances of people in their third age. However, the recent implementation of a European Directive has meant that the government was required to enact anti-age

discrimination legislation by 2006. The 2006 Equal Employment (Age) Regulations (henceforth Age Regulations) came into force on 1 October 2006 and cover age discrimination in employment and training across the whole age range. Yet the legislation will be more keenly felt among older people. The Age Regulations introduce a number of important new measures, the most controversial of which is a default retirement age of 65. In the realm of training, employers can still exclude older workers when a case can be made that such exclusion is 'in the interest of business'. Many experts in the field suggest that the day-to-day application of the legislation will largely be determined as case law builds up. Despite this, the main effect of the legislation will be cultural and may lead to a change in attitudes and conventions similar to those changes in attitudes associated with sex, disability and 'race' and, more recently, sexuality.

Pensions and Poverty in Old Age

Pensions are one of the central social policy issues, but they are also one of the most contentious because of their sheer scale and their escalating cost in an ageing society. Social security is by far the largest single expenditure programme, and over half of it is devoted to older people (see chapter 38).

Despite this, there is still a close association between low incomes and poverty and old age. Beveridge had intended that the national insurance (NI) basic pension (BP) scheme would overcome such poverty. Occupational pensions have raised the living standards of many pensioners, particularly couples, and the government has reduced the benefits of unemployed people more drastically than those of pensioners. Nonetheless, older people still form one of the largest groups living in poverty in the UK, and they are more likely to be poor than older people in other comparable EU countries (Walker and Maltby 1996). Many older people continue to live in poverty, defined by the government as living below 60 per cent of average (median) income after housing costs. Currently there are 2 million pensioners living in households with below 60 per cent median income before housing costs. However, pensioners were over-represented in the bottom two quintiles of the income distribution and, for pensioner couples, the older the age group of the head the more likely they were to be in the bottom two income quintiles of the income distribution. This reflects the increased likelihood of younger cohorts of pensioners having access to an occupational pension. Reflecting the higher proportion in the over-65 age cohorts owning their own home outright (68 per cent of pensioners compared to 28 per cent of the population as a whole), pensioners tended to be higher up the income distribution after housing costs. Single female pensioners were more likely to have lower incomes than their male comparators, reflecting the gendered nature of the occupational pensions structures. Similarly, those pensioners from an ethnic minority group were also likely to be at risk of low income.

Other data, derived from the Pensioner Income Series, shows that the incomes of the top 20 per cent of pensioners have increased by 76 per cent since 1979, whereas those of the lowest 20 per cent have risen by only 28 per cent. Indeed, average net income of pensioners grew by 64 per cent in real terms between 1979 and 1996/7 compared to 36 per cent for total average earnings for the same period, attributable to the increasing numbers of (mainly male) pensioners retiring with good occupational pensions.

The provision of pensions has played a crucial role in the creation of mass retirement, allowing employers to terminate working lives and to spread the cost over the whole population of working age. Beveridge had intended that a fund would be built up from the payments of contributions by employers and employees, yet it was decided to introduce the BP immediately, resulting in NI being financed on a pay-as-you-go (PAYG) basis (i.e. the NI contributions of those in employment go to pay the pensions of those in retirement). In effect, there is a social contract between the generations: those in employment pay taxes and contributions to fund the pensions of the previous generation in the expectation that the succeeding generations would do the same for them. Other important elements of state welfare provision, such as the NHS and social services, are financed on a similar basis.

In 1980, the Thatcher government, intent on cutting public expenditure, altered the up-rating link for the NI pension from earnings to prices, effectively reducing the value of the basic pension by more than one-third. This cut undermined younger generations' confidence in the state pension system, encouraging them to invest in private pensions. It is a salutary fact that, if this trend were to continue, the BP would be worth less than 10 per cent of average earnings in 2020. The Blair governments implemented further changes to the pensions system by enhancing the 'partner-ship' between the state and private sector, so that public expenditure by the state on pensions will shift towards the private sector. Improvements in the position of the poorest pensioners was seen as a priority through provision of the (means-tested) Minimum Income Guarantee (MIG), which became Pension Credit in 2005.

Pension Credit is made up of two compo-nents: a guarantee and a savings credit. The former raises the incomes of those pensioner couples whose pension and savings is less than £154 per week (and single pensioners with less than £100 per week) to these levels. Higher rates apply to those with disabilities, and all those 60 and over can claim. In May 2006, following a major review of pensions undertaken by the government-appointed Turner Commission, another White Paper on pensions, *Security in Retirement: Towards a New Pensions System* was pub-lished, broadly reflecting the Turner Com-mission's findings, and was latterly passed into law. In brief, the findings were that the current system should be simplified and means-testing kept to a minimum. It sug-gested that the BP should be uprated in line with national average earnings (rather than with the retail prices index) and that the current State Second Pension (which replaced SERPS) should become a flat rate supplement to BP. Further, it encouraged a raising of the state pension age incremen-tally to 68 by 2050 (the government reduced this to 2046) and the introduction of a new National Pension Savings Scheme (NPSS) from 2010.

Long-term Care

It is commonly assumed that older people, particularly those in their fourth age, are physically dependent. In fact, the vast majority of them are active and able to look after themselves without assistance from others – and increasingly so. For example,

75 per cent of those aged 90 and over were living in private households in 2001. The Community Care Statistics (2006) show the number of supported residents fell by 3 per cent on the previous year, despite growing numbers among these cohorts. Among people aged 80 and over, only 15 per cent are resident in care homes, nursing homes or hospitals, and for those aged 90 and over the proportion is 36 per cent. However, there is an association between advanced old age and disability and, because women live longer than men, they are more likely than men to be disabled. The numbers of women aged 80 and over resident in homes and hospitals is nearly five times that of men.

For most of the post-war period, the policy favoured by successive governments has been community care. In reality this has meant that families have been by far the main source of care for disabled older people and others needing support. Social policy researchers have demonstrated that 'family' care usually means care by female kin, although, in couples, care by older male spouses is not uncommon. However, socio-demographic changes are placing the family-based system of care under increas-ing strain. Greater longevity means that some caring relations across the genera-tions are being extended, leading to a wid-ening 'care gap' between the need for care among older people and the supply of both family care and formal care from the public, private and voluntary sectors.

The government's response in the 1980s to this growth in demand was to encourage the expansion of the private sector. This was achieved by means of social security subsidies for older people living on income support to enter private homes, while holding down expenditure on public serv-ices. The numbers of older people entering private residential homes nearly doubled between 1979 and 1984, and by 1994 had increased fivefold. Unfortunately, as a con-sequence, the social security budget for board and lodging payments rose from £10 million in 1978 to over £2,000 million in 1993. Under the 1990 NHS and Community Care Act, to curtail these escalating costs, local authorities were made purchasers of services from the private and voluntary sectors instead of direct providers.

Although additional resources were allocated to local authorities for the implementation of the 1990 Act, they were insufficient to keep pace with rising needs. There was an urgent need for a radical reappraisal of long-term care policy and the Royal Commission on Long Term Care, and its report (*With Respect to Old Age*) was published in 1999. This was a very progressive document and was one of the first to banish the notion that there was a demographic time bomb and that older people were a 'burden'. It suggested, in a nutshell, that the provision of long-term care should be split between living costs, housing costs and personal care. Personal care, it suggested, should be provided from general taxation according to need and the other costs according to a means-test. In 2000 the response was presented within the NHS Plan, which brought with it a distinction between nursing care that would be provided free (and paid by general taxation) and personal care, which would not. In Scotland, both would be provided free at the point of use. In March 2001, the National Service Framework (NSF) for older people was published. It sets out eight 'standards' addressing the healthcare needs of older people. Principal among these is the rooting out of age discrimination in the delivery of healthcare, the provision of person-centred care, promoting health and independence for older people and matching services to individual needs.

Emerging Issues

This chapter has emphasized that older people themselves do not readily conform to their caricature as passive burdens, often the popular perception. Surveys in Britain and other EU countries show a very different picture: the majority remain active, often making important contributions within families (for example, to childcare), and reject discriminatory labels such as 'the elderly' in favour of more active ones such as older people or senior citizens (Walker and Maltby 1996). Older people favour inclusion in society rather than the exclusion that sometimes afflicts them. When considering the older workforce, the main issue will be the effect of the Age Regulations. We may see a small yet significant cultural change in attitudes and conventions similar to those associated with sex, disability and 'race' and sexuality. However, this is dependent upon how case law develops. When considering pensions policy, it is clear that, at least for the next ten years or so, the state will only be responsible for provision of a non-means-tested flat rate BP, with the earnings-related element being provided through NPSS and other privately funded schemes (e.g. occupational pensions). In the field of the health and social care of older people, the push for the promotion of the eight NSF 'standards' to encourage the development of 'active ageing' will be the dominant priority for policy.

Guide to Further Sources

A 'must read' for all students of social policy is B. Bytheway, *Ageism* (Open University Press, 1995). This book contains some challenging and thought-provoking material. An excellent overview and research resource, containing descriptive text and many useful tables and diagrams, is E. Soule, P. Babb, M. Evandrou,

S. Balchin and L. Zealey (eds), *Focus on Older People* (Palgrave Macmillan/ HMSO, 2005). This is also available online as a pdf file.

J. A. Vincent, C. Phillipson and M. Downs (eds), *The Futures of Old Age* (Sage/ British Society of Gerontology, 2006) provides an up-to-date analysis addressing some of the major contemporary themes by some key social gerontologists.

A. C. Walker and C. Hagan Hennessy (eds), *Growing Older: Quality of Life in Old Age* (Open University Press, 2005) is a general overview of the path-breaking research conducted through the ESRC's *Growing Older* Programme.

S. Arber and J. Ginn (eds), *Connecting Gender and Ageing* (Open University Press, 1995) contains readings on the important issue of the gendered nature of old age. A. Walker and T. Maltby, *Ageing Europe* (Open University Press, 1996) is a general introductory comparative analysis of ageing and social policy in different EU countries.

Look at section 3, in particular, of L. Bauld, K. Clarke and T. Maltby (eds), *Social Policy Review 18. Analysis and Debate in Social Policy 2006* (Policy Press, 2006), which focuses on issues relating to 'older workers'.

Chapter 50

Disability

Mark Priestley

Overview

- There has been growing interest and development in disability policy since the 1970s.
- Disability has been viewed increasingly as an issue of human rights, citizenship and equality rather than one of care and rehabilitation.
- The claims and voices of the disabled people's movement have been instrumental in bringing about this change.
- Disabled people have often been active welfare consumers, taking control of resources to manage the support they need in place of traditional services.
- More countries have introduced policies to counter disability discrimination, based on civil and human rights, but legislation alone is insufficient to guarantee full equality.
- Transnational governance has become increased through institutions such as the European Community and the United Nations.

Introduction

Disability became increasingly prominent in policy debates during the latter part of the twentieth century, both in the UK and globally, culminating with agreement in 2006 on a United Nations Convention to protect the rights of disabled people throughout the world. The rising prominence of disability has been characterized by three significant themes. First, there has been a dramatic shift of policy thinking. Where disability was once seen as a deficiency within the person, it is now more likely to be viewed as a form of discrimination arising from deficiencies in society.

Second, there has been a corresponding move from policies for care and financial compensation towards policies for human rights and the removal of barriers to social equality. Third, and underpinning these developments, there has been a groundswell of self-organization amongst disabled people themselves, leading to greater representation in policy claims and greater involvement in the production of welfare.

Taking the first of these themes, most contemporary debates begin from a distinction between different models of disability, or different ways of thinking about the needs of disabled people. Traditional policy approaches often treated disability as an individual problem caused by physical, sensory or cognitive impairment. The solution was either to treat the person (through improved medical and rehabilitation services) or to compensate them for their 'limitations' (by arranging less valued social roles, such as sheltered employment, residential care, social security payments and so on). Thus, both the assumed cause of the problem and the policy response focused on the individual. The social model of disability adopts a different approach. From this perspective, the disadvantage experienced by disabled people is attributed to limitations in society rather than limitations within the person. As Oliver puts it:

> [D]isability, according to the social model, is all the things that impose restrictions on disabled people; ranging from individual prejudice to institutional discrimination, from inaccessible buildings to unusable transport systems, from segregated education to excluding work arrangements, and so on. Further, the consequences of this failure do not simply and randomly fall on individuals but systematically upon disabled people as a group who experience this failure as discrimination institutionalised throughout society.
>
> (1996: 33)

Until recently, this kind of thinking remained a fringe concern in policy-making – strongly advocated by disability activists (nationally and internationally) but at the margins of the policy community. By contrast, there is now much talk about the 'social model of disability' within policy institutions and within some parts of government. However, disability continues to raise a number of very challenging and controversial policy debates.

The Historical Context: Disability as an Administrative Category

Some understanding of history is essential in grasping the relationship between disabled people, social policy and the state. Today, in the UK and other developed economies, almost all aspects of disabled people's lives are subject to some kind of distinctive public policy (for example, there are specific policies concerning disabled people's education, health, housing, transport, employment, welfare benefits, family life and civil rights). Yet, prior to the emergence of the welfare state, people with significant impairments would have been largely undifferentiated from the greater mass of 'the poor'. A key point then is to understand why disabled people exist as a separate category for policy-makers at all.

Within critical disability studies, social model theorists evoked a broadly materialist account of British history to show how the growth of urban industrial capitalism created disability as a welfare 'problem' for the state. These arguments suggest that the emergence of competitive wage labour markets and factory production methods excluded many people with impairments from paid work and consigned increasing numbers to lives of poverty and economic dependency. As other policy historians have shown, the state's role in facilitating early industrial capitalism involved vigorous social measures to control the labour force and to remove incentives for idleness amongst the mass of the population. In this context, a key development for disabled people was the distinction made between the 'impotent' and the 'able-bodied' poor (or the 'deserving' and 'undeserving'). Whilst the idle poor might be rigorously disciplined, those deemed 'unable to work' were increasingly identified for the provision of limited welfare. The earliest English definitions of those 'not able to work' did not mention people with impairments, but by the time of the first Poor Law in 1601 it was already clear that a new category of disabled people was emerging – and that *inability to work* would become the key to deciding who was, and who was not, disabled.

Policing this distinction, and thereby entitlement to public assistance, required a whole new system of surveillance, regulation and control which brought responsibility for disabled people's welfare increasingly from the private into the public domain. It is not necessary to chart this history in any great detail here, and some of the key reading at the end of the chapter provides excellent overviews (for a British history, see Borsay 2005). Stone (1984) shows how disability has functioned as an important administrative category in the control of labour and in access to public welfare. In particular, she highlights the challenges that policy-makers face in providing any fixed definition of who disabled people really are. A key problem here is that the kind of disability definitions developed in countries like the UK, Germany or the United States have been interpreted differently in different circumstances.

A useful example is to consider why large numbers of disabled people considered 'unable to work' during times of high unemployment (like the 1930s) were quickly drafted into the labour force at times of greater need (for example, in munitions factories during the Second World War). Similar patterns are evident in more recent policy debates; for example, many of those deemed 'unable to work', and claiming disability benefits, in the lean times of the late 1970s and early 1980s were targeted in vigorous return-to-work policies under New Labour from 1997 onwards. Thus, it is important to view disability and disabled people as policy categories that are more flexible than fixed, determined not so much by a person's biology as by social, economic and political circumstances.

Policy Claims: The Disabled People's Movement

Although state responses to the needs of disabled people have been driven by economic and political forces, they have also been shaped by the claims and welfare struggles of disabled people themselves. Disability policy claims and protests have a long history, but the origins of the modern disabled people's movement lie in the political and welfare struggles of the late 1960s and 1970s. Since the early 1980s, disability activists have organized on an international scale under the umbrella of Disabled Peoples' International, which aims 'to promote the human rights of disabled people through full participation, equalization of opportunities, and development'. Within this global alliance, national and regional assemblies represent the interests of disabled people in more than 130 countries.

The development of disabled people's organizations in the USA, the UK and parts of mainland Europe has been well documented in the disability studies literature (see Campbell and Oliver's 1996 book for some fascinating insights into developments in Britain). There has been less awareness until recently about developments elsewhere, yet disabled people's organizations have been very active in developing countries. In recent years, high-profile initiatives like the African and Asia-Pacific 'Decades of Disabled People' have provided opportunities for self-advocacy and human rights campaigns with a significant impact on policy-making in those regions.

The claims of disabled people's organizations have focused on influencing both the content of social policies and the processes through which they are developed. Four underlying principles are worthy of note. First, there has been strong advocacy for the principle of 'nothing about us without us' (see Charlton 1998). Here the emphasis has been on ensuring that disabled people secure a voice in discussions about policies that affect them. Where such debates would once have been dominated by medical or social work professionals, and by welfare charities, it is now rare to find disability policy forums that do not involve disabled people as significant actors. Second, there have been demands to direct policy investment towards the removal of barriers that prevent disabled people from participating fully and equally in society (for example, the removal of physical barriers in the built environment or social barriers arising from negative public attitudes).

Third, and more specifically, there has been strong advocacy for policies that favour 'rights not charity'. Again there has been very significant success – for example with the introduction of disability anti-discrimination legislation in Europe and the UK, and with the introduction of a United Nations Convention. Finally, there have been claims to the greater involvement of disabled people in producing their own welfare solutions, resulting in policy changes towards greater choice and control for disabled people over their everyday lives. These two specific themes merit some further discussion.

Independent Living – New Modes of Welfare Production

The concept of independent living has been a prominent theme in disabled people's self-organization, and in claims to greater involvement in the production of welfare. Many of the early struggles were aimed at freeing disabled people from oppressive long-term residential institutions and developing new mechanisms to support community living. In Britain, as in many other countries, there have been significant closures of traditional institutions and the widespread implementation of 'community care'. However, policy claims have extended beyond this, targeting the lack of choice and control that many disabled people experience in their everyday lives and the power of professionals and social care agencies.

The movement for independent living has therefore been a key voice, not only challenging traditional social care policies, but offering new alternatives to support disabled people in practical ways. In particular,

this has involved claims to greater control over the financial resources for social care. Here the key claim has been to place more resources in the hands of disabled people themselves to organize and purchase their own support for daily living rather than relying on pre-defined 'services' (for example, by employing personal assistants to provide individual support with care and social activities rather than attending a day centre or receiving home help from a local social services department). Early independent living projects in Britain, Scandinavia and the USA were often run and controlled by disabled people themselves and provided new ways of thinking about welfare – blurring the traditional boundaries between purchasers, providers and consumers (see Barnes and Mercer 2006).

The success of such schemes, in offering disabled people more choice and control, gave rise to the emergence of new policies for 'direct payments', allowing people to arrange and purchase their own care and support in place of the social services they might otherwise be entitled to. Direct payments have brought new opportunities for self-determination and independent living and feature prominently in British government strategy. Although take-up remains relatively low and varies greatly in different parts of the country, there are ambitious expectations within government that individualized budgets might become the mechanism of choice for people seeking support to live independently. This in turn raises considerable questions about the future of traditional 'services' and the viability of long-standing policy investments in some public services and institutions.

Non-Discrimination: Policies for Civil Rights

As highlighted earlier, the rapid development of civil rights and anti-discrimination legislation has been a key feature of policy development in recent years, although different countries have taken different approaches (see Breslin and Yee 2002). While non-discrimination legislation was secured in the USA in 1990 (via the Americans with Disabilities Act) there was resistance to similar policies in the UK, especially from those concerned that providing equal rights for disabled people might impose unbearable costs on employers and service providers and thereby undermine the UK's economic competitiveness. However, there was also mounting evidence that disabled people experienced discrimination as being institutionalized throughout society and, by the mid-1990s, the government was persuaded to bring forward legislation.

It is not necessary to cover all the details of the Disability Discrimination Act here, but it is helpful to understand some of the basic policy principles. From the outset, it became illegal for employers to discriminate against disabled employees or for service providers to treat disabled customers less favourably, but only insofar as this might be seen as 'reasonable' or 'justified' (for example, not too costly for the employer). Over time, the legislation has been both strengthened and extended, most notably to cover discrimination in education and in requiring business premises and transport services to become more accessible.

In 2006, a more binding and general equality duty was placed on public authorities, mirroring policies to tackle institutional racism and gender inequalities. This means that all public bodies (such as government departments, local authorities, health trusts, schools and colleges, etc.) now have a duty to promote positive attitudes and equality for disabled people and to eliminate disability discrimination. There is also a greater emphasis on monitoring disability equality and encouraging participation by disabled people in public life. These developments shift greater responsibility onto public bodies to show how

equality is being promoted rather than relying on disabled people to prove that they have been discriminated against.

The mere presence of anti-discrimination legislation and guidance has little impact without enforcement. In Britain this was achieved with the creation of the Disability Rights Commission in 2000 as an independent body to promote disability equality in England, Scotland and Wales (in Northern Ireland a single body covered both disability equality and other dimensions of difference and discrimination). There have been significant debates about the extent to which disability discrimination policy should be included within a single equality agenda and, in 2006, the Equality Act paved the way for the abolition of the DRC and its incorporation within a new Commission for Equality and Human Rights. Although the move to mainstream disability issues has been widely welcomed, there remain concerns that established lobby groups (such as those representing gender or race equality) might overshadow the specific policy claims of disabled people.

The rights-based approach to policy shares much with the social model of disability discussed earlier but, on its own, offers a less radical strategy. The social model (as defined by its early authors) focused on the structural basis for disabled people's oppression, arising from the social relations of production and reproduction in modern capitalist societies. The implication was that real change could never be achieved without political struggle to challenge the very basis of disabling societies and institutions. By contrast, legal rights activists drew more heavily on a 'minority group approach' that emphasized claims within existing legal frameworks and constitutional law. Both social model and rights-based approaches recognize disability as a human rights issue, but the social model suggests that disability requires more far-reaching social and economic change to solve the problems disabled people face.

Globalization and Governance: UN and EU Influences

There are at least half a billion disabled people in the world – one in ten of the population – and this number is set to rise dramatically. Although the issues facing disabled people in rich technological countries, with developed welfare provision, are often different from those in poorer countries, disabled people remain amongst the poorest of the poor throughout the world. Access to resources is highly gendered, and the needs of disabled women and girls merit specific attention. Generational issues are also important and reduced life-chances for disabled children and disabled elders are evident. Global problems demand global responses and the increasing significance of transnational disability policy-making is particularly evident in the European Community and the United Nations.

There was little evidence of disability debates in the early development of European policy-making, although the mid-1970s saw some limited action programmes on vocational and social integration and a review of national policies. By the early 1980s there were signs of a broader socio-economic understanding (including acknowledgement that disabled people are amongst those most adversely affected by the economic cycle of a capitalist free market). The development of European disability policy since then has been marked by two key themes – a preoccupation with employment and the emergence of a rights-based approach. After continuing pressure from disability organizations, disabled people were finally made 'visible' as European citizens in the Amsterdam Treaty of 1997. Legal recognition established disabled people's claims as a legitimate concern of the European legislature, leading to the introduction of the first European disability rights legislation outlawing discrimination in employment.

As mentioned at the outset, similar developments have been apparent within the United Nations. It was in 1975 that the UN made its first Declaration on the Rights of Disabled Persons and 1981 was proclaimed International Year of Disabled Persons. In 1985, the Universal Declaration of Human Rights was extended to include disabled people and work began on a longer-term strategy under the slogan 'towards a society for all'. The adoption in 1993 of international *Rules on the Equalization of Opportunities for Disabled Persons* highlighted disabled people's participation in key areas of life (accessibility, education, employment, income, family life, culture, recreation and religion) and led more and more states to introduce anti-discriminatory legislation. However, the picture remains patchy, with different policy approaches and traditions in different countries, and varying levels of recognition and involvement for disabled people themselves in the policy-making process.

Emerging Issues

The passage, in 2006, of a new United Nations Convention has raised expectations and responsibilities for states across the world to ensure the participation and equality of disabled people in society. There has been much goodwill from governments but also major questions about the policy implications. Whilst there are apparently genuine commitments to make real positive changes to the human and social rights of disabled people, there are also concerns about the economic challenges. In resource-poor countries, the enormity of poverty reduction and human development challenges means that disabled people are often overlooked or under-valued in policy investments. In more economically developed welfare states, there are also financial pressures exacerbated by the challenges of disability equality.

There are major concerns about the number of people in developed economies who are out of work and claiming disability benefits (e.g. an estimated 2.7 million people on incapacity benefits in Britain) and a desire to 'help' them into work through benefits and support systems. For example, welfare reform proposals introduced in the British Parliament in 2006 identified disabled people as a key group (alongside lone parents and older workers). Policy objectives include supporting more people to remain in work and moving more disabled people from benefits into work. A much more proactive approach to gatekeeping benefits is likely for all but those with the most complex and severe impairments. The aim is clearly to reduce the number of people claiming disability benefits whilst being seen to increase support for 'severely disabled' people.

As discussed in this chapter, the claims of the disabled people's movement have been key to dramatic changes in the way we think about and develop disability policy. Yet, despite this history and substantial policy successes, or perhaps because of them, there are concerns about the future. As disability is mainstreamed within the single equality agenda, there may be fewer 'places at the table' of policy-making for disabled people but also greater scope for advocacy alliances with other oppressed groups.

Guide to Further Sources

For historical discussion of disability policy in modern welfare states, it would be useful to look at both D. Stone, *The Disabled State* (Temple University Press, 1984) and A. Borsay, *Disability and Social Policy in Britain Since 1750: A History of Exclusion* (Palgrave Macmillan, 2005). The former is helpful in understanding the relationship between disabled people, welfare and the state, while the latter provides a comprehensive history of policy development in Britain.

D. Mabbett, 'The development of rights-based social policy in the European Union: the example of disability rights,' *JCMS: Journal of Common Market Studies* 43/1 (2005): 97–120, shows how disability emerged in European policy-making, while M. Breslin and S. Yee (eds), *Disability Rights Law and Policy: International and National Perspectives* (Transnational, 2002) provides a number of useful contributions on rights-based policies across the world. The following three books all provide important insights into the emergence of disabled people's self-organization and the development of user-led policy alternatives to support independent living: C. Barnes and G. Mercer, *Independent Futures: Creating User-Led Disability Services in a Disabling Society* (Policy Press, 2006); J. Campbell and M. Oliver, *Disability Politics: Understanding Our Past, Changing Our Future* (Routledge, 1996); J. Charlton, *Nothing About Us Without Us: Disability Oppression and Empowerment* (University of California Press, 1998).

M. Oliver, *Understanding Disability: From Theory to Practice* (Macmillan, 1996) is useful as an introduction to different models of disability and their connection to theory and policy. The book also provides useful pointers to some of the influential ideas and writings that influenced policy change. M. Priestley, *Disability: A Life Course Approach* (Polity, 2003) links different disability models and theory with policy debates, both internationally and across the life course, and offers further learning resources for students.

There are also a number of established academic journals addressing disability issues in a diverse and critical way that would provide a wider reading of contemporary debates. Of these *Disability & Society* is widely regarded as the leading international title. Online, the Disability Archive UK also provides free access to several hundred papers by disability activists and researchers at <www.leeds.ac.uk/disability-studies> and is well worth a visit.

Chapter 51

Migrants and Asylum-seekers

Alice Bloch

Overview

- Britain has a long history of migration and ethnic diversity.
- People migrate for economic reasons, for social and familial reasons and/or to escape persecution, human rights abuses, war and conflict.
- Immigration and asylum policy has responded to public discourse focusing on different migrant groups at different times. Policy has been concerned with curbing immigration and is racialized.
- The links between immigration and social welfare became established as early as 1905 and are still interconnected.
- Immigration and asylum policy has resulted in a hierarchy of rights where some groups are included while others have been increasingly excluded from society.

Introduction

The term 'migrant' is used to describe both internal and international migrants. Internal migrants are people who move within the borders of a state, while international migrants move across international borders. The focus of this chapter is on international migration and social policy responses to migration and migrants. Though migration is often portrayed as a relatively recent phenomenon, Britain does in fact have a long history of migration and of ethnic diversity. Due to limitations in transportation technologies, early migration tended to be from other European countries, although as early as the sixteenth century, Africans were brought to Britain as slaves. Some migrants came to Britain for economic reasons; some,

like the French Huguenots, came as a consequence of religious persecution; while others came to Britain to join family members. During the nineteenth century, most migration to Britain continued to be from Europe. Migrants from Ireland formed the largest minority group, with migration from Ireland growing rapidly during the potato famine in the mid-nineteenth century. Britain also attracted migrants because it was the first industrial country, and so the growing economy provided economic opportunities for new migrants. By the start of the twentieth century, there were small numbers of Chinese, African, Indian and Caribbean migrants who had come as students, seafarers, performers and business people, as well as a diverse European migrant population, with the greatest numbers coming from Ireland, Germany, Poland and Russia.

A greater diversity of origin among migrants really began in the post-Second World War period, with migrants from colonial and Commonwealth countries coming to Britain for employment and then family reunion. Contemporary migration is a global phenomenon, which has been facilitated by globalization and improvements in transportation technologies. Global inequalities, the needs of the global economy, changing family structures including transnational families, war, conflict and human rights abuses all contribute to migration. The consequence has been increasing numbers of global migrants and an even greater ethnic diversity in countries of migrant settlement and Britain is no exception to this global trend. At the time of the 2001 Census, 7.9 per cent of the UK population described themselves belonging to an ethnic group other than White; a 53 per cent increase from 3 million people to 4.6 million people between the 1991 and 2001 Censuses.

One of the difficulties of exploring the relationship between migration and social policy is the interaction between changing patterns of migration and social policy responses, which creates a rapidly changing policy environment. In the UK there have been six immigration acts since 1993 and traditional migrant entry routes such as targeted labour market gaps, seeking asylum and family reunion have been severely constrained by policies of deterrence and restrictionism. Migration and migrants have become increasingly problematized as a challenge to the idea of national identity, social cohesion and security in public and official discourse. This chapter will define key terms relating to migration and asylum, explain the main reasons why people migrate and then consider the way in which responses to migration, including immigration controls and welfare provision, have shifted in response to different patterns of migration and cohorts of migrants. The chapter will conclude by identifying the current key and emergent issues in the social policy of migration and asylum.

Definitions

The term 'migrant' is often used generically, but for social policy analysis, it is important to understand who migrants are and the differing categories they fall into. Migrants come from different countries of origin, migrate for different reasons or different combinations of reasons, bringing with them different social, economic and cultural experiences and positions and, crucially, in the receiving country, their immigration status is linked to a set of legal and welfare rights entitlements.

'Immigrant' is the term used from the perspective of the receiving country to describe someone who is free to enter, work and settle in a country without any restrictions. Up until 1962, British subjects who were citizens of the UK and its colonies, and those who were Commonwealth citizens, such as people from the Indian sub-continent and the Caribbean, could enter and settle in the UK without restrictions. Migrants from Ireland have never been subjected to immigration control or controls on employment. Free entry and settlement in the UK is extended to citizens from countries in the European Union, though from 1 January 2007, although Romanian and Bulgarian nationals became free to enter Britain, they are restricted in terms of employment and are not entitled to settle permanently.

Another category, 'temporary migrants', includes people on temporary work schemes and student visas. Under these schemes, entry and/or permission to stay in the UK is dependent on obtaining a visa. Temporary migrants often face restrictions to the type of employment they can occupy and access to social services and benefits including social security and housing provision.

Since the late 1980s, the categories of migrant that have attracted the most political, public and policy attention are refugees and asylum-seekers. Britain has a long history of granting refuge to those experiencing persecution, and is a signatory to the 1951 United Nations Convention on the Status of the Refugee (Geneva Convention). Under the 1951 Convention, a refugee is defined as someone who, 'owing to a well-founded fear of being persecuted for reasons of race, religion, nationality, membership of a particular social group or political opinion, is outside the country of his nationality and is unable, or owing to such a fear is unwilling to avail himself of the protection of that country'. In the UK, people can arrive as 'programme refugees', which means they have refugee status on arrival or they can come to the UK and seek asylum. An asylum-seeker is someone who has applied for refugee status in the UK and is waiting for a Home Office decision on their case.

Refugees have the same rights to welfare, employment and family reunion as UK citizens, and until August 2005 were given indefinite leave to remain. However, since September 2005, refugees have been granted leave to remain for just five years, which will have longer-term consequences for settlement as temporary leave to remain makes people insecure and that impedes settlement and integration. Asylum-seekers have very few rights and entitlements, are not legally entitled to work and are excluded from mainstream social security. Destitute asylum-seekers can apply for subsistence support and/or accommodation support, which is administered by the National Asylum Support Service (NASS). Those who rely on NASS for accommodation are dispersed, on a no-choice basis, to locations around the country during their asylum claim and find themselves in areas where they can experience isolation, abuse and in some instances racist attacks. If a claim is rejected, an asylum-seeker may be given

'humanitarian protection' or 'discretionary leave'. These statuses recognize that someone would face serious risk and/or that it would be inhumane to return them to their country of origin even though their case does not meet the criteria of the 1951 Geneva Convention. People with 'humanitarian protection' and 'discretionary leave' have fewer rights than refugees, though they are allowed to work and access welfare and social services.

In addition to those with recognized statuses, some people enter the UK clandestinely as undocumented migrants or can become undocumented by, for example, not leaving the country once their visa has expired. Controlling or managing migration is one of the main concerns of the UK and other European governments and now only a minority can enter and settle in the United Kingdom without restrictions.

Why Do People Migrate?

Employment and economic opportunities are two of the key factors influencing any decision to migrate. Historically, one of the largest groups of migrants to Britain has been from Ireland. Technically, Irish migrants in the nineteenth century who came as workers were internal migrants because they were moving within the boundary of the nation-state. However, even since independence, migrants from Ireland have never been subject to immigration controls and in that respect they differ significantly from migrants from other former colonial countries, who have, since the early 1960s, been subjected to immigration controls. In the post-Second World War period, Britain was experiencing labour shortages, and so migrant workers were actively recruited from Ireland and the Caribbean as well as from Eastern Europe, where populations had been displaced during the war. The 1950s was a key decade of labour migration to the UK from Commonwealth countries, first from the Caribbean and then from the Indian sub-continent preceding increasingly restrictive immigration controls that began in the early 1960s.

People also move to join family members and these kinship networks have been an important facilitator of migration. The term 'chain migration' is used to describe the pattern of South Asian migration to Britain. This is where a migration chain emerges. First, one family member arrives in the UK, secures accommodation and finds a job. That person sends for the next family member, providing them with accommodation on arrival and often locating a job – and this carries on. The family and community are crucial in migration chains and often provide the financial and cultural capital that facilitates it. Once started, migratory movements often become self-sustaining and extended as spouses and children migrate in order to be reunited with their family.

Civil war, conflict, political oppression, discrimination and human rights abuses can also result in migration, and it is these motivations for leaving a country of origin that are most associated with refugees and asylum-seekers. Immigration controls and pre-embarkation checks make it difficult to enter the United Kingdom as an asylum-seeker legally, while the closed borders surrounding the European Union means that, increasingly, people who want to seek asylum find themselves dependent on people-smugglers, who plan their flight and often provide false documentation. The 1951 Geneva Convention was developed in response to conditions in post-war Europe and the limited grounds for claiming refugee status in the Geneva Convention means that poverty, generalized violence, displacement due to development projects or environmental disaster do not meet the international refugee definition. It is these factors, which are associated with economic and/or social disruption, that result in the

migration of people from the global South and East to the highly developed countries of the North and the West.

It is because of the limitations of the Geneva Convention that regional conventions, such as the 1969 Organization of African Unity Convention Governing Specific Aspects of Refugee Problems in Africa and the 1984 Cartagena Declaration on Refugees, emerged to reflect the specific context in South America. It is increasingly recognized, though not in the bureaucratic categories used by governments and policy-makers, that people often have more than one reason for migrating – or mixed motives – and that the reasons why refugees and asylum-seekers leave their country of origin overlap with the migration choices made by others.

The UK is a signatory to the Geneva Convention and has to meet international obligations. However, successive governments have also been under pressure at different times to control migration, and since the late 1980s this has been focused on asylum-seekers. The focus of asylum policy has been border controls, restricted rights and enforcement (detention and deportation) strategies. The public discourse has revolved around the dichotomy of 'deserving' refugees and 'bogus' or 'undeserving' asylum-seekers who are portrayed as coming to the UK to exploit the generous welfare system and employment opportunities. It is because of this that the rights of asylum-seekers have been gradually eroded. However, immigration policy has developed in a stepwise manner and policy trends in different periods can be identified and understood in the context of the migration flows, the prevalent economic situation and public discourse.

British Policy: Past and Present

Britain has a long history of controlling immigration which can be divided into three phases. First, was the period 1905 through to 1920, when the targets for control were Jewish immigrants from Eastern Europe and Germans who were considered alien enemies during the First World War. The second phase was 1962–88, which brought an end to virtually all primary migration from black Commonwealth citizens. The third phase has focused on the control of asylum-seekers.

The first period, from 1905, was important because the links between immigration and welfare were clearly made. Under the 1905 Aliens Act, entry could be refused if a migrant had no means of subsistence or deported if they were in receipt of Poor Relief within one year of entering Britain. In 1914, the Aliens Restriction Act was passed in response to anti-alien feeling, especially anti-German, generated by the outbreak of the First World War. Under this Act, aliens had to register with the police and the Home Secretary and immigration officers were given powers to control entry, deportation and employment. The 1919 Aliens Restrictions (Amendment) Act extended the terms of the 1914 Act to peacetime and included restrictions on employment even for some naturalized citizens.

The next major piece of legislation was the 1948 British Nationality Act, which gave British subjects, who were citizens of the United Kingdom and Colonies (UKC), and Commonwealth citizens the right to enter, settle and work in Britain. It also created a third category of citizens of Eire who were neither aliens nor subjects, but who had all the rights and duties of UKC citizens. This Act has been the only one since 1905 that does not increase controls on entry to the UK and/or restrict access to welfare and employment.

The second main phase of immigration controls started with the 1962 Commonwealth Immigrants Act and ended with the 1988 Immigration Act. This period was concerned with curbing immigration from

countries of the Commonwealth and New Commonwealth and brought primary migration among black Commonwealth citizens virtually to an end, though significantly not white Commonwealth citizens, which clearly demonstrated the racialized nature of these controls. The context for the second phase of immigration controls was the increase in numbers of people arriving from British colonies and Commonwealth countries in the period after the Second World War, first in response to Britain's need for labour to rebuild the war-torn economy, but then as refugees from independence struggles and post-colonial conflicts.

In 1945 Britain needed labour to rebuild the country, and initially Eastern Europeans from displaced persons camps were recruited purely on their ability to work. However, there was a need for more workers and so Britain actively recruited migrants from the Caribbean and the Indian sub-continent. The 1950s was the decade of labour migration from the Caribbean and, to a lesser extent, from the Indian sub-continent. Patterns of migration correlated with the demand for labour. Commonwealth migrants were often employed in unskilled or semi-skilled manual jobs and social mobility and economic success were elusive. Amid public concerns about immigration, the 1962 Commonwealth Immigration Act was passed. This Act was significant because, for the first time, restrictions on entry and settlement were placed on UKC subjects not born in the UK.

The 1968 Commonwealth Immigrants Act was rushed through Parliament in three days amid fears that East African Asians, as UK passport-holders, would exercise their right to come to Britain in the face of post-colonial Africanization policies. Under this Act, UK passport-holders were subject to immigration controls unless they had a parent or grandparent born, adopted, registered or naturalized in the UK. Such a policy effectively excluded East African Asians from entry to the UK, but not those of UK descent living in East Africa. The 1971 Immigration Act introduced the concept of partials and non-partials and, in effect, changed the status of Commonwealth citizens to aliens by allowing the right to abode only among those born in the UK or who had a parent born in the UK. Under the partial clause, nearly all non-white Commonwealth citizens were excluded from entry and the right to abode. The 1981 British Nationality Act went further and removed the right of citizenship to those born in the UK and only those able to satisfy the partial rule were automatically entitled to citizenship. The 1988 Immigration Act introduced the public funds test for dependents of people who had settled in Britain before 1973. Under the Act, all British and Commonwealth citizens who wanted their dependents to join them in the UK had to sponsor them and prove that they could do that without recourse to public funds.

The early 1990s saw an increase in the numbers of asylum-seekers entering Britain. As previous legislation had brought an end to virtually all primary migration – with the exception of family reunion – the focus of policy turned to this growing phenomenon. This third phase of immigration control has set out to control the entry of asylum-seekers to Britain and exclude them from social and economic participation in society. Table 51.1 shows the Acts from 1993 and their main effects. The cumulative effect of this legislation has been to marginalize and exclude asylum-seeking individuals and families through the incremental curtailment of social and welfare support which has been coupled with their exclusion from the regular labour market and penalty fines on employers taking on anyone without correct documentation which acts as a deterrent. The consequence has been an increase in destitution and homeless among asylum-seekers.

The European Union

Current asylum and immigration policy needs to be considered within the context of the European Union. The European Union has been gradually harmonizing policy and the focus has been on border controls, information-sharing, clear procedures for determining which asylum cases are eligible for refugee status, as well as the standards for the protection and treatment of asylum-seekers. With the expansion of Europe, securing borders has become more difficult as some migrants enter clandestinely with the assistance of smugglers or are trafficked for the purposes of exploitation.

At Tampere in 1999 a timetable was agreed for a common European asylum and migration policy. The essential elements included directives covering minimum standards on reception, asylum procedures and a revision of the Dublin Convention (specifying which member state is responsible for examining an asylum application to prevent refused asylum-seekers from moving to another member state). One concern has been that the harmonization of policies, especially on minimum standards, would lead to the adoption of the lowest common denominator. However, though these standards are now in place, not all member states have passed the necessary legislation to implement them so it is not yet clear what their impact will be.

Emerging Issues

Recent and key emerging areas in migration, asylum and social policy are schemes to manage migration, a focus on integration, social cohesion and national identity among those with rights to stay in the UK and the exclusion of others. In terms of managing migration, the Gateway programme for resettling refugees is likely to

Table 51.1 Immigration and asylum legislation since 1993

Legislation	Effect
1993 Asylum and Immigration Appeals Act	Local authorities no longer have to provide housing to asylum-seekers.
1996 Asylum and Immigration Act	This Act contained the Social Security (Persons from Abroad) Miscellaneous Amendment regulations which removed the entitlement of social security benefits for asylum-seekers who applied for asylum within the UK – that is in-country – rather than at the port of entry. Those who applied for asylum from within the country received in-kind support from local authorities, under the 1948 National Assistance Act, often in the form of vouchers instead of cash benefits. Also, anyone sponsored by relatives to come to the UK is excluded from claiming benefits for five years unless their sponsor dies.
1999 Immigration and Asylum Act	This Act removed asylum-seekers from the mainstream benefits system and introduced the National Asylum Support Service (NASS) to administer a virtually cashless voucher system, at less than the value of income support. The dispersal of asylum-seekers on a no choice basis to locations around the UK was also introduced.
2002 Nationality, Immigration and Asylum Act	Introduced Section 55 which allowed the Home Office to withdraw access to NASS support from those who do not apply for asylum 'as soon as reasonably practicable'.
2004 Asylum and Immigration Act	A failed asylum-seeker with a family can now have their support withdrawn if the person has failed without 'reasonable excuse' to leave the UK voluntarily. Local Authorities have a duty to provide for children under 18 under the Children Act 1989 and if necessary children will be separated from their family.
2006 Immigration, Asylum and Nationality Act	Asylum-seekers who are unable to travel back to their home countries due to medical situations or there being no safe route home are given board, lodgings and vouchers instead of any cash.

be expanded as part of a strategy to reduce the numbers of people arriving in the UK and claiming asylum. Other ways of managing migration and trying to ensure that those who do come to the UK bring with them skills that are needed or will do jobs, such as seasonal agricultural work, that others will not undertake are targeted work and employment schemes. In addition, the government has introduced a point system for prospective migrants modelled on the Australian system in an attempt to ensure that migrants to the UK are bringing valuable educational and employment skills.

It is likely that asylum-seekers will be increasingly excluded from society with greater numbers becoming destitute. The ever-increasing restrictions and management of borders are likely to see the continued rise in the numbers of people relying on people-smugglers to leave repressive regimes and poverty. For those with leave to remain, the emphasis of social policy will continue to be on integration, social cohesion and national identity in an effort to promote a more inclusive society, while others will be increasingly excluded and marginalized.

Guide to Further Sources

Some useful general texts on migration and policy responses in the UK are J. Solomos, *Race and racism in Britain*, 3rd edn (Palgrave, 2003); I. Spencer, *British Immigration Policy Since 1939: The Making of Multi-Racial Britain* (Routledge, 1997); S. Cohen, B. Humphries and E. Mynott (eds), *From Immigration Controls to Welfare Controls* (Routledge, 2003); R. Cohen *Frontiers of Identity: The British and Others* (Longman, 1994).

Useful analysis of refugees in the UK is provided by T. Kushner and K. Knox, *Refugees in the Age of Genocide* (Frank Cass, 1999); A. Bloch, *The Migration and Settlement of Refugees in Britain* (Palgrave, 2002); and R. Sales, *Understanding Immigration and Refugee Policy: Contradictions and Continuities* (Policy Press, 2007).

A useful introduction to the European Union is S. Lavanex, *The Europeanization of Refugee Policies: Between Human Rights and Internal Security* (Ashgate, 2001). The edited collection by C. Jones Finer, *Migration, Immigration and Social Policy* (Blackwell, 2006) explores key areas in migration and includes social policy case studies from Europe and the European Union.

Government websites, especially the Home Office (<www.homeoffice.gov.uk>) and National Statistics (<www.statistics.gov.uk>), contain useful policy documents, research reports and statistical data. The Information Centre about Asylum and Refugees in the UK (<www.icar.org.uk>) provides up-to-date information on asylum policy and asylum statistics as well as briefings on key topics.

Part VIII

International Issues

Chapter 52

The Role of Comparative Study in Social Policy

Margaret May

Overview

- Comparative analysis is a crucial and burgeoning constituent of social policy.
- The development of comparative policy reflects broader shifts both in the discipline and national welfare strategies.
- The study of comparative policy raises a number of distinct conceptual and methodological issues.

Introduction

The study of welfare provision inevitably involves some form of comparison between current practice and past or alternative ways of meeting need or improving existing policies. Such comparisons may not always be explicit, and the value bases may vary, but they are central to a discipline geared to evaluating welfare arrangements. This chapter focuses on the ways in which policy analysts have attempted to compare and contrast provision in different societies. It considers the aims of comparative study, the types of question most commonly asked, the special demands such enquiry places on students and researchers, and the key areas of current debate.

Why Comparative Social Policy?

Historically, the starting point for comparative analysis was the observation that in the post-war era many countries, especially those of the industrialized West, experienced a massive expansion in publicly financed and delivered welfare. This was underpinned, as the reports of Marsh in Canada, Van Rhijn in the Netherlands, Laroque in France and Beveridge in Britain showed, by a widespread belief in the state's duty and capacity to care for its citizens. Funding methods and forms of provision, however, varied considerably, as did the scale of state involvement. One stimulus to comparative analysis, then, was that of charting and explaining common trends and accounting for these differences.

A more pragmatic impetus came from reformers anxious to expand or improve provision and 'learn' from the experience (and 'mistakes') of others. Indeed, the fact that countries develop different responses to ostensibly similar problems was seen as a sort of natural experimental basis on which to build. Given the potential political and economic costs of innovation, governments too recognized the benefits of considering programmes developed elsewhere.

In practice, though, policy importation was highly selective, often serving simply to legitimate desired change, with reformers deploying comparative ammunition to substantiate or disprove their particular prescriptions.

Policy 'borrowing' along these lines has a long pedigree. But in the late twentieth century it gained new resonance as advanced industrial-capitalist societies became aware of the implications of an increasingly globalized economy. The extent to which economic change undermined the autonomy of nation-states and depressed public expenditure is hotly debated (see chapter 53). But it was clear that the combination of economic recession, high unemployment, changing work and family patterns, new political formations, rising consumer expectations and demographic fears inspired a widespread reassessment of the welfare settlements of the 1940s. While the pace and nature of restructuring varied, there was considerable commonality in the policies adopted and many governments engaged in some form of comparative exercise, if only to leaven domestic debate.

In the meantime, the post-war welfare order was internationalizing in other ways. The deregulation of national financial service markets meant pensions, health insurance and mortgages in many countries were increasingly provided by local subsidiaries of multinational conglomerates, with administration often outsourced to other parts of the globe. The General Agreement on Tariffs and Trade (GATT) negotiations liberalizing trade in services fostered similar developments, particularly in social care (see chapter 25). The spread of new information and other technologies hastened this process, as did the emergence of an international labour market for welfare personnel. Higher education institutions, for instance, moved into a global market, as did other services and 'back-office' provision such as medical screening and welfare data processing. Meanwhile, global communication systems enabled individuals to make their own policy comparisons and facilitated cross-national welfare lobbying. Together with the broader trends subsumed under the term 'globalization', these developments presented new challenges to comparative study and ones which continue to reverberate today.

Interest in cross-national analysis was also fuelled by other factors. One was awareness of the extent to which social policy was being shaped not only by the operation of global markets but the expanding remit of supranational entities such as the European Union, the World Bank and the International Monetary Fund (see chapters 36 and 37). Their interventions constituted a new focus for analysis, not least because they relied heavily on cross-national data. Adding to this during the 2000s, governments, especially in advanced industrial societies, expanded their investment in cross-comparative policy-formation. In the UK this was partly driven by Labour's commitment to evidence-based welfare. As significant was the emergence under the EU's open method of coordination of welfare benchmarking as a form of soft legislation and lever for change.

The resultant welter of statistics routinely produced by national and international bodies demanded careful appraisal, as did the many proposals to transplant provisions from one society to another. Welfare reform in North America, the Antipodes and much of Europe, East and West, in the late twentieth century involved remarkably similar shifts in the forms and role of state welfare. Different countries experienced a resurgence of 'neo-liberal' policies, moves to curtail or 'marketize' state services and a weakening of the class solidarity and social concerns that underpinned post-war welfare building.

More recently, welfare systems in much of the developed world seem to have metamorphosed again. In the face of intensified globalization and ongoing industrial change, social policy has been widely upheld as a means of securing rather than negating economic modernization. State welfare has accordingly been remodelled along the new 'enabling' nexus of active labour market and individualized work- and savings-oriented policies. Cross-nationally, public services have been redesigned on more 'personalized' lines. Equally significantly, there were also signs, albeit variable, of a repositioning of social policy in development strategies in other regions.

These still unfolding trends added a further twist to public debates about the direction and outcomes of welfare reform and the trade-offs between different measures. They also raised new questions about the nature and processes of policy diffusion, the extent to which national policy-making is structured by broad global rather than local factors and the sustainability of inherited welfare formations.

Approaches to Comparative Social Policy

Against this backcloth, comparative social policy thus centres on the complex task of examining welfare patterns in different countries, identifying commonalties and differences, explaining these and considering likely developments. More pragmatically, it is concerned with improving provision in one country by drawing on experience elsewhere and assessing the implications of different systems for individuals and the wider society.

In addressing these overarching concerns, analysts have tended to operate at different levels of abstraction. Some concentrate on country-specific studies, detailing the range and type of policies and delivery systems, but leaving the task of comparison to the reader. Others, while adopting an overt comparative approach, vary in the specificity of their focus. Many, especially those undertaking government-sponsored studies

or concerned to inform policy-making, concentrate on comparing programmes, usually in countries with broadly similar socio-economic and political structures. While adopting a similar 'micro' or 'single issue' approach, a second group starts from other points on the policy compass, exploring provisions for specific users, responses to particular 'problems' or policy processes. Whatever the starting point, 'micro' studies potentially involve comparing a number of interrelated elements:

- the extent and nature of the 'need'/ 'problem';
- the range of provision;
- the overall welfare context;
- policy-making processes;
- the aims of a particular programme(s)/ service(s)/benefit(s);
- their origins and development over time;
- entitlement criteria;
- the provider structure (statutory/non-statutory);
- the resource structure;
- the administrative structure;
- delivery/allocation processes;
- the regulatory structure;
- the 'efficacy' of current provision;
- pressures for change;
- policy proposals.

A further group of analysts follow a more 'macro' approach, attempting to characterize and compare 'whole systems' across a range of societies, often over time as well. This entails capturing the essence of a country's perceptions of and response to social need through considering:

- the general welfare milieu;
- policy-making 'styles';
- key forms of welfare 'input' or 'effort';
- predominant patterns of welfare production;
- predominant processes of welfare allocation;

- the main welfare output(s);
- the major welfare outcome(s).

Research Dilemmas

Exploring these issues within one's home country is far from straightforward. Cross-national study is even more problematic and presents major challenges in terms of like for like comparison. 'Social needs', for instance, are highly contested. Benefit systems and welfare services may have several, possibly conflicting, aims, not all explicated in legislation or government publications and which have to be 'read' from other sources. The purpose of one scheme may only be clear in the context of the overall scheme of welfare in a particular country. Providers may be governmental, non-statutory or 'mixed'. Establishing the resource structure involves examining funding arrangements (national or local taxation, direct and indirect; compulsory or private insurance; charging schemes; or combinations of these), staffing profiles and, in many instances, the role of non-paid carers or other helpers. Comparing administrative structures involves not only mapping formal organizational structures, but comprehending management cultures and the informal processes of 'street-level' delivery. Evaluating the efficacy of provision, whether in terms of take-up relative to 'need', enhanced individual well-being, decreased inequality, cost-effectiveness, or other possible criteria, is a highly value-laden and intricate process. Capturing stakeholder views including those of users is equally problematic.

Such difficulties are even more pronounced when comparing 'whole systems'. In many ways the techniques used are no different from those deployed in other studies and demand similar methodological sensitivity. But comparative study confronts additional dilemmas. The well-documented limitations of official statistics, for instance, are compounded by differing national conventions that may pre-empt direct comparison. Sources, categories and formats may vary; records for some programmes may not have been kept; there may be gaps in coverage, changes in definitions or methods of collecting and classifying data that in any case may not be freely accessible and then only in aggregate form. In many parts of the world welfare-related information may not be available.

The issues are not only a matter of accessing valid sources but of reliability and the complexities of undertaking research according to the investigative rules and epistemological traditions of another country. Social policy analysts are not 'culture-free' in either their interpretations or their research remits. Indeed, one salutary feature of comparative study is the discovery that burning issues in one society may not be so significant elsewhere and the extent to which, as social constructionists have long argued, 'social problems' may be differently perceived. Superficially, similar terms can carry very different meanings and local practices are easily misread. Traversing such cultural and linguistic frontiers demands methodological caution, especially in the contested arena of social policy.

Considerable effort has been invested in surmounting these hurdles. 'Safari' surveys of one or more countries by teams from another, for example, have given way to collaborative multinational projects designed to enhance cross-cultural literacy and combine differing research styles. Greater use is being made of sophisticated quantitative and qualitative techniques and fuller cross-national data sets have also been developed by non-governmental as well as governmental bodies, along with measures to improve access to micro-data. Nonetheless, comparative research remains fraught with difficulties and, given the complexities and cost of conducting alternative studies, heavily reliant on official sources.

Sensitively managed, however, it offers invaluable insights into policy formation and debate.

Foundations and Frameworks

One major contribution has been the development of classificatory frameworks specifying the key features of different kinds of welfare systems. Although differing typologies were advanced, until recently the most influential were variants on those developed by Wilenski and Lebeaux in the USA and Titmuss in the UK. Writing in the wake of the post-war settlements, the former distinguished two 'models of welfare': the 'residual', based on the principles of economic individualism and free enterprise, and the 'institutional', based on the notions of security, equality and humanitarianism.

These 'models' characterized both the historical development of social policy (which they saw as a mono-directional evolution from residualism) and the patterning of welfare in particular countries. In the first (typified by the USA), 'needs' were met primarily through the market or the family. The state provided an emergency 'safety-net' when these 'normal' supports broke down. Public welfare was, accordingly, highly selective, with low means-tested benefits, and widely perceived as stigmatizing. In contrast, the 'institutional' model (epitomized by Scandinavian countries) embraced universal, rights-based, non-stigmatizing, redistributive state welfare as a 'normal' function of industrial society. Using a similar categorization, Titmuss added a third ideal type, the 'industrial-achievement model'. Typified by the then West Germany, state welfare functioned as an adjunct to the economy with needs correspondingly met on the basis of work performance and status.

Such taxonomies formed the implicit template for other forms of macro-analysis, especially in English-speaking countries.

These entailed developing ways of plotting a country's welfare prowess, comparing quantitative aggregate data relating to the timing and coverage of national legislation and welfare expenditures. Equating high social spending with extensive welfarism, many studies similarly distinguished the welfare commitment exhibited in Scandinavia with that of America and fed into attempts to identify the pressures leading to increased welfare spending in Western states and variations between them.

Initially, purposive or teleological explanations prevailed, with state welfare perceived as safeguarding individuals against the shocks of industrial change and the vagaries of the market. From this evolutionary perspective, welfare statism appeared as the indispensable concomitant of industrial-urbanization and demographic change. Such thinking was increasingly contested by Marxist analysts who highlighted its role in maintaining labour discipline, productivity and social stability. From the 1970s it was also challenged from other perspectives. Focusing more on theorizing cross-national variations, many writers emphasized the correspondence between the spread of universal public welfare and the strength of social democratic or labour movements. Some, however, highlighted the role of different groupings and controversy was furthered by research on factors other than levels of political mobilization or power resources. Most influentially, a number of analysts pointed to the role of cultural and institutional structures and the 'path-dependent' nature of welfare arrangements.

From the late 1980s this intense cross-national debate shifted again, stimulated by the restructuring of state welfare and growing concern about its future. In trying to make sense of changing welfare arrangements within and between countries, researchers devised new classifications. Most influential was that advanced in 1990 by the Danish analyst G. Esping-Andersen, who developed a classification based not only on variations in the scale, scope and entitlements of public provision in capitalist countries, but also on differences in policy-making styles and processes and underlying patterns of class formation and political structures. It rested on a conception of state welfare as sustaining social citizenship along two related dimensions:

1 'Decommodification': the extent to which the state frees individuals from the operation of market forces and enables its citizens to lead a socially acceptable life independent of the labour market.
2 'Stratification': the extent to which state welfare differentiates between social groups and promotes equality and social integration.

Recognizing that the traditional gauge of welfare commitment, high social expenditure, often obscured these distributional issues, Esping-Andersen devised 'decommodification' indices to measure the accessibility, coverage and performance of social protection schemes in eighteen OECD states. His analysis led him to distinguish three ideal type 'welfare regimes':

1 *Social-Democratic Regimes*, epitomized by Scandinavian countries, where the pressure of a broad coalition of labour organizations and small farmers secured a state committed to full employment and generous, redistributive, universalist welfare benefits, incorporating both middle- and working-class interests.
2 *Conservative/Corporatist Regimes*, typified by Germany, France and Austria, where occupationally segregated benefits were introduced by conservative-dominated governments to secure both working- and middle-class support.
3 *Liberal Welfare Regimes*, exemplified by the United States and Anglo-Saxon

societies, where, in the absence of stable cross-class alliances, state welfare operated mainly on selective lines as a residual safety-net for the poor.

As with any ideal-type framework, some nations fitted these constructs more easily than others. But Esping-Andersen concluded that the welfare systems of developed countries could be incorporated within this schema, which also had a predictive value indicating that different regimes appeared to be moving along different trajectories.

The Changing Scope of Comparative Study

Whilst contributing substantially to our understanding of differences between welfare states, Esping-Andersen's work attracted extensive criticism, reinvigorating debate on the gestation of welfare systems and their potential for change. Equally salient here, it became the reference point for a new wave of cross-national research. Addressing major lacunae in his and earlier studies, this centred on four overlapping lines of analysis.

One stream of studies focused on his classification, questioning the allocation of nations within it, pointing to other welfare 'worlds' in developed economies and assessing the broader use of regime analysis. What emerged was a more complex scenario in which Esping-Andersen's threefold grouping of advanced industrial societies was often modified to include further 'regimes' such as those of the Antipodes, Mediterranean and Eastern Europe, and East Asia and 'outliers' or 'sub-categories' within 'regimes' (see chapters 54 and 55).

Debate over these adaptations was paralleled by controversy over whether taxonomies based on democratic welfare capitalism could (or should) be configured to include welfare systems in other parts of the world or whether different explanatory models were needed. As with development studies, some writers upheld the latter view, highlighting the ways in which 'Westernized' constructions inhibited comparative enquiry into provisions not only in low-income countries, but also in the fast-developing BRIC economies (Brazil, Russia, India and China) and led to inappropriate unidirectional prescriptions. Attempts were also made to recast Esping-Andersen's model, most notably by Gough and colleagues.

Utilizing a broader concept of 'welfare regime' encompassing non-state and non-market arrangements and focusing on 'well-being', Gough et al. distinguished three welfare regime 'families':

1 'Welfare state regimes'
2 'Informal security regimes'
3 'Insecurity regimes'

The second and third are differentiated from the first and each other by levels of reliance on informal employment, the nature and stability of social networks and governments and the ways in which formal and informal structures sustain rather than counter insecurity (see chapter 57). Within this framework, broad regional distinctions can be drawn between 'productivist welfare regimes (East Asia), clientistic 'partial or liberal informal security regimes' (Latin America), residual 'informal security regimes' (South Asia) and 'insecurity regimes' (sub-Saharan Africa).

Discussion of this and other reformulations of regime theory continue to dominate comparative study. In the context of the shifting axes of the global economy, they have also stimulated a proliferation of country-specific studies illuminating hitherto neglected welfare arrangements, particularly those of China, the Middle East and Muslim societies. These are adding new dimensions, still being explored, to notions of welfare variation.

But whatever the tack adopted, regime theorization built on and fed into a second line of analysis, that challenging the narrow statism of earlier studies. Partly because of their reliance on aggregate statistical data produced by governmental agencies, these focused on income transfer schemes as a proxy for a country's 'welfarism'. During the 1990s, however, research widened to encompass statutory services and variations in the state's fiscal and regulatory roles.

Equally fundamentally, increasing attention was paid to non-statutory welfare and cross-national differences in the policy 'mix'. Together these revealed a more complex picture of cross-national welfare activity. Public services did not always map neatly onto classifications based on income maintenance systems and some national patterns appeared to be programme-specific. When other forms of state intervention or non-governmental provision were factored in, the overall picture could change again, repositioning some countries in measures of welfare activity. Nonetheless, for many observers variation between regime clusters appeared greater than within them, making the notion a useful heuristic tool.

A third, interlinked set of writing opened up a different analytic front, emphasizing the need to assess social policies in terms of the impact not only on class but also on other social divisions. The lead here was taken by feminist-inspired studies that demonstrated the extent to which, irrespective of 'regime type', statutory welfare was contingent on private, unpaid gendered provision. For some, including Esping-Andersen, this meant adapting his typology; for others, it involved more radical retheorizing. This debate too is ongoing. But it has generated a wealth of research, bringing new insights into cross-national variations in women's welfare status and the gendering and re-gendering of welfare citizenship (see chapter 13).

It has also added to research into the welfare experience of other groups. Though bedevilled by the lack of reliable, compatible national data, there has been a surge of enquiries into the dynamics and impact of different welfare systems on ethnic minority and religious groups and provisions for economic migrants and asylum-seekers. More recently, partly prompted by concerns over demographic ageing, controversy has spilt over into cross-national assessments of provisions for the elderly, people with disabilities and children.

Expanding the comparative canvas involved more than a process of 'adding in'. It forced rethinking on the drivers and determinants of policy change cross-nationally and within different societies. Exploring these heightened awareness of ideational, cultural and temporal processes as well as political and institutional factors, and drew attention to the related economic discourse over 'varieties of capitalism' and the interplay between welfare, financial and employment 'regimes'. Above all, it contributed to a reconsideration of the aims and purposes of social policy and the development of new evaluations focused increasingly on 'well-being' processes and outcomes.

Emerging Issues

Such research has already filtered into national and international policy debates, and in many ways set the agenda for the immediate future. Looking forward, a number of issues relating to the tools, conceptual frameworks and, above all, the focus of comparative study stand out. In terms of the first, the main issues are those of developing higher-quality data and widening collaborative research. Moves in this direction are in train. But, despite initia-

tives like the UK's 2006 National Data Strategy and the International Data Forum, ways of minimizing the inherent difficulties of cross-cultural research are likely to be a source of continuing debate.

The use of regime-style analysis will also be high on the comparative radar. Given the inconsistencies within national welfare systems, a number of researchers already view programme-specific comparison as the best way forward. The most fruitful developments, however, are likely to lie with multi-country comparisons, more dynamic, 'Zwicky box'-style categorization and the use of new units of analysis. Typologizing clearly cannot encompass the range of empirically observed differences. But it is still the most effective way of gaining a holistic picture of the global patterning of welfare.

Whichever route is followed, comparative analysts will be under pressure to assess responses to the common challenges arising from the emergence in many regions of new social risks and the reconfiguration of long-standing ones. In turn, this is likely to lead to a reappraisal of the role of collective provision, particularly, the conjoining of social and economic policy.

The major challenge for comparative analysts, however, remains that of adumbrating the nature and direction of change in national social policies, assessing whether they indicate convergence or divergence and the relative influence of exogenous and endogenous factors. It means exploring their differential exposure to common pressures and the ways these are mediated by internal political processes and circumstances and the 'path dependencies' created by existing structures and funding mechanisms as against the systemic shifts that may flow from new political alignments. Finally and critically, it involves addressing the interconnections between welfare systems, the patterning of social divisions and changing constructions of citizenship.

Guide to Further Sources

Many of the issues addressed here are taken up elsewhere in this volume, and can be followed up in the suggested sources. P. Alcock and C. Craig (eds), *International Social Policy*, 2nd edn (Palgrave, 2007) provides a stimulating introduction to comparative analysis along with a number of country surveys. More detailed coverage of theoretical and methodological issues touched on in this chapter can be found in M. Hill, *Social Policy in the Modern World* (Blackwell, 2006); C. Crouch, *Capitalist Diversity and Change* (Oxford University Press, 2005); N. Manning, 'The origins and essence of US social policy', *Global Social Policy* 6/2 (2006): 155–72, and the many other contributions to this journal and others such as the *Journal of European Social Policy*.

The work of Gough et al. can be accessed at the Wellbeing in Developing Countries site, <www.welldev.org.uk>. Other gateways to current research and web sources can be found at <www.oecd.org> and on the SPA website at <www.spa.org.uk>.

Chapter 53

Globalization and Social Policy

Rob Sykes

Overview

- Globalization is a highly contested concept best understood as a number of interlinked processes.
- There are four main perspectives on globalization and its relationship with social policy developments.
- The simple 'globalization causes welfare retrenchment' argument is a gross over-simplification; a complex pattern of links between globalization and social policy change in different countries is emerging.
- There is a dynamic, two-way relationship between globalization processes and the development of national social policies.

Introduction

Today we hear a lot about globalization and the ways in which it is, supposedly, changing our world. Yet on closer inspection the various writers, politicians and political activists who talk about globalization and who, most often, express concern about its negative effects do not usually provide any clear definition of what they mean when they use the term, nor do they provide much evidence of how and why globalization is causing the problems they talk about. In short, debates about globalization might be said to have generated more political 'heat' than analytical 'light'. If we want to understand what the connections are between globalization and social policy, we need to cut through some of this 'hype' and try to answer two related questions:

1 What *is* globalization and how should we think about it?
2 What are the connections between globalization and social policy?

What is Globalization?

The term 'globalization' has been applied to a wide range of phenomena. Most commonly, it has been used as a generic term to refer to a variety of economic processes, such as an increasing internationalization of the production and exchange of goods and services, the deregulation of financial transactions, the spread of free trade on a worldwide scale and the restructuring and relocation of productive activities between different regions of the world. Globalization has also been implicated in a number of political processes, such as the weakening of nation-states and their loss of social and political autonomy, a decentralization process within national states and attempts to create new international political institutions to manage the new 'global politics'. In the field of social and cultural analysis, globalization has been associated with a massive increase in the availability and circulation of information, especially through the spread of the internet; with a greater interconnectedness between societies, so that distances in both space and time seem to be shrunk through telephonic communication, real-time television broadcasts, etc.; and with a threat to traditional cultures and social cohesion coupled with cultural homogenization, or so-called 'Macdonaldization', via the spread of global brands and products.

It has been argued that the spread of globalization means that the economic links between nation-states in the world market have become increasingly systemic, competitive and essentially corrosive of pre-existing political and economic relations. Globalization is increasingly seen as an intrinsic feature of the development of world capitalism, leading inevitably, unless resisted and checked, to the demise of autonomous, nationally managed economies, and, ultimately, to a loss of democratic control by ordinary citizens over their lives. This 'apocalyptic' version of the globalization thesis has now been largely discredited by more recent analysts. Nevertheless, a growing number of 'anti-globalizers', loosely organized members of a variety of social movements, protest in strikingly similar terms about the essentially negative effects of the spread of global capitalism, led, as these protesters see it, by bodies such as the World Trade Organization, the International Monetary Fund and even the European Union. Their concern is that the inhabitants of the poorer parts of the world, and the poorer and excluded of the richer countries, are consigned to poverty and exploitation if the forces of globalization are left unchecked. In this view, the welfare of all citizens –

except for those with the ability to pay for it – is under threat.

This brief review indicates the essentially contested character of globalization. The rest of this chapter summarizes four different perspectives on the connections between globalization and social policy (see box 53.1), then reviews these perspectives to see which appears best to explain the actual evidence on changes in welfare systems and social policy around the world. The chapter then suggests how globalization and social policy are best understood as related parts of a dynamic process, and concludes with a brief consideration of some emerging issues.

Mishra (1999) provides an example of the first perspective. He argues that the major effect of globalization is the decline of the nation-state in terms of its freedom to make policy, and in particular to pursue full employment and economic growth policies. These economic pressures tend to generate an increasing inequality in wages and working conditions both within countries and between countries, and increasing competition tends to exert a downward pressure on systems of social protection and social expenditure. Increasingly, as a result of these economic pressures from the globalized capitalist system, the ideological support for social protection systems becomes weakened, social democratic governments find their scope for welfare policy more and more limited and, indeed, democratic national political control tends to lose out to the forces of global economic powers. In sum, Mishra argues that globalization has empowered and privileged neo-liberal economics as a transnational force beyond the control of nation-states and governments.

Pierson (2001) provides an example of the second perspective. He asserts that the welfare state, rather than facing fundamental retrenchment and decline, is likely to be sustained in almost all countries in the future. This is not to say that there are not pressures on welfare states. These *are* likely

Box 53.1 Four perspectives on globalization and social policy development

1 *Globalization causes welfare retrenchment through capitalism's dominance*
   - internationalization of the world economy implies the demise of nation-state autonomy, a reduction of national governments' policy options and a weakening of labour movements – i.e. the main foundations of the national welfare state are fundamentally weakened;
   - development of global capitalism responsible for unemployment and rising inequality, creating worsening problems for welfare states;
   - both international trade and technological change create a significant decline in demand for unskilled, semi-skilled and traditionally skilled workers;
   - need for national economies to compete in world market exerts pressure for reduction in social expenditure by governments and private firms;
   - all the above create pressures to shift from social-democratic and collectivist to neo-liberal and individualist welfare ideologies – *overall retrenchment and decline of welfare states.*

2 *Globalization has little effect upon welfare states*
   - changes in the world economy are less widespread, smaller and more gradual than the full-blown globalization thesis suggests;
   - even if globalization has occurred, welfare states remain compatible with this process – globalized economies need to provide some sort of social welfare and political counterbalance to the effects of economic change;
   - 'threat of globalization' more an ideological ploy of national governments wishing to restructure welfare than an unchallengeable economic force;
   - *welfare states are changing, but this is due to factors other than globalization* (e.g. population ageing, technology, changes in family structures, new risks).

3 *Globalization's effects on welfare states are mediated by national politics*
   - external global forces are impacting upon national welfare state changes;
   - certain types of welfare state are more compatible with economic competitiveness than others, and can adapt better than others to the new environment;
   - worldwide competitive economic environment means that high-wage national economies will lose jobs to low(er)-wage countries unless checked;
   - particular character of the previous political and institutional arrangements (i.e. form of welfare state) in different countries will heavily affect responses to global challenges;
   - thus, *different welfare states will change in different ways* in responding to globalization – not simple welfare retrenchment or decline – and the support of different constituencies (unions, politicians, voters, etc.) will ensure continuation of welfare states in some form.

4 *Welfare states generated globalization and limit its future development*
   - globalization is largely a by-product of the development of democratic welfare states in the advanced economies;

- the guaranteeing of social rights within these welfare states allowed for the development of deregulation of national economies and the liberalization and re-regulation of the international economy, i.e. 'globalization';
- 'globalization' was an *unintended* consequence of national governmental social policy initiatives that were pursued for other motives;
- national rather than international bodies remain the key decision-makers in economic policy as well as welfare policy;
- the *future relationship between globalization and national welfare states depends upon the decisions of national governments.*

to lead to renegotiation, restructuring and modernization, but not to dismantling of welfare states. What Pierson calls the 'irresistible forces' playing upon welfare states are *domestic* forces, in particular the changed economies of advanced societies, the consequences of the 'maturation' of welfare states, and demographic change such as the ageing of populations especially in the Western capitalist economies. Globalization as an *exogenous* set of forces is, at best, of secondary significance.

Esping-Andersen and his associates (1996) provide a good example of the third perspective and argue that a nation's economic growth now appears to require economic openness, involving greater competition and vulnerability to international trade, finance and capital movements. Consequently, national governments are more constrained in their economic and other related policies. In responding to the dilemmas created by globalization, *different* national systems can and do respond in *different* ways, they argue. Far from foreseeing a system of 'competitive austerity', Esping-Andersen concludes that the welfare state is here to stay. Within the advanced economies, existing political alignments of clients, welfare state workers, trades unions etc. with a stake in existing welfare arrangements, imply that welfare state change will be limited and slow, even in the face of global economic changes and challenges.

The fourth and last perspective, represented by Rieger and Leibfried (2003),

turns the 'orthodoxy' that globalization threatens welfare systems on its head by suggesting that welfare states actually provided the vital precondition for the development of post-war economic liberalization, or what is more commonly known as 'economic globalization', and continue to constrain globalization now. They argue that a range of ad hoc measures focused on citizens' 'social rights' were developed in the West European nations in the 1950s and 1960s as part of the social democratic governments' attempts to regulate their economies to form a sort of welfare capitalism. Although it was not undertaken for this purpose, the development of welfare provisions allowed for the subsequent development of a free-market economy on an international scale. International trade and the 'globalizing' of the economy internationally had occurred before, but the difference in the post-Second World War period was that the welfare state was now able to lessen the social effects of free trade by countering the effects in terms of unemployment and lowering of incomes of certain groups. What is more, the role of national governments making decisions that are still domestically focused continues to be at the heart of global economic developments – the roles of bodies such as the WTO and the IMF are still much less important for global economic and political decision-making than national governments. Thus globalization is not some sort of inevitable and all-powerful 'external' process that governments and people have to respond to. Rather, they argue, we should still think of an international system that is made up of interdependent national economies, not some sort of totally globalized economy divorced from nation-states. National governments now have a threefold challenge: to reform their welfare state policies without alienating the various groups who have a stake in the status quo (welfare recipients, welfare workers etc.); to manage the socio-economic effects of globalization in their countries; and to maintain global market conditions. Whether each government can do this, and the ways in which they do it, are open questions.

Assessing the Perspectives

Having summarized the four perspectives, let us now look at the evidence regarding social policy developments to see which appears to offer the best guide to analysing the evidence.

Perspective 1: Globalization causes welfare retrenchment through the increasing dominance of capitalism in the world's economy. For this view to be upheld, we would expect the direct impact of economic globalization to have led to various countries experiencing substantial, and essentially similar, welfare state changes. In fact, there is little evidence of an essentially similar impact by globalization on all welfare states. Changes which have occurred, though they may have been indirectly related to globalization, have been mediated through national governmental policies and institutions, a process that has led to quite different outcomes, as we shall see below. Even in Central and Eastern European countries, where the situation after the collapse of the communist system may have seemed ripe for the neo-liberal characteristics of globalization to make the strongest impact, the evidence is

not that of unfettered forces of global capitalism causing welfare changes.

Perspective 2. Globalization has had little effect upon welfare states, though other social and economic processes have. In this case, we would expect globalization to have had little or no clear or direct impact on welfare state changes in individual countries. Any similarities in trends in welfare state policies between countries are, in this view, related to the choice of similar policy solutions by governments, rather than to the external constraints of globalization. Once again, the evidence seems to offer little support for this perspective. The significance of factors Pierson mentions, such as population ageing, the increasing costs of and demands for even bigger welfare systems, should not be undervalued. It is also clear, however, that factors in the international economy have also affected social policy change.

Perspective 3: Globalization affects welfare states but its effects and roles are mediated by national politics and policies. According to this view, we would expect to see policy changes that are path-dependent, but that may be quite significant. The nature of change will depend on the pre-existing national welfare ideology and the institutional framework of the welfare state in each country, but with similarities in trends within the same broad type of welfare state system.

The evidence on globalization and social policy change seems to support Esping-Andersen et al.'s view that existing welfare institutional arrangements and commitments in different countries significantly constrain the amount of change which can be and has been made in various countries around the world as governments seek to respond to the pressures of economic globalization (see also Perspective 4 below). Thus we see how different welfare states and different groupings of welfare states have responded in what have been called 'path-dependent' ways, i.e. which reflect pre-existing ways of delivering welfare and different sorts of welfare ideologies. These arrangements and commitments, and the constituencies they created of welfare users and welfare providers, coupled with the need for governments to sustain political support, mean that welfare state responses and adaptations to globalization will tend to be slow and piecemeal.

Perspective 4: Welfare states have generated globalization and limit its future development. This perspective is the least prescriptive of the range. Rieger and Leibfried suggest that what happens in the future with regard to *both* globalization's future development *and* social policy is an open question. What happens will depend, principally, not on the autonomous and 'external' impact of globalization, because globalization is not a process that is free of national governmental intervention. What happens will depend more upon the actions and policies of national governments, the responses of their national constituencies, and the possibility, for example, that certain countries may decide to retreat from full involvement in the global economy and return to protectionist trade policies to defend both their economic and social constituencies. In essence, we should be prepared for a variety of different responses and policy initiatives or, indeed for the whole complex interdependence to collapse.

Globalization and Social Policy as Parts of a Dynamic Process

So where does this brief review of theoretical perspectives and the evidence take us? Behind the hype about globalization causing welfare state collapse, or at best retrenchment, a rather more complicated 'reality' presents itself. It would certainly seem that economic globalization is presenting various welfare states with pressures upon their capacity to fund and sustain their welfare provisions, let alone expand them. On the political front, however, the picture of increasingly powerless governments whose autonomy is being significantly reduced by globalization appears exaggerated – governments around the globe are responding to globalization, albeit within a more heavily constrained range of policy options, in supporting, restructuring or retrenching their welfare states. In addition, in Europe the role of the European Union is increasingly important as a supranational body which could, simultaneously, be seen as promoting *and* resisting the pressures of globalization depending upon which area of its activities one looks at. Similarly, we need to consider carefully how other international organizations, such as the World Bank, the International Monetary Fund, the World Trade Organization, the International Labour Organization and others, are implicated in the interplay of pressures between globalization and national welfare state policy-making rather than simply accepting that these bodies represent and promote the unmitigated 'evils' of world capitalist globalization.

Dispassionate consideration of both the theories and evidence about globalization and social policy suggests that a more 'reciprocal' view of the links may offer a fruitful way forward, rather than thinking only in terms of how far and in what ways globalization causes social policy change. Research suggests that the character of globalization is being constructed and interpreted differently in different national systems, or types of welfare system. Different types of welfare state (or rather governments running welfare states) have different perceptions of globalization and the problems and opportunities it presents, connected to the ways in which these different types of national welfare system are themselves constructed and to their pre-existing welfare ideas and practices. So, the social-democratic welfare state of, say, Sweden brings to its perception and range of possible responses to globalization a quite different legacy from that of, say, the more market-focused USA, the post-communist Hungary or the quite distinct cultural and religiously infused welfare system of Japan. It could be argued that at the national level there are *different globalization processes*, since there are *different welfare state contexts*. National welfare systems have not only been developed to counter market failure, but are a reflection and a reinforcement of the specific social structural and labour market characteristics of a given country. Welfare systems constitute specific normative, ideological and cultural legacies in each country. Therefore, welfare states should be seen as important parts of the socio-economic and politico-cultural structures of countries which themselves shape the way that globalization influences these countries. Welfare state reforms apparently 'caused by globalization' could alternatively be understood as having either anticipated or even developed so-called globalization trends. For example, moves by national governments to reduce welfare costs as a major part of a rising public debt have, by their policies, contributed to the austerity which globalization is supposed to be generating.

Emerging Issues

Recently, much more attention is being paid by both academics and policy-makers to the links between globalization and social policy in the developing countries of Africa, Latin America and East Asia. Writers such as George and Wilding (2003)

point out that globalization has not yet penetrated these countries as much as the advanced industrial countries and, indeed, has tended to boost economic growth in these countries more than elsewhere. At the same time, a number of jobs have been exported to these countries from the advanced countries as a feature of globalized economics, and while this has been generally beneficial for those people gaining unskilled and semi-skilled jobs in, say, China and India, and for their export trade, it has been at the cost of job losses in the same sectors in the developed countries. Nevertheless, the political balance of power with regard to global decision-making still rests with the developed countries, not least within international organizations such as the WTO. Overall, it would appear that a key issue for the future of social policy in a globalized/izing world will be the potential for securing welfare outcomes not just in the developed but also in the developing countries.

Some have argued for the development of a global social policy approach. However, it is difficult to see which supranational agencies could command general support for developing this, especially in the aftermath of the Iraq war and the growth of ethno-religious tensions within and between countries, even if such a project could command the support of governments and citizens. A more likely prospect, at least in the short to medium term, is of national governments, plus certain transnational bodies such as the European Union, attempting to 'muddle along' in coping with economic and political pressures at home and abroad that characterize the relationship between globalization and social policy.

Guide to Further Sources

The best single-volume introduction to the variety of perspectives on globalization is D. Held and A. McGrew, *Globalization/Anti-Globalization* (Polity, 2002). Examples of the four theoretical perspectives outlined in the chapter can be found in the following texts: R. Mishra, *Globalization and the Welfare State* (Edward

Elgar, 1999); P. Pierson (ed.), *The New Politics of the Welfare State* (Oxford University Press, 2001); G. Esping-Andersen (ed.), *Welfare States in Transition: National Adaptations in Global Economies* (Sage, 1996); and E. Rieger and S. Leibfried, *Limits to Globalization* (Polity, 2003).

Chapter 54

Social Policy in Europe

Jochen Clasen

Overview

- European countries have consistently been the highest spenders on social policy within the economically advanced groups of OECD countries.
- European countries provide the most generous benefit levels within the OECD.
- Typically European (but not British) is the use of employment protection as a mechanism for securing income for wage earners.
- Typically European (but not British) is the involvement of social partners in social policy-making.

Introduction

Geographically, Europe is a rather vague entity. Its eastern border in particular is ambiguous. Russia is a European country, but is all of Russia part of Europe? Is Turkey European or Asian, or both? Politically, things are not much simpler. The idea that 'Europe' can somehow be regarded as synonymous with the European Union is unduly reductionist. Even if, in 2007, the EU covers 27 countries and thus represents most people who live in Europe, it excludes not only very small states such as Liechtenstein or Andorra, but politically important countries such as Norway and Switzerland.

From a British perspective, 'Europe' is often portrayed as both different from the UK and homogenous in its non-British character, as popular references to things 'European' with regard to food or football indicate. In some respects, the former notion might have some substance given the linguistic and partly cultural affinity of the UK with the USA, Australia, Canada and New Zealand as the economically advanced English-speaking 'family of nations' (Castles 1993). As for the latter point, however, culturally, linguistically and socio-economically Europe is a rather heterogeneous group of countries and regions. Since this applies to social policy too, it is rather difficult, if not impossible, to capture the variation of 'social policy in Europe' within the space constraints of this short chapter.

A less ambitious aim, therefore, is pursued here. First, adopting a macro-perspective, I ask to what degree social policy in European countries is different compared with social policy in other economically developed countries. Secondly, focusing on the European Union, I reflect on the diversity of social policy in Europe. Given that many readers of this volume are likely to be registered for a degree at a British university, it seems reasonable to ask how 'European' social policy in the UK is. In other words, are there traits which are 'typical' for European social policy, and, if so, do we find these traits in the UK?

European Social Policy – Does It Exist?

Is there such a thing as European social policy, or, more precisely, within the set of economically advanced countries in the world, is it possible to identify characteristics which are typical of social policy in Europe? Asking a similar question, and applying financial, institutional and ideological criteria, Baldwin (1996) firmly arrived at a negative conclusion. Indeed, using a perspective of public social spending as a point of departure, the range of social policy effort across European (and even EU) countries was very wide indeed in the 1980s and early 1990s. Equally, there was hardly any distinctively European pattern in which resources were distributed, i.e. as universal, insurance-based or means-tested support. Equally, the level of benefits, such as public pensions or unemployment compensation, was neither consistently higher nor lower in European countries than in other OECD countries. On average, Baldwin conceded, welfare spending might be more generous in European than in non-European countries, but he questioned how much, with so broad a range within the European social systems, the averages indicated.

Does Baldwin's verdict still apply today? If we take the European Union as a point of departure, the processes of enlargement in 2004 (adding ten countries) and 2007 (another two) have certainly created more rather than less diversity in the scope, depth and institutional range of social policy provision. However, if we consider the level of public social expenditure as a proportion of national income as a measurement of the

relative emphasis countries put on social policy and assess the thirty economically most advanced countries in the world (OECD-30), European nations have consistently been the highest spenders on social policy since 1980, with Sweden invariably at the top of the table (OECD 2007a). Similarly, throughout the past two decades there has always been a gap between the economically advanced European countries and the richer non-European countries such as the USA, Canada, Australia, New Zealand and Japan. Aggregate public social expenditure across the EU-15, i.e. member states prior to the EU expansion towards Central and Southern Europe in 2004, has been consistently higher than aggregate spending in these five non-European countries. Moreover, in 2003 each EU-15 country spent at least 20 per cent of their GDP on social protection, except for Ireland, where strong economic growth depressed the relative effort in public social spending. By contrast, no economically advanced country outside Europe reached this mark. Perhaps as a corollary, the average total revenue from tax and social insurance contributions as a percentage of GDP is significantly higher in European countries than in non-European OECD countries (OECD 2006a).

Of course, there are questions of comparability. Some social policy domains (such as education for example) are excluded and, while taking account of different sizes of national economies, measuring social expenditure as a share of GDP is always liable to fluctuations in national business cycles. Ideally, differences between such demographic patterns or unemployment levels should be considered in order to arrive at 'adjusted' levels of spending (Siegel, in Clasen and Siegel 2007). Moreover, recent analyses of 'net' social spending have pointed out that cross-national differences are less marked once the effects of taxation on benefit income, indirect taxation on consumption financed by benefits as well as tax breaks are considered (Adema and Ladaique 2005). If, in addition, voluntary social spending is considered, the variation in levels of net 'total' social expenditure between European and non-European OECD countries narrows considerably (ibid.: 32). However, such a broad measure might be less useful since it conceals redistributive efforts, which is a major objective of social policy. Thus, taking account of the effect of taxation, but leaving aside voluntary spending, differences between the higher European spenders and lower-spending non-European countries remain distinctive. Interestingly, using this measure of 'net publicly mandated social spending' indicates that continental European countries, such as France and Germany, rather than Nordic countries, are top of the OECD table as a result of the fact that the tax systems in Denmark and Sweden claw back more money handed out for social purposes.

European countries are often assumed to be providing the most generous benefits in the world. While the definition and measurement of 'generosity' is certainly complex, one indicator is the so-called 'net replacement rate', i.e. the level of net benefit income in relation to previous net earnings. The OECD provides such calculations for different risks, income levels and family constellations (OECD 2006b). A quick glance at, in this case, unemployment compensation during the first phase out of work indicates a significant degree of variation and, at first sight, little sense of a European pattern. However, it is noticeable that across eighteen different combinations of family types and earnings levels, the five most generous countries (out of thirty OECD countries) are always EU-15 countries (or Switzerland), albeit not always the same five. By contrast, while European countries, including the UK, can sometimes be found amongst the least generous five countries, this group is generally dominated by non-European countries.

Another often assumed trait of social policy in Europe is the emphasis on a broad rather than narrow notion of social citizenship. For example, in 2003 the vast majority of European countries distributed around 90 per cent or even more of their total cash transfers without an income test. By contrast, the bulk of cash benefits in Australia (over 80 per cent), New Zealand or Canada (close to 50 per cent) were income-tested (OECD 2007a). However, the picture is less than perfect given that means-testing is less prevalent in the US (15 per cent) than in some European countries such as Ireland (30 per cent) or the UK (22 per cent).

The role of publicly provided rather than privately purchased social policy is yet another characteristic associated with European social policy. In fact, the picture is much more blurred, which is partly due to the problem of delineating public (and thus assumed to be mandatory) and market-based private (and thus voluntary) social spending. The OECD (2007a) makes a distinction between voluntary private and mandated private protection expenditure, but difficulties remain. Nominally, private occupational pensions based on collective agreements, for example, can be fairly comprehensive and regulated in a way which makes them all but mandatory. Equally, sickness or disability benefits provided by employers are generally categorized by the OECD as private mandatory social spending, but not in all cases, thereby creating anomalies (De Deken and Kittel, in Clasen and Siegel 2007). This has considerable consequences, as the case of the Netherlands demonstrates, which the OECD (2007a) deems to have the second highest level of private voluntary social spending across thirty OECD countries, surpassed only by the USA. Other authors, however, consider the OECD's categorization of Dutch spending as a 'misnomer' (De Deken and Kittel, in Clasen and Siegel 2007). In short, in the absence of satisfactory conceptual clarity and good comparable data, it is difficult to substantiate the OECD's claim that market-based voluntary social protection is as relevant in some European countries (the UK, the Netherlands and also France) as it is outside Europe.

Turning to outcome measures of (not only) social policy, a consistent pattern emerges which indicates that some, but not all, European countries are maintaining relatively low levels of poverty and income inequality. Defining poverty as the proportion of individuals with below a certain percentage of median disposable income, statistics indicate that the four Nordic countries, but also West (Benelux, Austria, Switzerland, France) and Central European countries (the Czech Republic, Slovakia, Hungary) performed best across thirty-one economically developed countries. While all non-European countries were above the average (LIS 2007; see also OECD 2007b), the same applies to many European countries. The picture is similar for inequality (of disposable income; i.e. after tax and benefits), with North and West European countries, such as Denmark, Finland, Sweden and the Netherlands, having the lowest levels of inequality of all OECD countries. At the same time, however, there are several European countries, including the UK, Ireland, Greece, Italy and Spain, which have levels of inequality that are as high as economically advanced countries outside Europe (LIS 2007).

Finally, Baldwin (1996) pointed to institutional cross-national variation in, for example, the organization of healthcare or the role of family allowances. Here, his assessment of the absence of a European identity remains valid because of continuing diversity across and within countries, as well as within individual social policy arrangements (see chapter 52). This is perhaps most visible in pension systems which tend to be multi-tiered, with or without a minimum public pension, at times means-tested but often not, and

supplemented by mandatory or voluntary occupational systems. Categorizing healthcare systems too, a range of regulatory and financial models can be found across the OECD, but no distinctively European identity.

In sum, from a macro-perspective, social policy in Europe is distinctive in the sense of relatively high levels of public social spending, a broad notion of social citizenship and benefit rates which are typically, but not in all cases, more generous than in other economically advanced countries. Several European countries come out top in terms of reducing poverty and containing income inequality. However, there is no European social policy identity in the ways in which social protection is organized or in the mix between public and private provision.

Typically European and/or Typically British

Cousins argues that 'while we can see a distinctive *European social model*, we do not see a *single European welfare state* in any strong sense of the term' (2005: 240; emphasis in the original). Indeed, there is too much diversity of social policy arrangements even within the EU member states for it to be possible to postulate any sense of uniformity. However, while diverse in settings and outcomes, there are social policy characteristics which are either exclusively, or predominately, found in Europe. In the remainder of this chapter I shall address some of these and, in this context, reflect on the relative position of British social policy as typically (or atypically) European.

Social policy needs resources which are collected via direct and indirect taxation or social security contributions, sometimes referred to as 'payroll tax'. Typically European countries devote a greater role to contributory (social insurance) as opposed to tax funding of the welfare state, as indicated by the combined (employee and employer) share of social security contributions. For example, in 2000, marginal (combined) social security contribution rates for single persons on average earnings were below 20 per cent in all non-European OECD-30 countries, but typically between 30 and 45 per cent in European countries. The exceptions were Denmark, Ireland and the UK, as well as (at this particular income level) the Netherlands.

Typically European, and thus applying a broader understanding of social policy, is the use of employment protection as a mechanism of providing income security to workers. Across nineteen EU countries for which data exist, the UK had the lowest level of employment protection in 2004 (European Commission 2005: 190), followed by Ireland. Denmark too provides relatively little employment security but this is compensated by generous unemployment benefits and a strong profile of active labour market policies such as training. By contrast, the UK spends considerably less on active labour market policies than almost all other EU-15 countries (European Commission 2006: 132). Equally, the UK and Ireland focus benefit support on low-income groups and are significantly less generous to middle- and higher-income groups. This is also reflected in the relative scope of means-tested benefits, which is significantly above the EU average in Ireland, the UK and Malta (ibid.: 102). A quick glance at the generosity of other benefits (sickness and public pensions) underlines the fact that average (and better) income groups are invariably better protected in Northern and particularly in Western continental European countries compared with the UK (see OECD 2006a). In short, low levels of both job and income security, which are due to an only weakly regulated labour market, make the UK (and Ireland) somewhat atypically European and puts the countries firmly within the camp of eco-

nomically advanced 'liberal market economies' otherwise found outside Europe – in the US, Canada, Australia and New Zealand (Pontusson 2005).

In many European countries, trade unions and employers have long played pivotal roles in the administration of social policy, and in particular social insurance programmes, such as pensions, unemployment, injury or sickness insurance. The actual range and scope of involvement differs, of course. For example, employers and trade unions in Germany collaborate within quasi-public but legally independent and financially separate organizations of social insurance, at times joined by state officials. Social partners in Austria, Belgium, the Netherlands and Switzerland play similar roles. In France, employees and employer are jointly in charge of social insurance schemes such as the unemployment benefit and pension funds. In Sweden, Denmark and Finland trade union-affiliated organizations are solely responsible for administering unemployment insurance. Related to this, the idea of social security acting as a form of 'social wage', i.e. reflecting former earnings as a way of at least partially preserving accustomed living standards, is common in most European countries. In the UK, neither such arrangements nor the notion of social policy as part of industrial relations applies. Finally, collective bargaining is another important social policy instrument which Central and North European countries, but much less so the UK or Ireland, rely on as a means for securing not only income but regulating working conditions.

In sum, in the context of economically advanced countries in the EU, the UK (and Ireland to a lesser degree) is somewhat atypical in a European sense because of a notion of social policy which is narrowly focused on the redistribution of market income via taxation and benefits and services (Bonoli, in Classen and Siegel 2007), as opposed to a broader understanding which pursues social policy goals also via channels such as employment protection or collective agreements.

Emerging Issues

There is no European welfare state and there is no distinctive European social policy identity. But European countries engage more in social policy than in any other region of the world and, typically, apply a broader and more generous notion of social citizenship. Not all European nations are successful in combating poverty or containing income inequality, but the best performing countries in both respects are European. Not least as a result of improved efforts in some areas (such as education and health), the UK has moved from the edge to the middle of the range of European social policy as far as expenditure is concerned. However, in many other respects, and particularly with regard to the link between social policy and other policy fields such as industrial relations and employment protection, British social policy remains, for better or worse, somewhat atypically European.

A more European perspective thus serves as a reminder that social policy can (and perhaps should) be regarded from a broad perspective, involving more policy areas than the conventional classic social policy domains. Similarly, more nuanced data on social spending are gradually becoming available which, despite methodological challenges, allow for more meaningful cross-national comparisons within and beyond social policy in European countries (see chapter 52).

Guide to Further Sources

W. Adema and M. Ladaique, *Net Social Expenditure, 2005 edition*, OECD Social, Employment and Migration working papers, No. 29 (OECD, 2005) is an indispensable text for assessing social policy spending across countries. Similarly, the volume by J. Clasen and N. A. Siegel (eds), *Investigating Welfare State Change. The 'Dependent Variable Problem' in Comparative Analysis* (Edward Elgar, 2007) includes several contributions which reflect on the problems of conceptualizing and empirically comparing national social policy arrangements (including the contributions by G. Bonoli, J. De Deken and B. Kittel, and N. A. Siegel referred to in this chapter).

Very different but very useful texts are: P. Baldwin, 'Can we define a European welfare state model?', in B. Greve (ed.), *Comparative Welfare Systems: The Scandinavian Model in a Period of Change* (Macmillan, 1996), pp. 29–44; M. Cousins, *European Welfare States: Comparative Perspectives* (Sage, 2005); and J. Pontusson, *Inequality and Prosperity. Social Europe versus Liberal America* (Cornell University Press, 2005). F. G. Castles (ed.), *Families of Nations: Patterns of Public Policy in Western Democracies* (Dartmouth, 1993) remains a very useful approach to seeking similarities and differences across nations.

Issues of data, concepts and measurement can be followed in European Commission, *Employment in Europe 2005, DG Employment, Social Affairs and Equal Opportunities* (Office for Official Publications of the European Communities, 2005); European Commission, *Joint Report on Social Protection and Social Inclusion 2006* (Office for Official Publications of the European Communities, 2006); Eurostat, European Social Statistics. Social Protection Expenditure and Receipts, Data 1996–2004 (Office for Official Publications of the European Communities,

JOCHEN CLASEN

2007); OECD, *OECD Annual Revenue Statistics* (OECD, 2006a); OECD, *Benefits and Wages. OECD Indicators 2004* (OECD, 2006b); OECD, *The Social Expenditure Database; SOCX 1980–2003* (OECD, 2007a); and OECD, *Society at a Glance 2006* (OECD, 2007b).

OECD and related information can be accessed at <www.oecd.org/els/social/expenditure>, while data on income was drawn from LIS, *Luxembourg Income Study: Key Figures*, at <www.lisproject.org/keyfigures.htm> (accessed on 4/4/2007).

Chapter 55

Social Policy in Liberal Market Societies

Michael Hill

Overview

- Liberal market societies are defined as ones where social policy development has been particularly inhibited by political value systems that see social policy as a threat to the working of the capitalist market.
- While the US is seen as the archetypical example of a liberal market system, 'regime theory' identifies a group of other predominantly English-speaking nations with similar characteristics, including the UK.
- There are problems about this regime categorization as issues about the role of social insurance throw up complications and ambiguities.
- Within the liberal market regime group, an alternative grouping of nations engaging in direct resource transfers from the better off has been identified.
- Underlying the whole categorization problem is the fact that liberal market approaches to the management of the economy are now dominant in the economically advanced world.

Introduction

In exploring what is meant by 'liberal market societies', there is a need to clear out of the way potential misunderstandings about the use of the word 'liberal' in this context, as it is used in many different ways. One of its usages carries the particular connotation of freedom, but when linked in this way to the word 'market' it is only the freedom of markets that is being signified. The reference here, then, is to liberal economic ideas, which see the free market as the ideal device for allocating life-chances, and the primary role for the state as being to enhance economic efficiency. It is also important to

bear in mind that the usage here is not the same as the American usage of liberal to convey a progressive approach to social policy.

Characterizing Liberal Market Societies

Accordingly, when we look at social policy in liberal market societies, we are looking at an approach to social provision in which interference with the free working of the market has been kept to a relatively low level. This is, of course, in the modern world, in comparison with the other social policy models (see chapter 52).

The point about comparison is, of course, important. This label – 'liberal market societies' – is being used in comparative discussions of social policy to designate a particular social model or regime type distinguishable from others. The most influential contemporary usage is in the work of Esping-Andersen, who describes a type of welfare state in which means-testing is widespread, social insurance is little used and there is little redistribution through social policy. It may also be noted that there are comparable efforts by other writers to contrast the extent of government intervention in respect of industrial relations and the management of the economy as a whole.

The United States is often seen as the archetypical liberal market society. Its performance in respect of social policy – expressed either in terms of levels of expenditure or in terms of the incidence of poverty, inequality and ill-health – is markedly inferior to other societies of comparable prosperity. In dominant American political discourse, public social policy (often identified as 'welfare', with that word being given a special connotation to refer to reluctantly provided means-tested relief) is seen as a costly imposition upon citizens and upon the economy. As a consequence, whilst the relief of extreme poverty is not neglected, most social support (other than for elderly people) is only provided under conditions in which the behaviour of those getting it is regulated. In particular, there are expectations that efforts will be made to find paid work, and failure to do so may result in the termination of benefits.

American 'experts' (particularly economists) have taken a message around the world that freedom should involve minimum intervention into markets, and therefore residual social policy is designed only to prevent serious deprivation. They have had a strong influence upon the advice given by international organizations like the World Bank and the International Monetary Fund (see chapters 37 and 57).

However, in his regime typology, Esping-Andersen also links Australia, New Zealand, Canada, Ireland and the United Kingdom with the United States as liberal market social policy regimes. It may be noted that these are all societies in which English is the dominant language. The liberal market systems are sometimes referred to as 'Anglo-Saxon' regimes, an unfortunate usage, since the term is a pseudo-racial one unacceptable to the Irish and to many residents of these multiethnic societies. On the other hand, it is reasonable to accept that there are shared cultural influences across these Anglophone societies.

There are, however, other societies that some writers also include in the category. This brings us to a crucial point about the identification of liberal market social policy systems. In many respects the whole comparative social policy discourse is about the extent to which, in a wide range of modern societies with democratic systems of government, capitalist economic institutions are dominant and social policy involves a relatively marginal set of government interventions to modify its impact upon the welfare of citizens. In which case, why are some systems described as liberal market ones while others are labelled differently? Can we actually draw clear distinctions between regime types?

The crucial starting point for regime theory is an argument stating that, while in all democratic societies (indeed nearly all societies) governments give some attention to unmet needs (if only through Poor Law systems), in some societies redistribution of resources outside the market on the basis of need goes much further. Esping-Andersen explicitly explains this in terms of the significance of political movements, and describes the effects upon social stratification as reducing the effects of market processes (using a special term: 'decommodification'). But this is just referring to a tendency, shared by many societies, and in practice the boundaries of the liberal market category are hard to define (see chapters 52 and 54).

Some Problems About Defining Liberal Market Social Policy Systems

It is perhaps useful to go back to Esping-Andersen's defining characteristics to note how it uses a distinction between universal transfers and the use of social insurance on the one hand and social assistance on the other. The problem here is that social insurance is in fact found in some of the liberal market societies, but in modified and rather limited forms. Developments in its use – in the US in the Roosevelt era at the end of the 1930s and in the UK in the 1940s – have not been followed through. Hence, liberal market societies cannot be defined simply in terms of the presence or absence of social insurance. To be fair to Esping-Andersen, this is not quite his typologization; he uses the word 'modest' in relation to social insurance systems to qualify the classification. What then is meant by modest? Esping-Andersen uses some measures of the size of systems and the extent to which they effect redistribution to take this analysis further. We obviously cannot follow this through here, and can only note that choice of measures will be crucial and that it has not been difficult for Esping-Andersen's critics to seize upon alternative measures.

More difficult is the fact that there is not necessarily a clear link between the use of social insurance as a key social policy device and effective redistribution. While it has been argued that social insurance makes redistribution politically easier because everyone has a stake in the system, it is in fact the case that some social insurance systems redistribute very little. Moreover, in certain circumstances direct tax funding of a universal system may be a more effective redistributive device. This observation is particularly pertinent for some problems about the inclusion of the UK in the group of liberal market social policy regimes. As far as healthcare is concerned the universally available tax-funded NHS stands out as the key example of a social policy in the UK that largely frees up healthcare from market forces, and has a potential to address health inequalities more effectively than an insurance-based system.

Something of the same kind may be said about pension provision, though this is more complicated and therefore controversial. Many of the biggest and most comprehensive social insurance-based pension systems are not particularly redistributive. A feature of highly developed social insurance systems is that what pensioners get is principally determined by their previous labour market positions. Hence, even though the state may play a big role in making the system secure, it may have done very little to mitigate the effects of market forces. This means that we have to look for other, often more difficult to measure, indices of redistribution. Crucial here are (a) whether there is a guaranteed minimum (provided on a residency or citizenship basis regardless of previous labour market participation), (b) whether that minimum is set at a relatively generous level and (c) whether access to this minimum is governed by means-tests of any form. Hence the UK system satisfies the first two of those tests: there is a universally guaranteed minimum and that minimum is relatively generous (at least by the standards of other countries). This benefit is, however, a means-tested benefit (pension credit). But even the countries with strong social insurance pensions schemes underpin them in various ways with means-tests. The 'acid test' of relative generosity then depends upon the rules applying to those means-tests. We explore this topic further in the next section.

Is There a Sub-Group of Nations with 'Radical Systems'?

The analysis of the UK system in the last section indicates how interpreting the way social policy provisions relate to market systems is rather complicated. It is important to explore relationships between income differences in societies *before* government interventions and *after* them, suggesting that it is the size of the 'gap' between rich and poor and the extent to which policies close that gap that needs to be the object of attention rather than simply aggregate expenditure. Then income transfer policies may be examined in terms of their contribution to both the reduction of inequality and the eradication of poverty; these are alternative social policy goals which need to be interpreted in their wider political contexts. Income transfer systems may be compared in terms of *efficiency* (the relationship between outputs and inputs) and *effectiveness* (the actual redistributive achievement of systems). This raises questions about the wide range of influences on incomes, and the variety of policy options available to political actors who want the state to try to change the income distribution.

There are two possibilities here. One is that under certain circumstances markets may work, or have been made to work, in ways which minimize the need for government interventions *after* market processes. In this sense, Australia and New Zealand have been explicitly described as belonging to a 'fourth world of welfare capitalism', where political activity from the 'left' has been put not so much into the pursuit of equalization through social policy as into the achievement of equality in pre-tax, pre-transfer incomes. More widely, the success of governments in ensuring full employment may be seen to have a similar impact.

The other possibility is the operation of redistributive policy to have a direct impact upon eventually achieved incomes, without using the more indirect social insurance idea. It seems implicit in the notion of liberal market systems that such state-imposed interventions will be resisted as distorting the market too much. Hence, if within the liberal market group of nations identified above there are nations where such measures can be identified, it may be suggested that there is a need to identify yet another kind of 'regime'. It is in this sense that some comparative theorists have identified another regime group, which is called 'radical'. Its characteristic is a relative absence of social insurance, but some evidence of the use of means-tests to effect substantial redistribution. Australia and New Zealand are put in this category, and sometimes also the UK and Ireland. In the case of the UK, data on poverty throw doubt on the effectiveness of this, but the situation may be changing with the simplification of means-testing: the extensive use of tax credits to enhance the incomes of the working poor and the attempt to extend support in a comparatively straightforward way to the elderly poor in the form of pension credit.

Against this reclassification, it may be argued that, however effectively means-testing may redistribute, what remains crucially distinctive in the liberal market group of societies is the assumption that most citizens should develop their own forms of social protection – paying into private pensions systems, insuring against other contingencies (including even the risk of ill health) – with means-tested state benefits and services only for the poor. That assumption is rooted in an ideology that sees the operation of individual choice and self-interest in the marketplace as the best mechanism for the regulation of social life.

Why the Liberal Market Categorization Raises Important Questions

It is probably the case that, by now, some readers will be concluding that what we have here is an academic game in which scholars compete to offer alternative lists of nations. But taxonomies can be important for theory building, and in this case there are some crucial questions for social policy analysis about the extent to which the working of the market is, and can be, modified in the interests of welfare and redistributive goals. There is much contemporary debate about the viability of social policy arrangements that are not market-based. For example, in the area of pensions policy, international organizations like the World Bank have argued strongly for a model in which, beyond a state-guaranteed minimum, pensions should be provided through contributions to private marketized organizations. Justifications are offered for this in terms of the prime importance of tying social policy to economic goals. Nations looking to develop or strengthen pension systems (for example in East Asia – see chapter 56 – South America and Eastern Europe) are urged to adopt this model. But that approach is also challenged by a social insurance model (particularly developed in continental Western Europe but now also in Japan and South Korea). Significantly, the argument then centres not only on social goals but also on arguments about whether privatized pensions make the economic contributions claimed for them.

An important facet of the argument between the alternative social policy models concerns the impact of them upon competitiveness in the global economy. In fact there is an absence of strong evidence that the liberal market systems compete more effectively than others. Consider Esping-Andersen's list of the nations in that category. There are many simplistic journalistic assertions on this theme, many seeming to have cogency at some point in time but then losing force as nations rise and fall in the economic performance league. At the time of writing, Ireland stands out as a particularly strongly growing economy within the liberal market group, but surely that is explained by the special circumstances of that until relatively recently poorly developed economy. Efforts to test hypotheses about the impact of social policy upon economic growth run into considerable difficulties because of the multiplicity of factors that influence the latter.

Esping-Andersen's more recent work, building on his original theory, suggests that the nature of economic activity within a society is likely to be a crucial intermediary factor between social policy and growth. Where the neo-liberal model suggests that competitiveness can be achieved only through the driving down of wages and the removal of social protection, it is argued there is an alternative that involves a focus on preserving a highly trained and adaptable labour force. Social policy can make a contribution to this. Moreover, inasmuch as social protection systems contribute to social harmony, they generate a commitment to national problem-solving. Finally, since the welfare state is a system for the socialization of costs, then where it is absent the costs of economic change fall elsewhere with possibly more damaging consequences for the society (a key example here is, of course, the existence of high crime rates). Hence the relationship between social policy and growth is not as simple as neo-liberal theory suggests.

It is important to recognize that we have here not merely a set of arguments about competitiveness but also a conflict of discourses. The liberal market model embodies a set of principles: about the superiority of market arrangements, about the importance of growth and about the virtues of labour market participation. These are strongly defended by powerful actors – the beneficiaries of capitalist economic arrangements globally and within the most powerful nation in the world – against alternative discourses.

Emerging Issues

The era of an influential alternative social democratic discourse challenging the liberal market one is perhaps coming to an end (but see chapter 53). It was weakened by the fact that it never claimed to change capitalism but only to modify it, and that its more fiercely advocated 'cousin' (communism) ran into the sands both politically and economically. Perhaps now new green or feminist (see chapters 13 and 14) versions of this discourse are beginning to influence social policy a little. In the meantime there are grounds for the gloomy view (from a pro-social policy perspective) that the battle between the discourses has been won by the liberal market one.

Contemporary developments in social policy reflect the search for a compromise between the liberal market perspective and that viewpoint. Particularly in respect of social policies for people below pension age, there has been a strong shift, right across the world, towards policies that are seen as enhancing labour market participation. These may, of course, be simply revivals of older liberal market approaches, aiming to drive down labour costs and coerce people into work. But they may, for example, involve extensive attention to

training, to ensuring that care costs are supported and to minimizing discrimination against disabled people.

There is, however, another view that, although the evidence so far does not show that regimes with strong social policy systems cannot compete, the trends towards lower wages (and lower wage-related costs – such as social insurance contributions from employers) across the world will gradually eliminate the economic advantages of the economies with strong social policy systems. New competitors, particularly China and India, are also developing trained and highly adaptive labour forces, at much lower wage costs. The arguments for the liberal market approach to social policy are being taken very seriously by many nations, not solely those labelled in these terms by regime theory. Hence we have observed cuts to Dutch welfare benefits, earlier categorized by very high levels of income replacement, proclaimed as generating a 'Dutch miracle' of improved competitiveness. And even in Sweden there have been changes to the pensions system, involving the creation of a funded layer in which compulsory contributions go into private pension schemes. Traditional European welfare systems are on the defensive, making changes that may perhaps engender greater longer run changes.

Guide to Further Sources

The nature of comparative analysis of social policy is that classification systems explore individual type or regime categories in terms of their relationships to the alternatives. Hence this chapter, while it has avoided exploring any of the alternatives except inasmuch as they (as is the case with the Australasian 'fourth world' and the 'radical' regime type) are in a sense sub-types of the liberal market one, inevitably poses questions about contrasts. It is not possible therefore to direct readers to a literature on liberal market regimes and *nothing but* those regimes. The key sources for the exposition of the characteristics of the liberal market model of social policy are thus G. Esping-Andersen's very influential original work, *The Three Worlds of Welfare Capitalism* (Polity Press, 1990); R. E. Goodin, B. Headey, R. Muffels and H.-J. Dirven, *The Real Worlds of Welfare Capitalism* (Cambridge University Press, 1999), which, as well as offering a comparative analysis, explores the characteristics of one liberal market regime, the United States, and W. Arts and J. Gelisen, 'Three worlds of welfare capitalism or more?' *Journal of European Social Policy* 12/2 (2002): 137–58, which compares various approaches to regime theory.

The two key sources for the critique of the theory from the 'fourth world' perspective are F. G. Castles and D. Mitchell, 'Identifying welfare state regimes: the links between politics, instruments and outcomes', *Governance* 5/1 (1992): 1–26, and D. Mitchell, *Income Transfers in Ten Welfare States* (Avebury, 1991). D. Kangas, 'The politics of social security: on regressions, qualitative comparisons and cluster analysis', in T. Janoski and A. M. Hicks (eds), *The Comparative Political Economy of the Welfare State*' (Cambridge University Press, 1994) is another source on this issue.

No recommendations are included on the efforts to evaluate regimes in terms of competitiveness, on the grounds that this is a complex and often very technical literature. It is reviewed in chapter 13 of M. Hill, *Social Policy in the Modern World* (Blackwell, 2006). Esping-Andersen's work exploring issues about competitiveness and the future trajectories of welfare states is in his *Social Foundations of Post-Industrial Economies* (Oxford University Press, 1999) and his edited *Why We Need a New Welfare State* (Oxford University Press, 2002). Analyses of challenges to European welfare systems, shifting them in a more market oriented direction can be found in P. Taylor-Gooby's edited books, *European Welfare States under Pressure* (Sage, 2001) and *Making a European Welfare State?* (Blackwell, 2004).

Chapter 56

Social Policy in East Asian Societies

Michael Hill

Overview

- There is a case for looking at social policy in East Asian societies simply because of the increasing importance of those societies in the global scene.
- An examination of East Asia helps to enhance the explanatory power of comparative analysis.
- Comparative theory's claims to be of universal applicability means that examination of societies other than those for which it was developed provides an opportunity to test it.
- There are suggestions that new distinctively different regimes may be emerging in East Asia.
- The impact of rapid economic and demographic change raises crucial questions for social policy in this region.

Introduction

Early comparative social policy theory embodied a strong determinist element, suggesting that the growth of state social policy can be explained by industrialization, urbanization and democratization (in probably linked combinations). Such theory implied that differences across the world would be eroded by these processes. Later theory gave more attention to political differences between states, stressing differences in the extent of social policy development and the forms it takes. Nevertheless, regime theory works with a typology which seems to imply that each system will belong to one of a finite number of regime categories (see chapters 52 and 55). Hence a question that has been addressed by a number of scholars is 'Can regime theory be applied in East Asia, and if so how?'.

What Countries Are We Talking About?

There is an arbitrary character to any attempt to divide the world into regions for a discussion like this. Those divisions, moreover, tend to have an ethnocentric character in which societies that are seen to be alike to Western eyes are put together. The East Asian nations are, of course, the nations on the western side of the Pacific Ocean. The north-eastern Asian nations are the ones that get most attention from social policy scholars. Amongst them, there is one massive nation (China), another large one (Japan) and the divided nation of Korea (with important social welfare development in South Korea, and – as far as social policy scholars are concerned – no attention given to North Korea). There are two cities that were European colonies and are now quasi-autonomous Special Administrative Regions of China: Hong Kong and Macao. The latter is very small and has been little studied, though it is interesting to note as having an embryonic welfare system largely funded by taxes on gambling. Finally, in the northern group there is Taiwan, an island with a population of more than twenty million claimed by China but operating as an independent state, with now a democratic form of government and extensive social policies.

The nations to the south of that group have secured much less attention from social policy analysts, with the exception of the city-state of Singapore. Scrutiny of an atlas suggests there is no good reason to exclude discussion of Vietnam, Laos, Cambodia, Thailand, Malaysia, Indonesia and the Philippines from consideration here (and we could look even further south). In practice, with the partial exception of Malaysia, where limited developments have occurred along lines not unlike Singapore's, little attention has been paid to these countries. This may largely be explained in terms of the limited development of social policy.

So it is the social policy systems of Japan, South Korea, Hong Kong, Singapore and Taiwan that get most of the consideration in the discussions of social policy in East Asia, with even China getting less attention despite its importance (an issue to which we will return). Amongst these nations, Japan clearly has the most developed system. Moreover, as the one East Asian nation that has been a longstanding member of the Organization for Economic Cooperation and Development (OECD), the rich nations 'club' and main collator of statistics about their economic and social perfor-

mance, Japan features in many world-scale comparative analyses. In recent years Japan has been joined in the OECD by South Korea, so there is now some good comparative data on developments there too. The developments in Taiwan have quite a lot in common with those two, with all three nations using social insurance extensively. The disputed status of Taiwan means it has not been able to join the OECD.

Hong Kong and Singapore are of course small, though rich, and their social policy development has had some special features. In Hong Kong's case its colonial status meant that the UK encouraged some basic welfare development but kept costs low and did not let it develop social insurance. Singapore developed a rather distinctive approach of its own – a 'providence' fund – involving forced government-protected saving for social policy purposes.

So the debate about the characteristics of East Asian social policy is above all a debate about what is going on in Japan, South Korea, Taiwan, Hong Kong and Singapore, with some references to complex and hard to classify developments in China.

Fitting East Asian Societies into the Regime Model

The starting point for this discussion is to examine the arguments for the view that the East Asian nations can be fitted into Esping-Andersen's three-regime model (see chapter 52). Later sections go on to offer a case against that view and the various alternative perspectives. In Esping-Andersen's work one East Asian nation is included – Japan – and is seen as belonging in his 'conservative' category alongside European nations such as France, Germany, Austria and Switzerland. Esping-Andersen's original conclusions on Japan were challenged and he went back in later writing to defend his view. That defence is partly based upon his view that it is not helpful to multiply the number of specific regime categories, since he concedes that Japan is a marginal case between the conservative category and the liberal market one (see chapter 55). He goes on to stress the ways in which the pull between the two alternatives draws attention to strains and pressures within the Japanese system (particularly those relating to the role of the family in welfare). In that sense, one of the cases for regime theory is that it helps the analysis of these.

It is not surprising, given the controversy about Japan, that a rather similar argument has arisen about South Korea. That society is interesting inasmuch as there seems to be a struggle occurring around alternative perspectives on welfare that correspond with all three of the ideal-types in Esping-Andersen's model. There has been a strong emphasis upon the need to protect the market economy. There has been an emphasis upon the role of the family in welfare, and a strong interest in the use of social insurance, two characteristics of the conservative model. But there have also been significant advances towards universal and redistributive policies in relation to both pensions and healthcare. Again, therefore, the Esping-Andersen approach may be defended, not to assign South Korea to a regime category but to contribute to an analysis of a still evolving situation.

There has been consideration of the extent to which Taiwan shares the 'conservative' regime characteristics, while Singapore and Hong Kong have been categorized as rather more like liberal market ones.

Productivist Welfare Capitalism as a Fourth Regime Type?

There are two alternative approaches, using regime theory but identifying a fourth type. One of these is to suggest that these societies may be seen as ones in which the approach to social policy can be described as involving productivist welfare capitalism in which the orientation towards growth has been of key importance for social policy development. The difference here from the liberal market regimes, which that term seems also to describe (see chapter 55), is that the governments of the East Asian societies have been seen to be engaged in harnessing social policy in a particular effort to ensure rapid economic growth. Hence, for example, education policy has been stressed. Governments, particularly those in the countries that are still economically underdeveloped, have argued against rapid expansion of social care policies on the grounds that this could hinder the development project.

The very active state-driven developments (particularly characteristic of South Korea, Taiwan and Singapore) have implications for social policy different from those suggested in the delineation of either the conservative regime or the liberal market regime. The groups that first secured social protection in these societies comprised the military and civil servants. Measures to extend some insurance-based benefits to industrial workers followed next.

Securing the support of the emergent industrial 'working class' was important for the state-led growth so significant in these societies. Over much of the period between the Second World War and the severe financial crisis which shook East Asia in 1997, these societies experienced substantial growth with minimal unemployment. Hence, inasmuch as governments secured social support, they did it through their success in generating rapid income growth for the majority of the people. Data showing relatively low income inequality in South Korea and Taiwan offers additional evidence in support of this proposition. Egalitarian growth can be seen as a social policy goal not comprised within a regime theory premised upon the idea that social policy redistributes *after* market processes have had their impact.

A 'Confucian' Regime Type?

Another approach to the adaptation of regime theory has been to delineate a regime type with characteristics that are specifically Eastern. The main argument along these lines has been the suggestion that Confucian family ideologies lead to a greater delegation of welfare responsibilities to the family and extended family. It must, however, be said that the label 'Confucian' is not really appropriate outside Chinese societies.

However, wider problems about this argument are that (a) in any underdeveloped income maintenance system the family will, *faute de mieux*, have to take on greater responsibilities, and (b) the use of Confucian 'type' ideologies as a justification for inaction by the political elite is not evidence that political demands can and will be damped down in this way in the absence of evidence of the acceptance of that reasoning by the people.

Outright Rejection of Regime Theory?

It has alternatively been argued that the whole regime approach is inapplicable because it embodies 'Western' ethnocentric assumptions about the role of the state and about welfare development as a product of what has been described above as 'the truce' between capital and labour (see chapter 52). Support for that perspective is surely offered by the fact that all this analysis does not extend to far and away the biggest country in this region: China.

Communist China, without either a democratic system of government or capitalist economic institutions, developed forms of social protection. This was par-

ticularly evident in the urban areas where welfare was provided through the work units (sometimes called the 'iron rice bowl') to which individuals and families were expected to be attached for life. More recently, as attention has been given to the enhancement of economic growth, using capitalist institutional forms, issues about social protection have been addressed in various ways.

The question is then whether this transformation is something special to China, reinforced both by the legacy of work unit-based welfare and by Confucian ideas about family and community responsibilities? Or can regime models be used to describe what is going on in China in the evolutionary terms quoted above, involving choices between the conservative and the liberal market models? Chinese developments are complex, given the size of the country and the very uneven pace of development from place to place. The solution of welfare problems is to some extent delegated to local areas, hence we see special schemes being developed in big cities like Shanghai. There is some evidence that Chinese choices involve a mixture of social insurance for state employees, 'liberal' developments in relation to private enterprises and a continuing residual system in the countryside.

A Need to Build Other Analytical Considerations into Comparative Theory

Various points in the last three sections suggest that what may be problematical is not regime theory as a starting point, but efforts to follow it too closely in an analysis of contemporary developments (a conclusion that may apply to other societies as well as to the East Asian ones). Three modern theoretical developments that deserve further consideration here are (see also chapter 52):

- institutional theory (stressing that there may be crucial points in the evolution of systems where institutional choices are made);
- the impact of policy-learning and policy-borrowing when those choices are made;
- the 'pathways' set up by those initial choices that have a key impact upon subsequent developments.

In all the nations discussed here apart from Japan, key decisions about approaches to social policy were made (or in the case of China, are being made) in pre-democratic political systems. Moreover, even in the Japanese case some institutional arrangements imposed upon that country after defeat in war have been important. Elsewhere, authoritarian governments struggled with problems of securing or maintaining relatively high levels of popular support whilst at the same time facilitating economic growth. Social policy institutions were a specific product of decisions made outside democratic arenas, but making extensive use of expert advice.

The stories of Singapore and Taiwan show similar features, while in Hong Kong the issues were about maintaining British colonial rule in a colony with economic opportunities, but also massive social problems associated with the inflow of population from China (with accordingly massive social housing projects as a key social policy).

Taiwan provides an interesting case. The ruling group in pre-democratic Taiwan, the KMT, saw itself as the heir to Dr Sun Yat-Sen, the leading ideologist in the period in which the Chinese Empire was overthrown in the first two decades of the twentieth century. Sun Yat-Sen sought to fuse Confucian ideas with Western republican and socialist ones. The constitution the KMT adopted for China in 1946 embraced proposals originally made by Sun Yat-Sen, including article 155, which reads 'the state, in order to promote social welfare, shall establish social insurance', and article 157, which states: 'the state, in order to improve national health, shall establish . . . a public medical service system'. While it would be naive to explain social policy developments in terms of the KMT's assertion of its commitment to the principles of Sun Yat-Sen, the KMT was concerned to establish its legitimate rule and in this context set up a cluster of separate social insurance schemes.

The Taiwan story also illustrates the second theme: policy-borrowing from Europe. It is important in comparative studies not to lose sight of the extent to which policy-learning takes place over time and between nations. Initially this can be seen in terms of the central conflict explored in chapter 55 between liberal market approaches and the more state-led ideas (including in particular social insurance). Subsequently, the newly industrialized and increasingly democratic East Asian nations had the opportunity to observe the strengths and weaknesses of European policies adopted earlier in time and to learn from them selectively. They have, inevitably, been drawn into the new global debate about the economic costs of generous welfare benefit systems and have wanted to draw their own conclusions.

Early choices have a massive subsequent impact, particularly in providing 'pathways' that constrain changes of direction. Social insurance is particularly significant in this respect, in setting up long-run commitments and expectations. Japan, South Korea and Taiwan stand out as having gone down the social insurance road so that it subsequently influences later developments. A key Japanese example is the way it has moved on from some cost problems in its health insurance system to a form of care insurance (as has Germany). That topic is now on the Taiwan agenda. Conversely, the absence of an insurance approach in Hong Kong, but, rather, a social assistance orientation to income maintenance, has left the door open for new approaches to pensions influenced by the Singapore forced saving model. In the Chinese case, social insurance for state enterprise employees is a logical step forward from the work unit model for welfare, since it offers a way to collectivize risks that can no longer be carried by individual enterprises. As far as new private enterprise is concerned, the agenda is then open, but market solutions to welfare problems are inevitably attractive.

Emerging Issues

In exploring emerging issues, the comments above about existing pathways are important. But in East Asia there are two developments that may shift some or all nations dramatically away from any identified pathways. These are, first, economic and, second, demographic.

The very rapid economic transformation of China poses social policy issues not just for that country but also for its neighbours. As far as China is concerned, the dual system described above, of developing welfare institutions in the urban areas and a residual system in the rural areas, is threatened by both the intrusion into the former of foreign economic enterprises eager to operate with a minimum of constraints and the massive migration of rural workers to emergent jobs in the cities. The weakening central state apparatus is torn between aspirations to encourage growth without 'strings' and concern to maintain social welfare institutions. Any effort to forecast what will happen has to take on the difficult task of predicting how this vast society will democratize.

Outside China itself, it is important not to underestimate the impact of Chinese economic change on its near neighbours. A large adjacent growing low-wage economy threatens the standards of living of its neighbours, and consequently also social welfare provisions which impose tax costs. The Chinese challenge can be observed most directly in Hong Kong, now a Special Administrative Region belonging to China. Taiwan is claimed as Chinese territory; peaceful transformation there may take it into a relationship with China like that of Hong Kong. Alternatively, if China were to attempt to recover the territory by force, the negative impact of that upon the whole region would be devastating.

Demographic change needs to be related to economic change, but its effects can be examined separately. What is special about East Asia is that the worldwide demographic shift towards 'ageing societies' consequent upon the combination of falling birth rates and falling death rates is particularly dramatic in that region. At the moment, the most dramatic changes are occurring in Japan and South Korea, but in due course (as a consequence of its one-child policy) China's transformation will be massive. We therefore see both falling populations and a rapid growth in the number of elderly people relative to the numbers of prime age adults. It may be disputed that these are really problems (a topic beyond the scope of this chapter), but they (and particularly the latter) are seen to be problems by governments and opinion leaders in East Asia.

In Japan and South Korea (and increasingly in Taiwan) debate about this phenomenon centres upon issues about female roles. There are two traditional expectations of women – to bear children and to care for older people (generally their in-laws) – and a modern one of increased labour market participation. Ironically, inasmuch as there is a concern about insufficient prime age adults to meet the needs of the labour market, married women are the main source of extra labour. While politicians may exhort – as, controversially, has been the case in Japan – women to fulfil roles of child-bearers and carers, this surely can have little effect without attention being given *either* to securing new labour from other countries *or* to policies to reduce the pressures upon female labour market participants. These alternatives imply social policy changes. Those related to migration are complex and these countries are very reluctant to open their frontiers to migrant workers. Those relating to family life (which surely must be addressed, since it seems unlikely that governments can repress new female aspirations anyway) seem likely to engender new government initiatives in relation to social care at both ends of the life cycle. In respect of care of older people, Japan is already leading the way in this direction with the initiation of social care insurance.

These two emerging trends will of course interact very substantially, since what happens to the economy of the region will have a variety of impacts upon national labour markets and on the demand for female labour. However, studies of family policy suggest that while governments may succeed in reducing birth rates, they have considerable difficulty in increasing them. In any case the oppression of women consequent upon the combination of the three pressures discussed above is surely one that social policy needs to address.

Guide to Further Sources

The best sources for comparative accounts of all (or some) of the national social policy systems considered here are A. Walker and C.-K. Wong (eds), *East Asian Welfare Regimes in Transition* (Policy Press, 2005); M. Ramesh, *Social Policy in East and Southeast Asia: Education, Health, Housing and Income Maintenance* (RoutledgeCurzon, 2004). Also useful is a symposium in *Social Policy and Society* 3/3 (2004). The main sources of the alternative regime perspectives are on the productivist perspective: see I. Holliday, 'Productivist welfare capitalism: social policy in East Asia', *Political Studies* 48 (2000): 706–23 and 'East Asian social policy in the wake of the financial crisis: farewell to productivism?', *Policy and Politics* 33/1 (2000): 145–62, and Jones's thesis on the impact of Confucianism in C. Jones (ed.), *New Perspectives on the Welfare State in Europe* (Routledge, 1993).

An attack on the ethnocentrism of regime theory can be found in A. Walker and C.-K. Wong, 'The ethnocentric construction of the welfare state', in P. Kennett (ed.), *A Handbook of Comparative Social Welfare* (Edward Elgar, 2004). Accounts of developments which particularly bring out the institutional influences on recent social policy growth are, for Korea, H.-J. Kwon, *The Welfare State in Korea: The Politics of Legitimation* (St Martin's Press, 1999) and D.-M. Shin, *Social and Economic Policies in Korea: Ideas, Networks and Linkages* (RoutledgeCurzon, 2003).

An account of early developments in Taiwan is provided in Y.-W. Ku, *Welfare Capitalism in Taiwan: State, Economy and Social Policy* (Macmillan, 1997), while later ones are explored in Ku's contribution to the *Social Policy and Society* symposium cited above and in M. Hill and Y.-S. Hwang, 'Taiwan: what kind of social policy regime?' in the edited collection by Walker and Wong (2005).

Chapter 57

Social Policy in Developing Societies

Patricia Kennett

Overview

- The study of welfare arrangements in developing societies is a relatively new and expanding domain within social policy.
- A range of classification systems has been devised to explore and account for these arrangements.
- International institutions and overseas development assistance play a key role in shaping social policy in developing societies.
- From a social policy perspective the current development paradigm presents many challenges.

Introduction

An understanding of social policy in any part of the world can most successfully be achieved through analyses that incorporate historical, political and economic as well as social dimensions. This is particularly the case when attempting to understand social policy in less-industrialized societies, where the experiences of colonialism, independence and nation-building, the degree of influence exerted by international financial institutions, and the extent and nature of poverty and inequality have had a major impact on shaping social policy debates and systems of welfare.

There has often been a lack of a clear identity for social policy in less-industrialized countries and a much greater emphasis on the broader notion of social development. Since the 1950s the main tenet of development thinking has been premised, either explicitly or implicitly, on the role of modernization as a vehicle for facilitating economic growth through urbanization, industrialization and capital investment. The phrase itself, and the perceived strategies for achieving it, have implied the desirability of adopting a unilinear and universal development trajectory replicating and perpetuating the structures and systems dominant in Western industrial countries to the developing world. The development discourse has, until recently, tended to subordinate or subsume social policy within economic policy and to focus on homogeneity across developing societies, rather than diversity. The first section of this chapter will examine the conceptual distinctions that have been used to define, categorize and separate different parts of the world. It will then go on to distinguish patterns of welfare, focusing specifically on

Latin America and Africa. The role of international institutions and overseas development aid (ODA) in relation to the shaping of social policy instruments will then be considered. The discussion concludes with a consideration of the nature and extent of poverty and human development and the potential for social policy to centrally inform the development paradigm and contribute to improving the economic and social well-being of people in less-industrialized societies.

Concepts and Categories

A variety of imprecise and inconsistent conceptual distinctions have been used to categorize and differentiate areas of the globe, such as first/third world, developed/developing, North/South, industrialized/less-industrialized, which have usually involved poorer countries being contrasted, negatively, with the more developed, advanced, industrialized and richer countries of the North.

The World Bank's main criterion for classifying countries is the size of their economy measured by gross national income (GNI) per capita, with every country classified as either low income, middle income (sub-divided into lower-middle and upper-middle), or high income. In 2007, there were 545 low-income countries with a 2005 GNI of $875 or less, 48 lower-middle income countries with a GNI of between $876 and $3,465, 40 upper-middle income countries with a GNI of between $3,466 and $10,725 and 56 with a GNI of $10,726 or more. Those countries classified as low- and middle-income countries are generally understood to be 'developing societies'. In 1971 the United Nations established the Least Developed Countries group when 24 countries were identified as having a low per capita income, a low level of human resource development based on indicators of nutrition, health and educa-

tion and adult literacy, and a high degree of economic vulnerability. At the end of 2005, there were 50 countries designated by the United Nations as the Least Developed Countries (LDCs), of which 31 were in Africa, 4 were in the Arab Region, 14 were in Asia and the Pacific, and 1 was in Latin America and the Caribbean.

Since the 1990s, the United Nations Human Development Index (HDI) has provided a different approach to categorizing and ranking countries through the use of composite indices based on educational attainment, health and survival, economic resources and standard of living. In 2006, the HDI provided a ranking of 177 countries based on their average achievements, with 63 countries categorized as having high human development, 83 with medium human development and 31 with low human development.

Social Policy in Context

The developing world incorporates a range of diversity in terms of colonial history, political profile, social structure, levels of development and state and institutional capacity. As one might expect, social policy instruments are wide-ranging and more traditional welfare measures have come to include land reform, subsidy for food and water, and the regulation of the private sector. The choice and combination of instruments is likely to be unique to each country, as it involves the interplay of a range of forces, including ideological predisposition, institutional structures and the political and economic context.

A major factor impacting on the structures of provision and choice of social policy instruments has been the history and current context of geopolitical relationships between the North and the South which have been manifested through imperialism, colonialism, the institutionalization of relations of political and economic dependency,

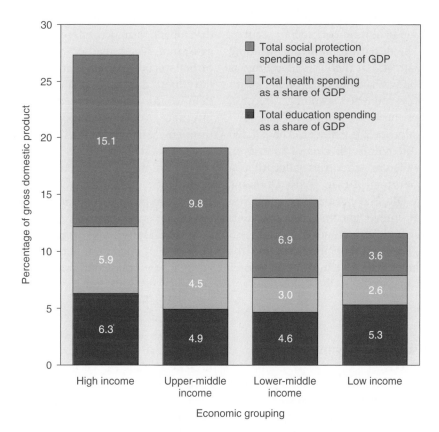

Figure 57.1 Social sector spending among country grouping classified by income
Source: P. Keyy and V. Saiz-Omenaca, 'The allocation of government expenditure in the world 1990–2001', unpublished paper, United Nations, Department of Economics and Social Affairs, Division for Social Policy and Development in UN, 2005, p. 118.

and development strategies and programmes which have in combination aggravated and perpetuated ethnic and religious tensions and conflict, and contributed to many of the negative aspects of social life in Africa, Asia and Latin America.

Figure 57.1 provides an overview of social security expenditure amongst groups of countries classified by income. It highlights the wide disparities in social sector spending between different groups of countries classified according to their level of economic development. High-income countries spend an average of 27 per cent of GDP on the social sectors, compared with 12 per cent in low-income countries. As figure 57.1 shows, the widest disparities in

expenditure between income groups are found in the area of social protection, which will include pensions, unemployment and disability benefits, for example. The development and maintenance of social security systems requires, in the first instance, an appropriate and complex infrastructure, state capacity and a formal labour market through which to raise and collect taxes to finance social sector programmes, and to implement these programmes. Poorer countries are usually characterized by limited state capacity and infrastructure, and budget and policy restrictions particularly from International Financial Institutions (IFIs). In addition, traditional labour structures, and massive and chronic levels of poverty and inequality, have militated against the evolution of social security systems. The disparities in health spending are not so great, but there is still enormous variation between economic groupings with high-income countries spending almost 6 per cent of their GDP on health and low-income countries 2.6 per cent. The pattern is a little different in the case of education, with low-income countries allocating a higher proportion of their Gross Domestic Product (GDP) (5.3 per cent) to education than upper-middle income (4.9 per cent) and lower-middle income countries (4.6 per cent). This highlights the trend towards growing investment in education in poorer countries.

Policy Issues and Regimes

While the aggregate data introduced above provides a useful starting point for analysing social policy in less developed countries, more important is an appreciation of the structures of welfare, its composition and the complex and changing patterns of relationships between different producers. Although patterns of social policy across the South vary depending on each country's distinctive historical pathway, focusing on Latin America and Africa, it is possible to identify two broad categories of social policy and welfare system which can be characterized as clientelistic and residual (see chapter 52). These different models can be linked to the levels of regulatory and institutional capacity achieved by particular states and the ways in which society has been organized. The clientelistic model, predominant in Latin America, emerged as a consequence of the power of elites and interest groups and their ability to 'colonize' the state apparatus. Welfare systems developed relatively early in Latin America compared to other developing regions and, by the 1980s many countries in the region

had longstanding, and in some cases well-developed formal welfare. Whilst social assistance has remained underdeveloped, formal social insurance programmes were introduced during the first half of the twentieth century and focused on providing insurance for specific groups of workers through earnings-related contributions. Barrientos (in Gough et al. 2004) highlights the importance of the extensive array of employment protection regulation, a particularly important component of the Latin American 'welfare mix'. Although there have been aspirations towards the universal provision of education and healthcare, the adverse economic conditions of the 1980s curtailed this ambition and significant gaps and inequalities in provision remain. The clientelistic model of welfare, which he categorizes as 'a liberal-informal welfare regime', can be characterized as occupationally stratified in terms of social insurance and employment protection and highly segmented in health insurance and healthcare provision. For the most part, this model benefits only a small proportion of the population who are in privileged positions in the formal sector. The majority of those in rural areas, and those who attempt to earn a living in the urban informal sector and their households (approximately 52 per cent of the population in Latin America) are excluded. Thus, the majority of the population must rely on informal support networks to protect them against social risk, and the sparse networks linked to national and international non-governmental organizations.

Residual social policy and welfare systems are most evident across much of Africa, particularly sub-Saharan Africa, the origins of which can be located in the history and experience of colonial rule through which the first limited social services were introduced. Akin Aina (1999) has argued that the expansion of formal social policy under the colonial administration was largely determined by economic factors and the exploitation of the resources of the colonies, as well as the maintenance of social order. Social policy provision was minimal, residual and discriminatory and more concerned with providing for the needs of, and thus supporting, the colonial administration. Following independence in the 1960s and 1970s, social policy was to play an important role in legitimizing many postcolonial governments, with the development of social programmes in education, housing, health, and price subsidies and controls. This was supported by the Keynesian model of development, dominant up until the 1970s, which incorporated a combination of international economic laissez-faire and state intervention to promote economic development, the social rights of the population, and social order. Social policy measures were seen as appropriate and desirable and, in tandem with economic growth, were key instruments for social development and the elimination of poverty.

The United Nations, and other international organizations, including the International Labour Organization (ILO), the World Health Organization (WHO) and the World Bank, supported community-based projects concerned with, for example, healthcare and education, as economic growth was measured, according to Midgley (in Hall and Midgley 2004), in terms of social outputs rather than per capita income growth. By the end of the 1970s, however, it appeared that this strategy was unsustainable. Political instability, drought, a drop in the price of primary commodities, defaults on loans, and corruption brought the African state to crisis point. According to Akin Aina (1999), social services and the social infrastructure decayed from sheer neglect and where they existed in rudimentary forms were appropriated by local barons and misused for political patronage. This resulted in a drastic reduction in expenditure and in public sector expenditure.

Development, International Institutions and Social Policy

By the early 1980s the perception that the relationship between macro-economic and social policy could be a positive one had been completely rejected and devalued. Most countries in South America and Africa were experiencing a decline in economic growth rates, high inflation levels, a growing debt burden and an increasingly competitive international environment compared to the 1970s. The debt crisis and economic decline became key issues across the globe, and rolling back the state, reducing public expenditure, privatization, the elimination of subsidies and opening up economies became fundamental components of the development paradigm.

The dominant discourse emerging at the global level was that the problems of development were primarily ones of economic (mis-)management, inefficiency and state corruption. From this perspective, improvements in social policy could only flow from improved economic performance. This was a reflection of the new economic orthodoxy emerging in the North which was subsequently transmitted to developing societies through the influential IFIs and promoted monetarist economic policy, deregulation and privatization. These themes were reflected at the global level and a consensus emerged on the most appropriate model of economic and political management for developing countries, including deregulation, privatization of state-run organizations, liberalization of the economy, the free market and retrenching of the public sector. There was also the commitment to channel aid through non-governmental organizations rather than through country governments (see chapter 37). This package of measures has often been termed the 'Washington Consensus', a phrase coined by economist John Williamson in 1990 when referring to appropriate development strategies for South America. Its strategies were promoted by global institutions and the most powerful state players and took the form of structural adjustment programmes through which loans to poor countries were conditional on policy changes proposed by the World Bank.

By the end of the 1990s there was recognition that structural adjustment had done little to improve the economic circumstances and social well-being of people in less-industrialized countries. A radical rethinking of the national and international policies needed to tackle the problems or poor countries that were failing to prosper was called for by civil society organizations and national governments in both the North and the South. There was a shift in the terrain of intervention from the economic to the political sphere as the term 'governance' became a dominant theme in international institutions. There was also a growing recognition and the emergence of a global discourse that social rights should be respected in the development process, and that poverty reduction should be adopted as a central objective of international development cooperation. More recently, IFIs, such as the World Bank, have begun to incorporate much more explicit references to poverty reduction and social development in their approach to concessional assistance to low-income countries.

The World Bank introduced its Poverty Reduction Strategy Papers (PRSPs) and the IMF its Poverty Reduction and Growth Facility (PRGF) in 1999. In 2000, 189 UN member states agreed a set of specific targets for reducing poverty, hunger, disease, gender inequality, illiteracy and environmental degradation, incorporated in the Millennium Development Goals. According to the OECD, the Millennium Development Goals provided a common framework for the international development community to guide policies and programmes and assess their effectiveness. In 2001 the Programme of Action for the LDCs was agreed in

Brussels. In 2006 the World Bank initiated a financial package for the Multilateral Debt Relief Initiative (MDRI), cancelling $37 billion in IDA debt of some of the world's poorest countries over 40 years. This is in addition to approximately $17 billion of debt relief already committed by IDA under the Enhanced Heavily Indebted Poor Countries (HIPC) Initiative.

A New Development Paradigm?

The current development paradigm, according to Eyoh and Sandbrook (2001), can be characterized as one of 'pragmatic neo-liberalism' and viewed as a more sophisticated version of the earlier neo-classical model it replaced. However, concern has been expressed with regard to an implementation gap between planning and action, and the failure of IFIs to translate their commitment to a social dimension into practice. What does appear to be apparent is that the current strategies outlined in this chapter suggest continuity rather than innovation, reformulation and recognition of the role of social policy in the development process. There is evidence of an intensified and more explicit intervention by the West into both the economic and political spheres of less developed countries. The 'new' development paradigm appears to be more about a reassessment of the process of policy formulation than a real innovation in the content of policies. But even here, whilst the emphasis is on country ownership, policy autonomy and the mainstreaming of poverty reduction policies, there remains a tension between national autonomy and policy conditionality imposed by the IFIs.

Many developing countries, particularly the LDCs, are highly dependent on external resources. However, there has been increasing concern that the amount of aid from richer countries is failing to reach specified targets or to match pledges made by national governments. In addition to concerns about the quantity of aid, the quality of ODA has also been called into question. Aid is often unpredictable, has numerous strings attached and usually involves the recipient in incurring transaction costs. According to the UN, international aid continues to be underused, inefficiently targeted and in need of repair. The practice of tied aid, linking development assistance to the provision of supplies and services provided by the donor country, remains widely prevalent, as does the economic conditionality imposed by IFIs. Pervasive and, in some cases, increasing levels of poverty and inequality highlights the necessity for the effective and efficient delivery of aid and the urgent need for reform of the institutional architecture and processes through which aid is delivered.

Emerging Issues: Globalization, Poverty and Human Development

The era of globalization has been marked by a technological revolution, an ideological and policy shift, a strengthening of the role of international institutions and a changing geopolitical landscape. Economic globalization has generated substantial prosperity for many parts of the world, particularly high-income OECD countries, while, at the same time, it has left large parts of the world behind in terms of economic integration and human development. Despite the steady rise during the 1990s in the number of developing countries adopting significant liberalization measures towards FDI, trade expansion has been concentrated in industrialized countries and a group of twelve developing countries. The majority of developing countries have not experienced significant trade expansion and, indeed, it is the LDCs that are most likely to have experienced a decline in their share of world markets. For the LDCs, trade liberalization has not been associated with poverty reduction.

Historically, the highest levels of income inequality have been found in Africa and Latin America, a situation that worsened during the 1980s and 1990s. In Latin America in the 1990s wealthier households accounted for more than 30 per cent of total income, while the poorest 40 per cent of households received only 9–15 per cent of total income. The largest income gap is in Brazil, and the lowest levels of income inequality can be found in Uruguay and Costa Rica.

According to the HDR (2005) 40 per cent of the world's population (2.5 billion people) live on less than $2 a day. In African LDCs, the proportion of the population living below $1 per day is estimated to have increased from 56 per cent during 1965–9 to approximately 65 per cent during 1985–95. Turning to the $2 a day poverty line, the incidence of poverty appears to have increased to over 82 per cent for African LDCs as a whole. The average incidence of poverty in Asian LDCs for the $1 a day poverty line fell from 35.5 per cent in the late 1960s to approximately 23 per cent in the late 1990s, and at the $2 a day poverty line declined from approximately 70 per cent to 68 per cent in those countries. Of the 37 LDCs for which poverty estimates are available over the relevant period, 23 show an increase (UNCTAD 2002).

Clearly, estimates on the extent of poverty in developing societies vary according to the definition applied and the methodology used to calculate the figures. The Chronic Poverty Research Centre estimates in its 2004–5 report that between 300 and 420 million people are trapped in chronic poverty, defined as those who 'remain poor for much or all of their lives, many of whom will pass on their poverty to their children, and all too often die easily preventable deaths'. However, some research suggests the figure could be even higher. Being in chronic poverty is not just about having a low income; it is about multidimensional poverty: hunger, illiteracy, dirty drinking water, no access to health services, social isolation and exploitation. Around a quarter to a third of the people living on less than US$1 are chronically poor. Sub-Saharan Africa has one of the highest levels of chronic poverty, while South Asia almost certainly contains the majority of the world's chronically poor.

The HDI is a composite covering three dimensions of human welfare: income, education and health. It is intended to provide a measurement that goes beyond income. Over the last decade, the HDI has been rising across all developing regions, though at variable rates and with the exception of sub-Saharan Africa. Eighteen countries with a combined population of 460 million people registered lower scores on the HDI in 2003 than in 1990, and there is real doubt if the Millennium Development Goals relating to the eradication of extreme poverty and hunger, reducing child mortality and universal primary education can be achieved by 2015.

The focus of this chapter has been on developing societies, which is a contested concept and a category that incorporates enormous diversity and heterogeneity. Whilst recognizing the specificity of individual developing counties, the chapter has also considered more general trends in social policy development, particularly in terms of the relationship between North and South and the role of international institutions. This chapter argues that a discursive reorientation of the neo-liberal development paradigm has taken place in which pro-poor policies have greater priority. However, there is little evidence to indicate that the practices of IFIs have changed significantly, or that aid is being provided in a more effective and appropriate way. The challenge for the international community, national governments and civil society is to overcome the democratic deficit evident in international institutions, strengthening the voice of developing country representatives, reforming the aid infrastructure and exhibiting a genuine commitment to social policy and social development. Social policy not only has the capacity to contribute to enhancing social capital and social cohesion but can also play a significant role in reinforcing the legitimacy of the political order and contributing to political stability.

Guide to Further Sources

The many issues and debates touched on in this chapter are explored in T. Akin Aina, 'West and Central Africa: Social Policy for Reconstruction and Development', in D. Morales-Gomez (ed.), *Transnational Social Policies. The New Development Challenges of Globalization* (Earthscan, 1999); I. Gough and G. Wood, with A. Barrientos, P. Bevan, P. Davis and G. Room, *Insecurity and Welfare Regimes in Asia, Africa and Latin America* (Cambridge University Press, 2004) (which includes Barrientos's chapter, 'Latin America: a liberal-informal welfare regime?'); D. Eyoh and R. Sandbrook, *Pragmatic Neo-liberalism and Just Development in Africa*, CIS Working Paper 2001–1 (University of Toronto, Canada, 2001); V. George and P. Wilding, *Globalization and Human Welfare* (Palgrave, 2002); A. Hall and J. Midgley, *Social Policy for Development* (Sage, 2004); P. Kennett, *A Handbook of Comparative Social Policy* (Edward Elgar, 2004) (which includes Perez-Baltodano's chapter, 'Globalization, human security and social policy: North and South); T. Mkandawire, *Social Policy in a Development Context,* Social Policy and Development Programme Paper No. 7 (United Nations Research Institute for Development, Switzerland, 2001); D. Morales-Gomez, *Transnational Social Policies. The New Development Challenges of Globalization*

(Earthscan, 1999); UNDP, *Human Development Report 2005. International Cooperation at the Crossroads: Aid, Trade and Security in an Unequal World* (United Nations Development Programme, 2005); and CPRC, *The Chronic Poverty Report 2004–2005* (Chronic Poverty Research Centre, University of Manchester, 2004).

International governmental and non-governmental organizations, such as the UNDP, the United Nations Research Institute for Social Development (<www.unrisd.org>), the World Bank (<www.worldbank.org>), the International Labour Organization (<www.ilo.org>), and the WHO (<www.who.int>), as well as Oxfam International (<www.oxfam.org>) and Save the Children (<www.savethechildren.org>), produce substantial amounts of material on developing societies much of which is relevant to the study of social policy.

Appendix 1

Careers and Postgraduate Study in Social Policy

Employment Prospects and Opportunities

Whatever the product or service being provided, the context or size of an enterprise, effective policy evaluation is central to decision-making and organizational success. In consequence, there is a high demand for graduates skilled in policy research, analysis, appraisal and data management, who are aware of resource and implementation issues and the complexities of meeting the needs of varying stakeholders, and who are able to make considered judgements. This appendix provides a brief indication of the consequent range of options open to those who have studied social policy as a specialism or as part of a combined programme. Exploring and evaluating these is in itself a form of policy analysis, raising many questions about current labour market developments that graduates may wish to investigate further and which impinge directly on the issues addressed in the *Companion*.

Bearing these points in mind, it can be seen that employment opportunities open to social policy graduates come from a number of sources. These include the annual First Destination Statistics compiled by University Careers Services, more general 'snapshot' and longitudinal surveys conducted by other agencies and data collected by degree providers. Together, they currently point to a buoyant graduate labour market and an increasingly diverse range of careers in the public, commercial and voluntary sectors open to those with the knowledge and skills gained from studying social policy.

In broad terms, these fall into two main groupings: first, occupations where an understanding of social policy is of direct relevance and is highly regarded by recruiters and, secondly, those where a greater emphasis is placed on the skills of policy analysis. This distinction, however, is a fluid one and there is considerable scope for movement between the two as well as within them in the early and later stages of a career.

Successful Career Planning

Recent studies show that competition for posts with the highest returns and development opportunities is intense. Given the possibilities and the patterning of employer expectations, forward planning – starting in the first, not the last, year of your programme – is essential. This involves researching the opportunities available, building a profile of your strengths and skills and playing to them. The ability to market yourself and draw on any paid or voluntary work you have undertaken alongside or prior to your studies is also vital. This appendix is intended to support this process and your personal development planning throughout your programme of studies. It should be used in conjunction with the advice of your tutors and careers service to enable you realistically to assess the main options open to you and capitalize on the competitive edge acquired through studying social policy.

Social Policy Career Pathways

Traditionally, most social policy graduates sought careers in the public services. This is still a popular choice and one that offers considerable opportunities for fast career progression. Salaries may not match those in the private sector, but public sector employers offer other benefits, such as funded pensions, flexible working and extensive training. As should be clear from this *Companion*, it is a misconception to equate this sector simply with direct service provision. Although social policy is a gateway to a career in social work or other caring professions, it also feeds into a growing range of management, advisory, research and administrative positions in national and local public sector agencies.

It also provides the expertise for pursuing similar posts with other employers, large and small, offering welfare and allied services. Voluntary and community organizations and social enterprises, for instance, have become significant economic players. They employ increasing numbers in research, policy development, marketing, fundraising and resource management, lobbying, project management, training and volunteer coordination as well as service delivery. A background in social policy is also of direct utility to commercial organizations trading in welfare, care and personal financial services.

The many changes instituted by recent governments mean that it is difficult to encapsulate the types of employment in statutory and non-statutory organizations that require social policy expertise. Indeed,

these can only be tracked by keeping up to date with the subject itself. For instance, new or changing structures (Foundation Hospitals, PCTs, Connexions), initiatives (the New Deals, Sure Start, Urban Regeneration, Neighbourhood Renewal, Community Safety), benefit and tax changes, e-governance and partnership working in its myriad forms all entail a host of 'front-line' and project management starter posts with good career progression opportunities. The government's public health agenda is generating cross-sectoral demand for a further range of advisory, health promotion, project management and support posts, while the expansion of vocational education in health and social care and the advent of citizenship courses have opened up opportunities in teaching at various levels and settings.

The advent of the 'evaluative state' and the increasing emphasis on user-involvement and consumer-oriented provision have been reflected in a parallel raft of employment opportunites. These include policy research and development and consumer information, advice and protection, as well as general management. Beyond these there is increasing cross-sectoral demand for graduates with a grounding in social policy in the fields of international aid and development, diversity management and corporate social responsibility (CSR). Though employment in the first often requires proficiency in one or more languages, international governmental and non-governmental agencies also recruit graduates familiar with comparative policy developments and analysis. An awareness of current policy, governance and community issues is also a sought-after basis for entering a career in diversity management or the fast-growing field of CSR.

With further changes in the pipeline, the current decade is likely to see a continuing growth in demand for staff with a knowledge of social policy. To assess the options fully, you will find it helpful to consider the various positions (summarized in job titles, descriptions and person specifications or competencies), career trajectories and rewards characteristic of both 'traditional' and 'newer' public services. Co-relatedly, you should also explore the relative merits of working for different levels and areas of government and the parallel posts in non-statutory agencies. Detailed reviews can be found in specialist career guides, but the main areas are summarized (in no particular order) below:

- employment services
- income maintenance services
- the health service
- housing
- adult care services
- childcare, early years and family services
- education and training/lifelong learning
- youth services
- connections
- community development
- immigration services
- leisure and sports services
- the police
- youth justice services
- criminal justice services
- legal services
- trading standards
- regeneration and planning
- economic development
- international aid and development
- information and advice services
- research and policy development
- corporate social responsibility

Generalist Career Pathways

Many social policy graduates opt for careers in other settings where their degree offers particular value. These include areas such as human resource management, counselling, and public and customer relations, with their affinities to many of the issues

addressed on social policy programmes. This also applies to the broad field of marketing, where social policy graduates can draw on their skills in research and needs analysis. Information from careers advisers shows that social policy graduates are recruited to a wide spectrum of occupations in these areas, working for large companies, small firms, voluntary bodies and public agencies. But graduate recruitment surveys also show that many employers do not ask for specific degree subjects. Rather, they seek individuals with a span of soft and transferable skills and, above all, the potential to develop them further. These areas typically pursued by social policy graduates include:

- financial services
- retail services
- leisure services
- employment services
- communication and media services
- legal services
- recruitment
- human resource management (HRM)
- counselling
- research
- policy analysis and development
- marketing, market research, public relations, advertising
- customer relations
- project management

Postgraduate Study and Further Training Opportunities

In considering your career options, you could also consider the value of further study. It may be that you wish to enrich your understanding of social policy and contribute to its development by undertaking your own research or by studying abroad. Alternatively, you may feel that you need to enhance your employability by gaining an additional qualification, or your chosen career may require you to develop further, specialist skills.

As with career planning, it is vital to research the costs, benefits and options available. Though the returns are often high, postgraduate study is expensive and time-consuming. State funding is limited; most students find it necessary to self-fund and study part time. Nevertheless, the available evidence suggests that many social policy graduates find this a worthwhile venture. Broadly speaking the main options are:

- vocational courses leading to professional qualifications;
- taught courses leading to: a Postgraduate Certificate (PG Cert), a Postgraduate Diploma (PG Dip) or a Master's Degree (MSc, MA, MBA, MPA);
- research courses leading to an MPhil or PhD

For some careers that social policy graduates might want to consider, a professional qualification is compulsory – for example, social work, teaching, the law. Increasingly, it is also an essential currency for gaining a foothold in some areas and prerequisite for moving from 'starter' to 'second step' posts in many fields. Career progression in HRM and marketing, for instance, is contingent on gaining a professional qualification. In other areas too, you may find it worthwhile extending your subject knowledge through a vocationally oriented course. These range from programmes geared to particular areas of employment such as housing or health promotion or specific organizational settings such as the voluntary sector through to broader courses in management. Many institutions run programmes that offer both professional accreditation and a Master's degree, and, for those with management experience, an MBA or MPA (Masters of Business/Public Administration) geared to specific services (such as the NHS or local

government) or general senior management posts.

You may, however, prefer the flexibility afforded by less overly vocational courses. Here too there is an ever-expanding range of programmes, enabling you to take your study of social policy further or move into cognate areas such as evaluative research or urban regeneration. Many taught programmes are offered on a credit-accumulation basis and can be studied in a variety of modes, institutionally, work- and web-based. They usually have to be completed within a set time, normally equivalent to between one and two years of full-time study. Postgraduate study by research demands a more extensive time commitment, particularly for a PhD, which usually requires three to four years of full-time study (five plus on a part-time basis). It involves the submission of a thesis based on a major piece of independent research advancing current knowledge. Many students register for an MPhil initially, transferring to a PhD after their first year if their progress is deemed satisfactory. Both require advanced methodological skills, gained through completing a postgraduate course in research methods during the first year of study.

Determining where to study

As with other career decisions, determining where to study hinges on a range of factors. Your careers service will hold a range of publications and be able to advise you on the processes involved, as will your tutors.

The application process

Unlike undergraduate study, there is no central application or clearing system (other than for teaching and social work). Instead, you have to apply directly to the relevant provider. Admissions tutors for vocational and taught Master's courses will want to assure themselves (through the application form and subsequent interview) that you have an appropriate background, and the ability and commitment to undertake advanced study. For an MPhil or PhD, selection hinges on the quality of the research proposal, which forms the core of the application process. This may be open-ended or it may involve you applying to undertake research in a pre-designated area. Either way, as with other applications, it is vital to seek your tutors' advice and ensure in advance that they are willing to provide references.

Sources of funding

Though various forms of sponsorship and support are available, they tend to be highly competitive and geared to particular forms of training. Most postgraduates rely fully or in part on their own sources. Nevertheless, it is worth considering the options available and bidding for one or a mix of them. Full details will be held by your careers service, but the main sources are:

- Public funding: through Research Council Awards (primarily for MPhil and PhD studies, applications for which should be made through the department at which you intend to study) and for teaching and social work.
- Institutional funding: bursaries, scholarships, studentships, teaching and research assistantships (again bid for directly).

- Employer support: the most comprehensive but most competitive are graduate traineeships, aimed at those with management potential. Many employers also provide assistance with fees, books or other costs and/or paid study leave.
- Assistance from charities: of varying amounts and based on differing criteria.
- Loans, including Career Development Loans, Professional Loan and Association of MBAs Loan Schemes (details will be available from careers services).

Studying, Working and Volunteering Abroad

You may also wish to consider, on graduating or later, to seek employment or study abroad. In terms of the latter, social policy in many countries is commonly taught within broad-based social or political science departments. These offer numerous opportunities for postgraduate study, but are subject to varied application processes and stiff competition for funds. In terms of employment, linguistic skills permitting, the range of subject-related and general options is, if anything, even wider than in the UK, as is the scope for volunteering. Many positions will, however, demand professional qualifications and these again should be tracked through the specialist literature.

Further Sources of Information

Your institution's careers service should be able to offer guidance on possible areas of employment, skills analyses, job search techniques and preparation for the selection procedures used by graduate employers. Trends in the graduate labour market are best tracked through the surveys produced by HESA (the Higher Education Statistics Agency), AGCAS (the Association of Graduate Careers Advisory Services: <www.agcas.org.uk>), AGR (the Association of Graduate Recruiters: <www.agr.org.uk>) and the IDS (Incomes Data Services: <www.ids.co.uk>).

Information and advice on employment and postgraduate opportunities can be accessed through a multiplicity of sources. The best starting points are: <www.

prospects.ac.uk>, <www.hobsons.com> and <www.guardian.co.uk/jobs>; and for overseas study, Association of Commonwealth Universities: <www.acu.ac.uk> and *Hobsons Guide to International Programmes in Europe*: <sites.hobsons.com/studyeurope>. These all provide case studies, links to more specific, specialist sources and information for those with particular interest or special needs. A useful starter for considering your skills base is P. Spicker, *Policy Analysis for Practice* (Policy Press, 2007).

Appendix 2

The Social Policy Association (SPA)

The SPA is the professional association for academics, researchers and students in social policy and administration. As an academic association in the social science field, it is a member of the Academy of Learned Societies for the Social Sciences and it has close collaborative links with other professional associations in cognate fields, such as the British Sociological Association (BSA) and the Social Research Association (SRA). It also has strong links with SWAP, the subject centre for social policy and social work, one of the Higher Education Academy's 24 discipline-based subject centres. The SPA works closely with SWAP and has been active in the development of the social policy benchmark statement, the range of which is reflected in the *Companion*.

The SPA is a membership organization and membership is open to all students, teachers and others working in the social policy field. All members pay an annual fee, with the cost of membership varying according to income bands. The benefits of membership include:

- free subscription to the leading social policy journals, the *Journal of Social Policy* (four issues per year) and *Social Policy and Society* (four issues per year);
- free copy of *Social Policy Review*, published annually by the Policy Press – an edited collection of articles reviewing developments and debates in social policy in Britain and internationally;

- a small grants scheme to support the setting up of seminars and conferences for members;
- *Policy World*: a popular newsletter published twice a year;
- subgroups for postgraduate students, international and comparative social policy analysis;
- an annual conference held in July each year in the UK;
- discounts on subscriptions to other leading academic journals – *European Journal of Social Policy*, *Policy and Politics* and *Social Policy and Administration*.

The majority of members of the SPA live and work in the United Kingdom, but the Association also has active members all over the world, including in particular Europe, North America, the Far East and Australia. The Association has growing links with social policy associations and scholars throughout the world.

The Association is managed by an Executive Committee made up of members elected at the Annual Conference, with members serving on the committee for periods of three years at a time. In addition, there are officers – a Chair, Secretary and Treasurer – also elected and serving on a three-year basis. Students of social policy are encouraged to join the Association and to contact staff members in their departments, schools or faculties. The SPA can be contacted through its web page <www.social-policy.com>.

Index

Page numbers in *italics* refer to figures; page numbers in **bold** refer to tables